**Environmental analysis
for management**

Environmental analysis for management

JAMES P. BAUGHMAN
Professor of Business History

GEORGE C. LODGE
Professor of Business Administration

HOWARD W. PIFER, III
Lecturer on Business Administration

All of the Graduate School of Business Administration
Harvard University

 1974

RICHARD D. IRWIN, INC. Homewood, Illinois 60430
Irwin-Dorsey International, London, England WC2H 9NJ
Irwin-Dorsey Limited, Georgetown, Ontario L7G 4B3

First Printing, March 1974

Case material of the Harvard Graduate School of
Business Administration is made possible by the
cooperation of business firms who may wish to remain
anonymous by having names, quantities, and other
identifying details disguised while basic relationships
are maintained. Cases are prepared as the basis for
class discussion rather than to illustrate either effective
or ineffective handling of administrative situations.

ISBN 0-256-01561-9
Library of Congress Catalog Card No. 73–87260

Printed in the United States of America

Preface

FOR CENTURIES, one of the defining characteristics of a good manager has been his ability to think and move faster than the economic, political, social, and technical norms of the environment in which he operates. It is precisely his ability to anticipate and lead among environmental hazards and opportunities and his skill in organizational modification that have been in demand. His environment has been generally encouraging and supportive of his behavior because his social benefits were perceived as greater than his social costs. In a social sense, managers and their organizations have been in a seller's market for 400 years.

Today, many managers and their organizations confront a buyer's market for their skills and, worse, a set of skeptical, even adversary, relationships unprecedented in their experience. Their environment is changing in ways they seem unable or unwilling to understand much less anticipate and at a pace too fast to follow much less to set.

Why? The simple answer is that there is plenty new under the sun. But there is more to the present state of affairs than that. An important part of the current dilemma faced by many managers is their unwillingness or inability to modify planning structures and techniques developed in past times when the environment was more stable. All too often, managers have fallen into a trap when formulating and implementing strategy. Their historic ability to think and move faster than their environment has led them to think in terms of situations in which the environment does not change at all. Consequently, there has been a propensity among managers to take economic, political, social, or technical factors

v

as "given" and to define the managerial task in a rather self-centered way: to optimize the "fit" between one's *own* activities and organizations and what are perceived as environmental constants.

There are often good reasons for this approach and many benefits in its application. For example, there are many occasions when an organization *should* take the market rate of interest and the minimum legal wage as environmental "givens" and manage its costs of capital and labor accordingly. Similarly, a firm may be well advised to operate *within* the technological "state of the art" thereby assuming that no breakthroughs are likely to disrupt its cost or price structures. There are also times when individual and collective behavior must *certainly* be held within a perceived ideological "consensus."

A danger in this approach is that it can make planning *too* easy. Problems are always easier to solve if they can be reduced or simplified. If factors can be excluded from consideration or if they can be positioned so that their influence is neutral or constant, so much the better for the problem-solver. But the hazards of oversimplification are manifest. In an environment characterized by accelerating inflation and militant workers, for example, managing as if the costs of capital and labor were fixed would clearly be irrational. Operating within the technological state of the art or within the traditional ideological consensus may deny either the possibility or probability of truly revolutionary change. Buggy whip manufacturers and horse traders who excluded horseless carriages from their thoughts probably slept easier than those who did not. But which was the wiser? Ecology was, for years, segregated as the preoccupation of "bird and bunny people." Today, it is the preoccupation of us all. It was, in short, a concern that simply could not be ignored and would not go away.

Environmental Analysis for Management is a casebook in coping with economic, political, social, and technical concerns that cannot be ignored and will not go away. It addresses situations in which managers have to deal with hazards and opportunities that are "environmentally intensive." That is to say, it considers problems that are very difficult for the manager or his organization to internalize; problems that do not lend themselves to self-centered, unilateral definition or solution; problems that inevitably evoke community-centered, multilateral action. The individual manager and his organization have a "stake" in the outcome, but they are *in and of themselves* unable to buffer the hazard or to benefit from the opportunity. Their only hope for constructive change turns upon their willingness and ability to engage in collective, non-adversary action with other "stakeholders" in seeking equitable solutions. Managing environmentally intensive problems most often turns out to be managing a complex set of conflicting relationships with other groups and organizations.

The cases deal with real problems of real organizations. Collectively, they bear evidence to the existence, importance, and persistence of environmental changes that underlie the more visible and transitory activities of purposive organizations. Individually, the cases emphasize the attention such changes should command in the strategic planning process of such organizations.

The cases present a spectrum of approaches to problem formulation and solution ranging from the philosophical to the scientific. The direction of influence also varies. At times, the organizational strategies and structures are varied in response to overwhelming environmental constancy. Throughout, however, the focus is upon the manager and the challenging task he faces in solving what often seem insoluable problems.

The concepts and cases contained in this book have been developed in two Harvard Business School courses: Planning in the Business Environment, which entered the required first-year curriculum of the MBA Program in 1963, and its successor, Environmental Analysis for Management, which took its present name in 1972.

The authors fully acknowledge their debts to the following present or former faculty colleagues whose contributions to those courses and to this book have been manifold: Raymond A. Bauer; Robert D. Behn; Norman A. Berg; David L. Birch; Ram Charan; Paul W. Cherington; Paul W. Cook, Jr.; Lawrence E. Fouraker; John D. Glover; W. Warren Haynes; Charles E. Johnson; E. Robert Livernash; Vincent E. O'Brien; George A. von Peterffy; Thomas C. Raymond; David C. D. Rogers; Lewis M. Schneider; Lawrence E. Thompson; and Nancy N. Wardell.

Our thanks also go to the more than 9,000 students who have suffered the growth pangs of "PBE" and "EAM" but who, we hope, have become better managers in the process.

Finally, we express our appreciation in this edition to Sue Hunt, Pat Potter, Judy Brown, and Joyce Milunsky who carried out the tedious, painstaking details of proofreading and editing.

February 1974   JAMES P. BAUGHMAN
                             GEORGE C. LODGE
                             HOWARD W. PIFER, III

Contents

IV   Unions and other interest groups

V   Environmental issues facing management

PART I

Introductory case series

Westinghouse Transportation Division (A)[1]

In June of 1963, Westinghouse Electric Corporation formally committed itself to trying to apply a "system approach" to one of the knottiest of urban problems, public transportation. Westinghouse had for decades acted as a supplier of electrical equipment for the manufacturers of rail rapid transit[2] vehicles. This pattern of acting only as a supplier was broken when Westinghouse decided to become the designer and prime contractor for a prototype of an automated rapid transit system. The Westinghouse system, called "Transit Expressway," was backed by top management as an answer to the transportation problems of medium-size U.S. cities. Contracts were signed with several agencies in June 1963, for the construction of a two-mile test track in Pittsburgh's South Park.

THE ORGANIZATION OF WESTINGHOUSE ELECTRIC CORPORATION

Westinghouse Electric Corporation, one of the world's largest electrical equipment suppliers, was founded with 200 employees in 1886 by

[1] This case was made possible by Westinghouse Electric Corporation. It was prepared by Christopher G. Russell, research assistant, under the direction of Professor John D. Glover, and Professor Thomas C. Raymond as a basis for class discussion rather than to illustrate either effective or ineffective handling of an administrative situation. The Transportation Division was not formally established until 1967.

[2] Rail rapid transit: operation of electrified rail vehicles on grade-separated rights-of-way.

George Westinghouse. From its inception, the company sold equipment for the rail transit industry, such sales at one time being a far larger percentage of total sales than in 1969, the time of the writing of the case. In 1969, the company employed about 100,000 people in the manufacture of 8,000 basic products. Annual sales of over $3 billion were derived from products as diverse as Christmas tree bulbs and nuclear reactors.

Westinghouse operated as a decentralized organization with many subsidiaries and divisions in widely spread locations. The company organized its products into six principal groups: (1) Electric Utility, (2) Industrial, (3) Construction, (4) Consumer, (5) Electronic Components and Specialty Products, (6) Aerospace, Defense, and Marine.

Each group was further broken down into from 10 to 15 product divisions. The Transportation Division, for instance, belonged to the Industrial Group.

THE TRANSIT EXPRESSWAY PROJECT

Transit Expressway was designed to overcome three problems that Westinghouse believed had prevented the construction of rapid transit systems in any but the largest U.S. cities. The transportation systems engineers at Westinghouse identified these problems as: (1) initial high capital costs, (2) high operating costs relative to the revenues derivable, (3) poor esthetic characteristics of the vehicles and their operation, (4) lack of a "systems approach" or comprehensive planning in the design of metropolitan transit systems.

The problem of high capital cost was to be tackled by designing vehicles lighter and smaller than traditional rail transit equipment, and thus more adapted to medium-size cities. The problem of high operating cost was to be attacked by developing an automatic control system for the trains, and also by using smaller, more economical vehicles. To ensure passenger comfort and convenience, the vehicles were designed to provide almost instant service, and to have the ride characteristics of a fine, air-conditioned automobile. In appearance, the Transit Expressway trains would resemble conventional rapid transit trains except that the vehicles would be smaller and would run on rubber tires rather than steel wheels. An artist's conception of the system appears in Exhibit 1. The drawing shows the rubber-tired vehicle running within a concrete "trough," the high outside curb being designed to prevent the escape of the vehicle. The drawing also illustrates one concept of the "systems approach," that mass transit systems should be coordinated with highway systems in order to minimize total costs. Right-of-way costs for transit systems are normally a substantial percentage of total construction costs (about 10 percent). The incremental right-of-way cost of putting Transit Expressway in a highway median strip was expected to be quite small; however, Westinghouse planners also anticipated that the lightweight supporting structure could be planned alongside many existing expressways.

Westinghouse intended Transit Expressway to fill a gap in the public transportation market that the company felt existed between the transportation services that could be provided by buses operating on public streets, and those services that could be provided by a conventional rapid transit system. Exhibit 2 shows that in many respects the characteristics of Transit Expressway were intermediate between those of bus operation and those of rail rapid transit. Transit Expressway vehicles, for instance, would have greater passenger-moving capability than a large bus. Nevertheless, each Transit Expressway car was designed to weigh only 8,575 pounds, the weight of two large automobiles.

Westinghouse's traditional rail rapid transit business

Westinghouse had been in the business of producing rail transit electrical equipment for more than 75 years. Westinghouse's early production of motors and controls for streetcars was eventually superceded by production of motors and controls for rail rapid transit systems—subways and elevated electric railways. Since 1946, Westinghouse's total production of such equipment for the U.S. market had exceeded that of any one of its competitors. In the years prior to 1969, the Transportation Division had averaged about $15 million in annual sales.[3] Westinghouse had high hopes that the development of the Transit Expressway system might greatly increase the company's sales to the transit industry. From a technical point of view, the rail rapid transit business had changed little in the previous 50 years. Powerful electric motors still drove steel wheels on steel rails, and, in effect, conveyed a "boxful" of people from one point to another. The motors (usually four 100 hp motors per car) had been improved somewhat to provide more power for less weight, and the heavy steel of the traditional car body had been replaced by lighter metals. Some transit cars had been air-conditioned, and more efficient electrical controls had been installed.

The marketing of rail rapid transit equipment followed a traditional and consistent pattern. The market for such equipment remained confined to a few large cities; New York and Chicago accounted for 85 percent of total purchases. Transit operators had ordered an annual average of 400 cars during the decade prior to 1969. The New York City Transit Authority's annual orders ranged from 100 to 400 cars.

---

[3] The estimate is based on ·the aggregate value of transit car business and the proportion of motors and control equipment supplied by Westinghouse. The company does not publish division sales figures.

The remainder of the market was provided by a few smaller cities—Boston, Philadelphia, and Cleveland.

The limited nature of the rail rapid transit market encouraged aggressive competition among the three, long-standing suppliers of rail vehicles—the St. Louis Car Division of General Steel Corporation, the Budd Company's Railway Division, and the Pullman-Standard Division of Pullman Inc. All of the car builders had considerable excess capacity. St. Louis Car was once the largest manufacturer of streetcars in the world. (No new streetcars have been sold in the United States since 1955.) Both Budd and Pullman experienced sharp declines in order for conventional railroad passenger equipment, and thus tried to expand their rail rapid transit business. In recent years, the Pullman Car Works in Chicago had occasionally operated at less than 10 percent of capacity. A Westinghouse spokesman said that due to the stagnation of the market, the competition among the car builders could be described as "cutthroat."

The transit authorities in the large cities had men trained in transit engineering who wrote specifications for the new equipment ordered. The car builders usually deferred to transit authority preferences in types of electrical equipment installed. One result was that transit authorities and car builders divided orders for electrical equipment among Westinghouse, General Electric Company's Transportation Systems Division, and an occasional smaller competitor.

The electrical and control equipment installed in a transit car represented a large percentage of the car's total cost. Transit vehicles cost about $125,000, and the electrical and control equipment accounted for up to 45 percent of the total value, or up to $56,000.

Mr. W. P. (Perry) Bollinger, general manager of Westinghouse's Transportation Division, described how Westinghouse worked with the car builders and the transit authorities in marketing its traditional transit equipment:

> We influence the specifications for transit equipment by working with the engineers of a transit authority. Usually, you're working with one or two guys, so there's no question who you're dealing with. We work with the car builder too, and since he's usually concerned with price, it then becomes a strategic battle as to who's going to give the most. That's a fairly straightforward business.

The marketing of Transit Expressway, Mr. Bollinger said, had proved to be considerably more complex than the marketing of the company's traditional rail transit products.

> An entire transit system (like Transit Expressway) costs many times more than a single-car order. Back at the buyer level, the decision

to buy cars is a lot easier than the decision to buy an entire transit system. New York, for example, buys cars on the basis of the state's borrowing power, plus commitments they get from the federal government, from HUD (Department of Housing and Urban Development). When a city wants to build a new transportation system, like San Francisco did, there is a tremendous selling job to do. It's necessary to go direct to the public and try to get them to agree to tax themselves more heavily. This makes it entirely different than just selling transit equipment.

ORIGINS OF THE TRANSIT EXPRESSWAY PROJECT

In the early 1960s numerous books and articles popularized the concept that the nation's major cities were being strangled by automobile congestion. This concern developed into substantial support for federal legislation to improve urban transportation, both through improved urban highways and through modern rail rapid transit systems.

The viewpoint favoring improved rail transit had strong advocates in Pittsburgh, the location of Westinghouse's executive offices. Patrick J. Cusick, Jr., executive director of the Pittsburgh Regional Planning Association, challenged local industry in 1962 to provide a modern transit system that could effectively compete with the automobile and so reduce rush-hour traffic.

John E. McNulty, marketing manager for the Westinghouse Transportation Division, described Westinghouse's gradual involvement, and the steps that led up to the construction of the prototype Transit Expressway system:

> This thing would not have been picked up if top management had not taken the initiative. Mark Cresap, president at the time, requested that some attention be given to the idea. The idea then just began to grow. It was timely. President Kennedy had just written a message to Congress on the subject of urban transportation.
>
> Westinghouse had a staff organization on transportation with a fellow named Charlie Kerr who followed the transit industry. Charlie was in his 60s, but he had unusual conceptual ability, and he set out to design a system. He set up all the original criteria, including the idea that the system should have the ride characteristics of a fine automobile, a Lincoln. He started with a concept of using a continuous, circulating belt. From this, he evolved to the idea of having an automated vehicle run on a loop.

Mr. McNulty said that Kerr's final concept was that of an integrated system of supporting structures and electronically controlled vehicles. The objective was a system with lower capital and operating costs than those associated with conventional transit operations, such operations often being hampered by the piecemeal acquisition of vehicles and electrical equipment. As Mr. Kerr saw it, the chief way to reduce operating costs was to use automated equipment; capital costs were to be reduced by designing lightweight vehicles and a lightweight "aerial" roadway.

The construction cost of the roadway was the largest single component (up to 65 percent) in the total cost of constructing a rapid transit system. Because of this consideration, Westinghouse engineered Transit Expressway to operate on a lightweight aerial structure rather than in a tunnel. The sketch in Exhibit 1 shows the vehicle in its anticipated mode of operation. In Exhibit 3, the Transit Expressway structure is shown compared to aerial structures for three other modern rapid transit systems. Preliminary estimates indicated that the precast concrete structure would cost from $2 million to $3 million per two-lane route mile. A tunnelized roadway was estimated to cost up to $10 million per mile.

DESIGNING FOR THE "CUSTOMER"

Transit Expressway was designed to attract passengers by providing a more desirable service than could be provided by the automobile. Mr. Kerr was credited with developing the following design criteria for Transit Expressway on the basis of what he felt the public wanted:

1. *Frequent service:* The modern commuter is not disposed to wait patiently for a train, because he feels that, as an alternative, he could always jump in his car and obtain instant transportation at the turn of a key. Transit Expressway was therefore to be designed to operate with maximum headways of 120 seconds between trains, 24 hours a day. A traveler would have an average wait of one minute under such circumstances. The desirability of having such frequent service reinforced the need for lightweight, automated cars in order to keep operating costs to a minimum.
2. *Comfort:* As automobiles have been provided with bucket seats, sound proofing, air conditioning, and tinted glass, they have contrasted ever more favorably with conventional mass transportation. Transit Expressway would reverse the trend. To avoid giving the impression of "mass" transportation, the vehicles would be relatively small, having only 20 bucket seats. No provisions were made for standees, as it was intended to provide greater capacity in peak hours by running ten-car trains, and reducing headways to 90 seconds. Sound levels in the cars were to be kept low, and the internal temperatures maintained within comfortable limits. The windows would be tinted to reduce glare and the heat of the sun.
3. *Appearance:* The cars, stations and roadway would be designed to be as attractive as possible. Again, the use of lightweight materials

would make it possible to avoid the ponderous designs of conventional transit systems. The "aerial" (to escape from the connotation of "elevated") structures would be designed to use graceful, single-pillar supports rather than a maze of steel posts.

4. *Safety:* Urban rapid transit systems were already classified as one of the safest forms of transportation in the world. A new type of rapid transit system, such as Transit Expressway. in which the motorman would be eliminated would have to be equally safe.

5. *Lightweight construction:* The need for lightweight construction was reinforced by the other criteria affecting appearance and cost. Lightweight metals and plastics were specified for the car bodies. Use of single axles with modern suspension would permit significant weight reduction over the standard double-axle, steel-wheeled truck. Use of rubber tires would further reduce weight and noise when compared to steel wheels, and they would also improve ride characteristics, and utilize present state-of-the-art automotive components.

6. *Cost:* Mr. Kerr envisioned the Transit Expressway as a mass-produced system of preengineered components. He considered his projected cost figures (on a mass-production basis) to be so attractive that there was no doubt in his mind that the system would have worldwide application. He did foresee, however, that such low costs would be obtainable in the first few years with only limited quantity production.

John McNulty, marketing manager for the division, continued his explanation of the project's development,

> Once Mr. Kerr had the design criteria set, the project was presented to Westinghouse top management. It was approved, and taken next to the Pittsburgh Regional Planning Association. With their blessing, it was finally taken to Washington, to HHFA (Housing and Home Finance Agency, later to become HUD). Mr. Weaver (Robert C. Weaver, administrator of HHFA) liked it, especially because HHFA was looking for a place to put its bets on urban transportation. I question whether the idea would have gotten the support that was forthcoming from the state and county had it not been for the federal interest. It was decided to construct a test track in South Park in order to further develop and evaluate the idea.

THE SOUTH PARK PROJECT

Transit Expressway was conceived as an ideal rapid transit system for a medium-size city. Westinghouse, understandably, hoped to sell the first complete system to Pittsburgh, and therefore planned to build the first prototype in Pittsburgh. Four different groups combined to fund the test and demonstration. The newly formed Port Authority of Allegheny County sponsored the project with the support of the Allegheny County Commissioners. The county commissioners made land available in South Park, a large, publicly owned recreational facility, located 11 miles south of the city's center. A two-mile test track was to be built with funds contributed by the state of Pennsylvania, the Port Authority and the federal government. The federal funds were to come from the HHFA Mass Transportation Demonstration Program.

Westinghouse also agreed to contribute heavily to the test because it stood to benefit from its success. Some contributions were also raised from other Pittsburgh-area companies like Bethlehem Steel which provided materials and engineering for the roadway. The following summarizes the financing:

Federal Housing and Home Finance Agency	$2,872,000
Port Authority of Allegheny County	886,000
Pennsylvania State Department of Commerce	200,000
Westinghouse Electric Corp. and others	1,042,000
	$5,000,000

The agreement between Westinghouse and the governmental agencies provided Westinghouse with three options if project costs exceeded $5 million. Westinghouse could (1) reduce the scale of the project, (2) request an additional authorization from the HHFA, or (3) absorb the extra cost itself.

THE MARKETING PLAN FOR TRANSIT EXPRESSWAY

Transit Expressway was not designed with the passenger-carrying capacity to enable it to replace existing rapid transit systems in the larger cities. The marketing department of the Transportation Division, therefore, saw the prime customer as the medium-size city which was beginning to experience severe traffic congestion, and the large city which might need to supplement an existing rail transit system. Twenty cities were estimated to be in or approaching this category (Exhibit 4).

Mr. Bollinger stated his conception of the market,

> There are many municipalities the size of Pittsburgh with a million or two population. Unlike New York and Boston, which may generate passenger capacities of 60,000 people per hour on a given line, these medium-size cities and some areas of the larger cities may require capacities of only 10,000 per hour. They'll never grow to be any more than that because of the nature of the way the cities are built. You need a different type of system for those passenger capacities, something you can afford to operate. You can't send a Cadillac to do a Chevy job.

The marketing department felt that the promotional campaign for Transit Expressway would have to be directed on a broad front rather than aimed at a specific group of prospective buyers. Although most of the medium-sized cities considered by Westinghouse had transit authorities, these authorities had neither the resources nor the authorization to spend large sums of money. The funds to build an entire transit system would have to be raised either through a municipal bond issue or through state and federal contributions.

Westinghouse planned to take its message on the advantages of the systems approach to all those the company thought might have some bearing on the issue. Advertisements were prepared both for popular magazines and trade journals. An 18-minute promotional film was developed for showing to groups of prominent individuals. Once the South Park test track was completed, Westinghouse planned to give demonstration rides to representatives of interested organizations and the general public in order to prove that a working prototype of the Transit Expressway system could actually be built.

No marketing surveys were conducted to determine if there was a demand for Transit Expressway, as it was felt the need was apparent in the congested highways of urban areas. John McNulty explained Westinghouse's attitude on this point:

> If we had done a market survey first to find out if there was a market for a system like ours, it probably would have told us that there was no market, no demand. Burnham (current Westinghouse president, Donald C. Burnham) has said that you have to throw the bait before the public in order to create a demand. Our Transit Expressway is the same as the electric toothbrush. The public didn't know it would want an electric toothbrush until it could see one. We built the South Park test track partly so that the public could see our system.

EXHIBIT 1
An artist's conception of Transit Expressway (1963)

EXHIBIT 2
Statistical comparison of three modes of transportation

Characteristic	BART transit car*	Transit Expressway	GMC bus†
Length	85'	23'4"	40'
Weight	70,000 lb.	8,575 lb.	20,000 lb.
Maximum speed.	80 mph	50 mph	60 mph
System speed‡	40–50 mph	30–40 mph	9 mph
Seating capacity.	80	20	40–50
Cost of vehicle.	$250,000	$65,000 (est.)	$35,000
Per-mile cost of roadway.	$6 million	$1.5 million	footnote§
Hourly passenger-moving capacity	40,000	8,000	3000–5000‖

* San Francisco's Bay Area Rapid Transit System was scheduled to go into operation in 1971, and to employ the latest technology applicable to conventional rail rapid transit. BART's system speed was to be twice that of existing rail rapid transit operations.

† General Motors Corporation manufactured over 90 percent of the transit buses sold in 1967.

‡ System speed is the average speed including stops for stations.

§ Buses operate on essentially free roadways, the cost being met out of automotive gasoline taxes.

‖ A bus line operating at capacity on city streets.

Source: Information supplied by the Westinghouse Electric Corp., the Massachusetts Bay Transportation Authority, and the Bay Area Rapid Transit District (San Francisco).

EXHIBIT 3
Aerial structures for rapid transit systems

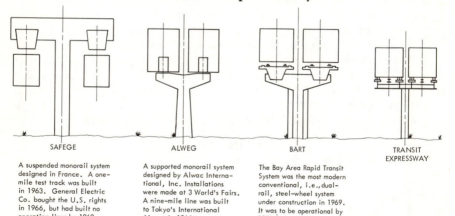

SAFEGE	ALWEG	BART	TRANSIT EXPRESSWAY

A suspended monorail system designed in France. A one-mile test track was built in 1963. General Electric Co. bought the U.S. rights in 1966, but had built no operating lines by 1969.

A supported monorail system designed by Alwac International, Inc. Installations were made at 3 World's Fairs. A nine-mile line was built to Tokyo's International Airport in 1964.

The Bay Area Rapid Transit System was the most modern conventional, i.e.,dual-rail, steel–wheel system under construction in 1969. It was to be operational by 1971.

Source: Westinghouse Electric Corporation.

EXHIBIT 4

Population statistics of the largest 20 urbanized areas

Urbanized area	Rank	Population			Population density (persons per sq. mile)			Population increase 1960–1966
		Central city	Suburbs	Total	Central city	Suburbs	Total	
Atlanta	21	487,455	280,670	768,125	3,802	2,387	3,125	23.7%
Baltimore	12	939,024	479,924	1,418,948	11,886	3,396	6,441	9.8
Boston	6	697,197	1,716,039	2,413,236	14,586	3,667	4,679	3.0
Buffalo	19	532,759	521,611	1,054,370	13,522	4,318	6,582	1.2
Chicago	3	3,550,404	2,408,809	5,959,213	15,836	3,273	6,209	8.2
Cincinnati	16	502,550	491,018	993,568	6,501	2,976	4,101	6.7
Cleveland	11	876,050	908,941	1,784,991	10,789	1,798	3,042	5.0
Dallas	17	679,684	252,665	932,349	2,428	688	1,441	20.8
Detroit	5	1,670,144	1,867,565	3,537,709	11,964	3,153	4,834	7.9
Houston	14	938,219	201,459	1,139,678	2,860	1,967	2,647	22.7
Jacksonville	63	201,030	171,539	372,569	6,657	2,113	3,344	9.8
Los Angeles	2	2,479,015	4,009,776	6,488,791	5,451	4,382	4,736	12.7
Miami	27	291,688	561,017	852,705	8,529	3,768	4,657	15.6
New York	1	7,781,984	6,332,943	14,114,927	24,697	4,018	7,462	6.7
Philadelphia	4	2,002,512	1,632,716	3,635,228	15,743	3,478	6,092	8.0
Pittsburgh	9	604,332	1,200,068	1,804,400	11,171	2,548	3,437	-1.2
St. Louis	10	750,026	917,667	1,667,693	12,296	3,500	5,160	8.5
San Francisco	7	740,316	1,690,347	2,430,663	15,553	3,232	4,253	11.7
Seattle	22	557,087	307,022	864,109	6,295	2,050	3,626	9.7
Washington, D.C.	8	763,956	1,044,467	1,808,423	12,442	3,740	5,308	26.7
Totals		27,045,432	26,996,263	54,041,695				
Average densities					10,028	3,295	4,963	

Note: Population changes 1960–1966 are calculated on the basis of Standard Metropolitan Statistical Areas.
Source: Automotive Safety Foundation 1964, *United States Statistical Handbook, 1968.*

APPENDIX

Aspects of the Pittsburgh environment

The following are excerpts from a *U.S. News & World Report* interview with Joseph M. Barr, mayor of Pittsburgh.

I think, if you were to be blindfolded, go into any city, and listen to its mayor, you would be unable to tell which city you were visiting. We are all in the same financial boat. All of us are going bankrupt, although some cities are too stubborn to admit it. Even small municipalities, when they run out of land to develop, are in trouble.

The key problem is that the city depends mainly upon real estate taxes for revenue. And that is a losing game. You cannot build a modern city on a real estate tax base. We have raised real estate taxes to the point where they cannot be raised much more, homeowners cannot take it any more. If we tried to raise real estate taxes now, our bridges would not be wide enough to accommodate all the people fleeing, bag and baggage, to outlying areas. We are killing the goose that laid the golden egg.

☆   ☆   ☆   ☆   ☆

The city has annexed only 2 square miles of land since 1930. Residents of other municipalities in Allegheny County, while they work here, use our roads, use our hospitals, pay almost nothing to the city. It is inequitable for an area of 55 square miles to support an area of 730 square miles, acting as a conduit or terminal for employment, health, education, entertainment, culture, traffic, sewage, and so on.

☆   ☆   ☆   ☆   ☆

Added to the fact that we cannot annex land, more and more land in Pittsburgh is tax-exempt, used by schools, hospitals, and other nonprofit organizations. One third of the real estate in Pittsburgh is now tax-exempt. Planned expansions of our colleges, hospitals, and similar organizations will increase this ratio in future years.

☆   ☆   ☆   ☆   ☆

We have experienced heavy outmigration. The population of the city today is 570,000. At its peak in 1950 it was 677,000. Our population will soon be back to the 1920 level.

During the 1950–60 period, we lost 92,000 people 20 to 44 years of age in middle income brackets. We have an increasing proportion of elderly people, many living on fixed incomes; and an increasing proportion of Negroes, many in lower income brackets. This is one factor in our reluctance to push up our real estate taxes.

☆   ☆   ☆   ☆   ☆

Actually, the Federal Government has been subsidizing outmigration and the development of suburbs. For a long time, the Federal Housing Administration would not approve home loans in the city because it feared deteriorating neighborhoods and declining property values. At the same time they approved thousands of home loans in the suburbs, and this was exacerbated by the Veterans Administration's GI home-loan program.

This, of course, speeded up deterioration and hastened outmigration. There is money for interstate highways and beltways serving the suburbs. There is money to develop water and sewer systems in suburbs. There is little or no money for housing, mass transportation, and other central-city problems.

✸ ✸ ✸ ✸ ✸

On mass transit, the Federal Government provided a small amount of money for "consultants." We are overrun with consultants trying to tell us how to solve our problems. But we are being nickeled and dimed on funds for equipment. When you have no money, all you do is keep studying something over and over again.

✸ ✸ ✸ ✸ ✸

We do not have home rule here. We have little power over the administrative structure of the city. If we want to set up a department of transportation, or to reorganize the city government, we must go to the legislature in Harrisburg. We have no power to impose new taxes, and cannot even raise rates on most taxes we are permitted to levy. We do not even have control over personnel practices and the wages we pay our policemen and firemen.

When we run into financial problems, we must go hat in hand to Harrisburg. We come back with the same hat in the same hand. The one-man, one-vote ruling has not helped us. It added more seats in the suburbs. The suburban legislators work with those from rural areas to block funds for cities. All someone has to do is raise the cry of "metropolitanism" and we are beaten. I served 20 years in the State senate. I think the group there now has less understanding of city problems than when I started.

✸ ✸ ✸ ✸ ✸

How can we solve our problems? We can't as long as we must depend on property taxes. There must be a redistribution of the tax burden.

Massive federal aid is needed for capital construction. Only the Federal Government has the money. We should have a six-year capital budget—a firm, unalterable commitment on such programs as housing, transportation, air and water pollution, schools—those items needed to rehabilitate our urban areas. This is the only way we can intelligently plan and build and show steady, measurable progress.

Westinghouse Transportation Division (B)[1]

WESTINGHOUSE's Transportation Division early experienced difficulties in staying within the terms of the $5 million contract for the Transit Expressway project at South Park. This departure from budgeted cost was expensive, as Westinghouse chose to make up the difference rather than diminish the scale of the project. Two major factors caused the variance from projected cost. First, the quality of the original design for the South Park vehicle was upgraded. Secondly, Westinghouse underestimated the lead time and the man-hours necessary to complete specific parts of the complex project.

The redesigned South Park vehicle carried 28 seated passengers, and up to 70 passengers with 42 persons standing. The length was increased to more than 30 feet. As a result of the alterations, the vehicle's weight more than doubled.

After accompanying John McNulty, Marketing Manager, on a tour of the South Park Project, the casewriter could testify both as to the comfort of the vehicle and the accuracy of the computer control. The operation of the vehicle was virtually without noise or vibration, whether observed from inside or out. The vehicle automatically decelerated for curves, not so much for safety's sake as to prevent discomfort to the

[1] This case was made possible by Westinghouse Electric Corporation. It was prepared by Christopher G. Russell, research assistant, under the direction of Professor John D. Glover and Professor Thomas C. Raymond as the basis for class discussion rather than to illustrate either effective or ineffective handling of an administrative situation.

passengers. Before beginning the test ride, Mr. McNulty laid one penny on the station platform and another penny on the floor of the car. After a two-mile circuit, the train stopped with both pennies exactly aligned.

REORGANIZATION

The budget on the South Park Project was overshot by a large enough margin that top management felt a reorganization was necessary. Prior to the reorganization in mid-1965, Transit Expressway had been a project of what was titled the "Transportation Systems Department." As a deficit operation, it had been kept separate (with its own manager) from the Traction Division which had been profitably turning out conventional rail transit motors and controls. At this time, the Traction Division, plus two other divisions, Industrial Equipment and Repair fell under the control of George W. Jernstedt, general manager. Westinghouse top management wished to combine the Transportation Systems Department with the Traction Department. The management team in the Traction Division generally opposed the incorporation of the Transit Expressway project. It was felt that Transit Expressway would only detract from the profitability of the division. There were also other considerations as Mr. Jernstedt explained, "It's confused things over here; there are so many political problems associated with urban transportation. I now spend as much as half my time on Transit Expressway."

In January 1967, Westinghouse top management went ahead with the plan to consolidate the Transportation Systems Department with the Traction Division to form the new Transportation Division. A new manager, Mr. W. P. (Perry) Bollinger, was placed in charge under Mr. Jernstedt's authority. Mr. Bollinger had come to Westinghouse Electric from Westinghouse Air Brake Co. (WABCO), a traditional supplier of transit equipment and, at times, a stiff competitor of Westinghouse Electric.

CASEWRITER:[2] I've gathered that things were a little out of control when you first came here; that you were brought in to do a job.

MR. BOLLINGER: Yes.

CASEWRITER: What do you do when you're the manager responsible for a profit center, and this type of project is given to you from the top? How are you held responsible for it?

MR. BOLLINGER: That's one of the reasons the whole thing was consolidated. Otherwise you had no hope of the project's ever being anything other than a loss situation. When you have a siuation like that, there's very little control over how big the loss will be. When everything was consolidated, the net result was profitable. Now we have annual objectives that are set on billings and profits. This is arrived at by a give-and-take negotiation that finally ends

---

[2] This interview took place in 1969.

as a commitment on the part of the general manager to produce a certain level of billings and profits for the whole division.

PROBLEMS WITH MARKETING TRANSIT EXPRESSWAY

The Transportation Division soon discovered that selling Transit Expressway was going to be considerably more difficult than had been expected, Mr. Bollinger said.

> It wasn't that there was lack of interested prospects for metropolitan rapid transit systems, we had inquiries from every major city in the country. Man, it was just what they wanted. "The mayor wants it, and he's going to have it, and come on out and give us a proposal and in no time at all you'll have a contract." That happened over and over and over again, but we never got any contracts. The problem is that the mayor may be as enthusiastic as can be, and he may even have a lot of friends in positions of power; but that doesn't mean anything is going to happen. This is one of the problems of our democracy; you've got to have public support to spend public dollars.

It came as a shock to the marketing department to discover that the customer was not whom he was assumed to be, that is, the transit authority, and the city government. John McNulty explained,

> Who is the customer? Not the public transit authorities. In Indianapolis and other cities, the authority members are real estate developers and lawyers by training. The Port Authority of Allegheny County (Pittsburgh) has no technical staff; they have to rely on consulting engineers.
>
> The consultant to the authority is normally the real customer, and it's a rare consultant who will take a risk on an innovative system. The consultant thinks he must protect his professional reputation. When he's faced with a project, he simply looks at what's existing and proven, and then simply cuts and pastes these items together. The only allies we have in an Authority who'll accept an innovating system are the architects and city planners. They're willing to take the risk, but don't usually have the influence.

There have been differing opinions within the Transportation Division as to the wisdom of keeping Transit Expressway as a proprietary product. Those longest associated with the project favored a more exclusive approach. After becoming responsible for the project in 1965, Mr. Jernstedt proposed to top management that Westinghouse's experience and designs be made available to the rest of the transit industry. His recommendation was rejected as "not timely." After the work at South Park was completed in 1966, Mr. Bollinger also suggested a more open approach. He specifically proposed having a large symposium, charging $100 a head for representatives from all interested companies in the transit industry, and providing them with detailed information on the South Park test. The object would have been to get more companies thinking in terms of Transit Expressway type systems, and perhaps selling more Westinghouse motors and controls as a by-product. The idea was finally rejected because it was felt the benefits might not offset the value of the information given away.

Another area of uncertainty within the Transportation Division was the extent to which the company had benefitted or would benefit from having taken a pioneering attitude toward Transit Expressway.

Mr. Bollinger offered qualified support for a pioneering approach, "If you wanted to minimize your risks, you'd never pioneer. Pioneering usually doesn't pay, but when it pays, it pays well." He went on to explain how he thought this applied to Transit Expressway:

> Let's say the system were bought the way we originally thought it would be; I mean, the customer purchasing an essentially turn-key operation. (Westinghouse was successful in atomic power with this approach.) I'm not sure it will happen, but let's say metropolitan transportation systems were bought this way. We could be at a competitive disadvantage in bidding on a system like that. We've made a substantial investment in Transit Expressway (estimated to be $4 million), and the competition hasn't made any. They could take a real dive on the job and not be out any more than we are.

Westinghouse's hopes for the future were raised by the initial federal support won from the Housing and Home Finance Administration. Mr. Bollinger commented on why he thought these hopes had proved optimistic:

> The Vietnamese war was surely part of the reason. We could build a metropolitan transportation system for a city the size of Pittsburgh every week for the money that's being put into that war. Now take a look at the current Department of Transportation activity. What there is of it is going into extensions of conventional systems. They've got $15 million this coming year to spend for R and D on technologically new systems. Why, those dollars wouldn't get you eight miles of track laid . . . a drop in the bucket. I'm not sure what the government's priorities will be when the war ends, but I doubt that urban transportation will be even second or third on the list.

CURRENT PROSPECTS FOR TRANSIT EXPRESSWAY SALES

"Two short years ago, most of us thought that we would sell a metropolitan transportation system on a turn-key basis," Mr. Bollinger said,

> Now some of us have doubts. We never asked ourselves, "Well fellas, how have they been sold in the past, and is there anything that's going to make that change?" Instead, we said, "This is the right thing to

do, we're the only ones that can provide a whole system, so they've got to buy the whole system from us." Well they don't have to buy the whole system from us. They can elect to do nothing at all, which is precisely what they have done.

The only cities where I can see any hope of selling a complete system within five years are Pittsburgh and Baltimore. In Baltimore, an independent consultant has made a study and recommended a system like Transit Expressway. We struggled to get that for some time. Until that happens you're not going to get anywhere. That hasn't happened yet in Pittsburgh, but, of course, we've got other things going for us here.

EXHIBIT 1
Public acceptance of Transit Expressway
(South Park test project)

1. Question 1 on survey of 2,500 riders: "What do you think of the ride?"

Possible response	Percent of total
"Quiet or very quiet"	78
"Noisy or very noisy"	14.5
"Can't say"	7.5

2. Question 2: "Would you object to Transit Expressway in your neighborhood?"

3. Question 3: "Would you object to Transit Expressway in business areas?"

Response	Question 2 (by percent)	Question 3 (by percent)
"Yes"	17.5	10.9
"Don't care"	8.2	5.7
"No"	64.6	80.6
"No response"	9.7	2.8

EXHIBIT 1 (*continued*)

4.   Question 4: "Would you use Transit Expressway instead of other existing transportation, public and private (given the conditions below)?"

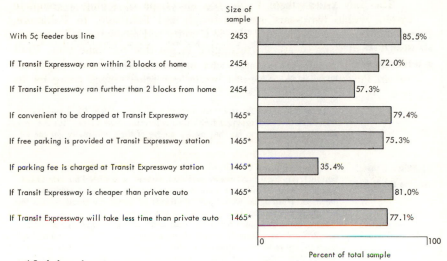

	Size of sample	
With 5¢ feeder bus line	2453	85.5%
If Transit Expressway ran within 2 blocks of home	2454	72.0%
If Transit Expressway ran further than 2 blocks from home	2454	57.3%
If convenient to be dropped at Transit Expressway	1465*	79.4%
If free parking is provided at Transit Expressway station	1465*	75.3%
If parking fee is charged at Transit Expressway station	1465*	35.4%
If Transit Expressway is cheaper than private auto	1465*	81.0%
If Transit Expressway will take less time than private auto	1465*	77.1%

Percent of total sample

* Includes only car owners.

Source: MPC Corporation, "Transit Expressway Report," developed under contract with the Department of Housing and Urban Development, 1967, p. 232.

APPENDIX

B\V   Transportation   outlook

April 26, 1969   WESTINGHOUSE TRANSPORTATION DIVISION (B)

Volpe maps out attack on mess in urban transit

Washington skeptics expected Transportation Secretary John A. Volpe to emphasize road building. Instead, the former federal highway administrator is going out of his way to promote mass transit.

Backed by a team of new advisers, Volpe is launching an early attack on the multitude of problems of urban transportation. Recently, he even raised the prospect of curtailing auto traffic in cities if those problems aren't relieved soon.

At the hub of the Transportation Dept.'s efforts are plans for a mass transit trust fund, now undergoing Administration scrutiny. Says Volpe: "It's the only sure way suggested so far that over a course of time will really get the job done."

$1-billion a year may be the ticket

Volpe's top urban adviser, former Seattle Mayor James Braman, now assistant secretary for urban systems and environment, sees a need for federal outlays of at least $1-billion a year to overhaul badly outmoded public transit networks. Washington would pay two-thirds of capital construction costs for new projects, probably by tapping auto excise taxes.

Local authorities, says Braman, "must know that federal aid is assured before they will be willing to embark on major expeditions" with planning lead times as long as 10 years. Braman would welcome state participation in a new federal-local arrangement, if they came in "as contributors, but not simply as middlemen."

A combination of guaranteed loans and direct grants to metropolitan authorities is the favored Washington approach. But direct subsidies to transit operators for new equipment are not ruled out.

New connections can unsnarl city

Braman's ideas run well beyond a trust fund. His newly created job is designed to coordinate auto, bus, rail, and air transportation plans for an urban setting. He will seek comprehensive planning on a regional scale to achieve balanced systems.

Federal authority for this approach already exists under the Demonstration Cities & Metropolitan Development Act of 1966. It provides for a comprehensive review of any federal loan or grant application to develop a transportation facility.

Braman sees massive concentration on urban road construction as the successor to the interstate highway program in the mid-1970s. He envisages a system of primary roads bringing cars to urban beltways ringing the inner city; the traffic load would feed into fringe garages or parking lots—not into already congested downtown areas. The rest of the trip to business or shopping centers would be by transit, with some center-city streets blocked to cars.

The road has a place in the future urban system, Braman indicates, but in downtown areas it would primarily carry shuttle buses.

The signs say 'no waiting'

All of this would be accomplished largely with today's technology. While he was mayor of Seattle, Braman asked Boeing Co. engineers to review promising new approaches such as dial-a-bus and personal rapid transit systems. They reported no breakthrough near enough on the horizon to justify holding up new planning for alternatives.

"Many cities are past the point of no return, others are fast approaching it," Braman says. "We can't wait; we have to begin now with what we have."

The changing environment of the transit industry[1]

Historical perspective

FOR MUCH of its 80-year history, the condition of the transit industry could be described as "sick." By the late 1960s transit operations had long been deficit-ridden; rolling stock had been permitted to deteriorate as a result; and the industry had been stagnant relative to the growth of other industrial sectors of the economy. In 1967, the basic product of the industry, transit vehicle miles, was almost identical with vehicle mileage in 1923.

The transit industry suffered directly and indirectly from technological advances in other industries. As a directly competitive technology, the private automobile offered the most serious threat. As early as 1923, the competitive effect of the automobile was becoming apparent. From then on, transit system operators found themselves catering increasingly

---

[1] Definitions of terms used in the text:

1. Transit: Includes urban, publicly and privately owned, motorbus lines, trolley-coach lines, electric street railways, and subway lines.
2. Rail transit: Excludes bus operations.
3. Rail rapid transit: Operation of electrified rail vehicles on grade-separated rights-of-way.
4. Rapid transit: Includes vehicles with rubber tires, such as a bus on an exclusive freeway lane.

This case has been prepared by Christopher G. Russell, research assistant, under the supervision of Professor John D. Glover, with the assistance of Associate Professor David C. D. Rogers.

to the poorer portions of the population that could not afford the generally superior transportation services offered by the automobile.

The technology of the transit industry in the 1960s remained much the same as the technology that prevailed in the 1920s. Partly for this reason, the productivity of labor in the industry showed little improvement over a 40-year period. The general rise in wage rates that prevailed throughout the economy was not accompanied by increasing productivity of labor in the transit industry. For various reasons, transit operators were unable to obtain fare increases that matched wage increases, and wages rose relative to revenues. Starting in the early 1930s, many insolvent transit companies passed into public control or ownership. Deficits often worsened thereafter as it became public policy to provide "service" to the economically disadvantaged by keeping fares low and running trains more frequently during off-peak hours.

Changes in urban land-use patterns also affected the transit industry adversely. Cities that matured in the age of rail transportation were built on a radial pattern. Residential "corridors" grew up around the transit lines that radiated from the downtown employment center. As personal incomes rose due to increased productivity, more people acquired automobiles. The automobile gave the urban population greater mobility, and permitted people to move away from the densely settled "corridors." The shift of the urban population toward a more uniform distribution complicated the task of transit passenger collection and distribution.

The urban automobile population swelled rapidly after World War II, while urban highway mileage increased at a much slower pace. Severe traffic congestion resulted in many cities. Although rapid transit systems were much more efficient movers of people than automobiles were, plans for improving public transit were kept in abeyance during the 1950s. Many cities waited to see if federal and state highway programs would reduce urban traffic congestion.

By the early 1960s, interest was renewing in public transit. The federal Mass Transportation Act was passed in 1964, providing two thirds of the capital cost of new transit projects. The Mass Transportation Act and the subsequent creation of a Department of Transportation did not initiate, however, the renaissance of the transit industry that some rail transit manufacturers expected. Financial and political difficulties complicated the construction and operation of new transit systems. The new federal legislation partially subsidized construction costs, but provided no assistance to systems that could not meet operating costs from revenues.

Political boundaries complicated the operation of metropolitan transit systems. Suburban dwellers, for instance, had generally not borne much of the cost of transit deficits, even though they benefited from public transportation services. The central cities, having attracted the elderly, the economically disadvantaged, and those in need of welfare assistance, found it difficult to bear the brunt of transit operating deficits, let alone the cost of constructing or modernizing a transit system. Despite all these difficulties, by 1967 several of the larger U.S. cities had undertaken new transit contruction in the belief that the ultimate benefits would offset the costs.

The dimensions of the transit industry

For the purposes of this note, the transit industry is defined as including the operators of urban transit systems, the suppliers of transit vehicles and their components, and the suppliers of external control systems for rail transit vehicles. Defined in this way, 1967 industry sales in the United States were roughly $1.8 billion. The gross investment in transit vehicles was approximately $2.8 billion. In 1967, there were $1,138 companies operating transit vehicles.

This note will focus on the operations of those 30 transit companies or authorities that were located in the 21 cities of over 500,000 population. It can be calculated from the figures in Exhibits 1 and 2 that nearly 60 percent of total motorbus passengers were transported in these few cities. All the electric rail transit systems of significance were operated in only five U.S. cities. Exhibit 3 provides selected statistics about the systems in these five cities plus recent trends in revenue passengers. By virtue of its size, the New York City Transit Authority dominates or influences all aggregations of rail transit statistics.

Only in a few cities, including Boston, Pittsburgh, Philadelphia, and San Francisco, did streetcar operations play a significant role in public transportation in 1967. In each of these cases, the streetcars operated largely on rights-of-way separated from automobile traffic.

Although the larger transit companies and authorities operate integrated bus and rail transit systems, it is useful to compare the two modes of public transit separately. It can be seen from Exhibit 4, that rail transit systems generate about one third the vehicle miles, revenue passengers, and operating revenues of bus systems. The number of rail transit vehicles is roughly one fifth of the number of buses however, indicating both the greater capacity and the more intensive usage of the average rail transit vehicle.

The transit industry is almost two industries in one, a rail transit industry wedded to a bus transit industry. The technologies of the electric traction motor and the internal combustion engines are profoundly different, and are suited to different kinds of transit vehicles. Because electrified vehicles receive their power from external sources, they are more adapted to operating on rails in large, interlocking, mass transportation systems. Gasoline or diesel-powered buses, having a self-contained power plant, are more adapted to operating as independent units. Because they run on rubber tires and compete with the automobile for use of public streets, buses rarely attain the speeds of electrified vehicles running on separate rights-of-way.

Buses had been produced as a sideline by the major automobile manufacturers. As such, buses have benefited from the enormous amounts of money that the automobile makers have invested in research on automobile technology. General Motors has a commanding position in transit bus manufacturing; it produced over 90 percent of transit motorbuses sold in 1967.

No one company comes close to dominating the manufacture of rail transit vehicles. Moreover, separate companies manufacture vehicle bodies and the electrical components. In 1967, three major manufacturers provided rail rapid transit cars[2] built to the specifications of the operators. These companies were St. Louis Car Division of General Steel Industries, Inc., Pullman-Standard Division of Pullman Inc., and the Budd Company's Railway Division.

The carbuilders manufacture the frame of the car; install running gear, electrical equipment, and interior furnishings according to the specifications of the operators. The traction equipment and controls alone account for 45 percent of the value of the finished car. A vehicle built by St. Louis Car might have wheel trucks built by the Rockwell Manufacturing Company, braking systems by Westinghouse Air Brake Company, motors by the Transportation Division of Westinghouse Electric Corporation, electric drive circuitry by the Transportation Systems Division of General Electric Company, and trackside train controls by the Sylvania Division of General Telephone and Electronics Company. The businesses of several of the electrical equipment manufacturers do overlap. Westinghouse Air Brake, for instance, makes control equipment as well as brake systems. Only Westinghouse Electric and General Electric, however, produce the full range of electrical equipment for transit cars.

Historical trends in the industry: 1888–1968

Prior to 1888, urban dwellers who wanted to get to work had to depend on their own legs or those of a horse. It is reported that in London as recently as 1854, over 200,000 people walked to jobs that were more than one hour away.[3] The electric streetcar was first operated

---

[2] Streetcars have not been manufactured since 1953.

[3] Lawrence Halprin, *Freeway* (New York: Reinhold Publishing Corp., 1966), p. 7.

in 1888 in Richmond, Virginia. Ten years later, Boston's streetcar operations had grown to such an extent that the Tremont Street line was put in a subway to avoid surface congestion.

Expansion was very rapid in the early years of the industry, and by 1910 it was capitalized at over $4 billion. Given the alternative means of transportation, there was a great demand for the services provided by electrified streetcars, and by subway and elevated trains running on separate rights-of-way. Equity securities in rail transit companies were in the "growth stocks" of the day. Privately generated funds dug the subways in New York (1904) and Philadelphia (1905) and erected the "Elevated" in Chicago, ringing the downtown with the famous "Loop" (1897).

The rail transit industry early faced the problem of operating in an environment susceptible to governmental regulation. Because of the services it rendered, the industry was open to public inspection and the attentions of the public's representatives. As the Institute of Rapid Transit pointed out in a brief historical outline, the industry played a role in attracting the public's unfavorable attention:

> It was a period when the theory of the "Trolley Trust" met wide acceptance. This idea gained credence from the notorious activities of a small minority of traction magnates such as Charles Yerkes, Chicago's "Goliath of Graft," and Philadelphia's P. A. B. Widener but, for the most part, was simply a natural outgrowth of the Tarbell-Steffens climate.[4] Nonetheless, municipal regulations increased. Franchises for new routes became more difficult to obtain and more subject to such onerous terms as requiring the company to pay 9 per cent of its gross revenues to maintain the public parks system, as in Baltimore. Concurrently with the deterioration in municipal relations, transit's public image began to slip.

Within 20 years, even prior to the impact of the gasoline engine, the urban rail transit industry was in trouble. In the first decade of the century, the industry had adopted a rigid fare system, five cents a ride. Rapid inflation during the First World War, plus overbuilding of street railways, made a five-cent fare unprofitable. By 1919, one third of the operating companies were bankrupt.

Automotive competition

Prior to the 1920s, electric streetcars had enjoyed a virtual monopoly in the field of local public transportation. By 1923, the competitive effect

---

[4] At the turn of the century a group of "muck-rakers," including Ida Tarbell and Lincoln Steffens publicized activities they felt jeopardized the public welfare just as Ralph Nader publicized the auto safety issue in the 1960s.

of the private auto was becoming significant. As Exhibit 5 shows, the rail transit sector of the industry reached an all-time high that year 15.7 billion passengers carried. In succeeding years, the public increasingly substituted the automobile for the streetcar, especially for pleasure riding on weekends and in the evenings. (Note quadrupling of automobile usage between 1922 and 1931 as given in Exhibit 7.) As early as 1927, it was apparent that the transit industry was stagnating. Exhibit 6 shows that streetcars, rapid transit vehicles, and even buses were delivered in decreasing numbers for almost a decade. *Moody's Public Utilities Manual* (1928) commented in a summary of the transit industry:[5]

> One cause of the great decline was of course the lack of suitable earning power on the capital invested in this business. Political ignorance and stupidity were for a long time the greatest handicap to which the industry was subjected; for politicians can never fully learn that wealth and capital have to be produced with much effort, and that capital will not flow into a business which does not pay a fair return.

In 1933, *Moody's Public Utilities Manual* pinpointed other reasons for the decline, including "the development in use of automobiles, the construction of auto highways, and the decreasing efficiency of urban transit [streetcars] as a result of growing traffic congestion."[6]

Between 1923 and 1930, fares had been revised upwards, but because of declines in passenger traffic, increased fares failed to produce increased revenues. The Great Depression neither slowed nor hurried the decline of the industry. The industry did benefit, as Exhibit 7 indicates, from the fact that auto travel did not increase for about five years during that period. The benefits from this easing of competition and from the decrease in average annual wages paid in the transit industry were offset, however, by the effects of the population's having decreased income. Many people who still had jobs walked to work. Others deferred traveling to stores and movies.

A trend began between 1935 and 1940 that would have great significance for manufacturers such as St. Louis Car Company and its suppliers of electrical equipment. As Exhibit 8 shows, the number of existing surface rail transit cars (largely streetcars) dropped by 13,420 units in five years while the number of trolley coaches and motorbuses owned increased by 14,024. The substitution of buses for streetcars offered a way of cutting costs at a time when the operating profits of transit companies were being tightly squeezed by falling patronage. Streetcar rolling stock and track replacement had been deferred in the early years of the depression, so that by the late 30s many companies faced the

---

[5] *Moody's Public Utilities Manual,* 1928, p. xxxi.

[6] *Moody's,* 1933, p. a 116.

necessity of replacing a substantial part of their equipment and trackage. Substitution of buses for streetcars was a way of reducing capital outlays in depressed times.

The coming of the Second World War brought a sudden resurgence for the transit industry. In order to increase the resources available for the war effort, the government encouraged the use of public transit and discouraged the use of the private automobile. Manufacture of buses and streetcars was expanded, as Exhibit 6 illustrates. The rationing of gasoline and rubber tires restricted the use of the existing auto population. As a result of such unusual conditions, operating income of transit companies reached an industry high in 1943.

The postwar inflation of transit wages; the growth of the auto population

The nation's return to a freer peacetime economy brought with it a dramatic decline in transit operating income. Rationing had forced people to build up large savings that they were now anxious to spend. Previously hemmed in by wartime restrictions, potential consumers now placed the automobile at the top of the list of things they wanted to buy. The automobile became a symbol of personal freedom.

The squeeze placed on the transit industry after 1945 was similar to that imposed during World War I, except that the government's fiscal policy during World War II had deferred inflation to the postwar period. The structure of the transit industry aggravated its sufferings. For one thing, the public and its representatives had grown accustomed to a rigid fare structure, and always opposed upward revisions. At the same time, rapidly rising wage rates bore heavily on the industry; the payroll was by far the largest operating expense. Many private companies that had not succumbed in the 20s and 30s now moved into public hands.

"Surface" transit operations suffered more than "rapid" transit from the postwar inflation and the inroads of the automobile. The surface streetcar networks were drastically pruned between 1945 and 1955, and there was no comparable increase in the bus population (Exhibit 8). The relatively stable statistic for the bus population conceals the fact that bus operations were dropped or curtailed in low population density areas, and large-seating-capacity buses were substituted on streetcar lines. Again, streetcar replacement usually meant a reduction in costs. Labor costs were reduced when large, one-man buses were used to replace two-man streetcars. Also, the "surface" or road for the bus was largely paid for by the gasoline taxes generated by the growing auto population. The municipal franchises of most street railway companies required them to maintain the street between the tracks, plow the snow in winter etc., in addition to bearing the capital cost of the track.

Transit industry trends in wages, revenues, and productivity

Even a superficial glance at the statistics in Exhibit 9 reveals that the transit industry remained in a stagnant-to-declining condition for many years. Total transit vehicle mileage, the basic output or product of the industry, was somewhat less in 1967 than in 1923. In the same 44 years, the U.S. population nearly doubled. The 58 percent rise in transit industry passenger revenues in those 44 years was almost entirely due to fare increases, but the fare increases failed to match the 96 percent rise in the consumer price index in the same period (compare Columns 7 and 11 in Exhibit 9). Between 1923 and 1967, the gross national product increased more than ninefold from $86.1 billion to $785 billion. Transit passenger revenues shrank from 7 percent of GNP in 1923 to 1.85 percent in 1967.

Employment in the transit industry declined nearly 50 percent from 1923 to 1967, but the increase in average wages paid (see Column 6) resulted in a doubling of total wages paid (see Column 9). The average wage in the transit industry has risen much faster than the consumer price index (see Column 17). The consumer price index rose 24 percent from 1955 to 1967, while the average wage in the transit industry rose 65 percent.

After 1945, the transit industry was caught in a cost-price squeeze. Wages, as a percentage of passenger revenues (Column 13), rose rapidly. Other costs such as debt servicing, maintenance, gasoline and electric power costs remained relatively fixed, given a particular scale of operation. Passenger revenue per vehicle mile (Column 19) represents the price at which the transit industry has been able to sell the basic service it generates. When the index for this price (Column 20) is compared with the consumer price index (Column 7), it can be seen that the transit industry has not been able to get price increases to match general inflationary trends.

It may be inferred from these data that the general demand for public transportation services has been relatively weaker than the demand for other consumer products and services. Another factor in retarding public transportation fare increases has been the desire of public transportation authorities (or their controlling political bodies) to provide low-cost "service" for the public, especially the less fortunate in society. Whatever the cause, the result has been that wages per vehicle mile (Column 15) have risen 179 percent in 44 years, while the consumer price index has risen 96 percent (Column 7), and passenger revenue per vehicle mile only 74 percent.

A final statistical measure of trends in the transit industry is obtained by calculating productivity per worker, as measured by vehicle miles per worker (Column 25). An index of this measure (Column 26) shows that productivity in the transit industry rose 74 percent from 1923 to 1968, while productivity per man hour in the nation's basic industries rose 258 percent (Column 23). From 1955 to 1967, the increase in productivity per man hour was 43 percent in the nation's basic industries, 35 percent in the rail rapid transit sector of the transit industry, and 10 percent for the entire transit industry. One can conclude from this that productivity increases in the rail rapid transit sector have been much greater than in the bus sector of the transit industry, but still fell behind general productivity increases in the nation's basic industries.

PUBLIC TRANSPORTATION AUTHORITIES

The example of the Massachusetts Bay Transportation Authority (MBTA) is useful in illustrating the problems faced by operators of public transit systems in medium-size cities. The MBTA was created by a Massachusetts act of 1964 to replace the Metropolitan Transit Authority (MTA). The act's objective was to make the transit district more widely inclusive, the MBTA being designed to initially include 78 cities and towns as opposed to the MTA's 14 cities and towns. The MTA itself had been designed to have a broader geographical base of support than its defunct predecessor, the privately owned Boston Elevated Railway Company.

By 1968, the MBTA had consistently run an operating deficit, called "net cost of service." Under the terms of the 1964 Act the "net cost of service" was assessed on the 78 cities and towns according to a prescribed formula. In a 13-month period ending September 30, 1967, the MBTA reported a net assessable cost of service of about $24.5 million. It can be seen from Exhibit 10 that about $22.4 million of the net assessable cost of service was attributed to local (bus) operations, and about $2.1 million was attributed to express (rapid transit) service. At the time, the rapid transit fare was $0.20 and the bus fare $0.10. When it became clear that the deficit for the period ending October 31, 1968, would come close to $30 million, the MBTA finally raised rapid transit fares to $0.25 and bus fares to $0.20.

The MBTA is afflicted by the fact that its subway tunnels have remained as permanent as the concrete they were made of, while population densities have shifted and technology has changed. Subway and surface rapid transit lines were added piecemeal as needs arose rather than as part of a grand metropolitan transportation plan or "system." The original backbone of Boston's subway, the Tremont Street line, was designed for streetcars. The increment was designed for larger rapid transit cars and the tunnels were constructed with a greater diameter. The final increment was designed for still larger rapid transit cars. As a result, the largest, most efficient cars could not be operated on two of the three lines, and the smaller cars could not be replaced by larger ones without rebuilding the tunnel network at an enormous cost. A similar condition exists in New York City, although to a lesser degree.

The mistakes of the past can be seen reflected in the operating costs presented in Exhibit 11. In 1966 and 1967, Montreal, Toronto, and Cleveland had new rapid transit cars, larger or more efficient than most of the cars used in Boston and New York. Toronto's cost of operation and maintenance was about $0.60 per car-mile as compared to New York's $0.83 and Boston's $1.52. Boston's extremely high costs stemmed to a considerable degree from the fact that it used streetcars in many of its subways. Boston's high labor cost—"Conducting Transportation"— reflected the relatively small size of Boston's cars.[7]

The MBTA's use of three different kinds of rapid transit cars also complicated things for the traveler, because many point-to-point trips entailed several vehicle transfers. The MBTA system was particularly inadequate for travelers who wished to move in directions other than to and from the downtown area. Such trips entailed much lost time in transferring from one line to another and in moving at oblique angles toward a destination.

Transit in other countries

Exhibit 12 gives selected data for several long-established rail rapid transit systems around the world. A breakdown of the operating statistics of several European transit systems is presented in Exhibit 13. In 1967, all were deficit operations, although the relative size of the deficit and the means of its financing varied with the city. The relative size of the deficit did not necessarily reflect on the efficiency of the operation, as fare structure and train scheduling could be made to vary according to the level of "service" the operator wished to provide.

When faced with growing automobile populations, the transit systems in the developed European countries experienced passenger declines similar to those in the United States. Although Exhibit 14 does not reflect the fact, it can be said that surface transit lines suffered more than the rapid transit lines from the automobile's inroads.

Around the world, many cities of medium size have seen fit to construct or extend rapid transit systems, even though the provision of such service is likely to require a subsidy (Exhibit 15). The two Canadian systems, Toronto and Montreal, were especially worth consideration by Americans because of the ways in which they differed from U.S. systems, despite their proximity.

The Toronto subway was begun in 1946, partially financed by transit surpluses generated during World War II. In 1953, Toronto became

---

[7] One man is required per car, be it large or small.

the first North American community to adopt a metropolitan form of government. This type of organization was believed by many to facilitate construction of projects, such as rapid transit systems, that have an impact on the entire metropolitan area. Under arrangements in effect in 1969, Metropolitan Toronto (the city and 13 suburbs) bore 70 percent of the cost of new transit construction, and the Toronto Transit Commission bore 30 percent.

With a population of 1.7 million in 1969, Metropolitan Toronto was similar in many respects to major U.S. cities. In per capita motor vehicle ownership, it was exceeded only by Los Angeles and Detroit. Toronto was significantly different from U.S. cities in not having large tracts housing minority groups in slum conditions. This factor in the United States kept suburban communities from wanting to join central cities in a unified metropolitan government. The relative absence in Toronto of tension caused by racial and economic disparities was thought by some observers to have contributed to the public's favorable attitude toward riding the transit system. The number of revenue passengers increased 15 percent from 1966 to 1967.

Most observers would agree that the public image of transit in Toronto was of a much higher quality than the image of transit in large U.S. cities. The greater homogeneity of the population, leading to widely held standards of cleanliness and public conduct, seemed to be a basic cause of the disparate public images. The TTC had little trouble with crimes committed on its premises, for instance. In the United States, crimes committed on the premises of public transit systems attracted increasing attention in the late 60s. It takes little imagination to guess at the public reaction to such headlines as appeared in two consecutive days of the *Chicago Tribune* in 1968 (Exhibit 16).

The continuing popularity of the Toronto subway attracted new housing construction all along the line. In the five-year period ending in 1963, 48.5 percent of all new high-rise apartments were reportedly built "within a short walking distance of the subway" (a two-block radius). The Toronto Transit Commission said that the subway "has in large measure been responsible for bringing in more than enough tax dollars to pay the annual amortization costs of the subway." TTC experts have also estimated that it would require 20 expressway lanes to carry the quarter million people that are carried daily on the Yonge Street subway.

The Montreal Metro, opened on October 17, 1966, was unique in its emphasis on the esthetic aspects of mass transportation. Each station was individual, bearing the stamp of a different architect. There were red stations, gray and yellow ones; stations with brick walls, stone walls, and some in sculptured relief. The French-speaking operators of the system proudly compared their stations to Toronto's, which they slighted as "tile bathrooms without fixtures." Montreal's blue and white trains were designed to be ultraquiet, running on rubber tires as did some lines of the Paris Metro. Fares were collected by automatic turnstiles to cut down on labor costs.

Several rather special factors made the construction of a rapid transit system easier in Montreal than it was in some U.S. cities. First, the use of the automobile was restricted in Montreal, as it was in New York, by geographical factors. The city was squeezed between the St. Lawrence River and the city's namesake, Mount Royal.

Montreal had a city population nearly double that of Toronto and the French-speaking residents of Montreal were apparently anxious to surpass the English-speaking rival city to the southwest. Jean Drapeau, who ran for mayor in 1960, seemed to have realized this. He was overwhelmingly elected on a platform calling for immediate construction of a subway system.

Urban transportation and the interstate highway program

As the automobile population swelled in the late 1940s and early 1950s, traffic jams became chronic in major cities. The answer to the problem seemed simple to many at the time—build more roads. The Federal Interstate Highway and Defense Program of 1956 proposed to spend $41 billion to build 41,000 miles of highway. Its advocates hoped that the program would free the automobile population from the limitations of its own numbers. Under the program, the federal government would foot 90 percent of the bill for new interstate highways; the states, 10 percent. Prior to the Act of 1956, the federal government had contributed 50 percent. About 5,300 miles of the total 41,000 miles were to be built in urban areas. The money to build the highways was to come from increased federal and state gasoline taxes, a form of taxation both easily collectible and of little concern to most drivers.

The states rapidly began construction of the rural portions of the Interstate Highway Program, postponing construction of the urban portions, as those promised to be both expensive and politically hazardous to build. The history of Boston's "Inner Belt" is typical of many urban highways in representing the difficulties associated with trying to relieve traffic congestion by building more highways.

The Inner Belt was first proposed as part of Boston's "Master Highway Plan of 1948." It was to be a circular highway, skirting the periphery of the central business district and intercepting all the radial highways at points a few miles from downtown. The objective in building the Inner Belt was to permit cars to travel to opposite sides of the city without having to pass through the congested central business district. The difficulty in building the highway was that it was impossible to design a route that did not either wipe out several thousand middle-class homes in Cambridge, several hundred upper-class homes in Brookline, or a goodly dozen of Boston's finest institutions in the Back Bay.

Theoretically, the Commonwealth of Massachusetts had the power of eminent domain to take whatever piece of land it wanted, provided just compensation was given. In actual fact, governors contemplating reelection or higher public office were loath to anger either significant portions of the population or the heads of large and wealthy institutions. Twenty years after the Inner Belt was first proposed, construction had still not begun, even though the Bureau of Public Roads had agreed to pay $45 million for a one-mile tunnel under some of Boston's institutions. Cambridge residents remained implacably opposed to the highway.

In regard to the development of urban highways, most major cities experienced difficulties similar to Boston's. By the early 1960s, there was widespread disenchantment with urban highways as the cure-all for metropolitan transportation problems. Many interested groups proposed alternative solutions: expanded rail transit systems, exclusive bus lanes on freeways, monorail systems, and computer control of automobile traffic. Stories on transportation problems in the cities were featured in many magazines (Exhibit 17); legislation was demanded to deal with the perceived threat to the cities.

Rapid transit proponents often spoke of their favorite mode of transportation as if, somehow, it were completely interchangeable with urban highways. They noted the destruction that urban highways often caused; they spotted the fact that state highway departments tended to push new roads through park lands. An implicit assumption in many of their discussions was that if only a modern rapid transit system existed, it would never be necessary to resolve conflicts over the use of open spaces. Highway advocates, on the other hand, frequently insisted that congestion could not be permitted to increase, and that the only way to deal with the malady was to build more highways.

Relationships between productivity, income levels, land-use patterns, and modes of transportation

Increasing urban populations and increasing personal incomes in urban areas were two factors often acknowledged as being related to urban traffic congestion. The indices presented in Exhibit 18 suggest that correlations do exist between increases in productivity, increases in the motor vehicle population, and the increasing percentage of the human population living in urban areas.

Since 1930, the increase in farm productivity per man-hour in the United States has closely paralleled the increase in the total value of farm machinery. Because farm productivity increased more rapidly than the increase of the general population and its demand for farm products, economic considerations pushed marginal farmers from their farms and pulled them toward the cities. The shift of the population from rural to urban areas was especially rapid in the years 1940–1967, the years when farm productivity per man-hour was rising most rapidly. Productivity per man-hour was also rising rapidly in the cities, but the prices of industrial products, unlike farm products, were not usually depressed by the population's limited ability to consume them. Increased productivity per man-hour could, therefore, generate increased personal disposable income. Exhibit 18 shows that from 1930 to 1967 there was a notable correlation between increases in industrial productivity per man-hour and increases in the index of automobile registrations.

Rail transportation, its technology and economics strongly shaped land-use patterns in the older cities in this country. All the major eastern cities that matured in the era of rail transportation developed collection and distribution lines flowing radially to and from their centers. A strong argument can be made that such cities were built on a radial pattern because it was the most efficient at the time. Because large quantities of goods could only be moved economically by rail, factories, markets and warehouses were best located near the heart of the city. Labor followed industry, and the population distributed itself along the streetcar and commuter rail lines radiating from the central business district.

The coming of the internal combustion engine freed vehicles, both passenger and commercial, from being tied to linear rail networks and catenary electric wires. With the development of large motor trucks by 1920, businesses no longer had to locate in downtown areas with the associated high rents and taxes. Workers who could afford automobiles began to move away from the densely populated "corridors" that characterized the surroundings of major streetcar lines. The population began to fill in the areas between the rail lines and gradually moved outward from the core city. As this occurred, a grid pattern of land-use began to be superimposed on the original radial pattern. As populations dispersed, the loading factors on transit company routes began to fall, and the cost-price squeeze began.

Rising personal income has clearly played a part in effecting a change in land-use patterns and mode of transportation utilized. Exhibit 19 shows that in 1967, automobile ownership increased rapidly with income up to a level of $5,000; from $8,000 to over $15,000, the rise in multicar ownership was most rapid. In Exhibit 20, personal consumption expenditures by categories are broken down for the years, 1930–1959. The rising relative importance of outlays for transportation seems to indicate both the consumer's preference for the services provided by the automobile and also the greater relative cost of using an automobile as compared to public transportation.

The automobile and public transit compared
as modes of transportation

A favorite exercise of rapid transit proponents in the 1960s was to compare the automobile with the rapid transit car as a means of moving a certain number of commuters from one point to another. The automobile came out very badly when such a comparison was based on almost any measure of cost or efficiency. Exhibit 21 shows that rail rapid transit cars could carry up to 20 times as many people per hour per track as could be moved per hour per lane on a freeway. Since it would have taken 20 lanes of freeway to move the number of people that could have been moved on one subway track, the freeway-automobile combination was an inefficient user of urban land by comparison. In addition, a subway tunnel would have removed no valuable land from the city's tax rolls.

The automobile also came out very badly when compared with rapid transit on the basis of cost per passenger-mile. Bureau of Public Roads calculations made in 1964, suggested that an average car used strictly for commuting would cost nearly $0.16 a mile, even if the car were depreciated over a ten-year period (Exhibit 22). For a family owning only one multi-purpose car, the cost of commuting was estimated at $0.11 per mile. By contrast, the passenger-mile cost of rapid transit in Exhibit 9 was calculated at $0.0385 for 1965.

The data suggest that the overwhelming preference of commuters for the private automobile at the time was not a result of cost minimization. The commuter who used an automobile was getting something he considered worth the extra cost. The extra "something" can be expressed in terms of factors such as time, convenience, and comfort. The automobile was able to provide nearly "portal-to-portal" transportation. Commuters using public transit often had to walk or make a series of vehicle transfers. Exhibit 23 suggests that in the eyes of many commuters the desirability of public transit fell off very rapidly with the distance that had to be walked to a transit stop. In the early decades of the 20th century, when average personal income was low, commuters had little extra disposable income to spend for "time and convenience." By the 50s and 60s, that was no longer true.

Comparisons of the automobile and public transit as modes of commuting transportation often overlooked the fact that the majority of automobile trips were not made in commuting to and from work. Exhibit 24 suggests that single-destination commuting trips in the 1960s were less than 40 percent of total automobile trips. Public transportation was especially noninterchangeable with the automobile as a means of transportation for the other 60 percent of all trips, inasmuch as such trips tended to have multiple destinations, shopping, business calls, etc. For multi-destination, nonscheduled trips, the margin of "time and convenience" that the automobile offered over public transportation was much greater than for commuting trips which took place daily at a regular time and had a single destination. Exhibit 25 graphically shows that transit trips were clustered much more closely around the commuting "rush-hours" in Chicago than were automobile trips. During these peak hours, 80 percent of the trips to and from the downtown area were made by public transit. Transit equipment and employees thus approached maximum productivity during only two hours of the working day.

From the 1920s to the 1940s, many urban travelers turned from public transit to the private automobile when the margin of "time and convenience" was sufficiently great and the cost differential was within their means to afford. After the Second World War, the proportion of the population that could afford an automobile increased greatly. From 1950 to 1967, vehicle registrations increased at a remarkably steady rate of 5 percent a year, as opposed to the population's average increase of 1.6 percent a year (Exhibit 26). The exhibit also shows that urban mileage driven very closely approximated registrations. At a 5 percent compounded growth rate, urban automobile mileage driven was therefore doubling every 14 years.

There were many indications that the construction rate of urban highways was failing to keep pace with the burgeoning auto population. Arthur E. Palmer, Jr., New York's transportation administrator estimated that in 1907 the average speed of a horse-drawn vehicle in Manhattan was 11.5 miles per hour, and that in 1966 the average speed of motor vehicles was 8.5 miles per hour. He commented, "The advantage of the motor vehicle as a flexible and freely moving mode of transportation has been lost in its own uncontrolled and unprovided-for abundance, like a herd of elk reduced to starvation by its own proliferation on a limited range."

New York, of course, could be described as a special example since it was one of the largest cities in the world, and because it was almost impossible to find land on which to construct further highways. There was evidence, though, that traffic congestion was rising even in Los Angeles, sometimes called the "Freeway Capital of the World," and blessed with a large supply of land occupied by low-density housing. Travel time studies conducted by the Southern California Auto Club indicate that of 14 point-to-point comparisons, 8 showed increased travel times from 1962 to 1963. The net area enclosed by a travel time of 30 minutes showed a reduction of 7 percent.

It became increasingly expensive to try to provide highways for the expanding urban automobile population. Right-of-way costs in particular soared as open areas were filled up, and increasing concessions were made to win the acquiescence of urban residents to new highway construction. Between 1946 and 1966, urban motor vehicle mileage driven increased 170 percent. In the same period, highway user taxes increased 440 percent (Exhibit 27). Over half of these taxes were produced in urban areas, and were allocated specifically to highway construction. In 1967, the Bureau of Public Roads estimated that the 5,300 urban miles of the interstate system represented 45 percent of total costs, but only 13 percent of total mileage.

The finances of major cities were put under severe pressure by the attempt to meet urban transportation needs by the highway-automobile combination. Cities bore many costs associated with motor vehicle traffic that were not reimbursed from gasoline taxes (Exhibit 28). Traffic controls, traffic police and highway maintenance were the largest of these factors. The true cost to the total community of operating an automobile as a mode of transportation was thus greater than the $0.11 to $0.15 a mile paid by the owner. Part of the hidden cost of automobile usage was carried by the personal property taxes of urban dwellers.[8] Suburban dwellers who drove downtown on urban highways largely outside their suburb did not bear any share of these costs in their own property taxes.

The Mass Transportation Act of 1964

By 1960, a significant portion of the population, reporters, social critics, urbanologists and congressmen were convinced that highway construction alone would not solve the "urban transportation problem." The alternative seemed to many to be improved rail rapid transit systems where such systems already existed, and new systems where there were none. Many economists, urban planners and those with an interest in the manufacture of electrical equipment argued that the federal government should aid the cities by providing transit operators with something equivalent to the "90–10" aid given for interstate highway construction. Between 1960 and 1963, several bills were introduced in Congress favoring federal subsidization of rapid transit. The first of these bills to become law, the Housing Act of 1961, provided $75 million in grants and loans for "demonstration projects" dedicated to the improvement of public transit. These bills were vigorously opposed by the "automobile and highway lobby," especially when some of the "rail-fans" suggested that public transit should get a cut of gasoline taxes. Apart from the respective merits of the opposing arguments, the "automobile and highway" lobby was a powerful political force with an important economic base. Automobile production did, after all, utilize 21 percent of all steel

---

[8] Subsidies to public transit also came from this source.

production, 49 percent of all lead, 61 percent of all rubber, 32 percent of all zinc, 13 percent of all aluminum and 58 percent of all upholstery leather sold in the country.

Forbes magazine in its October 1, 1968 edition, offered an explanation of how the "highway lobby" derived its political power:

> The highway lobby has behind it some of the most powerful state political machines in the U.S. In many states, the highway department produces the grease that keeps the machine running. Since the gasoline pump is one of the most efficient tax-collection agencies ever devised by man, in many states it takes in more money than any other state department. It has more contracts to give out; it has more favors to offer (like running a highway past someone's land even though common sense says it should be elsewhere). . . . It's also accepted practice for industry associations belonging to the Highway Users Association to ask key members of Congress to address their meetings for a fee that may run as high as $5000.

In May 1962, the Chamber of Commerce of the United States collected differing views on the question of subsidization of public transit. Viewpoints typical of several groups are presented in Exhibit 29.

The Urban Mass Transportation Act that was finally passed in 1964 provided less than the highway lobbyists feared it might, and less than the public transit interests wanted. The act of 1964, among other things, specified that, "The Administrator (Office of the Urban Transportation Administration, Department of Housing and Urban Development) . . . shall estimate what portion of the cost of a project . . . cannot reasonably be financed from revenues—which portion shall hereinafter be called "net project cost." The Federal grant for such a project shall not exceed two-thirds of the net project cost. The remainder of the net project cost shall be provided, in cash, from sources other than Federal funds."

The act (as amended) provided finance grants of $675 million to be drawn upon in fiscal years 1965–1969. The act also provided $140 million for research, development and demonstration projects. These funds were to be available for all forms of urban mass transportation.

The act did not set off a wild spree of rapid transit line construction, but it was moderately stimulating to the industry. Because most transit systems operated at deficits, they found it difficult to come up with their one-third share of the cost of undertaking a new project. Nevertheless, the act apparently stimulated the following activities: By 1968, five existing systems were extending their rapid transit lines; three entirely new projects were actually in, or approaching the construction stage; and five other projects were in the preliminary planning stage. Bus operators also experimented with "Freeway Fliers" and with increased service in areas where automobile ownership was low. Exhibit

30, developed by the Institute for Rapid Transit, shows rapid transit routes that were either under construction or planned in December 1968.

The U.S. Department of Transportation

In October 1966, President Johnson signed into law the act creating the new Department of Transportation. The 89th Congress declared that "the general welfare, the economic growth and stability of the Nation and its security require the development of national transportation policies and programs conducive to the provision of fast, safe, efficient and convenient transportation at the lowest cost consistent therewith and with other national objectives, including the efficient utilization and conservation of the Nation's resources."

The Department of Transportation (DOT) was designed to have broad responsibilities in the areas of ground, air, and sea transportation. Of specific interest to the urban transportation industry was the research conducted by DOT under the High-Speed Ground-Transportation Act (HSGT) of 1965. Although this research was largely concerned with intercity transportation, a great deal of the technology being developed was expected to have applicability to urban transport systems. Through 1968, the "HSGT" hardware programs were being applied to the vast Northeast Corridor which stretched from Washington north to Boston. It was expected that by 1980 there would be 25 such "corridors," containing 170 million people on about 10 percent of the nation's land area.

The following paragraphs include excerpts from annual reports of three major transit carbuilding companies; these passages give a feeling for how the companies responded to the federal rail transit legislation.

The Budd Company commented in its annual report for 1965, "The long-term prospects for an expanded market for the [Budd] Railway Division were enhanced by the passage of the Urban Mass Transportation Act of 1964 and the High-Speed Ground-Transportation Research and Development Act of 1965, which provide Federal support for demonstration and tests of transit and inter-city rail equipment."

Prospects did prove to be good for Budd. In 1966, Budd received a $26 million order for 61 high-speed cars for the New York–Washington run. In addition, Budd was awarded a $13.6 million contract to build 75 streamlined commuter cars for the Delaware River Port Authority.

In January 1967, Budd got an $18.8 million contract from the city of Chicago for transit cars. Budd also began work on a $57.3 million order for 270 cars for the Long Island Railroad. As of December 31, 1967, the company had a $115 million passenger equipment backlog, the largest in the company's history.

The Pullman-Standard Division of Pullman, Inc. was less successful than Budd in getting new passenger equipment orders. As the world's largest builder of railway equipment, it shipped 17,359 freight cars in 1965, but only 83 passenger cars. (The Pullman Car Works in Chicago had a capacity of 500 passenger cars a year.) The company's 1965 annual report noted hopefully, ". . . a rebirth of carbuilding activity is anticipated for this historic plant in the years ahead."

In 1966, Pullman delivered 21,646 freight cars, but the annual report for that year noted,

> Deliveries of public transportation equipment by the nation's three principal carbuilding companies continued to decline in 1966. As a result, the Pullman Car Works delivered only 12 new and rebuilt passenger cars during the year. . . . In addition, Pullman-Standard was awarded a contract to build 20 rapid transit cars for the Cleveland Transit Authority. These cars represent the first of this type of equipment to be constructed of stainless steel by this division. . . . Pullman-Standard's passenger carbuilding plant in Chicago is being maintained in anticipation of the resurgence of this type of business, as indicated by the numerous optimistic reports and forecasts by the federal government and many metropolitan transit authorities.

In 1967, the company's annual report noted without much comment that the company had delivered 20,218 freight cars, 32 rapid transit cars, and 20 commuter railroad cars.

The St. Louis Car Division of General Steel Industries, Inc., in 1966, delivered a pioneering order of 200 stainless-steel-composite rapid transit vehicles to the New York City Transit Authority. In 1967, the company received an order to build an additional 400 cars for the New York system, utilizing similar composite construction. Delivery also began late in the year on an additional order of all-aluminum cars for the Port of New York Authority Trans-Hudson system (PATH). A total of 206 PATH cars were ordered in the two-year period.

Rapid transit extensions and new systems

Boston provided a good example of how the new federal legislation was utilized by an existing rapid transit operating authority. When the Southeast Expressway was completed to Boston in 1959, the New Haven Railroad promptly ceased operations on its Old Colony Division, a commuter line that was closely paralleled by the new expressway. The addition of the erstwhile rail commuters to the existing highway traffic quickly reproduced the very sort of congestion that the expressway had been designed to alleviate. After much legal spadework, the Massachusetts Bay Transportation Authority (MBTA) was empowered to acquire the abandoned right-of-way. Under the terms of the 1964 Act, HUD agreed to cover two thirds, or $35 million, of the cost of converting the right-of-way into a rapid transit line and of providing 76 new, high-speed cars to be purchased from Pullman-Standard.

The Bay Area Rapid Transit (BART) system was, as of 1968, the most significant new project to be assisted by the 1964 act. San Francisco was the first American city in decades to build an entirely new transit system. Many believed that the city should have built a subway long before then, inasmuch as San Francisco, like New York, had natural obstacles to surface transportation. Rapid transit was first proposed for the Bay Area in 1900, for that very reason. Partly because it was con-stricted on three sides by water, the city's auto population density was the highest in the world, 7,000 per square mile.

By the 1950s, the San Francisco Chamber of Commerce was reporting that the city's economy was stagnating and that jobs were being lost in the central business district because of extreme traffic congestion. In 1953, the San Francisco Bay Area Rapid Transit Commission was set up to study the feasibility of constructing a rapid transit system. In 1957, at the recommendation of the commission, the state legislature created the Bay Area Rapid Transit District (BART). The district was given limited powers of property taxation in order to finance further study. BART's new directors soon made two important decisions. The first was to develop a system that would be more than competitive with the automobile through the use of the latest available technology. The second was to mount a massive promotional campaign to convince local taxpayers of the value of constructing the system. Where the pro-motional campaign was directed to businessmen, it emphasized the in-creased numbers of shoppers and workers who would be attracted to the central business district (CBD). Where the campaign was aimed at homeowners, it dramatized the increased speed and ease of movement that BART's 80-mph trains would bring. The most mentioned time saving was that to be offered by the underwater tube linking San Francisco and Oakland. Trains speeding through the tunnel were to make the trip in eight minutes. At that time, the trip across the Bay Bridge took 30 minutes by car; time required for parking had to be counted over and above that.

BART's directors decided to make their trains as alluring as possible to commuters. The cars were to be air-conditioned, with upholstered seats and carpeted floors. The windows were to be tinted and the interior paneled in soft colors. The cars will also be soundproofed and softly sprung. The track was to be nearly a foot wider than standard gauge in order to prevent lateral swaying.

In May 1966, the voters of the five Bay Area counties passed by a 61.2 percent vote (needed, 60 percent) a referendum permitting the issuance of $792 million in general obligation bonds. To the average homeowner in the five counties, this meant a voluntary $40 hike in his annual taxes.

In San Francisco, the initiative for action on transportation problems was local. In New York, action was initiated in 1967 by state governor, Nelson A. Rockefeller. The governor put considerable time and energy into the promotion of a $2.5 billion bond issue for transportation, bigger by $750 million than any previous issue. The issue was to provide $1.25 billion for highways, $250 million for airports, and $1 billion for mass transit (mostly for New York City). The governor's supporters raised nearly $1 million in promotional funds to ensure the overwhelming passage of the issue in the 1967 elections. When combined with matching federal funds, it provided $5.35 billion for statewide transportation, and $2.9 billion specifically for mass transportation in New York City. The money was to be spent in two phases: "Phase One" to be completed within ten years, "Phase Two" within an indefinite period. During Phase One, subway lines were to be extended and 500 high-speed, air-conditioned subway cars were to be purchased. Similar extensions and the purchase of an additional 500 cars were to take place in Phase Two.

In the general elections of November 5, 1968, voters in four U.S. cities passed judgment on proposed bond issues for rapid transit. Referenda for Los Angeles and Atlanta failed to pass; the referenda for Washington, D.C. and for the state of New Jersey passed by large margins.

The Los Angeles referendum posed the question as to whether a 90-mile, $2.5 billion rapid transit system should be partially financed by a hike in the Los Angeles county sales tax. A $750,000 campaign to win voter approval was launched by 75 top business and civic leaders. The proposal, nevertheless, failed to pass as only 45 percent of the voters voted in favor, and a 60 percent majority was required.

Atlanta had been involved in planning a rapid transit system for about a decade, but proper financing had never been obtained. The November 5 referendum rejected the most recent proposal, which was to issue $377 million in revenue bonds needed to start construction of a 40-mile system.

Several referenda were held in the counties surrounding Washington, D.C. to test voter approval of the suburban portions of the 95.3-mile, $2.3 billion regional rapid transit system. All these referenda received favorable votes.

Prospects for future change in the transit industry

As mentioned earlier, rising per capita income in the urban areas and the proliferation of the automobile contributed to the early decline of the rail transit industry, especially the street railways. By the late 1960s, it appeared that the same trends, extrapolated forward a decade or more, would favor a renaissance of the industry. In 1967, 75 percent of the nation's wealth was concentrated in the 2 percent of the total land area occupied by metropolitan communities. Demographic projections indicated that by 1980, more than 85 percent of the nation's population would reside in metropolitan areas; more than half of the total population being expected to live in 40 great urban complexes.

In the opinion of the casewriter, some of the relationships of factors in the external environment of the transit industry seemed to go something like this: Personal income had been steadily rising as a result of greater efficiency in the design, production, and marketing of goods and services; at the same time population had been increasing and shifting toward urban areas; urban automobile ownership had been increasing for all three reasons; as a result, more commuters wished to drive their cars to work; commuters and state highway departments were pushing for more urban highway construction; urban property owners were resisting highway construction; urban automobile ownership was outpacing urban highway construction; traffic congestion was increasing; government officials were noting the increasing cost of highway construction and the decreasing efficiency of urban vehicular distribution; remedial legislation came to be proposed.

One very important possible boost to the transit industry would be increased aid from federal and local governments. There were indications in 1968 that such aid might increase in the future. Alan S. Boyd, the nation's first Secretary of Transportation warned in September 1968 that the transit systems of the major cities were stagnating and needed to receive greater consideration relative to the urban highway program: "In our biggest cities, all the programs for improving downtown traffic will be of little value without a healthy, growing, mass transit system. . . . Everybody talks about balanced transportation. We've got about $4.5 billion a year going into the Highway Trust Fund. On the other side of the scale we have $175 million going into mass transit and $65 million for airports. We've got a bucketful of money for highways and only a medicine dropperful for the rest."

Also in September 1968, President Johnson signed legislation authorizing $190 million for urban mass transportation in 1970. This was up from $150 million for fiscal 1969. Funds were to be provided under the formula of "two thirds of costs exceeding net project cost." In testimony before a congressional subcommittee, George L. DeMent, president of the industry's influential trade association, the Institute for Rapid Transit, argued that the federal government should increase its contribution:

> We would like to point out that many of our cities have been handicapped by the two-thirds Federal, one-third local matching fund requirements under the Mass Transportation Act. If 90% Federal funds, with 10% local matching funds, could be made available for transit, as is

provided in the interstate highway program, it would enable much greater participation in the mass transportation program by cities throughout the country.

The "automobile-highway" lobby has persistently declared that the "90–10" type of aid the transit industry was asking for was not the same as the "90–10" aid provided for the interstate highway program. The 90–10 aid for transit, they pointed out, would have to come from general revenues largely derived from income taxes. The money for the 90–10 highway aid was derived strictly from gasoline taxes, and was thus a "user-tax." Groups like the American Automobile Association reminded voters and their representatives that it was traditional in this country to tax only those who benefited from services paid for by the tax.

Transit industry spokesmen attempted to show that entire metropolitan areas, even auto drivers as a group benefited from improved public transit. In 1968, the Southern California Rapid Transit District had Stanford Research Institute prepare a study seeking to prove that the benefits to the Los Angeles area from a transit system would far exceed the cost of construction ($2.5 billion for an 89-mile, five-corridor system). The following are excerpts from the "SRI" report:

> The total benefits to district residents expected to be generated by the proposed rapid transit project are estimated to be valued at $253 million annually. They are 87 per cent greater than the estimated annual costs of the project (for debt repayment), indicating a net annual benefit of $117 million.
>
> Of the total benefits, 44 per cent will accrue to travelers. These benefits (in 1968 dollars) will include: (1) Travel time saved valued at $40 million annually; (2) An expected $46 million savings in automobile operating costs; (3) A $23 million annual reduction in the cost of parking automobiles; (4) A cost savings of $3 million per year as some families avoid becoming two-car families or shift from two to one-car situations; (5) A reduction in highway accident costs valued at $5 million annually (in addition, 32 fatalities per year and 1,900 injuries should be avoided), and (6) Benefits to bus riders in improvements or fare reductions valued at $15 million.
>
> System users will pay an annual $50 million in transit fares and transit station parking fees in return for the benefits cited above, leaving a net traveler benefit of $85 million per year.
>
> Of the total benefits, 56 per cent—$109 million in 1968 dollars—will accrue to the community as a whole. Some of these benefits are: (1) Economic output amounting to $30 million per year through decreased structural unemployment; (2) An additional decrease in construction industry cyclical unemployment valued at $270 million over the seven-year period of system building, the equivalent of $24 million a year discounted over the life of the bond issue; (3) An increase in business productivity estimated to be worth a minimum of $15 million

per year; (4) Similar improvements in government productivity estimated at a minimum of $15 million, and (5) A much wider range
of choices and opportunities for both automobile drivers and non-drivers
in residential possibilities, travel habits and accessibility to the facilities
of the community. This is valued at $25 million annually.

Technology and the future of the transit industry

In an earlier study of the industry made in 1962, Stanford Research
Institute predicted that given certain conditions, rail transit might provide a $10 billion market over the next 20 years. The first condition
was that the government would have to find an equitable way to allocate
funds among different modes of transportation according to the economic
and social costs and benefits associated with particular modes. The second condition was that the latest technological advances would have
to be applied to new systems, and that improvements would have to
be made on present methods for the collection and distribution of transit
passengers at trip ends. If all these conditions were met, SRI predicted
a $10 billion market, as broken down in Exhibit 31. By 1969, visible
progress had been made toward meeting all three of SRI's preconditions
for the $10 billion market. The federal government had provided increas-
ing financial aid for public transit. Most major rapid transit systems
had provided large parking lots near their lines in order to facilitate
the collection of passengers. The provision of a large parking lot and
new rolling stock on the Chicago Transit Authority's Skokie line—Skokie
was a suburb of about 68,000 population—boosted average daily patronage from 1,500 to 7,500 between 1964 and 1966.

Research in the field of transit technology had been devoted to provision of more comfort and convenience for the passenger, reduction
of capital cost of equipment, and reduction of operating costs. In October
1968, General Motors Corporation announced it was building a prototype
gas turbine bus that would incorporate advances both in technology
and in customer comfort. By naming the test vehicle, "Rapid Transit
Experimental" (RTX) GM indicated that it thought of the bus as capable of providing more than just local transportation. The bus's 275-hp
turbine engine was smaller than a comparable diesel engine, and it
could give the bus a cruising speed of 70 mph at a somewhat lower
rate of fuel consumption. GM had been developing a gearless, noiseless
transmission for use in conjunction with the turbine engine. Besides
greater operating efficiency, the new power-train offered advantages to
passengers and bystanders. "RTX" was expected to be much quieter
than conventional buses, and the turbine engine was expected to emit
almost no air-polluting fumes. The bus was to have an air-suspension
system that could lower the front end by three inches for easier boarding.

The coach's interior was carpeted and its molded seats were angled outward toward large windows. Music could be piped throughout the vehicle.

Most of the research in the area of rapid transit technology had been devoted to reducing operating costs, particularly labor and maintenance costs. The cars on the newer systems, by 1969, were made of aluminum and stainless steel, relatively maintenance-free materials. Electric power costs were also lowered by the use of lighter-weight materials.

The four and one-half mile test track operated near San Francisco by the Bay Area Rapid Transit District was suggestive of things to come, because of its emphasis on the development of labor-saving technology, and because of its actual and potential use as a means for affecting the designs and operations of equipment suppliers. The $11 million test track was built in 1965 with two-thirds funding from HUD. Its purpose was twofold; to test and prove the automated equipment to be used for train control and fare collection, and to provide a sound basis for choosing between competitive bidders.

Electronic train control was believed to be necessary both to keep BART financially feasible, and to provide safe operation. Designers of the system calculated that it would be pushing human capabilities dangerously to expect motormen to maintain 90-second headways between trains moving at 80 mph.

Four companies built train control systems for evaluation on the BART test track. These were Westinghouse Electric Corp., General Electric Co., General Railway Signal Co., and Union Switch and Signal Division of Westinghouse Air Brake Co. The Philco Division of Ford Motor Co. was hired to evaluate impartially the systems of the four competitors. Westinghouse Electric Corp. won the competition, partly for the adjudged superiority of its design, and partly because it underbid its three competitors. Under the $26 million contract signed in April 1967, Westinghouse was to provide computerized control units for the 175 lead cars on the BART system. These car-borne control units were to be in constant communication with a central computer. (Mid-1969 BART developments are presented in the appendix to this case.)

BART as well as other transportation systems proposed at the time were intended largely to utilize current state-of-the-art technology. By contrast, however, the major transit systems existing in 1969 were utilizing the technology of about 1900–1920. Those systems were laid out at that time and many of their transit cars were either acquired or designed in that era (see Exhibit 32).

Major innovations in transit technology in the 20 years following 1969 were not expected to alter greatly the design of rapid transit cars from that of the BART system car. Once such a vehicle was made as comfortable as possible, and equipped with automated control to reduce costs and increase speeds, not much could then be done to improve its operation. The monorail, often touted in Sunday supplements as the future means of public transportation, was generally dismissed out-of-hand by transit experts. Its economics were said by many to be generally less attractive than the economics of conventional systems, and as of 1968, no simple switch had been designed for monorail tracks.

New technology was expected by some experts to have its most substantial impact on the rail transit industry in the area of tunnel construction. Although train operation was becoming automated in 1969, tunneling still remained nearly a "pick and shovel" operation. Exhibit 33 shows almost one half or more of total costs went for basic construction. The data also show that the cost of basic construction varied with the percentage of the system that was underground. Boring machines had been developed, but so far they could only operate where the subsoil consisted of rock or hard-blue clay. Where the subsoil was water soaked, as was often the case, sandhogs had to drive a pressurized caisson through the earth. Transit officials in Montreal suggested that if the city had not been blessed with firm subsoil, the subway system might never have been built. Looking to the future, in the late 60s, engineers at the Massachusetts Institute of Technology had become quite excited by the possibility of using lasers in the construction of tunnels.

One development that carbuilders and suppliers especially hoped for was a greater standardization of transit car specifications. William Van der Sluys, General Manager of passenger-car engineering, Pullman-Standard Division, said, "It would be wonderful if there were more standardization of vehicles, but the whole trend nowadays is the other way, and it's making transit cars extraordinarily expensive to build. There isn't even a basic body structure that can be repeated; each new car order has to be redesigned from scratch."[9]

James A. Miller, vice president and manager of the Railway Division of Budd Company agreed, "Manufacturers find themselves, not mass producing, but in a job-lot business. Our technical progress is being adversely affected by the need to fill so many varying kinds of orders."

---

[9] *Railway Age,* August 7, 1967.

EXHIBIT 1
Distribution of transit companies by population groups
(each company is counted only in the population group of the largest city it serves)

Population group	Number of cities in population group	Electric railways (incl. joint trolley coach and/or motor bus operations)	Trolley coach and motor bus operations combined	Motor bus (exclusively)
500,000 and over	21	9	1	20
250,000–500,000	30	2	1	43
100,000–250,000	81	0	0	88
50,000–100,000	201	0	0	133
Less than 50,000	5,112	0	0	426
Suburban and other. . . .		3	0	412
Total.		14	2	1,122

Sources: American Transit Association, *Transit Fact Book* (Washington, D.C., 1968); and Bureau of the Census, *U.S. Census of Population*, 1960 (Washington, D.C., 1961).

EXHIBIT 2
Revenue passengers carried on transit lines of the United States in 1967 distributed by type of service and population groups
(in millions)

	Grand total	Railway	Trolley coach	Motor bus
Subway and elevated	1,632	1,632	–	–
Surface lines: (by population group)				
500,000 and over	2,945	143	133	2,669
250,000–500,000	597	3	15	579
100,000–250,000	409	1	3	405
50,000–100,000	469	8	3	458
Less than 50,000	190	14	1	175
Suburban and other	374	27	0	347
Total.	6,616	1,828	155	4,633

Source: *Transit Fact Book*, 1968.

EXHIBIT 3

Statistical overview of existing rapid transit systems: 1965

	New York City Transit Authority	Chicago Transit Authority	Philadelphia Transportation Company	Massachusetts Bay Transportation Authority	Cleveland Transit System	Toronto Transit Commission	Montreal Transit Commission
City population (1960)	7,781,984	3,550,404	2,002,512	697,197	876,050	670,000	1,190,000
Pop. per square mile (city)	24,697	15,836	15,743	14,586	10,789	19,100	20,000
Single track miles							
Revenue	720	171	65	49	30	15	30
Nonrevenue (yards)	121	39	16	16	4	4	N.A.
Number of cars	6,700	1,160	493	280	88	170	369
Revenue car-miles (thousands)	314,686	44,349	14,923	8,987	4,258	9,348	N.A.
Miles per car	46,970	38,232	30,300	32,100	48,386	54,990	
Revenue passengers by year (thousands)							
1955	1,363,143	112,890	84,253	225,078	8,100	35,147	System opened Nov. 1966
1960	1,348,921	112,925	74,518	199,598	18,329	34,663	
1961	1,359,882	110,126	76,598	N.A.	17,789	32,993	
1962	1,383,368	114,068	72,619	N.A.	17,322	32,875	
1963	1,356,817	111,065	61,606*	N.A.	16,965	36,492	
1964	1,383,977†	111,218	67,149	N.A.	17,768	38,055	
1965	1,354,091	114,834	66,002	193,000‡	16,656	39,723	

* 19-day strike.
† Includes World's Fair Operation.
‡ Estimated by M.B.T.A.

Sources: U.S. Bureau of the Census, *Statistical Abstract of the United States: 1968* (Washington, D.C., 1968); and Institute for Rapid Transit, *Rapid Transit Reference Manual* (Chicago, 1967).

EXHIBIT 4
Comparison of rail and bus transit systems in the United States

Rail systems	1967	1965	1963	1961	1959
Number of operating companies	14	14	14	18	34
Miles of single track.	2,049	2,173	2,236	2,601	3,445
Number of employees	42,000*	N.A.	N.A.	43,700	47,700
Number of cars	10,645	10,664	10,634	11,419	11,983
Revenue passengers (millions).	1,828	1,882	1,899	2,003	2,005
Vehicle miles (millions)	434	437	436	455	470
Operating revenue (millions).	$404	$366	$349	$366	$365

Bus systems					
Number of operating companies	1,135	1,145	1,183	1,244	1,255
Route miles	57,200	55,800	54,300	52,200	49,700
Number of employees	N.A.	N.A.	N.A.	99,500	100,700
Number of buses	50,180	49,600	49,400	49,000	49,500
Revenue passengers (millions).	4,633	4,730	4,752	4,834	5,069
Vehicle miles (millions)	1,527	1,528	1,527	1,530	1,577
Operating revenue (millions)	$1,116	$1,036	$985	$945	$920

* Estimate by casewriter.

Sources: Moody's Investors' Service, Inc., *Moody's Transportation Manual* (New York, 1968), p. 66; and *Transit Fact Book*, 1968.

EXHIBIT 5

Trend of transit revenue passengers carried: Selected years 1912–1967
(millions)

Year	Grand total	Rail transit			Trolley coach	Motor bus
		Total rail transit	Surface	Subway and elevated		
1907	9,533	9,533	–	–	–	–
1912	12,135	12,135	–	–	–	–
1917	14,507	14,507	–	–	–	–
1919	14,916	14,916	–	–	–	–
1921	14,574	14,574	–	–	–	–
1923	16,311	15,650	–	–	–	661
1925	16,651	15,167	–	–	–	1,484
1927	17,257	14,901	–	–	–	2,356
1930	15,567	13,072	–	–	16	2,479
1935	11,264	9,612	–	–	–	1,652
1940	10,503.7	6,464.4	4,182.5	2,281.9	419.2	3,620.1
1945	18,981.9	9,636.0	7,080.9	2,555.1	1,001.2	8,344.7
1950	13,845.0	4,903.0	2,790.0	2,113.0	1,261.0	7,681.0
1955	9,189.0	2,586.0	845.0	1,741.0	869.0	5,734.0
1957	8,338.0	2,197.0	491.0	1,706.0	703.0	5,438.0
1959	7,650.0	2,025.0	378.0	1,647.0	517.0	5,108.0
1960	7,521.0	2,005.0	335.0	1,670.0	447.0	5,069.0
1961	7,242.0	2,003.0	323.0	1,680.0	405.0	4,834.0
1962	7,122.0	1,988.0	284.0	1,704.0	361.0	4,773.0
1963	6,915.0	1,899.0	238.0	1,661.0	264.0	4,752.0
1964	6,854.0	1,911.0	213.0	1,698.0	214.0	4,729.0
1965	6,798.0	1,882.0	204.0	1,678.0	186.0	4,730.0
1966	6,671.0	1,795.0	211.0	1,584.0	174.0	4,702.0
1967	6,616.0	1,828.0	196.0	1,632.0	155.0	4,633.0

* After 1940, total rail transit is broken down separately for surface, and subway and elevated operations.

Sources: For years 1907–1935: *Moody's Public Utilities Manual* (New York, 1940), p. 62. For years 1940–1967: *Transit Fact Book*, 1968, p. 7.

EXHIBIT 6

Trends of new passenger equipment delivered: Selected years 1912–1967

(in units)

Year	Grand total	Rail transit			Trolley bus	Motor bus
		Total	Surface	Subway and elevated		
1912	5,298	5,298	5,228	70	—	—
1917	2,565	2,565	2,153	412	—	—
1919	2,457	2,457	2,257	200	—	—
1921	1,185	1,185	1,160	25	—	—
1923	3,993	3,348	3,168	180	24	621
1925	3,662	1,491	1,331	160	—	2,171
1927	2,705	994	924	70	—	1,711
1930	2,334	608	608	—	112	1,614
1933	1,460	67	62	5	113	1,280
1936	5,863	575	399	176	545	4,743
1938	3,183	339	286	53	190	2,654
1940	5,254	652	463	189	618	3,984
1942	7,840	284	284	0	356	7,200
1944	4,151	284	284	0	60	3,807
1946	7,150	421	421	0	266	6,463
1948	9,165	726	478	248	1,430	7,009
1950	3,050	203	4	199	179	2,668
1952	1,992	19	19	0	224	1,749
1954	2,485	260	0	260	0	2,225
1956	3,135	376	0	376	0	2,759
1958	2,126	428	0	428	0	1,698
1960	3,222	416	0	416	0	2,806
1962	2,406	406	0	406	0	2,000
1963	3,858	658	0	658	0	3,200
1964	3,140	640	0	640	0	2,500
1965	3,580	580	0	580	0	3,000
1966	3,279	179	0	179	0	3,100
1967	2,548	48	0	48	0	2,500

Sources: For years prior to 1940, *Moody's Public Utilities*, 1940. For years after 1940, American Transit Association, *Transit Fact Book*, 1968, p. 13.

EXHIBIT 7

Annual total vehicle-miles of travel in the United States: Selected years
(in billions)

Year	Miles by type of vehicle			Miles by type of road		Total vehicle miles
	Passenger car	Buses	Trucks	Total rural	Urban	
1922	–	–	–	–	–	67.7
1925	–	–	–	–	–	122.3
1930	–	–	–	–	–	206.3
1931	–	–	–	–	–	216.2
1932	–	–	–	–	–	200.5
1933	–	–	–	–	–	200.6
1934	–	–	–	–	–	215.6
1936	–	–	–	–	–	252.1
1937	223.5	2.5	44.2	132.0	138.1	270.1
1941	275.8	2.8	55.0	170.0	163.6	333.6
1943	163.2	3.4	41.7	99.2	109.0	208.2
1946	280.6	4.1	56.2	170.8	170.1	340.9
1950	363.6	4.1	90.6	240.0	218.2	458.2
1955	492.6	4.2	108.8	330.5	275.1	605.6
1960	588.1	4.4	126.4	387.3	331.6	718.8
1963	645.4	4.5	155.6	420.0	385.4	805.4
1965	706.4	4.8	171.4	438.8	449.0	887.8
1966	744.8	4.9	173.9	460.7	469.8	930.5

Source: Automobile Manufacturing Association, *Automobile Facts and Figures* (Detroit, 1968), p. 49.

EXHIBIT 8

Trends in transit equipment owned by operating companies: 1935–1967

As of Dec. 31	Grand total	Rail transit			Trolley bus	Motor bus
		Total	Surface	Subway and elevated		
1935	74,844	50,466	40,050	10,416	578	23,800
1940	75,464	37,662	26,630	11,032	2,802	35,000
1945	89,758	36,377	26,160	10,217	3,711	49,670
1950	86,310	22,986	13,228	9,758	6,504	56,820
1955	73,089	14,532	5,300	9,232	6,157	52,400
1960	65,292	11,866	2,856	9,010	3,826	49,600
1961	64,014	11,419	2,341	9,078	3,593	49,000
1962	63,045	11,084	2,219	8,865	3,161	48,800
1963	62,189	10,634	1,756	8,878	2,155	49,400
1964	61,679	10,614	1,553	9,061	1,865	49,200
1965	61,717	10,664	1,549	9,115	1,453	49,600
1966	62,136	10,680	1,407	9,273	1,326	50,130
1967	62,069	10,645	1,388	9,257	1,244	50,180

Source: *Transit Fact Book*, 1968, p. 14.

EXHIBIT 9

Transit industry trends: Utilization, employment, wages, revenues, and productivity 1923–1967

Year	(1) Transit vehicle-miles (millions)	(2) Rapid transit vehicle-miles	(3) Passengers per rapid transit vehicle-miles	(4) Transit industry employment (in 000s)	(5) Rapid transit employment (in 000s)	(6) Average transit ind. wage	(7) Consumer price index (1923 = 100)	(8) Consumer price index (1955 = 100)	(9) Total industry wages (millions)	(10) Rapid transit total wages (millions)
1923	2,200	—	—	280	—	$1,510	100	—	$ 422	—
1927	2,400	—	—	270	—	1,660	102	—	458	—
1932	2,180	—	—	210	—	1,550	80	—	325	—
1937	2,500	—	—	215	—	1,730	84	—	356	—
1945	3,250	—	—	242	—	2,612	105	—	632	—
1947	3,340	—	—	255	—	2,970	131	—	790	—
1949	3,180	—	—	240	—	3,325	140	—	841	—
1951	2,910	—	—	208	—	3,760	152	—	872	—
1953	2,700	—	—	201	—	4,066	157	—	913	—
1955	2,450	382	4.60	198	66.0	4,364	158	100	864	$288
1957	2,290	388	4.45	177	54.5	4,746	165	104	840	260
1959	2,160	388	4.30	159	47.7	5,229	171	108	832	252
1961	2,080	385	4.40	152	43.7	5,642	176	111	856	247
1963	2,020	387	4.35	147	43.1	6,062	180	114	892	260
1965	2,010	395	4.30	145	42.6	6,645	185	117	964	284
1967	2,000	397	4.25	146	42.0	7,222	196	124	1,055	304

Note: Column 1 includes bus, streetcar, and rail rapid transit vehicle-miles. Column 7 was recomputed by the casewriter from sources given below in order to set 1923 equal to 100.

Sources: Unless otherwise noted, figures for columns are compiled from three sources:

1. *Transit Fact Book,* 1968.
2. *Moody's Transportation Manual* (1954–1967).
3. *Moody's Public Utilities Manual* (1920–1954).

Cols. 7 and 8: U.S. Bureau of the Census, *Historical Statistics of the United States, Colonial Times to 1957;* and *United States Statistical Abstract: 1968* (Washington, D.C., 1960 and 1968).

EXHIBIT 9 (continued)

Year	(1) Transit industry passenger revenue (millions)	(12) Rapid transit passenger revenue (millions)	(13) Total wages as a percent of total passenger revenue	(14) Total rapid transit wages as a percent of passenger revenue	(15) Total wages/ total vehicle-miles	(16) Total wages per vehicle-mile index (1923 = 100)	(17) Rapid transit wages/ vehicle-miles	(18) Rapid transit wages per vehicle-mile index (1955 = 100)	(19) Total pass. revenue total vehicle-miles	(20) Pass. rev./ per vehicle-mile index (1923 = 100)
1923	$ 925	—	46	—	$.19	100	—	—	$.42	100
1927	900	—	51	—	.19	100	—	—	.38	90
1932	620	—	52	—	.15	79	—	—	.28	67
1937	700	—	51	—	.14	74	—	—	.28	67
1945	1,314	—	48	—	.19	100	—	—	.40	95
1947	1,324	—	60	—	.24	126	—	—	.40	95
1949	1,420	—	59	—	.26	137	—	—	.45	107
1951	1,400	—	62	—	.30	158	—	—	.48	114
1953	1,460	—	63	—	.34	179	—	—	.54	129
1955	1,359	$404	64	71	.35	184	$.75	100	.55	131
1957	1,320	358	64	73	.37	195	.67	89	.58	138
1959	1,308	341	64	74	.39	205	.65	87	.61	145
1961	1,321	347	65	71	.41	216	.64	85	.64	152
1963	1,316	329	68	79	.44	232	.67	89	.65	155
1965	1,340	328	72	87	.48	253	.72	96	.67	160
1967	1,457	385	72	79	.53	279	.77	103	.73	174

Sources: *Moody's.*

EXHIBIT 9 (concluded)

Year	(21) Rapid transit passenger rev./ vehicle-mile	(22) Rapid transit revenue per vehicle-mile index (1955 = 100)	(23) Index of productivity man-hr. in basic industries (1923 = 100)	(24) Productiv./ man-hr. in basic ind. index (1955 = 100)	(25) Total vehicle-miles/ total workers	(26) Vehicle-miles per worker index	(27) Total rapid transit vehicle-miles/total workers	(28) Index	(29) Rapid transit pass. rev./R.T. vehicle-mile (Col. 21/ Col. 3)	(30) Rapid transit per pass.-revenue mile*
1923	—	—	100	—	7,857	100	—	—	—	—
1927	—	—	120	—	8,889	113	—	—	—	—
1932	—	—	131	—	10,381	132	—	—	—	—
1937	—	—	166	—	11,628	148	—	—	—	—
1945	—	—	193	—	13,430	171	—	—	—	—
1947	—	—	186	—	13,098	167	—	—	—	—
1949	—	—	202	—	13,250	169	—	—	—	—
1951	—	—	217	—	13,970	178	—	—	—	—
1953	—	—	230	—	12,433	172	—	—	—	—
1955	$1.06	100	250	100	12,374	158	5,788	100	23.0¢	4.6 ¢
1957	.92	87	259	104	12,938	165	7,119	102	22.2	4.15
1959	.88	83	277	111	13,576	173	8,134	116	21.5	4.10
1961	.90	85	295	118	13,702	175	8,810	125	22.0	4.08
1963	.85	80	320	128	13,723	176	8,979	128	21.8	3.90
1965	.83	78	346	138	13,862	177	9,272	132	21.5	3.85
1967	.97	92	358	143	13,689	174	9,452	135	21.2	4.57

* Rapid transit revenue per passenger-mile is obtained by dividing Column 29 by the average distance traveled by rapid transit passengers, approximately five miles.

Sources: *Moody's*
Col. 23: *Moody's Industrial Manual, 1968*; and *Historical Statistics of the United States.* U.S. Bureau of the Census.

EXHIBIT 10

Massachusetts Bay Transportation Authority
Statement of Net Cost of Service — Loss — by Express and Local
Fiscal Period September 1, 1966 to September 30, 1967

	Express Service	Local Service	Total
Income:			
Revenue from Transportation	$25,901,237.99	$17,381,588.22	$43,282,826.21
Revenue from Other Rwy. Operations	669,098.95	181,712.97	850,811.92
Non-Operating Income	3,536,901.14	949,326.19	4,486,227.33
TOTAL INCOME	30,107,238.08	18,512,627.38	48,619,865.46
Operating Wages and Fringe Benefits:			
Wages	20,301,501.87	26,911,293.18	47,212,795.05
M.B.T.A. Pensions	1,289,881.34	1,576,521.64	2,866,402.98
Social Security Taxes	770,356.18	941,546.43	1,711,902.61
Workmen's Compensation	125,949.93	293,883.18	419,833.11
Accident and Sickness Insurance	148,033.76	180,930.16	328,963.92
Group Life Insurance	177,253.64	216,643.29	393,896.93
Blue Cross — Blue Shield	701,313.43	857,160.80	1,558,474.23
Unemployment Insurance	7,122.60	8,705.40	15,828.00
Uniform and Work Clothes	97,233.99	127,072.63	224,306.62
TOTAL OPERATING WAGES AND FRINGE BENEFITS	23,618,646.74	31,113,756.71	54,732,403.45
Material and Other Items	2,441,305.00	2,999,571.00	5,440,876.00
Injuries and Damages	453,845.45	1,461,346.33	1,915,191.78
Depreciation	1,584,545.00	564,939.00	2,149,484.00
Interest on Unfunded Debt	1,183,732.00	1,013,332.68	2,197,064.68
Fuel	949,763.70	860,609.34	1,810,373.04
Taxes (Other than included above)	4,929.61	370,479.07	375,408.68
Railroad Commuter Subsidy	1,821,559.97	—	1,821,559.97
Middlesex & Boston Subsidy	—	397,160.00	397,160.00
TOTAL OPERATING EXPENSES AND TAXES	32,058,327.47	38,781,194.13	70,839,521.60
Fixed Charges:			
Interest on Funded Debt (M.T.A.)	3,109,851.94	1,101,770.50	4,211,622.44
Interest on Funded Debt (M.B.T.A.)	2,250,242.14	169,399.74	2,419,641.88
Payment on Funded Debt (M.T.A.)	2,292,108.98	1,713,587.44	4,005,696.42
Cambridge Subway Rental	405,007.92	—	405,007.92
Miscellaneous Debits (M.T.A.)	8,668.27	6,732.97	15,401.24
Bank Service Charges (M.B.T.A.)	13,102.23	1,014.68	14,116.91
TOTAL FIXED CHARGES	8,078,981.48	2,992,505.33	11,071,486.81
TOTAL CURRENT EXPENSES	40,137,308.95	41,773,699.46	81,911,008.41
COST OF SERVICE IN EXCESS OF INCOME	10,030,070.87	23,261,072.08	33,291,142.95
Less:			
State Financial Contract Assistance-M.T.A.	3,250,000.00		3,250,000.00
State Financial Contract Assistance-M.B.T.A.	1,467,348.75	63,590.63	1,530,939.38
Gas & Diesel Taxes Reimbursable	—	245,789.15	245,789.15
State Financial Contract Assistance on Railroad Subsidy	1,638,795.08	—	1,638,795.08
NET COST OF SERVICE — LOSS	3,673,927.04	22,951,692.30	26,625,619.34
Less — Unreimbursed Deficit	1,584,545.00	564,939.00	2,149,484.00
NET ASSESSABLE COST OF SERVICE	$2,089,382.04	$22,386,753.30	$24,476,135.34

Source: 1967 Annual Report of the Massachusetts Bay Transportation Authority.

EXHIBIT 11

Rail rapid transit cost of maintenance and operation
(before debt service, depreciation, and taxes)

	Boston MBTA 9-1-66 to 9-30-67	Chicago CTA 1-1-67 to 12-30-67	Cleveland CTS 1967	Montreal MTC 5-1-67 to 4-30-68	New York NYCTA 7-1-66 to 6-30-67	Philadelphia PTC 1967	Toronto TTC 1967
Revenue car-miles (in 000s)	9,540	45,314	4,149	24,213	316,264	14,931	16,418
Unit costs—cents per car-mile							
Maintenance—way and structures	35.00	10.21	9.32	13.70	16.37	8.55	15.08
Maintenance—car equipment	15.22	11.92	6.62	8.70	14.11	12.06	17.52
Power	14.53	7.98	9.59	5.41	11.06	13.40	8.90
Conducting transportation	87.14	32.87	30.22	20.34	41.66†	40.07	18.28
Subtotal (cents per car-mile)	151.89	62.98	55.75	48.15	83.22	74.08	59.78
Injuries and damages	43.07	3.12	1.06	0.50	1.79	N.A.	1.60
General and administrative	N.A.	12.24	12.80	6.09	6.11*†	N.A.	8.68
Total (cents per car-mile)	194.96	78.34	69.61	54.74	91.12	N.A.	70.06

N.A. = Not available.
* Includes operating rentals.
† Reflects increased cost of transit police protection and offset by credit received from city of New York.
Source: Institute for Rapid Transit, *Rapid Transit Reference Manual, 1967.*

EXHIBIT 12
Rail rapid transit around the world
(selected data, selected cities)

City (population 000)	Date of opening of first subway)	Total miles (subway miles)	Fare (cents)	No. of passengers yearly (daily average, 000s)	Gross 1962 receipts (000) (operating costs)	No. of cars (accommodation)*
New York (8,000)	October 1904	236 (134)	15	1,344,953 (3,675)	$273,700 (290,000)	6,850 200–300
London (transport area 10,041)	January 1863	226 (95)	3 a mile	674,000 (1,847)	76,500 (76,500)	4,150 140–144
Paris (transport area 6,223)	July 1900	116 (100)	11	1,214,298 (3,327)	65,000 N.A.	2,921 140
Chicago (metropolitan area 6,221)	October 1943	73 (17)	25	112,924 (309)	137,840 (126,200)	1,220 100
Boston (metropolitan area 2,589)	September 1898	49 (12)	20	212,000 (579)	40,180 (56,980)	450 Unknown
Berlin (3,350)	February 1902	55 (40)	9	250,000 (685)	42,500 (48,300)	857 90–150
Hamburg (2,180)	February 1912	44 (8)	7.5 to 15	142,091 (389)	7,200 (5,600)	530 150
Moscow (7,000)	May 1935	40 (35)	25	About 1,000,000 (2,730)	N.A.	Unknown 250
Tokyo (9,676)	December 1927	31 (28)	5 to 17	376,879 (1,033)	20,200 (20,200)	(As of May 1962) 523 120–150

* "Accommodation" denotes maximum capacity per transit car.
N.A. = Not applicable.
Source: Report of Teito Rapid Transit Authority (Tokyo: May 31, 1962).

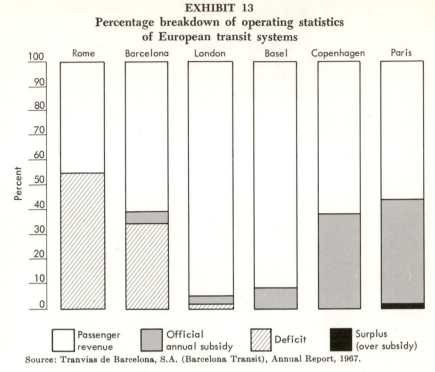

EXHIBIT 13
**Percentage breakdown of operating statistics
of European transit systems**

Passenger revenue | Official annual subsidy | Deficit | Surplus (over subsidy)

Source: Tranvias de Barcelona, S.A. (Barcelona Transit), Annual Report, 1967.

EXHIBIT 14
**The percentage decline in the number of surface passengers
on European transit systems, 1962–1965**

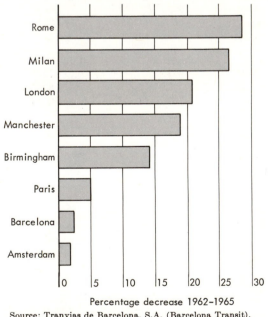

Percentage decrease 1962–1965

Source: Tranvias de Barcelona, S.A. (Barcelona Transit),
Annual Report, 1967.

EXHIBIT 15

Rapid transit construction around the world

City	Metropolitan population	Route mileage
Athens	1,900,000	15.9*
Baku	1,100,000	Under const.
Barcelona	2,000,000	16.4*
Berlin	5,000,000	58.3*
Brussels	1,300,000	Under const.
Budapest	2,100,000	2.3
Buenos Aires	4,000,000	19*
Cologne	1,000,000	Under const.
Caracas	1,500,000	Planning stage
Dusseldorf	900,000	Planning stage
Frankfurt	900,000	Under const.
Glasgow	1,900,000	6.6
Hamburg	2,300,000	46.1*
Hannover	600,000	Under const.
Kharkov	1,100,000	Under const.
Kiev	1,300,000	3.7
Kobe	1,400,000	Planning stage
Kyoto	1,200,000	Planning stage
Leningrad	3,900,000	15.2*
Lisbon	1,400,000	4.5*
London	11,000,000	244*
Lyon	900,000	Planning stage
Madrid	2,400,000	22.6*
Melbourne	2,100,000	Planning stage
Milan	2,600,000	7.5*
Montreal	2,200,000	15.2
Moscow	8,200,000	61*
Munich	1,200,000	Under const.
Nagoya	2,000,000	1.6
Osaka	8,300,000	16.8*
Oslo	500,000	15
Paris	7,800,000	117.2*
Rome	2,300,000	6.8*
Rotterdam	900,000	3.5*
Santiago (Chile)	2,000,000	Planning stage
Sao Paulo	5,000,000	Planning stage
Stockholm	1,200,000	32*
Sydney	4,000,000	Planning stage
Tiflis	800,000	6*
Tokyo	13,000,000	36.9*
Toronto	1,900,000	14.0*
Vienna	2,400,000	16.5*
Yokohama	1,600,000	Planning stage

* Adding new lines.

Source: Institute for Rapid Transit, *Rapid Transit Reference Manual*, 1967.

EXHIBIT 16
A negative element of public transit's image in the United States

EXHIBIT 17
Perception of an "Urban Transportation Problem" in the 1960s
by one opinion-forming magazine

Excerpt from article

Road Trap. The man who drives his auto to work, on the other hand, can rarely relax. He prizes the independence the auto gives him, but he pays for it dearly. With one foot on the brake and the other on the accelerator, he braves traffic jams so packed that, so the story goes, a Los Angeles driver was carried along for ten miles after he ran out of gas. He can expect no quarter from his own. A motorist lost ·on the Santa Ana freeway recently pulled his car onto the center island to take his bearings. Three hours later he was still there, trapped by a whizzing flow of motorists who refused to slow down enough to let him get back on the road.

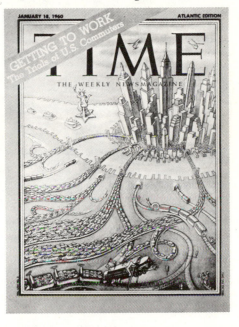

The total of U.S. cars is now 62 million, and it is growing faster than the population. Billions of dollars are being spent to build new roads and expressways that sometimes cost up to $30 million a mile. Los Angeles has spent $800 million in the last decade, Detroit $76.8 million since 1955, and Boston $125 million for a three-mile central artery. For every acre of floor space constructed, suburban plants now need two acres of space for their commuting workers' cars. Since cities, notably Los Angeles and Detroit, devote up to two-thirds of their downtown areas to streets and parking areas.

EXHIBIT 18

Comparative indices of industrial and farm productivity, the value of farm machinery, and motor vehicle registration°

Year	Index of truck reg.	Index of auto reg.	Index of industrial productivity/ man-hour	Index of farm product/ man-hour	Index of value of farm machinery	Percent urban population
1900	0	0	40	88	25	40
1910	3	2	51	90	65	46
1920	30	35	61	86	75	51
1930	100	100	100	100	100	56
1940	133	120	128	120	100	57
1950	236	175	154	183	207	64
1960	325	268	225	345	510	70
1967	440	350	325	500	665	73

* Statistics recalculated by casewriter from sources below so that 1930 is uniformly given an index value of 100.

Source: Bureau of the Census, *Historical Statistics of the United States*, and *Statistical Abstract of the United States, 1968* (Washington, D.C., 1960 and 1968).

EXHIBIT 19
Automobile ownership by income levels

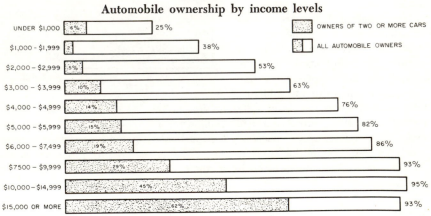

Source: Automobile Manufacturers Association, *Automobile Facts and Figures*, 1967.

EXHIBIT 20
Percentage distribution of personal consumption expenditures
1930–1959

Period	Total expenditure	Housing and Household operation	Clothing and shoes	Food and Alcoholic beverages	Transportation and travel	Other goods and services
1930–1934	100.0	30.8	10.8	24.9	8.5	24.9
1935–1939	100.0	27.7	10.5	29.0	9.4	23.4
1940–1944	100.0	26.0	12.2	31.7	7.1	23.0
1945–1949	100.0	24.7	11.7	32.2	9.2	22.2
1950–1954	100.0	26.9	9.7	28.5	12.2	22.7
1955–1959	100.0	27.7	9.0	26.0	12.6	24.7

Source: U.S. Housing and Home Finance Agency, *Housing Statistics, Annual Data* (March 1960), p. 38.

EXHIBIT 21
Passenger capacities per lane or track*

	Per lane/track per hour	Headway (minutes)	Effective capacity at various loading ratios	
Private automobile				
City street capacity	800		1,200 @ 1.50	1,600 @ 2.00
Freeway capacity	2,000		3,000 @ 1.50	4,000 @ 2.00
Transit bus (50 seats)				
City street	90	0.67	4,500 @ 100%	6,750 @ 150%
Freeway	180	0.33	9,000 @ 100%	13,500 @ 150%
Rail rapid-transit train				
six car train	30	2.00	21,600 @ 120	32,400 @ 180
	40	1.50	28,800 @ 120	43,200 @ 180
ten car train	30	2.00	36,000 @ 120	54,000 @ 180
	40	1.50	48,000 @ 120	72,000 @ 180

* Example of the number of persons carried in the peak direction on representative facilities are: eight-lane freeway—7,500 to 16,000 persons per hour; two-track rail rapid transit with six-car trains—12,000 to 43,000 persons per hour.

Source: Institute of Traffic Engineers, *Capacities and Limitations of Urban Transportation Modes*, (May 1965).

EXHIBIT 22
The cost of commuting by automobile

Depreciation.	$2,850.00
Gasoline and oil	799.00
Gasoline tax	361.50
Repair	871.00
Insurance	1,254.00
Parking, etc.	1,188.00
Tires	90.00
Accessories	75.50
Registration	152.00
Other taxes	324.00

$$\frac{\$7,865.00}{50,000 \text{ miles}} = \$0.1573 \text{ per mile}$$

Note: The estimates above were prepared in April 1964 by the Bureau of Public Roads. The figures given were for a second car used primarily for commuting. A daily, 20-mile round trip was assumed for a year of 250 working days. The figures are based on a ten-year, 50,000-mile life for the car.

EXHIBIT 23
Mode of transportation used with given distances to public transit

Distance to public transit	Means of transportation to work (percentage)			
	Automobile	Public transit	Walk	Total
Less than ¼ mile	68	28	4	100
¼ to ½ mile	72	24	4	100
½ to 1 mile	80	16	4	100
Over 1 mile	92	8	—	100
Average = ½ to 1 mile	82	14	4	100

Source: Automobile Manufacturers' Association, *Automobile Facts and Figures*, 1967, p. 64.

EXHIBIT 24
All automobile trips by destination

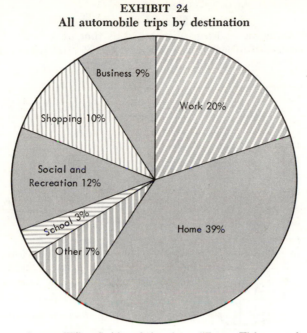

Source: Wilbur Smith and Associates, "Future Highways and Urban Growth," 1961.

EXHIBIT 25
Modal traffic peaks in Chicago
Daily internal trips distributed by time of arrival
(percentage distribution by hourly period, of total person trips
within each classification)

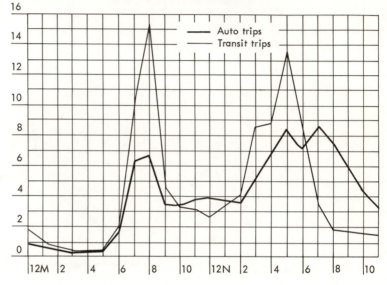

Source: Chicago Area Transportation Study, 1963.

Percentage of peak-hour commutation trips made by public transit

New York	Chicago	Philadelphia	Toronto	Boston	Cleveland
90	80	75	77	70	55

Source: "Hearings on Rapid Transit for the Nation's Capital" before the Committee on the District of Columbia, House of Representatives, February 17–March 17, 1965.

EXHIBIT 26
Population, vehicle registrations, and urban vehicle mileage

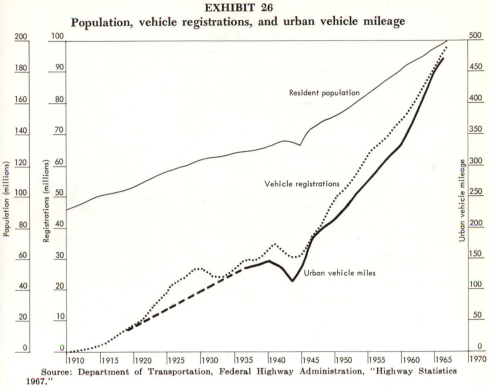

Source: Department of Transportation, Federal Highway Administration, "Highway Statistics 1967."

EXHIBIT 27
Special taxes on highway users
(millions of dollars)

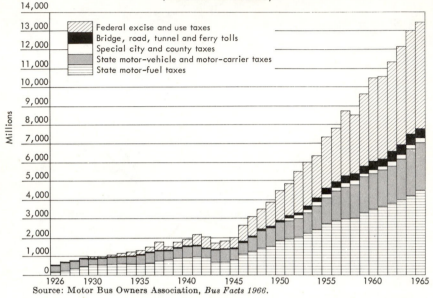

Source: Motor Bus Owners Association, *Bus Facts 1966*.

EXHIBIT 28
Roadway-related expenditures and revenues of large city governments of the United States, 1951 and 1961
(in millions)

	41 largest city total	Boston	Chicago	Los Angeles	New York	Phila-delphia
1951 Expenditures	$327	$10	$30	$15	$90	$15
Revenue	154	3	23	11	29	5
Difference	$173	$ 7	$ 7	$ 4	$ 61	$10
	43 largest city total					
1961 Expenditures	$676	$ 8	$68	$33	$211	$22
Revenue	305	2	57	11	80	5
Difference	$371	$ 6	$11	$22	$131	$17

Sources: 1951 data: U.S. Department of Commerce, Bureau of the Census, *Large City Finances in 1951*, 1960 data: U.S. Department of Commerce, Bureau of Census, *Compedium of City Government Finances in 1961*. From *Urban Transportation and Public Policy*, Lyle C. Fitch and Associates.

EXHIBIT 29

Examples of views on Federal Aid to Urban Transit collected by the Chamber of Commerce of the United States

U.S. Senator Strom Thurmond (on the floor of the Senate, June 27, 1960):

I heartily agree that rapid transit must be provided for. However, I say it is not the problem of the Federal Government. It is the problem of the cities involved. If the cities involved, which are cities with the greatest wealth in the United States, cannot go forward and undertake the responsibilities which are theirs, how can the Federal Government get the means from any other source except the rural people?

American Automobile Association (*Facts and Fallacies About Urban Transportation,* February 1962, p. 8):

Fallacy: Mass transit should be subsidized so it can compete on even terms with highway transportation which is heavily subsidized by the Federal and state governments.

Fact: Federal and state governments do not subsidize highway transportation. In fact, highway users are more than paying their own way. Special taxes levied on highway users by the Federal government support the entire "Federal-aid" highway program. Highway users also pay in full for construction, maintenance, policing and administration of other major rural and urban highways.

Transportation Center at Northwestern University—staff report: "Growth and Change in Metropolitan Areas and Their Relation to Metropolitan Transportation"—a research summary, p. 17:

Thus it may be that public transportation is desirable for aesthetic, national defence, health or political reasons entirely unrelated to its economic value. It may well be deemed socially desirable to provide public transportation for people who need to travel to and from their jobs but cannot afford or are unable to drive automobiles.

Whether these nonmarket virtues of urban mass transit justify subsidy is a matter for the citizenry . . . to decide.

Thomas R. Reid, civic and governmental affairs manager, Ford Motor Co., Indianapolis Rotary, May 1962:

There is really only one solution to the traffic problem, spread people over a greater area so they have room to move around without bumping into each other.

Source: Press release by the Chamber of Commerce of the United States (Washington, D.C., May 8, 1962).

EXHIBIT 30
Summary of rapid transit routes under construction
or planned for construction—December 1968

I. Extensions of already existing rapid transit systems

Chicago Transit Authority

Extension mileage: 14.7 miles on two expressway median strips
Number of cars: 150
Estimated cost: $69 million
Completion date: Early 1969

Cleveland Transit System

Extension mileage: 3.8 mile airport extension, opened November 15, 1968
Number of cars: 20
Estimated cost: $18 million

Note: Six extensions totaling 31.1 miles and costing an estimated $162 million were under study.*

Massachusetts Bay Transportation Authority (Boston)

	Cambridge Dorchester	Forest Hills Everett	Central Subway
Extension mileage..........	16.2	14.5	1.1
Number of cars.............	76	—	—
Estimated cost.............	$126.6 million	$141.5 million	$19.8 million
Completion data..........	1969	1970	1970

Note: Total program cost has escalated to $1 billion by December 1968, as a result of further line extensions, cost inflation, and earlier gross underestimates of cost.*

Metropolitan Transportation Authority (New York)

Under a $25 billion bond issue approved by voters in New York State, a vast rail transit improvement and expansion was to be carried out in metropolitan New York.

	Phase one ($ million)	Phase two ($ million)	Total ($ million)
Eastern Corridor...................	$ 806	$ 533	$1,339
Northern corridor.................	428	294	722
Southern Corridor.................	25	10	35
Central Business Dist..............	406	441	847
Total......................	$1,665	$1,278	$2,943
Completion Date:	By 1978	Indefinite	

* All such notes appended to the original by the casewriter.

EXHIBIT 30 (*continued*)

Southeastern Pennsylvania Transportation Authority (Philadelphia)

Broad Street Subway

Extension mileage............   7.6
Number of cars..............   90
Estimated cost.............. $109 million

Note: Construction expected to begin in late 1969 or 1970.[*]

II. New rapid transit systems under construction

Delaware River Port Authority (Philadelphia–Camden)

System mileage: 14.6   Opened in fall of 1968
Number of cars: 75   (Being delivered from the Budd Company)
Estimated cost: $80 million

San Francisco Bay Area Rapid Transit District

System mileage: 75.0   (Initial partial operation planned for early 1970)
Number of cars: 450   (Initial 250 cars scheduled to be ordered in 1969)
Estimated cost: $ 1.2   billion

Washington Metropolitan Area Transit Authority

System mileage: 97.2   (Groundbreaking fall 1968)
Number of cars: 800   (200 for the initial 25 mile system)
Estimated cost: $2.525 billion

III. Rapid transit systems being planned for construction

Metropolitan Atlanta Rapid Transit Authority

System mileage: 64.9 miles
Number of cars: 186
Estimated cost: $421 million

Note: Bond referendum rejected in November 1968 by voters.[*]

Metropolitan Transit Authority—Regional Planning Commission (Baltimore)

	Phase one	Phase two	Total
System mileage.............	27.0	44.8	71.8
Number of cars.............	105	527	632
Estimated cost.............	$394 million	$606 million	$1 billion

Note: System based on a concept similar to that of Westinghouse Electric
Corporation's Transit Expressway.[*]

Municipality of Metropolitan Seattle

System mileage: 47
Number of cars: 300
Estimated cost: $1.155 billion

[*] All such notes appended to the original by the casewriter.

EXHIBIT 30 (*concluded*)

Note: February 1968 bond referendum received a plurality but not the required 60 percent approval by the voters. Another referendum is planned for 1969.°

Port Authority of Allegheny County (Pittsburgh)

	Rail	Transit Expressway
System mileage	60.10	61.20
Number of cars	200	460
Estimated cost	$774,534 million	$739,338 million

Note: Engineering report dated December 1967, presented findings for both a rail and a Transit Expressway type of system.°

Southern California Rapid Transit District (Los Angeles)

System mileage: 61.73
Number of cars: 538
Estimated cost: $1.443 billion

Note: Referendum to provide necessary financing rejected by voters in November 1968.°

* All such notes appended to the oirginal by the casewriter.

EXHIBIT 31
Stanford Research Institute's projection of a $10 billion rapid transit market (1962–1982)

Transitway

Structure and track	$ 4,500,000,000
Stations	1,400,000,000
Shops, yards, and storage	400,000,000
Electrification	900,000,000
Signaling and control	500,000,000
Utility relocation	400,000,000
Engineering	900,000,000
Vehicles	1,000,000,000
Total	$10,000,000,000

Source: *Metropolitan Transportation and Planning*, January 1964, p. 16.

EXHIBIT 32
Age distribution of mass transit vehicles
(December 1964)

Year built	Number of transit vehicles					Percentage distribution	
	Rapid transit cars	Motor buses	Surface street-cars	Trolley coaches	Total vehicles	Rapid transit cars	Motor buses
Before 1900	0	0	0	0	0	–	–
1901–1920.	711	0	0	0	711	7.8	–
1921–1930.	{2,730	0	{1,560	{171	{48,691	{30.1	–
1931–1940.		610					1.2
1941–1950.	{3,451	16,010		{1,694		{38.1	32.5
1951–1960.		22,465					45.6
Since 1961	2,172	10,115	0	0	12,287	23.9	20.6
Total	9,064	49,200	1,560	1,865	61,689	100.0	100.0

Source: Tax Foundation, Inc., *Urban Mass Transportation in Perspective* (New York: 1968), p. 36.

EXHIBIT 33
Construction cost allocation for new rapid transit systems
showing areas of principle expenditures based on
engineering feasibility reports

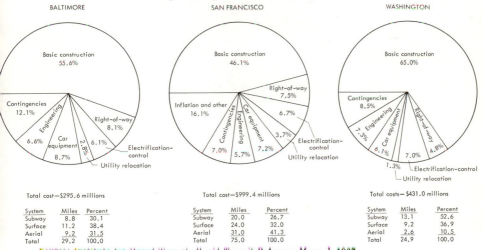

Source: Institute for Rapid Transit, *Rapid Transit Reference Manual*, 1967.

APPENDIX

TRANSPORTATION

Will car builders miss San Francisco train?

Transit system must order 250 ultramodern cars worth $50-million or more. But cars are so advanced that carbuilders are slow in bidding

When U. S. railroads stopped ordering passenger cars in the mid-1950s, three carbuilding companies, Budd Co., Pullman, Inc., and St. Louis Car Div. of General Steel Industries, Inc., chose to maintain their shops and forces.

They wanted to be ready for a rush of orders for rapid transit cars—estimated as high as $10-billion—that was always about to start "next year."

The years passed. They scrabbled along somehow, fighting each other

This is the big prestige order. The company that wins it could gain a huge advantage. And the winner may not be a carbuilder at all.

Too new? The cars that BART wants built are technologically so advanced that the chief problem in making them is not the fabrication of the metal, it's building the power, control, and braking systems. Says David G. Hammond, BART's chief engineer, "The specifications don't call for a car man-

panies, Rohr Corp. and Garrett Corp., in the act.

One company not planning to bid, at least so far, is Budd. Along with its subcontractors, Budd took a bath on the Northeast Corridor Project's high speed Metroliner cars when several subsystems failed to meet specifications.

Says a Budd official, "Although we do not intend to submit a bid to the Bay Area Rapid Transit for cars, we have a deep and continuing interest in the project which is one of the most advanced new rapid systems that has ever been planned. However, the proposed contract provisions present problems which, based on our own experience in the development and manufacture of highly advanced rail equipment, have led us to the decision not to bid on the cars. Although the technical problems are solvable, the commercial risks are too great."

First run. What bothers the car manufacturers particularly is the "inflexibility" of the contract language. "BART is asking the car makers to take responsibility that is far more than has ever been asked before," says another carbuilding company official. "The way the contract reads, BART could come in any time they wanted and stop production, or do anything they wanted to."

Bill R. Stokes, BART general manager, disputes this. "The specifications are based on performance," he says, "and not on how the manufacturer should do it, so the contractor has leeway. But the car manufacturers are looking over their shoulders at what happened to Budd and now they're getting gun-shy."

Manager Stokes and engineer Hammond realize that the BART car represents a significant advance in rail car technology; they also realize—no less than the executives at Budd, St. Louis Car, and Pullman—that if BART modifies specifications and adjusts contract terms for the car manufacturers, it will be setting a precedent for transit systems of cities that want to follow its lead, such as Washington, Baltimore, Atlanta, and Seattle.

Highly sophisticated car was designed for San Francisco Bay Area Rapid Transit District. Here model is examined by BART General Manager Bill R. Stokes.

mostly over replacement orders, building cars—with a few exceptions—for existing rapid transit lines. Always they were waiting for the big break, the time when the next generation cars would be ordered for brand-new transit systems, built from scratch, heralding a nationwide surge of orders.

At last, the moment has come, San Francisco and Oakland's Bay Area Rapid Transit District is asking for bids on 250 highly automated, very sophisticated transit cars. Cost: $50-million to $65-million, with the federal government paying $28-million.

ufacturer to be the prime contractor, they call for a qualified bidder. A company that is involved with subsystems, such as propulsion and braking, could come in as prime contractor with a car manufacturer as subcontractor."

Even more disturbing to the carbuilders is the fact that the specifications were not drawn up in the traditional manner. The contract, as it now stands, is more attuned to the aerospace industry than it is to the carbuilders. Indeed, when the bids are submitted June 3, BART would not be surprised to find two aircraft com-

Source: *Business Week*, May 3, 1969. Reproduced herewith by special permission of *Business Week* magazine.

A development affecting the structure of the industry

Car Novice Rohr Low Bidder on San Francisco Transit Units[1]

SAN FRANCISCO (UPI)—Rohr Corp., an aerospace firm, beat out experienced competitors by submitting a low alternate bid of $59 million for construction of America's newest and most complicated rail passenger cars.

The bid was for construction of 250 self-propelled cars, each carrying 72 passengers, to operate on the San Francisco Bay Area Rapid Transit District's 75-mile $1.3 billion system. The cars will attain speeds of 80 miles an hour.

Rohr, of Chula Vista, Calif., has never made rail cars before. Two other bidders, which have been making them for decades, were Pullman, Inc., of Chicago and General Steel Industries Inc., of St. Louis. Pullman's low bid was $2.4 million more than Rohr's and General Steel's was $4 million more.

The nation's third carbuilding firm, Budd Co. of Philadelphia, did not submit a bid.

Rohr Corporation was incorporated in California in 1940 as the Rohr Aircraft Corporation. In 1968, the company manufactured complete power package installations for jet aircraft, nozzles and motor cases for missiles and rocket boosters, satellite tracking antennas, large aluminum boat hulls, and Deep Submergence Rescue Vehicles.

The company reported record sales in 1968 of $261,936,000, and record earnings of $9,049,000. Sales had grown from $147.5 million in 1958, and the company had reported net income in excess of $2 million every year for a decade. At year-end in 1968, the company had a firm backlog of $420 million in orders.

Rohr Corporation prided itself on the application of advanced computer technology to its manufacturing operations. Rohr's 1968 annual report claimed that the company was one of the first to develop numerical control of machine tools, and that it was still a leader in the use of such technology. Rohr had also developed for its own use a computer-controlled warehousing system konwn as "Automove." In 1969, the company was investigating the possibility of developing and marketing similar systems for freight and mail handling firms and for airports.[2]

---

[1] *The Boston Herald*, June 6, 1969.

[2] *Moody's Industrial Manual*, 1968, p. 262; Rohr Corporation's annual report, 1969.

PART II

Economic policy and its impact upon management

The new economic game plan (A)

PRESIDENTIAL MESSAGE—AUGUST 15, 1971[1]

GOOD EVENING,

I have addressed the Nation a number of times over the past two years on the problems of ending a war. Because of the progress we have made toward achieving that goal, this Snuday evening is an appropriate time for us to turn our attention to the challenges of peace.

America today has the best opportunity in this century to achieve two of its greatest ideals: to bring about a full generation of peace, and to create a new prosperity without war.

This not only requires bold leadership ready to take bold action—it calls forth the greatness in a great people.

Prosperity without war requires action on three fronts: We must create more and better jobs; we must stop the rise in the cost of living; we must protect the dollar from the attacks of international money speculators.

We are going to take that action—not timidly, not half-heartedly, and not in piecemeal fashion. We are going to move forward to the new prosperity without war as befits a great people—all together, and along a broad front.

The time has come for a new economic policy for the United States.

[1] Text of President Richard M. Nixon's August 15, 1971 announcement of changes in economic policy as made available by the White House. Reproduced by permission.

Its targets are unemployment, inflation and international speculation. This is how we are going to attack them.

Unemployment

First, on the subject of jobs. We all know why we have an unemployment problem. Two million workers have been eased from the Armed Forces and defense plants because of the success in winding down the war in Vietnam. Putting those people back to work is one of the challenges of peace, and we have begun to make progress. Our unemployment rate today is below the average of the four peacetime years of the 1960s.

But we can and must do better than that.

The time has come for American industry, which has produced more jobs at higher real wages than any other industrial system in history, to embark on a bold program of new investment in production for peace.

To give that system a powerful new stimulus, I shall ask the Congress, when it reconvenes after its summer recess, to consider as its first priority the enactment of the Job Development Act of 1971.

I will propose to provide the strongest short-term incentive in our history to invest in new machinery and equipment that will create new jobs for Americans: A 10 percent Job Development Credit for one year, effective as of today, with a 5 percent credit after August 15, 1972. This tax credit for investment in new equipment will not only generate new jobs; it will raise productivity and it will make our goods more competitive in the years ahead.

Repeal of automobile tax

Second, I will propose to repeal the 7 percent excise tax on automobiles, effective today. This will mean a reduction in price of about $200 per car. I shall insist that the American auto industry pass this tax reduction on to the nearly 8 million customers who are buying automobiles this year. Lower prices will mean that more people will be able to afford new cars, and every additional 100,000 cars sold means 25,000 new jobs.

Income tax exemption

Third, I propose to speed up the personal income tax exemptions scheduled for January 1, 1973 to January 1, 1972—so that taxpayers can deduct an extra $50 for each exemption one year earlier than planned. This increase in consumer spending power will provide a strong boost to the economy in general and to employment in particular.

The tax reductions I am recommending, together with the broad up-turn of the economy which has taken place in the first half of this year, will move us strongly forward toward a goal this nation has not reached since 1956, 15 years ago—prosperity with full employment in peacetime.

Looking to the future, I have directed the Secretary of the Treasury to recommend to the Congress in January new tax proposals for stimulating research and development of new industries and new technologies to help provide the 20 million new jobs that America needs for the young people who will be coming into the job market in the next decade.

Reductions in federal spending

To offset the loss of revenue from these tax cuts which directly stimulate new jobs, I have ordered today a $4.7 billion cut in Federal spending.

Tax cuts to stimulate employment must be matched by spending cuts to restrain inflation. To check the rise in the cost of government, I have ordered a postponement of pay raises and a 5 percent cut in government personnel.

I have ordered a 10 percent cut in foreign economic aid.

In addition, since the Congress has already delayed action on two of the great initiatives of this Administration, I will ask Congress to amend my proposals to postpone the implementation of Revenue Sharing for three months and Welfare Reform for one year.

In this way, I am reordering our budget priorities to concentrate more on achieving full employment.

Cost of living

The second indispensable element of the new prosperity is to stop the rise in the cost of living.

One of the cruelest legacies of the artificial prosperity produced by war is inflation. Inflation robs every American. The 20 million who are retired and living on fixed incomes are particularly hard hit. Home-makers find it harder than ever to balance the family budget. And 80 million wage-earners have been on a treadmill. In the four war years between 1965 and 1969 your wage increases were completely eaten up by price increases. Your paychecks were higher, but you were no better off.

We have made progress against the rise in the cost of living. From the high point of six percent a year in 1969, the rise in consumer prices has been cut to four percent in the first half of 1971. But just as is the case in our fight against unemployment, we can and we must do better than that.

The time has come for decisive action—action that will break the vicious circle of spiraling prices and costs.

Wage-price freeze

I am today ordering a freeze on all prices and wages throughout the United States for a period of 90 days. In addition, I call upon corporations to extend the wage-price freeze to all dividends.

I have today appointed a Cost of Living Council within the Government. I have directed this Council to work with leaders of labor and business to set up the proper mechanism for achieving continued price and wage stability after the 90-day freeze is over.

Let me emphasize two characteristics of this action: First, it is temporary. To put the strong, vigorous American economy into a permanent straitjacket would lock in unfairness; it would stifle the expansion of our free enterprise system. And second, while the wage-price freeze will be backed by Government sanctions, if necessary, it will not be accompanied by the establishment of a huge price control bureaucracy. I am relying on the voluntary cooperation of all Americans—each one of you—workers, employers, consumers—to make this freeze work.

Working together, we will break the back of inflation, and we will do it without the mandatory wage and price controls that crush economic and personal freedom.

Freeing the dollar

The third indispensable element in building the new prosperity is closely related to creating new jobs and halting inflation. We must protect the position of the American dollar as a pillar of monetary stability around the world.

In the past seven years, there has been an average of one international monetary crisis every year. Who gains from these crises? Not the workingman; not the investors; and not the real producers of wealth. The gainers are international money speculators. Because they thrive on crises, they help to create them.

In recent weeks, the speculators have been waging an all-out war on the American dollar. The strength of a nation's currency is based on the strength of that nation's economy—and the American economy is by far the strongest in the world. Accordingly, I have directed the Secretary of the Treasury to take the action necessary to defend the dollar against the speculators.

I have directed Secretary Connally to suspend temporarily the convertibility of the dollar into gold or other reserve assets, except in amounts and conditions determined to be in the interest of monetary stability and in the best interests of the United States.

Now what is this action, which is very technical? What does it mean for you?

Let me lay to rest the bugaboo of what is called devaluation.

If you want to buy a foreign car or take a trip abroad, market conditions may cause your dollar to buy slightly less. But if you are among the overwhelming majority of Americans who buy American-made products in America, your dollar will be worth just as much tomorrow as it is today.

The effect of this action, in other words, will be to stabilize the dollar.

Now this action will not win us any friends among the international money traders. But our primary concern is with the American workers, and with fair competition around the world.

To our friends abroad, including the many responsible members of the international banking community who are dedicated to stability and the flow of trade, I give this assurance: The United States has always been, and will continue to be, a forward-looking and trustworthy trading partner. In full cooperation with the International Monetary Fund and those who trade with us, we will press for the necessary reforms to set up an urgently needed new international monetary system. Stability and equal treatment is in everybody's best interest. I am determined that the American dollar must never again be hostage in the hands of the international speculators.

Import tax

I am taking one further step to protect the dollar, to improve our balance of payments, and to increase sales for Americans. As a temporary measure, I am today imposing an additional tax of 10 percent on goods imported into the United States. This is a better solution for international trade than direct controls on the amount of imports.

This import tax is a temporary action. It isn't directed against any other country. It is an action to make certain that American products will not be at a disadvantage because of unfair exchange rates. When the unfair treatment is ended, the import tax will end as well.

As a result of these actions, the product of American labor will be more competitive, and the unfair edge that some of our foreign competition has had will be removed. That is a major reason why our trade balance has eroded over the past fifteen years.

At the end of World War II the economies of the major industrial nations of Europe and Asia were shattered. To help them get on their feet and to protect their freedom, the United States has provided over the past 25 years $143 billion in foreign aid. This was the right thing for us to do.

Today, largely with our help, they have regained their vitality. They have become our strong competitors, and we welcome their success. But now that other nations are economically strong, the time has come for them to bear their fair share of the burden of defending freedom around the world. The time has come for exchange rates to be set straight and for the major nations to compete as equals. There is no longer any need for the United States to compete with one hand tied behind her back.

New economic policy

The range of actions I have taken and proposed tonight—on the job front, on the inflation front, on the monetary front—is the most comprehensive New Economic Policy to be undertaken by this nation in four decades.

We are fortunate to live in a nation with an economic system capable of producing for its people the highest standard of living in the world; a system flexible enough to change its ways dramatically when circumstances call for change; and most important—a system resourceful enough to produce prosperity with freedom and opportunity unmatched in the history of nations.

The purposes of the government actions I have announced tonight are to lay the basis for renewed confidence, to make it possible for us to compete fairly with the rest of the world, to open the door to a new prosperity.

But government, with all its powers, does not hold the key to the success of a people. That key, my fellow Americans, is in your hands.

A nation, like a person, has to have a certain inner drive in order to succeed. In economic affairs, that inner drive is called the competitive spirit.

Every action I have taken tonight is designed to nurture and stimulate that competitive spirit; to help us snap out of that self-doubt and self-disparagement that saps our energy and erodes our confidence in ourselves.

Whether this nation stays number one in the world's economy or resigns itself to second, third or fourth place; whether we as a people have faith in ourselves, or lose that faith; whether we hold fast to the strength that makes peace and freedom possible in this world, or lose our grip—all that depends on you, on your competitive spirit, your sense of personal destiny, your pride in your country and in yourself.

We can be certain of this: As the threat of war recedes, the challenge of peaceful competition in the world will greatly increase.

We welcome competition, because America is at her greatest when she is called on to compete.

As there always have been in our history, there will be voices urging us to shrink from that challenge of competition, to build a protective wall around ourselves, to crawl into a shell as the rest of the world moves ahead.

Two hundred years ago a man wrote in his diary these words: "Many thinking people believe America has seen its best days." That was written in 1775, just before the American Revolution, at the dawn of the most exciting era in the history of man. Today we hear the echoes of those voices, preaching a gospel of gloom and defeat, saying the same thing: "We have seen our best days."

I say, let Americans reply: "Our best days lie ahead."

As we move into a generation of peace, as we blaze the trail toward the new prosperity, I say to every American: Let us raise our spirits. Let us raise our sights. Let all of us contribute all we can to the great and good country that has contributed so much to the progress of mankind.

Let us invest in our nation's future; and let us revitalize that faith in ourselves that built a great nation in the past, and will shape the world of the future.

Thank you, and good evening.

Managerial implications
of econometric models[1]

In RECENT YEARS economists have made increased use of a relatively new tool for analyzing the behavior of the overall economy—the econometric model. This kind of model, of which there are now a considerable number, attempts to depict in a set of equations the essential quantitative relationships that determine the behavior of such magnitudes as output, income, employment, and prices. Econometric models have been used for forecasting future economic conditions, estimating the impact of alternative government policies, and testing various hypotheses about the nature of the business cycle.

A simplified econometric model

The characteristics of an econometric model and the steps involved in its construction and use can best be explained by reference to a simplified version of an actual model. The following set of seven equations constitutes an econometric model and will serve to illustrate the main points.

$$C_t = c_0 + c_1 D_t \tag{1}$$
$$D_t = d_0 + d_1 Y_t - T_t \tag{2}$$
$$T_t = t_0 + t_1 Y_t \tag{3}$$
$$I_t = i_0 + i_1 R_t + i_2 K_{t-1} \tag{4}$$

---

[1] This note was prepared by Howard W. Pifer, lecturer on Business Administration, as a basis for class discussion rather than to illustrate either effective or ineffective handling of an administrative situation.

$$R_t = r_0 + r_1 Y_t + r_2 M_t \tag{5}$$
$$Y_t = C_t + I_t + G_t \tag{6}$$
$$K_t = K_{t-1} + I_t \tag{7}$$

These equations contain economic variables which are capitalized and coefficients estimated from historical data (for example, c_0, c_1, d_0, t_0, etc.). The subscript t refers to a given time period (for example, 1971) and $t - 1$ to the previous period (for example, 1970).

The variables included in these equations are defined as:

C = Consumption expenditures
D = Disposable personal income
G = Government expenditures
I = Net investment
K = Net capital stock
M = Money supply
R = Interest rate
T = Taxes
Y = Net income

The first equation states that consumption expenditures in the current period depend upon disposable personal income in the same period. Specifically, consumption consists of a fixed amount, c_0, and a percentage of total disposable income, c_1. The schematic diagram (Figure 1) depicts

FIGURE 1

the relationship between consumption expenditures and personal disposable income as well as the direction of influence—that is, changes in disposable income result in changes in consumption.

To assist in visualizing this simplified econometric model, sketch the relationships specified by each equation. In equation 2 personal disposable income is determined by the levels of both income and taxes during the period. Taxes depend on total income and are specified in equation 3 as a fixed amount, t_0, to represent exemptions and a variable amount, t_1, corresponding to the marginal tax rate. Net investment, according to equation 4, is determined by the current interest rate and the net capital stock available at the end of the previous period. Equation 5 relates the interest rate to both fiscal and monetary variables specifically, the current levels for total income and the money supply. The final two equations, called identities, are definitional statements which do not contain coefficients based upon historical data. Total income (or net product) is defined in equation 6 as the sum of consumption, net investment, and government expenditures. (The items that in the real world constitute differences between net income and product, primarily exports and imports, are omitted.) Also, the net capital stock at the end of the current period is equal to the last period's net capital stock plus current net investment as shown in equation 7.

Figure 2 provides a computed schematic representation of each equa-

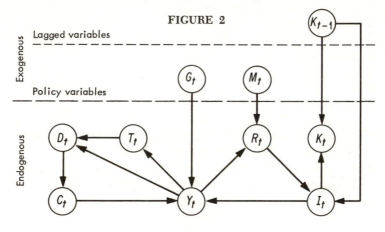

FIGURE 2

tion that has been specified. This set of seven equations defines a system in which the economic variables interact.

Within this system, three classes of variables have been defined. The first of these, lagged variables, consists of those variables whose values have been determined in previous periods. K_{t-1}, the net capital stock in the previous period, is an example of a lagged variable. The second category represents variables which can be directly controlled by the federal government and are often called policy variables. Both government expenditures and the money supply are assumed in the simplified model to be under the control of the federal government. Both lagged and policy variables are often defined as *exogenous* since their values are determined *outside* the model. The third category of economic variables are called *endogenous* variables and their values are determined *within* the econometric model. There are seven endogenous variables defined in this simplified model and illustrated in Figure 2—C_t, D_t, T_t, I_t, R_t, Y_t and K_t.

Constructing an econometric model

As a basis for an econometric model the investigator must first of all establish a conceptual framework that explains the way in which he believes the economy works. In the example, for instance, there are three components of final demand—consumption, investment, and government expenditures—that are determined by different sets of factors. Such a framework does not, of course, determine the exact relationships within the model. There is wide latitude left for the particular form the econometric model may take. For instance, it may be highly aggregative, containing only a few variables and equations, like the example, or it may be very disaggregative, containing many. Recently developed models may vary in size from a five-equation model to the very large Brookings model, which has over 300 equations in the complete version. The choice depends on how much the model builder wishes to explain and upon how much detail he thinks is needed to make the model perform reasonably well. Econometric models also vary with respect to the length of the unit time period; in practice, this period has varied from a quarter to a year.

There is also considerable latitude at the next step of model building—the formulation of the component equations. In the example, the first five equations represent the kind over which the model builder has discretion, for they embody hypotheses regarding economic behavior; the identities are based upon national income accounting conventions.

The investigator selects equations as a result of testing various economic hypotheses in historical data. Econometricians, those who build econometric models, have developed highly refined statistical methods for estimating the coefficients in their models. Their methods utilize the statistical technique of least-squares, often called regression analysis. Equations embodying given hypotheses may be estimated during the fitting and testing stage only to be subsequently discarded because they explain the historical data poorly. Others may be discarded if they do not provide adequate predictability when tested beyond the period of fitting.

The testing of hypotheses with actual economic magnitudes and the selection of a workable set of equations are the most important tasks of the model builder. He must decide not only which variables are to be included in each equation but also what form the variables are to take. Together, these two decisions constitute what is called specification. In the simplified model, the consumption equation might have contained, instead of disposable personal income, the components of income which accrue from wages and other nonwage sources. In specifying equations, the model builder is normally guided by economic theory, institutional knowledge of the economy, and results obtained by other research workers. But there remains a wide area of freedom for exercising ingenuity, which is reflected in different specifications among different models for equations explaining the same dependent variable. The task of specification is never really finished since new research may suggest other relevant variables and new forms. Revised specifications may also be required to reflect basic changes in the structure of the economy that make the old equations inapplicable.

Using an econometric model

After the equations have been selected and the coefficients estimated, an econometric model can be tested as a system. This means solving the set of equations for values of the unknown or endogenous variables. First, values of the inputs to the model are obtained. These inputs are all those variables assumed to be known at the time the model is processed; in the case of the simplified model, these are the previous period's capital stock, government expenditures, and the money supply.

After the values of the exogenous variables have been introduced into the system, the entire set of equations is solved simultaneously, and the outputs—the endogenous variables—are obtained. In the example, there are seven equations and seven unknowns, the endogenous variables. Clearly, the value for each endogenous variable depends on both the magnitude of the inputs and the estimated coefficients.

When the model is used for forecasting purposes, it is apparent that in addition to the lagged values, projections of all the policy variables must be included as inputs. In the example, there are only two such variables, government expenditures and the money supply. Values of both of these are uncertain and depend upon government policy. With exogenous values introduced, a solution is obtained for the first of the future time periods. Forecasts beyond the first period are made by further projecting the exogenous variables and using the necessary lagged values. In the simple model, K_t obtained in the first period becomes K_{t-1} in the second period. Successive solutions trace a path over time for all the endogenous variables.

Although the primary use of econometric models by corporations is for forecasting of future economic conditions, governments employ models to determine the economic impacts of alternative fiscal and monetary policies. In the simplified model, the two obvious instruments of government policy can be altered under an assumed new economic policy and the change in the endogenous variables can be obtained. The difference in the model's behavior under the assumed value of government expenditures and/or money supply represents the effect of the proposed change.

While the level of some variables can represent policy changes, the parameters in some equations are regulated by policy. By modifying the parameters t_0 and t_1 in equation 3 the probable effects of proposed changes in either level of exemptions and/or tax rates can be examined. This would involve changing the parameters of the tax equation to conform with the proposed changes in exemptions or rates and solving the model using the alternative tax functions.

The working of the simplified model

In the case of the simplified model, a verbal account of how the model would work if it were used to forecast the impact of a given increase in government expenditures is possible. In the case of models as complex as the Office of Business Economics (OBE) model that

FIGURE 3

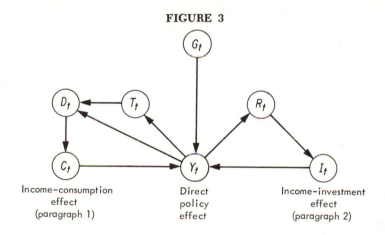

will be utilized in the fiscal policy simulation exercise (Figure 3 and below); verbal account is not possible.

1. The assumed increase in government expenditures will result in an increase in net income in equation 6. This, in turn, will increase taxes (equation 3) and also disposable income if the income effect exceeds the tax effect (equation 2) which then increases consumption (equation 1), and this increases income (equation 6), and so on, all within the same period.
2. The assumed increase in government expenditures will also result in an increase in the interest rate (equation 5) which will decrease investment which, in turn, decreases income, and the income-consumption interaction in paragraph 1 is again activated.

Thus, the initial increase in government expenditures should result in a net cumulative upward movement in production and income and in their components—consumption and investment. How far this cumulative movement will proceed depends on the spending behavior of consumers and investors. The higher the incremental spending out of additional income, the larger the total effect of the initial increase in government expenditures. However, the upward movement will always reach a limit, provided all the additional income is not spent.

This exhausts the effects of the increase in government spending on economic activity in the same period. However, there are additional effects in the next period, since the change in investment alters the capital stock (equation 7) which then affects next period's investment (equation 4), income, consumption, and so on.

Whether, how soon, and where the system will finally settle in response to the increase in government expenditures will depend on the initial state of the economy and on the particular behavior patterns reflected in the equation. If the system settles down to a unique income value, the effect of the additional government expenditures may be regarded as the resulting change in output. The ratio of the change in output to the initial change in expenditure is called the long-run multiplier. If the ratio is computed on the basis of the first period effect only, it is called the impact multiplier.

The above explanation of how the model works within a period illustrates the economic meaning of simultaneity. Mathematically, this is reflected in the fact that none of the equations can be used alone to obtain the total effect; the system must be solved as a whole.

It would be possible by different specifications of equations to remove the simultaneous character of the simple model. One could, for example, substitute D_{t-1} for D_t in equation 1. Consumption would then depend upon a lagged variable. In that case, the equation could be solved in isolation from the others since all values on the right would be known.

If the time period t is short enough, say a week, the substitution of lagged disposable income for current income is not unreasonable decisions to spend this week may well depend on last week's income and not on the current weeks'. When the time period is much longer—a quarter or more, as it is in almost all models—these behavioral lags become doubtful. That is, income earned within the quarter can clearly affect expenditures within the same period. Such interdependence also applies to other variables and points up the importance of simultaneity in a realistic model of economic behavior.

Forecasting errors

Needless to say, econometric models do not produce perfect forecasts of the future. There are several reasons for this. First, errors can be made in the projections of the exogenous variables. In our simple example, for instance, government expenditures may turn out to be different from those that had been projected. Second, the historical data to which the equations are fit usually contain errors; these will affect the estimates of the parameters.

These two sources of error should be distinguished from those that occur in the construction and solution of the model. To focus on these "model" errors, it is useful to regard an econometric model as a device that translates given inputs (exogenous variables) into certain outputs (the endogenous variables) and to explore the reasons this translation process may go wrong.

One reason for a model's failure to serve as a perfect translator stems from the fact that no conceivable set of equations can take full account of all the behavioral factors that influence given variables. While an equation may fairly represent the economic relationshpp over a long period of time, the actual behavior in a given period of time may be different from that which is predicted by the equation. This will cause differences between predicted and actual values.

Second, the various behavioral equations may not correctly specify the underlying economic relationships. In terms of the simplified model, for instance, consumption may depend not only on current disposable income but also on liquid assets held by consumers in the form of checking accounts. This is likely to result in incorrect estimates of coefficients.

A final class of errors that may be distinguished stems from shortcomings in our methosd of statistical inference. For instance, when two or more variables on the right-hand side of an equation tend to move closely together, it is difficult to calculate their separate effects on the left-hand term. This again affects the coefficients. Also in this class is the problem of bias in the coefficients when the equations are part of a simultaneous system.

The econometric approach is comparable in validity to alternative approaches—for instance, the "judgmental" method, which may also use econometric methods but which does not rely on an explicit set of simultaneous equations, or the "economic indicators" approach originally developed by the National Bureau of Economic Research. The particular promise of the econometric method stems from the fact that it provides explicit formulations of the cause—effect relationships in the economy which can be communicated and which are open to inspection and testing. In addition, compared with methods confined to predicting only directional change, the method has the clear advantage of quantification.

Living with a higher jobless rate[1]

CASTING a thin but menacing shadow over Phase II of President Nixon's New Economic Policy is an economic relationship known as the Phillips curve, which says that you can't get there from here. "Here" is an unemployment rate averaging close to 6% for 1971 and price inflation of roughly 4%. "There" is the President's twin target of 4½% unemployment and 2½% to 3% inflation by the end of 1972, or some time comfortably close to Election Day.

The Phillips curve is an analytical device that sums up the relation of various rates of inflation to corresponding levels of unemployment. It is always tilted strongly downward to the right, because a rapid inflation is generally associated with low unemployment, while relatively stable prices are likely to occur in times of high joblessness. The curve was devised by A. W. Phillips of the University of London in a 1958 study of prices and employment in Britain.

It is not the downward tilt of the curve that worries economists now. It is the suspicion that, in recent years, a combination of things has shifted the whole curve to the right. This would mean that for any given rate of inflation, the corresponding rate of unemployment would be higher than it was in the boom years before the recession. Another way of putting this is to say that structural unemployment, as distinct from cyclical unemployment in the U.S. has increased sharply.

---

[1] Reprinted from the December 25, 1971 issue of *Business Week* by permission of McGraw-Hill, Inc. Copyright © 1971 by McGraw-Hill, Inc.

The problem. If such a shift has occurred, the consequences for President Nixon's policies could be highly uncomfortable. Cyclical unemployment—the kind of joblessness that is generated by a general decline in the rate of economic activity—will respond to fiscal and monetary stimulation. As aggregate demand picks up, laid-off employees will be recalled, and new jobs will open up for others. Structural unemployment is more stubborn. It does not respond well to conventional measures—or even to the pickup in demand generated by a dollar devaluation. No amount of fiscal stimulus, for instance, is going to create jobs in the worked-out fields of Appalachia or bring aircraft employment in Southern California back to its old levels. To find a job, the structurally unemployed worker must either find a new skill or a new home, sometimes both.

Two major groups of people make up today's structural unemployment. In the first are low-skilled workers, primarily blacks, teen-agers, and women, who cannot compete successfully for jobs in a modern, technologically oriented world. In the second are skilled workers and professionals whose talents have been made obsolete by changes in technology, markets, or national priorities.

An increasing number of economists think that the cyclical unemployment of the recession has masked a significant increase in structural unemployment. As George L. Perry of the Brookings Institution and Robert A. Gordon of the University of California at Berkeley see it, the terms of the trade-off along the Phillips curve have distinctly worsened in the past 10 to 15 years, largely because the composition of the labor force has changed. A larger proportion of U.S. workers now fall into the groups with chronically high rates of unemployment. The policy problem is to find or create jobs for such people without committing the economy to a roaring inflation.

As a result of this widening in what Perry calls the dispersion of unemployment levels, his version of the curve has swung upward and to the right of the mid-1950s line, and there is no politically or socially acceptable trade-off point between the jobless rate and inflation. A sustained 6% unemployment rate seems only to buy the nation the same amount of inflation that 4½% or 5% yielded 15 years ago.

According to Gordon, the realities of this situation induced President Nixon to make his drastic policy turn last Aug. 15. "What the President did, in effect, was to take hold of that upper-left end of the curve," says Gordon, "and attempt to pull it down flat to the left by the use of the freeze and controls. This, theoretically, shifts the curve so that it is possible to drive unemployment down without incurring a politically impossible rise in inflation. If God is good to us, the Administration thinking runs, we wind up on the first Tuesday after the first Monday in November with 3% or less inflation and unemployment moving down toward 4½%. Economists don't know whether God is going to be that good to Mr. Nixon."

The rate. In fact, many economists are starting to talk of 5% as the "full-employment unemployment rate," in contrast to the 1960s figure of 4%. Chief economist Don R. Conlan at Dean Witter & Co., basing his conclusions in part on Perry's work, notes that "5% unemployment today is as inflationary as 4% was in 1966." The cyclical recovery in productivity of roughly 5% this year should carry through the first half of 1972 and help Nixon keep the curve bent down to the left by moderating price increases, Conlan believes, "but the structural problems in the labor force will be the same a year from now." Thus, he is not optimistic about chances for an early end to controls.

But neither Conlan, Gordon, nor practically any other economist re-

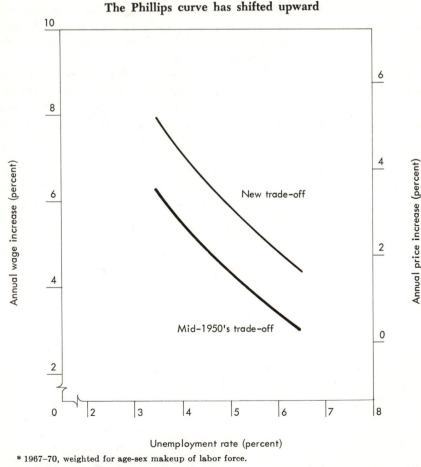

The Phillips curve has shifted upward

New trade-off

Mid-1950's trade-off

Annual wage increase (percent)

Annual price increase (percent)

Unemployment rate (percent)

* 1967–70, weighted for age-sex makeup of labor force.

Data: George L. Perry. Brookings Papers 3: 1970

gards 5% unemployment and the present Phillips curve as God-given and immutable. One school of thought, which the Administration adheres to, holds that the present incomes policy can permanently shift the curve by "breaking the spiral of inflationary expectations," as Council of Economic Advisers member Ezra Solomon put it recently in New York in an address before the First Annual Business Financing Conference, sponsored by *Business Week* and *Corporate Financing*.

"If the U.S. can be given some honest-to-goodness reality gains [in output per manhour, real wages, and employment]," Solomon said, "people will give up this quest for nominal or illusory gains, and we might go back to some more normal situation in which controls can be removed and the free market restored."

But Solomon, too, is fully aware of the structural unemployment barrier and the Phillips curve. In a question-and-answer session, he said that "if 4% unemployment was too optimistic a target then [in 1956], even 4.5% is too optimistic now." He later explained that he was "not suggesting 4.5% as the national target, but only as the practical limit of pushing on aggregate demand, given the present structure of the labor force, without causing the reemergence of pretty strong inflationary pressure."

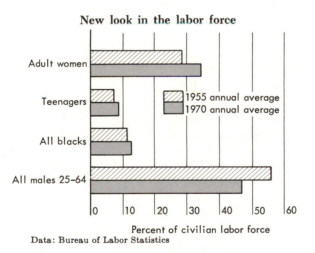

New look in the labor force

Adult women

Teenagers

1955 annual average
1970 annual average

All blacks

All males 25-64

0   10   20   30   40   50   60

Percent of civilian labor force

Data: Bureau of Labor Statistics

Solomon thinks the first job in handling the structural problem is to identify the components of today's 6% unemployment rate. "For example, in times when we've had a practically negative rate among adult white male workers, we've had 25% unemployment among black teenagers," he noted. Like Gordon, Solomon looks chiefly to manpower solutions, such as job training and better dissemination of job information to help solve this problem.

The aerospace workers are perhaps the clearest-cut example of what most people mean by structural unemployment. Like the cameramen in Hollywood today (. . .), the industrial workers displaced by automation in the early 1960s, and blacks driven out of the rural South by farm mechanization since the 1950s, they have clearly been structured out of their jobs by changes not caused by the business cycle. Their skills no longer fit the labor market.

New definitions.   But structural unemployment goes far beyond the old-fashioned definitions—so far, in fact, that many economists are hard put to define it, much less measure it. In a paper to be published next year as part of a study by the National Manpower Policy Task Force, a nonprofit research organization, Gordon offers this rather rigorous definition: "Structural unemployment exists in particular sectors of the labor market with differentially high unemployment rates if those differentials are not offset by relatively high wages or other advantages and workers in those sectors find it difficult or impossible to move to sectors with lower unemployment rates." Immobility, he emphasizes, "is an essential feature of the definition."

Gordon's cautious precision is understandable in view of the acrimonious debate of the early 1960s over the relative importance of structural and deficiency-of-demand factors in explaining the high jobless rates of that period. Economists still differ on the subject; some even avoid using the term "structural." But practically all take an eclectic view now. Most agree that the chronically long or repeated spells of unemployment that are typical for women, youths, low-skilled workers, and minority groups are structural.

An over-all number is harder to come by than a definition. But Gordon, who headed a 1962 Presidential committee that codified a nonpolitical system of reporting employment data, figures that frictional unemployment—normal quits and layoffs—and seasonal unemployment generally come to slightly under 3% of the civilian labor force. In a boom period, with the jobless rate at 4% and practically no cyclical unemployment, the 1% remainder would be structural. With the present labor force at 85-million, he thus figures conservatively that "more than 800,000 people" are now structurally unemployed, "people permanently deprived of the opportunity of getting a decent job they are willing to hold."

The numbers.   The details of reported unemployment in the structural sectors support this estimate. Bureau of Labor Statistics figures for November put teen-age unemployment at 17%, almost three times the 6% rate for all workers. Adult women had a 5.8% rate, compared with 4.4% for adult men and 3.4% for married men, the so-called "primary" group of breadwinners. The employment situation for blacks appeared to improve markedly, with a drop in the jobless rate to 9.3% from 10.7% in

October, while the white rate rose to 5.7% from 5.3%. But thousands of blacks have simply dropped out of the labor force in recent years into the large uncounted realm of "hidden unemployment."

Such figures take on added significance when they are calibrated against the demographic shifts in labor-force composition. Citing BLS data for 1956 and 1969, Gordon notes, for example, that the male percentage of the work force dropped from almost 68% to just over 62%.

The result, according to Carol S. Greenwald of the Federal Reserve Bank of Boston, is "a striking shift in the burden of unemployment from men to women and teen-agers." In 1970, Mrs. Greenwald wrote last summer in the bank's *New England Economic Review,* women and teen-agers accounted for 60% of the unemployed, against 43% during the 1957-58 recession. Citing a 1970 Brookings study by Robert E. Hall of the Massachusetts Institute of Technology, Mrs. Greenwald notes further that the high teen-age and female unemployment rates are largely functions of the frequency with which these individuals change jobs or move in and out of the labor force. She concludes that the BLS unemployment rate "has increasingly become a misleading measure of economic distress."

In his Brookings article, however, Hall carefully tried to fend off use of his figures on job turnover as the basis for negative value judgments about the needs or commitment to the work ethic among the groups he studied. "For many people," he wrote, "only low-paying, unpleasant jobs are available, either because of lack of skills or because of discriminatory exclusion." The key point, he concluded, is that "blacks and women seem to be excluded from work that offers an incentive to stay with a job permanently, and spend much larger fractions of their time in the labor force looking for new jobs than do white males."

Leaving questions of motivation and ethics aside, the cardinal fact for economists is that the wide dispersion in unemployment rates is a structural problem and requires structural solutions. So long as it persists at its current level, labor scarcities and supply bottlenecks will occur in "prime" work force sectors when the economy gets close to technical full-employment.

A massive new federal commitment to public-service employment and public works could push unemployment still lower, many economists agree. But this option, because of the Phillips curve, would involve the political risk of asking Americans to live with more inflation.

For the jobless, old skills are not enough

"I guess you could call me a high-priced migrant worker," says Thomas McCallum, a 51-year-old unemployed electrical engineer. For 20 years he worked for aerospace companies in New York, New Jersey,

Pennsylvania, Massachusetts, and Texas. Twelve months ago, he lost a $21,000-a-year job involving Air Force communications with the Mitre Corp. of Bedford, Mass., when a Vietnam-related contract expired. He is still willing to go anywhere for a job. But like thousands of other unemployed aerospace engineers and technicians vainly dispatching job résumés, he has found that there is no longer anywhere to go.

With the wisdom of hindsight, McCallum now realizes that "ever since companies stopped stockpiling engineers about 10 years ago, I've been hired for the life of a contract, then let go." He didn't mind. "I never had trouble finding a better job, and we have enjoyed seeing the country and making new friends." He recalls that he never felt insecure. "I always thought job security came from talent and experience," he says. "I was wrong."

Now McCallum insists that he will not sell his 1749 farmhouse in Londonderry, N.H.—bought two weeks before the Mitre job folded—unless he is reasonably sure that a job elsewhere will last. And he is more than ready to take a lower-paying job as long as it is secure.

Cold facts. The moment of truth came quicker for McCallum than for most aerospace casualties. "Reality usually sinks in when unemployment insurance runs out." McCallum says drily. But when he applied for unemployment compensation, he found he was ineligible. As a non-profit laboratory, Mitre had not been obliged to contribute to the unemployment insurance fund.

McCallum devoted several weeks to full-time job hunting while his wife, Sonia, went to work as a door-to-door saleswoman for Shaklee Products, makers of cosmetics and non-polluting detergents. Then he signed up at the Massachusetts Institute of Technology for a four-week course designed to turn unemployed aerospace engineers into urban technologists. The course led to several interviews with urban agencies, but no firm job offers. He is currently under consideration by the pollution control department of a midwestern city.

During the next few months, McCallum supplemented Sonia's $100 a week with an assembly line job at a Boston plastics factory. When that company closed, he picked apples at $10 a day in a New Hampshire orchard. A few weeks ago, he landed a TV repair job at a Montgomery Ward store in Nashua, N.H.

"I'm really grateful to the Ward's manager who trusted me when I said I needed this job," McCallum says. "Several places turned me down because they said I was overqualified."

Costs. Just the same, the TV repair job pays no more than a third of his former salary and the bills are piling up even though the McCallums watch their food purchases and do no entertaining. Some costs are inescapable. Mortgage payments run $220 a month. Another $200 goes to care for a son in a home for retarded children in Florida. The family has been using up the savings formerly earmarked for renovating the farmhouse, which needs it badly.

And aside from the financial pressures, McCallum says he still wants to work as an engineer, or at least in some sort of systems work for government agencies.

Unlike some engineering families struck by unaccustomed unemployment, the McCallums have drawn together rather than split apart since last winter. Their two sons in college not only pay their own tuition out of wages from odd jobs, but contribute to a family pool. A younger son in high school also contributes. "It's been a good experience in its way, as long as it doesn't last much longer," says Mrs. McCallum.

Good or not, the experience has left the boys with no great enthusiasm for technology. Michael, a bearded 20-year-old studying political science at the University of Massachusetts, explains his choice of a major with a small smile: "I'm going to get myself elected to some office so I can get Pop a steady job."

The silent screen. Across the continent, an unemployed movie cameraman shares McCallum's shock at discovering that an industry no longer needs his once valuable skill. "I rack my brain. Movies are all I know," says 51-year-old Robert H. Wyckoff. "I'm pretty old to start all over again. If I had the money, I'd buy a franchise and go into business for myself."

Wyckoff is a victim of changes in the California movie and television industry. New film-making technology, the trend to lower-budget productions and movie-making elsewhere, and reorganization of the industry have resulted in fewer jobs for skilled technicians. For some, like Wyckoff, this has resulted in no jobs at all.

This is a devastating experience for a man who averaged 44 weeks of work a year for 30 years, logging typical work days of 10 or 11 hours. Wyckoff earned $50,000 during his last full year of work, 1968. He has not worked regularly since.

Today, with his wife managing a friend's cookware shop (her first job in 25 years of marriage), the Wyckoffs' current annual income is $12,000. A good chunk of it goes to keep up payments on the $100,000 house in Bel Air still occupied by the Wyckoffs and their 13-year-old daughter. But the pool is unfilled and the yard unkempt. Their savings are gone and so are two antique cars, a beach home, and a power cruiser.

"We used to do a lot of entertaining," says Wyckoff, puffing nervously on a cigarette. "Now we've kind of dropped out socially."

A career. Wyckoff began work at 18 as a film loader for Warner Bros. He rose to assistant cameraman, camera operator, and finally in 1953, with TV production moving into high gear, he made fullfledged cameraman. For the next 15 years he was steadily employed, serving as director of photography for such TV series as *Sea Hunt, Get Smart,* and *Bewitched.* He varied the routine with an occasional feature film for the movie industry.

Wyckoff enjoyed the extra time and equipment used in shooting features, so in 1968 he began to pass up TV work to make himself more available for movie jobs.

By the time he realized that movie production was winding down, TV, too, was changing. There were fewer new shows, series were shorter, and shooting was moving abroad. "And once you're out of work, people begin forgetting you," Wyckoff says. "It's like your feet are in cement. It's so self-perpetuating."

Wyckoff has not shot a TV show since 1968. His one feature film was photographed in Hong Kong with a Chinese crew and shaky financial arrangements. When he received no pay for his first three weeks' work, he slapped a lien on the film and, after legal expenses, barely broke even. At first, he would work several days a month shooting commercials, but even this disappeared as advertising budgets shrank. He has not shot a commercial in six months.

Other troubles. Frank Calhoun of Chicago, a 39-year-old unskilled, unemployed, black janitor, represents a more complex type of structural unemployment. Political conservatives might argue that he symbolizes the culture of poverty rather than involuntary unemployment, since he quit his last job and refused another because it required weekend work. But many economists insist that a society that reduces unskilled job opportunities, pays low wages for the unpleasant unskilled jobs that remain, and provides welfare benefits for workers who reject those jobs will automatically produce large numbers of labor market dropouts. These economists say such unemployment—or, more typically, off-and-on employment—is built into the structure of today's economy as firmly as the job loss of the aerospace engineer or the movie cameraman.

A vocational school dropout, Calhoun made a stab at studying automotive body and fender repair under the GI Bill after Air Force service. "But I went for the money, to tell the truth," he says. "By the time I got interested, there were only eight months left and I didn't know anything. So I quit with three months to go."

Actually, Calhoun had wanted to be a baker. He had enjoyed baker's school in the Air Force, but when he came out he could not find a baker's job. So he became a janitor at the Merchandise Mart in 1957.

Up and down. Ten years later, with a wife and two sons to support, he quit for a better job as janitor at the Insurance Exchange, at a take-home pay of $238.50 every two weeks. Another step up, to night foreman of the janitorial staff at the Internal Revenue Service building, backfired when a hassle over a promised raise to $4 an hour resulted in Calhoun's firing. It also resulted in the union's discovery that he owed it $42.50

in dues, and—after payment of the back dues—in the building company's refusal to rehire him. "They told me that I wasn't ready from the beginning for this foreman's job," Calhoun says. "I wasn't qualified."

The janitors' union found him another job in a newspaper office three months ago. Because of transportation difficulties, he kept arriving a half hour after the 5 A.M. starting time. "The foreman called me on it a couple of times," Calhoun says. "I tried to explain, but he wouldn't listen. After a month I quit."

Since then, Calhoun has supplemented his $45-a-week unemployment check with pay from part-time cooking. The union offered him a $3.20-an-hour job cleaning a theater, but he did not want to work weekends. And he calculates that taxes and other deductions would reduce his pay to not much more than his unemployment insurance. Calhoun says his present income covers food and rent for his furnished room, all he needs since his wife and children left five months ago.

Calhoun knows that many janitors are being replaced by multipurpose machines that shampoo, buff, and strip floors, and that even buildings that still use janitors need fewer of them because of modern ventilation and filtering systems. But he is not worried. He figures that he can always find one job or another. And if he can ever put together the $750 for tuition, he plans to go to cooking school. "I most like to be cooking," he says. "You never go hungry."

Input-output:
Management's newest tool

THE WHITE ELEPHANT IS BECOMING
A CORPORATE WORKHORSE[1]

LAST FALL, the planning staff at Celanese Corp. was handed a tough assignment: to figure out what the upcoming strike against General Motors Corp., a major customer, would cost the chemical industry in lost sales. The planners had to calculate what would be lost not only in direct sales to GM, but in sales to the auto company's suppliers and to the suppliers of those suppliers. Celanese's forecast, pegged at different durations of the strike and now being verified, looks so accurate that the chemicals and fibers manufacturer expects soon to be probing still tougher questions, such as what will happen to its sales as housing starts begin to rise.

Two or three years ago, the best answer to such questions would have been rough estimates, at best. But that was before input-output analysis became an effective corporate tool. Invented nearly forty years ago, input-output analysis languished until the end of the 1960s. Then the Commerce Department began supplying information refined enough to fuel IO, as input-output is called in planning circles, and now the technique is really catching fire.

Some fifty major corporations—names like Union Carbide, Monsanto, Phillips Petroleum, National Steel, North American Rockwell, General

[1] George J. Berkwitt, *Dun's,* March 1971. Reprinted by special permission. Copyright © 1971, Dun & Bradstreet Publications Corporation.

Electric and Allied Chemical—are turning to IO to help them plan. Many more are investigating the concept. Two recent conferences, for example, were given over entirely to discussions on input-output. And input-output models have sprung up in about a dozen universities, including notably Harvard and Maryland. As Myron K. Peck Jr., senior mathematician for management information services at Monsanto Co., puts it: "Input-output isn't the answer to every forecasting problem. Nothing is. But for the services it performs, it is the best thing that has ever come down the pike."

The IO mosaic

What is all the excitement about? What is input-output analysis? In essence, input-output is a mosaic of the entire economy. Each tile in the mosaic is a kind of miniature portrait of the transactions between one product group, or industry sector, and another. Typically, it tells how much the one sector sold to the other; it tells what percentage of the total product of the buying sector is contributed by the selling sector; and it tells what percentage of "final demand"—that is, the ultimate use of all products—is represented by that sale.

Viewed another way, the input-output model is actually nothing more than a highly-faceted replica of the Gross National Product. "Anytime the government cuts a budget or gives the consumer more money to spend," says one corporate economist, "you can almost hear the IO model shake."

But its more local tremors are useful also. A chemical company like Celanese, for instance, can trace a change in demand in, say, automobile seat fabric all the way back to its impact on the sales of certain fibers. An aluminum producer can gage the impact on it from a change in, say, beer-drinking patterns.

Or the model can tackle broader questions. For instance, what was the actual balance of trade in imports and exports of steel in the first quarter of 1970? While raw steel weighed heavily on the import side, one IO model discovered that the American industry actually exported 1% more steel than it imported—through products that consumed U.S. steel in the manufacture.

To the user, the input-output model may be anything from a large wall chart to one or more volumes of computer printout. They all express the same basic information: for every industry sector included in the model, they give the dollar value of what that sector sells to every other sector and the percentage of its total output that is represented by what that sector buys from every other sector.

The idea of an input-output model was actually conceived back in the 1930s by Harvard economist Wassily Leontief. But as far as management was concerned, it was like an exotic new vehicle with no motor to propel it. Then about a year and a half ago, the Commerce Department came up with the motor: a set of inter-industry sales figures for 367 industry sectors—more than four times as many as in the previous government study. Now, individual agencies are refining that data still further.

Quite abruptly, a white elephant was transformed into a powerful workhorse. Categories that were too broad to be of use to any but macro-economists were refined to the point that they could be applied to individual divisions and product groups. For example, the old listing of "Livestock, Crops, Forestry and Fishery Products" was broken into twelve industry sectors. Fourteen headings under "Textiles and Apparel" became forty, expanding a thin sheaf of printout sheets to a four-inch thick binder.

Out in front

Now that the information is available, corporations are building in-house IO models that interface with the government figures. Not surprisingly, large companies with diverse product lines have taken the lead in constructing such models. And the chemical industry is out in front of everyone.

Take a look at the IO work going on at Monsanto Co. To date, the company has constructed four in-house models, two keying Monsanto to the national economy and two related almost entirely to internal operations. One of these is being used to forecast sales in Europe and to keep tabs on the company's performance there. Explains Monsanto's Myron Peck: "We needed the model to keep us healthy, to show us how far we are deviating from our projections."·

A second Monsanto model focuses on the impact of technological change on total demand for each of Monsanto's major product groups. A third model traces the flow of ten product groups through one Monsanto division and shows how the operations in other divisions affect that flow. This model, says Peck "tells us how to budget production and what to expect in profits for the next five years."

A fourth model, this one for the phosphates division, may have been one of the first to apply IO exclusively to one product group. "It is keyed to pounds of output instead of dollar value per unit of output," says Peck. "It tells us in pounds just what each department in the plant should be producing to meet final demand in any period. Any old-timer in the plant might have come up with an estimate," he adds, "but never this close."

Celanese's first IO model, constructed in 1967, is already out of date. "We learned from that effort that you just can't plunge in," says Dr. Elizabeth Rabitsch, a Celanese economist.

Now Celanese is rebuilding its IO forecasting capabilities, relying heavily on the U.S. government model for combined industry-economy data to aid in long-term planning assumptions. "The trick," says Dr. Rabitsch, "is to provide a series of links between a model such as the government's and a corporate model keyed into the company's own transactions."

Outside the chemical industry, some interesting IO projects also are underway. North American Rockwell Corp., for instance, uses input-output analysis as an acquisition tool. In fact, it was used, reportedly, in the formation of the company from the merger of North American Aviation and Rockwell-Standard. U.S. Steel, which uses input-output for a variety of market research projects, has produced an IO study of the screw machine industry.

Other companies are only beginning to build input-output models. Tenneco, for example, is just winding up an eighteen-month investigation of a wide variety of forecasting techniques. "Input-output looks as good if not better than the others," says William R. Glennon, manager of management sciences. Armco Steel Corp. is now constructing a "rudimentary" forecasting model. "We're converging on modern corporate planning techniques," says Paul Harmon, manager of economic research. "We expect to use IO when we get to the nuts-and-bolts stage of our strategic planning. It will be an outstanding tool when we are more diversified," Harmon adds. "It is always best with multiproduct companies."

Not everyone thinks that IO is for big companies only. One of the dissenters is S. William Yost, a vice president of the W. Tyler subsidiary of Combustion Engineering. "Of course, you can spend $200,000 on an IO model," Yost says. "But if you're selective, if you concentrate on the data most central to your own problems, you can spend considerably less." In fact, Yost is now experimenting with a model for a CE refractories division with sales in the $20-million-to-$30-million range.

Some noncorporate models

Some of the most dramatic results in IO are coming from noncorporate models. One is the Interindustry Forecasting Model at the University of Maryland. Last year, at the height of the tight-money period, the model was asked what would happen to capital expenditures if the 7% investment tax credit were suddenly repealed. Its answer: By 1975, there would be a slide of only 3% overall, while some industries would cut back much more drastically. Apparel manufacturers, for instance, would reduce expenditures by 40%; glass producers, 20%; special machinery manufacturers, 20%.

At Cambridge, Massachusetts-based consultant Arthur D. Little, an input-output model is used to measure the sensitivity of 147 industry sectors to changes in disposable income and capital outlays. To business-men traumatized by the recent economic slump, the findings were fasci-nating. Of the entire group, tht most sensitive were certain industrial commodities: iron, zinc, textile fibers, glass, aluminum and copper. Among the least sensitive were consumer nondurables, food and food processing, and consumer drugs.

IO got one of its biggest boosts last year with another study—this one industry-wide—of the dollar-and-cents effects of the GM strike. Cy-bermatics; Inc. of Fort Lee, New Jersey primed its IO model covering some 106 industry sectors to trace losses sector by sector, week by week as long as the strike continued. The figures were, for the most part, dead on target. The IO analysis showed that losses to steel, for instance, would be $62.3 million per week by the final week of the strike, while weekly losses for transportation would be $37.3 million and for rubber and miscellaneous products $14 million.

Of the government models in use, one of the most pertinent to busi-nessmen is being employed by the Federal Trade Commission. From now on, the FTC will be submitting both sides of a merger proposal to IO analysis. It is expected to provide one of the most effective methods yet for uncovering violations of antitrust.

Celanese Corporation[1]

ON SEPTEMBER 16, 1970, John W. Brooks, president and chief executive officer of Celanese Corporation, opened his copy of *The Wall Street Journal* and read with interest the articles describing the potential impact of the General Motors strike. The articles, which discussed the far-reaching implications of the United Auto Workers' strike against General Motors, were of particular interest to Mr. Brooks because Celanese produced many products that ultimately ended up in automobiles.

In 1969, Celanese had sales of approximately $8 million to the automobile industry, less than one percent of its total sales. Since few of its products were sold directly to the auto industry, the total dependence of Celanese upon automobile sales was unknown. However, the following insert in that week's *Time* magazine heightened Mr. Brooks' concern.

How the Strike Will Hurt[2]

What damage will the auto strike do to U.S. business? If the workers return to their jobs within a month or so, the impact will be minimal—except for the losses and layoffs suffered by G.M.'s suppliers. But if, as most authorities expect, the walkout lasts for six weeks or more, the effects could be unsettling. Last week Data Resources, Inc., an economic consulting firm headed by Harvard's Otto Eckstein, a former member of the President's Council of Economic Advisers and a member of *Time*'s Board of Economists, made some projections for *Time*. By analyzing 320 economic equations in a computer, Data Resources pro-

---

[1] This case was prepared by Howard W. Pifer, lecturer on Business Administration, as a basis for class discussion rather than to illustrate either effective or ineffective handling of an administrative situation.

[2] *Time*, September 28, 1970, p. 72.

113

jected what the economy would have looked like in this year's fourth quarter had there been no strike, and compared these results with what is likely to happen if the work stoppage lasts six weeks or twelve weeks. The figures listed below are in billions of dollars at an annual rate, except where otherwise stated.

		With strike	
	Without strike	*Six weeks*	*Twelve weeks*
GNP.	$1,003.3*	996.5*	987.2*
Corporate profits after taxes	$45.9	43.4	41.1
Unemployment rate (percent).	5.1	5.4	5.6
Total federal deficit.	$10.7	13.6	16.9
Consumer purchases of autos and parts	$40.6	35.8	29.5
Auto industry profits after taxes . . .	$2.8	1.9	.434

* Figures in billions of dollars at an annual rate, except where otherwise stated.

In addition, Eckstein's group also examined the effects of the hypothetical six- or twelve-week strikes on industries that are major suppliers to the auto companies. The figures listed below indicate the declines that those industries would be expected to sustain in fourth-quarter profits and production.

	Six weeks		*Twelve weeks*	
	Profits (percent)	*Production (percent)*	*Profits (percent)*	*Production (percent)*
Textiles.	8	2	18	5
Rubber	9	2	22	6
Steel	11	3	26	8
Nonferrous metals	4	2	9	5
Fabricated metals	3	2	7	5
Nonelectrical machinery	4	3	6	5
Electrical machinery	4	3	9	7

A significant proportion of Celanese and U.S. subsidiary sales were to the textile ($413 million) and rubber ($70 million) industries. Since these industries were major suppliers to the automobile industry, the above fourth-quarter losses in profits and production could have significant impact upon Celanese performance. With 1969 earnings of less than $80 million on sales of approximately $1.25 billion, a long shutdown in auto production could result in substantially lower earnings in 1970.

Corporate structure

Celanese Corporation, one of the United States' largest chemical companies, had been organized into five product groups—fibers, chemicals, plastics, coatings, and petroleum. In August 1969, Celanese reached an agreement to sell its interests in Champlin Petroleum Company and Pontiac Refining Corporation to a subsidiary of Union Pacific Railroad. Upon completion of the sale on January 5, 1970, operations were reduced to four product groups which essentially followed the SIC (Standard Industrial Classification) Codes (see Exhibit 1). For many years, Celanese annual reports have provided breakdowns of sales by product groups (see Exhibits 2 and 3).

Use of input-output analysis

Mr. Brooks was well aware of his planning staff's previous experience with input-output analysis and asked Corporate Planning if this technique could be used to estimate the impact that the automobile strike would have on Celanese sales and earnings.

Corporate Planning responded to the request of Mr. Brooks by outlining in a memorandum the procedure to be followed—(see Appendix).

In their ensuing discussion, Corporate Planning suggested that the technique could be applied but that the overall impact depended upon the length of the GM shutdown and its effect upon sales as well as production. While the shutdown would halt production, the reduction in shipments could be temporary and not materially affect automobile sales.

EXHIBIT 1
Celanese product groups

Celanese product group	Standard industrial classification codes	Input-output industry number	Input-output industry title
Chemicals	281	27.01	Industrial inorganic and organic chemicals
Plastics	2821	28.01	Plastics materials and resins
Fibers	{2823 2824	28.03 28.04	Cellulosic man-made fibers } Organic fibers, noncellulosic }
Coatings	2851	30.00	Paints and allied products

EXHIBIT 2
Celanese sales by product group and selected industries—1969*

	Estimated automobile ($ million)	Estimated textiles ($ million)	Estimated rubber ($ million)	Total ($ million)	Estimated market share (percent)	Estimated variable profit margin (percent)
Chemicals . . .	0.2	4.6	3.1	169.9	4	47
Plastics	0.4	2.2	1.8	113.6	6	50
Fibers.	–	405.5	64.5	556.3	20	48
Coatings	7.1	0.3	0.3	96.3	4	43
	7.7	412.6	69.7	936.1		

* Source: Celanese Annual Report, 1969. Includes U.S. subsidiaries and inter-company sales but excludes non–U.S. subsidiaries. Estimates derived from available government statistics.

EXHIBIT 3

Celanese sales by product group*
($ millions)

	1969	1968	1967	1966	1965	1964	1963	1962	1961	1960
Celanese Corporation and U.S. subsidiaries:										
Fibers	556.3	509.7	447.5	408.0	357.0	296.8	219.4	196.8	174.3	173.4
Chemicals	169.9	160.0	134.4	130.0	118.8	79.4	74.5	64.6	52.7	46.6
Plastics	113.6	105.7	93.7	113.5	93.1	87.7	73.1	66.1	65.5	54.6
Coatings	96.3	97.5	92.1	95.9	87.7	27.5	–	–	–	–
Petroleum	192.5	187.7	146.6	91.8	82.5	74.9	77.6	75.7	73.6	73.8
Subtotal	1,128.6	1,060.6	914.3	839.2	739.1	566.3	444.6	403.2	366.1	348.4
Non–U.S. subsidiaries:										
Fibers	146.1	141.2	115.0	106.7	95.8	87.6	71.6	60.6	63.9	59.4
Chemicals	31.4	25.8	27.4	23.5	23.7	21.1	20.7	19.3	16.8	13.5
Plastics	10.6	10.5	8.1	7.5	6.3	3.0	1.8	2.0	0.8	0.9
Coatings	–	49.9	51.2	51.4	12.2	–	–	–	–	–
Forest products	–	46.2	65.1	61.1	61.6	52.6	52.6	48.6	28.9	24.1
Subtotal	188.1	273.6	266.8	250.2	199.6	164.3	146.7	130.5	110.4	97.9
Inter-company sales	(66.8)	(78.4)	(71.1)	(67.2)	(63.3)	(29.8)	(30.9)	(29.2)	(28.1)	(28.1)
Total sales	1,249.9	1,255.8	1,110.0	1,022.2	875.4	700.8	560.4	504.5	448.4	418.2
Income before extraordinary items	76.3	57.8	59.3	66.6	64.3	54.0	41.8	37.5	30.8	33.3

* Source: Celanese Annual Report, 1969.

APPENDIX

MEMORANDUM

TO: John W. Brooks, president and chief executive officer
FROM: Corporate Planning Department
SUBJECT: Using input-output analysis to assess the impact of a GM
              strike[1]

The 1963 Input-Output Tables[2] provide a benchmark for estimating the impact of the automobile industry shutdown. In the I-O tables, the motor vehicles and parts industry is classified under the I-O industry number 59.03 (corresponding to the 4-digit SIC industry 3717). The principal product lines of a chemical and fiber producing company such as Celanese are classified under five different I-O industry numbers.

Sales of the chemical and fiber industries, in millions of dollars at 1963 producers' prices, are recorded in Volume I of the three-volume tabulation. Each horizontal row of the I-O table shows the distribution of sales (outputs) of one industry to each of the 366 other industries recorded in the table. Similarly, the entries in each vertical column show the distribution of purchases (inputs) of that industry from each of the 366 other industries. Volume I is known as the transactions table.

Reading across row 27.01 of the transactions table, one can see that in 1963 the sales of chemicals to the motor vehicle industry amounted to $15.7 million (see Table 1). Total sales of chemicals to other industries (total intermediate output) amounted to $10.6 billion. Gross Output, i.e. intermediate output plus sales to final markets, amounted to $12.6 billion.

It becomes apparent, when looking at this table, that the *direct* sales of chemicals and man-made fibers to the motor vehicle industry are very small. The *direct* sales of surface coatings for motor vehicles are fairly large. When reading across the row of industry number 30.00, one can see that in 1963 the sales of paints and allied products to the motor vehicle industry amounted to $182 million or almost 8 percent of total intermediate output.

The figures shown in Table 2 measure the direct requirements of materials per dollar of gross output in the motor vehicle industry. In

---

[1] Elisabeth K. Rabitsch, "Input-Output Analysis and Business Forecasting," presented to The Industrial Management Center's Advanced Seminar in Technological Forecasting: Concepts and Methods, November 15–20, 1970.

[2] The Office of Business Economics, Department of Commerce, published *Input-Output Structure of the U.S. Economy: 1963* as a three-volume supplement to the *Survey of Current Business* in 1969. This publication contained the full industrial detail for almost 370 industries. The November 1969 *Survey of Current Business* provided a summary version of these tables for approximately 80 industries.

other words, for each $1000 of output by the motor vehicle industry, a *direct* input of 40 cents worth of chemicals and $4.66 worth of paints and surface coatings is required. These figures are the "direct" input-output coefficients which are published in Volume II of the 1963 Input-Output Table.

The input-output method makes it possible to estimate the changes in total (direct and indirect) input requirements when final markets of a particular industry are expected to increase or decline.

The *indirect* (or inverse) coefficients shown in Table 3 provide a measure of the total requirements of materials per dollar of final sales of the motor vehicle industry. The *total* requirements of chemicals per 1000 dollars of final sales in 1963 amounted to almost $20, and those for paints and surface coatings to more than $9. In 1963, when final sales of the motor vehicle industry reached $23.5 billion, the total requirements of chemicals were estimated at about $470 million, and those of paints at over $200 million. The requirements of man-made fibers amounted to $74 million; these fibers are processed by the textile industry and the rubber industry, for example, to be consumed eventually in automobile production in the form of seat covers, wall linings, carpets, and tire fabrics.

TABLE 1
Inter-industry transactions
(in millions of dollars at producers' prices)

Industry number		Motor vehicles and parts 59.03	Inter- mediate outputs	Total final demand	Total
27.01	Industrial inorganic and organic chemicals.	15.7	10,573.9	2,039.3	12,613.2
28.01	Plastics materials and resins	10.7	2,939.4	299.6	3,239.0
28.03	Cellulosic man-made fibers.	—	769.6	40.8	810.3
28.04	Organic fibers, noncellulosic. . . .	—	1,359.8	135.5	1,495.3
30.00	Paints and allied products	181.9	2,363.0	99.0	2,462.1
	Intermediate inputs	27,850.8	—	—	—
	Value added.	11,486.7	—	—	590,388.7
	Total.	39,067.5		590,388.7	

TABLE 2
Direct requirements per dollar of gross output
(producers' prices)

Industry number		Motor vehicles and parts 59.03
27.01	Industrial inorganic and organic chemicals.	.00040
28.01	Plastics materials and resins	.00028
28.03	Cellulosic man-made fibers.	—
28.04	Organic fibers, noncellulosic.	—
30.00	Paints and allied products	.00466
	Intermediate inputs	.70598
	Value added.	.29402
	Total.	1.00000

TABLE 3
Total requirements per dollar of delivery to final demand
(producers' prices)

Industry number		Motor vehicles and parts 59.03
27.01	Industrial inorganic and organic chemicals.	.01992
28.01	Plastics materials and resins	.00684
28.03	Cellulosic man-made fibers.	.00117
28.04	Organic fibers, noncellulosic.	.00197
30.00	Paints and allied products	.00931
	Intermediate inputs	
	Value added	
	Total	

GWP, Inc. [1]

In August 1972 Milton Millward was given the responsibility for planning Great Western Plywood's (GWP) production capacity during the 1970s. GWP had created the special planning post for Mr. Millward in order to coordinate more closely its production capacity with the softwood plywood industry demand.

GWP was a major factor in the rather concentrated softwood plywood industry. In 1971 there were 184 producers of softwood plywood, mostly in the Western and Rocky Mountain states, the top ten of which produced 59 percent of the total. During 1971 GWP operated 16 plants throughout Oregon, Washington, and California and recorded sales of $94 million, representing approximately 8.5 percent of total industry sales. Recent industry statistics are detailed in Exhibit 1.

Great Western's earnings had always been sensitive to capacity utilization and the lead time on a decision to build a new plant was approximately 18 months. In response to rising labor and material costs, there was a strong trend in the industry toward automation and larger sized plants. While the average plant capacity in 1971 was 90 million square feet of plywood per year measured on a ⅜-inch basis, new plants being brought on line during 1971 ran as high as 160 million square feet, and 200-million-square-feet plants were under construction. GWP's exist-

---

[1] This case was prepared by Howard W. Pifer, lecturer on Business Administration, as a basis for class discussion rather than to illustrate either effective or ineffective handling of an administrative situation.

ing plants had a combined annual capacity of 1.4 billion square feet, and had operated at 96 percent of capacity in 1971.

SOFTWOOD PLYWOOD INDUSTRY

One of the company's problems, and that of the industry generally, was its dependency on the level of construction and the ups and downs that came with it. While efforts to find new uses for softwood plywood were being made, sales to the construction industries still constituted more than 50 percent of industry totals.

The softwood plywood industry reacted adversely to the residential construction slide in late 1969 and early 1970. Demand for softwood plywood sagged in 1969 and prices dropped. In 1970 housing starts quickened and the plywood market steadied. The dramatic upturn in housing during 1971 led plywood out of its sales slump, although it did not produce all the beneficial economic side effects for the forest products that had been forecasted.

Plywood markets

Softwood plywood had been channeled to a total domestic market that was divided roughly as follows: 50 percent for residential construction; 25 percent for industrial uses; 15 percent for local dealer sales to farmers, do-it-yourselfers, and small contractors; and 10 percent for general and industrial construction.

Of the 16.6 billion square feet estimated for 1972 softwood plywood production, the housing market was expected to take 8.7 billion. Roof and wall sheathing, subflooring and underlayment applications accounting for 69 percent of the housing total.

General construction was expected to require 2.3 billion square feet, of which 35 percent would go to concrete forming panels.

The industrial market for softwood plywood was pegged at 3.25 billion square feet in 1972; primarily for materials handling, transportation equipment, and products made for sale.

Anticipated over-the-counter sales and agricultural uses combined would account for another 2.35 billion square feet in 1972, 41 percent of that for do-it-yourself projects.

Plywood capacity

In 1970 the softwood plywood industry had produced at about 90 percent of its 16 billion square feet of rated annual capacity. By the end of 1971, at a cost of over $75 million, industry capacity had been increased to a new high of 17.1 billion square feet, boosting total industry investment in plant and equipment to over $1 billion.

Of the ten new plywood plants added in 1971, eight were in the South and two in the West, underscoring the spectacular growth achieved by the southern pine plywood industry in its eight-year history.

Geographic location

Oregon, Washington, and California had continued to lead all the states in producing softwood plywood. In 1965 about 93 percent of all softwood was produced in the West. By 1970 western production had dropped to 80 percent while the amount produced in the South increased to 20 percent of the total. In 1971 western and Rocky Mountain states produced 76 percent of the total with the remainder being produced in southern and Eastern Seaboard states.

The number of operating softwood plywood plants had remained stable between 1965 and 1970 when many smaller units were replaced by larger and more productive mills. Plant locations also shifted from the West to the southern states.

One reason for the growth of the southern plywood industry has been its comparative advantage in production costs. Average hourly earnings of production workers increased in 1970 to $4.50 in the West and to $2.50 in the South. The combined direct and indirect labor cost of producing a thousand square feet of western softwood plywood pushed upward to about $24 in 1970 or an estimated 14 percent more than 1969. Southern production costs were approximately $14 per thousand square feet in 1969 and remained almost the same in 1970.

Timber sources

A second reason for the comparative advantages of southern plywood has been higher yields from the log raw material. The net price of logs to plywood producers averaged $75 to $80 per thousand board feet. Residues salvaged from logs in the West averaged 10 percent of the log price paid by mills compared with 25 percent in the South. The character and size of yellow pine logs and the highly developed furniture market for wood residues in the South accounted for the difference in recovery percentages between the two regions.

The availability of timber in the future could become clouded as the pressures mounted for changes in use-priorities of the national forests. Multiple use had been a policy accepted by both conservationists and timber-using industries. The difficulty had been implementing the policy to the esthetic and ecological satisfaction of conservationists and the economic needs of all consumers and producers of wood products.

Outlook for 1975 and 1980

In the coming decade softwood plywood production had been forecasted by industry sources to grow at a compound annual rate of 3 percent to about 18.5 billion square feet in 1975 and to approximately 21.0 billion in 1980 (see Exhibit 2). An expanding plywood market in the 1970s depended upon a rising rate of housing construction. Growth in plywood production involved finding solutions to insuring availability of necessary quantities of timber raw materials on an economic basis.

In the 1961–70 decade, the softwood plywood industry adopted a wide range of new production technologies in its quest to develop new products, reduce costs, and conserve wood. The production process neared almost complete automation which most certainly would dominate industry operations in the 70s. Research into new construction applications was expected to be extended and composite products that were combinations of plywood and other complementary materials were being sought in the search for better building systems.

The exportation of softwood plywood gradually faded as the widespread domestic demand from the housing industry increased. By 1975 exports were forecasted to decrease to about 90 million square feet and then to 75 million square feet in 1980.

CONSTRUCTION INDUSTRY

The growth in the softwood plywood industry during the 1960s had been closely tied to residential construction, a highly volatile industry. New housing starts lagged behind the economic growth of the 1960s. The late 1960s high of 1.55 million starts in 1968 was far below the 1950 record of 1.95 million starts. Finally, in 1971, housing starts eclipsed the 1950 record with more than 2 million starts, representing more than a 40 percent increase over the 1970 total. This spectacular growth in housing starts was accompanied by a 13 percent increase in softwood plywood shipments, somewhat less than had been expected.

A prime reason for the weakening of the previously high correlation between housing starts and softwood plywood sales was the shift in the mix of housing starts. In 1966 single-family units had represented more than 65 percent of all housing starts. By 1971, this percentage had dropped to approximately 55 percent and the decline continued during the first four months of 1972 (see Exhibit 3). This decline was matched by a significant increase in the starts of multi-unit structures, especially apartments with more than four units.

This shift from single-unit structures to apartments had a significant effect upon the usage of softwood plywood, since plywood and wood veneer products represented a much higher proportion of the building materials included in single-family units than in apartments both in absolute dollars and relative terms. A recent study of the industrial impacts of residential construction stated that veneer and plywood products represented $500 of the construction cost per single-family unit and less than $200 per apartment unit. Veneer and plywood requirements per dwelling unit are detailed in Exhibit 4.

These trends were somewhat compensated by the rapid growth in manufactured housing which represented a major new market for softwood plywood. Manufactured, or industrialized, housing included both package units (complete housing packages made from factory-built components for on-site erection) and modular units (three-dimensional assemblies put together with other sections to form a housing unit). It was estimated that 60,000 modular units and 340,000 package units were erected in 1971, up substantially from 1970 levels of 33,000 modular and 270,000 package units.

CAPACITY EXPANSION DECISION

Faced with the significant short-run demand for softwood plywood, Mr. Millward was undecided whether to expand GWP's capacity. His concern focused on recent trends which could negatively impact the long-run potential for softwood plywood. Mr. Millward fully realized that GWP must not only forecast trends within the lumber industries, but also national economic policies and developments within the construction industries.

The economic policies of the Nixon administration, especially wage-price controls, imposed artificial constraints upon the basic demand structure within the industry. With the significant increase in residential construction and the limited plywood supply, many within the plywood industry feared a shift to close substitutes, preformed concrete and plastics, as replacements for wood products. The erratic oversupply and excess demand resulted in major price changes for softwood plywood. This uncertainty in prices hindered effective cost control by the construction industry and could reinforce the above-mentioned product substitutions.

To assist in the difficult task of relating its industry to the U.S. economy in general and the residential construction industry in particular, Mr. Millward contacted LCF, a nationally known consulting firm which specialized in conducting detailed industry studies. At their initial meeting Mr. Millward described his concerns with standard approaches for determining future capacity needs to Mr. George Goalsworthy, the project leader for LCF.

Input-output approach

At a subsequent meeting, Mr. Goalsworthy described an input-output (I/O) procedure which he recommended be employed to evaluate the uncertainties associated with forecasting GWP's future production capacity needs. In outlining his approach, Mr. Goalsworthy divided the capacity problem into four segments:

1. Forecasting the gross national product (GNP)
2. Determining the level of total softwood plywood industry output: converting GNP by components into final demand for lumber industry; converting final demand for lumber industry into total output for lumber industry; and converting total output for lumber industry into total softwood plywood industry output
3. Estimating GWP's dollar output from total softwood plywood industry output
4. Converting GWP's dollar output into GWP capacity needs.

After several exploratory discussions Messrs. Millward and Goalsworthy agreed on the above procedure and proceeded in its implementation.

Forecasting gross national product. Since the capacity decision required long-term projections of the economic climate, Mr. Millward proposed that GWP consider alternative economic scenarios. Since Great Western had previously relied upon published estimates of GNP, he selected two recent forecasts prepared by well-known economic consultants who forecasted significantly different future economic climates—Arthur D. Little (ADL) and Lionel D. Edie (Edie).

Arthur D. Little predicted a GNP of $1,096 billion 1958 dollars in 1980, while Edie predicted a GNP of $1,226 billion (see Exhibit 5). The Edie forecast, which exceeded the ADL estimate by 12 percent, assumed a higher proportion of durables to total personal consumption and a much higher proportion of capital expenditures to GNP. Their assumptions also differed on the physical amount of defense equipment required in 1980. ADL assumed a continuing increase in defense expenditures from 1963 to 1980, whereas Edie assumed that the requirements would return to the 1963 level. A partial compensation for this was the significant increases in federal nondefense and state and local government expenditures assumed by Edie.

Determining the level of total softwood plywood industry output. Having specified differing future economic conditions, Mr. Goalsworthy described the benefits of linking alternative economic conditions with the future demand for softwood plywood:

> Returning to our capacity forecasting problem, we can apply I/O analysis to the alternative GNP forecasts to obtain a 1980 forecast for the lumber and wood-products industry. By linking alternative I/O and

bridge tables (for example, the 1963 Department of Commerce, Office of Business Economics [OBE], and 1980 Department of Labor, Bureau of Labor Statistics [BLS] tables) which represent different assumptions about conditions within the lumber industry with our ADL and Edie GNP forecasts, we can look at a whole range of future levels of industry output.[2]

The 1963 Tables detailed actual GNP by components, final demand by industry, and inter-industry transactions. The 1980 Tables were based on BLS projections of these relationships and included estimates of both technological changes (I/O Table) and differing assumptions of future consumption behavior (Bridge Table). See the Appendix for an explanation of the BLS method of projection I/O coefficients.

Mr. Goalsworthy illustrated the kinds of behavioral and technological changes the Bureau of Labor Statistics projected by comparing the coefficients contained within the 1963 and 1980 Tables. The softwood plywood industry was included within I/O Industry Number 20 (lumber and wood products, except containers) and its sales were significantly impacted by shifts within the construction industries represented by I/O Industries 11 and 12 (new construction and maintenance and repair construction).

First, the 1980 BLS Bridge Table assumed that the overall percentage of final demand which was allocated to the construction industries would decrease from 17 percent in 1963 to 15.9 percent (see Exhibit 6). This decline was most notably evident in the investment sector (investment plus net inventory change) where more than 50 percent went into new construction in 1963 and was estimated to drop to 40 percent by 1980.

Second, shifts in construction technologies were also forecasted by BLS to reduce the amount of lumber and wood products which were required per dollar of final demand by the construction industries. In 1963 new construction required more than $.083 of lumber and wood products, including softwood plywood, per dollar of final demand. By 1980 this was forecasted to drop to $.077 per dollar of new construction. The decline in lumber uses within the maintenance and repair construction industry was forecasted to drop from $.056 to $.033 per dollar

---

[2] The total requirements table is often referred to as the I/O Table, whereas the percentage distribution of final demand by industry for each component of GNP is called the bridge table.

The 1963 I/O relationships were developed from corporate data, as part of the continuing program for the development of Input/Output Tables integrated with the National Income Accounts. The 1963 data were part of the second full-scale I/O study by OBE, the first covering the year 1958. With the completion of the 1963 I/O study, information on the technical structure of U.S. industries was now available for 1963 as well as for 1947 and 1958. The 1947 Tables were originally prepared by the Bureau of Labor Statistics and were subsequently made consistent with the OBE Tables.

of final demand. Reasons for these reductions in lumber inputs to the construction industries could be traced to the significant increases in the utilization of plastic and stone/clay products. In 1963 new construction required $.028 of input from the plastic-related industries (I/O Industries 28, 30, and 31) and only $.003 from stone and clay products (I/O Industry 36). BLS forecasted that these products would account for a total of $.157 per dollar of new construction in 1980.

Millward proposed that conversion of total output for the lumber and wood products industry into a demand for softwood plywood could best be done by using its 5.5 percent historical share of lumber products.

Estimating GWP's output from total softwood plywood industry output. Having reviewed both corporate and industry statistics, Mr. Millward suggested that the initial analysis assume that GWP's share of the plywood industry market would remain approximately 8.5 percent. Accepting this assumption, Mr. Goalsworthy noted that the geographic shifts occurring within the industry and GWP's centralized operations in Oregon, Washington, and California might result in future losses in market share.

Converting GWP dollar output into GWP capacity needs. The computation of GWP's capacity needs depended not only upon current levels of production capacity but also future plywood prices. This latter relationship resulted from the necessity to convert softwood plywood industry output measured in constant 1958 dollars into the 1980 price of plywood. After evaluating several different alternatives, Mr. Millward agreed to use the following formula for determining future capacity needs:

GWP 1980 capacity needs = Lumber industry 1980 output (1958 $)
 × Softwood plywood's share of lumber industry 1980 output
 × GWP's share of softwood plywood industry 1980 output
 ÷ Wholesales softwood plywood price per square foot (1971 $)
 ÷ Ratio of price index (1958) to price index (1971)

That is,

$$\text{GWP 1980 capacity needs} = \frac{\text{Lumber industry 1980 output } (.055)(.085)}{(\$0.069 \text{ per square feet})(100.0/137.4)}$$

or

GWP 1980 capacity needs = .0931 lumber industry 1980 output

The market shares assumed had been agreed to in previous meetings. The wholesale price of plywood was based upon 1971 shipments (see

Exhibit 1). Mr. Millward's major concern was the determination of future prices. Mr. Goalsworthy allayed these fears by noting that future inflationary trends could be eliminated by using constant 1958 dollars throughout the earlier stages of the analysis. If this were done, then LCF would only need to convert the 1971 plywood price into its 1958 counterpart by using the 1971 wholesale price index measured in 1958 dollars. Mr. Goalsworthy used the lumber and wood products wholesale price index which was 137.4 in 1971 (see Exhibit 1).

Implementation of input-output approach

Given the complexity of the proposed approach, Mr. Goalsworthy worked closely with Mr. Millward to explain the rationale for each step and developed detailed examples to clarify what assumptions were being made. To summarize the proposed methodology, LCF had prepared a complete example using the Arthur D. Little economic forecast and the 1963 Bridge and I/O Tables.

Using these assumptions for both the economic climate and the extent of behavioral/technological change, lumber output was forecasted to reach $18.7 billion. This could be translated into softwood plywood shipments of 20.5 billion square feet, quite close to industry projections made by the American Plywood Association (see Exhibit 2). Based on the above example, GWP would need to add approximately 340 million square feet of annual production capacity by 1980 (1.74 billion less current capacity) to maintain its market share.

Mr. Goalsworthy was encouraged with these results since they assumed that historically observed rates of softwood plywood usage would continue and, at the same time, agreed with projections being made by industry spokesmen. Having reviewed the test run of the I/O approach, Mr. Millward proposed that LCF evaluate different combinations of economic scenarios, Bridge and I/O Tables. In this way he could determine the relative impact of different assumptions.

In response to this request Mr. Goalsworthy evaluated all eight combinations of differing economic forecasts (ADL and Edie), Bridge Tables (1963 and 1980) and I/O Tables (1963 and 1980) and presented the results summarized in Figure 1.

FIGURE 1
GWP capacity needs for 1980

GNP forecast	Total lumber output*	Total softwood plywood shipments†	GWP capacity needs†	Bridge table	I/O table
ADL	$18.7	20.5	1.74	1963	1963
ADL	15.4	16.9	1.43	1963	1980
ADL	18.0	19.7	1.67	1980	1963
ADL	14.6	16.0	1.36	1980	1980
Edie	22.9	25.1	2.13	1963	1963
Edie	19.0	20.8	1.77	1963	1980
Edie	21.9	24.0	2.04	1980	1963
Edie	17.9	19.6	1.67	1980	1980

* Billions of 1958 dollars.
† Billions of square feet, ⅜-inch basis.

EXHIBIT 1
Softwood plywood industry statistics

Year	Pro- duction*	Ship- ments*	Value of shipments ($ million)	Whole- sale price index†	GWP market share (percent)
1967	12.8	12.9	784	108.2	8.25
1968	14.4	14.5	1,082	122.6	7.91
1969	13.5	13.4	1,086	135.6	8.20
1970	14.2	14.2	962	123.1	8.40
1971	16.2	16.0	1,107	137.4	8.49
1972 (est.)	16.8	16.6	1,180		

* Billions of square feet, ⅜-inch basis.
† Lumber and wood products (1958 = 100).
Source: Bureau of the Census, Bureau of Labor Statistics and Bureau of Domestic Commerce, *U.S. Industrial Outlook with Projections to 1980*, p. 22.

EXHIBIT 2
Softwood plywood demand forecast, 1971–80

		Percentage demanded by		
Year	Demand* (percent)	Residential construction	General construction	Other
1972	16.6	52.4	13.9	33.7
1973	17.2	53.9	13.4	32.7
1974	17.7	54.5	13.6	31.9
1975	18.5	53.8	13.8	32.4
1976	19.0	54.3	13.7	32.0
1977	19.5	55.4	13.6	31.0
1978	20.0	56.4	13.0	30.6
1979	20.5	56.8	12.9	30.2
1980	21.0	57.1	12.9	30.0

* Billions of square feet, ⅜-inch basis.
Source: American Plywood Association, *Forest Industries*, January 1972, p. 34.

EXHIBIT 3
New private and public housing starts

		Percentage in structures with		
Year	Housing starts*	1 unit	2–4 units	More than 4 units
1966	1,195.9	65.2	5.9	28.9
1967	1,321.9	63.9	6.4	29.7
1968	1,545.5	58.3	6.1	35.6
1969	1,499.0	54.1	6.5	39.4
1970	1,469.0	55.5	6.5	38.0
1971	2,084.5	55.3	6.4	38.3
1971 (1st 4 months)	592.3	54.3	6.6	39.1
1972 (1st 4 months)	722.9	53.2	7.2	39.6

* Thousands of units.
Source: *Construction Review*, June 1972, p. 16.

EXHIBIT 4
Veneer and plywood requirements per dwelling unit*

	Direct inputs	Indirect inputs	Total inputs	Percent of total unit costs
Single unit structures	$304	$193	$497	3.3
2–4 unit structures	203	98	301	3.0
Garden apartments	less than 131	N.A.	less than 153	1.5
High-rise apartments	less than 120	N.A.	less than 173	1.5

* Requirements based on the 1963 Input-Output Tables.
N.A. = Not available.
Source: *Survey of Current Business*, October 1970, p. 14.

EXHIBIT 5
Comparison of alternative 1980 GNP forecasts*

	Arthur D. Little		Lionel D. Edie	
	Dollars	*Percent*	*Dollars*	*Percent*
Gross national product	1096	100	1226	100
Personal consumption expenditures	722	66	784	64
Durables	104	9	166	14
Nondurables.	289	26	327	27
Services	329	30	291	24
Private investment	156	14	193	16
Residential	49	4	40	3
Plant	41	4	34	3
Equipment.	61	6	107	9
Change in inventories.	5	0	12	1
Government expenditures	215	20	244	20
Federal defense	104	9	47	4
Federal nondefense.	24	2	50	4
State and local	87	8	147	12
Net exports	3	0	5	0

* Billions of 1958 dollars.
Sources: Arthur D. Little and Lionel D. Edie.

EXHIBIT 6
Comparison of differences between 1963 and 1980 Bridge tables

	Percentage of GNP by component allocated to			
	I/O Industry 11		I/O Industry 12	
GNP component	*1963*	*1980*	*1963*	*1980**
Personal consumption	—	—	—	—
Investment.	57.3⎱	40.3	—	—
Net inventory change.	— ⎰		—	—
Net exports	—	—	—	—
Federal defense	3.5⎱	8.7	1.9⎱	3.2
Federal nondefense	16.6⎰		3.5⎰	
State and local.	26.0	28.6	5.9	6.3
Total GNP	11.1	9.6*	5.9	6.3*

* Percentages calculated assume that the distribution of GNP by component remains the same as 1963.

APPENDIX

Projection of input-output coefficients

Input-output coefficients reflect the relationships between producing and consuming industries. Any particular coefficient is the ratio of purchases from a producing industry to the total output of the consuming industry, that is, the purchases required per dollar of output. As the relationships between industries change over time—and more or less of certain inputs are required per dollar of output—the coefficients also change and these changes must be projected.

A change in a coefficient affects both the industry in which the change takes place and the industry which produces the intermediate good or service. Similarly, in projecting the input-output coefficients to 1980, two alternative approaches were utilized. The first approach consisted of detailed analyses of the input structures of industries. In the second method an aggregative technique was used to adjust the coefficients from the point of view of the industry as a seller of output to other industries.

Table 1 presents one measure of the net effect of the coefficient projections on the producing industries. The index of coefficient change for each industry is the ratio between that industry's intermediate output (assuming 1965 input-output coefficients) and the intermediate output (using 1980 coefficients), when both sets of coefficients are weighted by the 1980 industry output levels. An industry's index of change does not show how much the intermediate output of that industry actually is projected to increase or decrease; this change in intermediate output depends upon the growth rates of output of the consuming industries as well as the projected coefficient changes. The index for an industry does indicate whether the use of that industry's output is increasing or decreasing, on the average, per dollar of the consuming industries outputs from the point of view of a 1980 output distribution.

As noted above, input-output coefficients reflect relationships between producing and consuming industries and as these relationships change over time, the coefficients also change. There are several kinds of change in the relationship between industries which may be translated into a change in coefficients. The most notable of these is technological change whereby new or modified materials and processes are introduced into the production stream. Product mix change is another important cause of coefficient change; if the outputs of the products made by an industry change at different rates, then the input coefficients for the entire sector may also change. Price competition can also be the source of coefficient change; if the relative prices in two industries producing competitive products change, the relatively cheaper product may be substituted for the more expensive product.

The index of coefficient change for an industry as shown in Table 1 may have resulted from one or more than one of the sources of co-efficient change. The following paragraphs present a few of the basic considerations which were important in modifying the coefficients in selected industries.

The decline in the forestry and fishery products industry is primarily a function of the increased processing of wood in the consumer industries, that is, plywood, structural wood parts, etc. Increased fabrication of wood parts and components has the effect of making the stumpage input produced by the forestry component of this sector a smaller part of the total inputs of the wood processing industries, and thus resulted in the decline shown in Table 1.

A projected increase in the use of atomic power in addition to general declines in the uses of coal resulted in a substantial decrease in the coefficient ratio shown for the coal mining industry. However, in terms of absolute tonnage consumption, the 1980 estimate exceeds the 1965 use. The historical decline in coal used per kilowatt generated has slowed as the physical limit of this process is being approached.

The index for wooden containers shows a very pronounced decrease. This reflects the projected long-term decline of this industry due to inroads of competitive packaging materials. The chemical industry's small change is a result of relatively slow growth in basic chemicals, in part offset by more rapidly growing sales to selected customers such as agriculture (fertilizers and insecticides) and plastics and synthetics (raw materials for the manufacture of primary plastics and synthetics).

Increased use of synthetic materials is reflected in the coefficient ratios of those industries associated with these products. These industries are the plastic and synthetic materials and the rubber and miscellaneous plastic products industry, a producer of a wide range of fabricated products. On the other hand, the leather tanning industry shows a decline; this exemplifies the effect of the increased use of synthetic materials on older materials—in this case leather.

The primary iron and steel industry exemplifies two movements in technology and material use. First, increased competition from other materials has resulted in substitution. An example of this is the projected increase in aluminum, plastics, and fiberboard to replace steel in the manufacture of tin cans. Second, improved steels and better design concepts have decreased the quantity of steel per unit of product. In the case of tin cans, thinner steels permit a lesser total tonnage of steel per can. These trends are assumed to continue.

The ratio of coefficients for the nonferrous metals industry stands in contrast to that of primary iron and steel. Two distinct trends are present in this industry. First, aluminum, the largest single component, is assumed to continue its relatively high growth into other markets. Other nonferrous metals are presumed to grow, but at considerably lesser rates. These projections have the effect of moderating the total nonferrous industry so that the total industry coefficient continues to grow at a rate only slightly faster than its consuming industries.

TABLE 1
Index of coefficient change, 1965–80*

Industry number and title	Index of coefficient change, 1965–80
1. Livestock and livestock products	93.6
2. Other agricultural products	93.6
3. Forestry and fishery products	87.3
4. Agricultural, forestry, and fishery services	91.6
5. Iron and ferroalloy ores mining	101.7
6. Nonferrous metal ores mining	98.3
7. Coal mining	64.9
8. Crude petroleum and natural gas	94.7
9. Stone and clay mining and quarrying	99.9
10. Chemical and fertilizer mineral mining	108.2
11. New construction†	−
12. Maintenance and repair construction	74.1
13. Ordnance and accessories	112.3
14. Food and kindred products	105.2
15. Tobacco manufactures	98.3
16. Broad and narrow fabrics, yarn and thread mills	100.1
17. Miscellaneous textile goods and floor coverings	86.2
18. Apparel	98.1
19. Miscellaneous fabricated textile products	99.6
20. Lumber and wood products, except containers	91.5
21. Wooden containers	58.4
22. Household furniture	79.5
23. Other furniture and fixtures	107.0
24. Paper and allied products, except containers	97.7
25. Paperboard containers and boxes	97.1
26. Printing and publishing	80.6
27. Chemicals and selected chemical products	101.5
28. Plastics and synthetic materials	132.9
29. Drugs, cleaning, and toilet preparations	123.4
30. Paints and allied products	104.2
31. Petroleum refining and related industries	86.7
32. Rubber and miscellaneous plastics products	135.0
33. Leather tanning and industrial leather products	74.7
34. Footwear and other leather products	115.5
35. Glass and glass products	89.6

* The index of coefficient change for each industry is the ratio between that industry's intermediate output using 1965 coefficients and the intermediate output using 1980 coefficients, when both sets of coefficients are weighted by the 1980 industry output levels. The intermediate output of an industry is that part of its total output consumed by all intermediate industries.
† New construction has no coefficients since none of its output is sold for intermediate consumption.

TABLE 1 (*continued*)

Industry number and title	Index of coefficient change, 1965-80
36. Stone and clay products	103.6
37. Primary iron and steel manufacturing	78.0
38. Primary nonferrous metals manufacturing	106.9
39. Metal containers	92.9
40. Heating, plumbing and structural metal products	102.2
41. Stampings, screw machine products and bolts	89.7
42. Other fabricated metal products	95.0
43. Engines and turbines	93.5
44. Farm machinery and equipment	81.1
45. Construction, mining, and oil field machinery	86.2
46. Materials handling machinery and equipment	97.3
47. Metalworking machinery and equipment	86.6
48. Special industry machinery and equipment	114.1
49. General industrial machinery and equipment	95.2
50. Machine shop products	115.6
51. Office, computing, and accounting machines	139.4
52. Service industry machines	159.4
53. Electric industrial equipment and apparatus	104.6
54. Household appliances	100.4
55. Electric lighting and wiring equipment	100.2
56. Radio, television, and communication equipment	115.5
57. Electronic components and accessories	143.4
58. Miscellaneous electrical machinery and equipment	122.4
59. Motor vehicles and equipment	98.0
60. Aircraft and parts	95.4
61. Other transportation equipment	75.0
62. Scientific and controlling instruments	113.4
63. Optical, ophthalmic, and photographic equipment	148.1
64. Miscellaneous manufacturing	103.5
65. Transportation and warehousing	92.9
66. Communications: except broadcasting	144.3
67. Radio and television broadcasting	52.8
68. Electric, gas, water, and sanitary services	146.1
69. Wholesale and retail trade	122.6
70. Finance and insurance	96.0
71. Real estate and rental	78.8
72. Hotels: personal and repair services, except auto	106.7
73. Business services	128.5
74. Research and development	125.8
75. Automobile repair and services	116.9
76. Amusements	116.0
77. Medical, educational and nonprofit organizations	98.5
78. Federal government enterprises	94.2
79. State and local government enterprises	93.5
80. Gross imports of goods and services	126.7
81. Business travel, entertainment, and gifts	73.5
82. Office supplies	122.5

Excerpts from the Peterson Report (A)[1]

EARLY IN 1971, Peter G. Peterson resigned as the $125,000-a-year board chairman and chief executive officer of Bell and Howell to become the Assistant to the President for International Economic Affairs. President Nixon welcomed Mr. Peterson to Washington as "one of the ablest chief executive officers of this generation" and in February gave him his first assignment—that of assessing the competitiveness of American industry in world markets as background for the formulation of U.S. international economic policy in the 1970s.

Following the presentation of what became known as "The Peterson Report" to the president and the Council on International Economic Policy in early April, the president directed that it be given in briefing form to selected officials in the administration, members of Congress, and to groups outside the government. Subsequently, the president approved a series of specific work programs of the Council on International Economic Policy aimed at developing new policies and new legislative programs.

In December 1971, the Peterson Report was made publicly available in two volumes published by the Government Printing Office under the title *The United States in the Changing World Economy.* Volume I, entitled *A Foreign Economic Perspective,* contains Mr. Peterson's "personal overview of the origins and possible policy implications of the

---

[1] This case was prepared by Professor James P. Baughman from sources in the public domain as the basis for class discussion and is not intended to illustrate either effective or ineffective handling of an administrative situation.

137

new world economy." Volume II, entitled *Background Material,* contains text and exhibits "that provided the basis for briefings to the President and the Council on International Economic Policy during 1971."

In his report, Mr. Peterson concluded that the United States was falling behind in its ability to compete against Europe and Japan, partly because Washington had ignored the importance of foreign economic policy. He called for an end to what he regarded as the "soft" policies that the government, particularly the State Department, had followed through the 1960s. Instead, he advocated a new "hard" line in trade.

The Peterson Report appeared at a time when President Nixon was taking radical steps to defend the dollar and Peterson's work was widely credited as being the starting point for the dramatic changes in economic policy that the president announced on August 15, 1971. Early in 1972, Mr. Peterson was named Secretary of Commerce.

Much of the Peterson Report concentrates on "the essential importance of the quest for fundamental reform of the monetary system." The four excerpts which follow, however, are from those sections of the report which consider the problems of increasing the "competitiveness" of the United States in international trade and commerce. The first excerpt, "Balance of Payments," outlines the historical record of the persistent and deteriorating deficit in the American balance-of-payments and the dramatic increase in U.S. direct-investment overseas. The second, "Trade Trends," examines the strengths and weaknesses of American export and import portfolios and their effects on employment. The third and fourth, "A Strong Domestic Economy—Requisite for a Strong and Outward Looking Foreign Economic Policy" and "A Work Program for International Economic Policy," contain Mr. Peterson's prescription for increased "competitiveness."

EXCERPT 1

BALANCE OF PAYMENTS

Introduction

While a balance of payments problem is an international monetary problem, its roots often rest in policies that a country takes to meet domestic economic or political needs or security objectives. Thus, balance of payments problems are often really problems of defense spending, or aid, or trade, or investment abroad. We also find that these last four elements are interrelated and have cross effects (for example, investment abroad leads to later income, while in some cases inducing exports to the new foreign affiliate). Therefore, while the solutions to balance of payments problems will inevitably involve "bankers," those solutions may often be found in nonmonetary policies.

Domestic policies that touch off balance of payments troubles are often implemented with the knowledge that they may result in short-term instability in the international monetary system, and costs to domestic consumers. Under these circumstances, appropriate exchange rate adjustments can make very large contributions to equilibrium in the international economic system. Moreover, if the adjustment system can be made more flexible, adjustment will be more gradual and thus less politically sensitive.

Under the present monetary system, exchange rate adjustments have been infrequent as each country has pursued its own economic interests. We must formulate cooperative and constructive programs to deal with persistent balance-of-payments problems that have resulted.

The United States has run a basic balance-of-payments deficit in almost every year since 1950. According to the presumptions of a responsive monetary system, this should have resulted in an effective devaluation of the dollar. Yet, note that because of changes in effective prices of other currencies (mostly devaluations), the dollar has, in effect, been revalued since 1959 (Chart 40). The "comparative official dollar" had, in fact, risen 4.7 percent relative to other currencies at the beginning of 1970.

CHART 40
Movement in the effective rate of exchange of the U.S. dollar

Note: January 1959 = 100.

Balance-of-payments deficit problems have tended to be of two broad types:

1. *Long-term persistent problems.* These are caused by a variety of factors that can be influenced by longer-range policies concerning trade and export matters, defense expenditures, foreign investment, etc., as well as by fundamental domestic policies affecting relative prices, costs, and productivity.

2. *Short-term transitory problems.* Highly erratic movements have usually been caused by differences in interest rates between countries or by stock market investment flows. In recent years, anticipation of possible currency adjustments has also resulted in large international capital flows. Businessmen and bankers want to protect their short-term assets by moving out of currencies which may be devalued and into those which might be revalued; and speculators hope for quick profits by similar actions. Short-term movements have become an even greater problem during the 1960s because of growing amounts of mobile Euro-dollars (loosely defined as dollar balances held in banks overseas).

A variety of balance-of-payments measurements exist which indicate our net position—that is, the difference between our inflows and outflows. The current account and basic balances reflect persistent long-term movements and the liquidity and official settlements balances include the effects of short-term flows.

U.S. current account balance

The current account balance measures the difference between U.S. purchases of foreign goods and services, and sales of U.S. goods and services abroad. The definition commonly used in the United States also includes payment of pensions and personal and organized charitable remittances to foreigners, as well as the foreign exchange cost of our military disbursements in foreign countries.

This account was in surplus every year between 1960 and 1970, although there were wide variations as seen in Chart 41. Surpluses averaged almost $6 billion in the mid-1960s and shrank to about $2 billion in recent years; for 1971 the current account may show a $1 billion deficit.

U.S. basic balance

The basic balance adds private long-term capital movements and government grants and capital transactions to the current account balance. As Chart 42 indicates, since World War II we usually have had a basic balance deficit in the $1.5 to $3 billion range, but it is estimated this deficit will reach a record $8 to $9 billion in 1971. The persistence

CHART 41
U.S. current account balance
(merchandise, investment income, services, military, and
transfers, excluding government grants)

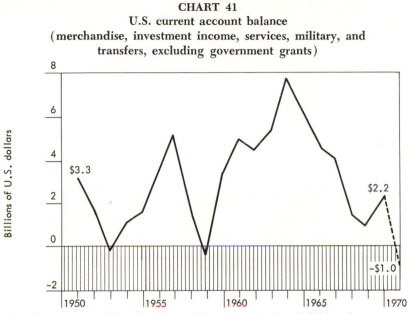

Note: Best measure of U.S. competitive position and transfer abroad of U.S. real resources.

CHART 42
U.S. basic balance

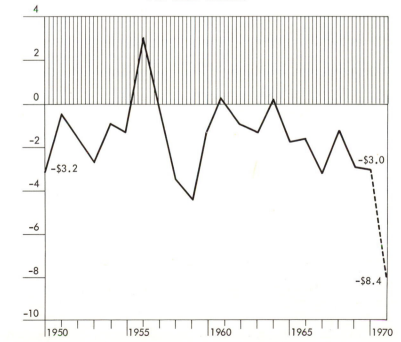

Note: Adds long-term capital movements to current account balance. Best measure of persistent features in U.S. payments position.

of this deficit has, of course, contributed significantly to the buildup of foreign reserves and U.S. dollars abroad.

The United States has a large net outflow on the capital account, mainly attributable to U.S. private direct and other investment abroad and government grants and loans. For example, in 1970 a current account surplus of $2.2 billion was outweighed by a deficit of $5.3 billion on the grants and long-term capital account, producing a basic balance deficit of about $3.0 billion.

U.S. balance of payments trends

One purpose of this overall presentation is to help predict the likely future—and understanding the past is, of course, one basis for doing that. Any reasonable prognosis of our future balance of payments requires an examination of the major components of the basic balance—which, it will be seen, is a composite of very different forces and trends.

Clearly, the chief contributor to our deteriorating basic balance has been our declining trade position. As Chart 43 illustrates, the trade surplus, which averaged over $5 billion annually in the early 1960s, was only slightly more than $1 billion in 1968 and 1969. The situation improved somewhat in 1970, but this was mainly because of an unusually large increase in exports of basic commodities. The deteriorating trend continued in 1971, with pre-August projections indicating a trade deficit for the year of about $2 billion.

Our worsening trade balance trends can be seen even more clearly when the data are adjusted to eliminate the influence on our trade of the various stages of the business cycle at home and abroad. The resulting long-term U.S. trade trend has been steadily worsening since 1964, and prior to the recent international currency adjustments, our adjusted trade deficit for 1972 was predicted at more than $3 billion. By comparison, those of West Germany and Japan have been sharply improving since the mid-1960s and would have probably reached surpluses of over $7 billion in 1972 without the currency adjustment actions that have been taken.

However, there are other divergent trends that also affect the balance in significant ways. A major deficit item has been government outlays abroad for the military, and for economic and military aid. As Chart 44 shows, these combined expenditures resulted in an outflow of $7.2 billion in 1970, or $3 billion more than in 1950.

The deficit on U.S. military expenditures has gradually increased from about $0.6 billion in 1950 to $3.4 billion in 1970. This is made up of gross U.S. military expenditures abroad of $4.8 billion, less foreign military purchases from the United States of $1.4 billion.

An analysis of the geographic composition of this deficit indicates

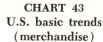

CHART 43
U.S. basic trends
(merchandise)

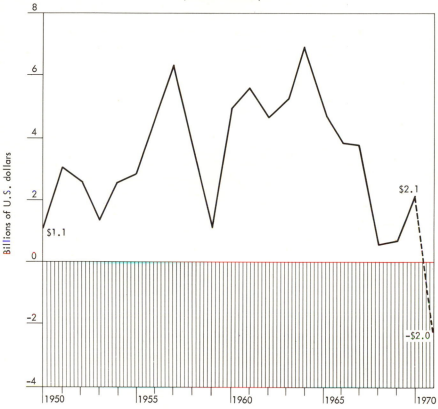

that $1.2 billion (or somewhat less if one takes credit for certain offsets) is in Europe, and that most of the remainder is in the Far East, including Japan. The military deficit in the Far East is expected to decline in the post-Vietnam period, probably to be offset to some extent by whatever we decide to do in additional economic support in Southeast Asia. A major part of our military deficit balance is almost $700 million paid to Japan for various bases, support services, products, and other miscellaneous items. Thus, one significant factor in America's basic balance in the 1970s will be the rate of progress made in defense burden-sharing. Foreign aid outlays in 1970 stood at $3.8 billion or about the same level as in 1950, when most aid was under the Marshall Plan.

Outlays for economic aid, about $1.9 billion, represent resources diverted by the United States. They do not, however, automatically add to our payments deficit because aid allocations increase U.S. exports

CHART 44
U.S. basic balance trends
(government)

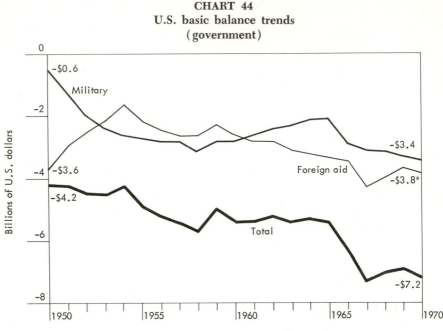

* Of the −$3.8 billion, −$1.7 billion are grants and −$2.1 billion are loans.

and because repayments of principal and interest on past U.S. loans show up as receipts in the current account. If these offsetting items are netted against the outflow for economic aid, part of the stated deficit would be eliminated.

As Chart 45 illustrates, our overall service transactions have remained at about a $1 billion deficit during the 1960s. But within the category there have been two important and diverging trends. Our earnings on fees and royalties—mainly from sales of our advanced technology abroad—tripled between 1960 and 1970 and, after considering the small amount paid to foreigners for their technology, this account showed a $2.2 billion surplus in 1970. On the other hand, our net payments abroad for travel and passenger fares have grown steadily, reaching a deficit of $2.3 billion in 1970. About $300 million annually is spent for travel to Canada and Mexico. This growth reflects a series of technological and marketing revolutions in the last decade—jet travel, tours, expansion of travel for business purposes, and growing U.S. affluence. Part of this deficit is compensated for in major ways in other accounts—such as the sale of U.S. jet aircraft to overseas airlines.

Perhaps the most surprising deficit compensators in our basic balance are private capital-related flows. As Charts 46 and 47 illustrate, income from our foreign direct investment has been greater than our new capital outflows, and the gap has been widening. The surplus was $1.6 billion

CHART 45
U.S. basic balance trends
(services)

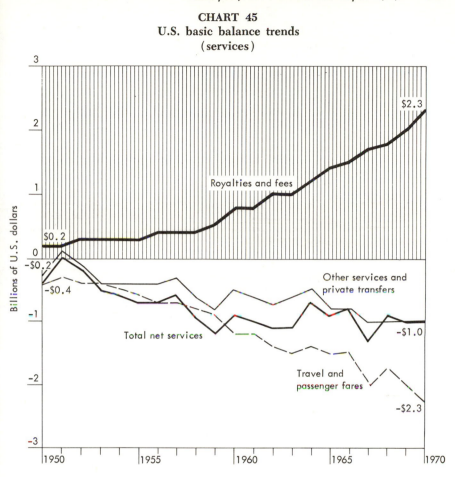

in 1970, compared with $0.7 billion in 1960 (Chart 47). If all private
U.S. investment income earnings abroad are counted, including bonds
and stocks and short-term assets, our gross income has more than quin-
tupled in 20 years—from $1.5 billion in 1950 to $8.7 billion in 1970.
(Chart 46. This does not include about $2.5 billion earned abroad in
1970 that was not brought back to the U.S., that is, "unremitted" earnings.) Deducting income, interest, and dividend payments to foreigners
who invest in the United States, the U.S. still had an investment income
balance of $4.5 billion in 1970. Another improvement in the private
capital-related account has been the recent acceleration of foreign direct
investment in the United States—which reached $1 billion in 1970, com-
pared with a small net outflow during 1963 and 1964. Furthermore,
in 1970, foreigners invested here $0.5 billion more than they took home
in direct investment income (Chart 46).

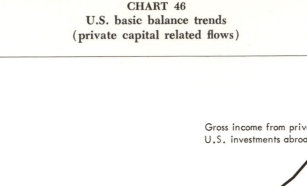

CHART 46
U.S. basic balance trends
(private capital related flows)

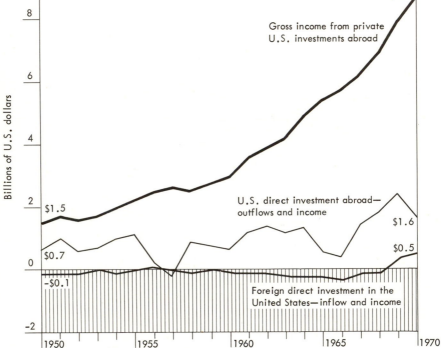

U.S. basic balance—regional composition

Another way of examining our basic balance is to break down these flows with our main economic partners. In 1970, as shown in Chart 48, and in recent years, our major deficits have been with Canada and Japan, and in both cases the trade and basic balances have been about the same. This similarity, however, hides fairly large nontrade movements: for instance, in 1970 we earned $300 million more from direct investment in Canada than we invested there. On the other hand, our net travel deficit with Canada amounted to nearly $200 million. In the Japanese case, we earned on a net basis more than $400 million in 1970 from selling services—but these earnings were offset by our military-related outlays in Japan of nearly $700 million. Private capital-related dealings with Japan are minute since Japan keeps out most direct foreign investment. Our relatively large trade surplus with the European

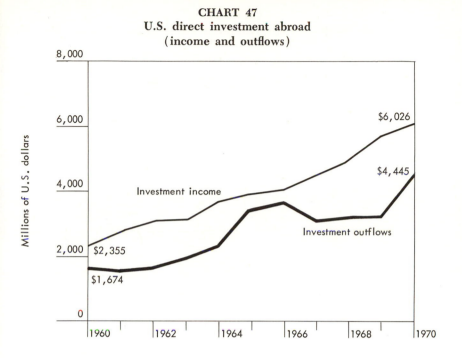

CHART 47
U.S. direct investment abroad
(income and outflows)

Community (EC)—$1.7 billion—was reduced to a much smaller basic surplus because of our military outlays there of $1 billion. Also in 1970, our new direct investment in the EC topped our investment income from there by $200 million. However, on the plus side, our net earnings from fees and royalties amounted to $500 million. With LDCs we have a basic balance deficit, as our trade surplus is more than offset by our economic and military aid outflows.

As mentioned above, the $5 billion jump in our 1971 basic balance deficit is mainly attributable to a worsening of our trade balance. On a country-by-country basis—estimated from data for the first six months of 1971—our growing deficit with Japan accounted for roughly half of the larger overall basic balance deficit (Chart 49). Declining surpluses with the EC and the United Kingdom were also important. Although our trade deficit with Canada grew, our basic balance position with Canada improved slightly.

While we expect to run basic balance surpluses with some countries and deficits with others, each country's own overall balance of payments position should be near zero. Such equilibrium is a sign of a well-functioning international monetary system. But the United States recorded by far its largest basic balance deficit in 1971—estimated at more than $8 billion—while other countries were recording large surpluses. As

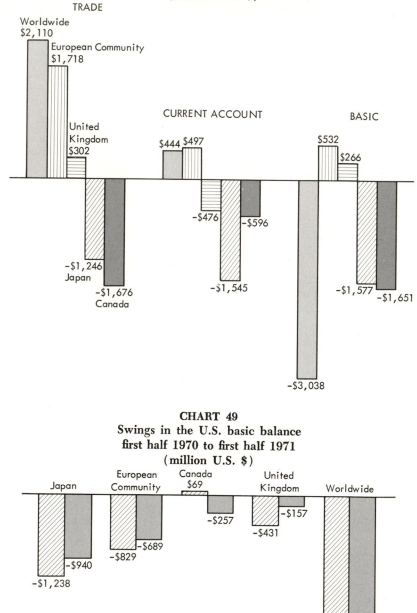

CHART 48
U.S. trade, current account, and basic balances, 1970
(million U.S. $)

TRADE

Worldwide
$2,110

European Community
$1,718

United
Kingdom
$302

-$1,246
Japan

-$1,676
Canada

CURRENT ACCOUNT

$444 $497

-$476

-$596

-$1,545

-$3,038

BASIC

$532

$266

-$1,577

-$1,651

CHART 49
Swings in the U.S. basic balance
first half 1970 to first half 1971
(million U.S. $)

Japan

European
Community

Canada
$69

United
Kingdom

Worldwide

-$257

-$431

-$157

-$689

-$829

-$940

-$1,238

-$2,080

-$2,596

Total [hatched] [grey] Merchandise

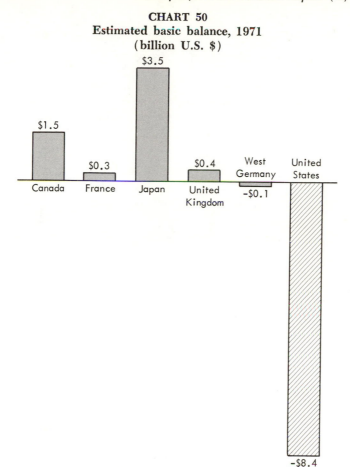

CHART 50
Estimated basic balance, 1971
(billion U.S. $)

Chart 50 indicates, Japan is expected to have the largest surplus—$3.5 billion—and Canada is next with $1.5 billion. Smaller surpluses are expected for numerous other countries, including $0.4 billion for the United Kingdom and $0.3 billion for France. This demonstrates that the international monetary system and exchange rate parities existing before August 15 failed to bring into equilibrium the payments positions between the United States and other countries.

U.S. liquidity balance

The liquidity balance formulation of the balance of payments measures the annual change in short-term claims of all foreigners (both private and official agencies) against U.S. reserves. The liquidity balance

CHART 51
U.S. liquidity balance

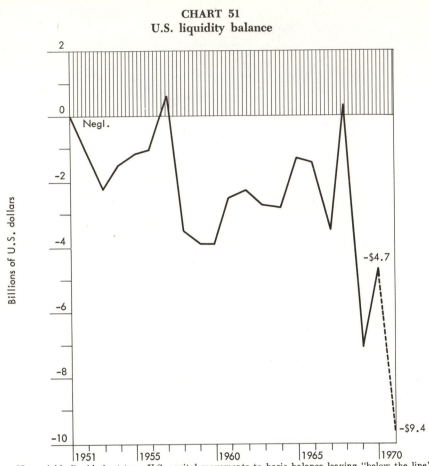

Note: Adds liquid short-term U.S. capital movements to basic balance leaving "below the line" liquid dollars held by both private and official foreigners and U.S. reserve assets. Best measure of potential short-term foreign claims against the U.S. dollar.

adds to the basic balance movements of U.S. private liquid short-term capital. Chart 51 shows the liquidity balance since 1951.

These capital movemtnts have been volatile and have had major and sometimes traumatic effects on both the level and distribution of world reserves. Further, the liquidity balance has been generally worsening: during much of the 1960s the deficit was about $4 billion; in 1969 and 1970, it was closer to $6 billion; and for 1971, the deficit will be about $9 to $10 billion.

U.S. official settlements balance

The official settlements balance adds liquid short-term private foreign capital movements to the liquidity balance. It measures changes in claims against us held by foreign official monetary agencies and in the level of U.S. reserves. It is probably the best indication we have of the pressure on the U.S. dollar in foreign exchange markets.

Large gyrations in world short-term capital movements occur because national economies may be in different phases of economic growth and cycles. In turn, these different phases often call for different national monetary policies—different rates of growth in money supply and rates of interest.

Money naturally flows where it can earn the highest rate of return for a given risk. Since the dollar is the principal transaction currency, vast capital movements most often are into or out of dollars. These short-term movements of billions of dollars have at times put heavy strain on the international monetary system, and have provided some countries more dollars than they wanted to absorb into their domestic reserves.

A world of rapidly growing economies requires adequate growth in global reserves, in order to keep pace with the growing level of exports and imports. It is generally agreed that several billion dollars of additional reserves are needed annually. U.S. deficits provided large portions of this annual growth in other countries' reserves in the 1950s and 1960s, and our own reserves were therefore reduced.

As Chart 52 illustrates, our official settlements balance has swung widely in recent years. In 1968 and 1969, the United States had a surplus because interest rates were higher here than in other major money markets. In 1970, when our interest rates dropped below foreign rates, short-term capital funds flowed abroad and we experienced a deficit of nearly $10 billion. In 1971, our large deficit—estimated at $30 billion—was only partially due to the interest rate differential. More important, especially after mid-April, was the fact that U.S. and foreign firms and banks were shifting from short-term dollar assets into German marks and other foreign currencies in anticipation of their revaluation.

Trends in U.S. liquid foreign assets and liabilities

While the liquidity and official settlements balances indicated *annual* changes in our payments position, Chart 53 shows *total*, foreign short-term claims against the dollar, both official and private, and our total reserves at the end of each three-month period. Foreign claims exceeded our reserves at the end of 1970 by $30 billion. This gap had widened to $37 billion by June 1971, and to almost $50 billion by September 1971.

However, only *official* liabilities could be submitted to the United States for redemption in gold prior to August 15, 1971. The United States can also use other reserve assets (that is, the SDRs or "Special Drawing Rights") to make foreign payments, or may draw some foreign currencies from the International Monetary Fund and use those funds

CHART 52
U.S. official settlements balance

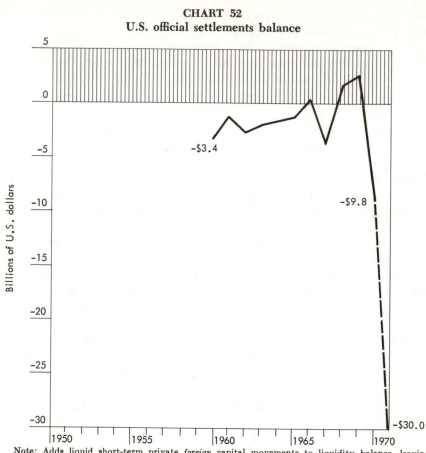

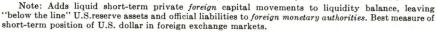

Note: Adds liquid short-term private *foreign* capital movements to liquidity balance, leaving "below the line" U.S.reserve assets and official liabilities to *foreign monetary authorities*. Best measure of short-term position of U.S. dollar in foreign exchange markets.

to repurchase dollars from foreign monetary authorities. Even so, as we moved through 1971 it was increasingly obvious that our remaining reserves were highly vulnerable. By the end of 1970 our liquid liabilities to foreign official agencies exceeded our combined reserve assets by $6 billion. By September 1971 the excess was $30 billion.

Including *near-liquid* liabilities in these figures, the shortfalls of our reserve assets on these two dates become $9 billion and $39 billion respectively.

U.S. foreign assets and liabilities

References to our balance-of-payments problems are often measurements of annual *cash flows* into and out of the United States. We have

CHART 53
Trends in U.S. liquid foreign assets and liabilities

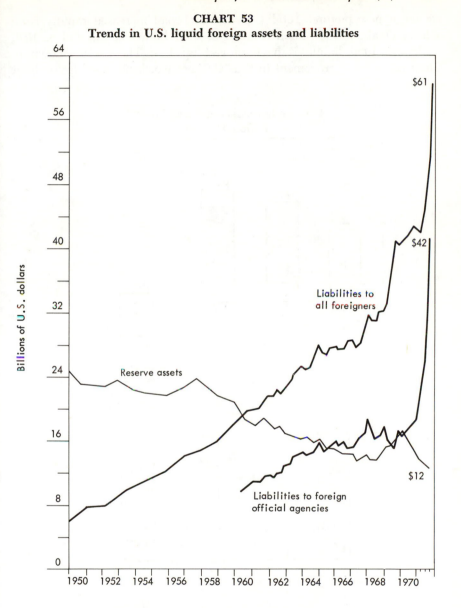

also discussed our position in official terms—that is, the U.S. assets held
by foreign official agencies in bank deposits, securities, and the like.
However, much of this nation's overall wealth is not in government
hands but in the hands of the private sector. We should therefore consider also an overall balance sheet of America's international position—
our overall net worth.

When we combine all private and official assets and liabilities abroad, we see a new picture. Total U.S. assets abroad increased rapidly from a level of about $86 billion in 1960 to $167 billion at the end of 1970 while our total liabilities have moved up less. The result, shown in Chart 54, is an improvement in the "U.S. net worth position" from about

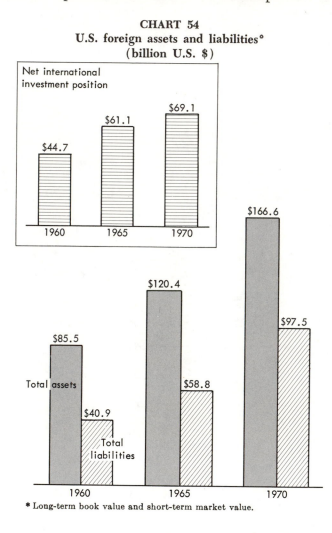

CHART 54
U.S. foreign assets and liabilities*
(billion U.S. $)

* Long-term book value and short-term market value.

$45 billion to $69 billion between 1960 and 1970. Remember that this figure includes for our net worth only the "book value" of our direct investments. Their market value would be much higher.

The question is often asked, "How can we have balance-of-payments difficulties and still have a net worth increasing at such a rate?" In the first place, much of this net worth is in private hands and therefore not available to offset official claims against our government's reserves.

Also, a substantial amount of earnings abroad (about $2.5 billion annually in recent years) is reinvested abroad, rather than being remitted.

Let us not leave a discussion of our balance of payments on such a high note since there are pressing problems.

To summarize briefly:

1. It seems that those who say there is some persisting imbalance in the international monetary and payments system are correct. We have seen the reluctance of most countries to revalue their currencies because of the effect it would have on their competitiveness and local jobs. We have seen how many countries like to see their reserves go up and dislike seeing them drop. So long as such efforts to preserve surpluses exist, and so long as deficit countries' currencies remain overvalued, it will be difficult to reach a sustainable pattern of world payments—and this, in turn, will invite trade and payments restrictions.

Exchange rate parity changes were seen as an essential adjustment mechanism in cases of fundamental payments disequilibrium. Exchange rate flexibility may also be helpful in coping with short-term capital flows. How far and in what ways is the world willing to use these avenues of providing a smoother and more stable payments pattern? What should we do to encourage appropriate exchange rate adjustments?

2. Efforts to resolve our balance-of-payments problems entail some costs and bring about conflicts with other goals. An effective devaluation of the dollar is supposed to improve our balance of payments mainly by reducing the dollar costs of our products abroad and increasing the prices we pay for foreign goods. Thus, while more jobs may be created here, our consumers' standard of living declines because of the higher prices that they have to pay for foreign goods.

In some instances, conflicts between balance-of-payments considerations and our national interests go beyond the desires of a smoothly functioning monetary system. For example, how far are we willing to go in modifying our policies in the field of foreign and security affairs to achieve an improved balance of payments? To put the matter differently, perhaps only an improvement in the balance of payments may permit us to continue our policies in the field of foreign and security affairs. Along this line, defense cost-sharing is a subject receiving increasing attention within our government. To what extent should its impact on balance of payments intensify these efforts?

3. We have also seen that various economies of the world can be out of phase with each other, and some say this leads the United States and other countries to make monetary decisions affecting money supply and interest rates that can have important short-term balance-of-payments effects. To what extent is it really practical to ask this country, or others, to distort in important ways the decisions they would otherwise make in the interests of promoting growth and price stability at home—

in order to help stabilize the international monetary system? In what specific ways would we expect ourselves and other countries to harmonize our stabilization polices? Or, are there new approaches to dampening the impact of large short-term swings of capital?

This brief examination of the balance-of-payments issue makes clear that there are a variety of problems involved: some monetary, some nonmonetary; some long-term, some short-term. It is a field in which important progress seems to be made only in an environment of urgency, if not in a time of crisis.

U.S. DIRECT INVESTMENTS ABROAD

American businessmen have made increasingly heavy investments abroad. We have seen some of the immediate effects on our own balance-of-payments position and have anticipated some of the long-range benefits to be gained by this broadening of the base for our national income. There are, however, other consequences here and abroad to be taken into account for the future.

During 1960–1970, U.S. direct investments in plant and equipment abroad more than doubled, to a total of $78 billion (Chart 55). The share going to Europe, where our investments have nearly quadrupled to more than $24 billion, has risen most rapidly—causing periodic con-

CHART 55
U.S. cumulative foreign direct investment abroad
(billion U.S. $)

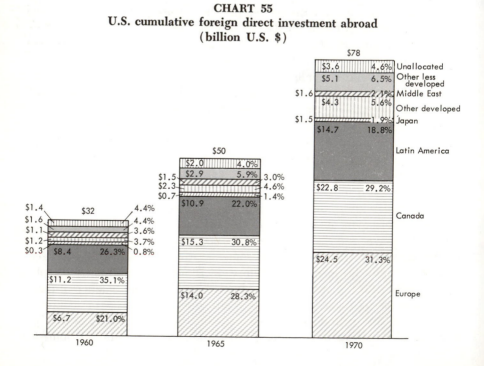

cern in important European quarters about a possible "American take-over" of existing businesses. (All studies in this field suggest that the preponderant amount of this U.S. investment is "new" investment and not the purchase of existing companies.) In only ten years the European share of total U.S. foreign direct investment rose from 21 percent to 31 percent. On an overall basis, a study covering the year 1964 showed that U.S. enterprises accounted for about 6 percent of total manufacturing sales in Europe—with U.S. representation somewhat stronger than that in "advanced" industries in which large firms play a dominant role: machinery and transport equipment (automotive, for example). A highly visible exception is the computer industry, in which U.S. companies have a larger market share.

Canada continues to be the largest single recipient of U.S. investment by a wide margin, but its share had declined from about 35 percent in 1960 to 29 percent of the total in 1970, or about the same as all of Europe. Thus, during the 1960s, the rate of increase of U.S. investment was obviously slower for Canada than for Europe. This concentration of U.S. investment in Canada is a major factor leading Prime Minister Trudeau to say that "living next to the United States is like sleeping with an elephant." On the other hand, we should not forget that 63 percent of Canada's manufactured goods are exported—which, of course, means Canadian jobs—and our investments in Canada contribute importantly to her export capability.

Latin America's share of total U.S. direct investment abroad has fallen sharply—from 26 percent in 1960 to less than 20 percent in 1970. Our total investment in Latin America, however, increased by about three-fourths during the 1960s and accounted for about 14 percent of total new U.S. investment abroad. But in the last year or so the rate of increase in U.S. investment in the region has slowed, due in part to the growing fear of expropriation of American assets, an issue with which we must deal. Some studies of a few years ago suggest that about 16 percent of Latin America's manufacturing output in U.S. owned—though this of course varies greatly by type of manufacturing (such fields as rubber and chemicals have stronger U.S. representation).

Note that small and relatively unchanged amount of U.S. investment in Japan in ten years—still less than 2 percent of total U.S. foreign investment and only slightly more than $1 billion. This is certainly not the result of a lack of interest or ardor by U.S. business. Rather, it reflects Japanese investment restrictions born of a traditional fear of control of their enterprises by "outsiders," and the special problems such outside interests present in an economy with such close interrelationships of labor, business, and government.

Direct foreign investments in the United States are less than $12 billion, about one sixth of what we have invested abroad, even though the U.S. GNP is of course larger than that of all Europe. Much could be said for increasing the amount of foreign investment in the United States.

U.S. investment trends (plant and equipment)

Chart 56 shows American companies were still investing more than six times as much in 1970 on domestic operations as abroad, but the

CHART 56
U.S. investment trends
(plant and equipment)

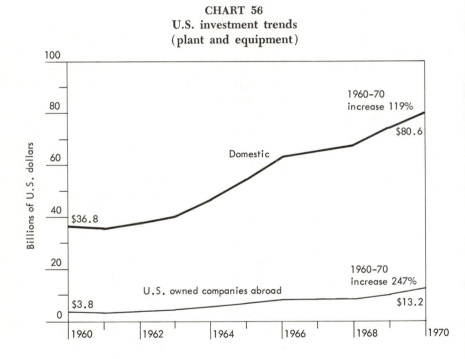

ratio is being reduced. The rate of growth of overseas investments over the past ten years is running at twice the rate of domestic expansion; whereas between 1960 and 1970 domestic investment in plant and equipment increased by 119 percent, investment by U.S.-owned companies increased by 247 percent. By and large, this is explained by the following factors: (1) more rapidly growing markets abroad, (2) the belief that some of those markets were less competitive than the U.S. market, (3) lower production costs, (4) movement behind trade restrictions, and (5) most important, if American firms are to participate in these foreign markets, competitive conditions require local production, which in turn requires a direct investment.

How much has direct investment abroad resulted in lower economies of scale in this country? Was it always a necessary condition to capturing these markets? To what extent does it continue to be? What is the effect on U.S. employment? How does this large investment affect export potential from the United States? Answers to these questions will help us formulate a trade and investment policy geared to market conditions in the 1970s.

U.S. direct exports versus sales of U.S.-owned foreign affiliates

Sales of our foreign affiliates are now about two and one-half times our direct exports of manufactured commodities, and nearly 75 percent greater than total U.S. exports. Moreover, foreign affiliates' sales have been growing almost twice as fast as our exports during the past decade, even though our exports have more than doubled in that period (Chart 57).

CHART 57
U.S. direct exports versus sales of U.S.-owned foreign affiliates

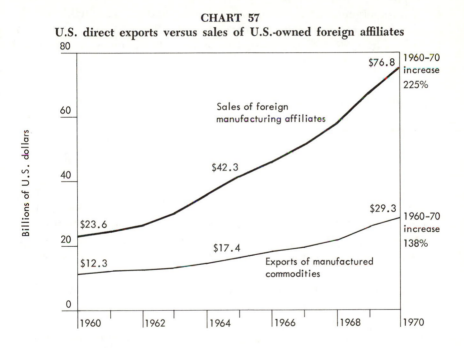

Several factors underlie this development.

1. Many foreign markets for our products are growing rapidly but, at the same time, are growing more competitive. Both the size of the markets and their competitiveness have made it attractive or necessary to invest abroad in order to tap them. Chart 58 shows that most sales of U.S. foreign manufacturing affiliates are in the local market abroad—78 percent in 1968. When we add another 14 percent of sales that go to third markets overseas, we find that

only about 8 percent of sales are back to the United States. This last figure has grown in recent years—though it appears on closer examination that a dominant portion of increasing exports to the United States by American affiliates abroad results from the U.S.-Canada Auto Agreement.

2. As foreign markets grow more sophisticated in their requirements, it becomes necessary to tailor products to meet specific customer needs in specific markets. This does not means that such plants necessarily limit U.S. exports of that product. Quite the contrary, the presence of a plant abroad to complete the final assembly often makes available an outlet for U.S. exports that otherwise would not have existed.

3. Some argue that the United States has not done enough to make exporting attractive to U.S. firms.

4. The emergence of the multinational corporation has facilitated the development of worldwide markets and sources. The multinational corporation, to be discussed, is a major phenomenon in the world economy.

The multinational corporation

Americans must come to know the new industrial type—the multinational corporation (MNC)—which will increasingly affect our way of life during the 1970s and 1980s. Here are some of its distinctive characteristics:

First, MNCs depend heavily on overseas income. There are many American companies now earning from one fourth to one half of their income abroad. The MNC is sensitive to policies affecting foreign investments—investments which, as we have seen, provide return flows of income that are a major positive factor in our balance of payments.

Second, the MNC has the resources and the scope to think and act with worldwide planning of markets and sources. Many international opportunities require capital and technology on a scale only large, multinational corporations can supply.

Third, since the MNC operates across national boundaries, it speeds up the transfer of know-how. It hastens changes—bringing important benefits but also accelerating adjustment problems.

Fourth, the development of the MNC has aroused serious concern among labor unions. They claim there are major U.S. job losses resulting from these companies which are characterized as "job exporters." As "evidence" of this, it is said that about 50 percent of the U.S. international trade transactions are "intracorporate"—which are assumed to result in lost U.S. jobs. Actually, as pointed out earlier, many of these transactions result in increased exports from the United States that would not have been possible without the foreign plant. One study shows that over half of all *exports* of manufactured products from the United States flow from MNCs and in turn about half of these go from the parent to the subsidiary plant abroad. A more recent study indicates that among America's larger MNCs, their positive net trade balance with their affiliates increased 85 percent from 1960 to 1970. Also, as mentioned above only about 8 percent of the output of U.S. foreign manufacturing subsidiaries is imported back to the United States (Chart 58).

CHART 58
Sales of foreign manufacturing affiliates of U.S. firms
(billion U.S. $)

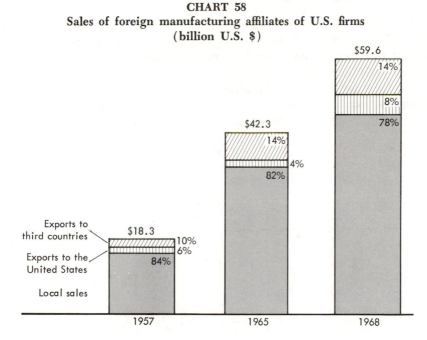

Fifth, the MNC is also a source of concern to some governments, since from its wide base it is often able to circumvent national monetary, fiscal, and exchange policies. The possibility of distortions arising from intracorporate pricing practices to take advantage of national variations in tax laws has also been cited with concern.

Sixth, studies indicate that MNCs tend to be companies that are growing at rates significantly higher than for all manufacturing industries as a whole—including their growth in domestic employment.

Not enough is known with certainty about the specific economic effects of MNCs, including their effect on jobs in this country. One thing, however, is already clear. These corporations are a major force in expanding both world trade and America's role in the world economy. Also, MNCs are an integral part of our technological and managerial expertise. To seriously restrict the activities of these corporations in their foreign operations would obviously be a major step back from the relatively open and interdependent world we have tried to help build.

EXCERPT 2

TRADE TRENDS

U.S. GNP—goods and services

In considering the future of trade, long-term data show that the United States is becoming an economy with a high proportion of its output in services. Goods are becoming less important in our total economic output, and employment has been shifting to services occupations.

By 1970, services made up about 40 percent of our output, but these industries employed about 60 percent of the labor force (Chart 14). This trend raises some important questions about the future structure

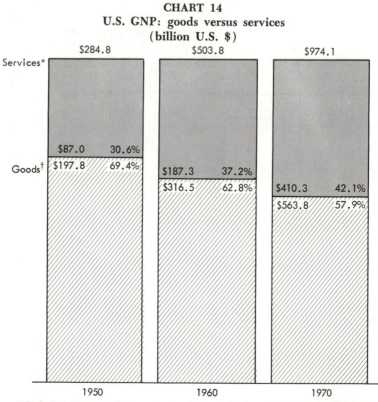

CHART 14
U.S. GNP: goods versus services
(billion U.S. $)

* Including transportation, communications, wholesale and retail trade, rentals, and other nongoods items.

† Including manufactures, construction, agricultural products, and inventory changes.

of our economy. Increasing productivity in services is much more difficult than in manufacturing. Some economists predict and view with equanimity the United States' international future as a "mature creditor"—engaged largely in services, drawing income from foreign investments, and importing more goods than it exports. Others are disturbed by this trend, and ask: To what extent is such an occurrence in our national interest? How dependent can a country be on services and goods produced by others and still be a world power? Will investment income grow sufficiently to make it possible to have balance-of-payments equilibrium with significant trade deficits? More positively, what kind of economy and, in particular, manufacturing capability do we want for the United States in the 1970s and 1980s? These are some of the kinds of questions that seem to deserve more study than they have received. In the meantime, our current analysis should note that most services are hard to export; thus a view of exports as a percentage of goods production (rather than of GNP) is revealing.

Exports in relation to production

One can understand why a country such as Canada is so concerned about American investment and trade policy when one sees that 63 percent of Canada's goods production is exported. Likewise, the share of United Kingdom production that is exported is four times the U.S. figure. The EC's external trade is only 22 percent of goods production, but half of the international trade of EC members is with other EC members. West Germany's export percentage, 37 percent of goods produced, is almost three times that of the United States. Japan's percentage approaches Germany's, with exports equal to 30 percent of goods produced (Chart 15).

A high ratio of exports to total goods produced makes countries more aware of their exchange rates. One of the main reasons for our balance-of-payments problems is that other countries have been reluctant to revalue their currencies—an action which would make their exports less competitive abroad. (In fact, over the past 15 years, there have been almost twice as many developed country devaluations as revaluations.) It is probably true that no one needs to have a balance-of-payments surplus who does not want it. Yet, many jobs are tied directly to exports and can be protected by the maintenance of undervalued currencies even if it is at the expense of higher domestic prices and a reduced variety of goods available to domestic consumers.

To the USSR these problems should seem less important, since the Soviet Union's ratio of exports to production is far lower than anyone else's (only 8 percent). But the Soviet Union is also less vulnerable to outside threats and pressures.

CHART 15
Exports in relation to production
(including agriculture, forestry, fishing, mining, quarrying, and manufacturing)

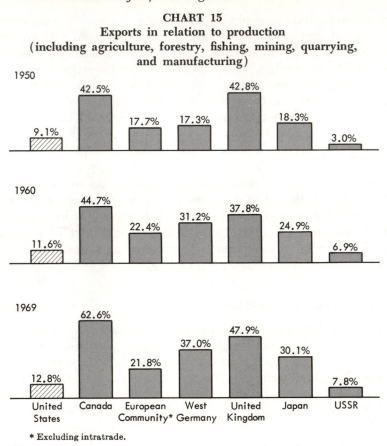

1950

42.5% 42.8%

9.1%   17.7%   17.3%   18.3%   3.0%

1960

44.7%   37.8%

11.6%   22.4%   31.2%   24.9%   6.9%

1969

62.6%   47.9%

12.8%   21.8%   37.0%   30.1%   7.8%

United States Canada European Community* West Germany United Kingdom Japan USSR

* Excluding intratrade.

U.S. foreign trade

U.S. exports in 1970 were about $43 billion and imports were about $40 billion, yielding a favorable trade balance of about $3 billion (Chart 16). For 1971, the balance has been projected as a deficit of about $2 billion, a reversal of normal U.S. experience, and the first trade deficit since 1893.

During the 1960s, both exports (8 percent growth annually) and imports (10 percent growth annually) have been growing faster than our economy. This expanding trade has been beneficial in many ways.

We are the largest individual trader in the world. Even though only a small percentage of our GNP is devoted to trade, we have a heavy impact on world total imports and exports. Our trade affects others more than it does us.

It is noticeable that, in the period covered here, our favorable balance has shifted from an average of about $4 to $5 billion in the first half

CHART 16
U.S. foreign trade

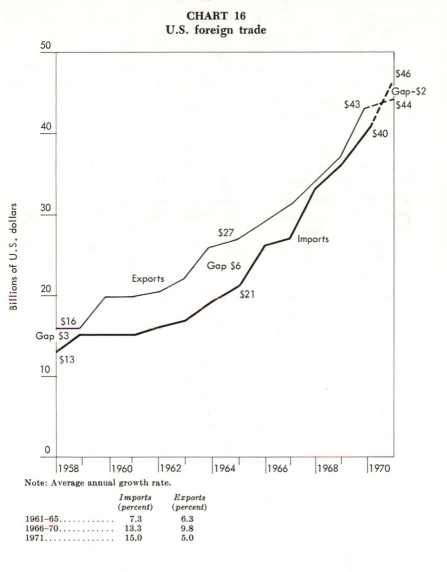

Billions of U.S. dollars

Note: Average annual growth rate.

	Imports (percent)	Exports (percent)
1961–65............	7.3	6.3
1966–70............	13.3	9.8
1971...............	15.0	5.0

of the 1960s to an average of about $2.5 billion in the five years ending 1970. If we were to take out certain items that some would say are not properly part of "exports"—aid-related transfers and add costs asso ciated with imports—for example, freight and insurance—we would see that the United States has run a trade deficit in recent years prior to the 1971 deficit experience.

Our trade, of course, has human as well as economic aspects. There are increasing and understandable concerns about the effect of our trade in general, and imports in particular, on U.S. jobs. It is estimated, for example, that between 600,000 and 750,000 jobs were lost between 1964 and 1971 as our trade balance shifted from a $6.8 billion surplus to an estimated $2 billion deficit. A precise calculation of the effects of U.S. trade on U.S. jobs is difficult to make and involves some conjecture. Most of the studies on job effects come to three broad conclusions (although these types of studies have received too little attention and are subject to many qualifications):

1. The net job effects are relatively small—in the range of a few hundred thousand jobs of a total U.S. work force of more than 80 million. This is partly a function of the relatively small percentage of our GNP accounted for by foreign trade—about 4 percent each for exports and imports and a much smaller fraction, of course, for the trade balance itself.
2. The figures in the most recent Department of Labor job impact studies show that trade has had a net favorable effect on U.S. employment.
    Thus, if trade both ways stopped (where there were alternatives to trade), our total employment would probably be reduced by a small amount. An exception in 1971 when, because of the trade deficit, there may have been a small job loss as a result of trade. But this should be reversed after the exchange rate realignments and new trading arrangements now being negotiated have had their effect.
3. On the whole, export-oriented jobs tend to be better paying than import-competing ones—reflecting the fact that our primary competitive advantage in international trade is in industries requiring high-level skills. There are, however, important exceptions to this general rule.

All this does not preclude dislocations and specific job effects in particular industries. Some of those whose lose jobs to U.S. imports seem to be arguing that one can restrict imports and save those jobs without affecting our exports, and our export-related jobs. But other countries can directly affect our exports to them in response to our actions against their exports to us. It is difficult to have everything our own way. Further, virtually every study of this subject concludes that *most* job effects result from changes and competitive factors within our own economy (that is, have nothing to do with foreign competition).

Nevertheless, job dislocations that do occur must be dealt with effectively and promptly. And clearly, our programs in this area must be handled on a far more comprehensive basis than any adjustment programs now in existence. At the same time, a major emphasis must be placed on what new job opportunities can be created in the 1970s to employ not just the workers who have been displaced but also the *much larger* number of new persons continually joining the work force. By 1980, a total of 100 million jobs will have to be provided in order to be at "full employment"—or almost 20 million more jobs than today. Thus the creation of new jobs and new industries must command our attention.

It is obvious to all that if our employment were higher, the United States would be better able to absorb the relatively small number of job dislocations caused by additional imports. Here is a point where foreign economic policy and domestic economic policy intersect.

U.S. foreign trade trends—by product categories

In considering trade policy for the 1970s and 1980s, we should study certain underlying economic forces. In what categories are surpluses strong? Declining? Why?

The analysis is not meant to imply that the United States should, as a matter of policy, seek surpluses in all sectors of foreign trade. The purpose of trade is to permit each nation to produce and sell according to its best comparative advantage; in some sectors the United States can be expected to show trade deficits as we make best use of trading opportunities. The crucial issue for national policy is not that of specific deficits, but of the overall balance; to that end, trends in major commodity groups provide some detail on the historical and projected 1971 overall performance. Understanding these trends should help us to predict better the future outlook.

U.S. foreign trade trends—agriculture

The U.S. agricultural surplus has grown recently, but the "green revolution" in the LDCs and preferential area trade restrictions impede U.S. exports. Besides, everyone seems to strive for self-sufficiency in food. Thus, despite U.S. comparative advantage, our favorable balance in agriculture is only about $2.5 billion (Chart 17).

There is much talk about adjustment to economic dislocations—that is, change in employment patterns caused by changing competitiveness, shifts in final demand, or productivity growth. The American farm is one example: In only 20 years, farm workers have dropped from 7.2 million to 3.5 million—from 12.2 percent to 4.4 percent of the labor force (Chart 18). Yet the fewer workers are producing 20 percent more, and the value of production per worker in constant dollars has grown from $2,700 in 1950 to $6,600 in 1970.

CHART 17
U.S. foreign trade trends
(agricultural products)

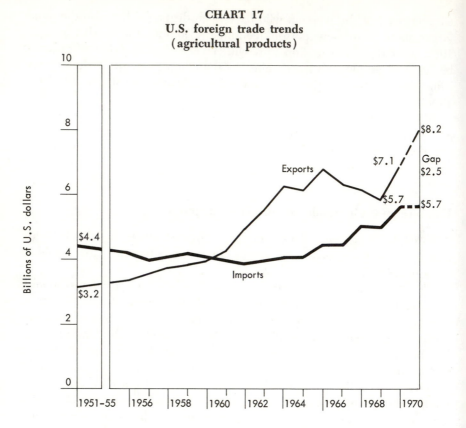

Given U.S. international comparative advantage in agriculture, it is worth another major effort to persuade other countries to reduce restrictions. Our lower prices would benefit other countries too, if we could mutually solve some of the political problems that underlie agricultural restrictions.

Despite foreign barriers, agricultural exports are a significant portion of the total value of U.S. production: almost 17 percent of total fruit production; 33 percent of the value of cotton and corn; 42 percent of tobacco; and more than 60 percent of wheat and soybean production are exported. This is both a tribute to the productivity of our agricultural sector, and a reminder of our vulnerability to trade retaliation in agricultural products if the United States were to implement restrictive trade quotas. Precisely because other countries can expand their agricultural production, most students of world trade expect U.S. agriculture would be one of the early victims of trade retaliation.

In analyzing our agricultural balance, note that the United States

CHART 18
U.S. agriculture

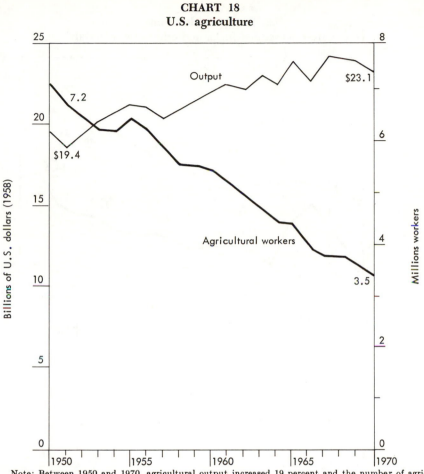

Note: Between 1950 and 1970, agricultural output increased 19 percent and the number of agricultural workers decreased 52 percent. Meanwhile, agricultural workers as a percent of total labor force
decreased from 12.2 percent in 1950 to 4.4 percent in 1970.

subsidizes agricultural exports under PL 480 at less than $1.0 billion
annually. This outlay is partially offset by foreign currency receipts of
about $330 million, making a net outlay of about $650 million.

U.S. foreign trade trends—minerals and resources

In minerals and resources (Chart 19) it is predictable that unless
there are some major breakthroughs in cleaner domestic energy resources—for example, a cheaper nuclear source—our trade deficit will
continue to increase and we will consume more and more relative to
what we produce. Some would say that oil imports, for example, could

CHART 19
U.S. foreign trade trends
(minerals, unprocessed fuels, and other raw materials)

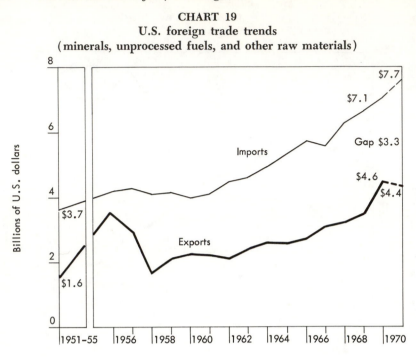

CHART 20
U.S. foreign trade trends
("nontechnology-intensive" manufactured products)

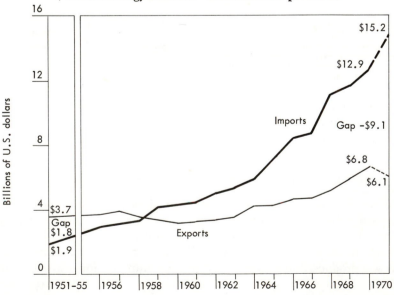

climb by $12 billion by the end of this decade, unless we find domestic alternatives.

U.S. foreign trade trends—manufactured products

A more rapidly widening gap in our trade balance is found in the so-called "nontechnology-intensive" manufactured products, and is probably an inevitable result of spreading industrialization. As countries begin production of products easiest for them, new sources of shoes, textiles, sporting goods, and the like appear (Chart 20).

With more countries becoming our competitors in products requiring less technology, it is likely that our exports of the future will depend increasingly on "technology-intensive" products (Chart 21). More than

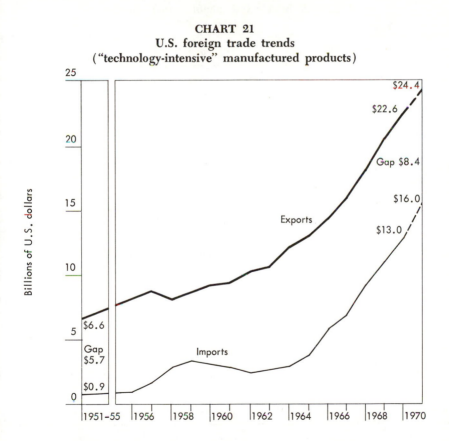

CHART 21
U.S. foreign trade trends
("technology-intensive" manufactured products)

half our foreign sales are in this category—and our favorable balance here is over $8 billion for 1971. It is expected that this 1971 "technology-intensive" surplus will about equal our "nontechnology-intensive" deficit.

There are, of course, important problems of definition in distinguishing "technology-intensive" or "nontechnology intensive" products. Some argue that at least one whole class of products included in the "technology-intensive" category—as defined by Dr. Boretsky (Department of Commerce)—does not belong in that category. (Automobiles are an often mentioned example.) Still others argue that while particular products of certain categories are "technology-intensive," others of that same category are not (certain chemicals would be an example). Such definitions are matters of judgment, and the reader should look at the specific product categories and arrive at his own conclusions (Chart 22). On balance, however, the trends are so powerful that it seems

CHART 22
U.S. trade in selected manufactured products
(million U.S. $)

	1970			Jan.-June 1970 balance	Jan.-June 1971 balance
	Exports	*Imports*	*Balance*		
Technology intensive:					
Fabricating machinery	$1,956	$ 900	$ 1,056	$ 506	$ 517
Motor vehicles and parts	3,549	5,479	−1,930	−1,045	−1,653
Aircraft and parts	2,659	275	2,384	1,345	1,776
Basic chemicals and compounds . . .	1,642	759	883	504	415
Power generating machinery (nonelectric)	1,395	782	613	356	281
Computers and parts	1,104	60	1,044	469	530
Scientific and professional instruments	857	356	501	255	282
Construction machinery	733	49	684	334	340
Telecommunications apparatus	661	1,104	−443	−157	−301
Synthetic materials	653	123	530	276	257
Electric power machinery	611	247	364	193	198
Medicinal and pharmaceutical products	421	87	334	179	140
Nontechnology intensive:					
Yarns, fibers, and fabrics.	603	1,136	−533	−254	−402
Clothing	200	1,267	−1,067	−434	−571
Footwear	10	630	−620	−297	−380
Paper and manufactures	622	1,087	−465	−225	−226
Iron and steel	1,270	2,032	−762	−128	−930
Nonferrous metals	964	1,652	−688	−299	−417
Furniture	54	231	−177	−93	−109
Wood manufactures	132	414	−282	−124	−165

safe to conclude that our trade position has been heavily dependent on higher technology products.

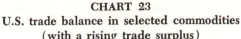

CHART 23
U.S. trade balance in selected commodities
(with a rising trade surplus)

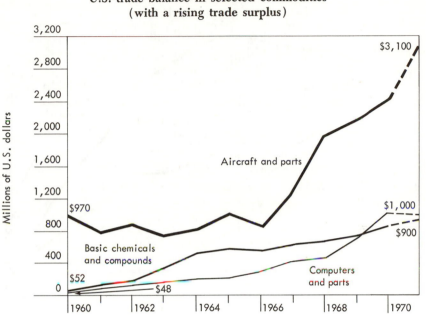

Charts 23 and 24 give examples of individual products that have rising or falling trade balances. While our trade surplus grew for aircraft, computers, and chemicals, there are rapidly growing deficits in motor vehicles, textiles, clothing, and footwear.

However, we should remember that in recent years the undervalued currencies of certain other countries have made us unnecessarily dependent on high technology products for which relative prices are often a less important competitive factor. Conversely, fairer exchange rates will make some of our "nontechnology-intensive" products much more competitive in world trade.

Chart 25 summarizes trade balance trends covering the four basic categories of products—manufactured and nonmanufactured—we have used in this analysis.

U.S. ratio of imports to consumption—manufactured products

Another way of viewing the penetration of foreign products into the United States is by specific market shares. Foreign goods do dominate some highly visible consumer categories: the foreign market share is in excess of 50 percent for amateur motion picture cameras, black and

CHART 24
U.S. trade balance in selected commodities
(with a declining trade balance)

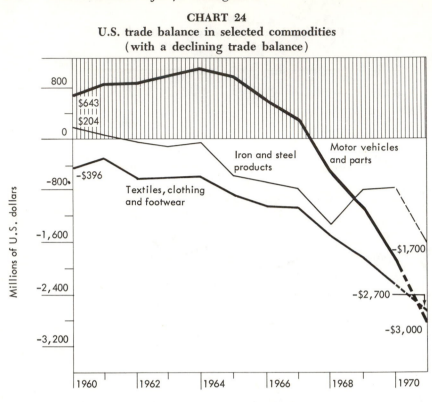

white television sets, motorcycles, radios, cassette recorders, and 35 mm still cameras (Chart 26).

It should be remembered that the numbers presented in this chart are aggregate market penetrations of some very large and diverse product fields. In the case of textiles, for example, there are a substantial number of specific and major product categories in which market penetration is well over 50 percent. The situation in steel is similar.

It would appear that the vast majority of consumers like the variety, richness, or lower prices of these imports. If restrictions were to limit the availability or increase the price of such products, consumers would no doubt feel that their "quality of life" had suffered. To illustrate this, studies of such products as shoes and television sets suggest that without imports, their prices in the United States might rise 30 percent. For tape recorders and a number of other key items, prices could rise as much as 50 percent. Aside from unfavorable consumer reaction, restricting these products would obviously add to inflationary pressures.

Industry and labor view import penetration as competition which causes significant adjustment problems. The speed of economic change can also aggravate this adjustment: in some of the cases, much of the

CHART 25
U.S. trade balance trends

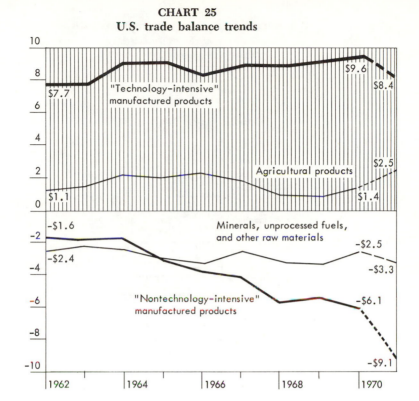

Billions of U.S. dollars

"Technology–intensive" manufactured products
$7.7
$9.6
$8.4

Agricultural products
$2.5
$1.1
$1.4

Minerals, unprocessed fuels, and other raw materials
-$1.6
-$2.5
-$2.4
-$3.3

"Nontechnology–intensive" manufactured products
-$6.1
-$9.1

1962   1964   1966   1968   1970

penetration took place within a period of ten years or less. At the same time, within most of these product categories we will see individual domestic companies that, by some combination of product innovation, quality, highly productive techniques, and effective marketing compete effectively. And in examples such as transistor radios or compact autos, consumer markets have been broadened by imports.

Market penetration is related to the rapidity with which technology, manufacturing know-how, capital, and goods are transferred around the world. It now takes much less time for a product first developed in one country to appear again in very similar form in another country. During the first quarter of this century, some studies suggest this process took about twenty years; by the second quarter of the century, this period had been shortened to ten years; and finally, in the 1960s, it has been shortened to three years.

Since, in the aggregate, imports are *still* a *small* fraction of our total output, in most product fields they are also a very small fraction of the market. On the other hand, it is also clear that since the mid-sixties the overall aggregate market share going to foreign products has increased significantly—approximately doubling.

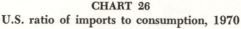

CHART 26
U.S. ratio of imports to consumption, 1970

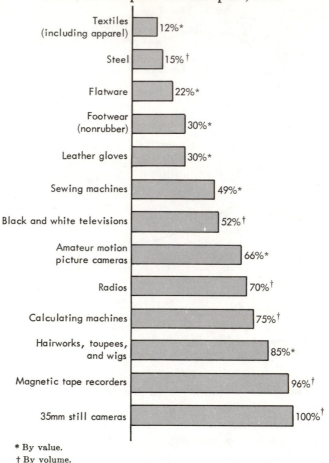

Textiles (including apparel)   12%*

Steel   15%†

Flatware   22%*

Footwear (nonrubber)   30%*

Leather gloves   30%*

Sewing machines   49%*

Black and white televisions   52%†

Amateur motion picture cameras   66%*

Radios   70%†

Calculating machines   75%†

Hairworks, toupees, and wigs   85%*

Magnetic tape recorders   96%†

35mm still cameras   100%†

* By value.
† By volume.

U.S. trade trends—by geographical area

In addition to analyzing our trading patterns by type of product, it is useful to review trade by geographical area.

In so doing, we should be careful not to conclude that our trade balance with all countries must be the same, or that it is "bad" if we have a deficit with some. It is inevitable that we should have some deficits in an expanding world of open trade, since our particular needs lead us to buy more products from some countries than from others.

On the other hand, it is true that bilateral trade barriers exist that seriously distort natural and open trading patterns. Thus, some trade negotiations are necessarily bilateral in nature and an understanding of the reasons for bilateral trading patterns can be important.

U.S. trade—with Canada

The logical starting place is Canada, our principal trading partner. Our exports to Canada, estimated for 1971, amount to about $10 billion and our imports about $13 billion (Chart 27). Our deficit has been

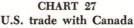

CHART 27
U.S. trade with Canada

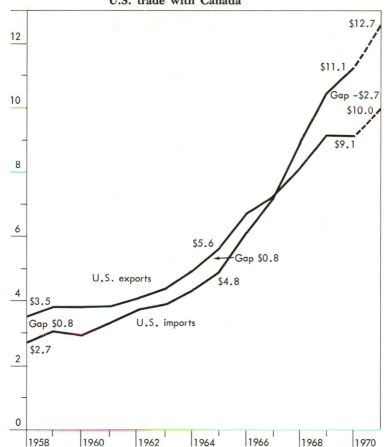

increasing for several reasons; the U.S.–Canadian Automobile Agreement has perhaps accounted for about half of it, and has played a major role in the declining "technology-intensive balance (Chart 28). We are

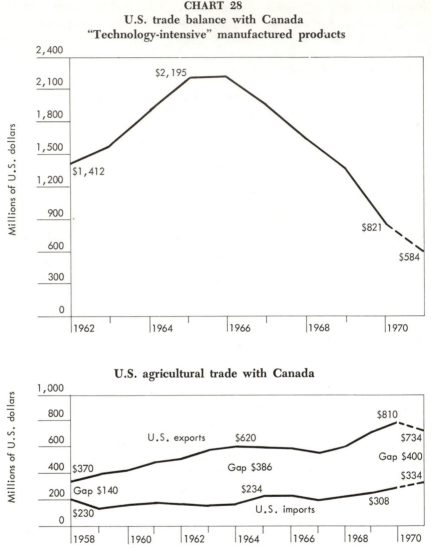

CHART 28
U.S. trade balance with Canada
"Technology-intensive" manufactured products

U.S. agricultural trade with Canada

Note: During 1958–70, about 19 percent of U.S. agricultural exports to Canada were goods for transshipment to third countries.

growing more dependent on Canada's oil and other raw materials. Also, the Canadian dollar has been undervalued in the past, although that problem recently has been eased. Our position in agriculture, however, showed a positive balance of over $500 million in 1970, which, after we deduct agricultural transshipments, leaves a net favorable balance of almost $220 million.

An important consideration is our heavy investment in Canada—over

$20 billion—and the resulting remittances that help our balance of payments. Also, as noted, 63 percent of Canada's production is exported. Since the United States has invested heavily in Canada, exports were certainly to be expected. Thus, our simple analysis focusing only on the total trade imbalance does not tell the full story.

U.S. trade with the European Community

Our trade with the EC shows rapid growth in both exports and imports, but very recently a shrinking positive trade balance of about $1.8 billion in 1970 and an estimated $0.5 billion in 1971 (Chart 29).

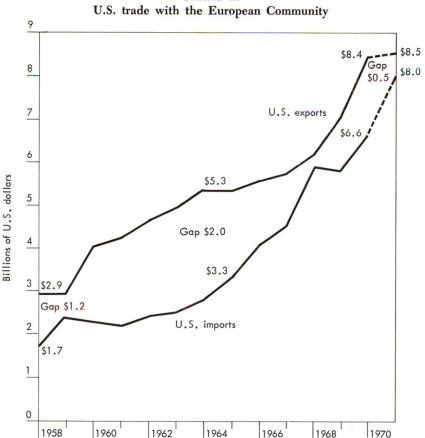

CHART 29
U.S. trade with the European Community

This balance is aided by a surplus in technology-intensive products with Western Europe estimated at $1.6 billion for 1971 (Chart 30).

CHART 30
U.S. trade balance with Western Europe
"Technology-intensive" manufactured products

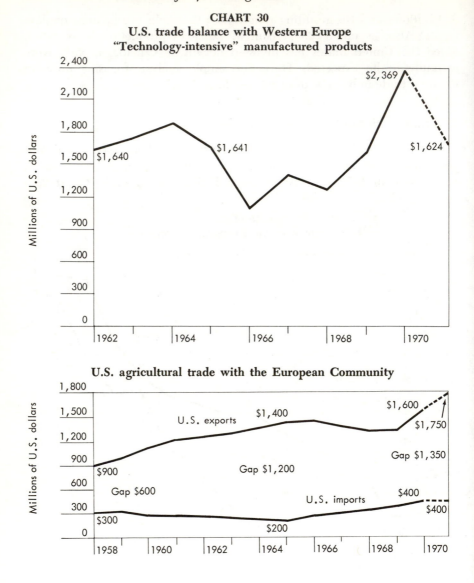

U.S. agricultural trade with the European Community

In most commodities, the EC countries have until now been good customers of and suppliers to the United States. There are, however, certain tendencies in the EC that are probably not in the economic or political interests of the United States, particularly for the future. The EC's variable import levy system for agricultural goods (under which a levy is applied against the imported product so that its final price in the EC tends to be at or above internal prices) is already restrictive and its impact on some U.S. products is probably large. For example, exports to Europe of a major commodity such as soybeans—which is not subject to the levy—have increased more than 55 percent since 1956. Exports of grains subject to levies, however, have grown much less—only 15 percent over this entire period. And, in recent years, shipments to the EC of U.S. grains under levy have declined 30 to 35 percent from their peak.

Another problem relates to preferential tariff treatment granted some 30 countries by the EC; in turn, these countries permit preferential access to their markets for EC manufactured products. The effects of these preferences on our citrus exports to the Community is a clear example of what from our standpoint is a discriminatory act, detrimental to both U.S. economic interests and the principle of a multilateral, open trading world.

To sum up: In 1950, the EC was an idea; by 1970, it had become the world's most important trading area. In 20 years it has changed both the political and economic shape of Europe and the world. The process of unification, while successful in overcoming old rivalries, has also created important new economic problems for the United States.

U.S. trade with Japan

The story is told by the almost vertical growth curves of trade with our No. 2 trading partner. Our exports to Japan have grown more than 17 percent annually during the past five years, and their exports to us have grown even faster. Japan is thus both a good supplier and customer. Only the Far East absorbs a larger portion of Japan's exports than does the United States which absorbs over 30 percent (Chart 31).

Much of the Japanese export effort is aimed at the United States, causing pressures on some of our domestic companies. Even our superiority in "technology-intensive" products does not show up in the U.S.-Japan trade balances. In fact, there is no other country in the world with which we have a negative balance on technology-intensive products. This deficit was more than $1 billion in 1970 and is estimated at more than double that for 1971. This particular deficit is larger than it would have been had Japan had fewer import restrictions on growth industries, such as computers and other advanced electronic products in which the United States excels (Chart 32).

Since Japan is an insular nation and a country poor in raw materials, it must import many basic commodities. The bulk of Japan's purchases from the United States—about 73 percent—are agricultural products and industrial raw materials, necessary for both domestic consumption and processing into exports. Japan, in turn, tends to sell us increasing

CHART 31
U.S. trade with Japan

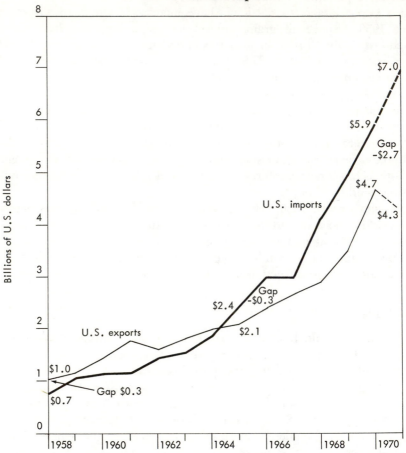

amounts of sophisticated products, reflecting numerous gains in their technology and know-how.

Japan's overall trade surplus is unusually large, given its amount trade—in 1970 Japan's trade surplus exceeded $4 billion—and it is growing rapidly. It was estimated to reach more than $7 billion in 1971. And in their five-year plans and projections, the Japan Economic Planning Agency and other research groups project favorable trade balances averaging about $11 billion by 1975.

Chart 33 shows Japan's trade balance and its foreign exchange reserves before August 15, 1971. Not only has the growth of trade surplus and reserves been substantial, but it has been accomplished during a period of full employment and rapid domestic growth—conditions which should tend to increase imports. It seems clear that an undervalued

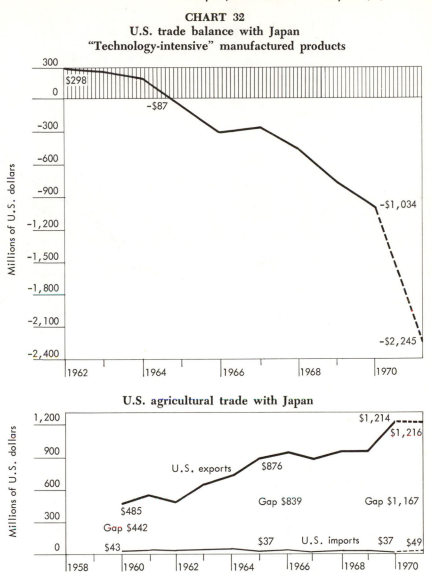

CHART 32
U.S. trade balance with Japan
"Technology-intensive" manufactured products

U.S. agricultural trade with Japan

currency contributed heavily to this situation—along with an apparent drive for "exports for exports sake."

Clearly, there is a large and growing dollar imbalance in our trading relationship with Japan. Is there also a lack of symmetry, or more accurately perhaps, even lack of equity, in Japanese-American commercial relationships?

As an example, examine the case of automobiles. Japan's automobiles

CHART 33
Japan: balance-of-payments trends

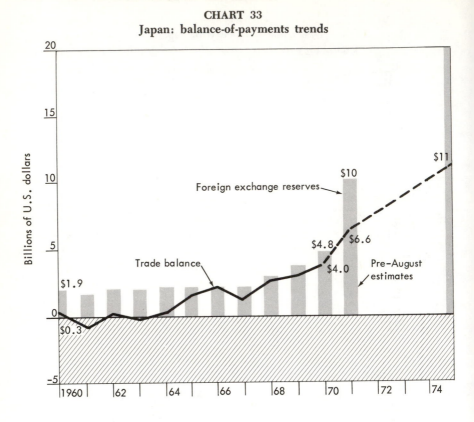

enter the U.S. market unimpeded, but for a modest tariff. Japan's auto exports to the United States are rising rapidly—from 69,000 automobiles in 1967 to 354,000 automobiles in 1970. In the first half of 1971, Japanese auto exports to the United States were up 124 percent over the previous year. Presumably because of lower transportation costs, the Japanese effort is aimed at our West Coast market. In the early months of this year, Japanese cars accounted for about 20 percent of new-car sales in the Los Angeles metropolitan area.

On the other hand, our automobile manufacturers face a variety of restrictions in Japan. Our two largest automobile manufacturers, General Motors and Ford, can own only a minority share of a company in Japan, on terms which are specified. They are also subjected to restrictions on the management composition of a Japanese affiliate.

If instead of investing, these U.S. manufacturers should want to export automobiles to Japan they confront extensive restrictions. Commodity and road taxes are aimed at the larger cars from the United States—taxes that result in a Cadillac that costs $8,000 in the United States being sold for $30,000 in Japan; even the Pinto which sells for about $2,000 in the United States, sells for nearly $5,500 when exported to Japan. General Motors, the largest exporter to Japan, accounts for only 0.1 percent of the very large Japanese market. To be sure, some of our most popular automobiles may not be suited to the Japanese market, but these artificial burdens clearly impede our exports to Japan.

There are a variety of other restrictions, quantitative and qualitative, often aimed at protecting growth industries of the future (fields where the U.S. would be in a strong position to export). These measures include informal agreements between the Japanese government and business officials—an elusive tactic known as "administrative guidance" that is effective because of the strong spirit of government-business cooperation existing in Japan—and the economic power the government can bring to bear against any violator. Obviously, we should consider all these restrictions in our trade negotiations. As will be shown later, we should also remember that Japan has already made some progress on its own in the direction of removing some of these restrictions.

Direction of trade

The well-developed pattern of trade that is apparent between the United States and the EC is in contrast to the thin flow of trade between Japan and the EC (Chart 34).

Japan sells over 30 percent of its exports to us, but only about 7 percent to the EC. Earlier we saw how much larger a percent of world trade the EC accounts for than does the United States. Thus, it becomes clear that Japan's share of U.S. imports is many times higher than Japan's share of EC imports. Looking at the reverse flow, only about 2 percent of the EC's external exports go to Japan, whereas 15 percent go to the United States.

Further growth of Japanese imports into the EC is impeded by non-tariff barriers, including quotas and less formal "safeguards." Many of the EC quotas are on textiles; others are on porcelain, cutlery, footwear, umbrellas, steel, and, in the case of Italy, motor vehicles. In 1969, for example, Italy imported 12 motor vehicles from Japan; and in 1970, only 481. Liberalizing negotiations are stalled on the issue of formulating the escape clause that EC countries could invoke against rising Japanese imports.

This asymmetrical trading pattern puts Japanese export pressure on the United States—while the EC undergoes a more "orderly" pattern of trade growth. Increased Japan-EC trade would be advantageous to the United States for another reason: lost U.S. sales in these two markets resulting from their increased competition would not be very great since, typically, we are not selling the same kinds of products.

CHART 34
Direction of exports, 1970
(billion U.S. $ and percent of countries' exports)

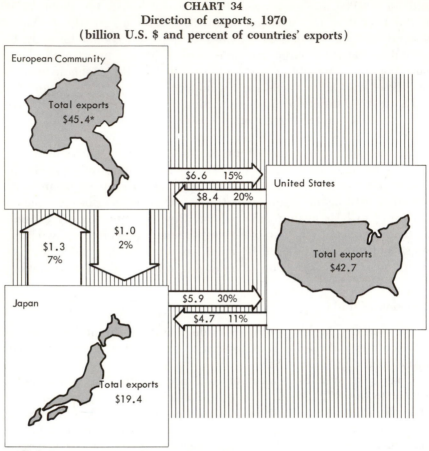

European Community

Total exports
$45.4*

$6.6   15%
$8.4   20%

United States

Total exports
$42.7

$1.3
7%

$1.0
2%

Japan

$5.9   30%
$4.7   11%

Total exports
$19.4

* Excluding trade within the European Community.

Free World trade with the USSR and Eastern Europe

The first striking feature of Chart 35 is the growth of Free World trade with Eastern Europe and the USSR, now totaling about $10 billion each way—imports and exports.

The second is the small U.S. share—only $350 million of exports—and less imports. Our allies are getting the dominant share of these sales.

The third feature is the tight hugging of the almost vertical lines, which is no accident. Trading with Communist countries usually requires barter, since they do not have sufficient convertible currency. Other Free World countries have set up special corporations and special financing arrangements for handling some of the unique aspects of trade with the Communist countries.

We all realize there are many political and national security considerations in East-West trade, particularly in high-technology products and

CHART 35
Free world trade with the USSR and Eastern Europe

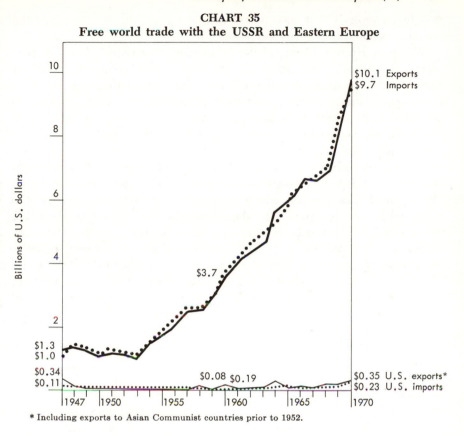

* Including exports to Asian Communist countries prior to 1952.

strategic materials. One specific contribution of our council will be to provide accurate economic input to this complex equation. In each case, the Council on International Economic Policy will be working closely with the National Security Council and the other interested government agencies.

EXCERPT 3

A STRONG DOMESTIC ECONOMY—REQUISITE FOR A STRONG AND OUTWARD LOOKING FOREIGN ECONOMIC POLICY

Increased competitiveness

I have earlier suggested the essential importance of the quest for fundamental reform of the monetary system if we are to attain a reasonably balanced and open international economic system. It may not be widely recognized that such a system also has a critical effect on what we have come to call "competitiveness."

We must try to understand the relationship between balance of payments equilibrium, fair exchange rates, and the "competitiveness" of our economy in international trade. We said earlier that fair exchange rates would make a major contribution toward achieving equilibrium in our overall payments balance. On the trade account, fair rates help establish our competitive position in two ways: they tend to set a price for our exports (in terms of other currencies) which makes it attractive for foreigners to buy our products, and they set prices for foreign goods in our market at which American industry can compete without suffering the artificial disadvantage which an overvalued dollar confers. By the same token, an exchange rate should not be set as to provide either an artificial advantage to exports or a bias against imports. The basic objective of a "fair" exchange rate is to assure overall external balance. In a state of external balance, we are thus "competitive" in the sense that as regards the trade account, we earn enough through exports of goods and services to pay for the products and services we import.

However, we should not assume that achieving balance of payments equilibrium is a sufficient economic goal. Desirable as it is, this does not achieve the larger purpose of *improving* the national purchasing power and the real income of our consumers.

Otherwise, we would need only to devalue constantly and thereby achieve balance. Repeated devaluations, however, would reduce our future "national purchasing power", that is, what we were able to buy for our consumers and industries for a given level of exports.

Our objective should be to *increase* our national purchasing power and the improvement in our consumers' standard of living. To achieve this, we will need to *increase* our competitiveness, our productivity, and, in general, enlarge the areas of comparative advantage vis-à-vis the rest of the world. The way to do this is to concentrate on the things we do best. This, in turn, will increase our *international* competitiveness.

Enough has been said above about the current realities to draw some major conclusions about the directions U.S. foreign economic policy should now take. Our situation in the world is not only different, but somewhat more precarious than in the past. Even for a nation as technologically advanced as ours, the world market has and will become increasingly competitive. We can meet this competition with methods that will leave our country and the world a better place to live in. But to continue dwelling successfully in the world, we must take conscious and deliberate steps to make our economy more competitive with those abroad.

First, as I indicated above, it is important to emphasize that development of those competitive strengths depends mainly *on our own efforts* rather than on the actions of other countries. A strong foreign economic policy for the United States begins in a strong domestic economy. But, as is the case with most fundamental truths, it tends to be overlooked in the preoccupation with the variety of specific issues with which we must deal, and it is vitally important that we not lose sight of it.

Indeed, without a strong domestic economic base in which our own people have a sense of their future, and confidence in their ability to find a productive role in the world economy, a positive foreign economic policy is probably impossible. In a world in which economics is becoming increasingly political, it is not possible to have inward looking foreign economic policies and outward looking foreign policies.

A second fact with which we must contend is the increasing propensity of Americans to question the value structure of our society. It is ironic that this comes at a time when the external demands of a more competitive world economy are rapidly increasing. Many believe that, in the past, too much emphasis was given to producing an ever larger quantity of goods and services while the "quality of life" was subordinated to this drive. Some charge that our past and present concerns about productivity and economic growth are concerns about production for production's sake, as if growth were an end in itself. The argument is made that we need no longer be concerned with growth, believing either that affluence is assured automatically, or that we should even take steps to hold growth in check while we concentrate our resources on problems of quality.

According to these arguments, one would logically be led to conclude that growth and the "quality of life" are irreconcilable concerns. I do not share this judgment. In my view, improvements in the "quality of life" in our society can best flow from an economic base which is strong enough to make these improvements realities. It is important that we reconcile these views since failure to do so will not only frustrate the achievement of our "quality improvement" goals but will also keep us from realizing the growth and productivity objectives which are necessary for our competitive position and an increased standard of living.

To achieve the appropriate balance in the pace and quality of growth, we need to find new ways to harness our productive potential to achieve our qualitative goals. For example, technology is, in itself, indifferent to the uses to which it is put. Decisions about how to use it rest with man and society and our task is to decide wisely, remembering that without constant efforts to sustain our growth potential and strengthen our international competitiveness, the resources necessary to implement the needed changes in our society which will improve life's quality will simply not be available. This is what the international division of labor is all about.

In the international division of labor, the United States has many comparative advantages, but the most obvious are in agriculture, management, capital goods, and advanced technology. In the past, our competitive position has also suffered in many product areas where we would have been price competitive at fairer exchange rates. Thus, with realigned rates, we might reasonably expect that comparative advantages could emerge in some areas of lower technological content. However, in its most meaningful sense of an improved standard of living through international trade, our continued competitiveness depends on more new investment in plant and equipment, more growth in research and development and more progress in training appropriate talent and manpower, particularly in the new skills U.S. workers will require as our society moves increasingly to more industrial sophistication and services.

This will not be an easy task. The challenge before us is difficult and will require both imagination and determination on the part of both government (the Congress and Executive) and the nation.

Investment

The president's initiative in August of this year, proposing a job development tax credit for new investment was the first, indispensable step in this direction. Its prompt approval by the Congress shows that awareness of the new realities of worldwide competition and the fundamental importance of new investment, in both the creation of new jobs and improvement of the nation's productivity, is growing.

The president was convinced that investment in new plant and equipment—where we are far from competitive in the incentives we offer as compared with all major Western industrial countries—is essential to our future. It is equally essential that our citizens as a whole—and industrial workers especially—understand that, without the investment we need to stay competitive, both productivity and jobs will suffer. One reason our workers earn higher incomes than any in the world is because the machinery they know how to use enables them to be the most productive. But other nations are putting similar machinery into use, and, unless we continue to improve our own, the real output (productivity) of our workers will decline and with it, jobs, income and, in the long run, the satisfaction which men derive and need from the knowledge that their work is useful, both to themselves and their society.

Technological opportunities

A second indispensable element in this process is the need first, to bring technology increasingly to bear upon the process of enhancing both the quality and quantity of our production and second, to deal effectively with the urgent social problems of our time.

A comprehensive approach is being taken in the administration's new technologies opportunity program. For example the exploration of new energy sources for the future could greatly reduce our dependence on imported oil. In the nuclear breeder reactor program recently announced by the president, we are striving to have a generous domestic supply of the cleaner kind of power.

We also need to stimulate our economy's industrial research and development efforts. Industry—to enhance its competitive position internationally as well as to produce more efficiently goods for the domestic economy—needs to do more to develop new products and processes. To achieve this goal, it is cearly appropriate that the federal government consider new methods for bringing forth the new technologies upon which productivity and competitiveness depend. Proposals, including new incentives for this purpose, will be submitted to the next session of Congress.

Thus, it is essential that we identify some of the promising opportunities in the 1970s where it makes good economic sense, good technological sense, and good social sense for America to invest as part of a national effort to discover and shape America's future. This does not mean America must lead in everything—which it cannot do and should not attempt to do—but rather it should lead in those things that make sense for America to lead in.

Manpower training needs

By 1980, full employment will require jobs for almost 100 million Americans, about 20 million more than today's level. The problem of finding jobs for this labor force will require both an economy growing at its full potential (which, in turn, means exploiting to the fullest our international opportunities) and a much improved system of fitting manpower skills to job requirements.

The United States today, for example, is oversupplied with technical manpower for its defense and space requirements. Yet there are shortages of laboratory specialists, medical assistants, computer technicians, and maintenance personnel for other complex equipment. Less than half of available jobs have been filled in these specialities.

The mismatch of technical skills to opportunities and what might be the current and perhaps continuing excess supply of college graduates is compounded by an apparent shortage of appropriate vocational training in high schools and post–high school education and training. It is estimated that eight of ten in high schools should be receiving occupational skill training, yet less than one of four are receiving it, and much of this training is not directed to anticipated needs in the labor force.

"Mid-stream" or mid-career training for adult employees is also limited. With rapid changes in the demand for labor brought about by innovations in technology, shifts of demand, and opening of international production, the labor force needs new ways to adapt to structural change.

The 70s hold much promise for the United States. If full employment can be reached, our GNP by 1980 will exceed that of 1970 by 50 percent, in real goods and services. The internal functioning of the labor market and its training institutions must be improved. Training itself needs to become more responsive to demand, and the flow of job information—matching skills to opportunities—requires improvement.

I believe we may be approaching a decade in which fundamental reorientation will be necessary to provide the career education, upgrading, and conversion of old skills to needed skills in the labor force of the 70s. Without it, the mistakes of the past could be repeated, paid for in abnormal unemployment and wasted opportunity.

Shaping the future

And finally, if we are to shape and indeed realize our future in this competitive world of the 1970s, are we not going to have to predict the future and define new strategies, in better ways than we ever have?

This does not mean that we have to embrace central planning like that practiced in the Communist countries, nor does it mean adopting the system of Japan or of any other particular country. It does mean, it seems to me, that we have to develop our own methods, define certain long-range economic and technological objectives, and create sufficient certainty in the intention to meet those objectives that our own private and public institutions can then generate the required long-range actions to do so.

Part of an effort to shape the future must be a concern with an organized program effort both to develop new sources of industrial material and energy (partly, through the technology of substitutes for natural materials) and the conservation of scarce materials to assure an ecologically balanced and attractive world. In 1970, the Congress created a National Commission on Materials Policy whose task is to inventory U.S. and world resource availabilities and needs, project these requirements into the future and make recommendations for an appropriate national materials policy. The president has directed that a task force of the council define the issues and cooperate fully with the commission in this review. We are acutely conscious of the need to construct a program which helps achieve in a balanced way our competitive, security, and ecological objectives.

It is not that the competitive challenge of the 1970s will not ask a good deal of all of us; it is rather—given a sense of national purpose—that we must make commitments about our economic future, and we must exert the will to compete and to lead.

EXCERPT 4

A WORK PROGRAM FOR INTERNATIONAL ECONOMIC POLICY

At the president's direction, the Council on International Economic Policy has undertaken a wide-ranging review of specific issues in our foreign economic relations the purpose of which is basically twofold: to enable us to construct a coherent strategy for the new era and to recommend new policies.

The following sections discuss the elements of the kinds of new programs which we now have under active consideration. However, I must emphasize that these proposals are still in the development and evaluation stage. Final decisions depend on presidential review of any new initiatives which may be proposed, either as changes in existing policy or as proposals to the Congress for its consideration.

Adjustment assistance

Adjustment to change is the essential feature of any healthy, dynamic economy in the modern world. In our society, with its relatively limited dependence on foreign trade, the magnitude of the adjustments which occur out of purely domestic structural changes is far greater than that directly attributable to the interaction of the rest of the world on our economy. These adjustments are often painful but, in the end, serve to make us stronger and more prosperous as a nation.

As regards adjustments due to import competition, while it may be true that they may be but a fraction of those which occur for domestic reasons, it is nevertheless a fact that the burden may be a heavy one for a particular industry to bear. Furthermore, a program to build on America's strengths by enhancing its international competitiveness cannot be indifferent to the fate of those industries, and especially those groups of workers, which are not meeting the demands of a truly competitive world economy. It is unreasonable to say that a liberal trade policy is in the interest of the entire country and then allow particular industries, workers, and communities to pay the whole price. This is particularly unacceptable at a time when unemployment levels are high and there is widespread concern over jobs. To correct the defects of the present program, several avenues are already being explored by a task force of the Council on International Economic Policy. The most important of these are summarized below.

1.   The broad national policy purpose of adjustment assistance should be to strengthen the U.S. economy by helping facilitate the processes of economic and social change brought about by foreign competition. The objective of an adjustment assistance program should be to make U.S. industry as a whole, including existing industries, more productive and competitive and thereby provide better paying jobs for American workers. When necessary, the program should be oriented toward encouraging the movement of workers and capital resources from activities no longer economically viable to those that are. In fact one index of the competitive strength of an economy is the proportion of its resources that are employed in activities in which the country excels.

2.   Adjustment assistance should be given a new focus. Early action mechanisms (including strengthened governmental information systems) should be developed to spot trade import problems and begin dealing with them at the earliest possible moment. This would entail not only identifying actual and potential import-impact areas, but also pinpointing foreign trade distorting or disruptive practices on a worldwide basis, which are likely to give rise to significant U.S. adjustment problems. As part of this effort, we need to speed up the process of making anti-dumping determinations and the decision-making process related to escape clause and unfair practices legislation.

3.   The program should be strengthened by building means for analysis of trade problems on an industry-wide basis, and providing a variety of assistance to encourage maximum self-assistance and market-oriented responses on the part of industry. Delivery of workers' benefits should be greatly accelerated. Finally, we need to determine whether and if the program could be broadened to include assistance to communities severely affected by foreign competition.

Clearly, the whole adjustment assistance effort is of great concern to organized labor. Developing a program which can be accepted by the unions, and communicated positively by union leaders to their membership will not be easy, but union support is critical to the program's success. Unions standing to lose membership through the retraining of their members for new crafts will have to be convinced that their workers will enjoy real benefits as a result.

Even when accelerated by a program of assistance, the adjustment process takes time—and in recent years some economic changes associated with increased imports have occurred very fast. When increasing imports have the potential to bring change faster than the adjustment system can cope with it—and thus to bring hardship—some have suggested that temporary orderly marketing mechanisms should be available. We are now exploring this possibility to develop criteria for invoking such mechanisms, and to see how these criteria can be internationalized so that such *temporary* protection could be available in all countries on an equitable basis.

However, if temporary mechanisms are used to restrict the volume of trade, it would seem to me to be desirable to consider the requirements of a concurrent, orderly adjustment program for the domestic industry which is gaining protection. By introducing a domestic adjustment program as well, we would ensure that the period of special protection is actually used to assist an orderly adjustment, and not used as a permanent crutch, at the expense of consumers at home and efficient producers in other countries.

Export expansion

We must be wary of an export expansion policy simply designed to celebrate exports for exports' sake. Export promotion policies must be viewed in the context of an overall fiscal and monetary policy designed to keep the economy on a full-employment growth path with reasonable price stability.

Nevertheless, within the context of such overall policy, exports can be an important generator of jobs. It is estimated that every billion dollars of (real) U.S. exports creates 60,000 to 80,000 jobs. In the absence of distorting incentives, these jobs are usually better paying than those in import-competing industries. If our exports were now in adequate surplus (that is, our trade balance had shifted from deficit to the size of surplus needed to bring our overall payments balance into equilibrium), the direct and indirect job effects of that surplus would have added between 500,000 and 750,000 men and women to the employed labor force. It is thus in the national interest to see to it that our exports are not at a disadvantage in responding to world demand, and that our exporters are equipped to take full advantage of the opportunities available.

The first export expansion imperative is a reformed monetary system to keep the dollar from becoming artificially overvalued again.

Also, other countries have long engaged in a variety of export-promoting measures. The United States needs more such measures of its own to correct certain international inequities and to realize our potential for growth in international markets. In our own export promotion, we shall also seek, in negotiation with other nations, to clarify and harmonize the international rules and limits that govern this national quest for markets.

Our council's work program includes action in five major areas: tax incentives, export financing, easing of regulations, East-West trade, and better government services.

Exports: Tax policies. Our tax treatment of exporters has been less favorable than that of other countries and should be improved. The creation of the Domestic International Sales Corporation (DISC) permits the deferment of taxes on some export earnings and should bring U.S. treatment more in line with that of other nations, as well as giving U.S. firms clearer rules within which to plan their export programs. Other aspects of tax policy as it relates to export competitiveness are under study. For example, if the United States should adopt a Value Added Tax (perhaps at least partially substituting for existing direct taxes), GATT (General Agreement on Tariff and Trade) rules would permit a system of border taxes and export rebates as is the custom elsewhere.

Exports: Financing. Special credits for exports are a common practice among trading nations and are provided in the United States by the Export-Import Bank. We are considering new ways to encourage the more flexible discounting of short-term export paper to make credits more widely available and to enlist the interest of smaller and medium-sized banks and businesses in export opportunities. We may also wish to expand government insurance of certain export risks.

Exports: Antitrust and other administrative restrictions. Our antitrust laws may contain inhibiting disadvantages to many potential exporters. the Webb-Pomerene associations have proved an ineffective offset to these disadvantages. Other possible checks to export expansion, such as excessive regulatory provisions, documentation and commodity controls, are being reviewed for possible removal or relaxation.

The Japanese example of promoting large trading companies, which specialize in export development, is well worth evaluating. There are countless small- and medium-sized U.S. firms which lack resources or know-how for dealing in highly competitive export markets. A trading company especially equipped to do so could place many of their products in these markets.

Exports: Communist countries. As I noted previously, the opportunities for the expansion of exports to the USSR and Eastern Europe are significant—although important political, as well as strictly economic, issues remain to be resolved before we can take maximum advantage of these opportunities. Our study will outline some of these for presidential decision. They include the desirability of offering "most favored nation tariff treatment to those Eastern countries with whom we reach satisfactory arrangements concerning our own exports, and the expansion of export financing possibilities for American firms doing business with eastern countries.

Exports: Goals and organization. Export expansion deserves a high national priority not only because of the jobs it creates, but also because of our growing need for imports and because a trade surplus will probably continue to be required to help finance our other external security and economic commitments. As a national goal, export expansion may well require the reorganization of many government services relating to it. Our commercial services need upgrading and expanding in many ways now under review.

There is an unfortunate asymmetry in the politics of trade policy; even though exporting and importing interests are almost equal in an economic, or dollar and cents, sense, they are far from equal in a political sense. Exporting interests have been perennially underrepresented in the public and political dialogue on trade policy. It is understandable that legislators come to feel there must be more injury than benefit to industry from trade. And the consumer, who also benefits in important ways from trade, is hardly heard from at all. If we are to have a balanced trade policy, it is important that these underrepresented groups be energized.

International investment

It is true, as I noted previously, that we do not know enough about multinational corporations. Accordingly, high priority is being given by a task force of the Council on International Economic Policy to obtaining the basic data and carrying forward hardheaded analyses. Yet we cannot wait for all of the facts to come in before formulating new policy initiatives.

Some of the specific issues which arise within this framework are the following:

Investment control. These controls were perhaps appropriate during the period when our balance of payments was under pressure, but their role is being reassessed in the light of important developments, following exchange rate realignment and in the context of a reformed monetary system.

Taxation. A crucial Labor argument about the multinational corporations relates to what is seen as their favorable tax treatment, since overseas earnings are not taxed by the United States until repatriated. There is also a widespread international concern over the tendency of the multinationals to maximize profits worldwide by exploitation of variations in national tax systems and manipulative inter-company pricing. This situation calls for review of U.S. tax practices and for new international understandings about both taxes and accounting procedures.

Extraterritoriality. Foreign criticism of American multinational corporations frequently stresses the affront to the foreign country's sovereignty which may result from the extraterritorial application of U.S. law to U.S. owned corporations. Some Canadians, for example, to whom the dominant role of U.S. investment is the subject of great political concern, have suggested that a government-to-government undertaking not to apply domestic legislation to corporations acting in the other's territory would greatly assuage political tensions and permit business to be conducted according to commercial criteria. Others argue that the application of American antitrust laws and practices abroad handicap the United States' competitive position in those countries.

Foreign investment in the United States. In general, the federal government treats foreign corporations the same as domestic corporations. In addition, the advantages that states, regional development areas, and some cities offer likely investors are generally available on a nondiscriminatory basis. Foreigners frequently allege, however, that our antitrust laws and most particularly the way they are administered, inhibit foreign investment in the United States. It also seems likely that insufficient information is available to the potential foreign investor about opportunities in the United States or that, at the very least, facilities for communicating available information are inadequate for the job. Thus, a more vigorous promotional campaign might yield dividends. The problem is not entirely dissimilar from what we experience in promoting U.S. tourism.

Expropriation and other forms of foreign harassment of, or discrimination against U.S. business. While expropriation policies of other governments create acute political problems, more subtle methods of harassment or discrimination—for example, with respect to tax advantages, rights of establishment, and access to convertible foreign exchange—pose equally serious problems. In the developed world, our friendship, commerce, and navigation treaties and the Organization for Economic Cooperation and Development Capital Movements Code provide some protection, but throughout the developing world the foreign corporation often has a less secure legal position. There would appear to be a manifest need for an international code to govern national treatment of foreign investments. It would be desirable for developing countries to subscribe to and honor such a code but failing this, a coordinated approach for the developed countries to such issues as expropriation (we plan to release in a matter of weeks a statement of U.S. policy on this subject), discriminatory practices, investment insurance, and dispute settlement would be desirable. At the same time, such a code governing national practices might well be supplemented by a code of good behavior for corporations.

The difficulties of negotiating such codes can hardly be overestimated but their importance for the fair treatment of international business in an open multilateral world can hardly be underestimated.

Legislative possibilities

The recent report of the President's Commission on International Trade and Investment Policy (the Williams Commission) recommends a major new initiative to liberalize international trade, including the eventual elimination of all tariffs and new arrangements to make trade in agricultural products responsive to factors of comparative advantage. Task forces of the Council on International Economic Policy are actively studying these recommendations and the possibilities for new legislative initiatives which would equip the president with the authority he needs to break through the sterile trade quarrels of the past and develop new arrangements to promote international commerce and finance in a growing domestic and world economy.

We are studying the kinds of presidential authority needed to deal with tariffs, (we should not forget that tariff reduction can be an effective antidote to regional preferential arrangements, for if there are no tariffs, of what value are tariff preferences?) the very important nontariff barriers, special problems in agriculture, and measures particularly needed to deal with trade issues involving less developed countries and the Eastern countries. We are considering the directions we should move in internationally and the kinds of authority we may require to negotiate agreements or codes relating to international investment issues. It may also be desirable to propose new legislation to deal with the temporary disruption of markets due to a rapid buildup of imports, and revisions in existing legislation concerning relief from import competition and unfair international trading practices (including antidumping and countervailing duty laws). Council task forces are attentive to the problem of discrimination abroad against U.S. exports and will propose measures to deal with it as needed.

Finally, we need to relate these issues to new programs designed to stimulate the competitiveness and development of America's economic strengths; to promote needed domestic adjustments and to deal constructively with our major domestic economic and social problems in an interdependent world economy.

The Williams Commission emphasizes the fact that "the [major new series of international] negotiations—and the preparations therefore—must involve the private sector and the Congress so as to ensure domestic consensus on U.S. objectives." I fully endorse this recommendation, and our study of new legislative proposals will include strategies for meeting this requirement. During the post-August 15 negotiations, for example, we have attempted to keep interested committees and members of Congress informed on the progress of the negotiations.

Excerpts from the Peterson Report (B)[1]

ONE of the major concerns of the Peterson Report[2] is the accelerating competition between the United States and Japan for world markets. In this excerpt, entitled "The Japanese Economic Miracle: A Special Review," Mr. Peterson traces the historical rise of Japan as an economic power and identifies the particular aspects of Japanese "competitiveness" that challenge American business aspirations.

THE JAPANESE ECONOMIC MIRACLE: A SPECIAL REVIEW

America's traditional and cultural ties have been with Western Europe. Our language and our impetus as a nation grew from our European heritage, as did most of our economic institutions. Throughout our history, most U.S. trade, investment, and security relationships bound us with the Atlantic nations.

America's familiarity with European ways of thought and action is obvious. Less familiar to us are the institutions and history of Japan, the country selected for description in this special review. It is because Japan is both culturally distant from Americans and because that nation

---

[1] This note was prepared by Professor James P. Baughman from sources in the public domain as the basis for class discussion and is not intended to illustrate either effective or ineffective handling of an administrative situation.

[2] For a fuller description of the history and nature of this document, see *Excerpts from the Peterson Report* (A).

has achieved a remarkable growth of output and trade that this special review is devoted to it.[3]

Only about ten years ago, if one had been asked to think aloud about Japanese products one would probably have mentioned very small market shares of Japanese photographic equipment, some electronic equipment, and toys—but certainly nothing as basic as steel or automobiles.

Today, the Japanese have passed the economies of West Germany, France, and the United Kingdom and rank behind only the United States and the Soviet Union in total output. Their growth rate of the past 20 years has surpassed everyone's expectations.

GOVERNMENT–BUSINESS PARTNERSHIP

Japan is a special kind of economic phenomenon. There is an assumption that the key objectives of government and business are essentially the same: the maintenance of Japan's economic health at home and the promotion of the nation's economic interests abroad.

The system of government–business interaction which underlies Japan's successful growth does not lend itself easily to description in Western terms. Japan's is neither an unplanned, free-enterprise economy like that of the United States, nor a centrally planned economy like those of Eastern Europe and the Soviet Union.

Many factors have brought about the Japanese phenomenon. Any list of them would have to include the insular psychology of an island nation, a homogeneous culture and sense of racial identity, and the need and will to recover from the devastation of World War II. The Japanese appear to have asked themselves, "What are the implications for us of trying to recover a powerful position in the world, while maintaining our low profile in overall foreign and defense policies?"

Part of the answer to this question has been a complex apparatus of interaction involving several government ministries such as the Ministry of Finance, the Ministry of International Trade and Industry (MITI), and the Bank of Japan; and formal hierarchial groups of industries, trade associations, and labor.

A major segment of Japanese government officials devote themselves to stimulating growth and improving business prospects—the Japanese government sees itself as a partner with business in facilitating economic growth.

The situation is far different from that in the United States—where it is probably true that major efforts of government officials are devoted

---

[3] A variety of sources were used to prepare this material. One of the most important was the Boston Consulting Group, which has specialized in a variety of studies of the Japanese economy.

not to growth and stimulation, but to restraint and regulation of business and labor: the role of the umpire.

The Japanese system includes a range of formal and informal channels of communication between government and industry. Thus, by the time a new policy decision is announced, widespread consultation has taken place, and a consensus has often been reached. Communication is facilitated by the close personal ties of business and government officials.

The Japanese recognize the need for broad, long-range economic planning, while avoiding overly detailed implementation. Plans of the Japan Economic Planning Agency are prepared in consultation with leading industry experts. While these plans lack legal sanction, they exert a powerful influence on the thrust and direction of the Japanese economy.

Japan is not a socialized economy in the sense of detailed government production plans. However, viewing the Japanese economy as a type of informal conglomerate is helpful. It is a form of business organization which, through strong financial management, can channel cash flows rapidly from low-growth to high-growth sectors.

The Bank of Japan is the financial center and, following guidelines of the Planning Agency, determines the nature and direction of growth by allowing companies in rapidly growing industries to employ more debt than they could safely incur by themselves.

UTILIZATION OF CAPITAL RESOURCES

Japan's high capital reinvestment rate (39 percent of GNP) was noted earlier. The Japanese system for the allocation of this capital deserves comment.

First, Japanese corporations employ large amounts of debt in their capital structure. In the Japanese steel industry, for example, debt currently accounts for nearly 80 percent of capital. For major Japanese corporations, debt-to-equity ratios often run 4 or 5 to 1, in sharp contrast to the *Fortune* average for 500 U.S. corporations of less than 0.5 to 1. This practice enables major Japanese corporations to expand capacity much faster than would be possible if they had to depend mainly on retained earnings or the underdeveloped Japanese security markets.

How can Japanese companies assume the level of risk associated with such heavy debt, and what are the implications for resource allocation within the economy? In brief, the government of Japan stands behind the debt position of major companies, ensuring both that financing will be available for rapid growth and that the government can play a central role in determining the nature and direction of that growth. As fewer guarantees apply to smaller or less efficient firms, the system encourages a rapid move toward concentration of production in the hands of the larger, more efficient producers.

Since the commercial banks of Japan provide the major source of funds to corporations via an aggressive lending policy, they are ultimately dependent upon the Bank of Japan. The fact is that no major company's loan is likely to be called unless the Bank of Japan wants it called. On several occasions in recent years, the bank has earmarked funds to be channeled through the commercial banks to major companies that have been, for all practical purposes, bankrupt. Major changes in management, organization, and operations have been the conditions attached to these financings.

Another institution characteristic of the Japanese system, conglomerate groupings called Zaibatsus, operate to decrease the financial risk of large companies.

These groups usually include, besides numerous manufacturing firms, a major commercial bank and an international trading company. Zaibatsus would normally dwarf any conglomerates in this country. The heads of the major companies review operating results, growth plans, and capital requirements much as do the heads of divisions of a U.S. conglomerate. They are usually in unrelated fields or in the relationship of supplier and user. Largely because of the dependence of Japanese companies on short-term debt, a bank in each Zaibatsu plays a central role.

Labor resources

A persistent myth about Japan is that of "cheap labor." It is commonly assumed that the growth of the Japanese economy is based primarily on low labor costs. Many countries of Asia have far lower labor costs and far more raw materials but none has the combination of Japan's efficient use and allocation of labor and capital resources, and a government-business partnership to promote growth.

Japan's labor rates have, of course, been low compared with those of some Western countries (Chart 67). However, in the sophisticated sectors of the economy—those like steel and machinery that are growing fastest and are most competitive in world trade—direct labor rates are at European levels. Wage increases of about 14 percent annually during 1965–70 in manufacturing sectors have been justified by high productivity rises of about 15 percent annually, or even more. In steel, Japanese annual growth in productivity of 18.5 percent outpaced wage gains. In the United States, on the other hand, wage gains exceeded productivity increases during the last half of the 1960s. As a result, the unit labor-cost gap continued to widen to the disadvantage of the United States. Productivity growth in Japan has also spurred major gains in Japanese real wages relative to the United States and other developed countries (Chart 68).

CHART 67
Average hourly earnings of wage workers in manufacturing, 1970

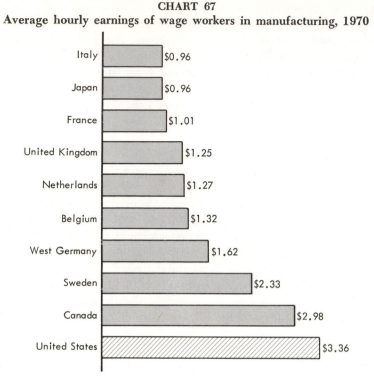

Italy	$0.96
Japan	$0.96
France	$1.01
United Kingdom	$1.25
Netherlands	$1.27
Belgium	$1.32
West Germany	$1.62
Sweden	$2.33
Canada	$2.98
United States	$3.36

Labor is indeed a critical factor in Japan's success—not so much because it is "cheap labor," but because it is efficient and flexible and because its organization in both companies and unions stimulates rather than impedes economic growth.

The "lifetime employment" system

Japanese workers are typically hired directly out of school and spend their careers with one company. This permanent employment system, which appears inflexible to the Western observer, has contributed importantly to Japan's economic miracle:

1. Since the worker enjoys lifetime job security, he more readily accepts technological change. If his job is displaced by automation, he knows he will be retrained by the company for another task.

2. Conversely, management is probably willing to expend larger sums to retrain a worker, knowing that such an investment is less likely to accrue to another company through the worker's leaving.

3. While the Japanese industrial labor force is unionized in about the same proportion as in the West, unions are organized by company

CHART 68

Index of real average hourly earnings of wage workers in manufacturing

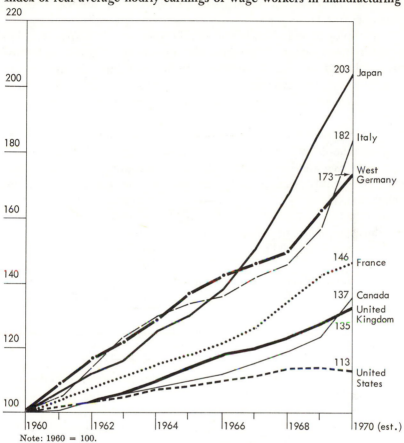

Note: 1960 = 100.

and not by trade. The union tends to identify its long-range interest with that of the company. In 1968, Japan lost 2.8 million man-days to strikes versus more than 49 million in the United States. Furthermore, virtually all strikes are of short duration. For all practical purposes, there have not been any major strikes for many years. In the last 15 years, the United States has lost more days per 1,000 nonagricultural employees than Canada, France, Germany, Sweden, or the United Kingdom—only Italy's rate exceeds the United States.

4. This company identification has important moral effects. Only if the company is successful can the employee enjoy a prosperous career and comfortable retirement.

5. Since wages are tied importantly to age, labor costs are a direct function of the average age of the work force. Thus, the fast-growing firm (or industry) recruiting large numbers of young workers directly

from school, has a relative cost advantage over the slow-growth enterprise. The slow-growth enterprise, therefore, encounters increasingly noncompetitive labor costs.

This employment system is not as inflexible as it first appears. Mandatory retirement age is 55—when the employee is given a lump-sum pension that is not really adequate to support him for the remaining 15 years of his life expectancy. He is therefore available to be rehired by his company (or a subsidiary or subcontractor) as a temporary worker.

Top management is not subject to early mandatory retirement: After being designated a director of the company, usually in his 40s or 50s, a Japanese executive is exempt from any mandatory retirement requirement. Presumably, this permits the selection of the most outstanding to stay past 55.

The effectiveness of worker training is dependent upon the literacy and education of the population. Japan's educational level is high: Illiteracy, for example, is negligible. A higher percentage of Japan's secondary school age population is in secondary school than in the United States— about 91 percent versus 78 percent. While college enrollment in the United States exceeds that in Japan, the Japanese college enrollment per thousand exceeds European levels.

The Japanese emphasize technical training. For example, Japan now graduates more engineers than the United States—with about half of the population. (The United States, however, still graduates more Ph.D.'s) Japan's vocational-technical educational system is highly developed, permitting them to direct the young into skills that will be in high demand in the future.

In the next pages, we shall review data on productivity and unit labor costs that are the composite result of many objective factors— capital input, training, increasing technology, longer work hours, etc. (In Japan, the average work week is about 49 hours, versus 37 to 39 in the United States). While it is hard to quantify in a chart, it is worth noting that a variety of foreign journalists visiting Japanese automobile plants, for example, refer to various worker motivational factors: "willingness to work," "discipline," "pride," "finishing up the work," etc.

Full-capacity policy

One consequence of the Japanese life time employment policy is that labor tends to be treated as a fixed cost. Also, because of the proportion of debt in its capital structure, the financial costs of a Japanese company are largely fixed. Therefore, a Japanese company is driven to operate at high capacity as long as its revenues cover variable or "out-of-pocket" costs. This can produce export prices which are extremely low.

In any economy where industrial output has consistently increased more than 20 percent annually for all industry, it is reasonable to place maintenance of market share as a primary corporate objective. These gains plus the effective commitment of the government to stimulate rapid economic growth have caused Japanese companies to add capacity in anticipation of market expansion. Given the capital costs of new facilities, much is done to ensure that they will be operated at capacity and available products moved onto world markets. This explains in part at least the tendency of Japanese exports to increase sharply and quickly when the increase in domestic demand slackens periodically, and helps explain some of the problems foreign competitors have with short-term Japanese pricing policies.

Their use of labor, capital, and good management practices has yielded Japanese productivity improvements unmatched by other industrial countries. The following charts add statistical substance to this conclusion.

In unit labor costs (Chart 69) the United States has an excellent performance from 1960 through 1965–66, when annual productivity increases equaled, or even exceeded, wage increases. More recently, we see that relative German costs have risen sharply, spurred by an inflationary boom and a substantial currency revaluation. In the case of Great Britain, we see a strong trend of rising unit costs, in spite of substantial devaluation.

The chart speaks eloquently of Japanese productivity performance— made even more remarkable by the fact that wage increases were about 14 percent annually between 1965 and 1970. An important question is how long Japan can continue this unique performance; inflationary pressures are building there too.

By very competitive export pricing and by tax and other incentives, Japan has been able to use its productivity growth to keep prices down for its export products (Chart 70) even though consumer prices have risen. Since consumer prices obviously include the cost of services (which in Japan have risen very rapidly), the disparity between export and consumer prices is necessarily overstated to some degree in these numbers. More analytical work must be done in order to establish valid comparisons of this type, based solely on the prices of comparable goods that are both consumed domestically and exported.

Japanese technology

The Japanese put major emphasis on high technology. Much foreign technology has been acquired through royalty agreements and various kinds of technical agreements. In some cases, it has been brought in by foreign companies as their equity in Japanese companies—but with

CHART 69
Unit labor costs in manufacturing
(1965 = 100)

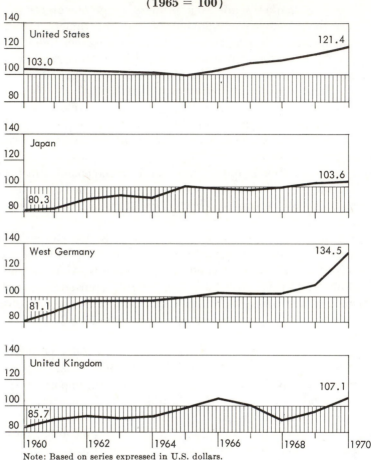

Note: Based on series expressed in U.S. dollars.

a handful of exceptions, the foreign firms have received only minority participation in such joint ventures.

Many American companies, knowing of severe investment restrictions (and in some cases import restrictions on these high-technology products), chose royalties as the most practical way to get revenue for their technology.

Thus, while most countries depend on direct foreign investment or domestic R and D to acquire advanced technology and know-how, Japan has purchased these needs outright through licensing agreements. Japanese royalty and management payments abroad were more than $650 million in 1970, and more than half was paid to the United States.

The comparison between Japanese royalty payments and those of

CHART 70
Consumer and export price indexes
(1960 = 100)

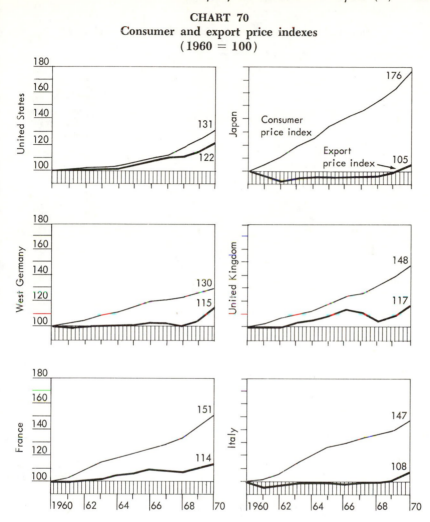

the United States and Germany is striking: from 1964 to 1970, while Japanese payments grew from $200 million to $650 million, U.S. royalty and management payments abroad increased from $108 million to $198 million; comparable West German payments totalled $192 million in 1967. Japanese royalty and management payments to foreigners were about six times greater than Japan's direct investment income payments to foreigners. A similar ratio for West Germany is roughly 1:1 and for the United Kingdom 1:2 (Chart 71).

In total, Japan has paid out $3.4 billion over the past ten years for access to a vast amount of foreign technology. The costs of developing this technology internally would have been much higher. In the future, Japanese plans suggest an increase in R and D investment from about

CHART 71
Japan: Direct investment versus technology purchases

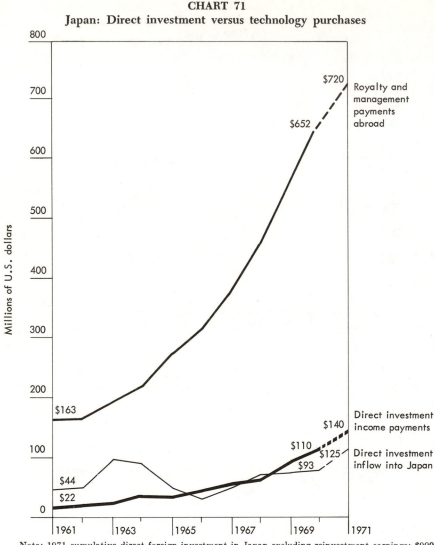

Note: 1971 cumulative direct foreign investment in Japan excluding reinvestment earnings: $900 million.

Japanese payments abroad for royalty and management were about six times that of direct investment income payments abroad during 1968–1971. The similar ratio for West Germany is roughly 1:1 and for the United Kingdom 1:2.

$3 billion in 1970 to nearly $13 billion in 1980. Clearly, Japan has decided to accelerate the development of its own technology.

Japanese export promotion policy

One common misperception about Japan is the view that Japan's growth is the result of exports. (As we have seen, Japan exports less of its production than some industrial countries.)

In fact, the export successes of Japan have been built upon high levels of domestic demand. From umbrella frames to motorcycles, the initial industrial growth has been to supply the rapidly expanding local market, with the export thrust following some three to five years later.

The cliché has it that "Japan exports to live," and there is truth in this. But it would be more accurate to say "Japan imports to live." The country's raw material position is well known; there is little in abundance and much that is lacking. Seventy percent of Japan's imports are industrial raw materials, including more than 80 percent of its coking coal, 98 percent of its iron ore, and 99 percent of its oil. Exports provide the foreign exchange to purchase the required imports. Exports are therefore of critical importance; they are not, however, the explanation for Japan's economic growth.

Perhaps the most effective export advantage enjoyed by Japanese companies in comparison to their U.S. counterparts is the Japanese trading company, which may well be the world's most efficient international marketing channel. These huge enterprises handle 88 percent of Japan's international trade, maintaining sales offices around the world and collecting market intelligence worldwide.

Each company markets hundreds of products and can efficiently fill its large ships with many small orders. It is estimated that the top 12 of these marketing enterprises handle 50 percent to 60 percent of Japan's exporting companies. In total, the trading companies handle about three fourths of all Japanese exports. Their huge sales volumes enable them to operate on small margins (the top five averaged a 0.15 percent return on sales in 1969). They also assist in export and raw material financing. The result is that small and medium-sized Japanese companies can sell their products to world markets at competitive prices. Small firms in the United States, conversely, are often unable to overcome high exporting costs and still sell their products at competitive prices.

Most large Japanese companies compete vigorously overseas (for example, Nissan and Toyota in North America). However, when a trading company handles the products of more than one company in an industry, it may allocate sales between them. Overseas competition in this case occurs between trading companies and not between individual producers. In addition, numerous competitors (both manufacturers and trading companies) often form joint ventures to exploit raw material sources. (Generally, the Japanese government does not attempt to extend its antitrust regulatory powers outside Japan and, indeed, often encourages various cooperative efforts.)

The continued existence of disparities in ocean freight rates will deter export expansion. This is particularly true in trade with Japan. Frequently the rate on the same commodity is higher from the United

States to Japan than vice versa. For example, the estimated ocean freight cost of an automobile imported from Japan is $70; and exported to Japan, $250.

For all the reasons mentioned above, Japan's competitive strength in exports has increased steadily in recent years. However, a coordinated government-business trade promotion campaign, including various financing and tax incentives, as well as an overall national commitment to exports, also explains Japan's successful export performance.

Industrial product specialization

Because so many of Japan's exports to the United States are highly visible (for example, home electronics products, automobiles, and motorcycles or basic industrial products (for example, steel), it would be natural to assume that the Japanese push exports of every product they make. However, Japan has not made the mistake of seeking unlimited objectives with limited resources. In fact, the Japanese have chosen selected products in which to pursue international competitive supremacy. In 1970, about 60 percent of Japan's exports were accounted for by four industrial groupings: transportation equipment (ships and cars), 17 percent; steel, 16 percent; electrical and electronic equipment, 13 percent; and textiles, 12 percent. No other industry accounted for as mu(h as 6 percent of the total.

The *London Economist* has made a historical study of Japan's industrial specialization. First, it pointed out that Japan thought of certain industries as "throw-away industries," not only because Japan was no longer competitive in these industries, but also because it was regarded as a mistake to try to gain a competitive position in those areas. Coal, paper pulp, nonferrous metals, and agricultural products are cited examples of such industries.

Second, the Japanese identified "early stage industrialization" activities (cotton textiles, sewing machines, bicycles, pottery, etc.) in which they no longer wished to compete in a vigorous way or invest precious capital. Companies in these fields had to release men, materials, and resources for more efficient and rapidly growing enterprises. It is, of course, exactly this transfer of resources from the less efficient to the more efficient sectors that facilitates rapid economic growth. A review of Japan's spending priorities for the 1970s shows a substantial scaling down of the Japanese textile industry as it shifts to other countries in Southeast Asia, and substantial expenditure for retraining today's textile workers.

Third, the Japanese focus on industries of the future and employ a variety of protective and incentive devices to develop their capabilities in these critical fields.

To make clear the modes of government–business interaction by which such goals are attained, we will examine briefly the cases of the Japanese steel and computer industries.

Government–business partnership: Two case studies

Steel. For many basic steel products, Japanese domestic prices are 20 percent to 40 percent below U.S. prices. Japanese government and industry have worked together to enhance the competitive strength of their steel industry; and low capital, material, and labor costs have been systematically combined with advanced know-how to make Japanese steel the world's cheapest.

At the end of World War II, with only three of 35 wartime blast furnaces still producing, and raw materials unavailable domestically, the Japanese Cabinet decided to make steel one of the priority industries in their recovery plan (along with coal, electric power, and chemical fertilizers). The Ministry of Finance granted special tax advantages to these critical industries, and helped them get capital by advising commercial banks to give them priority and low-interest rates on loans.

Steel plans were built on filled-in land next to deep water ports; and the Japanese set out to minimize transportation costs by building the world's largest and most efficient ships to carry ore directly to the plants and carry away finished steel exports.

As demand for steel rose following the outbreak of the Korean War, industry and government agreed on the First Rationalization Plan (1951 to 1955) to achieve scale investments and advanced techniques—$356 million was invested in these years. Sixty percent of machinery investment was spent on imported equipment—on which import duties were eliminated.

It is important to note that the government avoided the role of central planner and concentrated on defining general directions and creating incentives for growth. Liberal depreciation and reserve policies favored growth companies over stagnant ones.

When steel demand slackened in 1958, overcapacity and the high break-even cost nature of the industry led to plunging prices as firms strove to keep their facilities operating at full capacity. The Ministry of International Trade and Industry (MITI) took the initiative in achieving consensus among producers on temporary production cutbacks.

To meet the underlying need of avoiding excessive additions to capacity, MITI began in 1959 to prepare four-year demand forecasts and then allow companies to work out voluntary adjustments in their plans if planned additions to capacity appeared excessive. MITI in effect played a role of arbitrator for collusive action by the companies that would be illegal under U.S. antitrust laws.

While growth has been spectacular since 1960, problems of excessive capacity and price fluctuations have intensified. In the 1965 recession, Sumitomo, the third largest company, refused to agree to voluntary limits on production. The conflict lasted many months and was publicized as MITI's first failure to obtain consensus on steel production allocations. Similar disagreements have arisen recently with Sumitomo over the size and timing of capacity increases. As steel approaches a mature product phase in Japan and growth slows (the forecast for 1970–75 is less than 10 percent annually versus 16 percent in the 1960s), such problems of forging consensus will intensify.

More recently, spurred by MITI, the steel firms Fuji and Yawata merged to form Nippon, the largest steel producer in the world. MITI's announced objective was to increase the efficiency of two of the older but very large firms by integrating their manufacturing efforts.

Computers.   Japan entered computer development in the late 1950s, well behind then-current technology. In the early 1960s, the Japanese electrical companies sought out technical licensing agreements with U.S. companies involving manufacturing, engineering, and programming assistance. The surviving firms in the Japanese computer industry, Hitachi-Fuji and Nippon Electric were major recipients of this technology. However, since the mid-1960s, MITI has played an aggressive role in the industry's development—including protecting it from foreign competition. The rationale for protection is the classic "infant industry" argument, under which an embryonic domestic industry is allowed to establish economies of large-scale production while foreign suppliers, who are already producing in volume markets, are prevented from competing in the infant industry's home market.

The Japanese government supplied the computer industry with financial and tax incentives; the government also underwrote technological programs in support of this industry. In brief, MITI has been a catalyst and sponsor for the Japanese computer industry; this sponsorship has not dictated to the industry, but has provided crucial protection and stimulus.

Specific examples of government-business cooperation during the industry's development follow.

1.   The Electronic Industry Act of 1957 authorized financial assistance for computer hardware manufacturers, including direct subsidies for research and development, government loans to products just entering commercial production, and loans and accelerated depreciation for investments designed to "rationalize" operations (specialize production by firm) in accordance with MITI policy. These fiscal "carrots" which lubricate the consensus process have been rather modest in amount, but indicate to prospective creditors MITI's recognition of computers as an important development area. Such signals can be important in a manufacturing sector whose capital is 80 percent debt.

The act also authorized MITI to selectively exempt any portion of the electronics industry from the Antimonopoly Law. Cartels for production, R and D, and raw materials were permitted. Under this authority, MITI established a cartel in 1969 allocating the production of peripheral equipment. In a large-scale computer project sponsored by the government, five firms are cooperating to develop a large time-sharing system.

2.   After lengthy negotiations, the government allowed IBM to establish a 100 percent-owned subsidiary in Japan under severe restrictions and in return for the licensing by IBM of basic patents to all interested Japanese manufacturers. These restrictions include (*a*) market share ceilings, (*b*) requirements to export computers in amounts equivalent to sales in Japan, (*c*) prior announcement of new product introduction and clearance of manufacturing schedules, (*d*) approval of new plant facilities, (*e*) control of technology transfers, including approval of new laboratory facilities and their development. In spite of these restrictions and because of others, it should be said that IBM in Japan is very successful.

3.   In 1961, 70 percent of the Japanese computer market represented imported machines (not counting IBM's Japanese production). A wide range of import restrictions has reduced this share to 25 percent during the 1960s.

4.   In 1961 the Japan Electronic Computer Corporation, a joint marketing service and finance venture between the government and computer manufacturers, was set up to purchase from manufacturers and rent and service domestic computer systems for end users. (Foreign makers were forbidden from using the facilities of this corporation.)

5.   A further example of government support to the computer industry is the special levy on the import of large American computers. This special levy is transferred directly to an R and D fund which is allocated to the Japanese firms for the purpose of building a large-scale Japanese computer.

In all of these measures, business and government have cooperated closely. However, recent MITI attempts to spur further mergers and consolidations have been rebuffed by computer manufacturers.

In 1970 Japan was the world's second largest computer manufacturer. Like the steel industry, the computer industry in Japan exhibits planning and industrial support approaches quite foreign to U.S. practice.

Japanese natural resource requirements

For years, economists talked about the serious handicap suffered by Japan with its lack of raw materials. While the vulnerability implicit in dependence on others for critical raw materials still exists, the Japanese have made genuine progress in minimizing the economic effects of this lack of raw materials.

1. Japan could turn its full attention to making arrangements for foreign sources of raw materials without having to face the internal pressures resulting from closing down higher cost or lower-quality domestic production—difficulties which have been experienced in other parts of the world.

2. Raw materials have been obtained under long-term contracts (10–25 years) which provide low prices, a steady flow, and minimize price fluctuations.

3. The Japanese profited from development of natural resources in LDCs while maintaining a low political profile there. Rather than establish wholly owned subsidiaries, Japanese firms often extend loans to foreign mining firms to expand capacity and provide them with know-how through management contracts. The loans are usually tied to purchases in Japan, and repayment is in the newly mined output. Profits are earned through sales of machinery and equipment, on management contracts, and from interest on loans. The Japanese avoid the sometimes politically sensitive large-scale repatriation of profits. Also, repayment in kind seems less onerous to LDCs than cash repayments. Direct ownership, when it does occur, is usually through a minority share.

4. As the dramatic growth of Japan's steel industry illustrates, the disadvantage to Japan of the long distances over which raw materials must be transported has been overcome by super-sized ore carriers and tankers, by the tidewater location of most plants, an efficient sea transportation network (Japan is now the world's largest builder of ships), and the cartelized high-volume, long-term purchasing policy of Japan's producers.

As Chart 72 indicates, Japan is already the world's largest importer of iron ore, coking coal, copper ores, and crude oil and ranks second only behind the United States in imports of bauxite. It is also the world's most dynamic growth market for raw materials and will likely continue so at least through the mid-1970s, as Japan's 1975 projected requirements are about double the 1970 level. The Japanese are undertaking steps to assure adequate future supplies. Long-term contracts with foreign mineral producers—including many U.S. firms—are being concluded. Japan is expanding its fleet of super-sized ore carriers and tankers to keep shipping costs down. Tokyo's long-term economic plans indicate that greatly increased investment in raw materials will be one important use of their rapidly growing international reserves.

❋   ❋   ❋   ❋   ❋

No discussion of the Japanese economic miracle should leave the impression that Japan is without problems. Industrial pollution is high and budget projections for the 1970s show large increases in expenditures for environmental protection. Another problem is the potential limitation

CHART 72
Japan's selected raw materials requirements*

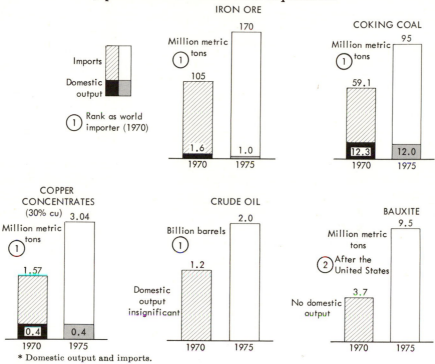

IRON ORE

COKING COAL

COPPER CONCENTRATES (30% cu)

CRUDE OIL

BAUXITE

* Domestic output and imports.

of power availability. Still another is the growing and largely neglected need for social services—such as housing, highways, and health. Again, projected Japanese budgets for the 1970s show increases of three times or more in some of these key areas. Labor unions may become more demanding and consumers may be less willing to save. Productivity increases may be harder to gain.

Yet, the Japanese have not only a unique government-business partnership, they also display a high degree of cohesiveness. They exhibit excellent morale, work hard, and have a sense of their future.

It would be a mistake to underestimate or overestimate their potential, just as it would be a mistake to believe we could or would want to transplant their whole system to the United States. Nonetheless, the developed countries of the world can undoubtedly learn from the Japanese experience.

Note on the Foreign Trade and Investment Act of 1972[1]

THE so-called "Burke-Hartke Bill" (House Resolution 10914 and Senate Bill 2592) introduced by Representative James A. Burke (Democrat, Massachusetts) and Senator Vance Hartke (Democrat, Indiana) represents an alternative to the approach advocated by the Peterson Report.[2] The following are "highlights of the bill" (which is still in committee in both the Senate and the House) as summarized by David J. Steinberg, Executive Director of the Committee for a National Trade Policy.[3]

HIGHLIGHTS OF THE BILL

1. The bill would impose quotas on all imports that are not now subject either to quantitative import restrictions or government-to-government export-control agreements. Exemptions would include goods not produced in the United States, and products where the competing U.S. industry "has consistently failed to make technological innovations required to remain competitive with foreign producers." Quotas in the

---

[1] This note was prepared by Professor James P. Baughman from sources in the public domain as the basis for class discussion and is not intended to illustrate either effective or ineffective handling of an administrative situation.

[2] For a fuller description of the history and nature of this report, see *Excerpts from the Peterson Report* (A) and (B).

[3] David J. Steinberg, *"Hartke-Burke" in a Nutshell: What It Is and What To Do about It* mimeographed release by the Committee for a National Trade Policy, 1972. These excerpts represent Mr. Steinberg's summary of the bill's provisions and are used with his permission. They do not represent his or his organization's opinion on the bill.

first year would be limited to average annual imports of the various product groupings in 1965–69. Product quotas would be set on a country-by-country basis, with provision for the shift of unfilled quotas from the shortfall country to either new or historical suppliers. Quotas in subsequent years would be raised or lowered to maintain the base-period ratio of imports to domestic production, or to meet special situations (for example, a finding that imports are "inhibiting the production of any manufactured product" and hence should be cut even lower than the 1965–69 level).

2. Authority to set these controls (final authority except for presidential decisions on the reallocation of unfilled quotas) would be delegated to a three-member Foreign Trade and Investment Commission, consisting of spokesmen for industry, labor, and the public. The commissioners would have six-year staggered terms. The new agency would replace the Tariff Commission and assume various trade-policy functions now administered by the Commerce, Treasury, and Labor departments (for example, antidumping and antisubsidy proceedings).

3. In addition to setting the import quotas described above, the commission would also have final authority (subject only to judicial review) to decide escape-clause cases (involving claims of industry-wide import injury). Findings of injury, and hence the need for government help, would not (as the law now requires) be subject to presidential decision. (The president would retain discretionary authority only in deciding whether to grant adjustment assistance to individual firms or groups of workers.) Quotas would be the only remedy for industrial injury from imports. On the other hand, the criteria for determining the contribution of imports to an industry's problem would considerably ease the injury test.

4. The bill would streamline antidumping and antisubsidy procedures.

5. The bill would tax in the year they are earned the earnings and profits of U.S. corporate subsidiaries abroad, even if not repatriated. The bill would repeal the federal tax credit (a direct credit against the company's U.S. tax) now given U.S. companies for payment of foreign taxes on income earned abroad from production or from patent royalties. Other tax provisions would slow allowable depreciation rates in foreign operations.

6. Another provision against U.S. foreign investment would authorize the president to prohibit any transfer of U.S. capital to another country whenever in his judgment "the transfer would result in a net decrease in employment in the United States." The president is also authorized to prohibit any holder of a U.S. patent from manufacturing the patented product abroad, or licensing its use outside the United States, when in his judgment "such prohibition will contribute to increased employment in the United States."

7.   The bill would delete Sections 806.30 and 807 of the U.S. Tariff Schedules. These sections permit U.S. firms shipping goods abroad for further processing to pay tariffs on the products reentering the United States only for the value added abroad.

8.   The bill would require that all goods containing foreign-made components be "clearly marked in a conspicuous place as legibly, indelibly and permanently as the nature of the article or container will permit . . . to indicate to an ultimate purchaser in the United States the English name of the country or countries of origin of the foreign made components." The same requirement would apply to the advertising of such products for sale in the United States.

A letter from Mr. Starrett[1]

THE L. S. STARRETT COMPANY

Since 1880
World's Greatest Toolmakers

Precision Tools · Dial Indicators · Steel Tapes
Ground Flat Stock · Hacksaws · Band Saws
Band Knives · Vises

Athol, Massachusetts 01331, U.S.A.
November 15, 1972

The Honorable Peter G. Peterson
Secretary of Commerce
Washington, D.C. 20230

Dear Secretary Peterson:

As the president of a precision toolmaking company, I am very involved and quite interested in the problems of low-cost, low-wage imports affecting U.S. manufacturing. I'm only going to speak for Starrett, but I do know that there are a host of other companies and industries that are just as concerned as I am.

---

[1] This case was prepared by Judith M. Brown and Professor James P. Baughman as the basis for class discussion and is not intended to illustrate either effective or ineffective handling of an administrative situation.

I've got several comments to make and some questions to ask. But before I continue, I'd like to tell you something about our company. My great-grandfather began as a New England farmer but his desire to invent useful tools led him to go into manufacturing in Athol, Massachusetts, in 1880. He eventually took out about 100 patents. Ever since then, our company has continually sought to broaden its product line and we now make over 3,000 tools. We sell almost exclusively to industrial supply houses, but our products end up in almost every factory in the United States.

We employ 1,701 people, a number of whom are highly skilled craftsmen who have been with us for many years. We are not unionized. Our 1967 Employees Stock Purchase Plan enables our people to become involved in Starrett as an enterprise, and we have made every effort to keep our facilities modern and efficient. Since we employ a significant number of the population of the Athol-Orange community, our position is one of importance to many more people than just those directly employed by Starrett. Enclosures 1–5 should give you a better idea of Starrett's position over a number of years. Enclosure 6 summarizes the opinions of a widely respected investment advisory firm about our company.

There are two aspects to the problem I would like to raise: foreign markets and the U.S. domestic market for our products. Let's take the foreign markets first. We are competing with manufacturers in foreign markets who are paying wages which are considerably less than ours. For a good example, let's take the Japanese, who are the most notorious. In a recent government report put out by an investigatory commission of the U.S. Tariff Commission, the stated figure for average hourly pay and fringe benefits in the United States was $3.97 in contrast to $0.98 in Japan. From our own information, we feel that this is substantially correct. While anyone can make a liar of me on an exception, generally speaking there is no technology that will overcome a cost difference such as the one just mentioned. This is especially true because in today's world of almost instant communication and transportation, most advanced technology in any field is readily available worldwide.

Actually, we ourselves have located plants overseas, strictly to be able to compete in foreign markets. At one time, in pre–World War II days, our exports contributed one third of our total business. Since World War II, however, exports have dropped to a trickle, and for only one reason: Our prices were too high for world markets because our costs were so much higher than those of the rest of the world. Because we cannot control what goes on in the rest of the world as far as wages and salaries are concerned, we had no choice except to abdicate the market or to go overseas and meet the competition. Last year, our overseas subsidiaries contributed 20 percent to our sales and 33⅓ percent to our income. In fact, during 1970 and 1971, our foreign operations' sales and earnings enabled us to keep our financial footing despite sharp declines in overall business conditions and our own domestic performance.

To be specific, our foreign operations are located in Sao Paulo, Brazil, and Jedburgh, Scotland. We also have warehouses in Canada and Mexico. We started these operations strictly to be able to compete in foreign markets and to replace the export business we had lost, *not* to manufacture abroad for importation back into this country.

In fact, we hadn't actually thought much about setting up a plant in Brazil until a local importer who was our representative there, an extremely energetic person, convinced us that it was worth looking into. In 1955–1956 my father sent me down there to examine possibilities. I was skeptical, because everyone kept telling me, "Brazil is the country of the future and always will be." But we went ahead anyway, investing $679,194 before production began in 1958; and we discovered that everyone had been wrong. Brazil's a tremendous, gung-ho country, growing by leaps and bounds—this is especially true of Sao Paulo, where we are located.

To date our operations in Brazil have been very satisfactory. We have crackerjack management there and a splendid relationship with the Brazilian government. We employ 170 people, all Brazilian nationals, and we're sympathetic to the government's desire for us to increase the percentage of the total Starrett product line made in Brazil. You see, although our primary reason for manufacturing in Brazil is to reach the rich domestic market of that particular country, we also use our organization there as an outlet for tools made in Athol and in Jedburgh. Furthermore, we are in Brazil to serve the rest of South America, which is no easy task, given Argentina's steep tariffs and the transportation problems in shipping to Chile and Peru. At any rate, we've done well despite inflation. In fact, we could almost say, thank God that Brazil has a military dictatorship, because without it the situation would be much worse.

Our reasons for establishing a plant in Scotland were similar. I went there in 1958 to help start the operations, and by 1960 we had invested $189,398. Today we employ 350 people in that plant. We were fortunate because we had good contacts in the United Kingdom. We spoke the same language. Our name and product line were well known there, and there was a good domestic market for our goods. At that time a Scottish location also gave us preferential access to the British Empire. Finally, we felt that we could serve the European tool and saw market better from Scotland, since we have always believed that the United

Kingdom would join the Common Market. The wage rate in Scotland is competitive, although it is not as low as is the Japanese rate.

Now to turn to the second part of the problem: the domestic market. This is the part I am most vitally interested in. I must stress again that when we went overseas we had no intention of importing back into the U.S. and that is still the case. Sometimes when we stock-out of a product here we may temporarily import from our inventories in Canada or Scotland. Occasionally we also supply some of the U.S. demand for metric tools from our Scottish plant, but we also make those tools in this country. So it is still fair to say that we do not manufacture overseas so as to import back into America.

Believe me, if money were our only concern, we could manufacture overseas, import from there, and turn our U.S. plant into a service and sales organization. We're not about to do that, unless we're forced by our governmental policies into importing into this country. We feel we have an obligation to our manufacturing people and indeed to the country to keep a healthy manufacturing organization alive in the U.S. If it comes down to import or die, however, of course we have to import. But we will fight it right down to the wire.

Again, we're faced with the same foreign competitors, only this time they are in our own backyard. Because of the giveaway trade policies of our government, we are faced with the same cost differential in this country which is making it an increasingly harder job to compete. The recent overall balance of trade is ample evidence of this; however, there has been for a number of years a manufacturing balance of trade not in our favor.

With this letter I include three pages from our current catalog which illustrate three of our best tools (Enclosures 7–9). On each page I have noted our selling price and the selling price for a comparable tool offered in the United States by our main Japanese competitor, Mitutoyo. These are only examples. Every tool we make is vulnerable to being undersold.

Let me tell you about our No. 120 dial caliper (Enclosure 10). It sums up the whole damn problem. Dial indicators of this type originated in Switzerland and Germany and sales broadened out from the Common Market area to encompass the United States and the rest of the world. At the time these started to come into the States in quantity in the 1950s we did not feel we could compete price-wise, because of our then manufacturing capabilities. Our answer to the problem was to ignore it and leave this area to foreign manufacturers. Brown & Sharpe, an American firm with a Swiss subsidiary, then began to import the tool into the United States and it soon became one of their most popular tools here. Even though no one was making it in this country, using this tool as a leader, both domestic and foreign manufacturers were becoming more important suppliers to our distributors because of it. We knew that the tool was useful and, because the demand was here, and because our distributors had to have suppliers who could give them a quality tool, we felt that this should be manufactured here in this country. We knew we could match the European price so we decided to make it in Athol rather than simply importing the tool, which would go against our grain. We tooled up the best way we could and found that it would cost us $20.00 to make this tool and about $8.00 to sell it. We introduced it in September at various trade shows and listed it in our catalog at $45.00 (without a case). This is the list price to the ultimate consumer. The distributor, however, pays us $32.06 for it, so that, if all of our cost figures work out, we should make a $4.00 profit on this tool.

Just as we completed this complex and costly process of setting up production and distribution systems, however, a Japanese firm began to import a competitive dial caliper and to sell it for $33.50. Given our costs, we just can't beat this price. But what really scares us is that Mitutoyo (our competitor) is selling the same caliper in Europe and South America at even lower prices. We just don't know *what* their *real* costs are. We really don't know whether or not it's within the realm of possibility to compete with this company.

Now, we intend to give this tool the best push we can; but if we fail, we fail. If things get bad, we could go partially offshore. We could continue to do the heavy and exotic machining in this country to take advantage of the lower unit costs of large lots. We could then finish the hand operations in Brazil, thereby cutting our overall costs and enabling us to approach the Japanese price. As a last resort, we could ship all the machinery necessary to produce the caliper to our foreign plants, make it abroad, and import it back into this country. We don't want to do this. We have tried to make a new product here, but unfair competition could very well push us out of this country.

Now, whom does this hurt most? Well, it hurts those people in the higher-paid manufacturing jobs, not the lower-paid jobs, as has been commonly assumed, because the higher-paid people show a greater wage differential between their wages and those of foreign competitors. The result of this foreign threat has been that a number of companies have gone out of business and a number of other companies have set up overseas for the purpose of shipping back to this country. Once a U.S. manufacturer does this, he pretty nearly forces his other domestic competition to do the same or be forced out of business.

These facts convince me that our whole trade policy is wrong. The only answer, as I see it, is a border tax which would be applied country by country. A formula should be devised to make up the difference between the hourly wages being paid in a particular country and the minimum wage which we are forced by federal law to pay in this country. This would not be protectionism as such—I define protectionism as not allowing foreign competitors into our market at all. We like competition and we need it, but fair competition. Fair competition to us means that whatever rules and regulations we are forced to operate under in this country should be equally applied to those competitors who want to come into this country and sell against us. We ask no more than the same treatment when we go into their countries. How ridiculous it is that we wouldn't allow anyone in this country to set up shop on Main Street and pay employees $.80 an hour, yet we're welcoming products from coolie labor countries which do just that!

Now let me comment on a couple of points which are germane to this whole situation. We have before us in Congress the Burke-Hartke Bill, which in effect says that any U.S. company with overseas subsidiaries will have to pay through the nose to keep them. This policy will make it unprofitable to operate overseas. The bill proposes this under the guise of meeting foreign imports. What its authors are really saying is that whether you go overseas to meet foreign competition in foreign countries (as Starrett has done) or whether you go overseas to ship back into this country (which Starrett has not done) makes no difference at all. You can't do either, says Burke-Hartke. Effectively this would mean that no U.S. company could set up overseas to meet foreign competition in foreign lands. So American companies would just abdicate that market. The Burke-Hartke Bill seems to imply that if we do all the manufacturing here, we can still export, which is bunk. That is the reason companies went overseas to begin with.

Now, I happen to agree with the thought that these off-shore subsidiaries should not be allowed to ship back into this country merely because they can product overseas more cheaply. To prevent this type of practice would be desirable, except that as long as foreign-owned companies are not controlled (and in the Burke-Hartke Bill they are not), then we are merely opening our doors to ruinous trade. I can sympathize with the manufacturer who does go overseas and sends back goods into this country because current government policies make it almost mandatory to do so, especially in some areas like radio and TV. But if a border tax was put on that treated equally everything coming into this country, whether produced by an American subsidiary or not, then this would eliminate the necessity of shipping back into this country. It would then be up to the domestic plant to compete.

The so-called productivity issue has also been in the limelight recently. Productivity in this country is not all that bad. I define productivity as the best usage of men, machines, and capital culminating not in cost per hour, but in units per hour. It's true that our productivity has not been increasing at the same *rate* as other countries, but when you're operating at the high edge of the state of the art in any particular field, you are not going to increase productivity as much percentage-wise as is a country which is starting off at a low level. According to a report given by Gene Beaudet, Editor-in-Chief of Iron Age, U.S. productivity is still about 20 percent greater than that of competing industrial nations. The report goes on to say that what hurts most is not our output per man-hour, but the cost of that man-hour.

Of course, the root cause of all this is inflation—particularly wage and salary increases that have outstripped productivity and thereby have increased our prices over a long number of years. This is not something that an individual company can fight, however, but must be met nationwide by the government. What we must do, then, is to face facts as they are and look at what we need to do to insure fair competition. Hopefully the government can bring our inflation under control, but I see no signs of it under either a Democratic or Republican administration.

In a nutshell, I say that the true answer to our problem is to make every company and country that wants to sell in the United States, whether foreign or domestic, abide by the same rules. For foreign countries this means a border tax to equalize any differences. This tax would be different, country by country, and would take care of so-called multinational firms who are shipping back into this country. It would also be automatically self-liquidating if and when the competing country came up to our legislated levels, such as the minimum wage. Incidentally, the minimum wage would merely let us operate under the same rules, but would still put most U.S. companies at a disadvantage, because no one in high technological industries is paying anywhere near the minimum rate. This rate, however, does give us a rational basis from which to work. We're not afraid of foreign technology or marketing techniques. Everything comes down to a price differential, which in turn is based on wage differentials.

I hope this letter prompts you to reply—or better still to do something to influence policy along the lines I suggest. I hope you won't say: "Why don't you stop making precision tools and get Adjustment Assistance so that you can turn to manufacturing something like popcorn that sells well in this country." This assistance bit is, to my way of thinking, a political ploy to avoid meeting the real issue head on. In our case, and I think our case is typical of most companies in the country, we like what we're doing, we are expert at it, we have built up a work force that is skilled in this area, and if we wanted to make popcorn we'd have done it long before now. Enclosed is a copy of a letter another tool firm sent to their congressman, who read it into the Congressional Record (Enclosure 11). It suggests the seriousness of the problem.

Sincerely,

D. R. Starrett
President

DRS/jb
Enclosures

THE L. S. STARRETT COMPANY

Consolidated Statements of Income and
Retained Earnings and Additional Paid-In Capital

YEARS ENDED JUNE 30, 1972 AND 1971

Income and Retained Earnings	1972	1971
Net Sales	$32,383,792	$28,704,315
Costs and Expenses:		
Cost of Goods Sold	18,324,304	16,341,513
Depreciation	842,138	796,541
Selling, General and Administrative Expenses	6,807,927	6,619,832
Interest Expense	37,375	47,172
Provision for Federal and Foreign Income Taxes	2,860,000	2,247,000
Total Costs and Expenses	28,871,744	26,052,058
CONSOLIDATED NET INCOME FOR THE YEAR	3,512,048	2,652,257
Less — Dividends Declared and Paid ($.83 per share in 1972, $.80 per share in 1971)	1,642,133	1,587,995
— Charge attributable to 35,754 shares in 1972, 29,813 shares in 1971, of stock purchased for treasury	507,448	389,671
Net Increase in Retained Earnings for the Year	1,362,467	674,591
Retained Earnings — At Beginning of Year	17,870,026	17,195,435
Retained Earnings — At End of Year	$19,232,493	$17,870,026
Earnings per share — based on average number of shares outstanding	$1.78	$1.34

Additional Paid-In Capital		
Additional Paid-In Capital — At Beginning of Year	$ 4,305,082	$ 4,274,551
Add — amount attributable to options exercised for 56,209 shares in 1972, 7,139 shares in 1971, under 1967 Employees' Stock Purchase Plan	646,404	88,166
— adjustment of excess of cost of assets acquired from The Herman Stone Company in 1970	—	6,204
	4,951,486	4,368,921
Less — charge attributable to 35,754 shares in 1972, 29,813 shares in 1971, of stock purchased for treasury	77,994	63,839
Additional Paid-In Capital — At End of Year	$ 4,873,492	$ 4,305,082

ENCLOSURE 2

THE L. S. STARRETT COMPANY

Consolidated Balance Sheet June 30, 1972 and 1971

ASSETS

	1972	1971
CURRENT ASSETS:		
Cash	$ 1,054,122	$ 1,054,942
Short Term Investments — at cost, which approximates market	3,599,244	2,258,000
Accounts Receivable (less allowance for doubtful accounts of $164,100 in 1972, $159,500 in 1971)	5,160,828	4,406,020
Inventories	14,065,803	13,958,491
Total Current Assets	23,879,997	21,677,453
PROPERTY, PLANT AND EQUIPMENT — at cost:		
Land	329,508	330,848
Buildings (less accumulated depreciation of $3,081,565 in 1972, and $2,980,445 in 1971)	4,036,370	4,024,434
Machinery and Equipment (less accumulated depreciation of $7,860,281 in 1972, and $7,306,357 in 1971)	3,392,047	3,331,766
OTHER ASSETS:		
Cash Value of Life Insurance	143,000	138,000
Deferred Charges and Miscellaneous Assets	363,742	421,487
	$32,144,664	$29,923,988

LIABILITIES AND STOCKHOLDERS' EQUITY

	1972	1971
CURRENT LIABILITIES:		
Accounts Payable and Accrued Expenses	$ 1,963,124	$ 1,901,731
Accrued Federal, State, Foreign and Local Taxes	2,546,400	1,896,300
Long-term Debt Due Within One Year	34,323	33,760
Employee Deposits for 1967 Stock Purchase Plan	230,724	647,603
Total Current Liabilities	4,774,571	4,479,394
LONG-TERM DEBT:		
5⅞% Mortgage Payable	171,613	202,560
RESERVE:		
For Unusual Risks of Foreign Operations	600,000	600,000
STOCKHOLDERS' EQUITY:		
Common Stock — (1,993,996 shares outstanding in 1972, 1,973,541 shares in 1971)	2,492,495	2,466,926
Additional Paid-In Capital	4,873,492	4,305,082
Retained Earnings	19,232,493	17,870,026
Total Stockholders' Equity	26,598,480	24,642,034
	$32,144,664	$29,923,988

Notes to Financial Statements

YEARS ENDED JUNE 30, 1972 AND 1971

PRINCIPLES OF CONSOLIDATION: The consolidated financial statements include the accounts of The L. S. Starrett Company and all of its subsidiaries (all of which are wholly-owned), namely Rhode Island Tool Company, Inc., The L. S. Starrett Co. of Canada Limited and Herramientas de Precision, S.A. de C.V. (Starrett) (Mexico), for the years ended June 30, Industria e Comercio L. S. Starrett S.A. (Brazil) for the years ended April 30, and The L. S. Starrett Company Limited (Scotland) for the years ended May 31. All significant intercompany items have been eliminated.

The financial statements of the foreign subsidiaries have been translated into U. S. dollars as follows: property, plant and equipment and depreciation thereon at the average rate of exchange in effect at the time of construction or acquisition and all other assets, liabilities, income and expense at the prevailing rates of exchange at June 30, 1972 and 1971. The net underlying assets of the foreign subsidiaries, included in the consolidated balance sheet of the Company at June 30, 1972, amounted to $6,170,000 and $5,400,000 at June 30, 1971.

ENCLOSURE 2 (*concluded*)

Notes to Financial Statements (*Continued*)

INVENTORIES: Inventories are valued on the lower of cost or market basis, cost in general being average cost, except that the principal U. S. materials used in the manufacture of flat stock and saws are valued on the last-in, first-out basis. Inventories at June 30 consisted of:

	1972	1971
Finished Goods	$ 4,500,558	$ 4,541,917
Goods in Process and Finished Parts	6,948,677	6,678,410
Raw Materials and Supplies	2,616,568	2,738,164
	$14,065,803	$13,958,491

PROPERTY, PLANT AND EQUIPMENT: The cost of depreciable property, plant and equipment is depreciated over the estimated useful lives of the assets. Depreciation for U. S. assets is computed generally on the 200% declining balance method and substantially all other assets are depreciated by the straight-line method.

STOCKHOLDERS' EQUITY: 5,000,000 shares of no par common stock are authorized with an assigned value of $1.25 per share. Transactions during the years were as follows:

	Shares	
	1972	1971
Common stock issued:		
Balance, beginning of year	2,201,606	2,194,467
Issuances, 1967 Employees' Stock Purchase Plan	56,209	7,139
Balance, end of year	2,257,815	2,201,606
Treasury stock:		
Balance, beginning of year	228,065	198,252
Purchases	35,754	29,813
Balance, end of year	263,819	228,065
Shares outstanding, end of year	1,993,996	1,973,541

1967 EMPLOYEES' STOCK PURCHASE PLAN: Under the plan, the average purchase price of the optioned stock outstanding at the end of 1972 and 1971 is $14.36 or $13.44, respectively, per share, or 85% of the market price exactly two years from the date the options were granted, whichever is lower. Changes under the plan were as follows:

	200,000 shares available under the Plan		
	On Option	Options Exercised	Unoptioned
Balance, July 1, 1970	80,551	48,779	70,670
Options Granted	14,914	—	(14,914)
Options Exercised	(7,139)	7,139	—
Options Cancelled	(11,970)	—	11,970
Balance, July 1, 1971	76,356	55,918	67,726
Options Granted	50,055	—	(50,055)
Options Exercised	(56,209)	56,209	—
Options Cancelled	(8,715)	—	8,715
Balance, June 30, 1972	61,487	112,127	26,386

PENSION PLANS: The Company has non-contributory pension plans covering substantially all domestic employees and contributory plans covering certain employees of foreign subsidiaries. The total pension expense for 1972 and 1971 was $507,000 and $476,000, respectively. The Company's policy is to fund pension costs accrued.

INVESTMENT CREDIT: Investment credit of $34,000 in 1972 was used to reduce Federal Income tax expense.

ENCLOSURE 3

THE L. S. STARRETT COMPANY

Consolidated Statement of Changes in Financial Position

YEARS ENDED JUNE 30, 1972 AND 1971

	1972	1971
SOURCE OF FUNDS		
Net Income	$3,512,000	$2,652,000
Depreciation	842,000	797,000
Acquisition of The Herman Stone Company	—	6,000
Issue of Stock — Employees' 1967 Stock Purchase Plan	716,000	97,000
Other	187,000	103,000
	5,257,000	3,655,000
USE OF FUNDS		
Payment of Cash Dividends	1,642,000	1,588,000
Plant and Equipment	1,047,000	1,707,000
Purchase of Company Stock	630,000	491,000
Decrease in Long-Term Debt	31,000	34,000
	3,350,000	3,820,000
INCREASE (DECREASE) IN WORKING CAPITAL	$1,907,000	$ (165,000)
Consisting of Changes in:		
Cash	$ (1,000)	$ (123,000)
Short Term Investments	1,341,000	(1,565,000)
Accounts Receivable	755,000	(95,000)
Inventories	107,000	1,562,000
Accounts Payable	(61,000)	75,000
Accrued Taxes	(650,000)	(26,000)
Long-Term Debt Due Within One Year	(1,000)	306,000
Employee Deposits for 1967 Stock Purchase Plan	417,000	(299,000)
	$1,907,000	$ (165,000)

ACCOUNTANTS' REPORT

To the Stockholders and Directors of
The L. S. Starrett Company

One Boston Place
Boston, Massachusetts

We have examined the consolidated balance sheet of The L. S. Starrett Company and subsidiaries as of June 30, 1972 and 1971, and the related statements of income and retained earnings, additional paid-in capital and changes in financial position for the years then ended. Our examination was made in accordance with generally accepted auditing standards, and accordingly included such tests of the accounting records and such other auditing procedures as we considered necessary in the circumstances.

In our opinion, the aforementioned consolidated financial statements present fairly the financial position of The L. S. Starrett Company and subsidiaries at June 30, 1972 and 1971, the results of their operations and the changes in their financial position for the years then ended, in conformity with generally accepted accounting principles applied on a consistent basis.

TOUCHE ROSS & CO.
Certified Public Accountants

August 4, 1972

THE L. S. STARRETT COMPANY

Ten Year Review

EARNINGS

Year Ended June 30	Net Sales	Income Before Fed. Inc. Taxes	Net Income After All Charges	Dividends Paid
1972	$32,383,792	$6,372,048	$3,512,048	$1,642,133
1971	28,704,315	4,899,257	2,652,257	1,587,995
1970	32,691,873	7,713,620	3,822,620	1,579,025
1969	31,965,736	7,639,559	3,668,559	1,374,377
1968	33,130,369	8,285,115	4,190,115	1,208,470
1967	32,865,668	7,888,336	4,138,336	1,163,971
1966	28,079,829	5,766,891	3,010,166	815,854
1965	22,455,280	3,464,176	1,623,923	618,792
1964	19,780,323	2,613,184	1,216,044	738,383
1963	19,352,348	2,774,876	1,187,404	693,044

FINANCIAL STATISTICS

Year Ended June 30	Working Capital	Property, Plant & Equipment Net	Stockholders' Equity	Book Value Per Share*	Common Shares Outstanding*
1972	$19,105,426	$7,757,925	$26,598,480	$13.34	1,993,996
1971	17,198,059	7,687,048	24,642,034	12.49	1,973,541
1970	17,362,510	6,781,189	23,965,255	12.01	1,996,215
1969	15,570,940	5,467,762	20,970,500	10.78	1,944,783
1968	14,568,021	5,495,207	19,979,944	9.97	2,003,112
1967	12,713,034	5,787,109	17,403,911	8.60	2,024,158
1966	10,759,664	5,688,518	14,556,693	7.16	2,032,588
1965	9,761,748	6,045,019	12,561,795	6.12	2,052,370
1964	10,286,168	6,491,732	18,599,770	6.30	2,950,180
1963	9,447,652	6,713,134	18,182,937	6.15	2,958,216

*Based on shares outstanding at the end of each year
adjusted for the 1965 and 1968 two-for-one stock splits.

ENCLOSURE 5

THE L. S. STARRETT COMPANY

Simplified Income Statement

FOR THE YEAR ENDED JUNE 30, 1972

Money paid to us by our customers	$32,384,000
This money was used as follows:	
Wages and salaries to all employees including Social Security Taxes and other benefits	$13,134,000
Cost of materials and supplies used to make the goods sold (steel, forgings, castings, boxes, paper, pipe, wire, cutters, drills, oil, etc.)	7,848,000
Other operating costs (depreciation, electric power, advertising, office expenses, etc.)	3,659,000
Federal Income, State and Local Taxes	4,109,000
Four quarterly dividends paid our stockholders during the year	1,642,000
Common Stock purchased for the treasury	630,000
Retained In The Business to Strengthen And Develop The Company	1,362,000

DIRECTORS

JOHN N. ENGELSTED, Chairman of the Board, O. S. Walker Company, Inc., Worcester, Massachusetts
WALLACE FINDLAY, Executive Vice President and Treasurer of the Company
WALTER W. HASKINS, Retired. Formerly Western Sales Manager of the Company
CARL O. NEWTON, Vice President and Director of Sales of the Company
DOUGLAS R. STARRETT, President of the Company
ROBERT W. STODDARD, Chairman of the Board, Wyman-Gordon Company, Worcester, Massachusetts
ROBERT M. TYLER, Private Investments. Formerly General Manager of Athol Manufacturing, Division of Emhart Corporation
LLOYD B. WARING, Vice President, Kidder Peabody & Co., Incorporated, Boston, Massachusetts
GEORGE B. WEBBER, Vice President in Charge of the Webber Gage Division of the Company

OFFICERS

DOUGLAS R. STARRETT, *President*
WALLACE FINDLAY, *Executive Vice President and Treasurer*
CARL O. NEWTON, *Vice President and Director of Sales*
GEORGE B. WEBBER, *Vice President in Charge of Webber Gage Division*
ROGER MOORE, *Clerk*

SOLE TRANSFER AGENT AND REGISTRAR — The First National Bank of Boston
    Address in Boston — P.O. Box 644, Boston, Massachusetts 02102
    Address in New York — First National Boston Clearance Corporation
                61 Broadway, New York, New York 10005

COUNSEL — Ropes & Gray, Boston, Massachusetts

LISTED — New York Stock Exchange

ENCLOSURE 6
Selected financial and marketing information,
the L. S. Starrett Company, 1963–1972

Item	1963	1964	1965	1966	1967	1968	1969	1970	1971	1972
Cash flow per share ($)	0.65	0.62	1.12	1.81	2.41	2.48	2.28	2.29	1.75	2.18
Earnings per share($)	0.40	0.41	0.79	1.48	2.05	2.09	1.89	1.91	1.34	1.76
Capital spending per share	0.32	0.15	0.19	0.22	0.43	0.27	0.40	0.95	0.87	0.53
Average annual P/E ratio	17.7	18.5	10.1	6.4	6.4	9.7	11.7	8.6	11.8	9.8
Average annual dividend yield (percent)	3.5	3.3	3.5	4.3	4.4	3.0	3.2	4.9	5.1	4.8
Funded debt ($ million)	—	—	5.2	3.2	1.9	0.3	0.3	0.2	0.2	0.2
Net worth ($ million)	18.2	18.6	12.6	14.6	17.4	20.0	21.0	24.0	24.6	26.6
Percent earned on total capital	6.6	6.6	10.6	17.8	21.9	20.8	17.4	15.9	10.7	13.2
Percent earned on net worth	6.6	6.6	12.9	20.7	23.8	21.0	17.5	16.0	10.8	13.2
Percent all dividends to net income	58.0	61.0	38.0	27.0	28.0	29.0	37.0	41.0	60.0	47.0

Note: Sales mix: Precision measuring tools, 75 percent; metal-cutting saws, 20 percent; ground flat steel, 5 percent.
Sales by end user: Metalworking, 65 percent; automotive, 10 percent; aviation, 5 percent; other, 20 percent.
Shareholders: 3,540. Employees own about 50 percent of common; directors own about 7 percent of common. No preferred stock.

ENCLOSURE 7

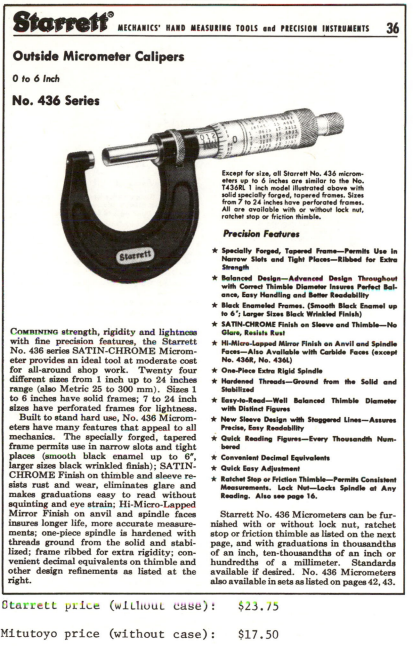

Starrett®
MECHANICS' HAND MEASURING TOOLS and PRECISION INSTRUMENTS   36

Outside Micrometer Calipers

0 to 6 Inch

No. 436 Series

Except for size, all Starrett No. 436 micrometers up to 6 inches are similar to the No. T436RL 1 inch model illustrated above with solid specially forged, tapered frames. Sizes from 7 to 24 inches have perforated frames. All are available with or without lock nut, ratchet stop or friction thimble.

Precision Features

★ Specially Forged, Tapered Frame—Permits Use in Narrow Slots and Tight Places—Ribbed for Extra Strength

★ Balanced Design—Advanced Design Throughout with Correct Thimble Diameter Insures Perfect Balance, Easy Handling and Better Readability

★ Black Enameled Frames. (Smooth Black Enamel up to 6"; Larger Sizes Black Wrinkled Finish)

★ SATIN-CHROME Finish on Sleeve and Thimble—No Glare, Resists Rust

★ Hi-Micro-Lapped Mirror Finish on Anvil and Spindle Faces—Also Available with Carbide Faces (except No. 436R, No. 436L)

★ One-Piece Extra Rigid Spindle

★ Hardened Threads—Ground from the Solid and Stabilized

★ Easy-to-Read—Well Balanced Thimble Diameter with Distinct Figures

★ New Sleeve Design with Staggered Lines—Assures Precise, Easy Readability

★ Quick Reading Figures—Every Thousandth Numbered

★ Convenient Decimal Equivalents

★ Quick Easy Adjustment

★ Ratchet Stop or Friction Thimble—Permits Consistent Measurements. Lock Nut—Locks Spindle at Any Reading. Also see page 16.

COMBINING strength, rigidity and lightness with fine precision features, the Starrett No. 436 series SATIN-CHROME Micrometer provides an ideal tool at moderate cost for all-around shop work. Twenty four different sizes from 1 inch up to 24 inches range (also Metric 25 to 300 mm). Sizes 1 to 6 inches have solid frames; 7 to 24 inch sizes have perforated frames for lightness.

Built to stand hard use, No. 436 Micrometers have many features that appeal to all mechanics. The specially forged, tapered frame permits use in narrow slots and tight places (smooth black enamel up to 6", larger sizes black wrinkled finish); SATIN-CHROME Finish on thimble and sleeve resists rust and wear, eliminates glare and makes graduations easy to read without squinting and eye strain; Hi-Micro-Lapped Mirror Finish on anvil and spindle faces insures longer life, more accurate measurements; one-piece spindle is hardened with threads ground from the solid and stabilized; frame ribbed for extra rigidity; convenient decimal equivalents on thimble and other design refinements as listed at the right.

Starrett No. 436 Micrometers can be furnished with or without lock nut, ratchet stop or friction thimble as listed on the next page, and with graduations in thousandths of an inch, ten-thousandths of an inch or hundredths of a millimeter. Standards available if desired. No. 436 Micrometers also available in sets as listed on pages 42, 43.

Starrett price (without case): $23.75

Mitutoyo price (without case): $17.50

Source: Catalog No. 27 (4th ed.),
        The L.S.Starret Co. and interviews.

ENCLOSURE 8

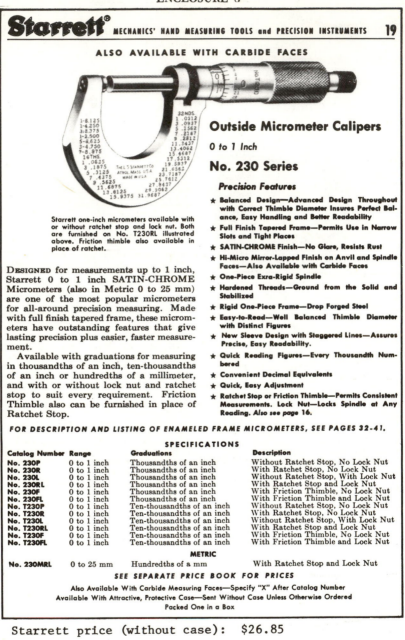

Starrett® MECHANICS' HAND MEASURING TOOLS and PRECISION INSTRUMENTS   **19**

ALSO AVAILABLE WITH CARBIDE FACES

Outside Micrometer Calipers

0 to 1 Inch

No. 230 Series

Precision Features

★ **Balanced Design—Advanced Design Throughout with Correct Thimble Diameter Insures Perfect Balance, Easy Handling and Better Readability**

★ **Full Finish Tapered Frame—Permits Use in Narrow Slots and Tight Places**

★ **SATIN-CHROME Finish—No Glare, Resists Rust**

★ **Hi-Micro Mirror-Lapped Finish on Anvil and Spindle Faces—Also Available with Carbide Faces**

★ **One-Piece Extra-Rigid Spindle**

★ **Hardened Threads—Ground from the Solid and Stabilized**

★ **Rigid One-Piece Frame—Drop Forged Steel**

★ **Easy-to-Read—Well Balanced Thimble Diameter with Distinct Figures**

★ **New Sleeve Design with Staggered Lines—Assures Precise, Easy Readability.**

★ **Quick Reading Figures—Every Thousandth Numbered**

★ **Convenient Decimal Equivalents**

★ **Quick, Easy Adjustment**

★ **Ratchet Stop or Friction Thimble—Permits Consistent Measurements. Lock Nut—Locks Spindle at Any Reading. Also see page 16.**

Starrett one-inch micrometers available with or without ratchet stop and lock nut. Both are furnished on No. T230RL illustrated above. Friction thimble also available in place of ratchet.

DESIGNED for measurements up to 1 inch, Starrett 0 to 1 inch SATIN-CHROME Micrometers (also in Metric 0 to 25 mm) are one of the most popular micrometers for all-around precision measuring. Made with full finish tapered frame, these micrometers have outstanding features that give lasting precision plus easier, faster measurement.

Available with graduations for measuring in thousandths of an inch, ten-thousandths of an inch or hundredths of a millimeter, and with or without lock nut and ratchet stop to suit every requirement. Friction Thimble also can be furnished in place of Ratchet Stop.

FOR DESCRIPTION AND LISTING OF ENAMELED FRAME MICROMETERS, SEE PAGES 32-41.

SPECIFICATIONS

Catalog Number	Range	Graduations	Description
No. 230P	0 to 1 inch	Thousandths of an inch	Without Ratchet Stop, No Lock Nut
No. 230R	0 to 1 inch	Thousandths of an inch	With Ratchet Stop, No Lock Nut
No. 230L	0 to 1 inch	Thousandths of an inch	Without Ratchet Stop, With Lock Nut
No. 230RL	0 to 1 inch	Thousandths of an inch	With Ratchet Stop and Lock Nut
No. 230F	0 to 1 inch	Thousandths of an inch	With Friction Thimble, No Lock Nut
No. 230FL	0 to 1 inch	Thousandths of an inch	With Friction Thimble and Lock Nut
No. T230P	0 to 1 inch	Ten-thousandths of an inch	Without Ratchet Stop, No Lock Nut
No. T230R	0 to 1 inch	Ten-thousandths of an inch	With Ratchet Stop, No Lock Nut
No. T230L	0 to 1 inch	Ten-thousandths of an inch	Without Ratchet Stop, With Lock Nut
No. T230RL	0 to 1 inch	Ten-thousandths of an inch	With Ratchet Stop and Lock Nut
No. T230F	0 to 1 inch	Ten-thousandths of an inch	With Friction Thimble, No Lock Nut
No. T230FL	0 to 1 inch	Ten-thousandths of an inch	With Friction Thimble and Lock Nut
METRIC			
No. 230MRL	0 to 25 mm	Hundredths of a mm	With Ratchet Stop and Lock Nut

SEE SEPARATE PRICE BOOK FOR PRICES

Also Available With Carbide Measuring Faces—Specify "X" After Catalog Number
Available With Attractive, Protective Case—Sent Without Case Unless Otherwise Ordered
Packed One in a Box

Starrett price (without case): $26.85

Mitutoyo price (without case): $20.50

<u>Source</u>: Same as Enclosure 7.

ENCLOSURE 9

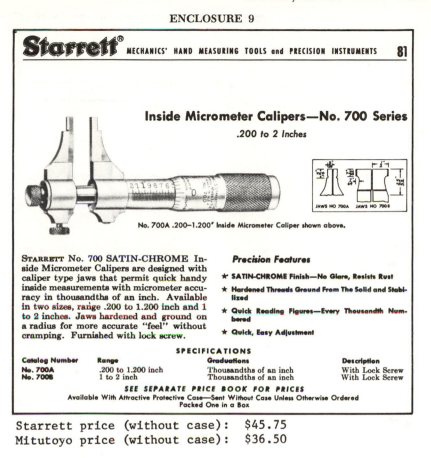

Starrett® MECHANICS' HAND MEASURING TOOLS and PRECISION INSTRUMENTS   **81**

Inside Micrometer Calipers—No. 700 Series

.200 to 2 Inches

JAWS NO 700A   JAWS NO 700B

No. 700A .200–1.200" Inside Micrometer Caliper shown above.

STARRETT No. 700 SATIN-CHROME Inside Micrometer Calipers are designed with caliper type jaws that permit quick handy inside measurements with micrometer accuracy in thousandths of an inch. Available in two sizes, range .200 to 1.200 inch and 1 to 2 inches. Jaws hardened and ground on a radius for more accurate "feel" without cramping. Furnished with lock screw.

Precision Features

★ SATIN-CHROME Finish—No Glare, Resists Rust

★ Hardened Threads Ground From The Solid and Stabilized

★ Quick Reading Figures—Every Thousandth Numbered

★ Quick, Easy Adjustment

SPECIFICATIONS

Catalog Number	Range	Graduations	Description
No. 700A	.200 to 1.200 inch	Thousandths of an inch	With Lock Screw
No. 700B	1 to 2 inch	Thousandths of an inch	With Lock Screw

SEE SEPARATE PRICE BOOK FOR PRICES
Available With Attractive Protective Case—Sent Without Case Unless Otherwise Ordered
Packed One in a Box

Starrett price (without case): $45.75
Mitutoyo price (without case): $36.50

<u>Source</u>: Same as Enclosure 7.

ENCLOSURE 10

---

2   **Starrett®** NEW TOOLS

Dial Caliper (American Made)
No. 120

Direct Reading. Measures Inside, Outside and Depth Dimensions in Thousandths Of An Inch Over Full 6-Inch Range

★ **Knife edge contacts for inside and outside measurements**

★ **Depth rod with cut-out for gaging small grooves and recesses**

★ **Useful for scribing lines parallel to work edges**

★ **One-hand use with thumb-operated fine adjusting roll**

★ **Hardened stainless steel rack for lasting accuracy**

★ **Positive split gear anti-backlash control**

American made in a full six inch range, this four-way dial caliper has knife edge contacts for inside and outside measurements, and a rod connected to its slide for obtaining depth dimensions. The rod contact is cut out to provide a nib for gaging small grooves and recesses.

By placing the front end of the reverse side of the movable jaw against the edge of a work piece, parallel lines may be scribed against the front end of the fixed jaw. The movable jaw is set to the required measurement by setting the bar and dial to the proper reading. After setting, the movable jaw should be clamped in position with its lock screw.

All readings are taken directly from the bar (.100″ graduations) and dial indicator (.001″ graduations—.100″ range per revolution). Measurements may be made with one hand, a thumb roll being provided for fine adjustment. Knurled thumb screws lock the movable jaw and adjustable indicator dial at any setting.

Made of hardened stainless steel, with sharp black bar graduations on a no-glare satin background, No. 120 is built for long service life. It has a hardened, ground and stabilized stainless steel rack with teeth pointing downward to shed foreign matter, and a positive split gear anti-backlash control.

Catalog Number	Size	Bar Graduations	Dial Indicator Graduation	Range Per Revolution	Price Each
No. 120	6″	.100″	.001″	.100″	$45.00
No. 120	Attractive, protective case extra				3.50

Overall Length, Jaws Closed	Bar Dimensions Width	Thickness	Approximate Jaw Depth Outside	Inside
8″	⅝″	⅛″	1½″	¾″

Sent with case unless otherwise ordered

Packed one in a box

Starrett price (without case): $45.00

Mitutyo price (without case): $33.50

SHIN-NIHON TOOLS CO., LTD.

Osaka, Japan

June 2, 1971

Messrs. Armstrong Bros. Tool Co.
Chicago, Illinois
U.S.A.

Dear Sirs:

We know your company very well as the leading manufacturers of tools for industrial machinist use and we have been wanting to write you for long time. We are very interested in establishing business relation with your esteemed firm.

First of all, we wish to explain you about our organization as follows:—

Recently, four leading manufacturers of handtools in Japan, namely Asahi Kinzoku Kogyo Co., Aigo Kogyo Co. Ltd., Mishima Mfg. Co. and Toyo Kiko Mfg. Co. have formed a group name Shin Nihon Tools Group, according to suggestion and financial help of Japanese government. The purpose of their forming group are: 1) Rationalize of distributing system. 2) Level up of production technique. 3) Modernize of equipments by financial help of government.

Before, each manufacturer used to handle sales of their products respectively. It was very uneconomical and inefficient and they could not render good service to the customers. In order to solve such problem, it has been decided to establish a sales organization to handle their products intensively. We are the company who have been established for that purpose under joint investments of the above makers. We are formed by experts of tools and foreign trade, and so we are very sure that we shall be able to render you very quick service.

For your reference. We are sending you a leaflet of our products. As you will find in the leaflet, there are wide range of tools and we are very sure there will be some items which you are interested.

Among all the items mentioned on the leaflet, tools for industrial use, such as Striking face wrench, structural box wrench, hook spanner and spanners for heavy industrial use are very well accepted among the customers. In fact, we have been delivering large amount of these items to American Government according to Federal Specification. We are proud of our quality of these items.

We know well that these lines are of your products, as we have one of your catalogue, and we are very sure you are manufacturing these items.

We have heard that production cost of these items in U.S.A. are very expensive compared with those in Japan. Now we wish to propose you one idea as follows:

If you find the quality of our products quite well which is well compared with your products, and if you find our prices are lower than your production cost of your products. You may pick up our products with your own brand. It will be more profitable for you. If you agree with our above proposal, please write us by return so that we shall send you our quotation and samples.

Thanking you in advance for your favorable reply.

Yours faithfully,

Source: *Congressional Record*, June 28, 1971.

Alloy Steel, Inc.[1]

Mr. Gerald Burmeister, president of Alloy Steel, Inc. (ASI) since mid-1971, is deeply concerned with a question that has plagued ASI for five years. He is wondering whether or not to invest in new technology for refining high-alloy-content metals which would replace or supplement his present process. "Electro-slag remelting (ESR) looks appealing but we have so much vacuum-arc remelting (VAR) capacity that we're just not sure if ESR is right for us. This is a very important decision; it will affect our operations for many years," Mr. Burmeister stated.

Electro-slag remelting (ESR)

ESR is a process used mainly for refining high-alloy-content metals to meet stringent specifications. Developed in the 1930s by Robert Hopkins, an American inventor, the process has only recently become popular in the U.S. Present worldwide ESR capacity exceeds 500,000 net tons per year with a major portion found in the USSR. A 1970 survey showed the following distribution:

[1] This case was prepared by James H. Leonhard, Judith M. Brown, and Professor James P. Baughman as the basis for class discussion and is not intended to illustrate either effective or ineffective handling of an administrative situation.

Country	Capacity (net tons/year)
USSR.	400,000
U.S.	40,000
U.K.	26,000
Sweden.	18,000
W. Germany	14,000
Austria	8,000
France	8,000
Japan	2,000
Total.	510,000

It should be noted that the USSR uses ESR for "alloy steels" as well as high-alloy steels, whereas only the latter are produced by ESR or VAR (vacuum-arc remelting) in the United States with VAR being by far the more popular. Exhibit 1 lists some of the major domestic users of ESR and presents their capacities and products.

Present U.S. capacity stands at about 63,000 net tons, but no recent figures for the other countries are available. It is predicted that by the mid-70s the U.S. capacity will approach 400,000 net tons while the USSR will increase to 600,000 with Western Europe and Japan increasing capacity by tenfold.

ESR and VAR are similar processes but have some important differences. In both cases electric current flows through a previously produced ingot called the electrode and the heat generated causes the electrode to melt. The molten droplets fall through a slag (ESR) or a vacuum (VAR) and are solidified below in a copper mold. The purpose of both processes is the removal of impurities (dissolved gases and nonmetallic particles) and the control of grain size and grain distribution. This refining process is necessary in the production of many high-alloy steels made for critical applications.

The use of a molten pool (slag) rather than a vacuum changes the final product significantly according to ESR users. Some of the claimed advantages over VAR are listed below:

1. Increased yields only 1 to 2 percent loss with ESR versus 5 to 6 percent for VAR.
2. Due to the molten interface with the slag and the walls, the surface of ESR-produced ingots is smoother than the VAR product.
3. The ESR ingot solidifies more slowly and more uniformly, thereby creating a superior thermal balance and permitting better grain-size control. This eliminates VAR defects and is important for control of mechanical properties.
4. While the VAR electrode must be the exact chemical composition of the desired final ingot, the ESR process allows limited alloy additions during remelt. Thus, ESR has more flexibility in the final product.

5. Fewer and better-dispersed impurities remain with ESR.
6. ESR is a simpler process to use.
7. It is claimed that ESR is less expensive than VAR. This is discussed below.

Costs

While there are differences of opinion, everyone in the field agrees that ESR is no more expensive to operate than VAR, and most assert that it is less expensive. For example the Soviets claim that it is twice as expensive to produce a VAR product of the same quality.

The capital costs of an ESR furnace are undoubtedly less. Consarc, a manufacturer of both ESR and VAR units, reports a cost of $192,000 for a 24-inch ESR furnace versus $240,000 for the same size VAR furnace. Carpenter Technology has recently installed two 25-ton ESR units (3000 ton/year capacity) at a cost of $600,000.

Production costs are more difficult to gauge, but Consarc reports savings of about $2.00 per ton for ESR over VAR (Exhibit 2) and Boehler-Darvo, another ESR manufacturer, estimates a $20 per ton savings. While Carpenter Technology has not divulged its production costs, the firm has stated that ESR-produced high-purity tool and die steels will be marketed at no premium over their present VAR products, indicating expected savings with ESR. Tests at Carpenter Technology have also shown ESR products to be superior to VAR with respect to more uniform structure and fewer and better dispersion of impurities.

Company performance and history

After discussion of the ESR question, Mr. Burmeister was asked by the casewriter to comment on his company's performance in the past three years. He began:

> Sure our performance has been poor, especially in 1971 when we lost $2.3 million, but we've done all we could in reducing costs. Our organizational and operational changes were significant, but no one else seems to be doing their part. The cost of labor and materials is rising, but that productivity figure is no better than it was eight years ago and prices have not kept pace either. ASI has always been in the forefront of technology in the production of tools steels and other high alloy steels. We've got the most modern equipment but with the depressed markets of recent years causing low capacity utilization, we just can't take advantage of it. Government, Business, and Labor must work together for the common good if our industry is to continue to survive.

Since its 1915 founding in Lewisburg, Pennsylvania, ASI has specialized in tool steels and other high-alloy-content steels produced in various forms such as ingots, billets, bars, and discs. The company has continued to grow throughout its history and presently includes two domestic and one foreign subsidiary as well as eleven affiliates and licencees in eight countries. While warehouses and sales offices are maintained in 12 major U.S. cities, domestic manufacturing is concentrated in Lewisburg.

Present equipment at Lewisburg includes three electric furnaces, two vacuum induction furnaces having capacities of 2000 pounds and 60,000 pounds, eight vacuum-arc remelt (VAR) furnaces and numerous rolling mills, hammers, and presses. ASI is capable of producing many types of high alloy content ingots as well as finished products. Most of their equipment was installed between 1956 and 1971 when ASI carried out a $40 million expansion program to meet predicted sales of $75–80 million in 1971. Unfortunately, actual 1971 sales were only $41.6 million, thus leaving ASI with much excess capacity. For instance, in 1967 the newly completed melt shop was running at 60–70 percent capacity with sales of $50 million. Exhibit 3 and 4 are ASI's recent income statements and balance sheets. Exhibit 5 summarizes the past ten years of operation.

Exhibit 6 places ASI in the total steel industry with less than 0.02 percent of total steel shipments. However, net sales represent 0.21 percent of total steel revenues due to the high price of the company's products. The illustration below describes ASI's position with respect to the rest of the steel industry.

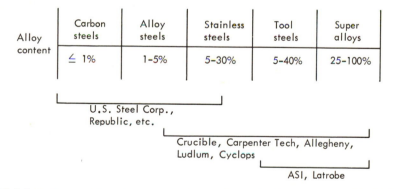

Alloy content	Carbon steels	Alloy steels	Stainless steels	Tool steels	Super alloys
	≤ 1%	1–5%	5–30%	5–40%	25–100%

U.S. Steel Corp., Republic, etc.

Crucible, Carpenter Tech, Allegheny, Ludlum, Cyclops

ASI, Latrobe

Exhibit 7 provides forecasts of total steel shipments in 1985. This indicates a continued rising demand for steel, and there is no reason to believe specialty steel will not follow a similar trend.

The specialty steel industry

Specialty steel, which encompasses stainless steels and tool steels, constitutes only about 1 percent of total net steel industry shipments in the United States[2] but it accounts for approximately 7 percent of

---

[2] Total net industry shipments = 87 million tons in 1971.

total steel industry dollar sales. Historically tool steels have represented 10–11 percent of specialty steel shipments.

Specialty steels are designed and produced for use in extreme environments requiring exceptional hardness, toughness, tensile strength, heat, corrosion, or abrasion resistance. They contain substantial amounts of costly alloys such as chromium, nickel, molybdenum, or cobalt. Frequently products are made to order and are generally sold by the pound rather than by the ton.

The particular properties required demand advanced technology, making specialty steels difficult and expensive to manufacture. Sophisticated equipment such as vacuum-arc furnaces make this a moderately capital-intensive industry. Additionally the cost of alloying materials has continued to rise and the labor necessary to produce a ton of specialty steel can be as much as 20 times the amount needed for a ton of carbon steel.

The industry is composed largely of comparatively small companies with major carbon steel producers accounting for no more than one third of specialty steel shipments. Changes in the volume of production quickly affect profits in these small companies. This is a result of high fixed costs, characteristic of the industry, and the accompanying need to maintain high operating rates to minimize production costs.

Another factor affecting plant efficiency is the percent yield from raw steel. Yield is determined by dividing shipments by production and runs about 70 percent for carbon steel. Due to more complex processing, specialty steel yields are significantly lower with stainless about 60 percent and tool steels 55–60 percent.

Market prices of alloy steels have risen rapidly in the past five years. Exhibit 8 is representative of the price increases. Due to the small size of the industry relative to carbon steel, price increases are not scrutinized by the government, giving specialty steel producers some freedom to match costs and revenues. Additionally customers are usually more concerned with quality and service than with price.

Markets

The bulk of tool and alloy steels are purchased by two industries, aerospace and machine tool. Both of these industries have been depressed in the last two years but indications are that they are recovering somewhat. Aerospace, hurt by reduced space spending, cancellation of the SST, and the slowdown in the Viet Nam war will get a boost from the Space Shuttle and the new U.S.–Soviet joint space efforts. The table below shows the aircraft parts industry and Exhibit 9 illustrates projected trends to 1980 in the machine tool industry.

Forecasts of value of shipments for selected industries
($ millions)

Industry	1971 (actual)	1972	1975	1980
Tools and dies.	$2,010	$2,200	$2,100	$2,700
Aircraft equipment	6,800	6,800	6,100	5,800

Domestic competition

Domestic producers of specialty steel range in size from Bethlehem Steel to J. L. Jessup. Exhibit 10 provides a comparison of these companies. Of course figures for the larger corporations include products other than specialty steel and cannot be directly compared. Competition among domestic producers is mainly on the basis of quality and service. Prices are equal for the same products, thus a company that can produce a high-quality item and provide good service should not suffer from domestic competition.

Foreign imports

A major problem facing specialty steelmen is the rising percentage of apparent domestic consumption[3] captured by foreign imports. Imported specialty steels, competing mainly on price differentials, captured nearly 22 percent of apparent consumption in 1971. Exhibits 11 and 12 detail the historic trends of imports, exports, and shipments for *tool steel* and show the rising percentage imports have captured. The sources of the imports are broken down in Exhibits 13 and 14 for high-speed tool steel and alloy tool steel with Sweden alone accounting for over 30 percent of tool steel imports in 1971.

Mr. Burmeister expressed his view of the import situation in the following comment:

> We feel our products can compete with anyone's, but foreign producers using unfair trade practices have hurt sales tremendously in the past three years and are a major problem for us. What can you do when they don't submit a dollar bid but merely state that their price will be 20 percent below the lowest domestic bid? How can we compete with that? We're also experiencing indirect competition from imported manufactured goods which have reduced our customers' requirements for ASI's products. I don't know when the government is going to wake up, but if they don't do something soon the United States will

---

[3] Apparent consumption = Industry shipments + Imports − Exports.

be dependent on foreigners for these high technology steels, which would dangerously threaten our national security. The government has only irritated our problems with their voluntary steel quota plan; our industry must be protected by strictly imposed quotas and tariffs to bring foreign imports back into fair competition. The government has the ultimate responsibility for stemming the import tide.

Foreign producers have been able to increase their exports of specialty steel to the United States for a variety of reasons. Once their level of technology caught up with the United States and the quality of their goods was equal, the foreign producers were able to take advantage of the lower cost of labor they enjoy. Additionally, most other countries aid their exporting companies through financial aid, tax incentives, encouragement of export cartels, and similar devices, none of which are practiced in the United States. Finally, duties and tariffs on U.S. goods are notably higher than the United States imposes on its imports, thus exacerbating the U.S. trade deficit in specialty steel.

Voluntary restraint programs

By 1968, when imports of all steel products had reached almost 17 percent of apparent consumption, domestic steelmen were in an uproar. They demanded fixed quotas on all steel imports. The U.S. government was unwilling to impose quotas and instead negotiated voluntary quotas with Japan and the European Economic Community (EEC), the major sources of imports. This agreement, known as the Voluntary Restraint Program (VRP), ran three years and amounted to letters of intent in which both parties agreed to limit tonnage exported to the United States to 5.75 million tons in 1969 and to allow no more than a 5 percent growth in exports per year. Additionally, they asserted their intention to "try to maintain" the same product mix as in the past.

While imports of all steel products did in fact decline from 17,900,000 tons in 1968 to 14,034,000 tons in 1969, the product mix was not maintained. Specialty steel imports (stainless and tool steel) jumped from 189,193 tons to 197,477 tons. Foreign producers had thus minimized the expected decline in dollar sales by exporting higher-priced specialty steels (while the quantity of imports declined by 22 percent the value only fell 12 percent). This, combined with the fact that four of the major producers of tool steel (Sweden, Canada, Austria, and the United Kingdom) did not sign the agreement, caused domestic producers like ASI to suffer more than they had prior to 1968.

A new agreement was negotiated in the spring of 1972 to run for three years. Exhibit 15 illustrates the limits of the agreement. Some important differences exist between this new VRP and the first one.

1. The United Kingdom sent a letter of intent in addition to Japan and the EEC.
2. Japan agreed to limit annual growth in exports to 2.5 percent in 1973 and 1974.
3. The EEC and the United Kingdom will limit export growth to 1 percent in 1973 and 2.5 percent in 1974.
4. Specific limits were placed on specialty steel imports as detailed in Exhibit 15.
5. The signer agreed to try to maintain product mix.

Unfortunately for specialty producers some key problems remain, such as the fact that Sweden, Canada, and Austria, who accounted for 60 percent of 1971 tool steel imports, were still not included. Also, there is no restriction on third-party imports, for example, Japan to Canada to the United States. Further, the program is still purely voluntary, especially in regard to product mix. Another problem is that the higher-priced tool steel is included under "alloy steel" leaving open the possibility that exporters will switch to these more profitable items. And finally, no detailed breakdown was made of the various grades of specialty steel.

In late May 1972, the State Department sent notification to Sweden of its intention to negotiate and include that country in the VRP. To date Sweden has not replied, but indications are that it will resist any curbs on its exports.

A further development threatens to delay or invalidate the entire program. The Consumers Union has filed a lawsuit charging that the VRP violates the Sherman Antitrust Act and names the Secretary of State, U.S. Steel Corporation, the American Iron and Steel Institute, and leading Japanese and European companies as defendents. Consumers Union claims that customers cannot buy as much foreign steel as they want and that U.S. mills can "charge artificially high prices" as a result. The Justice Department has warned that VRP is not immune from antitrust since the Justice Department was not involved in the negotiations.

Meanwhile, specialty steel producers continue to lobby for imposed quotas and higher tariffs as the only effective way to save the domestic industry. The U.S. government is resisting this solution, fearing it would touch off retaliatory measures by foreign governments on U.S. exports.

A professor at a well-known eastern business school was heard to remark, "It sure looks like the government is selling out the specialty steelmen to save the large carbon steel producers. It makes sense when you compare the size of the industries. Why should the government, or the major steel companies for that matter, be concerned about 1 percent of the industry when sacrificing it will save the big boys?"

Other factors affecting ASI performance

In addition to depressed markets and import competition, ASI in recent years has been squeezed by rising labor and materials costs without complementary price and productivity increases. Exhibits 16, 17, and 18 illustrate this dilemma. ASI's employment costs and materials costs have risen faster than the rest of the steel industry, but neither productivity nor prices has followed suit. Thus, while the whole steel industry has suffered somewhat, ASI has been more severely harmed. Mr. Burmeister has thus far been unable to find a solution to this set of problems.

EXHIBIT 1
Domestic ESR capacity°

Company	Number of furnaces	Annual capacity (net tons)	Metals produced
1. Cabot Corporation	4	14,000	Cobalt-, nickel-, and iron-based superalloys; corrosion resistant alloys
2. Carpenter Technology	4	12,000	Tool and die steels
3. Cyclops Corporation	1	1,750	Specialty steels
4. Cybermetals.	2	1,250	High-strength aircraft, stainless and alloys, tool steels
5. International Nickel Co. (Huntington Alloy Products Division)	1	4,500	Nickel and nickel-base alloys
6. Simonds Steel.	2	8,500	High-speed tool and die steels, stainless
Total	14	42,000	

Note: * Total U.S. capacity is 47,075 tons.

EXHIBIT 2
Annual cost comparison—VAR and ESR
(based on twin, 24-in. furnace for each process)

Unit cost	VAR* ($/ton)	ESR† ($/ton)
1. Direct labor	$17.12	$13.71
2. Manufacturing overhead (140 percent of direct labor)	24.00	19.20
3. Power costs (1.2¢/week)	8.39	12.13
4. Cooling water cost	1.25	1.17
5. Depreciation (10-year straight line based on installed cost)‡	17.12	11.96
6. Building depreciation (20-year straight line)§	0.89	0.71
7. Slag cost	–	8.00
Total (above material cost)	$68.77	$66.88

* VAR based on 2800-ton production.
† ESR based on 3500-ton production.
‡ VAR installed cost = 480,000; ESR = 384,000.
§ Assumes 1000 sq. ft./furnace at $25/sq. ft. Capital cost = $50,000.

EXHIBIT 3
ALLOY STEEL, INC.
Income statements (1970–71)

	1971	1970
Net sales	$49,234,939	$53,698,081
Other income	511,862	564,548
Equity in affiliated companies	184,322	228,442
Total	$49,931,123	$54,491,071
Costs and Expenses:		
Cost of sales	$39,732,369	$41,580,351
Selling and administrative	7,492,557	7,550,845
Depreciation	2,113,749	2,197,693
Pensions	1,697,886	1,679,059
Taxes (other than income)	1,364,498	1,420,003
Interest	1,272,611	1,288,359
Sundry–Net	20,182	17,874
Total	$53,693,852	$55,734,190
Loss before taxes and extraordinary gains	$ (3,762,729)	$ (1,243,119)
Taxes on Income:		
Federal: Current	(748,000)	(1,393,235)
Deferred		471,235
State and local	(18,500)	3,560
Total	$ (766,500)	$ (918,440)
Loss before extraordinary gains	(2,996,229)	(324,679)
Extraordinary gains	238,202	215,877
Net Loss	$ (2,758,027)	$ (108,802)
Loss per share (based on average number of shares outstanding)		
Before extraordinary gains	($2.10)	($.23)
Extraordinary gains	.17	.15
Net Loss	($1.93)	($.08)

EXHIBIT 4
ALLOY STEEL, INC.
Balance sheets

	1971	1970
Assets:		
Cash	$ 5,723,277	$ 5,004,704
Note and accounts receivable	6,391,865	6,675,583
Estimated Federal Income Taxes recoverable	875,000	1,310,000
Inventories (LIFO)		
Finished goods	4,280,677	4,383,695
Work in process.	5,584,039	5,862,066
Raw materials and supplies	2,118,219	2,230,761
Total Inventories.	$11,982,935	$12,476,522
Prepaid expenses	945,885	1,182,996
Total Current Assets	$25,918,962	$26,649,805
Investments:		
Affiliated companies, at equity	1,722,378	1,431,979
Subsidiary not consolidated.	–	153,792
Other at cost	59,261	173,327
Total Investments	$ 1,781,639	$ 1,759,098
Property, at cost:		
Land	616,107	628,387
Buildings and improvements	8,249,534	8,501,713
Machinery and equipment.	40,292,319	39,724,223
Construction in process	361,392	240,647
Total.	$49,519,352	$49,094,970
Less depreciation and amortization.	20,914,949	18,921,052
Net property	28,604,403	30,173,918
Cash surrender value of life insurance	664,099	605,981
Deferred charges	754,425	1,312,779
Total Assets.	$57,723,528	$60,501,581
Liabilities:		
Current Liabilities:		
Current maturities on long-term debt.	$ 1,500,000	$ 1,500,000
6 percent notes payable—banks	1,850,000	–
Accounts payable	4,817,780	4,790,044
Salaries and wages.	3,478,861	3,804,897
Deferred Income Taxes.	316,156	316,156
Other taxes	133,559	205,285
Total Current Liabilities.	$12,096,356	$10,616,382
Long-Term Debt (less current maturities):		
6⅞ percent notes payable—insurance companies (due		
1973–1983)	14,950,000	16,350,000
6 percent note payable—bank (due 1973–1978).	515,000	615,000
Total Long-Term Debt	$15,465,000	$16,965,000
Deferred Income Taxes.	2,363,404	2,363,404
Shareholder's Equity:		
Preferred stock—400,000 shares authorized, $10 par value—		
none issued	–	–
Common stock—authorized 4,750,000 par value $2.50—		
issued and outstanding 1970 and 1972, 1,424,039	3,560,598	3,560,598
Capital surplus	6,708,744	6,708,744
Retained earnings	17,529,426	20,287,453
Total Equity	$27,798,768	$30,556,795
Total Liabilities and Equity.	$57,723,528	$60,501,581

EXHIBIT 5

Summary

	1971	1970	1969	1968	1967	1966	1965	1964	1963	1962
Net sales*	49,234	53,698	63,862	54,751	60,402	61,689	51,072	41,475	38,321	38,197
Net income* (loss)	(2,758)	(109)	1,084	2,910	3,098	3,758	2,601	1,814	2,093	2,335
Net income per share (loss)	(1.93)	(0.08)	.76	2.06	2.21	2.71	1.95	1.33	1.53	1.73
Cash dividends*		213	853	845	836	1,040	830	820	816	674
Net working capital*	13,823	16,033	16,500	17,160	14,731	1,322	11,588	10,763	13,010	10,641
Current ratio	2.2	2.5	2.6	2.5	2.5	2.2	2.3	2.9	3.3	2.8
Net worth (equity)*	27,799	30,557	30,879	30,428	28,129	25,523	22,805	20,840	19,896	18,330
Capital expenditures*	462	422	3,483	10,734	6,132	2,080	1,753	3,347	6,078	2,589
Depreciation*	2,114	2,198	2,133	1,593	1,457	1,580	1,425	1,424	1,043	832
No. shares outstanding*	1,424	1,424	1,424	1,413	1,400	1,382	1,382	1,368	1,368	1,347
No. employees	2,170	2,039	2,500	2,785	2,438	2,549	2,345	2,118	2,104	2,093

* Note: = 000 omitted.

EXHIBIT 6
Shipments

Year	Shipments (net tons)	Percent of tool steel	Percent of total steel shipments
1971	19,890	25.523	0.0228
1970	23,036	26.091	0.0254
1969	30,974	27.192	0.0330
1968	28,601	26.874	0.0312
1967	31,760	28.812	0.0378
1966	34,792	28.615	0.0386
1965	28,991	24.498	0.0313
1964	22,683	22.183	0.0268

EXHIBIT 7
Forecasted steel shipments

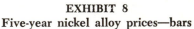

Year	Forecast (total steel shipments in net million tons)
1972	95
1975	103–107
1980	110–118
1985	115–130

Source: *33 Magazine*

EXHIBIT 8
Five-year nickel alloy prices—bars

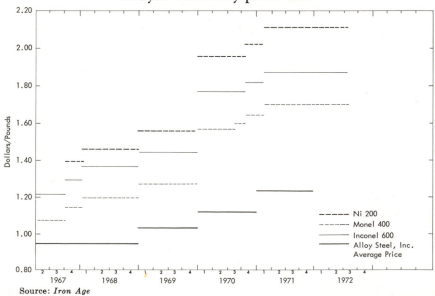

Source: *Iron Age*

EXHIBIT 9
Net new machine tool orders

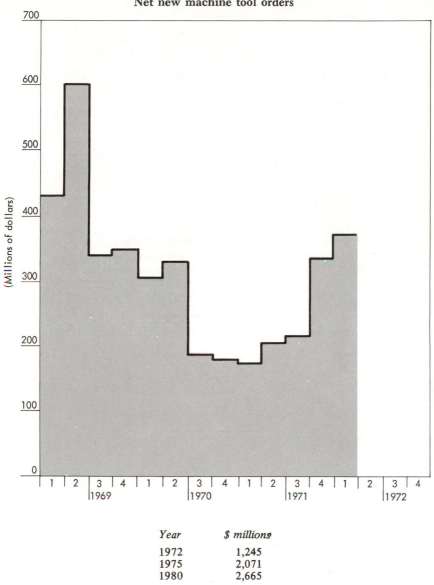

Year	$ millions
1972	1,245
1975	2,071
1980	2,665

EXHIBIT 10
Specialty steel producers—1971 results

Company	Steel shipments (net tons)	Net sales ($ millions)	Net income ($ millions)
Bethlehem Steel.	12,577,000	$2,993.30	139.200
Allegheny-Ludlum	365,954	487.30	1.419
Cyclops Corporation	1,251,483	338.80	4.153
Carpenter Technology	N.A.*	149.90	4.055
Latrobe	16,790	41.58	(0.777)
Columbia	N.A.		
J. L. Jessup	N.A.		
ASI	19,890	49.20	(2.758)

Note: * N.A. = not available.

EXHIBIT 11
U.S. foreign trade in total tool steel
(high-speed and alloy tool steel—net tons)

Year	Net industry shipments	Imports	Exports
1971	78,010	12,759	3,617
1970	88,337	17,635	2,159
1969	113,921	15,253	2,725
1968	106,366	15,162	1,606
1967	109,929	18,859	1,639
1966	121,345	17,614	1,775
1965	118,242	12,954	1,652
1964	102,379	9,081	2,275

EXHIBIT 12
U.S. foreign trade in tool steel
(high-speed and alloy tool steel)

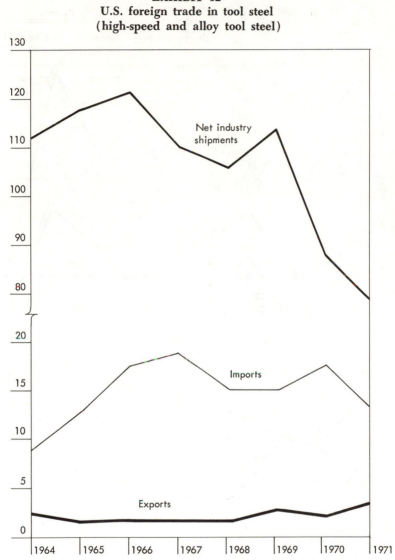

EXHIBIT 13
U.S. imports of high-speed tool steel by country of origin

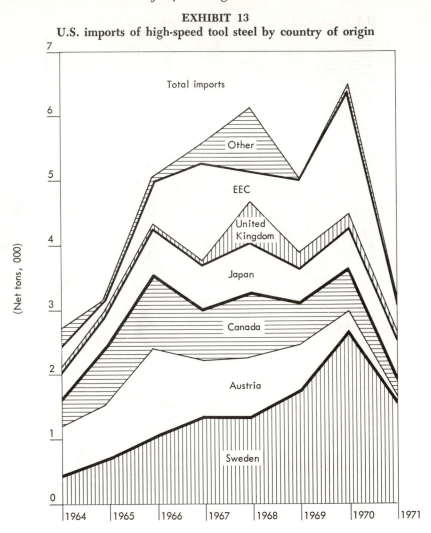

EXHIBIT 14
U.S. imports of alloy tool steel by country of origin

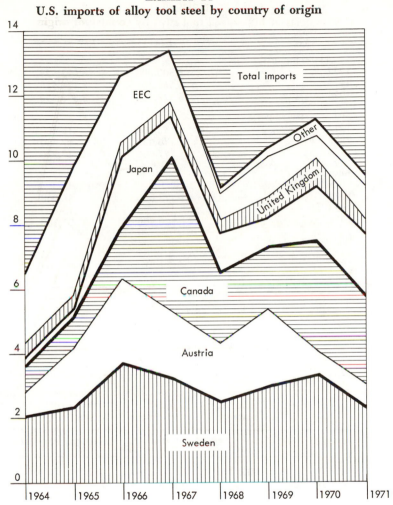

EXHIBIT 15
1972 VRP agreements—detailed limits
(net tons)

Year	Japan	EEC and U.K.
Total steel imports		
1972	6,500,000	8,093,573
1973	6,662,500	8,174,510
1974	6,829,000	8,378,810
Stainless steel imports		
1972	82,400	18,600
1973	76,000	17,430
1974	77,900	17,930
Alloy steels (includes tool steels)		
1972	172,000	86,000
1973	156,700	75,400
1974	160,500	77,300
High-speed steel		
1972	985	132
1973	1,010	109
1974	1,035	111

EXHIBIT 16
Indexes of revenue elements
(1964 = 100)

Year	Average prices/ton Industry	ASI	Employment costs/ton Industry	ASI	Materials, supplies, and services/ton Industry	ASI	Shipments/ employee (tons/emp.) Industry	ASI	Shipments/ employee (1964 = 100) Industry	ASI
1964	100.0	100.0	100.0	100.0	100.0	100.0	153.5	10.730	100.0	100.
1965	100.0	96.6	97.4	88.9	103.3	99.4	158.8	12.336	103.4	115.
1966	105.9	97.2	105.7	87.8	110.6	98.6	156.2	13.627	101.8	127.
1967	104.3	104.2	110.2	105.0	105.6	101.9	150.8	12.951	98.2	120.
1968	107.4	105.0	108.0	106.4	117.7	107.5	166.5	10.650	108.4	99.
1969	111.5	113.1	114.2	119.5	121.0	117.8	172.4	12.376	112.2	115.
1970	113.0	126.8	120.0	132.0	129.8	146.0	170.9	11.301	111.2	105.
1971	123.3	135.5	125.8	150.8	144.0	159.5	178.8	9.164	116.3	85.

EXHIBIT 17
Estimates of unit cost and revenue elements alloy steel inc. 1964–1971
($/ton shipped)

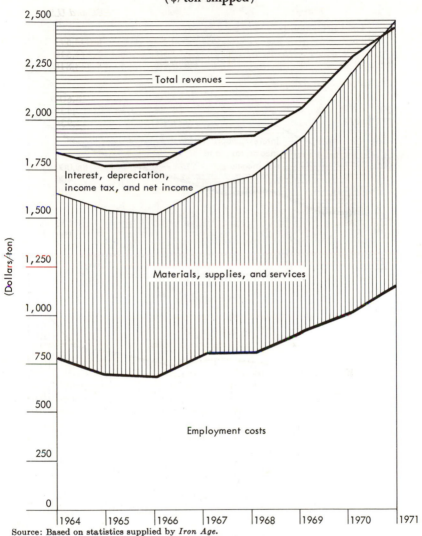

Source: Based on statistics supplied by *Iron Age*.

EXHIBIT 18
Estimates of unit cost and revenue elements total steel industry 1964–1971
($/ton shipped)

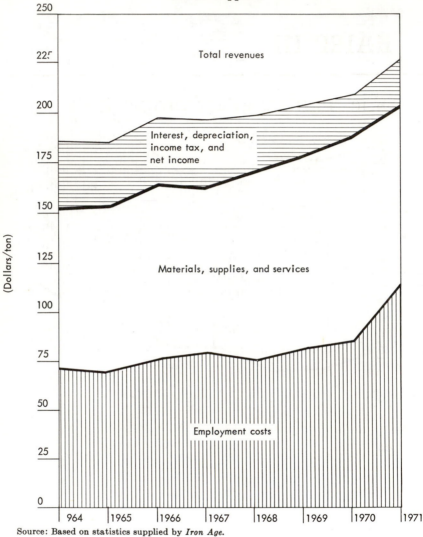

Source: Based on statistics supplied by *Iron Age*.

PART III

The regulation of competition

United States *v.* Aluminum Company of America

In 1937 the government brought suit to have the Aluminum Company of America (Alcoa) dissolved on the ground primarily that it had a monopoly in the manufacture and sale of virgin aluminum ingot. This antitrust action was not the first in which Alcoa had been involved. In 1912 the government had obtained a consent decree that forced Alcoa to dissolve certain contracts in restraint of trade between it and other companies, and that further enjoined Alcoa from entering into any agreements which would result in regulated prices on finished aluminum products.

The suit was tried by Judge Francis G. Caffey in the United States District Court for the Southern District of New York. The proceedings continued from 1938 to 1941 and a judgment favoring Alcoa was entered in 1942.

The case was appealed by the government but the Supreme Court refused to hear it since less than six of the judges considered themselves qualified to pass impartial judgment. Instead, the Supreme Court referred the case to the Second Circuit Court of Appeals which reversed the previous decision in favor of the company. The decision of the Second Circuit Court written by Judge Learned Hand stands out as a significant development in the interpretation of antitrust legislation.

The basis of many previous decisions under the Sherman Act had been Section 1, which proscribed contracts, combinations, and conspiracies in restraint of trade. Section 2, which dealt with monopolizing and attempts to monopolize, had been invoked far less frequently in judicial proceedings, and its use in this instance accounts to a great extent for the importance of the Alcoa case.

UNITED STATES v. ALUMINUM COMPANY OF AMERICA et al.[1]
CIRCUIT COURT OF APPEALS, SECOND CIRCUIT

Excerpts from decision of Judge Learned Hand

Alcoa's monopoly of virgin ingot

Alcoa is a corporation, organized under the laws of Pennsylvania on September 18, 1888; its original name, Pittsburgh Reduction Company, was changed to its present one on January 1, 1907. It has always been engaged in the production and sale of ingot aluminum, and since 1895 also in the fabrication of the metal into many finished and semifinished articles. It has proliferated into a great number of subsidiaries, created at various times between the years 1900 and 1929, as the business expanded. . . . Aluminum was isolated as a metal more than a century ago, but not until about 1886 did it become commercially practicable to eliminate the oxygen, so that it could be exploited industrially. One, Hall, discovered a process by which this could be done in that year, and got a patent on April 2, 1889, which he assigned to Alcoa, which thus secured a legal monopoly of the manufacture of the pure aluminum until April 2, 1906, when this patent expired. Meanwhile Bradley had invented a process by which the smelting could be carried on without the use of external heat, as had theretofore been thought necessary, and for this improvement he too got a patent on February 2, 1892. Bradley's improvement resulted in great economy in manufacture, so that, although after April 2, 1906, anyone could manufacture aluminum by the Hall process, for practical purposes no one could compete with Bradley or with his licensees until February 2, 1909, when Bradley's patent also expired. On October 31, 1903, Alcoa and the assignee of the Bradley patent entered into a contract by which Alcoa was granted an exclusive license under that patent. . . . Thus until February 2, 1909, Alcoa had either a monopoly of the manufacture of virgin aluminum ingot, or the monopoly of a process which eliminated all competition.

. . . Alcoa—either itself or by a subsidiary—also entered into four successive cartels with foreign manufacturers of aluminum by which, in exchange for certain limitations upon its import into foreign countries, it secured covenant from the foreign producers, either not to import into the United States at all, or to do so under restrictions, which in some cases involved the fixing of prices. These cartels and restrictive covenants and certain other practices were the subject of a suit filed by the United States against Alcoa on May 16, 1912, in which a decree was entered by consent on June 7, 1912, declaring several of these covenants unlawful and enjoining their performance; and also declaring invalid other restrictive covenants. . . .

---

[1] 148F-2J 416 (1945), reviewing 44 F. Supp. 97.

None of the foregoing facts are in dispute and the most important question in the case is whether the monopoly in Alcoa's production of virgin ingot, secured by the two patents until 1909, and in part perpetuated between 1909 and 1912 by the unlawful practices, forbidden by the decree of 1912, continued for the ensuing twenty-eight years; and whether, if it did, it was unlawful under Section 2 of the Sherman Act. It is undisputed that throughout this period Alcoa continued to be the single producer of virgin ingot in the United States; and the plaintiff (government) argues that this without more was enough to make it an unlawful monopoly. It also takes an alternative position: that in any event during this period Alcoa consistently pursued unlawful exclusionary practices, which made its dominant position certainly unlawful, even though it would not have been, had it been retained only by natural growth. Finally, it asserts that many of these practices were of themselves unlawful, as contracts in restraint of trade under Section 1 of the Act. Alcoa's position is that the fact that it alone continued to make virgin ingot in this country did not, and does not, give it a monopoly of the market; that it was always subject to the competition of imported virgin ingot, and of what is called secondary ingot; and that even if it had not been, its monopoly would not have been retained by unlawful means, but would have been the result of a growth which the Act does not forbid, even when it results in a monopoly. We shall first consider the amount and character of this competition; next, how far it established a monopoly; and finally, if it did, whether that monopoly was unlawful under Section 2 of the Act.

From 1902 onward until 1928 Alcoa was making ingot in Canada through a wholly owned subsidiary; so much of this as it imported into the United States it is proper to include with what it produced here. In the year 1912 the sum of these two items represented nearly ninety-one per cent of the total amount of virgin ingot available for sale in this country. This percentage varied year by year up to and including 1938: in 1913 it was about seventy-two per cent; in 1921 about sixty-eight per cent; in 1922 about seventy-two; with these exceptions it was always over eighty per cent of the total and for the last five years 1934–1938 inclusive it averaged over ninety per cent. The effect of such a proportion of the production upon the market we reserve for the time being, for it will be necessary first to consider the nature and uses of secondary ingot, the name by which the industry knows ingot made from aluminum scrap. This is of two sorts, though for our purposes it is not important to distinguish between them. One of these is the clippings and trimmings of sheet aluminum, when patterns are cut out of it, as a suit is cut from a bolt of cloth. The chemical composition of these is obviously the same as that of the sheet from which they come; and, although they are likely to accumulate dust or other dirt in the factory, this may be removed by well known processes. If a record of the original composition of the sheet has been preserved, this scrap may be remelted into new ingot, and used again for the same purpose. . . . Nevertheless, there is an appreciable sales resistance even to this kind of scrap, and for some uses (airplanes and cables among them), fabricators absolutely insist upon virgin: just why is not altogether clear. The other source of scrap is aluminum which has once been fabricated and the article, after being used, is discarded and sent to the junk heap; as for example, cooking utensils, like kettles and pans, and the pistons or crank cases of motorcars. These are made with a substantial alloy and to restore the metal to its original purity costs more than it is worth. However, if the alloy is known both in quality and amount, scrap, when remelted, can be used again for the same purpose as before. In spite of this, as in the case of clippings and trimmings, the industry will ordinarily not accept ingot so salvaged upon the same terms as virgin. There are some seventeen companies which scavenge scrap of all sorts, clean it, remelt it, test it for its composition make it into ingots and sell it regularly to the trade. . . . The judge (Judge Caffey in the District Court) found that the return of fabricated products to the market as secondary varied from five to twenty-five years, depending upon the article; . . .

There are various ways of computing Alcoa's control of the aluminum market—as distinct from its production—depending upon what one regards as competing in that market. The judge figured its share—during the years 1929–1938, inclusive, as only about thirty-three per cent; to do so he included secondary, and excluded that part of Alcoa's own production which it fabricated and did not therefore sell as ingot. If, on the other hand, Alcoa's total production, fabricated and sold, be included, and balanced against the sum of imported virgin and secondary its share of the market was in the neighborhood of sixty-four per cent for that period. The percentage we have already mentioned—over ninety—results only if we both include all Alcoa's production and exclude secondary. That percentage is enough to constitute a monopoly; it is doubtful whether sixty or sixty-four per cent would be enough; and certainly thirty-three per cent is not. Hence it is necessary to settle what we shall treat as competing in the ingot market. That part of its production which Alcoa itself fabricates, does not of course ever reach the market as ingot; and we recognize that it is only when a restriction of production either inevitably affects prices, or is intended to do so, that it violates Section 1 of the Act. . . . However, even though we were to assume that a monopoly is unlawful under Section 2 only in case it controls prices, the ingot fabricated by Alcoa necessarily had a direct effect upon the ingot market. All ingot—with trifling exceptions—is used to fabricate intermediate, or end, products; and therefore all intermediate, or end, products which Alcoa fabricates and sells, *pro tanto* reduce the demand for ingot itself. . . . We cannot therefore agree that the computation of the percentage of Alcoa's control over the ingot market should not include the whole of its ingot production.

As to secondary, as we have said, for certain purposes the industry will not accept it at all; but for those for which it will, the difference in price is ordinarily not very great; the judge found that it was between one and two cents a pound, hardly enough margin on which to base a monopoly. Indeed, there are times when all differential disappears, and secondary will actually sell at a higher price: i.e., when there is a supply available which contains just the alloy that a fabricator needs for the article which he proposes to make. Taking the industry as a whole, we can say nothing more definite than that, although secondary does not compete at all in some uses, (whether because of sales resistance only, or because of actual metallurgical inferiority), for most purposes it competes upon a substantial equality with virgin. On these facts the judge found that every pound of secondary or scrap aluminum which is sold in commerce displaces a pound of virgin aluminum which otherwise would, or might have been, sold. We agree: so far as secondary supplies the demand of such fabricators as will accept it, it increases the amount of virgin which must seek sale elsewhere; and it therefore results that the supply of that part of the demand which will accept only virgin becomes greater in proportion as secondary drives away virgin from the demand which will accept secondary. . . . At any given moment therefore secondary competes with virgin in the ingot market; further, it can, and probably does, set a limit or ceiling beyond which the price of virgin cannot go, for the cost of its production will in the end depend only upon the expense of scavenging and reconditioning. It might seem for this reason that in estimating Alcoa's control over the ingot market, we ought to include the supply of secondary, as the judge did. Indeed, it may be thought a paradox to say that anyone has the monopoly of a market in which at all times he must meet a competition that limits his price. We shall show that it is not.

In the case of a monopoly of any commodity which does not disappear in use and which can be salvaged, the supply seeking sale at any moment will be made up of two components: (1) the part which the putative monopolist can immediately produce and sell; and (2) the part which has been, or can be, reclaimed out of what he has produced and sold in the past. By hypothesis he presently controls the first of these components; the second he has controlled in the past, although he no longer does. During the period when he did control the second, if he was aware of his interest, he was guided, not alone by its effect at that time upon the market, but by his knowledge that some part of it was likely to be reclaimed and seek the future market. That consideration will to some extent always affect his production until he decides to abandon the business, or for some other reason ceases to be concerned with the future market. Thus, in the case at bar Alcoa always knew that the future supply of ingot would be made up in part of what it produced at the time, and, if it was as far-sighted as it proclaims itself, that consideration must have had its share in determining how much to produce. How accurately it could forecast the effect of present production upon the future market is another matter. Experience, no doubt, would help; but it makes no difference that it had to guess; it is enough that it had an inducement to make the best guess it could, and that it would regulate that part of the future supply, so far as it should turn out to have guessed right. The competition of secondary must therefore be disregarded, as soon as we consider the position of Alcoa over a period of years; it was as much within Alcoa's control as was the production of the virgin from which it had been derived. . . .

We conclude therefore that Alcoa's control over the ingot market must be reckoned at over ninety per cent; that being the proportion which its production bears to imported virgin ingot. If the fraction which it did not supply were the produce of domestic manufacture there could be no doubt that this percentage gave it a monopoly—lawful or unlawful, as the case might be. The producer of so large a proportion of the supply has complete control within certain limits. It is true that, if by raising the price he reduces the amount which can be marketed—as always, or almost always, happens—he may invite the expansion of the small producers who will try to fill the place left open; nevertheless, not only is there an inevitable lag in this, but the large producer is in a strong position to check such competition; and, indeed, if he has retained his old plant and personnel, he can inevitably do so. There are indeed limits to his power; substitutes are available for almost all commodities, and to raise the price enough is to evoke them. . . . But these limitations also exist when a single producer occupies the whole market: even then, his hold will depend upon his moderation in exerting his immediate power.

. . . It is entirely consistent with the evidence that it was the threat of greater foreign imports which kept Alcoa's prices where they were, and prevented it from exploiting its advantage as sole domestic producer; indeed, it is hard to resist the conclusion that potential imports did put a ceiling upon those prices. Nevertheless, within the limits afforded by the tariff and the cost of transportation, Alcoa was free to raise its prices as it chose, since it was free from domestic competition, save as it drew other metals into the market as substitutes. Was this a monopoly within the meaning of Section 2? The judge found that, over the whole half century of its existence, Alcoa's profits upon capital invested, after payment of income taxes, had been only about ten per cent, and, although the plaintiff (government) puts this figure a little higher, the difference is negligible. The plaintiff does indeed challenge the propriety of computing profits upon a capital base which included past earnings that have been allowed to remain in the business; but as to that it is plainly wrong. . . . A profit of ten per cent in such an industry, dependent, in part at any rate, upon continued tariff protection, and subject to the vicissitudes of new demands, to the obsolescence of plant and process—which can never be accurately gauged in advance—to the chance that substitutes may at any moment be discovered which will reduce the demand, and to the other hazards which attend all industry: a profit of ten per cent, so conditioned, could hardly be considered extortionate.

. . . Having proved that Alcoa had a monopoly of the domestic ingot market, the plaintiff had gone far enough; if it was an excuse, that Alcoa had not abused its power, it lay upon Alcoa to prove that it had not. But the whole issue is irrelevant anyway, for it is not excuse for monopolizing a market that the monopoly has not been used to extract from the consumer more than a fair profit. The Act has wider purposes. Indeed, even though we disregarded all but economic considerations, it would by no means follow that such concentration of producing power is to be desired when it has not been used extortionately. Many people believe that possession of unchallenged economic power deadens initiative, discourages thrift and depresses energy; that immunity from competition is a narcotic, and rivalry is a stimulant, to industrial progress; that the spur of constant stress is necessary to counteract an inevitable disposition to let well enough alone. Such people believe that competitors, versed in the craft as no consumer can be, will be quick to detect opportunities for saving and new shifts in production, and be eager to profit by them. In any event the mere fact that a producer, having command of the domestic market, has not been able to make more than a fair profit, is no evidence that a fair profit could not have been made at lower prices. . . . True, it might have been thought adequate to condemn only those monopolies which could not show that they had exercised the highest possible ingenuity, had adopted every possible economy, had anticipated every conceivable improvement, stimulated every possible demand. No doubt, that would be one way of dealing with the matter, although it would imply constant scrutiny and constant supervision, such as courts are unable to provide. Be that as it may, that was not the way that Congress chose; it did not condone good trusts and condemn bad ones; it forbade all. Moreover, in so doing it was not necessarily actuated by economic motives alone. It is possible, because of its indirect social or moral effect, to prefer a system of small producers, each dependent for his success upon his own skill and character, to one in which the great mass of those engaged must accept the direction of a few. These considerations, which we have suggested only as possible purposes of the Act, we think the decisions prove to have been in fact its purposes.

It is settled, at least as to Section 1, that there are some contracts restricting competition which are unlawful, no matter how beneficent they may be; no industrial exigency will justify them; they are absolutely forbidden. Chief Justice Taft said as much of contracts dividing a territory among producers, in the often quoted passage of his opinion in the Circuit Court of Appeals in United States v. Addystone Pipe and Steel Co. . . . The Supreme Court unconditionally condemned all contracts fixing prices in United States v. Trenton Potteries Company. . . . Starting, however, with the authoritative premise that all contracts fixing prices are unconditionally prohibited, the only possible difference between them and a monopoly is that while a monopoly necessarily involves an equal, or even greater, power to fix prices, its mere existence might be thought not to constitute an exercise of that power. That distinction is nevertheless purely formal; it would be valid only so long as the monopoly remained wholly inert; it would disappear as soon as the monopoly began to operate; for, when it did—that is, as soon as it began to sell at all—it must sell at some price and the only price at which it could sell is a price which it itself fixed. Thereafter the power and its exercise must needs coalesce. Indeed it would be absurd to condemn such contracts unconditionally, and not to extend the condemnation to monopolies; for the contracts are only steps toward that entire control which monopoly confers: they are really partial monopolies.

❋   ❋   ❋   ❋   ❋

We have been speaking only of the economic reasons which forbid monopoly; but, as we have already implied, there are others, based upon the belief that great industrial consolidations are inherently undesirable, regardless of their economic results. In the debates in Congress Senator Sherman himself . . . showed that among the purposes of Congress in 1890 was a desire to put an end to great aggregations of capital because of the helplessness of the individual before them. . . . That Congress is still of the same mind appears in the Surplus Property Act of 1944, and the Small Business Mobilization Act. . . . Throughout the history of these statutes it has been constantly assumed that one of their purposes was to perpetuate and preserve, for its own sake and in spite of possible cost, an organization for industry in small units which can effectively compete with each other. We hold that Alcoa's monopoly of ingot was of the kind covered by Section 2.

It does not follow because Alcoa had such a monopoly, that it "monopolized" the ingot market; it may not have achieved monopoly; monopoly may have been thrust upon it. If it had been a combination of existing smelters which united the whole industry and controlled the production of all aluminum ingot, it would certainly have monopolized the market. In several decisions the Supreme Court has decreed the dissolution of such combinations, although they had engaged in no unlawful trade practices. . . . We may start therefore with the premise that to have combined ninety per cent of the producers of ingot would have been to monopolize the ingot market; and, so far as concerns the public interest, it can make no difference whether an existing competition is put an end to, or whether prospective competition is prevented. The Clayton Act itself speaks in that alternative: "to injure, destroy or prevent competition." . . . Nevertheless, it is unquestionably true that from the very outset the courts have at least kept in reserve the possibility that the origin of a monopoly may be critical in determining is legality; and for this they had warrant in some of the congressional debates which accompanied the passage of the Act. . . . This notion has usually been expressed by saying that size does not determine guilt; that there must be some exclusion of competitors; that the growth must be something else than natural or normal; that there must be a wrongful intent, or some other specific intent; or that some unduly coercive means must be used. At times there has been emphasis upon the use of the active verb, monopolize. . . . What engendered these compunctions is reasonably plain; persons may unwittingly find themselves in possession of a monopoly, automatically so to say: that is, without having intended either to put an end to existing competition, or to prevent competition from arising when none had existed; they may become monopolists by force of accident. Since the Act makes monopolizing a crime, as well as a civil wrong, it would be not only unfair, but presumably contrary to the intent of Congress, to include such instances. A market may, for example, be so limited that it is impossible to produce at all and meet the cost of production except by a plant large enough to supply the whole demand. Or there may be changes in taste or in cost which drive out all but one purveyor. A single producer may be the survivor out of a group of active competitors, merely by virtue of his superior skill, foresight and industry. In such cases a strong argument can be made that, although the result may expose the public to the evils of monopoly, the Act does not mean to condemn the resultant of those very forces which it is its prime objective to foster. . . . The successful competitor, having been urged to compete, must not be turned upon when he wins. The most extreme expression of this view is in United States v. United States Steel Corporation,[2] . . . repeated in United States v. Interna-

---

[2] Justice McKenna for the majority said, p. 451: "The Corporation is undoubtedly of impressive size and it takes an effort of resolution not to be affected by it

tional Harvester Corp. . . . It so chances that in both instances the corporation had less than two-thirds of the production in its hands, and the language quoted was not necessary to the decision; so that even if it had not later been modified, it has not the authority of an actual decision. But, whatever authority it does have was modified by the gloss of Cardozo, J. in Swift & Company v. United States, . . . when he said p. 116: "Mere size . . . is not an offense against the Sherman Act unless magnified to the point at which it amounts to a monopoly . . . but size carries with it an opportunity for abuse that is not to be ignored when the opportunity is proved to have been utilized in the past." Alcoa's size was magnified to make it a monopoly; indeed, it has never been anything else; and its size, not only offered it an opportunity for abuse, but it utilized its size for abuse, as can easily be shown.

It would completely misconstrue Alcoa's position in 1940 to hold that it was the passive beneficiary of a monopoly, following upon an involuntary elimination of competitors by automatically operative economic forces. Already in 1909, when its last lawful monopoly ended, it sought to strengthen its position by unlawful practices, and these concededly continued until 1912. . . . Meanwhile not a pound of ingot had been produced by anyone else in the United States. This increase and this continued and undisturbed control did not fall undesigned into Alcoa's lap; obviously it could not have done so. It could only have resulted, as it did result, from a persistent determination to maintain the control, with which it found itself vested in 1912. There were at least one or two abortive attempts to enter the industry, but Alcoa effectively anticipated and forestalled all competition, and succeeded in holding the field alone. True, it stimulated demand and opened new uses for the metal, but not without making sure that it could supply what it had evoked. There is no dispute as to this; Alcoa avows it as evidence of the skill, energy and initiative with which it has always conducted its business; as a reason why, having won its way by fair means, it should be commended, and not dismembered. We need charge it with no moral derelictions after 1912; we may assume that all it claims for itself is true. The only question is whether it falls within the exception established in favor of those who do not seek, but cannot avoid, the control of a market. It seems to us that the question scarcely survives its statement. It was not inevitable that it should always anticipate increases in the demand for ingot and be prepared to supply them. Nothing compelled it to keep doubling and redoubling its capacity before others entered the field. It insists that it never excluded competitors; but

---

or to exaggerate its influence. But we must adhere to the law and the law does not make mere size an offence or the existence of unexerted power an offence. It, we repeat, requires overt acts and trusts to its prohibition of them and its power to repress or punish them. It does not compel competition nor require all that is possible." The minority through Day, J. agreed, p. 460: "The act offers no objection to the mere size of a corporation nor to the continued exertion of its lawful power, when that size and power have been obtained by lawful means and developed by natural growth, although its resources, capital and strength may give to such corporation a dominating place in the business and industry with which it is concerned. It is entitled to maintain its size and the power that legitimately goes with it, provided no law has been transgressed in obtaining it."

we can think of no more effective exclusion than progressively to embrace each new opportunity as it opened, and to face every newcomer with new capacity already geared into a great organization, having the advantage of experience, trade connections and the elite of personnel. Only in case we interpret exclusion as limited to manoeuvres not honestly industrial, but actuated solely by a desire to prevent competition, can such a course indefatigably pursued, be deemed not exclusionary. So to limit it would in our judgement emasculate the Act; would permit just such consolidations as it was designed to prevent.

*   *   *   *   *

We disregard any question of intent. . . . In order to fall within Section 2, the monopolist must have both the power to monopolize, and the intent to monopolize. To read the passage as demanding any specific intent, makes nonsense of it, for no monopolist monopolizes unconscious of what he is doing. So here, Alcoa meant to keep, and did keep, that complete and exclusive hold upon the ingot market with which it started. That was to monopolize that market, however innocently it otherwise proceeded. So far as the judgment held that it was not within Section 2, it must be reversed.

*   *   *   *   *

Remedies

Although the Circuit Court rendered its decision finding that Aloca had illegally monopolized the aluminum ingot market under Section 2 of the Sherman Act, no relief was decreed. The court returned the case to the District Court for the determination of appropriate remedies. The reason for not specifying a remedy was that during the war period the federal government had erected aluminum plants the capacity of which exceeded Alcoa's productive capacity. The court felt that the ultimate disposition of the government plants would be a factor of great importance in prescribing the final remedy.

The government had demanded, among other things, that Alcoa be dissolved. The court pointed out that "dissolution is not a penalty, but a remedy; if the industry will not need it (dissolution of Alcoa) for its protection, it will be a disservice to break up an aggregation which has for so long demonstrated its efficiency." The disposal agency (War Assets Administration) should have complete discretion to dispose of government plants in any way it saw fit, uninfluenced by views expressed by the circuit court. The district court could then evaluate the effects of the disposal program, and determine appropriate remedies which would "secure the establishment of those competitive conditions which the Antitrust Acts demand."

Procter & Gamble and Clorox[1]

As the 1957 fiscal year came to a close, the management of the Procter & Gamble Company had good reason to be pleased. The Cincinnati-based household products maker had just recorded the highest sales ($1.2 billion) and earnings ($67.8 million) in its 120-year history, up 11 percent and 14 percent, respectively, from the year before. In doing so, the company moved up two notches on the *Fortune* 500 list, becoming the 29th largest U.S. industrial corporation.

Leading the way were P&G's soaps, detergents, and cleansers, whose combined $514 million domestic sales had captured more than half the market. Foremost among these were Tide and Cheer laundry detergents and Ivory and Camay hand soaps. Other P&G market leaders included Crisco shortening and Gleem and Crest toothpastes.

These products had been backed by an $80 million advertising expenditure and $47 million more spent on sales promotion, making Procter the nation's largest advertiser. As the largest buyer of television time in the country, the company received the highest volume discounts available, reportedly as much as 25–30 percent.

In addition, 1957 had seen P&G expanding into new markets with

---

[1] This case was prepared entirely from publicly available documents by Jonathan T. Carder, research assistant, under the direction of Howard W. Pifer, Lecturer on Business Administration. It incorporates material from two earlier cases, *Federal Trade Commission* v. *The Procter & Gamble Company* and *The Procter & Gamble Company in U.S.* The case is intended to serve as the basis for class discussion rather than to illustrate either effective or ineffective handling of an administrative situation.

the introduction of Comet, an abrasive cleanser, and the acquisition of the Duncan Hines baking mix business and the Charmin Paper Mills.

One big question mark, however, overshadowed all this. In May 1957, Procter & Gamble had notified the Federal Trade Commission of its intention to acquire the assets and business of the Clorox Chemical Company, the nation's leading liquid bleach maker. As of July, the FTC had still not responded, and P&G was uncertain as to whether it should go ahead and finalize the deal with Clorox.

Methods of entry

In its expansion into new markets in 1957, P&G had taken three different routes. The company's introduction of Comet household cleanser was the result of internal product development—Comet was created and manufactured in Procter's own facilities.

In the case of Charmin Paper Mills (and Duncan Hines), P&G had made what might be termed a "toehold" acquisition of a very small firm in its industry. Charmin's 1956 sales of $23 million made it a dwarf beside industry giants Scott Paper and Kimberly Clark, each with household paper products sales in excess of $200 million. In discussing the purchase, P&G president Neil H. McElroy commented, "Although this is an entirely new business for us, it is a logical extension of our interest in cellulose products made from cottonseed linters and wood."

The Clorox acquisition represented the third type of entry into new markets—buying an established industry leader. Clorox in 1957 was the acknowledged bleach king, with its $40 million in sales accounting for 48.8 percent of the domestic liquid bleach market.

Procter had been approached by the Clorox owners who wanted to dispose of their business for estate purposes, "in exchange for the marketable securities of a big company."[2] P&G decided to enter this market, which tied in nicely with its detergent sales, via the Clorox route after a study by its promotion department stated: "We would not recommend that the Company consider trying to enter this market by introducing a new brand or by trying to expand a sectional brand. This is because we feel it would require a very heavy investment to achieve a major volume in the field, and with the low available (i.e., profit margin) the payout period would be very unattractive."[3]

Unlike its competitors, all essentially regional bleach producers, Clorox had an already existing national network of 13 plants, as well as a strong nationwide brand image.[4] The Purex Corporation, Clorox's

---

[2] From testimony before U.S. Supreme Court, February 1967.

[3] From Trade Regulation Reports (No. 316; August 17, 1967).

[4] Because of high shipping costs and low sales price, it was not feasible to ship household liquid bleach more than 300 miles from its point of manufacture.

closest rival with 15.7 percent of the liquid bleach market, also had 13 plants but distributed to less than half of the national market. P&G's study predicted that Procter's sales distribution and manufacturing setup could increase Clorox's share of the market in areas where it was low. It concluded, "Taking over the Clorox business . . . could be a way of achieving a dominant position in the liquid bleach market quickly, which would pay out reasonably well."

The Clorox acquisition

On August 1, 1957, Procter and Gamble acquired Clorox in a stock transaction valued at $30.3 million. On October 7, 1957, the FTC filed a complaint charging that Procter & Gamble had violated Section 7 of the Clayton Act, as amended by the Celler-Kefauver Act.[5] The allegation was that Procter's acquisition might substantially lessen competition or tend to create a monopoly in the production and sales of household liquid bleaches. The following table summarizes the litigations that ensued:

Year	Month	Event
1957	December	Federal Trade Commission evidentiary hearings begin.
1960	June	FTC hearing examiner concludes that the acquisition was unlawful and orders divestiture.
1961	June	On appeal, the commission reverses, holding that the record as constituted was inadequate, and remands to the examiner for additional hearings.
1962	February	Hearing examiner again holds the acquisition unlawful and orders divestiture.
1963	November	FTC affirms the examiner and orders divestiture.
1966	March	Court of Appeals for the Sixth Circuit disagrees and dismisses the FTC's complaint.
1967	April	Supreme Court announces that the Court of Appeals has erred, confirms the commission's findings, and orders Procter to divest Clorox. The vote is 7 to 0, with two abstentions.
1967	October	Purex sues Procter for $523.5 million, claiming P&G's illegal acquisition and subsequent operation of Clorox severely damaged Purex sales, profits, goodwill, and customer acceptance.

---

[5] "No corporation engaged in commerce shall acquire directly or indirectly, the whole or any part of the stock . . . or assets of another corporation engaged also in commerce, where . . . the effect of such acquisition may be substantially to lessen competition, or tend to create a monopoly."

The following are excerpts from the opinion of the Supreme Court, as delivered by Justice William O. Douglas:[6]

Clorox's position

At the time of the acquisition, Clorox was the leading manufacturer of household liquid bleach, with 48.8% of the national sales—annual sales of slightly less than $40,000,000. Its market share had been steadily increasing for the five years prior to the merger. Its nearest rival was Purex, which manufactures a number of products other than household liquid bleaches, including abrasive cleaners, toilet soap, and detergents. Purex accounted for 15.7% of the household liquid bleach market. The industry is highly concentrated; in 1957, Clorox and Purex accounted for almost 65% of the Nation's household liquid bleach sales, and, together with four other firms, for almost 80%. The remaining 20% was divided among over 200 small producers. Clorox had total assets of $12,000,000; only eight producers had assets in excess of $1,000,000 and very few had assets of more than $75,000.

In light of the territorial limitations on distribution, national figures do not give an accurate picture of Clorox's dominance in the various regions. Thus, Clorox's seven principal competitors did no business in New England, the Mid-Atlantic States, or metropolitan New York. Clorox's share of the sales in those areas was 56%, 72%, and 64% respectively. Even in regions where its principal competitors were active, Clorox maintained a dominant position. Except in metropolitan Chicago and the West-Central States Clorox accounted for at least 39%, and often a much higher percentage, of liquid bleach sales. (See Exhibit 1.)

Since all liquid bleach is chemically identical, advertising and sales promotion is vital. In 1957 Clorox spent almost $4,700,000 on advertising, imprinting the value of its bleach in the mind of the consumer. In addition, it spent $1,700,000 for other promotional activities. The Commission found that these heavy expenditures went far to explain why Clorox maintained so high a market share despite the fact that its brand, though chemically indistinguishable from rival brands, retailed for a price equal to or, in many instances, higher than its competitors.

FTC findings

The Commission found that the acquisition might substantially lessen competition. The findings and reasoning of the Commission need be only briefly summarized. The Commission found that the substitution of Procter with its huge assets and advertising advantages for the already dominant Clorox would dissuade new entrants and discourage active competition from the firms already in the industry due to fear of retaliation by Procter. The Commission thought it relevant that retailers might be induced to give Clorox preferred shelf space since it would be manufactured by Procter, which also produced a number of other products marketed by the retailers. There was also the danger that Procter might underprice Clorox in order to drive out competition,

---

[6] Reproduced by permission from *Trade Regulation Reports* (No. 316; August 17, 1967).

and subsidize the underpricing with revenue from other products. The Commission carefully reviewed the effect of the acquisition on the structure of the industry, noting that "[t]he practical tendency of the . . . merger . . . is to transform the liquid bleach industry into an arena of big business competition only, with the few small firms that have not disappeared through merger eventually falling by the wayside, unable to compete with their giant rivals."

Further, the merger would seriously diminish potential competition by eliminating Procter as a potential entrant into the industry. Prior to the merger, the Commission found that Procter was the most likely prospective entrant, and absent the merger would have remained on the periphery, restraining Clorox from exercising its market power. If Procter had actually entered, Clorox's dominant position would have been eroded and the concentration of the industry reduced. The Commission stated that it had not placed reliance on post-acquisition evidence in holding the merger unlawful.

Court of Appeals' view

The Court of Appeals said that the Commission's finding of illegality had been based on "treacherous conjecture," mere possibility and suspicion. It dismissed the fact that Clorox controlled almost 50% of the industry, that two firms controlled 65%, and that six firms controlled 80% with the observation that "the fact that in addition to the six . . . producers sharing eighty per cent of the market, there were two hundred smaller producers . . . would not seem to indicate anything unhealthy about the market conditions."

It dismissed the finding that Procter, with its huge resources and prowess, would have more leverage than Clorox with the statement that it was Clorox which had the "know-how" in the industry, and that Clorox's finances were adequate for its purposes. As for the possibility that Procter would use its tremendous advertising budget and volume discounts to push Clorox, the court found "it difficult to base a finding of illegality on discounts on advertising." It rejected the Commission's finding that the merger eliminated the potential competition of Procter because "there was no reasonable probability that Procter would have entered the household liquid bleach market but for the merger." "There was no evidence tending to prove that Procter ever intended to enter this field on its own." Finally, "there was no evidence that Procter at any time in the past engaged in predatory practices, or that it intended to do so in the future."

The Court of Appeals also heavily relied on post-acquisition "evidence to the effect that the other producers subsequent to the merger were selling more bleach for more money than ever before" that "there [had] been no significant change in Clorox's market share in the four years subsequent to the merger," and concluded that "this evidence certainly does not prove anti-competitive effects of the merger." The Court of Appeals, in our view, misapprehended the standards for its review and the standards applicable in a Section 7 proceeding.

Clayton Act—probabilities

Section 7 of the Clayton Act was intended to arrest the anticompetitive effects of market power in their incipiency. The core question is whether a merger may substantially lessen competition, and necessarily requires a prediction of the merger's impact on competition, present and future. The section can deal only with probabilities, not with certainties. . . . And there is certainly no requirement that the anticompetitive power manifest itself in anticompetitive action before Section 7 can be called into play. If the enforcement of Section 7 turned on the existence of actual anticompetitive practices, the congressional policy of thwarting such practices in their incipiency would be frustrated.

All mergers are within the reach of Section 7, and all must be tested by the same standard, whether they are classified as horizontal, vertical, conglomerate[7] or other. As noted by the Commission, this merger is neither horizontal, vertical, nor conglomerate. Since the products of the acquired company are complementary to those of the acquiring company and may be produced with similar facilities, marketed through the same channels and in the same manner, and advertised by the same media, the Commission aptly called this acquisition a "product-extension merger":

> By this acquisition . . . Procter has not diversified its interest. in the sense of expanding into a substantially different, unfamiliar market or industry. Rather, it has entered a market which adjoins, as it were, those markets in which it is already established, and which is virtually undistinguishable from them insofar as the problems and techniques of marketing the product to the ultimate consumer are concerned. As a high official of Procter put it, commenting on the acquisition of Clorox, "While this is a completely new business for us, taking us for the first time into the marketing of a household bleach and disinfectant, we are thoroughly at home in the field of manufacturing and marketing low priced, rapid turn-over consumer products."

Anticompetitive effects of merger

The anticompetitive effects with which this product-extension merger is fraught can easily be seen: (1) the substitution of the powerful acquiring firm for the smaller, but already dominant, firm may substantially reduce the competitive structure of the industry by raising entry barriers and by dissuading the smaller firms from aggressively competing; (2) the acquisition eliminates the potential competition of the acquiring firm.

Oligopoly—price leadership

The liquid bleach industry was already oligopolistic before the acquisition, and price competition was certainly not as vigorous as it would have been if the industry were competitive. Clorox enjoyed a dominant position nationally, and its position approached monopoly proportion in certain areas. The existence of some 200 fringe firms certainly does not belie that fact. Nor does the fact, relied upon by the court below, that after the merger, producers other than Clorox "were selling more bleach for more money than ever before." In the same period, Clorox increased its share from 48.8% to 52%. The interjection of Procter into the market considerably changed the

---

[7] A pure conglomerate merger is one in which there are no economic relationships between the acquiring and the acquired firm.

situation. There is every reason to assume that the smaller firms would become more cautious in competing due to their fear of retaliation by Procter. It is probable that Procter would become the price leader and that oligopoly would become more rigid.

Barriers

The acquisition may also have the tendency of raising the barriers to new entry. The major competitive weapon in the successful marketing of bleach is advertising. Clorox was limited in this area by its relatively small budget and its inability to obtain substantial discounts. By contrast, Procter's budget was much larger; and, although it would not devote its entire budget to advertising Clorox, it could divert a large portion to meet the short-term threat of a new entrant. Procter would be able to use its volume discounts to advantage in advertising Clorox.[8] Thus, a new entrant would be much more reluctant to face the giant Procter than it would have been to face the smaller Clorox.

Possible economies

Possible economies cannot be used as a defense to illegality. Congress was aware that some mergers which lessen competition may also result in economies but it struck the balance in favor of protecting competition.

Potential competition

The Commission also found that the acquisition of Clorox by Procter eliminated Procter as a potential competitor. The Court of Appeals declared that this finding was not supported by evidence because there was no evidence that Procter's management had ever intended to enter the industry independently . . . The evidence, however, clearly shows that Procter was the most likely entrant. Procter had recently launched a new abrasive cleaner (Comet) in an industry similar to the liquid bleach industry, and had wrested leadership from a brand that had enjoyed even a larger market share than had Clorox. Procter was engaged in a vigorous program of diversifying into product lines closely related to its basic products. Liquid bleach was a natural avenue of diversification since it is complementary to Procter's products, is sold to the same customers through the same channels, and is advertised and merchandised in the same manner. Procter had substantial advantages in advertising and sales promotions, which, as we have seen, are vital to the success of liquid bleach. No manufacturer had a patent on the product or its manufacture, necessary information relating to manufacturing methods and processes was readily available, there was no shortage of raw material, and the machinery and equipment required for a plant of efficient capacity were available at reasonable cost. Procter's management was experienced in producing and marketing goods similar to liquid bleach. Procter had considered the possibility of independently entering but decided against it because the

---

[8] (Casewriter's footnote) Purex, like Procter & Gamble a multi-product firm, received volume discounts as high as 15 percent on its television advertising in 1957.

acquisition of Clorox would enable Procter to capture a more commanding share of the market.

Threat at edge of industry

It is clear that the existence of Procter at the edge of the industry exerted considerable influence on the market. First, the market behavior of the liquid bleach industry was influenced by each firm's predictions of the market behavior of its competitors, actual and potential. Second, the barriers to entry by a firm of Procter's size and with its advantages were not significant. There is no indication that the barriers were so high that the price Procter would have to charge would be above the price that would maximize the profits of the existing firms. Third, the number of potential entrants was not so large that the elimination of one would be insignificant. Few firms would have the temerity to challenge a firm as solidly entrenched as Clorox. Fourth, Procter was found by the Commission to be the most likely entrant. These findings of the Commission were amply supported by the evidence.

The judgement of the Court of Appeals is reversed and remanded with instructions to affirm and enforce the Commission's order.

Concurring opinion

Justice John M. Harlan concurred in the Supreme Court's decision, but did not share the majority opinion's view that a "summary will demonstrate the correctness of the Commission's decision," nor that "the anticompetitive effects with which this product-extension merger is fraught can easily be seen."

One area of Justice Douglas' opinion which Justice Harlan severely criticized was Douglas' quick dismissal of Procter's contention that the merger could be justified by marketing economies, especially the discounts it received on large advertising expenditures. Said Harlan:

> The Commission's analysis of the economies involved in this case is critical and I regret that the Court refrains from commenting upon it. The Commission—in my opinion quite correctly—seemed to accept the idea that economies could be used to defend a merger, noting that "(a) merger that results in increased efficiency of production distribution or marketing may, in certain cases, increase the vigor of competition in the relevant market." But advertising economies were placed in a different classification since they were said "only to increase the barriers to new entry" and to be "offensive to at least the spirit, if not the letter, of the antitrust laws." Advertising was thought to benefit only the seller by entrenching his market position, and to be of no use to the consumer.
>
> I think the Commission's view overstated and oversimplified. Proper advertising serves a legitimate and important purpose in the market by educating the consumer as to available alternatives. This process contributes to consumer demand being developed to the point at which economies of scale can be realized in production. The advertiser's brand

name may also be an assurance of quality, and the value of this benefit is demonstrated by the general willingness of consumers to pay a premium for the advertised brands.

Undeniably advertising may sometimes be used to create irrational brand preferences and mislead consumers as to the actual differences between products,[9] but it is very difficult to discover at what point advertising ceases to be an aspect of healthy competition. . . . It is not the Commission's function to decide which lawful elements of the "product" offered the consumer should be considered useful and which should be considered the symptoms of industrial "sickness." It is the consumer who must make that election through the exercise of his purchasing power. In my view, true efficiencies in the use of advertising must be considered in assessing economies in the marketing process, which as has been noted here are factors in the sort of Section 7 proceeding involved here.

I do not think, however, that on the record presented Procter has shown any true efficiencies in advertising. Procter has merely shown that it is able to command equivalent resources at a lower dollar cost than other bleach producers. No peculiarly efficient marketing techniques have been demonstrated, nor does the record show that a smaller net advertising expenditure could be expected. Economies cannot be premised solely on dollar figures, lest accounting controversies dominate Section 7 proceedings. Economies employed in the defense of a merger must be shown in what economists label "real" terms, that is in terms of resources applied to the accomplishment of the objective. For this reason, the Commission, I think, was justified in discounting Procter's efficiency defense.

Justice Harlan also criticized the court's opinion for making no effort to "embark upon the formulation of standards for the application of Section 7 to mergers which are neither horizontal nor vertial," leaving "the Commission, lawyers, and businessmen at large as to what is expected of them in future cases of this kind." Harlan suggested the following "four guides" be used to determine the legality of conglomerate or product extension mergers:

> First, the decision can rest on analysis of market structure without resort to evidence of post-merger anticompetitive behavior.[10]
> Second, the operation of the pre-merger market must be understood as the foundation of successful analysis. The responsible agency may presume that the market operates in accord with generally accepted

---

[9] The commission found, for example, that Clorox was identical to other liquid bleaches. Procter contended, and the court of appeals concluded, that Clorox employed superior quality controls. The evidence seemed to indicate that the regional and national brands were very similar, but that some local brands varied in strength.

[10] Harlan argued, "Only by focusing on market structure can we begin to formulate standards which will allow the responsible agencies to give proper consideration to such mergers and allow businessmen to plan their actions with a fair degree of certainty."

principles of economic theory, but the presumption must be open to challenge of alternative operational formulations.

Third, if it is reasonably probable that there will be a change in market structure which will allow the exercise of substantially greater market power, then a *prima facie* case has been made out under Section 7.

Fourth, where the case against the merger rests on the probability of increased market power, the merging companies may attempt to prove that there are countervailing economies reasonably probable which should be weighted against the adverse effects.

Clorox divestiture

In May 1968, Procter & Gamble began the divestiture of Clorox, selling 1.2 million, or 15 percent, of the Clorox shares to the public, at $27.50 per share.[11] The second and final leg of the divestiture was completed on January 2, 1969, when Procter received 1,721,518 shares of P&G common from its shareholders in exchange for the remaining 6.8 million shares in the Clorox Company.[12]

In a report given at the Procter & Gamble 1967 Stockholder's Meeting, President Howard J. Morgens discussed Clorox's operations while a part of P&G:

> In the last year before we acquired it, Clorox had met earnings of $2,500,000. . . .
> . . . Throughout the period of Procter & Gamble ownership, Clorox advertising and promotion expenditures have been constantly reduced. In no full fiscal year under our ownership did the expenditure per unit equal that of the former company.[13]
> . . . Also the average price of Clorox last fiscal year was about the same as it was at the time of our acquisition—even though the general price index rose sharply during the same period. At the same time, Clorox earnings have increased markedly. In the fiscal year ended June 30, 1967, Clorox had net earnings of $10,800,000.

Significant increases in Clorox's sales volume in 1962 and 1963 were attributable to the company's conversion from glass to plastic bleach bottles. The higher cost of plastic packaging and the conversion cost were offset by higher selling prices and lower unit delivery cost, the latter resulting from the lighter weight of plastic bottles. In the years following 1963, reductions in the cost of the plastic bottles contributed to lower cost and lower selling prices.

In total, Clorox earned nearly $72 million while a Procter subsidiary. Since apparently almost all of this income was remanded to the parent

---

[11] After federal income taxes of $7.8 million, P&G reported a net profit of $19.4 million on the transaction.

[12] P&G common closed at $86, down ½, for the day.

[13] This was achieved in spite of the fact that by 1967 all major television networks had discontinued, or were discontinuing, volume discounts.

in the form of dividends (see Exhibit 2), a rough ROI calculation (leaving aside Clorox's terminal value) would indicate an annual rate of return in the neighborhood of 13.5 percent on P&G's $30.3 million investment. (Exhibit 3 is Clorox's balance sheet at the time of divestiture.)

At the time of divestiture, Clorox estimated that it had approximately 46 percent of total 1967 national household bleach sales. This market included dry bleaches, which accounted for roughly 13 percent of total Clorox sales.

Although Procter & Gamble continued to manufacture a dry bleach product in the United States, and a liquid bleach, "ACE," in Italy, it came to an agreement with Clorox whereby P&G would not compete in the manufacture or sale of a sodium hypochlorite liquid bleach in the United States for a period of five years after the completion of divestiture.

Procter and Gamble in 1972

As the 1972 fiscal year drew to a close, the management of the Procter & Gamble Company had good reason to be pleased. Sales had increased an average of 7.2 percent in each of the past 15 years, rising in 1972 to $3.5 billion. Earnings had done even better, growing 9.6 percent per year to $276.3 million in 1972. Procter had reached 21st place on the *Fortune* 500 list. (See Exhibit 4 for a 15-year summary of P&G's operations.)

P&G's product line had also grown handsomely in this period. Joining the old standbys was a veritable army of new items including Head and Shoulders shampoo, Folger's coffee, Mr. Clean liquid household cleanser, Pampers disposable diapers, Scope mouthwash, Secret deodorant, and Zest soap. The sales breakdown by product areas in 1972 was:

Product area	Percent
Laundry and cleaning products	43
Personal care products	27
Food products	23
Other	7

The company's advertising expenditure in 1971 was estimated at $275 million, maintaining it as the largest national advertiser. (Sears, Roebuck & Company, in second place, spent $200 million on national advertising.) Approximately $190 million of Procter's total went to measured television advertising.[14]

Comet

In the 22 months following the 1957 introduction of Comet, Procter & Gamble had spent $7.2 million advertising and promoting it. Within

---

[14] All 1971–72 advertising and market share estimates are from *Advertising Age*, August 28, 1972.

20 months of its first appearance on the market, Comet had grabbed 36.5 percent of a $53-million abrasive cleanser market previously dominated by Colgate's Ajax. By 1972, Comet's market share had increased to over 50 percent, while Ajax's had slipped to 32 percent. In 1971, P&G spent an estimated $5.8 million on media advertising for Comet.

Charmin

As for Charmin Mills, it had figured prominently in Procter's march into the household paper products business. Mr. Whipple's "squeezably soft" tissues had been wiping up in the single-ply toilet paper market, attaining first place with a 16.2 percent share by 1972. Bounty paper towels had also done well, ranking first in some areas and "absorbing" a respectable 14 percent of a $480 million market. Neither product was yet distributed west of the Rocky Mountains. In all, paper products were estimated to account for 10 percent of P&G's sales in 1972.[15]

Clorox in 1972

Clorox on its own had shown all the earmarks of becoming a miniature Procter & Gamble. When it parted company with P&G in 1969, Clorox took with it all 12 executives that the parent had loaned it, including Clorox President Robert B. Shetterly. Once out of the Procter womb, Clorox began a Procter-like diversification by acquisition into other household (Liquid-plumber, Jifoam cleaner, Formula 409), food (B in B mushrooms, Cream of Rice), and pet care (Litter Green cat litter) products. Latest acquisition was Martin-Bower Corporation, with $89 million sales in the institutional and fast-food supply business.

In the bleach industry, Clorox sales continued to grow despite a competitive scar in 1969 when the introduction of enzyme laundry products caused a cutback in total bleach usage in the United States. Clorox met the competitive threat by nearly doubling its 1970 advertising expenditure, to $15 million, from 1969's $8 million, and reversed the decline in the liquid bleach market. In 1971, ad spending was raised to $19 million with over $6 million of this backing Clorox liquid bleach. For fiscal 1972, analysts estimated that liquid bleach sales would account for 57 percent of Clorox $185 to $190 million total sales, with sales of the company's two, new, dry, powdered bleaches accounting for 12 percent.[16] The bleach market in 1972 was believed to be a $212 million

---

[15] In the national baking mix market, Duncan Hines now held the No. 1 spot with 35 percent, followed by General Mills' Betty Crocker with 27 percent.

[16] Martin-Bower's sales are not included in the $185 to $190 million total sales.

retail market, of which $170 million was in liquid bleach and $42 million in dry bleach.

Legal problems

Despite the company's many successes, the outlook for Procter & Gamble in 1972 was not entirely rosy. One problem was the Supreme Court's refusal in April 1972 to review a key procedural issue in the $523 million 1967 antitrust suit brought against the company by Purex. Procter had appealed to the Supreme Court to rule Purex couldn't use the court decisions from the Clorox case as evidence of an antitrust violation in its private damage suit. The high court refusal left standing a lower court ruling in favor of Purex, apparently clearing the way for trial of the Purex charges.

Another headache for Procter was a number of restrictions the FTC had placed on P&G after the company's acquisition of coffee maker J. A. Folger & Company. Perhaps the most binding of these was that Procter was forbidden to acquire before 1974 any "household consumer product corporation engaged in interstate commerce" without prior FTC approval. It seemed likely too, that even after 1974, the FTC would be keeping a close eye on Procter's acquisitions.

With these problems in mind, Procter's management mulled over the possible new markets it might enter in the future in order to sustain its steady growth. A second question that arose was how to enter these markets.

EXHIBIT 1

Market shares of liquid bleach brands in 1957 as shown by the Nielsen food index for nine territories*

Section of the country	Clorox	Purex	Fleecy White	Hilex	Linco	Roman Cleanser	All others
New England	56.0	—	—	—	—	—	44.0
Metropolitan New York	64.3	—	—	—	—	—	35.7
Middle Atlantic	71.6	—	—	—	—	—	28.4
East Central	42.4	5.0	5.2	0.9	0.7	27.2	18.5
Metropolitan Chicago	28.6	0.1	18.9	0.1	50.3	—	2.0
West Central.	34.5	20.6	9.0	25.8	2.1	—	8.0
Southeast	52.6	16.0	5.7	—	—	5.3	20.4
Southwest	48.4	39.6	3.9	—	—	—	8.1
Pacific	39.2	42.4	—	—	—	—	18.4
National	48.8	15.7	5.9	4.0	3.3	2.1	20.2

* Percent of total sales of liquid bleach on a consumer dollar basis.
Note: No figures given if the brand listed is not sold in the area.
Source: Trade Regulation Reports 1966 (71,715) *Procter & Gamble Company* v. *Federal Trade Commission.*

EXHIBIT 2

Clorox Company sales, income, and retained earnings
(in thousands of dollars)

	(11 mo.) 1958	1959	1960	1961	1962	1963	1964	1965	1966	1967	(8 mo.) 1968
Net sales	38,736	46,908	51,382	53,150	63,801	70,619	76,224	76,408	77,889	82,514	56,947
Net income	2,362	3,565	4,141	4,149	4,764	6,217	8,752	9,229	9,855	10,796	7,919
Profit margin (percent)	6.1	7.6	8.1	7.8	7.5	8.8	11.5	12.1	12.7	13.1	13.9
Retained earnings (at beginning of period)	N.A.	N.A.	N.A.	N.A.	N.A.	N.A.	N.A.	948	1,177	1,332	128
Plus: Income	2,362	3,565	4,141	4,149	4,764	6,217	8,752	9,229	9,855	10,796	7,919
Less: Dividends	N.A.	N.A.	N.A.	N.A.	N.A.	N.A.	N.A.	9,000	9,700	12,000	7,900
Retained earnings (at end of period)	N.A.	N.A.	N.A.	N.A.	N.A.	N.A.	N.A.	1,177	1,332	128	147

N.A. = Not available.
Source: Prospectus for the Clorox Company, May 22, 1968.

EXHIBIT 3
CLOROX COMPANY
Balance sheet, February 29, 1968

ASSETS

Current Assets:

Cash	$ 1,397,949
Marketable securities	4,763,077
Accounts receivable.	3,399,247
Inventories, at lower of cost (first-in, first-out) or market	2,053,816
Total Current Assets.	$11,614,089
Property, Plant, and Equipment—at cost	
(less accumulated depreciation).	$ 5,380,470
Goodwill*	18,476,976
Other Assets	570,134
Total.	$36,041,669

LIABILITIES

Current Liabilities:

Accounts payable.		$ 4,158,190
Accrued liabilities.		3,863,231
Total Current Liabilities.		$ 8,021,421
Deferred Income Taxes.		$ 317,000
Shareholder Equity:		
Common stock (issued and outstanding).	$ 8,000,000	
Additional paid-in capital	19,556,008	
Income retained in the business.	147,240	$27,703,248
Total.		$36,041,669

* "Goodwill of $18,476,976, as shown above, represents the excess of market valuation of the Procter & Gamble shares . . . over the net assets of (Clorox) Chemical Co. when exchanged therefore in 1957. The Company has not amortized the amount of goodwill because it is considered that there has been no diminution of value."

Source: Prospectus for the Clorox Company, May 22, 1968.

EXHIBIT 4
Procter & Gamble Company and subsidiary companies financial review 1957–1972

Fiscal year ended June 30	1957	1958	1959	1960	1961	1962	1963	1964	1965	1966	1967	1968	1969	1970	1971	1972
Net sales (millions of $).	$1,156	1,295	1,369	1,442	1,542	1,619	1,654	1,914	2,059	2,243	2,439	2,543	2,708	2,979	3,178	3,514
Net earnings (millions of $).	$67.8	73.2	81.7	98.1	106.6	109.4	115.8	130.8	133.2	149.4	174.1	182.6*	187.4	211.9	237.6	276.3
Net earnings as per- cent of net sales. . . .	5.9	5.7	6.0	6.8	6.9	6.8	7.0	6.8	6.5	6.7	7.1	7.2*	6.9	7.1	7.5	7.9
Net earnings per share†.	$.86	.89	.99	1.18	1.28	1.30	1.38	1.49	1.53	1.74	2.04	2.15*	2.25	2.60	2.91	3.38
Common dividends per share.	$.463	.50	.525	.60	.663	.725	.775	.838	.90	.963	1.05	1.15	1.25	1.325	1.40	1.50

* Excludes an extraordinary profit of $19,403,000 ($0.23 per share) on sale of 15 percent of the company's investment in The Clorox Company.
† Based on average number of common shares outstanding during the respective years. All per-share figures have been adjusted to give effect to the stock splits in 1961 and 1970.

Source: Procter & Gamble Annual Report, 1972.

Merger guidelines[1]

Purpose

The purpose of these guidelines is to illustrate the Department of Justice's standards used in determining whether to challenge corporate acquisitions and mergers under Section 7 of the Clayton Act. (Although mergers or acquisitions may also be challenged under the Sherman Act, commonly the challenge will be made under Section 7 of the Clayton Act.) The responsibilities of the Department of Justice under Section 7 are those of an *enforcement agency*. These guidelines are subject to change at any time without prior notice.

General enforcement policy

The primary role of Section 7 enforcement is to preserve and promote market structures conducive to competition. Market structure is the focus of the department's merger policy chiefly because the conduct of the individual firms in a market tends to be controlled by the structure of that market. Emphasis on market structure generally is adequate for the purposes of a statute that requires only proof that a merger "may

---

[1] This is an abridged version of the "Merger Guidelines" issued by the Antitrust Division of the Department of Justice under the Democratic administration of President Lyndon B. Johnson in May 1968.

be substantially to lessen competition, or to tend to create a monopoly." An enforcement policy emphasizing a limited number of structural factors also facilitates both enforcement decision-making and business planning which involves anticipation of the department's enforcement intent.

In certain cases, the structural factors used will not be conclusive. This is sometimes the case, for example, where basic technological changes are creating new industries, or are significantly transforming older industries, making current market boundaries and market structure uncertain. The department in these cases may not sue despite nominal application of a particular guideline, or it may sue even though the guidelines do not require the department to challenge the merger. Since there is incomplete knowledge of structure-conduct relationships for conglomerates, structural criteria will not be solely used in these guidelines.

Market definition

A market is any grouping of sales in which each selling firm enjoys some advantage in competing with those firms whose sales are not included. A market is defined both in terms of its product dimension ("line of commerce") and its geographic dimension ("Section of the country"). It is ordinarily measured by the dollar value of the sales for the most recent twelve-month period.

Line of commerce. The sales of any product or service which is distinguishable in commercial practice from other products or services will ordinarily constitute a relevant product market. The sales of two distinct products to a particular group of purchasers can also be a single market where the two products are reasonably interchangeable.

The department seeks to prevent mergers which create a power to behave noncompetitively in the production and sale of any particular product, even though that power will ultimately be limited by the presence of other products that are less than perfect substitutes. The department also tries to prohibit mergers between firms selling distinct products which may enhance the companies' market power because the products compete enough to influence the production, development or sale of each.

Section of the country. The total sales of a product or service in any commercially significant section of the country, or aggregate of sections, will make up geographic market if there are significant regional sales of the product.

Because data limitations will often make precise delineation of geographic markets impossible, any merger which appears to be illegal in any reasonable geographic market is challenged even though in another reasonable market it would not appear to be illegal.

HORIZONTAL MERGERS

Enforcement policy

For horizontal mergers, the department's enforcement of Section 7 of the Clayton Act has the following purposes: (*a*) preventing the elimination of any independent company likely to have been a substantial competitive influence in a market; (*b*) preventing any company from obtaining a position of dominance in a market; (*c*) preventing significant increases in concentration in a market; and (*d*) preserving significant possibilities for eventual deconcentration in a concentrated market.

In horizontal mergers, the department emphasizes the size of the market share held by both the acquiring and the acquired firms. The larger the market share held by the acquired firm, the more likely it is that the firm has been a competitive influence or that concentration in the market will be significantly increased. The larger the market share held by the acquiring firm, the more likely it is that an acquisition will lead it to a position of dominance or of shared market power.

Market highly concentrated

In a market in which the shares of the four largest firms amount to approximately 75 percent or more, the department will ordinarily challenge mergers between firms accounting for, approximately, the following percentages of the market:

Acquiring firm (percent)	Acquired firm (percent)
4	4 or more
10	2 or more
15 or more	1 or more

Market less highly concentrated

In a market in which the shares of the four largest firms amount to less than approximately 75 percent, the department will ordinarily challenge mergers between firms accounting for, approximately the following percentages of the market:

Acquiring firm (percent)	Acquired firm (percent)
5	5 or more
10	4 or more
15	3 or more
20	2 or more
25 or more	1 or more

Market with trend toward concentration

The department applies stricter standards where there is a significant trend toward increased concentration. Such a trend is considered to be present when the aggregate market share of any grouping of the largest firms in the market from the two largest to the eight largest has increased by approximately 7 percent or more over a period from any year five to ten years prior to the merger up to the time of the merger. The department will ordinarily challenge any acquisition by such firms whose market share amounts to approximately 2 percent or more.

Nonmarket share standards

The following are two cases in which a challenge by the department can ordinarily be anticipated: (a) acquisition of a competitor which is a particularly competitive factor in the market; and (b) a merger involving a substantial firm and a firm which, despite an insubstantial market share, possesses an unusual competitive potential or has an asset that confers an unusual competitive advantage.

There may also be certain horizontal mergers between makers of distinct products regarded as in the same line of commerce where some modification in the minimum market shares subject to challenge may be appropriate.

Failing company

A merger which the department would otherwise question will ordinarily not be challenged if (a) the firm faces the clear probability of a business failure, and (b) efforts by the failing firm have failed to elicit a reasonable offer of acquisition more consistent with the purposes of Section 7. The department does not regard a firm as failing merely because the firm has been unprofitable for a period of time, has lost market position, has poor management, or has not fully explored the possibility of overcoming its difficulties through self-help.

The difficulty in assessing these factors will lead the department to apply this standard only in the clearest of circumstances.

Economies

The Department will not normally accept as a justification for an acquisition subject to challenge under its horizontal merger standards the claim that the merger will produce economies because (a) a challenge is unlikely to be made to mergers of the kind most likely to involve companies operating significantly below the size necessary to achieve significant economies of scale; (*b*) if there are potential economies, they can normally be realized through internal expansion; and (*c*) there are severe difficulties in establishing the existence and magnitude of economies claimed for a merger.

VERTICAL MERGERS

Enforcement policy

The department believes that anticompetitive consequences can be expected whenever a vertical acquisition in a supplying or purchasing market raises barriers to entry in either market or to disadvantage existing nonintegrated or partly integrated firms in either market in ways unrelated to economic efficiency.

Vertical mergers tend to raise barriers to entry (*a*) by foreclosing equal access to potential customers, reducing the ability of nonintegrated firms to capture competitively the market share needed to achieve an efficient level of production, (*b*) by foreclosing equal access to potential suppliers, thus either increasing the risk of a price or supply squeeze on the new entrant or imposing the additional burden of entry as an integrated firm; or (*c*) by facilitating promotional product differentiation, when the merger involves a manufacturing firm's acquisition of firms at the retail level. Besides impeding the entry of new sellers, vertical mergers also inhibit the expansion of presently competing sellers by conferring on the merged firm competitive advantages, unrelated to real economies of production or distribution.

The department believes that the most important aims of its enforcement policy on vertical mergers can be stated by guidelines framed primarily in terms of the market shares of the merging firms and the conditions of entry which already exist in the relevant markets.

Supplying firm's market

In determining whether to challenge a vertical merger for lessening competition in the supplying firm's market, consideration must be given to (*a*) the market share of the supplying firm, (*b*) the market share of the purchasing firm, and (*c*) the conditions of entry in the purchasing firm's market. According, the Department will ordinarily challenge a merger or series of mergers between a supplying firm, accounting for approximately 10 percent or more of the sales in its market, and one or more purchasing firms, accounting *in toto* for approximately 6 percent or more of the total purchases in that market, unless there are clearly no significant barriers to entry into the business of the purchasing firm or firms.

Purchasing firm's market

Challenges will be made to most of the vertical mergers which may have adverse effects in the purchasing firm's market since adverse effects in the purchasing firm's market will normally occur only as the result of significant vertical mergers involving supplying firms with market shares in excess of 10 percent. Vertical mergers can be challenged on the ground that they raise entry barriers in the purchasing firm's market or confer upon the purchasing firm a significant supply advantage over unintegrated or partly integrated existing or potential competitors.

If the product sold by the supplying firm is either a complex one in which innovating changes have been taking place, or is a scarce raw material whose supply cannot be readily expanded to meet increased demand, the merged firm may have the power to use any temporary superiority, or any shortage of the product, to put its competitors at a disadvantage by refusing to sell the product to them (supply squeeze) or by narrowing the margin between the price at which it sells the product to their competitors. The department believes that the increase in barriers to entry arising simply from the increased risk of a possible squeeze is sufficient to warrant prohibition of any merger between a supplier possessing significant market power and a substantial purchaser of any product meeting the above description. The Department will ordinarily challenge a merger or series of mergers between a supplying firm, accounting for approximately 20 percent or more of the sales in its market, and a purchasing firm, or firms, accounting *in toto* for approximately 10 percent or more of the sales in the market in which it sells the product whose manufacture requires the supplying firm's product.

Nonmarket share standards

Certain mergers, not liable under the market share standards, can still be challenged under Section 7. The most common such instances are acquisitions of suppliers or customers by major firms in an industry in which (a) there has been, or is developing a significant trend toward vertical integration by merger which would probably raise barriers to entry or impose a competitive disadvantage on unintegrated or partly integrated firms, and (b) it does not clearly appear that the particular acquisition will result in significant economies of production or distribution unrelated to advertising, etc.

The acquisition by a firm of a customer or supplier which increases the difficulty of potential competitors in entering either of their markets or puts competitors of either firm at an unwarranted disadvantage will be challenged.

Failing company

The standards set forth in paragraph 9 apply to a vertical merger.

Economies

The department will not normally accept as a justification for an acquisition the claim that the merger will produce economies, because (a) substantial potential economies of vertical integration can normally be realized through internal expansion into the supplying or purchasing market, and (b) barriers preventing entry into the supplying or purchasing market by internal expansion usually result in no challenge being made to the acquisition of a firm or firms of sufficient size to overcome or adequately minimize the barriers to entry.

CONGLOMERATE MERGERS

Enforcement policy

Conglomerate mergers are mergers that are neither horizontal nor vertical.

At the present time, the department regards two categories of conglomerate mergers as having sufficiently identifiable anticompetitive effects for specific guidelines: mergers involving potential entrants and mergers creating a danger of reciprocal buying.

Enforcement action will also be taken against other types of conglomerate mergers that on specific analysis appear anticompetitive.

Mergers involving potential entrants

Since potential competition often limits the exercise of market power by leading firms and is a likely source of additional competition, the department will ordinarily challenge any merger between one of the most likely entrants into the market and:

1. Any firm with approximately 25 percent or more of the market;
2. One of the two largest firms in a market in which the shares of the two largest firms amount to approximately 50 percent or more;
3. One of the four largest firms in a market in which the shares of the eight largest firms amount to approximately 75 percent or more, provided the merging firm's share of the market amounts to approximately 10 percent or more; or

4. One of the eight largest firms in a market in which the shares of these firms amount to approximately 75 percent or more, provided either (*a*) the merging firm's share of the market is not insubstantial and there are no more than one or two likely entrants into the market, or (*b*) the merging firm is a rapidly growing firm.

The firm's capability of entering on a competitively significant scale relative to the capability of other firms and the firm's economic incentive to enter are important.

The department will also ordinarily challenge a merger between an existing competitor in a market and a likely entrant, undertaken for the purpose of preventing the competition that such entry might create.

Unless there are exceptional circumstances, the department will not accept as a justification for a merger the claim that the merger will produce economies, because the department believes that equivalent economies can be normally achieved either through internal expansion or through a small firm acquisition or other acceptable acquisitions.

Mergers creating danger of reciprocal buying

The department will challenge reciprocal buying (that is, favoring one's customer when making purchases of a product which is sold by the customer). Unless reciprocal buying is unlikely, the department considers reciprocal buying possible whenever approximately 15 percent or more of the total purchases in a market in which one of the merging firms sells are accounted for by firms which also make substantial sales in markets where the other merging firm is a more substantial buyer than all or most of the competitors of the selling firm.

The department will also ordinarily challenge (*a*) any merger undertaken to create reciprocal buying arrangements, and (*b*) any merger creating the possibility of reciprocal buying where one (or both) of the merging firms has within the recent past, or after the merger, actually engaged in reciprocal buying, or attempted directly or indirectly to induce firms with which it deals to engage in reciprocal buying.

The department will not ordinarily accept as a justification for such a merger the claim that the merger will produce economies, because the Department believes that equivalent economies can be achieved through other legal mergers.

Mergers which entrench market power and other conglomerate mergers

The department may bring suit where an acquisition of a leading firm in a relatively concentrated or rapidly concentrating market may increase the market power of that firm or raise barriers to entry in that market. Examples include: (*a*) a merger which produces a very large disparity in absolute size between the merged firm and the largest remaining firms, (*b*) a merger of firms producing related products which may induce purchasers, concerned about the possible use of leverage, to buy products of the merged firm rather than those of competitors, and (*c*) a merger which may enhance the ability of the merged firm to increase product differentiation in the relevant markets.

The conglomerate merger area involves novel problems that have not yet been subjected to as much analysis as have horizontal and vertical mergers. The conglomerate merger field as a whole is one in which the department considers it necessary to carry on a continuous study of the ways in which mergers may have significant anticompetitive consequences in circumstances beyond those covered by these guidelines. For example, the department has used Section 7 to prevent mergers which may diminish competition resulting from technological developments that may increase interproduct competition between industries whose products are presently relatively imperfect substitutes. The department may identify other categories of mergers that can be the subject of specific guidelines.

Failing company

The standards set forth under the heading, "Failing company," are normally applied by the department in determining whether to challenge a conglomerate merger; except that in marginal cases involving the application of points 3 and 4 in the section entitled "Mergers involving potential entrants," the department may not sue even though the acquired firm is not "failing" in the strict sense.

United States of America v. International Telephone and Telegraph[1]

On July 2, 1971, the Federal District Court of Chicago announced that it had ruled against the Justice Department in the *Canteen Case*, finding no violation of the Clayton Act in International Telephone and Telegraph's 1969 acquisition of the Automatic Canteen Corporation. In fact, Judge Richard B. Austin had decided that ITT actually spurred competition in the food business by applying time-and-motion studies to vending-machine repairs and cost analysis to cafeteria menu planning.

The news was encouraging to the management of ITT, then involved in arduous negotiations with the Antitrust Division of the U.S. Department of Justice. These negotiations were aimed at reaching an out-of-court settlement on not only the Canteen acquisition, but also ITT's 1969 acquisitions of Grinnell Corporation and Hartford Fire Insurance Company, both of which were contested by the Justice Department.

The trial court's decision, however, once again raised two familiar questions in ITT's mind:

1. Could ITT, which had now received favorable District Court decisions on both Canteen and Grinnell, win any or all of its three antitrust cases if the Justice Department appealed them to the Supreme Court?

2. Should ITT pursue a harder bargaining line in its settlement nego-

---

[1] This case was prepared by Jonathan T. Carder, research assistant, under the direction of Howard W. Pifer, lecturer on business administration. It was developed entirely from publicly available documents and is intended to serve as a basis for class discussion rather than to illustrate either effective or ineffective handling of an administrative situation.

tiations, expecting the Justice Department to be more willing now to make concessions?

Corporate history

The history of ITT can be divided into two distinct periods: "before Geneen," and "after Geneen."

Before Geneen. On June 16, 1920, Col. Sosthenes Behm and his brother Hernand incorporated the International Telephone and Telegraph Company (with assets consisting of the Puerto Rico Telephone Company, the Cuban Telephone Company, and a half interest in the Cuban American Telephone and Telegraph Company) as a communications service company in the Caribbean.

Under the leadership of Colonel Behm and his successors, ITT grew to become in 1959 a worldwide factor in the telecommunications field, with revenues of $765 million and earnings of $29 million, occupying 51st place on the *Fortune* list of the largest industrial corporations. At this time, 80 percent of the company's earnings came from outside the United States, primarily from the manufacture of telecommunications equipment and the operation of telecommunications utilities.

After Geneen. Harold Sydney Geneen came to ITT from Raytheon, where he had served as executive vice president and director. A registered CPA in New York and Illinois, Geneen had initially worked for two accounting firms, then moved up to chief accountant at American Can (1942–1946) and later to vice president and controller at Jones & Laughlin Steel (1946–1950) and Bell & Howell (1950–1956) before joining Raytheon.

If ITT's growth in its first 39 years could be called impressive, then its growth since the arrival of Harold Geneen to the ITT presidency in June 1959 must be termed phenomenal.

Along with instituting a system of tight management controls, the British-born Geneen embarked the company on a policy of broad diversification both as to business activities and geographical markets. In the next decade ITT acquired 85 companies in the United States and 75 in other countries, so that in late 1969, according to data ITT submitted to a House Antitrust Subcommittee: ITT owned at least 50 percent of the stock in each of 114 companies in the United States, Canada, and Mexico; 158 in Europe; 30 in Latin America; 15 in Africa and the Middle East; and 14 in the Far East and the Pacific. These 331 corporations were major subsidiaries such as Aetna Finance, Avis Rent-A-Car, Continental Baking, Levitt & Sons, and Sheraton Corporation—firms that had an additional 708 lower-tier subsidiaries of their own.

Seemingly undaunted by the three antitrust suits, ITT had continued its acquisitions into the 1970s, highlighted by at least 17 more additions in the United States in 1970 alone. For the year ended December 31, 1970, the company reported sales of $6.4 billion and earnings of $353.3 million, putting ITT in eight place on the *Fortune* list. Only 19 percent of revenues and 15 percent of net income came from telecommunications. In addition, 65 percent of net earnings were derived from United States and Canadian operations. (Exhibit 1 summarizes ITT's operations under Geneen. Exhibit 2 divides ITT's sales and earnings by product groups. Exhibits 3 and 4 provide data on ITT acquisitions.)

Antitrust problems

By 1967, ITT's acquisitive nature had come under the scrutiny of the Justice Department's Antitrust Division. After the Federal Communications Commission had approved the proposed merger of ITT and the American Broadcasting Company on December 31, 1966, the division insisted on a reopening of hearings by the FCC. When the commission on June 22, 1967, again upheld the merger, the Justice Department filed an appeal in the District of Columbia Court of Appeals, arguing that the merger would eliminate ITT as a potential entrant into broadcasting as a network operator and as a substantial factor in CATV operations. The department also maintained that the merger would lead to violations of the integrity of ABC's news and public affairs programming.

The Court of Appeals still had not ruled on the case by the end of 1967, more than two years after the directors of ITT and ABC had approved the merger. Invoking a provision in the merger agreement that either party could withdraw if the merger were not completed by December 31, 1967, ITT chose to withdraw from the merger rather than renegotiate the terms of the merger (necessitated by changes in ITT and ABC's stock prices) and face further litigation.

The real clash, however, came in 1969, when the Antitrust Division filed suits against three ITT acquisitions:

1. Canteen Corporation of Chicago, Illinois, the nation's largest food-vending company, with 1968 revenues of $322 million;
2. Grinnell Corporation of Providence, Rhode Island, the nation's largest supplier of fire-protection sprinkler systems, with 1968 sales of $341 million;
3. Hartford Fire Insurance Company of Hartford, Connecticut, the nation's second largest fire insurance company, with $1 billion in premiums.

The suits were the result of the vigorous antitrust policy of the new division chief, Assistant Attorney General Richard W. McLaren. Mc-

Laren, formerly an antitrust lawyer and chairman of the American Bar Association's antitrust section, had accepted the Nixon appointment on the condition that he be given a free hand to attack the spreading tide of conglomerate mergers,[2] an area that had escaped litigation under his predecessor, Donald F. Turner.

Unlike Professor Turner, McLaren took the position that Congress had intended that the antitrust laws should be applied to all classes of mergers, including conglomerates, and believed the Supreme Court would share this view. McLaren also convinced the Nixon administration that if it did not crack down on conglomerate mergers, there was a strong likelihood that Congress would take action. ". . . (T)his Administration had no alternative," said McLaren.[3] With this mandate of sorts, Richard McLaren then seized upon the ITT-Canteen merger as an opportunity to test his policy in court.

In contesting the ITT and other conglomerate acquisitions, McLaren emphasized two basic concepts: *potentiality,* referring to a situation where an acquiring company was a possible entrant into the acquired firm's market; and *reciprocity,* referring to a company's ability to use its large-scale purchasing power to promote its own sales. The following excerpts from a memo to Deputy Attorney General Richard G. Kleindienst dated October 13, 1970, summarized McLaren's views on the three ITT cases:[4]

> . . . . In Grinnell, the main thrust of our case is that because of its acquisition by ITT, Grinnell will be entrenched as the dominant firm in the manufacture and in the installation of automatic sprinklers.
>
> All of Grinnell's manufacturing competitors are relatively small companies, and the competitive installers of automatic sprinkler systems are small regional or local contractors. Grinnell clearly dominates both the manufacture and installation of sprinkler systems. At the trial, witnesses testified that ITT's ability to finance sprinkler jobs and to obtain advantages through its insurance contacts (Hartford) and real estate construction jobs (Levitt) will make it very difficult for them to compete. In fact, the principal competitor testified that he considered seeking a similar merger in order to survive. From the evidence in the record, we will argue that the merger will create barriers to the entry of new competition and will entrench Grinnell in its dominant position.
>
> In Canteen, we will argue that the food service business is becoming

---

[2] A "conglomerate" merger is one in which there are no important horizontal or vertical relationships between the acquiring and acquired corporations (for example, ITT's acquisition of Continental Baking).

[3] "Antitrust—The Then and The Now," *Mergers & Acquisitions,* Vol. 4, No. 5, September–October 1969, p. 5.

[4] Attorney General John N. Mitchell had disqualified himself from the cases because his former law firm had done work for ITT. Kleindienst, therefore, as No. 2 in the hierarchy, had to approve all Justice Department actions regarding the ITT cases.

increasingly concentrated and that the merger with ITT provides an increased opportunity for practicing reciprocity, since ITT buys from the same industries which utilize food service of the type offered by Canteen. We will also argue that as the merger wave continues, the opportunities for reciprocity of this type will spiral. Documents indicate that the food service industry is quite susceptible to reciprocity.

In the Hartford case, we are also urging a reciprocity theory—that ITT's immense purchasing power spread across the breadth of the economy cannot help but exert a powerful effect on Hartford's insurance business. Insurance is largely a fungible commodity, and most of ITT's suppliers require it. It is to be expected that these suppliers will favor ITT-Hartford in their insurance purchases even if no pressure is applied. We also allege vertical foreclosure of other insurance firms from ITT's substantial insurance purchases; elimination of potential competition (ITT is already in life insurance); triggering of other mergers; and entrenchment of Grinnell, as described above.

In addition to the theories described above, we expect to argue that the three acquisitions are not only part of ITT's program of acquiring large leading companies, but are part of a general marger trend which, if continued, will have substantial anticompetitive effects upon the economy as a whole. . . .

ITT's arguments

In the Canteen and Grinnell District Court hearings, ITT argued that it did not and would not engage in reciprocity, that it was "not really all that big" (to quote McLaren), and would not use its power in other fields to benefit Canteen and Grinnell. In addition, ITT argued that the Justice Department was really just attacking it on bigness grounds, and that there was still plenty of competition in the industries involved.

Meanwhile, in out-of-court discussions with McLaren and his staff, the company's attorneys had maintained initially that the Antitrust Division's policy was not supported by the law, that there was no justification for it in cases and legislative history, and that since the division had little chance of winning the cases, they should settle for an injunction against reciprocity and certain future acquisitions.

Later, as it became clear that McLaren would not be dissuaded from pursuing the cases by this argument, ITT's lawyers attempted to work out a compromise whereby the company would be able to keep Hartford, whose enormous cash flows figured importantly in ITT's long-range planning. Their approach was that leaving aside the question of who would win the case, the most that the Antitrust Division could get out of the court, and the most it should really ask for or want, would be the items outlined in the following letter:

Hollabaugh & Jacobs,
Washington, D.C.,
November 25, 1970

Honorable Richard W. McLaren,
Assistant Attorney General, Antitrust Division,
Department of Justice, Washington, D.C.

Dear Mr. McLaren: As I mentioned to you during our conference Monday afternoon, I sincerely believe that the proposed settlement package which we left with you affirmatively meets the issues and theories raised in the Government's complaints in the three ITT cases. Moreover, I believe that the proposals suggested in the package are consistent with the underlying objective of Section 7 of the Clayton Act.

ITT offered substantial divestiture consisting of the major portion of Canteen's commercial and industrial in-plant feeding operations in the United States; the extensive domestic operations of ITT Levitt and Sons, Inc.; and three life insurance companies which were owned by ITT prior to its acquisition of Hartford. There were certain minor exceptions relating to ITT Levitt and the life insurance companies. Beyond this substantial divestiture, ITT has offered various injunctive provisions, extensive in scope, which would deal effectively with the alleged anticompetitive effects pleaded in the Government's three complaints. These provisions, in summary, include prohibitions relating to reciprocity and reciprocity effect; prohibitions against Hartford's lending money to, providing financing for, or making investments in any ITT system company in the United States (without prior consent of the Department of Justice or the United States District Court); prohibitions against transferring to Hartford and to Canteen certain ITT business; prohibitions to assure that there will be no anticompetitive package selling of Grinnell and ITT products, or the installation of Grinnell sprinkler systems in ITT facilities (all without prior consent, etc.); and a prohibition that would prevent Hartford from supplying possible sales leads to Grinnell unless such information was supplied to competitors of Grinnell. In short, ITT has endeavored to deal with the issues of reciprocity, reciprocity effects, vertical relationships, inter-company dealings and other issues presented by the Government's complaints in these cases.

While as I indicated above, it is our belief that the package left with you Monday deals with the issues in the Government's case, I now wish to state that in an effort to resolve this very burdensome litigation, ITT is prepared to supplement the extensive package left with you Monday with the following additional divestitures: (*a*) complete divestiture of ITT's interest in Canteen; and (*b*) complete divestiture of Grinnell's Industrial Piping Division. This is the Grinnell Division which is engaged in the "power piping" business referred to in the Government's complaint in the Grinnell case and involves total sales of about $50 million. This is already a separate operating entity and we believe that it can be successfully divested as a going business.

The proposed divestitures represent assets of approximately $500 million and annual revenues of approximately $600 million, plus insurance companies having an excess of $2 billion of life insurance in force and annual premiums of $26.7 million. We believe this suggested divestiture is responsive to your expressed concern about "aggregate concentration" despite the fact that ITT is of the view that Section 7 of the Clayton Act does not extend to this issue. It should also be noted that ITT faces an imminent loss of its Chilean assets of approximately $200 million.

You also mentioned the subject of ITT's proposed acquisition of the O. M. Scott Company and indicated that you intend to investigate this acquisition. It is ITT's belief that this proposed acquisition does not violate any of the merger guidelines enunciated by the Department of Justice or the Federal Trade Commission, or impinge on any of the general areas of concern spelled out in the Attorney General's speech before the Georgia Bar Association on June 6, 1969. Certainly, it was not ITT's intention to violate any of those guidelines and ITT will cooperate fully in any such investigation.

As ITT has informed you, it is not their desire to engage in continual confrontations with the Department of Justice. They are anxious to resolve this litigation and get on with the urgent business of helping the economy move forward.

Very truly yours,

Ephraim Jacobs.

(Exhibit 5 is a more detailed delineation of the settlement package. It was included with the Jacobs letter.)

McLaren, however, was not interested in this proposal. As he later commented, "I thought that we would take the cases up and we would win them and get more than that."[5]

The *Grinnell* case was the first to reach trial, and in December 1970, a Connecticut District Court ruled against the Justice Department and dismissed the complaint against ITT. Perhaps comforted by the fact that the Antitrust Division had never lost a case in the Supreme Court since the Celler-Kefauver Amendment was passed in 1950, McLaren prepared his appeal for the Supreme Court.[6]

Apparently Richard McLaren was not the only one aware of the Supreme Court's record of generally reversing trial court merger decisions. In a letter dated April 16, 1971, to Deputy Attorney General Kleindienst, ITT counsel Lawrence E. Walsh admitted that "one must realize that if the government urges an expanded interpretation of the vague language of the Clayton Act, there is a high probability that it will succeed." Walsh added that this would represent a major expan-

---

[5] *Hearings Before the Committee on the Judiciary, United States Senate, 92d Congress, Second Session on Nomination of Richard G. Kleindienst of Arizona to be Attorney General,* p. 132.

[6] The Celler-Kefauver Act amended Section 7 of the Clayton Act to cover acquisitions of assets, as well as stock, when the effect of the acquisition or merger may be substantially to lessen competition or tend to create a monopoly.

sion of the antitrust laws, and therefore should not be pursued until the Justice Department had sounded out the Secretary of the Treasury, the Secretary of Commerce, and the Chairman of the President's Council of Economic Advisers for their views on the matter. It was further requested that the department delay the submission of the jurisdictional statement in the *Grinnell* case long enough to permit ITT "to make a more adequate presentation on this question."

Included with the Walsh letter was a memo from ITT's attorneys to the Justice Department advocating a comprehensive review of administration policy toward diversification by merger. Citing Professor Turner as a reference, the attorneys argued that a ban on diversification (that is, conglomerate) mergers "would sacrifice vital national goals— economic growth and full employment, American competitiveness in world markets, and the balance of payments—to the unrealized fear of dangers to (domestic) competition."

It was contended that diversification by merger is often the only established means of stimulating competitiveness in established industries:

> . . . Through diversification, scarce management skills, additional re-
> sources of capital and know-how, and, most important, the will and
> ability to plan for growth, can be brought to bear in new indus-
> tries. . . . ITT itself is a case in point. ITT stimulates the profit growth
> of each of its profit centers by helping them develop short-range and
> long-range plans for growth and by assisting them through a central
> management staff of over 1,000 industrial and operations specialists.
> Since 1960, ITT's earnings have grown at a steady compound rate
> of 11% a year. The improved competitiveness of the companies ITT
> has acquired is illustrated by the growth and development of subsidiaries
> like Avis and Sheraton.[7]

Stressing ITT's expropriation problems in Cuba and Chile, and the company's national importance as the third largest corporate contributor to the U.S. balance of payments, the memo's authors also maintained that the risks of foreign operations must be balanced by a stable economic base in the United States:

---

[7] Profitability ratios for Avis (in percent):

	1964	1965	1966	1967	1968
Net income to assets	4.0	3.0	3.1	2.8	2.6
Net income to sales	6.1	4.0	4.0	2.8	2.8
Assets to sales	150	130	129	100	107

Source: *Investigation of Conglomerate Corporations* a report by the staff of the Anti-trust Subcommittee of the Committee of the Judiciary, U.S. House of Representatives, 1971, pp. 124–25.

. . . This need for a stable domestic base is the basic reason for ITT's diversification program. If this diversification into the United States economy is prohibited, the ability of ITT and other United States companies to assume the substantial risks of doing business abroad in a competitive world market will be substantially impaired.

Although he eventually authorized the Grinnell appeal, Solicitor General Erwin N. Griswold, a former dean of the Harvard Law School, did so reluctantly, because:

. . . there was grave doubt in my office by member of my staff and myself about the Grinnell case. We felt that it would be very difficult to win it, not only because the law with respect to conglomerate mergers is far from clear, but also because in this particular case there had been sharp conflict in the evidence before the District Judge, and the District Judge had found all the acts against us. And all experience shows that it is extremely difficult to win an antitrust case or another type of case in the Supreme Court when you have to attack the findings of fact.

Meanwhile, ITT had taken a new tack. On April 29, Felix G. Rohatyn, an ITT director and partner in the Wall Street investment banking firm of Lazard Freres and Company, with the assistance of Dr. Raymond Saulnier of Columbia University (formerly chairman of Eisenhower's Council of Economic Advisers) and Dr. Willis J. Winn, dean of the Wharton School, had made a presentation to the Justice Department to the effect that a Hartford divestiture would cost the ITT stockholders approximately $1 billion,[8] and ITT would be greatly weakened, particularly in its overseas operations, to the detriment of the U.S. balance of payments. Rohatyn, also chairman of the New York Stock Exchange Surveillance Committee, added that so massive a divestiture might unsettle U.S. securities markets, with possible impact on some financial organizations.

A change of mind[9]

Unlike the previous ITT approaches, Rohatyn's apparently had an impact on McLaren. Perhaps concerned that ITT would meet the same

---

[8] It was argued that the shares of ITT and Hartford could have been expected, on the basis of historical values and the performances of other securities, each to sell at a lower earnings multiple than the shares of ITT were selling at that time. It was thus estimated that an ITT shareholder holding one share of ITT (after divesting Hartford), and one share of the divested Hartford, would then have securities with a combined value of only $52, as compared with the $64 per share price of ITT on April 29.

[9] For the record, the now-famous meeting between ITT lobbyist Dita Beard and Attorney General Mitchell took place on May 1, 1971, at the mansion of Kentucky Governor Louie B. Nunn. It was alleged by columnist Jack Anderson

fate that had befallen Ling-Temco-Vought, a conglomerate that had nearly gone bankrupt when forced to divest itself of certain of its subsidiaries, McLaren asked Richard Ramsden, a former White House Fellow and currently a partner in the Wall Street investment management firm of Brokaw, Schaenen, Clancy and Company, to assess the validity of ITT's claims.

Ramsden concurred that a divestiture of Hartford would likely cause a severe financial hardship to ITT, and because of changes in the law and accounting practice, entail a loss to ITT stockholders in excess of $1 billion. Bruce MacLaury, a Treasury official in attendance during the Rohatyn presentation, expressed a similar view.

On June 17, McLaren presented the following memo to the deputy attorney general, which was immediately approved:

> Department of Justice,
> Washington, D.C.,
> June 17, 1971

> Memorandum for the Deputy Attorney General
> Re: Proposed Procedure in ITT Merger Cases

> *Background.* We have three anti-merger cases pending against ITT: the *Grinnell* case (sprinkler systems), which was tried and lost in the District Court and is now on appeal to the Supreme Court; the *Canteen* case (vending and food service), which was tried and is now *sub judice;*[10] and the *Hartford Fire Insurance Co.* case, which is set for trial in September.

> About six weeks ago, representatives of ITT made a confidential presentation to the Department, the gist of which was that if we are successful in obtaining a divestiture order in the ITT-Hartford Fire Insurance Company case, this will cripple ITT financially and seriously injure its 250,000 stockholders. Esessentially, this is because ITT paid a $500 million premium for the Hartford stock but took its assets in at book value in a so-called pooling of interests transaction. It cannot now sell its Hartford stock without (a) suffering a serious loss as opposed to what it paid but, at the same time (b) incurring a large capital gain tax. A "spin-off" to its own shareholders would be a—and probably the only—feasible alternative; however, a spin-off would leave ITT with the large preferred dividend commitment it made in acquiring Hartford ($50 million a year), but without the earning power which was counted on to cover that commitment. The result, we are told, would be a loss of well over $1 billion in ITT common stock value, a weakened balance sheet, and reduced borrowing capacity.

that at this meeting the Attorney General gave his assurance of a reasonable settlement of the antitrust suits, while Mrs. Beard gave her assurance of a $400,000 ITT contribution to the 1972 Republican National Convention. (Exhibit 6 is a memo from Mrs. Beard to the head of ITT's Washington office said to confirm this. Mrs. Beard later denied under oath having written the memo.)

[10] Being tried.

We have had a study made by financial experts and they substantially confirm ITT's claims as to the effects of a divestiture order. Such being the case, I gather that we must also anticipate that the impact upon ITT would have a ripple effect—in the stock market and in the economy.

Under the circumstances, I think we are compelled to weigh the need for divestiture in this case—including its deterrent effect as well as the elimination of anticompetitive effects to be expected from divestiture—against the damage which divestiture would occasion. Or, to refine the issue a little more: Is a decree against ITT containing injunctive relief and a divestiture order worth enough more than a decree containing only injunctive relief to justify the projected adverse effects on ITT and its stockholders, and the risk of adverse effects on the stock market and the economy?

I come to the reluctant conclusion that the answer is "no." I say reluctant because ITT's management consummated the Hartford acquisition knowing it violated our antitrust policy; knowing we intended to sue; and in effect representing to the court that he [(sic) it] need not issue a preliminary injunction because ITT would hold Hartford separate and thus minimize any divestiture problem if violation were found.

Perhaps equally guilty is the trial judge, who listened sympathetically to defendants' plea that granting our motion for preliminary injunction would cost Hartford stockholders the $500 million premium ITT was paying for their stock. Obviously, if such a premium is being paid on an unlawful acquisition, the acquiring company may lose that and more if forced to divest, and will so plead if found guilty. This highlights our continuing need for amendment of the Expediting Act to permit us to appeal from District Court orders denying our motions for preliminary injunctions in such cases.

Proposed Procedure. In order that we do not lose the deterrent we have developed in this field, I propose the following terms of settlement of the ITT cases:

1. *Grinnell*-divestiture. This would require a joint motion in the Supreme Court to refer the case back to the District Court for entry of consent order—which was the procedure the Department followed in *National Steel Corporation.*

2. *Canteen*-divestiture by consent order.

3. *Hartford*-divestiture along lines of *LTV*, including particularly:

　　a. Prohibition for 10 years of (i) acquisition of any corporation with assets of $100 million or more; (ii) acquisition of any corporation with assets of $10 million–100 million without approval of the Department, or permission of the court; and (iii) for a period of an additional five years, prohibition of any acquisition of any corporation with assets over $10 million except on a showing that it will not tend to lessen competition or create a monopoly.

　　b. Prohibition against engaging in systematic reciprocity.

　　c. Divestiture of Avis and Levitt.

Finally, in all three cases, I think we should have the right to approve

ITT's press releases: We want no great protestations of innocence, government abuse, etc. etc.

I recommend that you approve a program along the lines of the foregoing—allowing, of course, for some leeway in negotiating.

Richard W. McLaren,
Assistant Attorney General,
Antitrust Division.

In discussing his change of attitude, McLaren said later:

I went into this settlement on the basis that I thought there was a chance of winning. I also knew there was a chance of losing; right? Say it is 60 to 40. All right, as a lawyer, I analyzed it.

A 60 percent chance I win, and then I think later when I get all this information, can we really afford to win, and then have these disastrous consequences, or is it the other way around?

On the other hand, we have got a 40 percent chance that we will lose. All right, if I lose, my whole program goes down the drain, so I look for some sort of a solution where we could purge their violation, and where we would still . . . have a program, and we still have a deterrent.

And if you pare away all of these things, . . . take away Avis, take away Levitt, take away Grinnell . . . , take away the two insurance companies and Canteen, if that had been the ITT case we were dealing with at the time we filed the Hartford, we would not have sued them for acquiring Hartford. . . ."[11]

With Kleindienst's approval, McLaren then dictated his terms over the phone to Rohatyn. One week later, department officials met ITT's lawyers to hammer out a final settlement. At this time, however, in the words of ITT senior vice president and general counsel, Howard J. Aibel, "That (McLaren's) bargining position was unacceptable to ITT."[12] It was estimated by ITT officials that McLaren's proposed divestiture involved subsidiaries with sales near $1.2 billion, and assets in excess of $900 million.

With respect to Levitt and Canteen, ITT wanted to keep those properties bought or constructed after the acquisition. With respect to Grinnell, ITT argued that it should only be forced to divest the Fire Protection Division. ITT also protested that there was no good antitrust reason why it should be forced to divest Avis, and asked about the negotiability of the provision of no acquisitions over $10 million. McLaren told ITT

---

[11] *Kleindienst Hearings,* pp. 330–31.

[12] In June 1972, the SEC charged Aibel with violating securities law in connection with the 2664 shares of ITT he sold on June 18, 1971. The SEC claimed Aibel had sold the stock on the basis of insider information not available to the general public. Aibel consented to a permanent injunction barring him from further violations of securities laws.

the department would negotiate on details, but that the basic provisions of the proposal were firm.

On June 29, Felix Rohatyn went to Kleindienst's office, complaining that McLaren was taking a rigid attitude with respect to the settlement negotiations, and that the nature of the negotiations was unreasonably punitive. Kleindienst replied that he would not inject himself into the settlement negotiations, that this was a problem between ITT's attorneys and Mr. McLaren and his staff.[13]

Quo vadis?

On July 2, after hearing that the District Court had found no antitrust law violations in ITT's acquisition of Canteen, the management of ITT paused to reassess its position. It was clear what President Geneen thought of the Justice Department's antitrust policy: "Our *#!6#?! Government is about to run the country down the drain."[14] Nevertheless, if ITT took a harder bargaining position, was it prepared to run the risk of more courtroom battles, and the possible loss of Hartford?

Meanwhile in Peru and Chile, the governments were nationalizing ITT's telephone business. In Washington, ITT's Continental Baking had just agreed to run corrective ads on its Profile Bread, and was still arguing with the FTC over the truth of its Wonder Bread and Hostess Cake advertising claims. In New York, ITT had just filed suit against General Telephone and Electronics for antitrust law violations regarding GT&E's purchases of telephone equipment.

Within this environment, ITT's management thought once again about those two familiar questions. . . .

---

[13] *Kleindienst Hearings,* p. 99.
[14] *Forbes* interview, May 15, 1971, p. 189.

EXHIBIT 1

INTERNATIONAL TELEPHONE AND TELEGRAPH CORPORATION AND SUBSIDIARIES CONSOLIDATED

1959–1970 summary*

(dollar amounts in thousands except per-share figures)

	1970	1969	1968	1967	1966	1965	1964	1963	1962	1961	1960	1959
Results for year:												
Sales and revenues	$6,364,494	5,474,743	4,066,502	2,760,572	2,121,272	1,782,939	1,542,079	1,414,146	1,090,198	930,500	811,449	765,640
Income before extraordinary items	$353,307	234,034	180,162†	119,221†	89,910	76,110	63,164	52,375	40,694	36,059—	30,570†	29,036
Per common share	$3.17	2.90	2.58	2.27	2.04	1.79	1.55	1.35	1.21	1.09—	.98†	.95
Profit margin (percent)	5.6	4.3	4.4	4.3	4.2	4.3	4.1	3.7	3.7	3.9	3.8	3.8
Return on stockholders' equity (percent)	13.0	11.8	12.2	11.7	11.5	10.8	9.9	9.1	8.6	8.0	7.4	7.2
Dividends per common share	$1.07½	.97½	.87½	.77½	.69⅛	.61⅞	.55	.50	.50	.50	.50	.50
Range of common stock price (rounded)	$60–31	61–46	63–45	62–36	40–29	34–24	31–26	28–21	29–16	31–22	24–16	23–14
Year-end position:												
Total assets	$6,697,011	5,192,587	4,022,400	2,961,172	2,360,435	2,021,795	1,668,853	1,469,168	1,235,781	1,088,310	923,944	932,269
Long-term debt	$1,458,806	1,145,383	931,772	744,675	433,834	428,134	309,795	293,408	266,815	182,509	148,478	165,512
Stockholders' equity	$2,923,628	2,081,309	1,652,092	1,143,568	820,007	739,620	659,429	592,429	483,531	465,061	415,814	415,088
Stockholders' equity per common share	$18.08	16.88	16.83	17.39	16.78	15.69	15.06	14.29	14.11	13.76	13.26	13.36
Year-end statistics:												
Shares of common stock outstanding (000's)	67,820	65,371	59,059	49,940	42,168	40,530	38,720	36,924	33,258	32,750	31,362	31,060
Employees	392,000	353,000	293,000	236,000	204,000	199,000	185,000	173,000	157,000	149,000	132,000	136,000

* The above data are as reported in the ITT Annual Reports for the respective number of years, except that number of shares and per share amounts have been adjusted for two-for-one stock split effective January 26, 1968.
† Extraordinary credits in 1968, 1967, 1961, and 1960 amounted to $12,242, $3,539, $7,620, and $7,902 respectively.
Sources: ITT Annual Reports and *Moody's Handbook of Common Stocks*, 1968, 1972.

EXHIBIT 2
ITT principal product groups—1970
(dollar amounts in millions)

	Sales and revenues		Net income	
Manufacturing:				
Telecommunications equipment	$1,244	19%	$ 52	15%
Industrial and consumer products	1,849	29	71	20
Natural resources	287	5	30	5
Defense and space programs.	316	5	8	2
	$3,696	58	$161	45
Consumer and business services:				
Food processing and services	$1,241	19%	$ 30	8%
Consumer services	808	13	19	6
Business and financial services.	386	6	21	6
Hartford Fire*	–	–	88	25
	$2,435	38	$158	45
Utility operations.	233	4	34	10
Total.	$6,364	100%	$353	100%

* Hartford's $1 billion in annual premiums was not included in ITT's 1970 sales and revenues.
Source: ITT 1970 Annual Report.

EXHIBIT 3
Partial list of U.S. acquisitions by ITT
during period of January 1, 1960 to July 1, 1971

Year	Company	Product
1960	Division of L. C. Miller Co.	Electromagnetic vibration equipment
1961	Suprenant Mfg. Co.	Specialized wire and cable
	American Cable & Radio Corp.*	Communications equipment
	Jennings Radio Mfg. Corp.	Vacuum capacitors and switches
1962	National Computer Products, Inc.	Diodes and other electrical components
1963	General Controls Co.	Automatic industrial controls
	Bell & Gossett, Inc.	Pumps and heating equipment
	John J. Nesbitt, Inc.	Heating and air conditioning equipment
	Cannon Electric, Inc.	Electrical connectors
1964	Gilfillian, Inc.	Ground control radar
	Hayes Furnace Co.	Furnaces
	Aetna Finance Co.	Consumer financing and life insurance
	Terryphone Corp.	Communications systems
	Barton Instrument Co.	Measuring devices
1965	Division of Clevite Corp.	Semiconductors
	Henze Instrument & Valve Co.	Industrial valves
	Avis, Inc.	Motor vehicle rentals
	National Auto Renting Co.	Motor vehicle rentals
	Kerby Microwave	Microwave products
	Documat Inc.	N.A.
	Press Wireless	Newspaper and communication services
	Hamilton Management Corp.	Mutual funds and life insurance
1966	Electro Physics Labs	Electronic equipment
	Wakefield Corp.	Abrasives
	Jabsco Pump Co.	Specialty industrial pumps
	APCOA	Parking facility operator
	Brooks Equipment Corp.	N.A.
	Consolidated Electric Lamp Co.	Incandescent and fluorescent lamps
	H. W. Sams & Co.	Printing and publishing
1907	Amplex Lustra Corp.	Incandescent and fluorescent lamps
	Cleveland Motels	Motor inns
	National City Truck Rental	Truck rentals
	Means Motor Livery Corp.	Motor vehicle rentals

* Previously controlled but not consolidated.
N.A. = Not available.

EXHIBIT 3 (*continued*)

Year	Company	Product
1967 (cont.)	Simon Worden White assets of H. K. Porter	N.A.
	Modern Life Insurance	Life insurance
1968	Levitt and Sons, Inc.	Residential construction
	Massachusetts Trade Shops Corp.	N.A.
	Sheraton Corp. of America	Hotels and motor inns
	Bailey Technical School	Technical school
	Rayonier, Inc.	Chemical cellulose and lumber
	Applied Institute of Technology	Technical school
	Jasper Blackburn Corp.	Electrical transmission equipment
	Pennsylvania Glass Sand Corp.	Mining and manufacturing of silica
	Sterling Design Co.	N.A.
	ETC, Inc.	Solderless electrical terminals
	Bramwell Business College	Business school
	Continental Baking Co.	Bread and bakery products
	Transportation Displays, Inc.	Advertising services
	Texas Tool & Machine Co.	Industrial equipment
	Peters & Russell, Inc.	N.A.
	Gotham Lighting Corp.	Architectural lighting equipment
	Speedwriting, Inc.	Assorted consumer services and study courses
	State Auto Parks	Auto parks
	Gremar, Inc.	N.A.
	Pennway Co.	N.A.
1969	Thorp Finance Corp.	Consumer loans
	Temple School, Inc. and six others	Business schools
	Hopkins Airport Hotel, Inc.	Hotel
	United Homes Corp.	Residential construction
	Liberty Investors Benefit Insurance Co.	Insurance
	Marquis *Who's Who*	Publishing
	Decca Systems, Inc. ⎫ Decca Radar, Inc.† ⎭	Navigational equipment
	Joseph B. Giglio Enterprises, Inc.	Avis franchise
	Canteen Corp.	Food vending
	Electronics Institute of Technology	Technical school
	Avis Option Cities	Avis franchises
	Pascal Lease, Inc.	Avis franchise
	United Building Services	Cleaning services
	C&S Lighting Maintenance Co.	Commercial lighting installation and service
	Industrial Credit Co.	Financing

† Fifty percent interest.

EXHIBIT 3 (*concluded*)

Year	Company	Product
1969	Wadsworth Land Co.	Land holdings
(cont.)	Industrial Cafeterias, Inc. and Menumat	Food service
	American Electric Mfg. Corp.	Street lighting
	G. K. Hall Corp.	Publishing
	American Building Services, Inc.	Janitorial services
	Southern Wood Preserving Co.	Pressure treated timber
	Grinnell Corp.	Fire protection sprinklers
1970	Alton Canteen Co.	Food vending
	Pearson Candy Co.	Candy products
	Jacques French Restaurant and affiliated companies	Restaurants and specialty foods
	Ace Industrial & Institutional Services	Janitorial services
	Hartford Fire Insurance Co.	Fire insurance
	Thermotech Ind.	Thermoplastic and thermosetting molding
	Abbey International	Life insurance and financing
	Maintenance Division, Service Group, Inc.	Building maintenance
	Hoffman Specialty Mfg. Corp.	Heating and plumbing specialties
	Gwaltney, Inc.	Pork products
	Erie Canteen Co.	Food vending
	Bldg. Servicing Co. of Texas	Janitorial services
	General Creosoting Co.	Power and telephone poles
	Landis Financial Group	Financing
	B & B Stores, Inc.	N.A.
	South Bend Window Cleaning Co., Inc.	Building maintenance
	White Glove Bldg. Maintenance Co., Inc.	Building maintenance
1971	Michie Co.	Publishing
	Roquemores of Miami, Inc.	Distributes automotive parts
	H. M. Harper	Industrial fasteners
	Eurofund International	Closed-end investment company
	O. M. Scott Co.	Lawn care products
	Peninsula Plywood Corp.	Plywood
	Charlestown U-Drive-It, Inc.	Vehicle rentals
	First State Insurance Co.	Insurance
	Cameron & Calley	Property and liability insurance
	Odyssey Press and Pegasus	Publishing

Sources: *Investigation of Conglomerate Corporations*, a report by the staff of the Antitrust Sub-committee of the Committee of the Judiciary, U.S. House of Representatives, 1971; *Mergers and Acquisitions*, 1966–1972; and Standard and Poor's *Standard Corporation Descriptions*, 1972.

EXHIBIT 4
Major U.S. acquisitions by ITT°
during period of January 1, 1962 to July 1, 1971
(in millions of dollars)

Year	Company	Price paid	Asset value	Annual sales prior to merger
1965	Avis, Inc..	$ 55.8	$ 63.6	$ 44.6
1968	Levitt and Sons, Inc.	91.6	91.0	93.6
	Sheraton Corp. of America	193.2	282.8	287.0
	Rayonier, Inc..	293.1	296.3	156.7
	Pennsylvania Glass Sand Corp.	112.5	46.3	25.1
	Continental Baking Co.	279.5	186.5	621.0
1969	Thorp Finance Corp..	46.5	120.2	18.9
	Canteen Corp..	245.0	140.9	322.2
	Grinnell Corp..	251.3	184.4	341.3
1970	Hartford Fire Insurance Co..	1,065.1	1,723.1	1,002.3
1971	O. M. Scott Co..	110.0	40.0	67.3

* Acquisitions for which ITT paid over $40 million in cash or stock.
Source: *Investigation of Conglomerate Corporations*, 1971; *Mergers and Acquisitions*, 1966–1972; and
Standard Corporation Descriptions, 1972.

EXHIBIT 5
Supplement to Jacob's letter detailing proposed settlement package

1. *Divestiture of Canteen's Commercial and Industrial In-Plant Feeding Operations in the United States.* Canteen would agree to divest itself of such portions of its existing United States commercial and industrial in-plant feeding business on a local market bases as the Government deems sufficient to avoid any possible market domination by Canteen. The divested operations would be sold outright, or converted into independent distributors who would be franchised to use the name Canteen, but in whom Canteen would have no equity interest. Divestiture of the commercial and industrial in-plant feeding and vending business would eliminate any possible market domination by Canteen, would establish a new independent competitor or competitors, and would eliminate any possibility of "reciprocity" and "reciprocity effect" as alleged in the complaint. Canteen would be left with only the school, hospital, institutional feeding, public restaurants, and miscellaneous vending business, which provides no basis for the practice of "reciprocity" or the existence of "reciprocity effect"—and such portions of its commercial industrial in-plant feeding business as does not dominate any market.

2. *Divestiture of ITT Levitt and Sons, Incorporated.* ITT would agree to divest all of its interest in the domestic operations of ITT Levitt and Sons, Inc., the residential building developer (with the exception of a small subsidiary, ITT Levitt Development, Inc., which is currently engaged of disposing of land owned or acquired by Rayonier Corporation in the counties

EXHIBIT 5 (*continued*)

of Flagler and St. Johns, Florida). Levitt is a substantial user of capital and its customers in many cases look to Levitt for assistance in financing and securing insurance for the homes, as the Government pointed out in its briefs in the Hartford case. In addition, Levitt purchases building materials and appliances for use in its homes. The divestiture of Levitt would, therefore, eliminate a substantial basis for the allegations of "reciprocity" and "reciprocity effect" claimed in the Government's complaints. It would also re-establish as an individual entity a leading company in an industry in which there has been a significant number of mergers.

3. *Divestiture of ITT's Existing Insurance Underwriting Operations in the United States.* ITT would agree to divest itself of all of ITT's United States insurance underwriting operations existing at the time of the acquisition of Hartford (including all employer-employee group insurance underwriting) with the sole exception of an adequate consumer credit life/accident and health insurance operation directly associated with the loans made by ITT's consumer credit companies. ITT would also retain its small ITT Variable Annuity Insurance Company which is just beginning operations. These consumer related operations provide no basis for the practice of "reciprocity" or the existence of "reciprocity effect" alleged in the Government's complaints.

Specifically, this means that ITT would:

a. Divest itself completely of ITT Life Insurance Company of New York (formerly Modern Life Insurance Company).

b. Divest itself completely of ITT Midwestern Life and ITT Hamilton (except for some form of residual organization to underwrite credit/life accident and health for ITT's consumer credit companies involving insurance in force of approximately $423.5 million and annual premiums of approximately $13.8 million).

This divestiture would involve life insurance in force of approximately $2 billion and total annual premiums of approximately $26.7 million.

4. *General Injunction Against Reciprocity.* An injunction prohibiting any reciprocity activities by ITT, Canteen, Grinnell, or Hartford, identical to the recent Consent Decrees entered in the cases of *U.S. Steel, Inland Steel, Bethlehem Steel, General Tire and Rubber Company, PPG Industries*, etc.

5. *Anti-Reciprocity Publicity.* A nationwide saturation advertising campaign of full page advertisements in leading magazines, newspapers, trade journals and business publications giving notice that ITT and its subsidiaries do not, and will not, practice reciprocity nor recognize "reciprocity effect"—at an advertising cost to ITT of over $200,000. The text of such advertisements and the media schedule will be subject to the prior approval of the Department of Justice. In addition, a direct mailing of the ITT policy against reciprocity will also be made to ITT customers and suppliers in the same manner as in the other recent Department of Justice Consent Decrees (U.S. Steel, etc.). ITT is also willing to make a similar direct mailing of such notices using any other mailing lists desired by the Department of Justice.

6. *Additional Injunctive Provisions Involving ITT, Hartford, Canteen and Grinnell.* A total prohibition against Hartford Fire Insurance Company making any loans to, providing financing for, or making investments in, any other

EXHIBIT 5 (*concluded*)

ITT System company in the United States without the prior consent of the Department of Justice or the United States District Court.

7. A total prohibition against transferring to Hartford Fire Insurance Company (or any subsidiary of Hartford) any insurance coverage of ITT presently written by United States insurance companies other than Hartford, without the prior consent of the Department of Justice or the United States District Court. (Or a provision prohibiting transfer of any such coverage in the U.S. except after open competitive bidding with at least two other responsible bidders and prohibiting any preferential treatment of Hartford in the bidding procedures or award.)

8. A total prohibition against transferring to Canteen any ITT food service contracts presently held by other United States food service companies, without prior consent of the Department of Justice or the U.S. District Court. (Or a provision prohibiting transfer of any such food service contract in the U.S. except after open competitive bidding with at least two other responsible bidders and prohibiting any preferential treatment of Canteen in the bidding procedures or award.)

9. A total prohibition against awarding to Grinnell any ITT automatic sprinkler installation contract in the United States, without the prior consent of the Department of Justice or the U.S. District Court. (Or a provision prohibiting award of any such contract in the U.S. except after open competitive bidding with at least two other responsible bidders and prohibiting any preferential treatment of Grinnell in the bidding procedures or award.)

10. A mandatory injunction prohibiting the sale of ITT products in mechanical packages or systems along with Grinnell sprinkler systems, power piping systems or pipe hangers without prior consent of the Department of Justice or the U.S. District Court, or requiring a price breakdown in any package quotation to enable the customer to select only portions of the package.

11. A mandatory injunction prohibiting Hartford from supplying possible sales leads or other marketing assistance to Grinnell unless the same information is provided to any other interested sprinkler companies.

EXHIBIT 6
The Beard Memorandum

PERSONAL AND CONFIDENTIAL

ITT

Washington Office
Date: June 25, 1971

To: W. R. Merriam
From: D. D. Beard
Subject: San Diego Convention

I just had a long talk with EJG.[1] I'm so sorry that we got that call from the White House. I thought you and I had agreed very thoroughly that

---

[1] Edward J. Gerrity, ITT vice president

EXHIBIT 6 (*continued*)

under no circumstances would anyone in this office discuss with anyone our participation in the Convention, including me. Other than permitting John Mitchell, Ed Reinecke,[2] Bob Haldeman[3] and Nixon (besides Wilson,[4] of course) *no one* has known from whom that 400 thousand commitment had come. You can't imagine how many queries I've had from "friends" about this situation and I have in each and every case denied knowledge of any kind. It would be wise for all of us here to continue to do just that, regardless of from whom any questions come; White House or whoever. John Mitchell has certainly kept it on the higher level only, we should be able to do the same.

I was afraid the discussion about the three hundred/four hundred thousand commitment would come up soon. If you remember, I suggested that we all stay out of that, other than the fact that I told you I had heard Hal[5] up the original amount.

Now I undersand from Ned[1] that both he and you are upset about the decision to make it four hundred in *services*. Believe me, this is not what Hal said. Just after I talked with Ned, Wilson called me, to report on his meeting with Hal. Hal at no time told Wilson that our donation would be in services ONLY. In fact, quite the contrary. There would be very little cash involved, but certainly some. I am convinced, because of several conversations with Louie[6] re Mitchell, that our noble commitment has gone a long way toward our negotiations on the mergers eventually coming out as Hal wants them. Certainly the President has told Mitchell to see that things are worked out fairly. It is still only McLaren's mickey-mouse we are suffering.

We all know Hal and his big mouth! But this is one time he cannot tell you and Ned one thing and Wilson (and me) another!

I hope, dear Bill, that all of this can be reconciled—between Hal and Wilson—if all of us in this office remain totally ignorant of any commitment ITT has made to anyone. If it gets too much publicity, you can believe our negotiations with Justice will wind up shot down. Mitchell is definitely helping us, but cannot let it be known. Please destroy this, huh?

[2] Lt. governor of California
[3] White House aide
[4] Congressman Bob Wilson (California), the man in charge of the 1972 Republican Convention arrangements
[5] Harold S. Geneen
[6] Gov. Louie Nunn of Kentucky

The views on bigness are contradictory[1]

**THE DILEMMA FOR U.S. BUSINESS: HOW TO GAIN
THE ADVANTAGES OF SIZE WITHOUT RUNNING
AFOUL OF THE THEORY THAT BIGNESS IS BAD**

THE government took a giant step this week in making firm a policy that big corporations are bad corporations.

In a surprise trade-off in settling the three outstanding antitrust cases against International Telephone & Telegraph Corp., the Justice Dept. established antitrust guidelines that say clearly to managers of huge concerns that the only way they can make significant acquisitions without inviting a challenge from the antitrusters is by shedding other assets to stay at their present size. ITT agreed to rid itself of $1-billion worth of annual business in order to retain Hartford Fire Insurance Co., with its $1-billion yearly premium income (box, page 61).

The settlement conforms to Assistant Attorney General Richard W. McLaren's view of his job as chief of the Antitrust Div.: to keep newcomers from joining the league of giants. By accepting the settlement, McLaren stopped short of establishing firm legal precedent. But he got the results he wanted in a case involving one of the most prominent of all conglomerates.

While his predecessors in the Johnson Administration had felt that the antitrust laws did not stretch to conglomerate mergers, McLaren

---

[1] Reprinted from the August 7, 1971 issue of *Business Week* by special permission. Copyright © 1971 by McGraw–Hill, Inc.

immediately announced his intention to go after these combines of disparate interests. Conglomerate mergers "raise barriers to entry and discourage smaller firms from competing," he has said. In addition to the three ITT cases, he settled a suit against Ling-Temco-Vought's acquisition of Jones & Laughlin Steel on a similar get-rid-of-something-else basis, scared off the White Consolidated-White Motor merger after an initial court win, and has kept moldering in district court a case to force Northwest Industries to divest itself of the B. F. Goodrich stock that it acquired in an abortive takeover attempt.

It is a campaign that has subjected McLaren to an unusual amount of personal abuse, including a pasting from within the hierarchy of his own party: Representative Bob Wilson (R-Calif.), chairman of the GOP congressional committee, lashed out at him for his "devotion to tearing down big business."

This week's trailblazing deal comes as debate over U.S. antitrust policy quickens. Two opposing currents of criticism are swirling around McLaren's division:

That antitrust policy has been too lax. Ralph Nader and his allies in the "new populism" attack on big institutions are the leaders in this charge, which has been well promoted onto the front pages and the best-seller lists. Dramatizing arguments long made in dry journal articles by economists and law professors, these critics argue that bigness is bad because it leaves the consumer at the mercy of the producer and may inhibit political and social freedom. They want the country's biggest corporations broken up into relatively tiny entities, none with more than one-eighth of a market.

That American enterprises need to be bigger to compete successfully with swiftly growing enterprises abroad. Peter G. Peterson, the top White House aide on international economic matters, has convinced President Nixon that one reason for trade troubles is the way Washington controls the overseas business arrangements of U.S. corporations and prevents new combinations of resources at home. He points to the creation of Nippon Steel Corp.—the world's largest—as evidence that U.S. companies are losing their once-dominant position in international business.

McLaren thinks it is unjust to dismember companies now that long ago were allowed to get big. "That's saying if you are successful and compete hard and build up your company to be the biggest in the industry, Uncle Sam should move in and break you up." But he has been equally cool to suggestions from Peterson, Commerce Secretary Maurice Stans, and Housing & Urban Development Secretary George Romney that U.S. companies faced with new aggressiveness from foreign competitors be given some freedom from antitrust enforcement. The first test of whether he is winning this interagency battle will come within the next two weeks, when Justice announces whether it opposes the merger of the National and Granite City steel companies. Within the Administration, the issue in this case is whether a merged company will better be able to compete with foreign steel.

Differences of definition

The root controversy in all this discussion is how to define "competition." No one wants little government autocrats parceling out the nation's economic resources. All agree that the public gets the best deal when choice is left to the free play of a competitive marketplace. But to Ralph Nader, competition can almost be measured by a formula: a large number of smallish competitors in a market, none with a big chunk of the total business. To General Motors Chairman James Roche, on the other hand, competition is the vigorous year-in, year-out fight to win buyers from another large and capable company.

The distinction is fundamental. The populists worry about an industry's or a corporation's structure—what it is and, thus, what it could do. The businessman is concerned with a company's performance—what it is doing now. A company may engage in no anticompetitive acts and still be "anticompetitive," at least potentially, by virtue of its size or position in a line of business.

The law reflects the same dichotomy. The 1890 Sherman Act basically looks at performance: It is a long list of prohibitions against specific kinds of collusive dealings. The 1914 Clayton Act, on the other hand, looks at structure. It is the weapon used against new aggregations of market power, and it provided the basis for the suits against ITT.

The question of just how competition should be measured is focused most sharply in the attacks on conglomerates. These multi-line companies dominate no individual markets and raise none of the traditional objections to big mergers—that a competitor is being eliminated, for instance, or that a major customer will be locked into a single source of supply.

Instead, the cases are rooted in the American tradition's deep distrust of big institutions, in the belief that sheer size can constitute a social ill. McLaren has argued that would-be competitors will stay out of the way of an ITT simply because they are afraid of taking on such a giant.

But Federal District Judge Richard B. Austin, in his decision in the Canteen case, one of the three settled this week, decided that ITT actually spurred competition in the food business by applying time-and-motion studies to vending machine repairs and cost analysis to cafeteria menu planning. He lauded the "vigor, enthusiasm, motivation" that ITT engendered in Canteen employees.

For his part, ITT Chairman Harold Geneen, knowing that Washington is peering over his shoulder, has been highly sensitive to the anticompetitive possibilities in his company, especially the opportunities for reciprocal dealings. ITT Avis, for instance, often loses out to higher-bidding Hertz for the rent-a-car concession at an ITT Sheraton hotel.

But Geneen has designed his company as a pool of talents. He claims this breadth of expertise "adds competition the economy would not otherwise enjoy" by using "the very untraditional outlook such a company brings to an industry" to build a smaller outfit into a zesty competitor for the No. 1 spot. "We're risk takers," says ITT Vice-President Richard H. Smith. "How many guys will gamble a $300-million plant" such as the one ITT built for Rayonier, or "take on GE and Sylvania," as ITT does in its not-very-successful flashbulb business?

The willingness to risk large resources in the interest of competition is, in fact, a principal argument of all the conglomerates. N. W. Freeman, head of Tenneco, Inc., brags of how he gambled $50-million in new capital on the chance that J. I. Case Co. could be turned around from a money-losing producer of agricultural equipment into a black-ink maker of construction equipment—and won. The implication is that such risk-takers may be the very ones who should be buying up other companies.

Recent research by University of Pennsylvania economist Oliver E. Williamson suggests that the managers of conglomerates operate "a miniature capital market" that is more astute at allocating resources than are the banks—which don't know as much about an industry's growth potential as the companies in the field know—or single-line companies, which tend merely to reinvest in the same old areas. A conglomerate, he reasons, has a better feel for the total economy, and so can put its assets where new business is developing.

Dominance of market

Although the attack on bigness is seen most clearly when it strikes at the conglomerates, most of the collected evidence against corporate giantism applies to the operations of classic oligopolies, where a few large companies dominate a market. A blue-ribbon task force on antitrust policy appointed by President Johnson near the end of his term took aim on such concentration as the No. 1 evil in the American industrial scene. It singled out, particularly, makers of autos, flat glass, synthetic fibers, airplanes, organic chemicals, and soaps. The task force reflected the economists' deep-seated belief that the best form of competition is price competition. A long line of theoretical economists has reasoned that oligopoly operates, in fact, much like monopoly, allowing producers to charge as much for their goods as the market will pay. Empirical studies made since the end of World War II have supported this theory by suggesting that companies in concentrated industries do, in fact, have higher profits than those in fields that have many competing sellers.

But more recent work, primarily by the conservative economists at the University of Chicago, challenges those conclusions. Economist George J. Stigler headed a Nixon-appointed antitrust task force that rejected the break-them-up approach. He says the difference between high-profit and low-profit industries may come from nothing more than the owners of small companies draining off money in extra-large salaries and expense accounts that otherwise would show up on the bottom line. And work published only 10 months ago by a Stigler associate, Yale Brozen, suggests that high profits do not continue year after year in concentrated industries.

Another argument holds that just as there are "natural monopolies," such as utilities, there are "natural oligopolies." Almarin Phillips, University of Pennsylvania economics professor, points to the aerospace industry as one of these. There, he says, huge resources must be committed at the very frontier of scientific knowledge, and massive managerial mistakes are inevitable. Thus the number of healthy companies will get fewer and fewer. It was Phillips' analysis that persuaded Justice to approve the McDonnell-Douglas merger in 1967. And Boeing now says it can never again manage on its own a project as big as the 747.

Computers and buses probably are other fields where the technological investments are so high in relation to the number of units that can be sold that oligopoly seems inevitable. But even when they are not inevitable, oligopolies are so individual that it is impractical to try to squeeze them into a single mold. For example, note the contrast between the operating policies and present conditions of two areas most often mentioned in discussions of industrial concentration:

Automobiles. General Motors Corp. is in the odd position of being both the favorite whipping boy of the populists and, along with Sears, Roebuck & Co., the businessman's ideal of a company that manages its giant size efficiently. Bigness gives GM some economies of scale in the complex business of manufacturing a car that are not available to American Motors or even Chrysler Corp. For example, GM uses a single set of dies to produce all the inner door panels for its standard-size cars and thus can amortize that cost over many more units. Perhaps more important, a big and expensive distribution network, such as GM can provide, is almost essential to success in the auto business.

Detroit insists that the savings from such advantages of bigness are passed on to buyers of cars. The relatively flat price curve over the years proves it, the auto makers say. Detroit knows its customers are fickle; each year from one-third to two-thirds of car buyers are switching brands, so prices must be competitive.

The U.S. auto industry has been slow to catch on to some consumer trends, notably the demand for real economy cars. But, as McLaren says, "imports have kept Detroit humping." Foreign cars cause some growls in the board room, but staff economists point to them as fresh proof that Detroit does not exercise any suppressive control over the market.

Steel. The steel industry, on the other hand, gets generally poor marks from other businessmen and is bearing up poorly under the attack of foreign producers. Agreeing with the smaller steel companies, F. J. Robbins, president of Bliss & Laughlin Industries, says: "Basic steel finds it hard to compete in world markets because it is such a fragmented industry. Perhaps the bigger outfits should absorb the smaller, troubled ones."

But Joseph B. Lanterman, president of Amsted Industries, which has diversified out of its reliance on steel operations, does not agree. "Bigness is not automatically a great thing for the consumer," he says. "Look no further than U.S. Steel. They are so bogged down by red tape that they are unable to change direction or products."

The smaller steel companies do not seem to feel free to fight with their gloves off. "Bethlehem and U.S. Steel still run the show," says an economist at one of the other major steel producers. "There's a little less discipline than there once was, but it's no secret who calls the shots." Price increases have averaged about 4.5% a year over the past 25 years—twice the rate of auto price increases.

Paradoxically U.S. Steel, which the Supreme Court in 1920 refused to dismember because it reasoned that a steel company had to be big to compete with foreign producers, agrees that combines of the smaller companies are not the answer to foreign competition. "They won't make any difference at all," says U.S. Steel's Chairman Edwin H. Gott. The problem in steel is not just the size of the company, but the size and efficiency of the individual mills.

The executives of big companies know the tremendous advantages of being big in business, but they also know that the comfortable safety of size can dampen a venturesome spirit. When William T. Ylvisaker, president of fast-growing Gould, Inc., sat down to talk about bigness in Chicago last month, he insisted: "Bigness should be encouraged—it takes a large company with a lot of money and good people to develop better products." But minutes later he was musing that "the big guys get static, immobile, busy guarding their own interests. These big companies tend to become less creative, less flexible."

Clearly there are thresholds of size efficiency. But economists insist that scale efficiencies in production can be reached by companies far smaller than the biggest U.S. companies, and businessmen tend to agree. Paul A. Miller, the Eaton Corp. group vice-president in charge of the truck component operation, says: "If you're talking about a basic model of an axle or a transmission, it takes 12,000 to 15,000 units per year to make the program viable. With that much volume, it can stand on its own two feet." A top executive at Reliance Electric Co. figures a company can stay in the business of making small a.c. motors if it gets orders for a half-million units a year, far below the annual production at Westinghouse and General Electric.

Factors beyond in-plant assembly line efficiencies give the bigger company a leg up. Businessmen assume that the public benefits from these efficiencies through lower prices, while economists worry that the savings get siphoned off in wasteful operations or in high profits and never reach the customers. Canada, in fact, is considering a new law under which Ottawa would approve large mergers only if specific cost savings are passed on to buyers.

Businessmen agree, though, that the individual company can get special benefits from size.

R&D advantages are the most important to Amsted's Lanterman. "We get the capability and expertise to pursue research at a level that none of our single parts could. . . . You can make two and two add up to five."

Personnel considerations are the biggest plus for Eaton Chairman E. Mandell de Windt. "We can afford to continually recruit and attract young guys. And we can put them through a formal program which small companies can't."

Staff expertise—the favorite argument of the conglomerators—can make all the difference in the success of an individual entity, Tenneco's Freeman points out. He lists tax men, computer experts, advertising professionals, and "a substantial office in Washington with representation at all branches of the government that benefits all of our corporations. Not a single one of them on their own could afford it."

Distribution is "much more efficient the bigger we get," says an executive at TRW, Inc. The company supplies valves from its German plant for Ford Pinto engines made in Germany and valves from its British plant for the Pinto engines that are assembled in England.

Borrowing is a lot easier for bigger companies. "If we had been solely in the aerospace industry during the credit crunch of last year," says the Signal Companies' president Forrest N. Shumway, "our troubles would have been far worse than they were." Garrett Corp. is a major Signal component in the aerospace business, he notes, but "Garrett's borrowing capacity is unrelated to its own activities, because it has this umbrella."

Shumway readily concedes that there are some disadvantages that come with size: "A smaller entity can move faster," he says. Says John T. Gurash, chairman of INA Corp.: "There is no doubt that on sheer efficiency (if you could truly measure it) the big companies are more difficult to run efficiently. There is a lot of wasted motion in big companies."

As the debate goes on in the U.S. over the pluses and minuses of corporate bigness, most of the rest of the world is solidly in the corner of giantism. With government approval and often with the government as marriage broker, industrial goods producers in Japan, Britain, and the Common Market have been joining at an awesome pace.

Originally these mergers were designed to combine entities that were inefficiently small into units that had at least a slim chance of viability. The British pulled five Scottish shipyards together into Upper Clyde Shipbuilders, Ltd., which nevertheless went bankrupt last summer. Germany put 50 coal mines from 26 different owners together into Ruhrkohle AG, which still has trouble keeping customers who are being wooed by foreign producers selling below Ruhrkohle's costs.

But the overseas merger wave has now taken a new turn toward consolidations of the big. And the goal is clear: to get the smaller foreign producers to Uncle Sam-size.

Nippon Steel Corp. is the result of last year's combine of Fuji and Yawata Iron & Steel companies, parts of the old Nihon monopoly that was broken up at the end of World War II. So strong was political support within Japan for the merger of the two biggest companies in the industry—with combined sales of $3.7-billion—that the legislature threatened to disband the nation's antitrust commission when the members indicated they might not approve.

The Japanese take national pride in having the world's No. 1 producer in so basic an industry as steel. But the politicians also see the merger as a good way to go after more export sales. "Before the merger," explains Nippon President Yoshihiro Inayama, "two large companies, Fuji and Yawata, were engaged in fierce, futile, cutthroat competition that resulted in many wastes. In eliminating that competition, we indeed achieved rationalization."

While Europeans are not likely to be quite so blunt about the advantages of eliminating competition, similar producing toward industrial combines goes on there. The French created their largest company by combining Renault and Peugeot auto makers, and then topped that last fall with a blend of the Pechiney Aluminum Co. and Ugine-Kihlmann, the steel-chemicals outfit. Managers of the new $2.7-billion-a-year giant are clear about what they want from the merger: better footing to compete in third markets with Aluminum Co. of America, Anaconda, and Reynolds.

The Dutch put two chemical producers together into the $2-billion AZKO, which includes among its holdings U.S. American Enka, International Salt, and Organon. The merger broadens the product lines of the two partners and lets them put more energy into the fierce competitive fibers business, where they must sell against Du Pont and Monsanto. The Swiss put under one roof the Ciba and Geigy drugmakers to create a company that accounts for more than 7% of Switzerland's gross national product.

Dealing under two flags

Trans-border mergers have come off, too, including the "union" earlier this year of Italy's Pirelli and England's Dunlop Rubber Co., making a tire giant outranked only by Goodyear and Firestone. Others: the German-Belgian photographic combine Agfa-Gevaert; the German-Dutch plane builders VFW-Fokker.

The European push for mergers can actually help U.S. companies, according to James Rahl, the Northwestern University law professor who is the ranking authority on the antitrust implications of American business operations in Europe. Rahl sees American managers as better deal makers than Europeans, as being able to buy a company while rival European bidders are still fulminating. And Americans operate under elastic corporate charters. If a French company wants to merge with a foreign entity, for instance, it must disband and create a new corporation—and stockholders must pay huge capital gains taxes. The Common Market is only beginning to put teeth into antitrust enforcement, waging its first case against an American company—Continental Can—for buying a European competitor.

Americans are under special restraints from Washington in operating abroad—most notably the "extraterritorial" reach of the U.S. antitrust laws. Under this concept, the Justice Dept. can knock down a U.S. company's participation in a deal that takes place totally in other countries. No other government has such a cross-border reach over its business.

The question, of course, is whether the traditional U.S. rules put American companies at too much of a disadvantage in world markets. "It is becoming increasingly evident that even the United States market cannot be treated as an independent unit with its own 'rules of the game,'" says James Leontiades, an international marketing expert at the University of Pennsylvania's Wharton School. He sees the rise of the multinational firm as "adding an important new dimension; that is, the optimum size for a strictly domestic firm may be quite different from that of the multinational company."

Meanwhile, the constraints on the multinationals are increasingly onerous. Gillette's attempt to buy the German appliance maker Braun, for instance, has been hung up over Justice Dept. charges that possession of Braun's electric razor knowhow might keep Gillette from developing its own, competitive electric shaver in the U.S. market.

Needed: A reliable yardstick

The public never knows of most of the deals that the antitrust law scotches because they are stopped right in corporate headquarters by antitrust counsel. Celanese, for instance, backed off from taking a minority position in a foreign joint venture when it realized that it could not keep the overseas company out of the U.S. market; using Celanese knowhow and lower overseas wage and operating costs, the foreign supplier could have undersold Celanese here. And ITT has backed away from a couple of foreign deals because owning a small overseas outfit in an industry might preclude buying a bigger U.S. outfit later in the same field.

This week's settlement wth the Justice Dept. may change that balance for ITT, since it can make most big U.S. acquisitions only with a nod from Washington. The conglomerate "remains substantially free to pursue its course of buying foreign firms—except as they have an impact on the domestic market," McLaren explains. ITT this week, in fact, was negotiating a setup in which it would take an interest in several Italian auto-parts companies.

"This whole antitrust thing is so screwed up," complains Eaton's chairman de Windt. "It's so fuzzy at the moment that you have to assume that you can't do anything. You don't know what you can do and what you can't do. . . . This situation certainly has to be clarified."

But businessmen will probably never get the firm yardstick they want to measure business policies. The enforcers insist that any rigid formula would force them to move against combines that really do spur competition. The Nader-backed report on antitrust lambasted McLaren for not moving against Honeywell's absorption of General Electric's computer business, for instance—a union of a No. 3 and a No. 5 in a concentrated industry. McLaren applauded the deal because of the specific situation: The combined company still has worldwide computer sales only one-seventh as large as those of IBM.

McLaren now fears that Congress will take a renewed interest in antitrust legislation, which was quescent as long as the ITT cases were alive and there was a chance that the Supreme Court would clarify the existing law.

On Tuesday, three days after the compromise with Geneen was announced, the House Judiciary Committee sent to the printer its long-awaited report on conglomerates, which will be made public late this month.

It contains suggestions from committee chairman Emanuel Celler (D-N.Y.) for a new, all-embracing agency that would review every proposed merger in any field. This merger agency would take on work not only from the Justice Dept. and the Federal Trade Commision but also from such industry regulators as the Civil Aeronautics Board and the Interstate Commerce Commission.

The guide that Celler would give this agency "is a pretty rigid proposition," McLaren complains. "You would have to get too specific, so that a company of *x* dollars of sales cannot buy a company of *y* dollars of sales."

"You have to be more flexible than that to make it work," McLaren adds. He is afraid that any set formula would, for instance, would have banned the Honeywell-GE computer deal.

Lee Loevinger, Kennedy's antitrust chief and a champion of conglomerates who differs with McLaren on many points, seconds him on this score: "I'm very wary of this business of just drawing a line and saying you can't go beyond it. It's the lazy man's way of enforcing antitrust."

Senator Philip Hart (D-Mich.), head of the Senate's antitrust subcommittee, agrees that as long as Justice can stop the mergers it wants to stop, it is best not to tamper with the laws. "Once you start fooling around amending antitrust legislation, you always worry that you will come out with something weaker than we have now," an aide explains. And without enthusiasm from Hart, Celler won't press for any action soon on his proposals.

Corporate political clout

But the overriding reason that antitrust enforcement will never present a simple black-and-white choice to business is that Americans use it not just as an economic regulator but as a way to move toward political and social egalitarianism.

Even the Supreme Court, in a 1958 decision spelling out the basic principles of antitrust legislation, said that it rested on a Congressional belief that competition is the best way to distribute resources "while at the same time providing an environment conducive to the preservation of our domestic political and social institutions."

Attorney General John Mitchell defends his department's antitrust policy by arguing that mergers concentrate political and economic power in too few hands in too few metropolitan centers. "We do not want our middle-sized and smaller cities to be merely 'branch store' communities," he says.

Washingtonians know that political clout is not the sole province of big business. The retail druggists are a classic example of small businessmen who win the bulk of their governmental battles because each tends to be an important chamber of commerce force in his home town.

But it is also true that big business tends to use its size to political advantage. W. R. Grace & Co. keeps in its Washington office a "grass-roots file," a district-by-district listing of every company installation, down to local sales offices for garment companies. One government anti-trust man comments that when a speech lauding Harold Geneen is inserted in the Congressional Record, "We just get swamped with copies of that being sent on by 200 different Congressmen from districts where ITT is a factor."

Nader refers to a 1962 Ling-Temco memo that gives as one reason for the upcoming merger with Chance-Vought the belief that, with a broader geographic base, more Congressmen will support the company. Geographic influence "represents a significant additional factor considered by the government in awarding contracts."

But the ability to field a lot of advocates is not equivalent to having one's way. Nader's own summation of political interference in antitrust decisions shows no case where the pressure clearly controlled the outcome. Moreover, those who ask companies to take on more responsibility for the social environment say that the visibility of the corporate giants makes them more effective vehicles for change. Those companies are the ones the White House approaches to create jobs for the long-term unemployed, for instance, or to search out manufacturing suppliers owned by minority businessmen.

Signal's Shumway says that only the combined strength of his various units enables the company to undertake such projects as putting $50,000 into a black-owned business in Watts, training Mexican-Americans to take technicians' jobs at Texas refineries, and depositing spare funds in a minority-owned savings and loan association.

In addition to these social goals, Loevinger points to the escalating public demands for safer products and cleaner air and water. He concludes: "The kind of things we're asking business to do today take size and money. You can't do the job without that."

What ITT gave up to keep the best of the lot

Just at the time it won the second of three antimerger cases brought against it by the government, International Telephone & Telegraph Corp. started negotiating the deal with the Justice Dept. in which it gave up most of what it had won. The prize: The conglomerate gets to keep Hartford Fire Insurance Co., far and away the most profitable of the three acquisitions under attack.

"ITT didn't settle because they thought I was going to lose," antitrust chief Richard McLaren says. In fact the company feared that if all three cases were consolidated before the U.S. Supreme Court, the justices might come out with a keep-some-sell-some compromise decision that would force it to give up Hartford, since it is the biggest of the three acquisitions.

To keep Hartford's $1-billion annual premium income, ITT is giving up another $1-billion in annual sales: Canteen and the fire protection business of Grinnell-the two companies that federal district courts had said ITT could keep—plus Avis, Levitt, Hamilton Life Insurance Co., and Life Insurance

Co. of New York. McLaren says that all the components of the deal are "insurance-related," implying that their retention by ITT would be directly anticompetitive. But the fact that they equal Hartford's annual sales indicates that the antitrusters were at least as interested in total size as in the business specifics.

McLaren, too, recognizes that Hartford's enormous cash flow makes it the choice property of the package. And despite ITT insistence that it is making the deal just to keep Hartford, he still hopes that the company will change its mind over the next three years and exercise its option to sell the gem and keep Avis, Levitt, and the two smaller insurance companies. Canteen and the Grinnell line must go in any event.

Corporate executives trying to apply the ITT settlement to their own planning will find the most useful part of the agreement the precise definitions of the kinds of future deals that the conglomerate must clear with Justice. Washington is trying to keep out of the hands of big companies any subsidiaries that are important factors in oligopolistic industries. As spelled out in the ITT consent order, an oligopolistic market is one where the four top companies get 50% or more of the total business—a definition that covers almost all U.S. manufacturing except for such light industry as soft-drink bottling and women's wear. And a "leading firm" is pinpointed as one with at least $25-million in sales and at least 15% of any market with total annual sales of $100-million or more. That is the most precise outline yet of the kind of merger that will get the finecomb treatment from the antitrust analysts.

Federal Power Commission and Consolidated Edison[1]

IN JUNE OF 1972, Charles Luce and his staff wearily faced still another skirmish in their eight-year battle to obtain permission to construct a pumped storage facility at Cornwall on the Hudson River. The plant, utilizing water pumped up to a reservoir on Storm King Mountain, was to be used to generate electric power for the citizens of New York City some 40 miles away. Luce, chairman of the beleaguered utility, had inherited the Cornwall project when he took over Consolidated Edison in August 1967.

Because the Cornwall plant was to be situated on a U.S. navigable waterway, permission to construct it had to be obtained from the Federal Power Commission (FPC) which exercises, among other things, jurisdiction over such nonfederal hydroelectric facilities. Because the project would use water from a New York river, permission also had to be obtained from the state; initially given, this approval was being challenged in a suit to the New York courts claiming that water antipollution laws would be violated by Cornwall. At this same time, Con Ed was also dealing with the Atomic Energy Commission (AEC) on licensing of Indian Point #2, a nuclear facility, which like Cornwall was part

[1] This case was prepared by Nancy N. Wardell, research assistant, under the supervision of Professor George C. Lodge as a basis for class discussion rather than to illustrate either effective or ineffective handling of an administrative situation.

Authorization of this case for teaching purposes does not indicate that the Federal Power Commission agrees with the interpretations and assumptions contained therein since these are the work of the casewriter and not the Federal Power Commission staff.

of the overall Con Ed plan to construct an enlarged electric-generating system.

As a public utility, Con Ed is legally obligated to supply New Yorkers with sufficient power. The increasing demand for electricity in the 60s had been putting great strains on Con Ed's existing capacity, much of which was obsolete. Use of electricity for commercial and residential purposes as well as for mass transit, sewage disposal, and pollution control make it vital to the well-being of the New York economy. The dramatic blackout in November 1965, not only brought activities in the Northeast to an abrupt halt but also drew attention to the fact that the nation's power supply, and New York's in particular, could no longer be taken for granted.

Why pumped storage?

The area served by Con Ed consists of the five boroughs of New York City and about 70 percent of Westchester County, a total of some 600 square miles. In the mid-1960s many of Con Ed's plants needed to be retired. But this potential loss of capacity was accompanied by a growth in overall demand for electricity by Con Ed's 3 million electricity customers, so not only did Con Ed need replacement plants but also additional capacity.

In the utility business, meeting demand for electrical energy is complicated by the fact that there are fluctuations. Demand peaks in the daytime, for example, when air conditioning and mass transit use large amounts of power. Nighttime demand may be as much as 40 percent less than daytime. Likewise, there is a seasonal imbalance; summer demand is much higher than winter. The Cornwall project had been conceived of by Con Ed as a way of meeting increased demand and also as a way of compensating for the fluctuations in usage. In a pumped storage facility, excess or unused nighttime electricity is used to pump water uphill to reservoirs; during the day as the peak demand time approaches, the water is released to flow downhill through turbines thus generating electricity on short notice and with minimal pollution. While electricity from fossil fuel or nuclear plants cannot be stored, pumped storage is, in essence, a method of storing electricity for those times when it is needed. The energy thus stored can be made available quickly (within minutes).

In the late 1960s as New Yorkers became increasingly concerned about air quality, pressure was brought to bear on Con Ed to reduce its contribution to the city's air pollution. Accordingly, old plants which did not have proper stack gas emission controls either were being remodeled or phased out, and the company had turned to cleaner-burning fuels like gas or to nuclear plants as well as to projects like Cornwall. A hydroelectric plant like Cornwall had several advantages: It was expected to take less time to build and to get licensed than a nuclear plant, and to cost less money, and it is relatively nonpolluting. A nuclear plant takes about ten years to construct and get licensed, a traditional fossil fuel plant about seven and a pumped storage about four, assuming, that is, that all goes well.

Consolidated Edison

Con Ed is one of the country's oldest and largest utility companies, formed by an amalgamation of smaller companies. Once the giant of the industry, Con Ed's rates are now the highest while its generating capacity has dropped to sixth and its growth rate is among the lowest in the country. The region it serves has over 9 million people; land is scarce, people are sensitive to air, water, and land pollution and in May of 1971 in an effort to head off summer power shortages, Luce launched a conservation of electricity campaign under the slogan, "Save-a-Watt." Many other utilities criticized Con Ed for what they regarded as an embarrassing break with tradition—a utility advertising in an attempt to reduce rather than increase its load.

Con Ed's revenues come from sales of electricity, gas, and steam and have gone from $655 million in 1960 to over $1 billion in 1971. The increase in revenue, however, has not been accompanied by a corresponding rise in dividends for the company's some 300,000 stockholders. The company has over 24,000 employees and a total of over 4.2 million customers.

Despite a 1971 decision to discontinue all sales promotion, the company predicted that normal load growth would be at least 5 percent per year. Meeting this growth has not been helped by the breakdowns in equipment which have occurred with a frequency that enrages many New Yorkers, causing the chairman of the New York State counterpart to the FPC, the PSC (Public Service Commission) to comment, "half its capacity is junk . . . half of it is off the line half the time."[2]

Against this backdrop of general ill-will from New Yorkers, Con Ed was attempting to replace and increase its generating capacity. The Cornwall project, initiated in 1963 and planned for completion before 1970 was to become a symbol of frustration for the company and its foes.

The government

In June of 1972, the chairman of the Federal Power Commission, John N. Nassikas, remarked, "Any regulatory action which substantially

---

[2] Economic Priorities Report, *The Price of Power*, Vol. 1, No. 2, May/June 1972, p. 48.

affects private interests—if it is to be effective in the public interest, to win acceptance, and to withstand the rigors of judicial review—must have a compelling basis."

The regulation of the electric and natural gas industries has and will continue to affect substantially both public and private interests. Mr. Nassikas, like Mr. Luce, inherited the Cornwall project when he accepted his new position in August 1969. Just prior to his tenure, and increasingly thereafter, the U.S. energy outlook had gone from rosy to black. Supplies once perceived as adequate were being seen as scarce and there was growing concern over the U.S. competitive position vis-à-vis other countries whose energy supplies might be more reliable.

Traditionally the FPC has served as a surrogate for marketplace competition; since utilities are monopolistic, the FPC has controlled prices just as competitive forces are believed to control them in nonmonopolistic industries. The FPC's jurisdiction over price is limited to wholesale prices for electricity and gas sold interstate; state utility-regulatory agencies, like New York's PSC, control the retail rates.

Today, the role of the FPC is not only recognized as substantially affecting the public interest but it is also being questioned. Is there a compelling basis for the FPC itself?

The historical context

In 1920 when the Federal Power Commission was established to regulate hydroelectric projects, and subsequently in the 1930s as its responsibilities were expanded to include regulation of interstate wholesale sales of electricity and natural gas, the tenor of the times was characterized by a distrust of big business and a belief by Congress that government regulation of competition was a requisite good.

A former chairman of the Federal Trade Commission, the agency which had conducted investigations into the operating practices of the gas and electric industries, commented:

> The Federal Power Act of 1935 was passed as the investigation by the Federal Trade Commission was drawing to a close after several years during which the Commission was relentlessly exposing *the evil practices and conditions that had possessed the industry*. The Act naturally addressed itself to the correction and elimination of those practices and conditions. . . .[3]

The Federal Power Act gave the FPC the jurisdiction over the electric utilities industry and its authority was extended to the natural gas industry by the Natural Gas Act of 1938.

---

[3] E. L. Davis, "The Influence of the Federal Trade Commission's Investigations on Federal Regulation of Interstate Electric and Gas Utilities," *The George Washington Law Review*, Vol. 14, No. 1, December 1945, pp. 21, 22, and 26. (Italics added.)

The Federal Power Commission was established well before atomic energy was developed. After World War II, when the atom was directed toward peacetime uses including electricity production, a special agency was created both to promote and regulate atomic energy. This agency, the Atomic Energy Commission (AEC), is similar to the FPC in that it has appointed commissioners and permanent civil service staff. The AEC has jurisdiction over nuclear power plants; companies wishing to build a nuclear plant to produce electric energy must have the approval of the AEC. Subsequent sale of this nuclear-produced electricity is regulated at the wholesale level by the FPC and at the retail level by the particular state utility regulatory agency wherein the retail sale is occurring.

Regulatory powers of the FPC

The Federal Power Act and the Natural Gas Act give broad regulatory powers to the FPC over the *interstate* transportation and *wholesale* sale of electric power and natural gas and over *hydroelectric* power developments on streams under the control of Congress. Under both acts its statutory duties may be broadly categorized into four (arbitrarily selected) categories: rule making, investigations, rate making, and adjudication of applications and complaints.

Rule making. The commission is empowered to "prescribe, issue, make, amend and rescind such orders, rules and regulations, as it may find necessary or appropriate to carry out the provisions of the Act." It is also empowered to set out rules governing procedure and practice in the electric utility and natural gas industries.

Rule making can cover such issues as accounting practices for electric utility companies (all public and private utilities must use FPC accounting rules) or reporting procedures as did a recent rule prescribing the use of computerized data processing by companies in reporting statistics to the FPC.

Rule making might be termed quasi-judiciary in the sense that it lays down rules which are inherently policy statements governing the behavior of the industries it regulates.

Investigations. The commission can conduct those investigations it sees fit in order to carry out the statutes. As early as 1945 the commission began hearings into the natural gas industry (based on an order issued September 22, 1944).[4] Today the Federal Power Commission is carrying out the Natural Gas Survey, an attempt to ascertain precisely what are the natural gas resources in this country. The survey has encountered some congressional and consumer group criticism on such grounds as either it should have been conducted by some other governmental group

---

[4] FPC Docket No. G-580.

which did not regulate the gas industry, such as the USGS (United States Geologic Survey), or it should have more representatives of consumer groups.

In the spring of 1972 the commission completed the 1970 Electric Power Survey, a four-volume study of the electric power industry in all regions of the nation, considering projected supplies, demands, and possible courses of action for policymakers and the companies.

Rate making. The commission must approve rate changes made by electric or natural gas companies involved in interstate sales. As long as electric rates were declining, the FPC did not insist that the utilities file for rate decreases. However, electric utilities have been increasingly requesting rate increases, claiming increased cost of service. The commission has also experienced many requests for rate increases from the natural gas industry; the nature of its activities has changed as well since it now must consider how to regulate new types of gas such as imported, liquefied natural gas.

Applications and complaints. Hydroelectric power projects may not be built, electric power utilities may not dispose of or acquire electric facilities, natural gas pipeline companies may not construct a pipeline without commission approval. Growth in the demand for energy is accompanied by an ever-increasing flow of applications to the FPC for new or expanded facilities.

Just as companies may file an application for permission to do something, so may individuals, states, municipalities or state commissions file a complaint if they feel that the utility has not done what it should under the Federal Power Act. (The same holds true for the Natural Gas Act, except that it has not authorized "any person" to file such complaints.) While some applications and complaints can be handled informally without a hearing, they often become very lengthy and involved. The Cornwall case was to become one of the latter variety.

To handle the volume of applications and other matters, the FPC has a staff of about 1,100 persons, including five commissioners, appointed for staggered terms by the president. The resources, in terms of personnel and budget, available to the FPC are summarized in Exhibit 2 as is the formal caseload, exclusive of uncontested applications and work such as review of other agencies' projects. Some 90 percent of the FPC's budget is spent on personnel and approximately 96 percent of the staff are career civil service employees, subject to civil service regulations and protection.

The FPC is responsible for ensuring the nation has an adequate and reliable power supply; as power outages occur, questions keep being raised by various government bodies about the adequacy and reliability of the electric power supply. In testimony before the Joint Congressional

Committee on Defense Production in September of 1971, Mr. Nassikas addressed the issues of electric and natural gas supplies. In the electric energy area, Mr. Nassikas pointed out that the FPC, the state public service commissions and the major operating utilities, through the established nationwide group of nine electric reliability councils and twenty-two power pools, are acting to coordinate electric utility system planning and operation as well as contingency programs to render emergency or stand-by capacity.

He also noted that: "With respect to the supply and availability of fossil fuels specifically for electric utility use, we are working with other agencies of Government, as well as industry, in order to help stimulate the production of all types of fuels, to ensure their delivery at needed points of consumption. . . ."[5]

The FPC, however, has no formal authority over these fuels, other than natural gas, which are essential to a utility's ability to function. Natural gas, sought after as a fuel because of its nonpolluting qualities and its low price, is now in short supply. In the natural gas area, Chairman Nassikas has testified before more than a dozen different congressional committees interested in the availability of that fuel.

The FPC since the passage of the National Environmental Policy Act has been required to pay even more attention than before to the environmental aspects of electricity generation. Prior to NEPA, the FPC had required that projects include appropriate recreational facilities, protection of wildlife, etc., but with the formalization of environmental procedures in an act, the FPC must require applicants to submit an Environmental Impact Statement if the project will affect the environment.[6] New projects almost always have an effect and ascertaining precisely what this effect is can be technologically difficult, time consuming, and in the case of esthetic effects, subjective. The procedures for compiling Environmental Impact Statements are under almost constant change as new court decisions are made.

One FPC staff member working on environmental aspects of applications commented to the casewriter: "We get geared up for a new procedure and then along comes a Court decision which changes things. In the last two years we have had three different sets of procedures.

---

[5] Statement of John N. Nassikas, Hearings Before the Joint Committee on Defense Production, Congress of the United States, September 23, 1971, p. 25.

[6] *Environmental Impact Statements* are statements, required under section 102 (2) (c) of NEPA, which attest to the effects, both positive and negative, on the environment of a project. The effects include aspects such as thermal, air, water, and land pollution. Statements are compiled by the company making the application and are routed by the regulatory agency through its own staff and to other governmental groups which would have knowledge as well as jurisdiction over some aspect of the projected impact.

Each one has slowed down processing from four to six months. We are now years behind."

Additionally, the FPC is now expected to comment on the environmental impact of projects subject to the jurisdiction of *other* governmental agencies such as the AEC or the Army Corps of Engineers. One staff member's sole job now is to review other agencies' environmental statements. Recent court decisions have focussed on the procedures used in fulfilling the requirements under NEPA and the trend appears to be moving towards requiring even more information, not less.

A recent FPC ruling (The Green County decision) was overturned by a circuit court and is on appeal to the Supreme Court by the FPC. If the FPC is again overruled, it would no longer be permitted to use an industry-provided environmental impact statement, but would be required to do its own field research on the subject.

The complexity of environmental procedures mirrors the tangled web of energy regulation as a whole. At least 40 government agencies or congressional committees have become involved in energy regulation or policy. Critics have suggested that the area of regulation is more complicated than it has to be because of the government's preference for and financial support of atomic energy. Some 85 percent of energy research money provided by the federal government goes into atomic energy; new technologies or ways of improving the efficiency of or reducing the polluting effects of older technologies receive the left-over 15 percent.

The preferential treatment accorded atomic energy, critics contend, means that even the energy regulators are treated preferentially with the AEC being the glamor agency and the FPC being the whipping post when crises occur.

History of the Cornwall application

In January of 1963, Con Ed applied to the FPC for a license to construct the Cornwall plant. Plant facilities were to be situated both at the base and up the face of Storm King Mountain, with power being transmitted to New York by means of 25 miles of high-tension lines strung across the Hudson and down Westchester County from ten-story towers. A reservoir to hold the water pumped in from the Hudson was to be constructed at the top and would require flooding of 240 acres of woodland including 70 acres of Black Rock Forest owned by Harvard University.

Con Ed did not leak out any details of the project prior to its official announcement because of the problem of accumulating land. But initial community reaction was minimal due in part to the efforts of Mr. Vilas,

Con Ed's Director of Community Relations. He knew intimately the people on top of Storm King Mountain whose summer homes would be covered by the reservoir and he had been a member of the Hudson River Conservation Society for over 20 years. His close personal contacts helped smooth over many ruffled feelings. The remaining ruffled feelings were smoothed over by the economic benefits which would accrue to Cornwall: a tripling of assessed valuations, a halving of the tax rate, a thousand new jobs for the construction of the plant and many permanent jobs in the completed plant.

Cornwall town fathers supported the project vigorously before the FPC and the high level of their enthusiasm prompted a local newspaper, the Middletown *Times-Herald Record*, to look into the matter. The reporters were denied access to the village records and the paper sued for the right to inspect the books. After obtaining a court order permitting it to do so, the paper discovered some $160,000 in payments over a four-year period by Con Ed to the Cornwall village attorney. The paper described the attorney's payments as covering "extensive lobbying and public relations activities on behalf of the proposed hydroelectric plant in Cornwall."[7] In addition, Con Ed, under a 1963 contract with Cornwall, had made payments which included $2.8 million for a new water system for the town.

In the initial briefs filed before the commission, the opponents of Cornwall pointed out the ugliness of the project and the need for places of peace and beauty in our hectic society: "the excavation into Storm King is in effect a quarry with no possibility of concealment, littered over with electrical equipment and an enormous gantry crane which will not blend, no matter what color it is painted."

Carl Cramer, the author and historian declared: "We believe that ugliness begets ugliness and that nature's beauty, once destroyed, may never be restored by an artifice of man. . . . We would offer the peace and healing our river gives, as it has always given, to those who seek its waters for respite from the tension of their lives. We believe that the time for opposing those forces that would defile the Great River of the Mountains is now."

The supporting briefs noted the need for power generated by Cornwall and that no one was challenging the power market for the electricity. It also noted that there was "evidence that the power plant as presently terraced into the mountain, together with the natural stone, shrubbery, and camouflage to be employed will be relatively inconspicuous and unobtrusive to those passing above it on Storm King Highway."

On March 10, 1965, the Federal Power Commission voted three to one to allow Con Ed to build the Cornwall plant, stating: "Whatever

---

[7] Middletown *Times-Herald Record*, March 28, 1968.

may be the negative aspects of adding this on Storm King Mountain, on balance we do not believe it outweighs the public interest in the effective utilization of an unusually fine pumped-storage site."[8]

This comment led the *New York Times* to editorialize:

> It was inevitable that the Federal Power Commission, an agency created to foster the growth of the electric power industry, would give greater weight to arguments based on engineering and economic considerations than those based on esthetics. Surely such an agency should not continue to have the final word . . . in dealing with sites of great natural beauty.[9]

The FPC decision was challenged immediately by the Scenic Hudson Preservation Conference. SHPC was a coalition of some 45 conservation organizations, including national ones like the Sierra Club and local ones like the Palisades Nature Association.

SHPC was under the direction of Leopold Rothschild, a New York attorney, who from the beginning had stated the group's position succinctly: "The life of the Hudson itself is at stake. This is a real test case. If Con Ed is allowed to get away with it, there will be others attempting the same thing."[10]

In an unprecedented move, the SHPC and three Westchester County towns appealed the FPC decision to the Second Circuit Court of Appeals in New York City. That court, in December 1965, set aside the license granted by the FPC and directed the commission to hold hearings again with the instructions that "the Commission's renewed proceedings must include as a basic concern the preservation of natural beauty and of national historic shrines, keeping in mind that, in our affluent society, the cost of a project is only one of several factors to be considered. The record as it comes to us fails markedly to make out a case for the Storm King [Cornwall] project on, among other matters, costs, public convenience and necessity, and the absence of reasonable alternatives."[11]

The FPC's response indicated the commission's feeling that the competing claims of adequate power and environmental protection were finally being recognized:

> The decision of the Court of Appeals in *Scenic Hudson* was quickly recognized as a landmark in judicial regulation of the administrative process. . . .The Scenic Hudson opinion creates the framework within which the competing social claims of an adequate and reliable supply of electric power and the protection of scenic resources and our natural environment must be resolved.[12]

---

[8] *The New York Times*, March 10, 1965.

[9] Ibid.

[10] *Newsweek*, December 21, 1964.

[11] *Scenic Hudson Preservation Conference* v. *Federal Power Commission*, 354 F 2d, 620 (1965).

[12] FPC, Opinion No. 584, p. 3.

Con Ed petitioned the United States Supreme Court to review the decision of the court of appeals, but in May 1966, the Supreme Court declined.

The Cornwall case was reopened. Over 60 expert witnesses testified before the commission, over 675 exhibits were introduced into the record, and in the 100 days spent on the hearings, over 19,000 pages of record were amassed.

By this round, Con Ed planned to put the entire plant underground and to spend considerable sums to landscape a waterfront park for the people of Cornwall. While the battle was being waged, Con Ed had been forced to build a 500,000-kilowatt conventional generating plant at Staten Island and to delay the retirement of older generating stations. Con Ed had imposed six rate hikes in ten years on its customers, claiming, in part, that higher rates were needed because of higher costs associated with running old and inefficient generating stations. Con Ed's earnings were not helped by the fact that it had already spent over $14 million on the nonexistent Cornwall plant. (The SHPC had spent over $1 million in keeping it nonexistent.)

In considering what alternatives Con Ed had to the Cornwall plant, the FPC delved into the question of nuclear alternatives. Con Ed's history here had been fraught with problems as well. Its first nuclear plant had been placed in operation at Indian Point in August 1962. Five years later in the 1966–67 electric rate hearings before the PSC, the New York City Housing Authority strongly questioned the company's prudence in building Indian Point because of the high costs of the project and because it was close to a highly populated area. Thereafter the Con Ed record with respect to atomic energy became open to public debate. Negotiations for Indian Point #2 were begun in 1965 with a target completion date of 1969; by 1972 the plant was still not licensed.

In assessing the nuclear and other alternatives, the FPC first considered the cost aspect. In the early 1960s depending on what combination of fuels was used, the Cornwall project was projected to cost between $119 million and $172 million. (By 1970, this cost was projected at $234 million.) A nuclear alternative during the same time period was estimated to cost "in excess of $192 million *more* [over the $234 million] . . . with the annual cost differential growing in the later years."[13] A combination of nuclear-gas turbine capacity was another alternative, but it too would cost far more than a pumped-storage project, about 158 million *more* than Cornwall.

In addition to cost factors were siting issues. The FPC noted that:

> Nuclear units require considerable acreage of open land and an abundant supply of cooling water, limiting sites to relatively undeveloped areas

---

[13] FPC, Opinion No. 584, August 19, 1970.

adjacent to major rivers or tidal waters. Sites available along the Hudson are limited by the terrain, by present use of industrial parcels along the river, and by the desirability of obtaining at least twenty-five acres for a nuclear plant site.[14]

The FPC noted that one site was possible but it questioned the reliability of a nuclear unit versus a hydroelectric one given the outage problems inherent in nuclear units. Accordingly, the commission decided that "an all nuclear unit is not a feasible alternative to Cornwall."[15] The nuclear-gas turbine alternative was deemed not equivalent to Cornwall and in addition the FPC said, "We stress that [its] reliability quotient . . . is far less than Cornwall's."[16]

The FPC considered as well the possibility of alternative conventional or pumped-storage hydroelectric sites. The Con Ed witnesses testified that they had conducted "extensive surveys for conventional hydroelectric or pumped-storage sites within a radius of 100 miles from New York City,"[17] without locating a suitable site and the FPC's own staff surveys were in agreement with this. None of the opponents, or intervenors, proposed any alternative sites to Cornwall.

The "practicality and cost of purchasing" power was considered as an alternative to Cornwall, and the commission concluded that the quantities required, particularly in the time frame that these would be needed (without delays), would not be available. It said, "Finally, if load growth exceeds plant expansion, present sellers may themselves become seekers of purchased power."[18] The commission indicated that it was not wise to depend, for example, on being able to purchase power from Canadian plants that were not yet even completed.

Because coal is a highly polluting fuel, the idea has been raised that it should be burned right at the mine mouth with the resultant electricity being transmitted by long transmission lines from Pennsylvania or West Virginia to New York. Assuming that the lines could be built underground in the urban areas surrounding New York and the city itself, this, of course, would solve New York's problems with air pollution. However, the FPC concluded that New York's problem shouldn't be resolved at the expense of non–New Yorkers. Air pollution created in mine-mouth operations, they said, is just as negative a factor when it is rural air pollution as when it is urban.

Having decided that the record "clearly establishes that [Cornwall] offers more reliable cleaner and cheaper electricity than any other feasible alternative," the commission looked to the question of "whether,

[14] Ibid. Sec. 115.
[15] Ibid., Sec. 121.
[16] Ibid., Sec. 113.
[17] Ibid., Sec. 122.
[18] Ibid., Sec. 136.

and if so to what degree, the project will create detrimental aesthetic and environmental conditions."[19]

All the participants in the case could agree on just one thing: It is extremely difficult to balance technological versus social values.

The Sierra Club president, David Brower, argued against society's preoccupation with "commodity purposes" alone and said the case was a confrontation between those who would develop and those who would preserve. A Yale art historian and architect, Vincent J. Scully, Jr., evaluated the aesthetic importance of Storm King in eloquent terms:

> . . . it is a mountain which should be left alone. It rises like a brown bear out of the river, a dome of living granite, swelling with animal power. It is not picturesque in the softer sense of the word, but awesome, a primitive embodiment of the energies of the earth. It makes the character of wild nature physically visible in monumental form.[20]

Professor Scully referred to the Con Ed recreation proposal as "suburbanization of the mountain."

According to FPC procedures, cases are initially decided by a "hearing examiner" who serves in the role of a judge. Once his decision has been made, the five commissioners must either accept, amend, or reject his decision. Thirty days after the commissioners issue their decision, unless further challenged by interested parties, the decision takes effect. In August 1968 the presiding examiner issued his decision, which was to permit construction of the Cornwall facility. But before the commission had concluded its review of this decision, the city of New York intervened and asked that the question of the relationship of the Cornwall plant to a nearby water aqueduct supplying New York City be considered. In November, the commission reopened the proceedings and, after more review, a Supplemental Initial Decision, again authorizing the construction, was issued by the presiding examiner in December 1969. This decision, too, did not go unchallenged and interested parties again argued for and against the plant.

Parties filed briefs on exceptions and briefs opposing exceptions to both the initial decision of August 6, 1968, and the supplemental initial decision of December 23, 1969. In May of 1970 oral arguments were held before the commission.

In July 1970, the commissioners toured the site in person, viewing it from a helicopter, by boat, on foot, and by automobile, assessing the previous assertions made by FPC staff members, Con Ed staff, and opponents of the plan. Counsel for the various interested parties were invited to be present and counsel for the village of Cornwall, Scenic Hudson, Con Ed, John S. Tamsen pro se, representatives of the Palisades

---

[19] Ibid., Sec. 141.
[20] Ibid., p. 42.

Interstate Park Commission and the city of New York Department of Water Resources attended. In addition, the Orange County Government, the Cornwall Taxpayers Water Protection Association, the Putnam County Historical Society and the Hudson River Sloop Restoration, Inc. all offered their assistance during the viewing. In August the FPC approved the Cornwall application.

Intervenors again challenged the decision, but the appeals courts upheld the FPC's decision. In the summer of 1972, the final impediment to Federal approval was removed when the U.S. Supreme Court refused to review the lower court's decision. But state approvals were still lacking. A suit filed in a state court had been won by the conservationists; the certificate of approval for the project issued by the New York Department of Environmental Conservation had been set aside. But in June of 1972 an appellate court set aside the state court's decision. The opponents, however, had no intention of dropping the fight and planned to appeal the reversal, saying the appeal would be made because of: "The danger to the New York City Aqueduct, supplying 40 percent of our water supply, the water supply of Chelsea and Poughkeepsie, as well as the marine resources of the river."[21]

But if the FPC's role in Cornwall was over, it had other issues to contend with that more than filled the void left by Cornwall. The right of the FPC even to exist was being challenged. In the June 16 issue of *Science,* the magazine of the prestigious American Association for the Advancement of Science, Glenn T. Seaborg stated the case for the AEC to subsume all the other federal regulators of energy industries:

> To develop and utilize these energy technologies in the most economic and expeditious manner, the coordination of the U.S. energy programs must be the responsibility of a *single government agency,* . . .
>
> The Atomic Energy Commission has developed over several decades a superb research base, with excellent laboratories and a tradition of successfully managing large projects in the public interest. . . . *No other agency of the federal government* is in a more favorable position to launch a unified program for meeting the energy needs of the American people than is the Atomic Energy Commission. It should be transformed into the U.S. Energy Agency.[22]

For his part, Luce could ignore the FPC's problems, being faced now with the fact that delays to date have run the projected costs of the Cornwall project to $400 million, more than double the initial projected cost. And it still does not exist except on the drawing boards.

---

[21] Alexander Saunders, chairman of SHPC, *Wall Street Journal,* July 1, 1972.

[22] *Science,* June 16, 1972, Vol. 176, No. 4040. (Italics added.)

EXHIBIT 1
Federal Power Commission

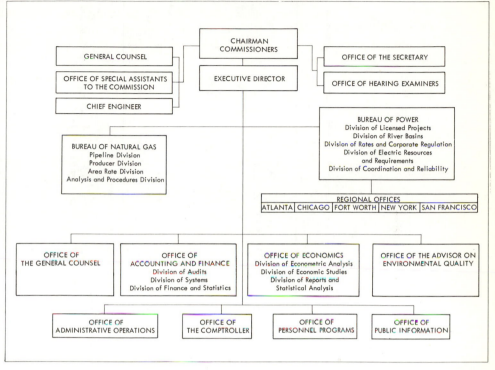

Note: Organization Chart—Revised April, 1971.

EXHIBIT 2
Budget, personnel, and workload for the FPC 1965–1973
(estimate)

	1965	1966	1967	1968	1969	1970	1971	1972	1973
Expenditures (in thousands of dollars):									
Actual.	$13,081	$14,067	$14,220	$14,563	$15,666	$17,848	$19,820	$21,583	$22,798
Adjusted actual*.	13,081	13,595	13,305	12,933	13,060	12,593			
Percent change from 1965 (adjusted actual).	—	+3.9	+1.7	-1.1	-0.2	-3.7			
Personnel (in numbers of people):									
Average	1,111	1,092	1,131	1,109	1,090	1,097	1,182	1,171	1,191
Percent change from 1965.	—	-1.7	+1.8	-0.2	-2.8	-1.3	+6.3	+5.4	+7.2
Workload† (in number of cases heard):									
Completed by June 30.	33	24	29	53	43	39			
Pending as June 30.	63	92	91	96	115	125			
Total for year.	96	116	120	149	158	164			

* Of these expenditures, personnel compensation has been adjusted to allow for pay increases and all expenditures have been adjusted for inflation, since 1965. (These remarks, however, do not apply for data for year 1971 through 1973.)

† Formal case workload, not including some 2,000 uncontested cases per year which are not heard by a hearing examiner.

Sources: *A New Regulatory Framework: Report on Selected Independent Regulatory Agencies*, The President's Advisory Council on Executive Organization, January 1971, p. 186. Data for 1971 through 1973 provided by the FPC, March 1972. Data for 1972 and 1973 represent estimates as of February 2, 1972.

APPENDIX A

LEGISLATIVE SUMMARY

1880   Legislation preliminary to the establishment of the Federal Power Commission began in the 1880s with several Rivers and Harbors Acts giving the federal government, or branches such as the secretary of war, control over various aspects of U.S. waterways.

      Initially these acts were intended to prevent obstruction of navigable waterways.[1]

1906   A United States Department of Agriculture Report, *Report of the Forester,* for the fiscal year 1905–1906, established the principle that the use of water power should no longer be free, and that charges should be calculated per mile according to the length of ditches and pipelines, or per acre for land used such as for areas flooded by reservoirs, and for the conservation of the water supply. Not everyone agreed with the concept of charges.

1920   The debate over the appropriate way to handle the nation's water power supply raged for a decade and culminated in the Federal Water Power Act of 1920.[2] The act established the government's right to regulate waterpower (hydroelectric) projects and to limit licenses to fifty years or less. The act was to be administered by a Federal Power Commission consisting of three men, the secretary of war, the secretary of the interior, and the secretary of agriculture.

1928   In 1928, Senator Walsh of Montana called for a Senate investigation of the gas and electric industry. Subsequently the Federal Trade Commission was authorized to investigate these two industries.[3] The investigations (which lasted several years), uncovered ample evidence of abuses, primarily in accounting practices, which resulted both in higher rates to consumers and over-valued stock prices.

1930   On June 23, the Federal Power Commission was reorganized to become an independent commission with five full-time commissioners (serving five-year staggered terms, only three of them to be of the same political party), replacing the three secretaries. The commissioners were to be appointed by the president. The

---

[1] Rivers and Harbors Acts, 23 Stat. 133 (1884); 26 Stat. 426, 454 (1890).

[2] 41 Stat. 1063, (1920) 16 U.S.C. 791.

[3] S. Res. 83, 70th Cong., 1st Sess. (1928) and extended by S. J. Res. 115, 73d Cong., 2d Sess., (1934).

commission's function—hydroelectric regulation—remained the same.[4]

1934   A Senate Joint Resolution, No. 74 (April 14) directed the Federal Power Commission to look into the question of electric rates being charged and the quality of service provided to commercial and industrial consumers.

1935   The Public Utility Act[5] was passed. Title I was the Public Utility Holding Company Act (to be administered by the SEC); and Title II became Parts II and III of the Federal Power Act, thereby establishing firmly the principle of federal government regulation of interstate commerce in electric energy. The Public Utility Holding Company Act was designed to prevent financial abuses such as has been uncovered by the Federal Trade Commission investigations. It pertained primarily to security transactions and acquisitions of securities and assets of other companies. The SEC's job was to look after the interests of the utility *security holders* while the FPC was to look after the utility *rate payer*. In broad terms the FPC was given regulatory powers over the interstate transportation and sale of electric power wholesale in addition to licensing of hydroelectric sites.

Title II of the Public Utility Act subsumed the Federal Water Power Act of 1920 into Part I of the "Federal Power Act,"[6] and added Parts II and III to the Federal Power Act. Part I essentially gives the Commission authority to license and supervise hydroelectric projects. Under Part II the commission is given jurisdiction over utilities owning or operating facilities involved in the transmission or sale (wholesale) of electric energy in interstate commerce. (The FPC does not regulate retail sales; individual states do that.) Part III pertains to administrative and procedural aspects.

1938   The Natural Gas Act[7] was passed, giving the FPC jurisdiction over rates in interstate commerce. Interstate transportation of natural gas has occurred for only about ten years prior to the passing of the Natural Gas Act. (The seamless pipe, developed in 1925, had greatly spurred pipeline construction.)

1942   February 7, the Natural Gas Act was amended giving the FPC authority to issue certificates for the construction of pipelines, pipeline extensions and all new operations since February 7, 1942,

---

[4] 46 Stat. 797 (1930), 16 U.S.C. Secs. 792, 793, 797.
[5] 49 Stat. 803 (1935) 15 U.S.C. Sec. 79a *et seq.*
[6] 49 Stat. 838 (1935) 16 U.S.C. 791a-825r.
[7] 52 Stat. 821 (1938) 15 U.S.C. Sec. 717 *et seq.*

as well as a "Grandfather clause" certificate for facilities already in operation.

1954 The Supreme Court ruled in *Phillips Petroleum* v. *Wisconsin,* that the FPC had jurisdiction over prices charged by independent producers selling to companies in interstate sale of natural gas. To the present time, the original acts have been amended and in addition, the Federal Power Commission has had duties prescribed to it both directly and indirectly under other federal statutes ranging from the Tennessee Valley Authority Act (1938) by which the FPC was to approve contracts for TVA extension of credit, to Flood Control Acts, the Atomic Energy Act (1954), and The National Environmental Policy Act (1970).

APPENDIX B

MAJOR REGULATORY POWERS OF THE FPC[1]

Natural gas

The commission exercises the following responsibilities with respect to the natural gas industry in *interstate* and *wholesale* (*not* retail) commerce:

Facilities.   Issues certificates authorizing natural gas pipelines to construct or abandon, extend, acquire, or operate transportation and storage facilities;

Sales.   Investigates the need for and, when appropriate, directs pipelines to sell (or stop selling) natural gas to local distributors;

Rates.   Investigates and regulates the rates, charges and services for natural gas transported or sold for resale in interstate commerce;

Information gathering.   Gathers, analyzes, maintains, and publishes information on natural gas pipelines subject to commission jurisdiction;

Accounting.   Promulgates and enforces a uniform system for financial accounting and reporting;

Import/export.   Regulates transportation and purchase of gas in submerged lands of the Outer Continental Shelf and gas imported or exported.

Electric power

The commission exercises the following responsibilities with respect

---

[1] The itemization of responsibilities is summarized from: *An Informal Explanation of the Organization & Work of the FPC, 1971,* pp. 10–13, 20–24.

to the electric power industry in hydroelectric projects and in interstate, wholesale commerce.

Rates.   Regulates the rates and services of public utilities selling electricity in *interstate* wholesale commerce and reviews and, upon a satisfactory finding, confirms and approves proposed rates for the sale of electric power from certain federal and international hydroelectric projects.

Hydroelectric facilities.   Issues and administers permits and licenses for the planning, construction, and operation of nonfederal hydroelectric projects on waters or lands subject to federal jurisdiction;

Conservation.   Requires, under licenses issued for water power projects, the conservation and development of the land and water associated natural resources (fish, wildlife, and outdoor recreation), and the preservation of historic, scenic, and other aesthetic values;

Safety.   Periodically inspects licensed projects during construction and in operation regarding their physical safety;

Interconnects.   Promotes and encourages voluntary interconnections of electric transmission facilities and coordinated operation within and between regional districts which the commission is directed to establish;

Accounting.   Promulgates and enforces a uniform system for financial accounting and reporting by interstate public utilities;

Public information.   Publishes a variety of statistics and reports concerning the electric power industry generally. These give impartial information to consumers, assist state regulatory agencies, and provide information concerning individual utilities on a comparable basis;

Securities.   Regulates certain issuances and sales of securities by electric public utilities and regulates their merger or consolidation and their disposition or acquisition of facilities; regulates the holding of interlocking positions between electric public utility companies and between public utilities and electric supply companies or companies authorized to underwrite securities;

Cost.   Allocates the costs of certain federal hydroelectric projects, participates in the allocation of costs of others, and studies plans for reservoir projects;

International.   Authorizes the exportation of electricity to foreign countries and issues permits for maintaining facilities at international borders for the transmission of electric energy between the United States and a foreign country.

Consolidated Edison (A)[1]

CONSOLIDATED EDISON COMPANY of New York is a favorite target for criticism from customers, public officials, the press, and even some business consultants. After citing the giant utility company's difficulties with customers in 1966, *Fortune* magazine labeled it "the company you love to hate." In August 1968, the *Wall Street Journal* noted that Con Ed "seems to have a unique capacity for alienating its 4.2 million customers, including the biggest customer of all, the city."

The article in the *Journal* presented a list of complaints that has become standard for Con Ed critics: "Con Ed charges the highest electric rates of any big-city utility, contributes a major share of New York's air pollution, noisily chops 40,000 holes in the streets each year, inefficiently operates an aging system that produces nearly 1,900 neighborhood power failures annually—and is rude in the bargain."[2]

To top it all off, the company's financial record has been mediocre. Since 1964, operating revenues and net income have grown at barely 5 percent a year, and Con Ed's return on its rate base is under 6 percent—well below the performance of other large utilities. (See Exhibit 1 for financial data.)

---

[1] This case was developed as part of the Program on Business Leadership and Urban Problems at the Harvard Graduate School of Business Administration. It was prepared in 1970 by Efrem Sigel, assistant in research, assisted by Howard Cox and Francisco de Sola, under the supervision of Professor George C. Lodge, as a basis for class discussion rather than to illustrate either effective or ineffective handling of an administrative situation.

[2] *Wall Street Journal,* August 1968.

Management conceded that its rates are high and that service needs improvement, but Con Ed points out, in defense, that the problems of doing business in New York City are without parallel: the company's bill of $193 million for state and local taxes is several times that of other large utilities, and the city requirement that many of its transmission lines be placed underground adds considerably to the costs of construction and maintenance.

Nevertheless, disappointing operating results and the volume of criticism have forced Con Ed to examine its own house. The board of trustees recognized the need for change when it named Charles F. Luce chairman of the board in August 1967. Mr. Luce had been undersecretary of the Department of the Interior, having previously served as administrator of the Bonneville Power Administration, a public power authority. His appointment constituted a sharp break with the past at Con Ed, which had traditionally promoted its chief executives from within. It reflected the board's view of the seriousness of the situation.

In a year as chairman, Mr. Luce had committed the company to programs of air-pollution control and equal employment, had adopted a new moto ("Clean Energy"), changed the color of the trucks from orange to blue, instituted a cost-cutting program, and retained a consulting firm to study the company's internal organization. A year of these efforts, however, did not appear to have had much impact on Con Ed's public image or operating results. Mr. Luce was, therefore, in the midst of a thorough review of company problems in order to determine which ones were most important and whether there was an underlying pattern to the company's difficulties. He then hoped to develop a specific plan for meeting those problems in the years ahead.

Consolidated Edison's purpose

Con Ed is the largest investor-owned utility in the country in terms of electric revenues, number of electric customers, and total assets; it is second in total operating revenues. It serves some 4.1 million customers in New York City and Westchester County and, in 1967, had operating revenues of $931 million and assets of $3.7 billion. Though electricity accounts for the bulk of its sales, Con Ed actually furnishes three different kinds of energy: electricity to the five boroughs of New York City and most of Westchester; gas to Manhattan, the Bronx, and two wards of Queens; and steam to midtown and downtown Manhattan.

A recent report to the chairman of Con Ed defined the company's mission as follows:

1. Sales distribution and service. To sell and distribute power to individual customers and service their needs on a continuing basis.

2. Facilities development. To provide required generating and transmission facilities.
3. Production mission. To operate and maintain generating and transmission facilities.
4. Support activities. Functions such as finance and public relations which are not related to a specific mission.

Because of its size and the fact that its operations are confined to a small and concentrated geographical region, Con Ed plays an important role in the political and economic life of the New York metropolitan community. (Con Ed serves 600 square miles, compared to 94,000 square miles for California's Pacific Gas and Electric. Yet, the company has 66,000 miles of underground transmission lines—more than any other company in the world. This underground system is so expensive to maintain that Con Ed spends twice as much on transmission and distribution facilities as it does on generating plants.) The company is New York City's largest real estate taxpayer, and in 1967 paid a total of $139,745,000 in local taxes. Conversely, the city and its related agencies are the largest single customer of Con Ed, spending $70 million a year for electricity alone. In recent years, Con Ed has averaged more than $250 million annually in construction expenditures; one executive estimates that by itself the company provides 15 to 20 percent of all employment in building trades in New York City. And, with some 25,000 employees, Con Ed also ranks as the second largest private employer in the metropolitan area. All employees, except for about 5,000 professionals and supervisors, are members of Local 1-2 of the Utility Workers Union of America, AFL-CIO. Con Ed has a union shop provision under which all workers must join the union within 30 days after becoming permanent employees.

Company history

Con Ed's economic importance in New York City and its close ties—both financial and political—with various city and state governmental agencies are reflected in the company's 147-year history and, particularly, in the series of continuing battles it has fought with elected officials and other economic interests in the metropolitan areas.

Con Ed's roots go back as far as 1823, when landowner-clergyman Samuel Leggett and a group of influential New York businessmen incorporated the New York Gas Light Company. Despite problems of production and transmission, and the costliness of the new fuel, numerous gas companies sprang up and battled each other vigorously for franchises, which were granted by the city governments. The 1850s brought a 30-year period of stability and relative peace, marked by rapid construction of lines and mains. By the 1880s, however, the gas companies faced the spectre of a new competitive light source—electricity. Thus, in 1884, the largest gas companies of New York joined together to form the Consolidated Gas Company of New York. But even this giant could not stop the spread of electricity, and by 1900, the electric companies were well on the way to winning the lighting race.

The leaders of the gas industry responded to this threat by quietly buying up the stocks of electric companies. As both gas and electric companies spread outward from Manhattan in the first decade of the 20th century, the two industries gradually intertwined. A small group of New York financiers played an important part in this process of stock transfer and acquisition. The final impetus toward unity came through the efforts of two pioneers in New York City lighting, Harrison Edwards Gawtry of the Consolidated Gas Company and Anthony Brady, representing the growing electric industry. By the start of the depression, Consolidated Gas already controlled the largest central station organization in the world—including the New York Edison Company, the Brooklyn Edison Company, the United Electric Light and Power Company, the New York and Queens Electric Light and Power Company, the Bronx Gas and Electric Company, and the Westchester Light Company. Following the addition of a few more companies to this complex, the Consolidated Edison Company of New York finally emerged in 1936.

Con Ed's birth was marked by vigorous political battle over its very right to exist; the scars of the battle are still very much felt today.

The specific controversy involved Con Ed and the then mayor of New York, Fiorello LaGuardia, but its roots were historic. The inefficiencies of municipal regulation and the corruption accompanying the grant of franchises had led to the growth of state and local regulation of utilities in the early 1900s. It was in 1921 that the current New York State regulatory agency, the Public Service Commission, was created to supplant various inefficient district commissions. And, in the 1930s, came stricter federal regulation in the wake of disclosures of financial manipulations and conspiracy among utilities and utility holding companies. In 1934, Mayor LaGuardia took office to find that the city was facing a financial crisis. Unable to obtain special revenue-raising powers from the state legislature, LaGuardia turned on the New York utilities and demanded that the companies cut the city's power and light bill. This demand broadened into a general attack which was to last six years. The mayor sought to control the utilities which, he believed, were overcharging the public for their services. To do this, he proposed that the city buy its own power plants, which would serve as a "yardstick" to measure the cost of providing power. LaGuardia's proposal was not an isolated case but was part of a wider demand for public power in the United States. In 1933, for example, Congress had created the TVA to provide electricity to millions of customers in the Tennessee Valley.

LaGuardia's purpose was not only to hold down electric rates but also to curb what he viewed as the inordinate political power of the utilities. In a pamphlet published in 1935, he stated:

> The fight for a yardstick municipal plant in this city is bound to be a bitter struggle in which the utility interests use their great wealth and power to defend themselves against any threat to their profits. They will misrepresent the issue and produce irrelevant examples of small public power plants that have sold out to private systems in various parts of the country. They will take the same set of figures that I have used and twist them to different conclusions. They will bring quiet pressure to bear upon those businessmen who oppose them. But in the long run these tactics will be of no avail because the facts are overwhelmingly against them and in favor of a yardstick plant.

The mayor's commissioner of water supply, gas, and electricity claimed that "their (utility company's) charges are 30 to 40 percent higher than the average charges for street lighting paid by other municipalities in the United States" and said that the utilities could cut rates by 30 percent "without thereby impairing the right of the company and its stockholders to a fair net valuation."

But Con Ed was not idle in defending itself. Chairman Floyd L. Carlisle rebutted the mayor's charges, contending that reductions would seriously impair the company's financial stability and make further rate reductions extremely difficult. The company counsel, Joseph M. Proskauer, testified before a legislative committee that the mayor's bill for a municipal plant "gives cities the right to the most unfair competition that was ever heard of." The net effect of permitting the public power plants, he argued, would be a duplication of lines and equipment, "a waste for which somebody has got to pay, and that somebody is always the taxpayer."

In 1937, the chairman of the Federal Power Commission, Frederick R. McNinch, joined the fight, charging that New York City's power rates were too high. The head of the New York State Public Service Commission, Milo Maltbie, sharply disagreed and defended Con Ed. Though the controversy raged for six years, LaGuardia was unable to get a bill empowering the city to take over power plants and to set up a municipal regulatory commission. A compromise was struck over the city's power bill, however. In 1935 and 1936, the company filed rate reductions amounting to $7 million annually.

In sum, the company had been "up against the wall," as one executive put it, and found itself severely discomfitted by the glare of public attention which had focused on it for six years. Its accounting practices and valuation procedures had been roundly criticized, and the very quality of the services it offered had been derided. The mayor and his allies, on the other hand, could never muster the necessary support for the establishment of a municipal power plant.

Memories of the dispute have lingered. One Con Ed executive feels, for example, that "the wisest decision the company ever made was to buy the city's subway power plants in 1959." (The company paid the full book value of $126 million for the three 50-year old plants, even though some observers thought their real economic worth was considerably lower. When asked about the purchase at a stockholder's meeting, Harland Forbes, then chairman, stated, "I don't know about the income point, but I do think it was a very great value to eliminate the city of New York from competition in the power field. I think that's where the value lies.") The purchase appeared to eliminate the threat of city-owned power intervening in the company's operations. If the mayors after LaGuardia did not call for public power plants, however, they felt no hesitancy about holding Con Ed up to public scrutiny and ridicule. Thus, Mayor Robert F. Wagner was following a time-honored practice in November 1961 when he blasted both the Public Service Commission and the company on the occasion of a rate increase. Wagner accused the commission of "holding a grab-bag for the utilities" and called the increase "rate gouging." Mayor John V. Lindsay also has sustained a running battle with the company.

Influence of company history on personnel and practice

The long period of consolidation which preceded the formation of Con Ed in 1936 left its imprint on the procedures by which the company chose its executives and the qualities which were important to advancement in the company. The record shows that the competing utilities were put together by a small group of New York financiers for whom, presumably, personal contact and past association were an important aspect of business dealings. Indeed, the list of the trustees of the old Consolidated Gas Company reads like a "Who's Who" of the New York financial community: Samuel Sloan, William Rockefeller, George F. Baker, James Stillman, Hugh Auchincloss, and George Whitney, among others. In the same way, generations of families sometimes became involved in the utilities: Anthony Brady was succeeded by his son, Nicholas Brady; while Harrison Gawtry's son, Lewis Gawtry, also followed his father, both assuming important positions in Con Ed.

The tradition of personal association and family involvement shaped the company's development; in many ways it became like a family to its employees. Thus, the senior executives at Con Ed have generally been engineers who patiently worked their way up the company ladder.

Ralph Tapscott began as assistant chief electric engineer at New York Edison and became chief executive officer at Con Ed in 1942; Hudson Roy Searing, who started as a telephone operator at New York Edison in 1909, succeeded him. Later came Charles E. Eble, chairman until 1967, who began his career as a $6-a-week messenger boy and rose to the top after 40 years with the company. In 1966, Thomas O'Hanlon wrote in *Fortune* that "most Con Edison executives have spent their lives within the protective womb of the company—an environment they will not now, in their later days, permit to change. Old and embattled, proud and thin-skinned, the men who lead Con Edison look upon the company as their own personal creation." Occasionally, however, the company has looked beyond its ranks for chief executives.

"It is curious," recalled Franklin E. Vilas, director of community relations, "that outsiders with vast governmental experience were brought in when the company was undergoing periods of crisis. Take George Cortelyou—he was very well versed in Washington power circles and was extremely influential in bringing the company out of the crisis period it was in during the thirties. And now, when the company is suffering the same ills, they bring Charles Luce in." Mr. Cortelyou served three presidents—Cleveland, McKinley, and Roosevelt—and was the first head of the Department of Commerce and Labor, chairman of the Republican National Committee, postmaster general, and secretary of the treasury.

At lower levels in the company, a similar spirit of inbreeding has prevailed. For years, employment was based on personal contact, political favoritism or ethnic preferences, with a heavy reliance on Irish New Yorkers. For example, Bernard Gallagher, senior vice president for personal and industrial relations, noted that "five or ten years ago, 90 percent or so of our new employees were referred to us by persons already employed by the company. We never discouraged this sort of thing, but we did not hire persons whose skills and abilities were not up to par."

Some aspects of this employment policy persist even today. When asked how Con Ed recruits new engineers, Kenneth Bellows, assistant vice president, explained:

> We use the old school tie system. We ask men from the different colleges, not professionals from the personnel department, to be like Con Ed ambassadors. . . . The area we recruit is from Philadelphia to the middle of New York, such as Cornell and all of New England. We don't hop all over the country. It is not economically sound, especially with the fine group of colleges that we have in this area.

The worst effect of such inbreeding, according to Con Ed's detractors, has been to make the company peculiarly insensitive to the criticisms of outsiders. The critics say that the company has dealt with a number of recent problems by denying that there is any problem at all. These areas of controversy include Con Ed's technical performance, its high rates, its dealings with communities and individual customers, and its relations with the press and governmental bodies.

The 1965 blackout and aftermath

Con Ed's most recent round of public woes began in November 1965 when a massive power blackout struck the entire northeastern United States. As the *New York Times* reported:

> At 5:17 on November 9, the lights went out somewhere in the Niagara frontier, in Buffalo, Rochester, Syracuse, Utica, Schenectady, Troy and Albany . . . . Within four minutes, a line of darkness had plunged across Massachusetts all the way to Boston. It was like a pattern of falling dominoes—darkness sped southward through Connecticut, northward into Vermont, New Hampshire, Maine and Canada.

The breakdown in the northern New York State–Canada area caused this region to draw power from New England and southern New York, at the very time—early evening—when Con Ed's territory was experiencing its own peak demand. This "swing" in the power flow—going north, instead of south into the city as was needed—caused the blackout. The New York–Pennsylvania–New Jersey–Maryland system ties also failed, and the Con Ed operator in charge at headquarters on West 65th Street was unable to cut the city off from the interstate ties in time. For periods of up to 14 hours, an area with a population of 25 million was without the power to run elevators or subways, light homes, drive factory machinery, or operate life-saving equipment in some hospitals. A total of 600,000 people were stranded in the New York City subways alone.

The press and public officials were swift to demand explanations for the failure and, in New York, laid part of the blame at Con Ed's door for lack of safety measures and adequate reserve capacity. The *New York Times* accused the 65th Street operator of negligence for reacting so slowly to the power "swing." Con Ed defended the operator and charged that its efforts to provide reserve power in a generating station at Cornwall-on-the-Hudson had been hampered by the efforts of conservationists.

President Johnson ordered an investigation by the Federal Power Commission, and by December 7, the FPC had completed its report. It concluded that there "can be no absolute assurance that outages of the November 9th magnitude will not recur." But it faulted the power companies involved for a lack of safety devices and suggested that a swifter reaction by the Con Ed operator could have mitigated much of the power failure. The FPC recommended more automatic monitoring equipment and more closely knit power grids as part of the answer.

The report did nothing to still public criticism of Con Ed. The company had a bad time of it for a number of reasons. First, two smaller power failures had preceded the big outage of 1965. In 1959 and 1961, parts of central Manhattan were blacked out at peak load hours on hot summer days. Then, the company had minimized the importance of the blackouts, calling them "the happenstance of a group of feeder failures serving a single area at a particular time." Con Ed continued, "This was entirely unforeseeable, and the mathematical chances are negligible that a similar situation will develop again." Secondly, the blackout coincided with the election of John V. Lindsay, New York City's first fusion mayor in 20 years. From the markedly unfriendly tone of communications between Con Ed and the city administration in recent years, it would appear that the power failure was an inauspicious beginning for relations with a new mayor.

Rate increases obtained by Consolidated Edison

A final reason for the criticism leveled at Con Ed after November 1965 was that the blackout came in the midst of a series of rate increases by which the company has raised electric charges some $100 million since 1958. Sixteen months before the blackout, in July 1964, the Public Service Commission had approved a $27 million increase. Scarcely 8 months after it, in July 1966, Con Ed filed yet another increase, this one amounting to $32 million annually. High rates for satisfactory service were bad enough, critics charged, but high rates from a utility as negligent as Con Ed were intolerable.

Since 1958, when the current series of rate hikes began, the city of New York has grown increasingly vehement in its opposition to them. The city itself is a huge consumer of power; it feels an obligation to represent the interests of millions of its residents, many of them poor; and it claims high electricity costs are to the detriment "not only of the ordinary user of electric current but also of commerce and industry and the general economy of the city." (Some observers would add that it is good politics for elected officials to take a stand against Con Ed and in "the public interest.")

After Con Ed filed its increase of July 1966, the city asked that the new rates be suspended pending public hearings. On November 25, 1966, the commission ordered public hearings, but allowed the increase to stand in the interim. Should the hearings show that the increase was not justified, the commission said, the amount would be refunded with interest. Public hearings began in December and continued through July 1967, with the record running to more than 4,000 pages of testimonies, exhibits, and schedules.

The principal opponents of the rate increase were the city of New

York and the New York City Housing Authority. Although the issues in the hearings were often highly technical, there were four main points of contention:

1. *The rate base.* The return of a utility is defined as net income on electricity sales before deductions of interest, divided by the electric rate basis—which is essentially the total capital employed in the electricity operations. Obviously, the larger the rate base of a utility, the larger the return to which it is entitled. The Housing Authority sought to exclude from the rate base about $70 million of investment in Indian Point I, Con Ed's first nuclear-powered generating facility, which had cost a total of $142 million. It contended that a conventional plant would have cost only $70 million and that Con Ed's customers should not have to foot the difference for an "imprudent" investment. This was particularly so, according to the authority, because Con Ed had not taken advantage of federal aid for Indian Point and had not invited other utilities to participate in the investment, thereby spreading the risk.

2. *Operating expenses.* The Housing Authority challenged the treatment of various general expenses which it said should not be charged to consumers.

3. *Rate classifications.* The city maintained that the schedule of increases filed by the company discriminated against residential customers and asked that it be set aside.

4. *Rate of return.* Financial experts for the city contended that a "fair" rate of return for Con Ed would be between 5.85 and 6 percent—rather than the 6.2 to 6.3 percent allowed by the Public Service Commission in a 1961 hearing.

For each of these points, the company had a rebuttal. Con Ed defended its investment in Indian Point as sound and said it would result in future benefits to consumers. As evidence, it pointed to what it said were prospective lower operating costs for the company's second nuclear-powered plant (Indian Point II). Con Ed also maintained that its treatment of various expenses, including contributions to civic or business organizations, followed standard accounting practice. On the question of rate schedules, the company said that judgment was crucial and referred to past procedures of allocating costs and setting rates. Finally, the company supported its quest for a higher rate of return by reference to the results shown by other utilities. It also pointed out that even if the new rates took effect, its return on electricity operations would not exceed 5.7 percent, which, it said, "is substantially less than a fair and reasonable rate of return."

Though each side in the hearings had its experts and its cited references, the main point at issue lay beneath the surface. This was an assumption by the city and also by many of Con Ed's customers, that while the company might technically justify each separate point in a rate schedule, taken as a whole, the rate increases were indefensible. In its brief, the city stated that "it is an established fact, admitted by Con Ed itself, that many of the leading electric utilities in the nation have been reducing their rates during the past three or four years." Thus, no matter how many battles the company might win before regulatory agencies, it could not still public criticism of its activities. In March 1968, the Public Service Commission rules in favor of Con Ed on almost all of the points at contention. Yet, barely three months later, Mayor Lindsay was again demanding redress—this time for what he claimed were $20 million in excessive charges for Con Ed's gas rates over the past five years. And once again, the Public Service Commission duly ordered hearings.

In discussing rates in an interview, Mr. Luce conceded that the company would have to weigh carefully the political effect of any further requests for increases. "Ultimately," he explained, "you have to have the support of your customers, and that means convincing them you're doing a reasonably good job. It doesn't matter what court victories or regulatory victories you win if your customers don't have a favorable opinion of you."

The chairman said he thought that customers were concerned "not so much with the cost of service but the type of service—the impersonality of the company, the inaccurate billing, the delay in hooking up service, etc." He added, "If you perform well on the service side, I think people will accept the cost."

Community relations

Another area in which Con Ed has had increasing problems is in its relations with the various communities it serves. The problem has two dimensions. One concerns the company's attempts to introduce new technology in the form of huge generating plants—attempts which have often run afoul of local political sentiment or the wishes of conservationists. The other dimension concerns the company's relations with individual customers, including the service it provides and its activities in the Black and Puerto Rican communities of New York City.

Central to the company's plans for future generating capacity is its concern to cut down on pollution of New York City's air. The traditional fuels for generating plants, coal, and oil, both contain relatively high amounts of sulphur. When consumed, these fuels give off sulphur dioxide, which is a major air pollutant. A study by the New York City Council in 1965 found that Con Ed discharges 15 percent of particulate emissions (soot) and nearly half of the sulphur dioxide in the city.

By the end of 1967 the company had cut back on both pollutants by 33 percent. Local Law No. 14 required that by 1971 the sulphur content of coal and oil burned in the city must not exceed 1 percent, but Con Ed takes pride in reporting that it achieved this goal by early 1968. In the long run, however, the company feels that the only way to avoid air pollution is through nuclear-powered facilities. Con Ed awarded contracts for its fourth nuclear plant in January 1968 and simultaneously announced plans for a fifth.[3] By 1980, Mr. Luce has said, nuclear fuel will generate about 75 percent of Con Ed's electricity, compared to the present figure of 4 percent. Nevertheless, nuclear power brings with it a whole set of new problems. Not the least of these is obtaining community and governmental approval for the erection of a plant.

In 1962, Con Ed applied for a license from the Atomic Energy Commission to build a nuclear-powered plant at Ravenswood, Queens, which would have been the first such plant in a heavily populated area. The proposal touched off more than a year of angry controversy, with critics charging that Con Ed had paid insufficient attention to safety factors. In January 1964, Con Ed withdrew the application and said it would put the plant near its Indian Point facility, 24 miles upstream from New York City.

At about the same time, Con Ed ran into trouble in its attempt to build a pumped-storage plant with a capacity of 2 million kilowatts at Storm King Mountain, Cornwall, New York. The design called for a powerhouse and pumping station on the Hudson, a reservoir 1,000 feet up on the mountain side, and transmission lines connecting the power source to the New York City system. Functionally, the plant was to serve as a huge storage battery; when power demands in its system were low, Con Ed would use excess capacity to pump water uphill into the reservoir. At times of peak need, this stored water would flow down again to generate electricity. Use of the new facility would enable the company to avoid using its oldest and least efficient generating equipment during peak load times. Moreover, it would enable Con Ed to put 2 million kilowatts of power on the line in less than a minute to meet an emergency—much less than the time needed to start up conventional steam-powered turbines.

Though the Cornwall plant made sense from both an economic and an engineering standpoint, the company had not reckoned with another kind of criteria: the project's effect on natural beauty. Storm King Mountain is located in an historic region of the Hudson River Valley, and, in recent years, restoration of the valley has become an important con-

---

[3] As of August 1968, Con Ed has one nuclear facility in operation at Indian Point, a second nearing completion, and a third started, both at the same site. Contracts for the generating unit of a fourth have been awarded, but the site is as yet undetermined. A fifth is planned for the same site.

cern to many individuals. Con Ed's plans thus encountered opposition from conservationists, nature lovers, fishermen, historians, and Hudson Highland residents, who banded together in a group called the Scenic Hudson Preservation Conference. They contended the facility "would cut a huge gash in the mountainside, lessen the natural beauty of the area, possibly damage marine life in the Hudson River, and scar the countryside with overhead transmission lines."[4] (In defense, Con Ed pointed out that its revised plans called for the generating station to be placed entirely underground, and for the reservoir to be located between Mt. Misery and White Horse Mountain, not on Storm King itself.)

Despite Scenic Hudson's opposition to the project, the Federal Power Commission voted in March 1965 to approve Con Ed's plans. But the conservationists were not through. They appealed the FPC decision to the U.S. Circuit Court, which in December 1965 set aside the FPC order. The court found that the commission had failed to consider adequately "the over-all public interest" and remanded the case to the FPC with the instruction that "the Commission's renewed proceedings must include as a basic concern the preservation of natural beauty and of national historical shrines." Two and a half years later, Con Ed was still waiting for the second decision.

The immediate problem facing the company was where to locate its fourth and fifth nuclear plants. Con Ed was hoping to build a nuclear plant on Fort Slocum, or Davids Island, in the western Long Island Sound, but before it could do so it needed approval from the Atomic Energy Commission, which in the past had refused to license plants so close to heavily populated areas. The company was also considering several locations on the Hudson, near its Indian Point facility. These plans were opposed by conservationists who said such a clustering of plants would raise the water temperature and kill thousands of fish. At one site Con Ed was also stymied by the refusal of the largest property owner—a Catholic fraternal organization—to sell its land. When the company threatened the society with condemnation proceedings, members reacted by writing to their congressmen and contacting the hierarchy of the Roman Catholic church.

Customer relations

The second dimension of community relations is Con Ed's dealings with individual customers. Here the company is handicapped by past practice and by the immense problem of doing business in New York City. Many of New York's apartment buildings are 50 years old and more, and were built with electric meters inside the individual apart-

---

[4] *Consolidated Edison and the Conservationists* (Northwestern University School of Business, 1966), p. 2.

ments. Thus, the company can only determine electricity usage by gaining entrance to the apartment. Failing this, it has to fall back on billing for "estimated" usage. The mechanical problems are compounded by the changing population which Con Ed serves: as middle-class families head for the suburbs, the company is increasingly left with lower-class customers who use less electricity and pay bills less regularly. (In 1965, electricity usage by Con Ed's residential consumers was less than half the national average.) The net amount of uncollectibles that were written off went from $1.7 million in 1962 to $4.5 million in 1967, and the latter figure represents a loss of $0.51 on each $100 of sales revenue. "And this doesn't even begin to reflect the costs involved in mailing reminder notices, disconnect notices, and the expenses of maintaining our credit and collection operations," said George E. Smith, assistant general manager for credit and collections in the Customer Accounting Department. As might be expected, uncollectibles were highest in several of the city's poorest areas: East Harlem had losses on 93 out of 1,000 customers, and the Brownsville–East New York–Canarsie section of Brooklyn had losses on 99 per 1,000.

Con Ed has 4 million gas and electric accounts, and each month it sends over 100,000 disconnect notices—7 percent of all its bills—to customers who have ignored three previous "reminders" to pay. After the dispatch of the disconnect notices, Con Ed's collectors take over. The company maintains a staff of 150 whose job is to show up at the customer's residence and demand payment. Mr. Smith noted that 40 percent of collectors' calls are made in two-man teams now because "our men have been physically assaulted in some of the neighborhoods and they refuse to go into these areas alone." All in all, the company disconnects about 350 customers a day. In many cases, of course, collectors are denied access to a customer's property. Then the company has no choice but to get a court order and the aid of a marshal to disconnect and remove the equipment from a customer's premises. As William E. Wall, Con Ed vice president, explained, "At the point that we have a marshal with an axe to break down the door, the guy opens the door and gives you $10, and you've already spent $100." Max M. Ulrich, vice president for customer accounting and customer relations, commented, "This is a city with an extraordinarily mobile population. If you compare the number of final bills we issued each year for the past several years to the number of customers we had, you'll get an idea of the extent of population mobility we face. By law, of course, we must provide service to anyone who requests it, yet it's becoming a Herculean task to collect the monies that are owed us."

C. Wesley Meytrott, vice president for sales, illustrated another aspect of customer relations by pointing to a long series of complaints from a woman in Queens about the noise caused by Con Ed's street repairs. An agreement with a local contractor called for the work to be done in the mornings and on Sundays, but there was no telling that to the resident. "What do I do?" asked Mr. Meytrott. "I get hundreds of these complaints a year."

But the problems from the company's point of view are only part of the story. Con Ed's reputation as an infrequent and inaccurate biller is legendary, and the mere mention of the company to the average New Yorker is enough to generate one horror story after another. One Westchester customer said the company had sent him only estimated bills for a year. Then, when they finally got around to reading the meter, tried to apply a newly approved rate increase retroactively to the balance. "I took that one all the way to the Public Service Commission before they backed down," he claimed. Critics also note that Con Ed's exposure to bad debt loss is cushioned by its practice of requiring deposits from any customer who has not had a previous account, or whose credit references are "inadequate." Such deposits totaled $29.6 million at the end of 1967, and the company was paying customers 4 percent a year for the use of their money—well below the prime rate charged for loans by commercial banks. Realizing this, Con Ed applied to the Public Service Commission for permission to raise the interest on deposits to 5 percent. The PSC said legislation would be necessary, but when Con Ed sponsored such a law it was bottled up in the 1967–68 session of the state legislature.

Relations with minority groups

Beyond the problem of uncollectibles and service, relations with the city's growing minorities were a source of continued concern to Con Ed. Mr. Luce had stepped up the company's equal employment program, and, in 1967, 30 percent of all new employees were Blacks or Puerto Ricans. In other steps, Con Ed—with the cooperation of the union—took on 97 high school dropouts in a special training program, initiated a part-time employment program for 137 youngsters still in school, and agreed to participate in a summer job program for ghetto youth.

Another project that Con Ed was considering was direct involvement in housing in the ghetto. According to Dean M. Bressler, in charge of urban affairs for the Community Relations Department, the company had received several proposals from other firms to operate in rehabilitating or putting up new housing. But Con Ed was unsure about whether or not to concentrate on residential or commercial/industrial development, and did not know what the reaction of community groups would be to the company's involvement.

Press relations

Con Ed has never enjoyed a good press, but after the 1965 blackout, the company received brickbats from all sides. Nothing was more devastating than the *Fortune* article which appeared in March 1966. Reporters from the magazine had spent six months researching the company, and Con Ed executives had cooperated fully. They felt the company could not help but gain from coverage in a prestigious business publication. When the article appeared, however, it blasted Con Ed as an old, hidebound corporation which had high rates, legions of dissatisfied customers, and close ties to various city and state politicians.

A year later, the *Nation* revived many of the same themes in an article entitled "Con Edison: The Arrogance of Power." It labeled Con Ed "a defiant oligarchy, relentlessly pursuing an inflexible, public-be-damned policy." And only recently the *Wall Street Journal* took off after the company with a front-page article headed, "Unhappy Utility." Referring to the continuing criticism of Con Ed by public officials and the press, Mr. Meytrott argued:

> Utilities have always been sitting ducks for politicians. We're whipping boys, with no effective way to respond. When we make a mistake, everybody screams. When the Transit Authority or some other city or public body makes a mistake, it's on the 42nd page of the *Times*. For instance, if our operational necessities dictate a short service interruption, the *Times* puts it on the front pages. If the Transit Authority stops service temporarily on a line, you have to search every page of the *Times* to even find news of the interruption.

Political environment

The friction between Con Ed and various public bodies stems in part from the sheer number of governmental units with which the company must deal, and, in part, from its vulnerability to political determination of its revenues and costs. In New York City and Westchester County, Con Ed serves more than 50 cities, towns, and villages. It reports to the New York State Public Service Commission, and, through it, to the legislature, and also comes under the jurisdiction of the Federal Power Commission.

Both operating revenues and operating costs are highly influenced by the actions of political bodies or regulatory agencies. One of the largest expenses incurred by Con Ed is its tax bill—$193 million in 1967, exclusive of federal income taxes. Most of this item consists of local real estate taxes, which now come to $102 million more per year than they did in 1958. (The company points out that six rate increases since 1958 total $100 million, so state and local taxes have actually gone up more than rates.)

On the other hand, the rates Con Ed can charge must be approved by the Public Service Commission, a state body. Thus, the company is in a squeeze; an important part of its costs are determined by New York City property taxes, while all of its rates are subject to Public Service Commission approval. This situation has historically dictated close contacts by Con Ed with all parties. It maintains a registered lobbyist at the state capital in Albany, during the legislative session, and Mr. Wall described the company's activities there as "pretty standard lobbying." The company's representative "will have a reception, take a few guys to dinner, buy tickets to their fund-raising functions, and try to make friends." The image of a utility using naked power and forcing its will on legislators is a myth, he said, because "that kind of arm-twisting just can't work." Some observers feel the company's approach is not quite that benign, however, and at least one legislator said he thought the company had the power to make things uncomfortable for those who attacked it.

As for relations with the Public Service Commission, Wall said the notion that they are "patsies" for Con Ed "is just not true." Dealings with the commission are professional and conducted at arm's length. "I would no more think of buying a commissioner lunch than I would of running out naked on Irving Place," Mr. Wall said. Nevertheless, company officials do try to maintain cordial relationships with commissioners, and some have acquaintanceships of long standing. It's a common practice in the utility industry throughout the country for utility executives to attend conventions of regulatory officials, and even to host them at cocktail hours and dinners.

In New York City, Con Ed's influence flows naturally from its economic power. According to the *Fortune* article, Con Ed and the construction contracts it lets annually were traditionally regarded as part of the patronage which political leaders dispense. No one knows exactly how the system worked, but it is obvious that Con Ed and political leaders have had much to gain from each other. Con Ed has needed the approval of the city's Department of Water Supply, Gas, and Electricity for permission to build or repair transmission lines and to dig up the city streets. In the past, politicians have looked to the economic power of Con Ed to provide jobs and, more importantly, contracts to friends and contributors. The practice of contracting out also insured excellent relations between the company and the powerful New York City Central Labor Council, AFL-CIO, since the jobs created are filled by members of the building trades unions. Today, however, though company executives have extensive contact with city officials, they describe such relationships as strictly business; one executive said all meetings were "on a ten o'clock in the morning, across-the-desk basis."

In the spring of 1968, Con Ed's name was dragged into the papers during the trial of Henry Fried, a building contractor, and James L. Marcus, formerly Mayor Lindsay's commissioner of water supply, gas, and electricity. The two were accused, with others, of conspiring to pay and accept bribes in return for city contracts. (Marcus pleaded guilty and Fried was convicted by a federal jury.) The original indictment alleged that Fried had paid money to Marcus and others in order to obtain city permission for Con Ed to rebuild transmission lines over city-owned land on the Croton Aquaduct in Westchester County. A statement by Mr. Luce in July 1968 declared, "So far as our investigation can find, Mr. Marcus did not obtain any money, either directly or indirectly, from Consolidated Edison," and noted that the company was still seeking approval to rebuild the transmission line. At the same time, Mr. Luce revealed that a vice president of Con Ed had been relieved of his duties in January 1968 for failing to report to his superiors that Mr. Fried had contacted him with the bribery plan.

Following the Marcus trial in August 1968, 13 individuals, including Mr. Fried, and 14 companies were indicted on charges of rigging bids for almost $50 million worth of utility contracts, including $34 million in contracts awarded by Con Ed.

The Marcus case and its aftermath spurred the new management to look closely at its dealings with contractors and city officials. After the first indictments, Mr. Luce canceled all the contracts Con Ed had with companies owned by Mr. Fried, and then moved to strengthen competitive bidding as a way of selecting contractors. A large proportion of Con Ed's construction work is done by outside contractors, a situation which in the past encouraged contractors to seek special relationships with the company. (Such relationships had a political dimension, because construction firms, being privately held, are often in a better position than large corporations to make donations to political parties or individual politicians. In return for performing this favor for their customers, such firms can then obtain preference when it comes time to give out contracts.) Referring to such understandings between Con Ed officials and the construction companies, Mr. Luce stated, "I believe we've got this stopped, though I have no doubt that it's a matter of constant vigilance to keep people who do business with the company from obtaining special treatment."

In one sense, however, upsetting the old ties between Con Ed, its contractors, and the city has proved extremely disruptive. Noting that the delay in approval of the transmission lines "has cost us millions of dollars," the chairman said, "I've kidded Lee Rankin (corporation counsel to the city of New York) as to whether or not we can afford to deal with the city in an honest fashion. I don't want to do business any other way, but I suspect the new policy so far has been a rather costly one."

Regulatory environment

At the state level, the key agency for Con Ed is the Public Service Commission, which has wide authority to regulate and prescribe rates for gas and electric companies, telephone companies, and common carriers. It consists of five members appointed by the governor for ten-year terms. The governor may name a sixth, or even seventh, member if the Commission certifies that such additions are necessary to its workings. The chairman of the PSC receives $32,000 a year, and the other commissioners receive $29,000—which is more than the chairman of the Federal Power Commission and various other federal agencies receive.

At present, all five members of the PSC are Republicans who were appointed by Governor Nelson Rockefeller. The PSC chairman is James A. Lundy, a former borough president of Queens who ran on the Rockefeller ticket for state controller in 1958 and was defeated. Another member is Ralph A. Lehr, the former Republican committee chairman from Erie County (Buffalo) who was appointed in 1959. A profile in the *New York Times* the day after his selection began, "An amiable, lackluster upstate politician has come up with one of the better plums in the New York State government pie. . . . For years Mr. Lehr's friends have regarded him as the prototype of a professional politician."

The other commissioners are Edward P. Larkin, the former presiding supervisor of the town of Hempstead; Frank J. McMullen, a state assemblyman for 16 years; and John S. Ryan, a former member of the commission's legal staff. According to a *Times* study, Mr. Larkin was appointed because party leaders wanted to get him out of the way in order to run a stronger candidate in Hempstead town elections in 1959.

Complaints about the PSC have focused on the competence and probity of its members and staff; as state senator Paul Bookson said in 1967, "I seriously question whether they are acting in the public interest."[5] A series in the now-defunct *World Telegram & Sun* in 1960 concluded that the last three New York governors—two Republicans and a Democrat—"have repeatedly used the regulatory board as a place to pay off political debts." More recently, a reporter for the *Buffalo Courier Express* went over the seating list for the June 1967 fund-raising dinner of the Republican State Committee and discovered the names of three out of five of the commissioners. "This is customary for an affair of this type," the paper stated. "But ticket sales reached deep into the PSC's staff. Among the PSC staffers paying $150 a ticket were the commission's supervising hearing examiner and his wife; its chief

---

[5] *Nation*, March 27, 1967, p. 404.

public information officer; the PSC's director of utilities and his wife; the commission's assistant director of utilities and the chief of the electrical bureau in the commission's Division of Utilities." Also attending the dinner were top executives of six out of seven private utilities operating in New York State, as well as a "director or two" of Con Ed.

Members of the commission staff, however, strongly defended its proceedings in an interview. Norman Abell, the assistant director of the Division of Utilities, explained that "this is a commission that has to balance interests." Noting that the public service law guarantees utilities a fair and reasonable return, Mr. Abell said the commission "shouldn't be pro-consumer any more than it should be pro-utility." John D. McKechnie, director of the utilities division, concurred. "Any commission could force rates down till they were so erosive that a company's service would go to pieces," he said. "Or, they could favor investors. A good point is usually somewhere in between."

As for the charge that the PSC has been politically dominated, Mr. Abell contended, "The mere fact that a man has been in politics doesn't detract from his ability to make fair decisions—just the opposite. It helps keep the commission from being too scholastic. If you had a bunch of accountants and engineers, they might lose touch with public sentiment."

Conflict with New York City

Among the many problems confronting Con Ed's management, one of the most urgent is its relations with the city government—a matter that has both political and economic overtones. In May 1968, Mayor Lindsay released a consultant's report to the Mayor's Council on Consumer affairs entitled, "The City and Electric Power." The mayor announced that he would seek state legislation "enabling the city council to create a new regulatory agency to supplant the Public Service Commission in the regulation of gas and electric rates for the City of New York."

The report also recommended that the city consider alternate sources of power supply if Con Ed would not lower its rates. Dr. Timothy W. Costello, deputy mayor for administration and chairman of the Council on Consumer Affairs, explained the reasons for the recommendation. "The point is that Con Ed will adjust its rates only in relation to the ability of its customers to go elsewhere. A good example was Co-op City, a large housing development in the Bronx. Con Ed gave them a very good rate when they threatened to install their own generators. This is what we're interested in with the city." (See Exhibit 3 for full list of recommendations.)

The report was given immediacy by two sets of negotiations that the city was conducting with Con Ed at the time of its release. One was for renewal of the contract to supply power to public buildings and street lights, currently valued at $30 million. Con Ed had originally asked for an increase of $1 million a year, and the city had called this excessive. The other was Con Ed's request for permission to rebuild the transmission line on the city-owned property in Westchester. Under the old contract, Con Ed paid the city $214,000 a year in rental for the right-of-way. To renew the agreement, the city was asking for a ninefold increase in rent and, also, for "wheeling rights"—the right to use any excess capacity in the line to bring in power from other sources upstate, such as the New York State Power Authority. The authority, a public agency, generates hydroelectric power in northern New York for sale to publicly owned electric agencies and also to private companies.

In a letter to Dr. Costello, Mr. Luce took strong exception to the request for the ninefold rental increase. "It is, indeed, a strange position for the Consumer Protection Division of the city to advocate because, under universally accepted principles of rate making, the inflated rental must ultimately be paid by the city's electric consumers." He also noted that previous agreements with the city had made no mention of wheeling rights and added, "In any event, we do not forsee there will be excess capacity in this line for leasing to others. In fact, we probably will be required to construct additional transmission capacity, over and beyond this line, to bring into New York City all of the power necessary to meet load growth."

The deputy mayor pointed out in reply that the request for a ninefold increase in rent was based on the fact that the new line would carry nine times as much power—which was, he said, the only detailed information Con Ed had provided. He also noted that the city has an obligation to its taxpayers to obtain the best possible deal in commercial agreements with profit-making corporations. As for the city's request for wheeling rights, Dr. Costello stated, "What the city is seeking is substantially what the United States regularly insists on when it grants rights-of-way to private utilities. I am sure this practice and the public policy reasons behind it are familiar to you."

In discussing the controversy, Mr. Luce recalled that the only reason Con Ed needed a right-of-way at all was because it had agreed to oblige the city by putting generating stations outside city limits. For the city to then turn around and make exorbitant demands on the company "is a very unfair thing," he stated.

Moreover, the chairman explained, obtaining wheeling rights would be an empty privilege because there was no excess power for sale in the state. Con Ed expected no surplus capacity in the line, and the city had no transmission lines which tied in to the proposed cable. Yet, granting the request would probably hurt Con Ed in the money markets since the provision "would be misunderstood in the financial community." In sum, said Mr. Luce, the city's demand "simply casts another shadow on our financing but gives the city no comparable advantage."

Nevertheless, the alternative was also unattractive. Con Ed had another route for the line, but it was less desirable technically and might prove even more costly. Mr. Luce, therefore, had to decide how important the present negotiations were to future relations with the New York City government and what concessions, if any, he might make. Referring to his relations with public officials, the chairman had said, "We can't afford feuds or vendettas with the city. So, our strategy must always be to try to minimize the areas of difference, because there are always so many more things you have to work with them on. You keep your cool and be professional. When the mayor blasts us on gas rates, we have to recognize that he's just plying his trade."

Company organization and financing

In January 1968, Mr. Luce contracted with Cresap, McCormick and Paget, a management consulting firm, for a study of Con Ed's internal structure "to make sure we are organized so as to best achieve the goals of greater economy, better service, and higher earnings."

At present, Con Ed is organized along functional lines, with vice presidents based at headquarters in charge of such departments as: data processing, purchasing, finance, system and electrical engineering, industrial relations, sales, customer accounting, and public relations. Line departments, such as production and sales, are further broken down into a series of branch offices or substations which carry on the job of selling or transmitting power. For example, a district sales office in Harlem would sell electric or gas service, arrange for installation of service, answer questions about rates, and refer complaints about service to the proper department.

Both the sales and the engineering departments carry on planning activities, which are particularly important to Con Ed because of its huge capital budget and the long-time between initiation and completion of a construction project. Thomas Duncan, senior vice president for engineering, described the planning process (Exhibit 4):

> Well, in planning we go through these stages:
> 1. We develop a load forecast, a forecast of the customer's demands. We take into account such things as population, trends in the economy, special electric-using devices and use these things to come up with projections, both long- and near-term. In all of these things we consult with sales.

2.   Once we have these projections, we have to determine facilities requirements. We take into account such things as the economies of existing plants, when some plants have to be retired, and our reserve requirements. Just how much reserve we'll need is a judgment matter. Sure we have the probabilities of outages (breakdowns in part of the system), but this goes beyond a mathematical matter. We have to use some judgment. It takes about six years to go from concept to operation.

3.   Then, we go into our capital budgeting. We have a five-year rolling budget that gets updated each year. We also include such things as the purchase of commercial buildings, the modernization of buildings, the purchase of our transportation fleets.

4.   Then we have to design the facilities. We have to decide what type of capacity it should have, where it should be, what effect it will have on the environment. We have to decide what sort of exterior appearance the facility should have. And we have to get community approval.

5.   Then, we have to build it.

With capital expenditures of more than $250 million a year, financing is a constant preoccupation for Con Ed. The company now pays out about 75 percent of earnings in preferred and common stock dividends; retained earnings plus depreciation, thus, provide only half of the annual capital needs. (In 1967, $118.6 million out of $255.9 million was generated internally.) The balance comes from investors, in the form of long-term debt, preferred stock, or equity. Since 1963, debt has averaged 53 percent of the company's total capitalization, with preferred stock and common stock representing 15 percent and 33 percent, respectively. In 1967, Con Ed raised $40 million from the sale of preferred stock and $80 million from the sale of bonds.

This heavy dependence on the capital markets makes Con Ed—like all utilities—particularly vulnerable to the movement of interest rates. "Unlike a manufacturing company," said Mr. Duncan, "we can't postpone a plant for six months and tell consumers 'you'll just have to buy shoes elsewhere.' We're required by law to meet the load demand." This requirement caused increasing strain for the company in the mid-60s, when strong growth in the economy, plus large federal deficits, combined to push interest rates to new highs. In several cases, the interest cost to Con Ed of new money was higher than its average return on total capital. Almost as important as the overall level of interest rates is Con Ed's own credit rating. In 1966, Moody's downgraded Con Ed bonds from AA to A, reflecting poorer coverage of the company's interest obligations. Between 1958 and 1966, the company's ratio of before-tax earnings to debt service costs plunged from 5.18 to 2.88.

Charles B. Delafield, vice president and treasurer, explained that "this company has had a long record of inadequate earnings." As a result, he said, "We've had to do some financing that other companies wouldn't have to do." This included the issuance of $90 million of convertible preference stock, as well as some equity offerings. "If I had my choice," said Mr. Delafield, "I'd keep at least the same proportion of common stock, but I'd do away with preferred and run the debt ratio way up. I wouldn't mind a ratio of 60–40, or even 62–38." But the present level of earnings ruled out this choice, he explained, because coverage of interest expense would be too low.

To illustrate Con Ed's difficulties in appealing to investors, company officers themselves have frequently compared its financial performance to that of other utilities. A financial consultant to the company submitted evidence of this sort in the 1968 gas rate hearings before the Public Service Commission. It showed that Con Ed's return on total capital and on book value of the equity was well below that of 11 other utilities (see Exhibit 5). (The utilities were judged to be comparable because, like Con Ed, each sells both gas and electricity, and each has annual revenues exceeding $100 million.)

In late 1968, Con Ed was planning to sell another $60 to $80 million of bonds, as part of a program to raise $240 to $250 million by the end of 1969. The five-year capital budget, 1968–72, projected total needs of $1.4 billion, of which $680 million was to come from external sources (see Exhibit 9). In light of these needs, both Con Ed's lowered bond rating and its earnings record were a source of concern, according to Mr. Delafield, "because we're facing a constantly shrinking market for our offerings." The largest portion of Con Ed bonds are taken up by state and other government pension funds, but many of these are restricted, either by statute or by their own operating rules, from acquiring anything but AA bonds. As a measure of the added cost to Con Ed of the A rating, Mr. Delafield pointed to the recent issue of $50 million worth of debt by Commonwealth Edison, another large utility. "They sold $50 million at a yield of 6.7 percent. I think if we had gone to the market at the same time with $80 million, we might have broken the 7 percent mark, or we'd have been right around 6.95."

One possibility for the company was to delay its offerings in the hope of getting lower interest rates, but Mr. Delafield remarked that "If you need $250 million within 18 months, you don't have much leeway. You have to space these issues out somewhat. I've found over the years that it's better to raise the money when you need it and play the averages, rather than to try to outguess the market."

As for the impact of political controversy on the company's financing and relations with investors, Mr. Delafield said he had no doubt that "the hostility and bad press which this company has had have added to our problems" of raising money. He mentioned one example: In 1966, the company had an issue of preferred stock coming to market at the same time that it had filed a rate increase with the Public Service Commission. "Two out of the three institutional buyers we had lined up told me that their purchase was subject to getting approval from the commission," Mr. Delafield stated.

Challenge to management

The selection of Mr. Luce as chairman in August 1967 sent tremors through the entire Con Ed organization. As one executive put it, "Most of the top management is Republican, and many of these people have put in years combatting the spectre of public power in New York. Imagine their concern at the selection of a Democrat and a public power man to head the company."

At the time of his selection, Mr. Luce was 49. His early training was legal: After graduating with honors from the University of Wisconsin Law School in 1941, he held a Sterling Fellowship at Yale Law School for a year, and then moved to Washington, D.C., where he was a law clerk to Justice Hugo Black. He then spent two years as an attorney for the Bonneville Power Administration and practiced law in Walla Walla, Washington, for 15 years.

In 1961, Mr. Luce was named administrator of the Bonneville Power Administration by Interior Secretary Stewart Udall. In five and a half years as administrator, he improved the agency's financial results and was the principal architect of one of the largest electric power transmission programs undertaken in the United States—the Pacific Northwest–Pacific Southwest inter-tie. He also helped bring about the development of the Hanford nuclear generating plant, which was the world's largest nuclear-steam plant, with 800,000 kilowatt capacity, at the time of its completion in 1966.

In 1966, Mr. Luce was named undersecretary of the Interior by President Johnson, and he took office in September 1966. Within a year he had accepted the post of chairman and chief executive officer at Con Ed.

Originally, Mr. Luce had felt that one of Con Ed's major needs was better public relations in order to refurbish its tarnished image. But a few months on the job convinced him that many other changes had to take place as well. In newspaper advertisements in early October 1967, Mr. Luce spelled out what the company was doing to improve customer service, control air pollution, and cut costs. The chairman later took his case to numerous civic organizations and meetings in the New York metropolitan area. One of his principal themes was that Con Ed has a responsibility to help shape the urban environment in which it operates—a responsibility which includes providing equal employment, upgrading housing, and improving the general aesthetics and cleanliness of the city.

In discussing the problems of the city, Mr. Luce drew attention to what he called "deteriorating educational facilities and opportunities." Inferior schools, he said, make the company's labor problems more critical because "we need excellence and high standards of performance," and also stimulate the flight to the suburbs. "The main reason people don't live in the city, I think, is the city educational system," Mr. Luce maintained.

Con Ed tries to make up for these deficiencies with its own training courses, he explained, and said there was "no doubt" that the company could make its greatest contribution to combatting poverty through its employment programs. In addition to his employment efforts at Con Ed, Mr. Luce serves as head of the Manpower Task Force of the New York Urban Coalition, an organization which seeks to channel the resources of industry into programs for combatting urban poverty.

Mr. Luce also identified housing as a central problem and expressed the hope that Con Ed could "help build better houses or renovate old houses." Asked whether or not a corporation acting in such a way might not arouse hostility and harm its interests, he conceded that there was "a great danger" in direct involvement in urban problems. "But the danger is even greater if you don't act," Mr. Luce said.

Looking at his own role in guiding the company, Mr. Luce said the two greatest challenges were "to communicate, one, a service orientation, a customer orientation, a community orientation to our people, and two, a burning desire to operate this company as efficiently as possible. . . . We've made some progress, but compared to the total distance of the track we have to cover, we've barely rounded the first turn."

Map of Consolidated Edison electric service areas

EXHIBIT 1

CONSOLIDATED EDISON

Balance sheet

(data in $ millions)

	Dec. 31, 1967	Dec. 31, 1966	Dec. 31, 1965	Dec. 31, 1962	Dec. 31, 1957
Assets:					
Utility plant at original cost*	$4,237.2	$4,042.7	$3,875.6	$3,191.0	$2,060.2
less reserve for depreciation	804.0	775.0	706.1	591.2	398.5
Net plant	3,433.2	3,267.8	3,169.5	2,599.8	1,661.7
Investments at cost or less	5.9	5.3	6.3	5.7	4.5
Current assets	223.5	223.5	178.4	181.2	138.2
Deferred charges†	20.1	20.7	22.7	40.0	21.9
Total assets	$3,682.7	$3,517.3	$3,377.0	$2,826.7	$1,826.3
Liabilities:					
Long-term debt	$1,841.6	$1,786.0	$1,711.0	$1,439.1	$ 899.7
Capital stock	1,274.1	1,234.8	1,185.4	946.8	456.7
Surplus	367.9	340.5	321.7	261.5	352.1
Total Capitalization	3,483.7	3,361.2	3,218.1	2,647.4	1,708.6
Deferred Federal Income Tax	15.5	16.4	17.3	20.0	17.5
Current liabilities	173.6	129.9	130.0	150.4	88.8
Deferred credits	6.8	6.7	8.6	5.8	4.5
Reserve for injuries	3.0	3.0	3.0	3.0	6.8
Total Liabilities	$3,682.7	$3,517.3	$3,377.0	$2,826.7	$1,826.3

Operating Revenues:					
Electric.	$778.0	$721.7	$693.6	$583.7	$441.8
Gas	104.4	105.3	104.3	103.6	81.5
Steam	44.6	39.2	38.4	34.2	26.4
Other	3.8	3.5	3.9	3.7	2.9
Total Operating Revenues.	$930.8	$869.7	$840.2	$725.2	$552.7
Operating Revenue Deductions:					
Operations	$352.7	$330.3	$328.4	$290.3	$238.0
Maintenance	87.9	83.7	78.9	72.5	55.1
Depreciation.	89.8	88.3	83.6	68.8	46.4
Taxes, other than Federal Income . .	193.6	178.7	160.1	129.3	87.7
Federal Income Tax	16.3	14.1	17.7	29.8	39.4
Federal Income Tax deferred in prior years for accelerated amortization	(.9)	(.9)	(.9)	(.9)	3.7
Total Operating Revenue Deductions . .	$739.4	$694.2	$667.7	$589.8	$470.3
Operating Income	191.4	175.5	172.5	135.4	82.4
Income deductions	68.5	65.2	60.7	44.7	25.7
Net Income	122.9	110.3	111.8	90.6	56.7
Dividends on preferred stock—applicable to year	26.8	24.2	21.6	19.7	9.6
Net income for common stock	96.1	86.1	90.1	70.9	47.1

* Of this amount, electric plant was: 1967, $3.8 billion; 1966, $3.6; 1965, $3.4; 1962, $2.8; 1957, $1.7.
† Of this amount, nuclear research and development costs were as follows: 1967, $7.0 billion; 1966, $7.7; 1965, $8.4; 1962, $10.6.
Note: Totals may not add because of rounding.

EXHIBIT 2
Public service regulations

Authority of commission (Article 4, Sec. 66, Public Service Law): "The commission shall have general supervision of all gas corporations and electric corporations. . . ."

Provision for hearing (Article 4, Sec. 71): "Upon the complaint in writing of the mayor of a city, the trustees of a village or the town board of a town . . . or . . . not less than twenty-five customers . . . as to . . . the rates, charges or classifications of service . . . the commission shall investigate as to the cause for such complaint."

Rate-fixing power (Article 4, Sec. 72): "After a hearing and after such an investigation as shall have been made by the commission or its officers . . . the commission may, by order, fix just and reasonable prices, rates and charges for gas and electricity. . . ."

Reasonable return (Article 4, Sec. 72): "In determining the price to be charged for gas or electricity, the commission may consider all facts which in its judgment have any bearing . . . with due regard among other things to a reasonable average return upon capital . . ."

Burden-of-proof provision (Article 4, Sec. 72): ". . . At any hearing involving a rate, the burden of proof to show that the change in rate or price if proposed by the person, corporation or municipality operating such utility, or that the existing rate or price, if on motion of the commission or in a complaint filed with the commission it is proposed to reduce the rate or price, is just and reasonable shall be upon the person, corporation or municipality operating such utility. . . ."

Salaries of Public Service Commissions and other selected public officials:

Official	*Salary*
PSC chairman	$32,265
PSC member	29,160
New York state legislator	15,000
New York City borough president	35,000
Chairman, Federal Power Commission	28,500
Member, Federal Power Commission	27,000
United States congressman or senator	30,000

EXHIBIT 3
Recommendations from "The City and Electric Power" °

Because of the enormity of the power problem in New York City, its limitless importance physically, economically and socially, the city must come to grips with power problems directly and not through intermediaries.

A New York City Power Commission should be initiated to be a watchdog, a partner, an innovator, or a catalyst, whatever the needs may be. It might be a cabinet officer, but it must be given full authority to act for the city in this area. It must be potent, or it shouldn't exist at all.

Assuming that such a Commission exists (or that a cabinet officer is given this responsibility), it will be referred to as the "commission" in the following recommendations:

1.   The Commission shall check on Consolidated Edison's progress in complying with the Federal Power Commission's recommendations for providing for an uninterrupted power supply. It shall make regular reports to the mayor at stated intervals until compliance is achieved, which should be by a certain date.

2.   The city should cooperate with Consolidated Edison in modernizing building and electric codes and eliminating restrictive practices which prevent the use of modern technology and least expensive methods in the construction and operation of its facilities. It should also cooperate in eliminating unnecessary requirements which make electrical installations for consumers more expensive.

3.   To safeguard public health, safety and aesthetic values, the Commission shall work with Consolidated Edison in the location of additional generation, transmission and substation facilities and, when agreed upon, to assist in obtaining public acceptance therefore. Appropriate decisions should be made in the planning stage, not after commitments are made.

4.   The city should re-examine its tax policy as it affects Consolidated Edison. It is out of line with other cities and with other utilities. The city should decide whether it wants the taxpayer directly or the rate-payer indirectly to pay the bill. Since the two groups are not the same, the city must exert leadership with Consolidated Edison in both a meaningful dialogue and a conclusion that is in the public interest.

5.   The city should designate the Transit Authority and the Department of Water Supply, Gas and Electricity to examine sources of supply other than Consolidated Edison for the city's own electric load. This study should include the possibility of purchasing power from the New York State Power Authority and other sources, as well as the possibility of the city's generating its own power. This study should be made promptly since the contract with Consolidated Edison for supplying electric energy for street lighting, public buildings, etc., expires June 30, 1968, and the initial term of the Transit Authority contract expires in 1969. Therefore, the problem of renewal of existing contracts will have to be faced in a relatively short time. Long-term solutions such as purchasing power from the State Power Authority or the

° A report to the New York City Consumer Council on Consolidated Edison's rates, service, and reliability by C. Girard Davidson, 1968.

EXHIBIT 3 (*continued*)

city's building its own generating facilities obviously cannot be accomplished before the existing contracts expire. The study, therefore, should recognize that interim solutions such as purchasing power from Con Ed on short-term contracts or even on published rate schedules may be necessary.

6. The jurisdiction now exercised by New York State Public Service Commission over electric, gas and steam utilities operating in the City of New York should be transferred to a Public Service Commission to be established by the City of New York.

7. Con Ed's high electric rates are out of line with other cities and must be reduced. The company's new management must reverse the former disregard for frugality and the wasteful practices in the company's operation. The city must set a deadline for substantial rate reductions, and if Con Ed does not comply, the next step in the following recommendations should be undertaken.

    a. Con Ed's management should be given a reasonable but fixed time in which to reduce electric rates substantially. The city through the Commission or cabinet officer with authority, should work conscientiously with Con Ed to assist it in reducing rates and giving better service as recommended in 2, 3, and 4 above.

    b. If rates are not lowered substantially by a certain date, the city should assist Con Ed further by entering into partnership arrangements with it and providing part of the service where municipal financing results in lower costs. For example, the city could obtain the necessary authority and then construct generating and transmission facilities and lease them to Con Ed. The lease payments from Con Ed would amortize the revenue bonds issued by the city to pay for the cost of the facilities, but the use of municipal credit would result in lower cost financing and thus give lower rates to New York City's electric users.

    c. In the event neither of these steps results in Con Ed's bringing electricity to New Yorkers at reasonable rates, then obviously the city should purchase, own and operate all of its electric facilities as Mayor LaGuardia advocated some years ago. The city of Los Angeles and other municipal operations have proved that this type of operation ultimately results in the lowest cost power to consumers.

EXHIBIT 4
Five-year forecast

	Actual 1967	Estimated 1968	1969	1970	1971	1972
perating data:						
System energy requirements						
Electric (millions of kwh)	29,030	30,600	31,900	33,350	34,900	36,600
Gas (thousands of mcf)	62,944	65,500	70,400	75,400	80,400	85,700
Steam (thousands of M lbs.).	35,506	35,600	36,800	37,850	38,950	40,100
Peak demand						
Electric (net mw).	6,147	6,850	7,150	7,450	7,750	8,050
Gas (thousands of mcf per day). . . .	365	500	525	550	575	600
Steam (thousands of M lbs. per hr.) .	10.5	12.5	12.8	13.2	13.5	13.8
Capability						
Electric (Net Mw–summer)						
Production	7,488	7,681	8,028	9,081	9,429	9,464
Firm purchase or sales (net).	120	610	843	470	270	500
Total	7,608	8,291	8,871	9,551	9,699	9,964
Gas (thousands of mcf per day)						
Natural gas	476	500	525	550	575	600
LP (air gas)	41	0	0	0	0	0
Total	517	500	525	550	575	600
Steam (thousands of M lbs. per hr.) .	12.7	13.5	13.6	13.6	13.5	13.8
Customers at year end (thousands)						
Electric	2,920	2,945	2,960	2,980	3,000	3,020
Gas.	1,247	1,244	1,241	1,238	1,235	1,232
Steam	2.5	2.6	2.6	2.7	2.7	2.7
inancial data (millions of dollars):						
Construction expenditures						
Electric	$235	$278	$255	$206	$230	$268
Gas.	11	19	21	18	23	21
Steam	3	5	7	3	4	3
Common.	7	8	7	8	8	8
Total construction expenditures . .	$256	$310	$290	$235	$265	$300
(total 1968–72 incl. $1,400 million)						
Financing required for construction . .		$185	$170	$115	$135	$165
(total 1968–72 incl. $770 million)						
Interest charged to construction (credit)	$ 6.0	$ 11.7	$ 13.1	$ 12.8	*	*
Investment tax credit	$ 6.8	$ 7.6	$ 9.4	$ 4.6	*	*

* Amounts not determinable but should be in excess of amount stated for 1970.

EXHIBIT 5
Comparative financial data
Consolidated Edison and similar electric utility companies

	1963	1964	1965	1966	1967
Percent earned on average total capital:					
Consolidated Edison	5.4	5.4	5.6	5.4	5.7
Average of 11 other companies in the industry	6.7	6.9	7.0	7.1	7.2
Percent earned on common stock equity:					
Consolidated Edison	8.5	8.0	8.6	8.1	8.8
Average of 11 other companies in the industry	11.6	12.1	12.3	12.4	12.6

Consolidated Edison (D)[1]

FALL of 1972 found Con Ed in continuing difficulties.

Repeated power shortages plagued its 9 million users in New York City and Westchester County.

Public and private watchdog agencies simultaneously hounded the company to make more power and to halt the pollution accompanying power production.

Federal-State controls over power-plant siting seemed inevitable. Some were suggesting that the needs and pressures of the future required governmental control over all power production in the Northeast.

Financing the ever-spiralling costs of new plants was becoming increasingly difficult as utilities in general, and Con Ed in particular, continued to show poor financial performance.

1969 revision of plans

Shortly after the New Year, Charles F. Luce, chairman of Con Ed's board, made his third "Report to the People of New York City and Westchester County." His full-page report printed in the area's news-

[1] This case was prepared by Professor George C. Lodge entirely from published sources for use as the basis for classroom discussion rather than to illustrate either effective or ineffective handling of an administrative situation.

Distributed by the Intercollegiate Case Clearing House, Soldiers Field, Boston, Mass., 02163. All rights reserved to the contributors. Printed in the U.S.A.

Revised, September 1972.

papers was a frank discussion of the company's plans and problems. Noting that more capacity was essential, he said:

> To provide a site for future nuclear generating facilities, Con Edison has purchased Fort Slocum, an 80-acre island in Long Island Sound about one-third mile off New Rochelle. In the 1970's it would make an ideal location for up to 4,000,000 kw of nuclear generation.
>
> Looking even further into the future, we have asked that planning for Welfare Island not preclude the location of a nuclear power generator under the island in the late 1970's. Such a generator would produce not only electricity, but also steam to heat and cool the skyscrapers of Manhattan. We want eventually to get all of our smokestacks out of Manhattan. A nuclear generator placed underground on Welfare Island could enable us to remove the four smoke stacks near the United Nations.

In discussing the power failures of the preceding summer, he said: "Altogether, about 5 percent of our customers were affected by outages or low voltage, or both. *We deeply regret these local failures. We are determined to strengthen our distribution system so they won't recur.*"

The summer, however, got off to an inauspicious start with recurring shortages, ranging from brownouts, to blackouts, to air conditioning cutbacks and subway delays. Several of Con Ed's generating plants broke down and the company was unable to construct adequate reserve power production units.

During the summer of 1969, Luce wrote federal, state, city, and county officials asking them to review the company's revised Ten-Year Plan (see Appendix A for excerpts) and in particular urging them to consider a "coordinated approach to the power problems of the metropolitan area."

A summary of events from then until 1972 follows:

1969

June   The company's inability to supply full power became apparent once again.

July   Luce wrote a letter to Mayor Lindsay outlining Con Ed's plans and requesting the city's cooperation for the proposed expansion of the fossil-fueled Astoria plant. Stressing that the expansion was the only timely alternative, Luce promised the plant would use a "new grade of fuel oil which is almost free from sulphur" and, whenever available, natural gas. Luce reviewed the company's 1965 contract with Westinghouse for Indian Point No. 2 construction and their 1967 contract for Indian Point No. 3 He also discussed the 1968 purchase of components from GE and Associated Electric Industries for Indian Point No. 4, and the delays attendant upon Cornwall. Pointing out that Indian Point No. 2, initially scheduled for June 1969, would not be ready until June 1970, and Indian Point No. 3, initially scheduled for June 1971 would be postponed until 1973, Luce said that there would be "gaps in our power planning." He claimed that despite the addition, at great cost, of light, oil-fired turbines at existing plants and purchases of power, there would still be supply problems, and that Astoria expansion was thus critical.

August   Luce announced that the company was applying to the Public Service Commission (PSC) for an increase in its electric rates—a 14 percent raise for residential and 16.9 percent for commercial customers.

September   Con Ed common stock hit an 11-year low when 1.9 million additional shares were offered to stockholders. A feeder cable at the East 14th Street substation failed, knocking out the stock ticker at the New York Stock Exchange.

November   PSC hearings on Con Ed's request for rate increase began. Luce argued "fair-rate-of-return" principle. Rate of return was about 5.6 percent, lowest among major U.S. utilities, which average 7 percent. The price of electricity in New York, however, is about 17 percent higher than the average in the rest of the country.

New York City published "Master Plan" calling for a reordering of national and regional priorities to meet urban problems. Militants broke up a lunch of 1,500 discussing plan.

Luce proposed a new state agency with exclusive jurisdiction over approval of electric power plant site location. He said Con Ed's proposed, new oil- and gas-fired units at Astoria, New York, will require three approvals from federal agencies, four from New York State agencies and at least 20 from New York City agencies.

Con Ed financial vice president predicted that $800 to $900 million in outside financing will be needed in the next five years to meet Con Ed's $1.5 billion construction budget. (*Wall Street Journal*, November 19, 1969.)

December   FPC examiner ruled for a second time in favor of Con Ed's right to build Cornwall pump storage station. Scenic Hudson Preservation Conference and the city of New York vow to carry the battle to the courts. "It's been difficult to plan future power facilities with this project in limbo," says Luce.

Mayor Lindsay urged that "giant corporations and utilities" be brought under increased public supervision. Mentioning Con Ed, he proposed that the federal government provide incentives and penalties to compel "these corporations" to become more responsive to human needs. (*New York Times,* December 4, 1969.)

The Public Service Commission warned of "brownouts again next summer." (*New York Times,* December 4, 1969.)

In its review of Con Ed's ten-year operating plans, the FPC said, "There is reasonable assurance . . . that Indian Point nuclear unit No. 2 will have passed its shakedown period" by the summer of 1972 and that in 1973, No. 2 will be increased in capacity. "Indian Point No. 3 is expected to produce power by 1973." ("A review of Consolidated Edison Company 1969 Power Supply Problems and Ten-Year Expansion Plans," Bureau of Power, FPC, December 1969, p. 37.)

1970

January   Big fish kill at Indian Point. Fish were trapped by a faulty underwater screen device (not nuclear leakage or thermal pollution).

February   Joseph C. Swidler, a Democrat and former TVA adviser, became chairman of the PSC. Sixteen days later the PSC rejected Con Ed's request for a 13 percent rise in steam rates.

In its 1969 annual report, Con Ed stated, "We [encourage] . . . gas sales. . . . We advertised gas heating not only to increase gas earnings, but also because gas is a cleaner fuel than oil . . . every oil furnace we convert to gas helps reduce New York City's air pollution problem."

Indian Point No. 2 was estimated to be on line by the end of 1970 and Cornwall by 1978.

March   Northern States Power Co. of Minnesota held public meetings to let "customers share in deciding where plants should be, what kind of fuel they should burn, how sites should be landscaped, and how waste should be removed." (*Business Week,* March 29, 1970, p. 142.)

Luce predicts brownouts during summer. (*Wall Street Journal,* March 17, 1970.)

April   Con Ed profits fell in first quarter of 1970. Nixon administration and Sen. Muskie reported drafting legislation calling for increased state regulation of power production.

May   New York attorney general sought $5 million damages and the closing down of Con Ed's nuclear power plant for thermal and chemical pollution of the Hudson River. (*Wall Street Journal,* May 13, 1970.)

June   Indian Point nuclear plant went out for rest of the summer because of a defective pipe in the cooling system. Power was thus cut by 3 percent, 260,000 kw.

July   "Big Allis," a 1,000,000-kw generator in Ravenswood, Queens, broke down again and will be out of commission until late fall, cutting power an additional 13 percent. Con Ed imported power from Canada and the TVA, and reduced voltage to stretch capacity. Subway schedules in New York disrupted due to power shortage. Mayor appeals for reduced driving to hold down air pollution in an atmospheric inversion (*New York Times,* July 30, 1970).

August   Chairman of the Federal Power Commission (FPC) again authorized Con Ed's Cornwall plant. Conservationists vow to continue the fight.

               Mayor allowed 800,000 kw expansion of Con Ed's Astoria plant. Company had requested 1.6 megawatts. Plant burns natural gas and low sulphur fuel. (*New York Times,* August 23, 1970.) Two borough presidents demanded public hearings "on this matter that is so vital to . . . daily health and safety." (*New York Times,* August 25, 1970.)

               Committee to stop Con Ed's pollution project was formed, including George Wald of Harvard and Stephen Dyers, director of the cardiopulmonary laboratory at St. Vincent's Hospital. Committee plans three steps: a lawsuit against Con Ed to keep it from building the Astoria plant, the collection of signatures on a petition to Mayor Lindsay, and a request to the FPC and PSC to put Con Ed into a receivership of trustees for failing to provide adequate electric power. (*New York Times,* August 12, 1970.)

               Senator Edmund Muskie said it was "ridiculous" that there was no national power policy and added that a national grid would provide "an obvious part of the answer." (*New York Times,* August 30, 1970, Sec. 3, p. 1.)

September PSC approved $90 million of the $119 million electric rate increase, increasing residential rates by 4 percent and commercial rates by 14.5 percent.

               Heat wave forces utilities from Virginia to New York to slash voltages by 5 to 8 percent. The blackout hit 65-square blocks. Mrs. Josephine Priese of Queens had company from California and Canada so she had stocked up on meats and frozen foods. The food spoiled; her friend, Mrs. Marie Smith of Montreal, said, "I'll be glad to get back to Canada. You can have New York." Roy LaMotto, owner of a flower shop, said, "I've got flowers for a wedding on Saturday. Look at my roses. They look like balloons. I can't sell any of this now." Many small storeowners said their losses would be covered by insurance. (*Wall Street Journal,* September 24, 1970, p. 4.)

December   Hearings before AEC for a license to operate Indian Point No. 2 begin.

1971

February   A 20-block strip of midtown Manhattan went black on February 7. In the Northeast, fuel stocks were dangerously low and coal and oil prices were climbing.

Business Week (February 13, 1971) analyzed Con Ed's situation and blamed the problems on bad planning, ranging from underestimates of demand to overestimates of supply. *BW* noted Con Ed is unable to tap the excess reserves of midwestern utilities because transmission lines in Ohio and Pennsylvania cannot carry the necessary power through their system. *Business Week* claimed that Con Ed's forecasting has been hampered by a lack of sufficient local data and by concentration on new construction rather than on the increased power needs of remodeled buildings.

Con Ed president, Lou Roddis, indicated that capital costs for nuclear plants have gone from $130 per kw in 1967 to more than $260 in 1970 and are expected to reach $500 per kw by 1980. (*BW*)

In its 1970 annual report, Con Ed estimated the following schedule for new capacity:

> 1971—Indian Point No. 2, 873,000 kilowatts
> 1972—oil-fired units, 640,000 kilowatts
> 1973—Indian Point No. 3, 965,000 kilowatts
>   oil-fired units, 240,000 kilowatts

March   Joseph C. Swidler, chairman of PSC, is reported to have asserted that the proper way to tackle the power problem is to set state and national priorities for growth that the power industries and authorities could then serve. (*New York Times,* March 17, 1971.)

The State Power Authority announced plans to build a $150 million pumped-storage plant at an unnamed site, presumably in the Catskills or Berkshire foothills, to provide power for New York City and the southeastern part of the state. Previously SPA has sold wholesale electricity primarily to upstate areas.

New York City's municipal services administrator, Milton Musicus (who also heads a city committee on power needs), stated, "Judging by the slippage in bringing new generating capacity into service, I have no confidence that the company [Con Ed] will be able to realize its 10-year program to meet the city's power need." (*The New York Times,* March 17, 1971.)

May   Dr. Ernest Sternglass, professor of radiation physics at the University of Pittsburgh School of Medicine, argued that nuclear reactors at Indian Point and Brookhaven National Laboratory on Long Island "appear to have increased infant mortality in surrounding areas." (*New York Times,* May 12, 1971.)

Rep. John M. Murphy, Democrat from Staten Island, said he felt that one of the major problems facing Con Edison in its day-to-day operations was the fact that they "dumped the old-timers too soon. [They] knew the ropes. They knew how to get even the most routine jobs done without the red tape that ties up present management." (*New York Times,* May 16, 1971.)

November   In testimony before the Federal Price Commission, Luce said:

> As a result of this earnings squeeze, which started in the middle sixties and is being felt severely today, utility common stocks have lost favor with the investing public. The price-earnings ratio for such stocks has declined sharply, and investors no longer see in them a real potential of earnings growth. The last four common stock issues Con Edison has sold have had to be sold at substantial discounts below book value, and our stock sells in the market well below book value. Its market price today is little more than half what it was in 1965.
>
> An even more critical aspect of the earnings squeeze is that it has resulted in the interest coverage of most companies declining precipitously.
>
> Some companies have found themselves unable to sell bonds either because they could not meet the coverage

requirements of their mortgage indentures or because such a sale would result in a lowering of their bond ratings. A number of companies have been de-rated, resulting in increased interest costs and restriction of the market for their bonds. . . . the rating agencies have made clear that the fate of Con Ed's single "A" rating depends on the outcome of our pending electric rate case.

                ◦   ◦   ◦   ◦   ◦

The electric industry is perhaps the most capital-intensive industry in the country. To accommodate the present rate of load growth, the industry is committed to a five-year construction program costing $55 billion. This program must be financed principally by selling stocks and bonds to the public.

December   Investment in Cornwall reached $20,670,000 with approvals still not given.

1972

January   Luce issued his Annual Report to the People (see Appendix B).

February   In its 1971 annual report, Con Ed stated, "The key to adequate power reserves in 1972 is Indian Point Nuclear Unit No. 2. Environmental protection costs for 1972 are estimated to be $140 million."

New York State Department of Environmental Conservation ordered suspension of testing of circulating water pumps at Indian Point No. 2 pending hearings on the Hudson River ecology. (*New York Times,* February 29, 1972.)

PSC expressed interest in the idea of redesigning electricity rates to make heavy peak-demand users pay more, instead of less, for their power. Currently costs are spread evenly with reductions being given to quantity users (except for residential) who are primarily industrial. (*New York Times,* February 6, 1972).

April   Con Ed issued $150 million bond issue and explained that between 1972–1976, the utility would require $3.08 million for capital expenditures. (*New York Times,* April 12, 1972.)

A problem was discovered in the emergency core cooling system at Indian Point No. 2. It was clear the plant would not be functioning during the summer of 1972.

The president of PECor, a subcontractor on Indian Point No. 2 asked the AEC to hold up licensing because of "inadequate, incomplete and questionable design" of parts of the nuclear reactor. (*Wall Street Journal,* April 3, 1972.)

Stockholders at the annual meeting (May 15) were told that Indian Point No. 2 would not be available and that there might be "intentional outlying area blackouts to save service in high-density areas." (*New York Times,* May 17, 1972.)

May　　The Public Service Electric and Gas Co. of Newark, New Jersey, announced plans to build a huge, floating nuclear plant anchored out in the ocean and protected by an immense breakwater. Environmentalists aren't convinced the plant will be safe and seashore residents question the new addition to their beaches. Public Service decided on the idea after being frustrated in attempts to find suitable power plant sites in the highly populated state. There were many unanswered questions: Who owns the ocean coastline and who should receive property taxes from the plant? What damage would marine life incur? What if there were an accident? Would the plant be obsolete even before it was completed? Gulf Oil Company was building a nuclear plant cooled by helium in lieu of water (the ocean's vast water supply being another prime reason for the New Jersey plant). "We studied floating plants," a Gulf spokesman said, "but we concluded, 'Who needs them?'" (*Wall Street Journal,* May 24, 1972.) Contractor for the floating power plant is Offshore Power Systems, a joint venture of Westinghouse Electric Company and Tenneco Inc.; financial commitment by the two companies to date is $210 million for a factory.

June　　Supreme Court refused to hear appeal on Cornwall thereby upholding FPC's decision to approve the project.

Federal Trade Commission (FTC) decided to launch an investigation into how the FPC sets natural gas prices, and subpoenaed the records of 11 companies. (*Business Week,* June 24, 1972.)

PSC announced that Con Ed was the only major electric utility out of seven to have discontinued all sales promotion advertising in 1971. Although Con Ed's institutional advertising tripled, PSC said such appeals for "conserving gas or electricity were clearly in the public interest and would be considered a legitimate cost." (*New York Times,* June 25, 1972.)

July　　Felica Salmonese, who runs a delicatessen in Brooklyn, checked her store after the latest Con Ed power failure.

"Look, all my potato salad is gone. All my rice pudding is gone. All my salad is gone. I make it all myself." "Who's gonna pay us for all the ice cream we threw out," asked her husband Louis. (*New York Times,* July 19, 1972).

The New York PSC "announced it would begin an unprecedented investigation of possible regulations that would cut down consumption of electricity in New York City. The commission said it might limit the amount of electricity Consolidated Edison Co. can sell for heating and air conditioning or else limit the company to supplying only properly insulated buildings with power for those uses." The idea of such changes was supported by the environmentalists, but rejected by many power company executives. "Many utility executives . . . scoff at the ideas." Donald Cook, chairman and president of American Electric Power Company and a leading industry spokesman, asserted that "the standard of living of any people has a direct correlation with the amount of energy utilized by that society. Unless we say that our standard of living is as high as it should be, that poor people should remain forever poor, we must come to the conclusion we must make available the amount of power our society ask for." (*Wall Street Journal,* July 27, 1972).

The AEC granted Con Ed permission to operate Indian Point No. 2 at 20 percent for testing purposes; the company had requested permission for 50 percent. Full licensing cannot occur until completion of an environmental impact study currently in progress.

PSC's chairman, Joseph C. Swidler (a former FPC commissioner), announced adoption of a "strong but not absolute policy to discourage promotional advertising. Those utilities which cannot justify such advertising will not be permitted to include them as operating expenses . . . which means when rates are calculated these costs would be charged against profits." (*New York Times,* July 2, 1972.)

The role of government

In the light of these circumstances, Con Ed faced a variety of proposals for increased governmental intervention into electric power generation.

1. In 1970, Mayor Lindsay had appointed a watchdog Committee on Public Utilities for "all utility problems" in New York. The committee, headed by Milton Musicus, was to coordinate its efforts with the Federal

Power Commission and the state Public Service Commission, and to require monthly reports from Con Ed. After the February 7 blackout and a conference with Mr. Luce, Mr. Musicus said the city was appealing to the state and federal governments to make additional power supplies available to Con Ed. He said the city was considering requesting legislation to enable the Power Authority to sell electricity for use in the city. The subsequent announcement by the PA that it would build a hydroelectric plant triggered speculation about an increased and perhaps very altered role for the PA in the future.

2. On February 8, 1971, President Nixon asked Congress to enact a "comprehensive and wide-ranging program" to protect the environment against pollution. He addressed the issue of power plant siting and said:

> The power shortage last summer and continuing disputes across the country over the siting of power plants and the routing of transmission lines highlights the need for longer range planning by the environmental concerns well in advance of construction deadlines. . . .
>
> I propose a power plant siting law to provide for establishment within each State or region of a single agency with responsibility for assuring that environmental concerns are properly considered in the certification of specific power plant sites and transmission lines. (*Congressional Quarterly*, February 12, 1971.)

3. Sen. Henry Jackson (Democrat, Washington), chairman of the Senate Interior Committee, proposed legislation which would bar funds from all federally aided projects in states that fail to establish "comprehensive" plans for land use.

At the same time Sen. Edmund Muskie (Democrat, Maine) proposed the creation of regional boards with power to license all siting and construction of power plants. Members of the board would be appointed by governors, but they would need to follow federal guidelines. In hearings before Muskie's intergovernmental relations subcommittee, Luce argued that the last thing Con Ed needed was still another layer of regulatory jurisdictions. He cited the difficulty and delays Con Ed had experienced trying to obtain clearances for a critically needed 25-mile transmission line. Approvals were required from:

> . . . five municipalities in Westchester County, a minimum of three in Rockland County, the Hudson River Valley Commission, the Federal Aviation Agency, the Corps of Engineers, the New York State Highway Department, the East Hudson Parkway Authority and the Palisades Interstate Park Commission. . . . A number of these agencies not only have the power to hold hearings but do hold hearings to consider the advisability of the line. (*Wall Street Journal*, April 3, 1970.)

4. Perhaps the most radical proposal for the reorganization of the U.S. power industry and its regulation comes from John T. Miller, a Georgetown University law professor. Writing in the *Fordham Law Review* (May 1970), Miller argued that Con Ed had the same four options in 1970 that it had had in 1965, when an FPC examiner first pointed them out: The company could construct transmission lines to bring in power from sources outside New York City; it could build conventional thermal plants within the city; it could build nuclear plants in the area; or it could construct pumped-storage hydroelectric projects where feasible. In addition, he made the following suggestions.

A The problem

There are several ways in which the present difficulties might be overcome. A great variety of legislation has been introduced in Congress from time to time dealing with one facet of the problem or another. The piecemeal approach encourages hope in the resolution of some part of the tangle, but it serves to divert recognition from the fact that the problems are intertwined. A more direct, time-saving answer might be found in a statutory reorganization of the interstate electric power industry, a redrafting of the spheres of regulatory responsibility, and a reallocation of regulatory resources. This should only be done on the basis of a thoroughgoing congressional study in which it will first be necessary to identify the problem. At the risk of oversimplification, it might be summarized in a series of propositions like the following.

1. Future supplies of interstate electric power must be planned and provided on a regional basis in the interest of conservation of natural resources, enjoyment of economies possible only with the most modern power generation and transmission equipment, reduction of competing demands on the capital markets at a time of high interest rates, and the provision of adequate service at the lowest reasonable cost to consumers.

2. To provide a sensible base for future planning, existing generation and transmission facilities should be operated in terms of regional supplies and market requirements.

3. All public interest aspects of each new interstate generation and transmission project should be heard, considered, and resolved in one forum after which, subject to court review, the decision of that forum as to facilities to be built and on what terms shall be final.

4. Jurisdiction over interstate generation and transmission facilities and service through such facilities should be separated from jurisdiction over distribution facilities and service and lodged in a single federal authority. Furthermore, the interstate facilities should be segregated by ownership and/or contract from distribution facilities and operations to permit effective licensing and rate regulation.

5. Competition should be eliminated from the electric power industry only to the extent necessary to accomplish effective regulation and

a clear statutory exemption should be provided where competition must be eliminated for that purpose.

6. State regulation should be made more effective by the remedy adopted for better regulation of interstate activities in the electric industry.

B. A possible remedy

The following remedy has been drafted to meet the problem as just visualized. Little of it is novel. Most of it reflects regulatory concepts employed in other industries and proposals previously suggested to Congress. It is intended to apply to the investor-owned sector of the industry, except where otherwise specifically provided.

1. *Federally chartered regional corporations.* Congress shall enact a statute providing for the chartering of investor-owned regional public utility corporations empowered to engage in the generation and transmission of electric energy in interstate and foreign commerce. There should be but one such corporation for each region. The geographical extent of each region might be specified by the enabling statute, subject to amendment after public hearing by the federal agency assigned overall regulatory jurisdiction.

2. *Transfer of existing interstate facilities.* The law should define generation and transmission in interstate and foreign commerce and require that all such facilities, together with their related easements, located within a region shall be transferred to the local, federally chartered regional public utility corporation at book value in exchange for its securities, to the end that but one investor-owned firm is engaged in such activities in each region.

3. *Capitalization and consideration.* The capitalization of the regional public utility corporation shall be such as to enable it to pay for the acquired facilities by the "roll-over" of a proportional part of the debt of the transferring firm and an appropriate amount of equity securities without increasing the cost of electricity to the ultimate consumer or injuring the investor. Equity securities might be authorized for sale to the distribution companies or to the public to obtain funds for working capital requirements. Equity securities obtained in this manner from a regional public utility corporation by a public utility holding company or by a public utility shall be redistributed to the shareholders of such firms in a manner designed to eliminate every holding company relationship from the interstate electric industry and forbid its recrudescence.

4. *Management.* The boards of directors of the regional public utility corporations might be chosen initially by the Federal Power Commission regional advisory councils of the industry, and thereafter in the usual manner by the shareholders.

5. *Federal regulation.* A federal agency—probably the Federal Power Commission—shall be granted complete licensing, financing, and rate jurisdiction over the regional public utility corporations. A "grandfather" license or certificate of public convenience and necessity will

issue immediately upon transfer of existing jurisdiction facilities to the regional public utility corporation, giving it all the authority needed to own and operate such facilities. Wholesale contracts shall be negotiated within a specified time between the regional public utility corporation and the firms which it shall supply with power for resale, which whole-sale contracts shall be filed with the Commission and subject to its rate jurisdiction. No new generation or transmission facilities shall be constructed in interstate or foreign commerce except by a regional public utility corporation and only after issuance of an authorizing order of the federal agency based upon application, notice, and hearing. The final order shall be subject to court review. The initiative for proposing new plans shall rest with the regional public utility corporation, the federal agency being empowered to require interconnections and wholesale service only upon application or in emergency situations whenever such action is required by the public interest. This will not adversely affect existing service, nor require the construction of substantial additional generation or transmission facilities by the regional public utility corporation.

6. Local hearings. In order to provide appropriate consideration of matters of local interest such as air and water pollution, aesthetics, safety, and potential injury to health, hearings shall be afforded on application to construct generation and transmission facilities before an examiner of the federal agency appointed under the Administrative Procedure Act,[1] who shall hear the proceedings in the geographical area most directly affected by the proposed facilities.[2] There shall be no other public hearing on the same project before any other federal, state or municipal body. When issues are raised as to matters such as safety of nuclear reactors or pollution of water and air, jurisdiction over which is now vested in another federal agency, such agency shall be given a reasonable opportunity to study the issue and to submit recommendations thereon, through expert and policy witnesses, in the proceedings before the examiner.

7. Eminent domain. The regional public utility corporation shall enjoy the power of eminent domain, enforceable in federal courts, for the construction of generation and transmission facilities authorized by the federal agency.

8. Cooperation with state regulatory authorities. The federal agency shall collect cost and market data from the regional public utility corporations and from all of their wholesale customers, which data shall be made readily available to state regulatory agencies for use in regulating retail rates and services in the electric industry.[3]

---

[1] See 5 U.S.C. Sec. 3105 (Supp. IV, 1969). Hearing examiners serving at the Federal Power Commission hold office under this statute.

[2] "In fixing the time and place for hearings, due regard shall be had for the convenience and necessity of the parties or their representatives." 5 U.S.C. Sec. 554 (b) (Supp. IV, 1969).

[3] "A Needed Reform of the Organization and Regulation of the Interstate Electric Power Industry," pp. 635, 636, 662–66.

APPENDIX A

Excerpts from Con Edison's *Revised*
Ten-Year Program to Meet Growing Energy Needs
and Reduce Air Pollution, 1969–1979[1]

SYSTEM PROJECTIONS

During the next decade Con Edison's Electric load is expected to increase from 7,350,000 kilowatts to 10,850,000 kilowatts, and the Company's net generating capacity will grow from 8,172,000 kilowatts to 14,037,000 kilowatts. Table 1 outlines peak electric loads and capacity available by years through 1979. Tabe 2 shows planned additions to electric generating capacity and Table 3 lists the planned electric capacity retirements.

DELAYS WHICH AFFECTED THE PROGRAM OF 1966

1. Indian Point No. 2 nuclear unit was originally scheduled for service in 1969, but it is doubtful that it will be ready before the summer of 1971 for various reasons, including design revisions required by the Atomic Energy Commission and labor problems at the construction site.
2. Indian Point No. 3 nuclear unit was originally planned for 1971. Interventions before the Atomic Energy Commission and other delays have adversely affected the schedule. It appears that a construction permit may not be granted by the AEC before late this summer and that the project cannot be completed before 1973.
3. Our Cornwall project was first announced in 1962 for service in 1967. Interventions initially by conservation groups and lately by the City of New York led to hearings before the Federal Power Commission in 1964, 1966, 1967 and 1969. A Federal Court remanded the initial license granted by the FPC in 1965 for further hearings. The Commission has not yet rendered its decision and further review by the Courts is anticipated. It now appears that the project cannot be placed in service before 1977–78, a loss of ten years in providing its benefits to the people of New York City and Westchester County.
4. When the Cornwall plant was delayed beyond 1972, Nuclear No. 4 was rescheduled for 1974 service date. The accumulative effect of delays on Indian Point Units 2 and 3 clearly show that the 1974 date cannot be attained and it is now scheduled for 1976.

---

[1] July 22, 1969.

5. These delays in the operation of new capacity will postpone the deactivation of older fossil fuel generating units in the City of New York which had been planned for 1971 and 1972.

NEW GENERATING FACILITIES

Because of various delays and the continued rapid growth of load, we have been forced to take a number of alternate steps from the former program, in order to provide adequate and reliable service to the people of New York City.

Gas turbine units can be manufactured and installed more quickly than other types of capacity, although they are definitely a second choice to a peaking facility such as the Cornwall pumped storage plant, particularly from a system reliability point of view. We have, however, had to install about 175 megawatts of additional gas turbines during 1968–69 and plan 900 megawatts of this type of capacity in 1970. Gas turbines are not designed for base load operation and because of their inherently high operating cost, can be used only for a few peak load days and at times of emergency need for capacity. The amount of such capacity that can be absorbed on any system is limited. We are adding these gas turbines because it is the only capacity we can install and have operational in 1970.

Con Edison has joined with Central Hudson Gas and Electric Corp. and Niagara Mohawk Power Corporation in the construction of a 1200 Mw. oil fired base load plant at Roseton, N.Y. on the Hudson River north of Newburgh for service before the summer of 1973. Our share of this capacity will be 480 Mw. for four years and 360 Mw. for the next four years.

Following the postponement of the Bell nuclear unit, previously mentioned, from which Con Edison expected to purchase 600 Mw. of capacity starting in the summer of 1973, we are now planning a joint project with Orange and Rockland Utilities, Inc. for 1973 on their system. This will be a 600 Mw. oil fired unit, of which 400 Mw. will be our share.

The next large generating capacity addition for the Con Edison system is required in 1974. Recent experience shows that it requires four to five years from date of authorization to place a fossil unit in service and from six to seven years for a nuclear unit. Nuclear No. 4, and 1115 Mw. unit outside of New York City, was planned for a 1974 service date but this date cannot now be attained, and 1976 appears to be the earliest service date possible for such a unit. After study of many possible alternates, the company has concluded that the capacity requirement for 1974 must be met by an oil and gas fired plant of approximately 1200 to 1600 Mw. located in New York City for reasons which are described later.

OTHER POSSIBLE SOURCES OF POWER

Canadian power

Con Edison has investigated other possible sources of generating capacity such as the planned Canadian hydroelectric development. Recent inquiry in this regard determined that essentially the entire output of the Churchill Falls plant now under construction in Labrador, will be required for anticipated load growth in Canada. Only short term capacity could be made available. This could not be utilized because of the transmission required.

Mine-Mouth plants

Mine-Mouth generating plants in Pennsylvania to supply this area have been studied frequently. These studies all show that additional high capacity transmission lines are required since the strong high voltage network existing and being planned throughout the Northeast, for reliability purposes, cannot also be used for importing large blocks of power such as 1,000,000 or 2,000,000 kilowatts. The required new, long transmission links to the city, a considerable portion underground, make this alternative unattractive economically and uncertain for a specific service date because of the difficulties that will be encountered in obtaining the extensive right-of-way necessary for both the overhead and underground sections. This right-of-way will be particularly difficult to obtain because it is through areas which are not being served by the lines.

LOCATION OF FOSSIL FIRED CAPACITY FOR 1974

The only feasible alternate for a source of new capacity for 1974 is to locate additional conventional capacity in the City. It is proposed to install about 1,200–1,600 Mw. of new capacity, fired by 0.37 per cent sulfur oil or natural gas whenever natural gas is available. Such an addition on very low sulfur fuel oil would contribute substantially to the improvement of air pollution control in the City. For instance, this capacity using 0.37 per cent sulfur oil would emit only about one-quarter the amount of sulfur dioxide that would be emitted by equivalent capacity of the older, less efficient equipment (proposed to be deactivated) on 1 per cent sulfur oil.

Studies have been made of several possible sites and it is concluded that the Astoria plant in Queens is the most desirable. It is close to the center of load on the system and reasonably remote from the concentration of buildings in Manhattan. From the standpoint of thermal discharge, Quirk, Lawler and Matusky Engineers, have reported that at the Astoria location more than 1600 Mw. of capacity may be installed and still comply with the proposed criteria of the New York State Water Resources Commission.

ESTIMATED STACK EMISSIONS

Table 4 is a comparison of the estimated stack emissions associated with the 1966 Ten Year Program and those in the current program. It shows that by 1974 the emission of both SO_2 and particulates under the current program including the enlarged plant at Astoria will be less than contemplated under the 1966 program.

TABLE 1

Estimated electric load and capacity—summer peak*

(megawatts)

	1969	1970	1971	1972	1973	1974	1975	1976	1977	1978	1979
Load:											
Maximum 1-hour net distributed load	7,350	7,725	8,075	8,400	8,725	9,075	9,425	9,775	10,125	10,475	10,850
Capacity:											
Estimated installed capacity.	8,172	9,072	9,945	9,945	11,265	11,975	12,043	12,881	13,761	14,037	14,037
Estimated firm purchases from other utilities	710	445	420	400	0	0	0	0	0	0	0
Estimated capacity usable for Con Edison system.	8,882	9,517	10,365	10,345	11,265	11,975	12,043	12,881	13,761	14,037	14,037

* July 22, 1969.

TABLE 2
Program of electric capacity additions*
prior to summer peak in year indicated

Year		*Net capacity (megawatts)*
1970	Gas turbines at Astoria Plant	450
	Gas turbines at undetermined location	450
	Total	900
1971	Nuclear Unit No. 2 at Indian Point Station	873
1973	Increased capacity in Unit No. 2 at Indian Point Station	92
	Nuclear Unit No. 3 at Indian Point Station	965
	Roseton Plant (Con Ed share)	480
	Bowline Point Plant (Con Ed share)	400
	Total	1,937
1974	Increased capacity in Unit No. 2 at Indian Point Station	35
	Expansion of Astoria	1,200†
	Total	1,235
1975	Increased capacity in Unit No. 2 at Indian Point Station	33
	Increased capacity in Unit No. 3 at Indian Point Station	35
	Total	68
1976	Increased capacity in Unit No. 3 at Indian Point Station	33
	Nuclear Unit No. 4	1,115
	Total	1,148
1977	Pumped-storage Units No. 1, 2, 3, and 4—Cornwall Plant	1,000
	Roseton Plant—(decrease in Con Ed share)	−120
	Total	880
1978	Pumped-storage Units No. 5, 6, 7, and 8—Cornwall Plant	1,000

* Subject to periodic revisions dependent upon changing conditions including variations in Construction Schedules.
† Depending on detailed studies the additional capacity may be as great as 1600 MW.
July 22, 1969

TABLE 3
Program of electric capacity retirements
prior to summer peak in year indicated

Year		Net capacity (megawatts)
1973	Hell Gate Station—all units	617
1974	Kent Avenue Station—all units	92
	Sherman Creek Station—all units	199
	Hudson Avenue Station Units No. 1, 2, 3 and 4.	234
	74th Street Station Unit No. 3 (effective capacity)†	0
	Subtotal.	525
1976	East River Station Units No. 1 and 4*	239
	59th Street Station Unit No. 7†.	32
	Waterside Station Unit No. 1†.	39
	Subtotal.	310
1978	East River Station Units No. 2 and "S"*.	75
	Hudson Avenue Station Units No. 5, 6, 7, and 8*	510
	Waterside Station Units No. 10, 11, 12, and 13†	107
	59th Street Station Unit No. 8†.	32
	74th Street Station Unit No. 4 (effective capacity)†	0
	Subtotal.	724
	Total	2,176

* Associated boilers are expected to be retained for the steam system.

† Boilers at the stations noted produce steam for high-pressure turbines. The exhaust from these turbines can be utilized either to generate power from low pressure turbines or to provide steam for the distribution system. Only the low-pressure turbines cited are to be retired; the boilers are expected to remain in service.

TABLE 4
Estimated stack emissions

	1966 program		Current program	
	SO_2 (1000 tons)	Particulates (tons)	SO_2 (1000 tons)	Particulates (tons)
1966	340	11,350	–	–
1967	278	11,050	–	–
1968	277	10,230	–	–
1969	233	5,880	168	7,236
1970	192	5,760	181	7,772
1971	122	4,660	152	6,516
1972	109	4,380	169	7,344
1973	112	4,530	125	5,380
1974	121	4,840	91*	4,079*
1975	130	5,220	98*	4,354*
1976	100	4,090	86*	3,875*

* Assumes Astoria expansion at 1600 Mw.
July 22, 1969.

APPENDIX B

Report to the people of New York City and Westchester County[1]

As 1972 begins we reaffirm our commitment to the goals of Con Edison as published when I joined the Company almost five years ago:

—To provide the best possible service at rates as low as the cost of doing business will permit.

—To protect the environment in every practicable way, and to design and maintain our properties to intrude as little as possible on the appearance of the communities we serve.

—To employ and promote without discrimination, and to take positive steps to qualify the underprivileged for useful jobs.

Progress since 1967 toward achieving these goals has been substantial, though not as rapid as we would have liked. *It now requires 6–10 years and sometimes longer to plan, license and build generating units and high voltage transmission lines, and to resolve environmental controversies surrounding them.*

Here is where we stand on various programs that we think are of special interest to you:

Power supply. Con Edison has the largest construction program in its history, a program designed to meet load growth of about 450,000 KW per year, and in addition to retire in this decade about 2,000,000

---

[1] Charles F. Luce, chairman of the board, Consolidated Edison Company of New York, Inc.

KW of obsolete in-city generating capacity. *To finance this program, with related transmission and distribution facilities, will require about $3 billion in the next five years.*

Here are the new generating stations under construction and when we expect they will be ready for commercial operation if there are no further licensing delays:

—350,000 KW of peaking turbines to be mounted on two barges anchored on the Brooklyn waterfront ("The Narrows"), July 1972.

—800,000 KW representing Con Edison's share in two units at Bowline Point near Haverstraw, July 1972 and May 1975.

—1,840,000 KW in two nuclear generators at Indian Point near Buchanan, July 1972 and November 1974.

—480,000 KW representing Con Edison's initial share in two units at Roseton near Newburgh, November 1972 and May 1973.

—800,000 KW addition to our Astoria Plant, June 1974.

In addition, we are building extra high voltage transmission interconnections with other utilities that, subject to the timely issuance of permits, will double our power import capability by 1974.

For the second half of the 1970's and early 1980's we hope to construct the 2,000,000 KW pumped storage hydroelectric Cornwall (Storm King) project; a 1,200,000 KW oil-fired station on the lower Hudson, perhaps at Ossining; and at least 700,000 KW of additional peaking gas turbines. We also hope to purchase under long term contracts in excess of 1,000,000 KW of capacity from the Power Authority of the State of New York, and 500,000 KW or more from Hydro Quebec.

For the latter part of the 1980's we presently foresee as new sources a series of nuclear plants, possibly island-based or barge-mounted, advanced design gas turbines, and perhaps a beginning on fuel cells magnetohydrodynamic generators (MHD), and breeder reactors. *If new opportunities for purchase can be found, whether of base-load or peaking power, we will take advantage of any that would be in the interest of our customers.*

This revised 20-year Advance Program recently transmitted to the appropriate Federal, State, City and County governmental agencies can provide our customers with reliable electric energy and, at the same time, make it possible to improve further the environment of the metropolitan area. Like all such plans, it will of course be subject to change from time to time to adapt to changing conditions and technology.

As an integral part of long range planning we have increased our direct participation in research and development five-fold in the past five years, and have encouraged an industry-wide coordinated research and development program. In years ahead we foresee even greater expansion of R & D commitments.

We welcome suggestions from any citizen or groups of citizens for improvements in our long-range planning.

The summer of '72.   To get ready for the summer of 1972, we are taking as many machines out of service for overhaul this winter as can be spared.

In the meantime Big Allis has been performing well, and we are pushing hard for completion this summer of three new generating units: Indian Point No. 2, Bowline Point No. 1 and "The Narrows." All three are essential if we are to have adequate reserves this summer. *We are more optimistic than the PSC about our chances of completing them on present schedules but we recognize that despite our best efforts further delays may occur.*

The environment.   We continue to strengthen programs for environmental protection. We have recruited a highly competent staff of environmental and research experts to assist our designers and operators. In the past five years Con Edison has increased power sendout by 29%, yet has reduced its sulfur dioxide and particulate emissions by more than 50%. In the next five years we expect to increase power sendout by another 28%, and reduce by more than half the remaining emissions in New York City. By spring none of our more than 100 boilers will be burning coal, since all conversions from coal to oil will have been completed by then. This is solid progress. According to the latest published figures we now account for a relatively small share of the total air pollutants emitted in New York City. *Further, the energy we provide is the key to many other environmental improvements: better mass transit, sewage treatment, solid waste disposal, etc.*

Perhaps the most complex of the many environmental problems we have faced is the method by which to cool Indian Point No. 2 and No. 3. Based on the best information and expert advice available to us, both units have been built with "once through" river water cooling. To modify the units to add cooling towers would itself create environmental problems, for example, scenic damage and possible air pollution from saline water vapor. It would, moreover, cost electric consumers an estimated $18 to $20 million per year in higher rates. The New York Department of Environmental Conservation has approved the construction of "once through" cooling for Indian Point No. 2, but reserved decision on No. 3. The AEC, which must independently examine the matter, has not yet ruled as to either unit.

"Save-A-Watt."   Inevitably there will be pressure on the environment from the addition of new facilities required to meet the people's needs for electricity in the next two decades, however carefully the facilities may be designed. Moreover, the increased use of *any* form of energy further depletes the world's diminishing resource base.

In 1971 we therefore discontinued our sales department, and began a "Save-A-Watt" educational campaign on the need for saving energy of *all* kinds and how to do it. Further, we're trying to modify our pricing policy by asking the PSC to reduce the quantity discount for large users of electricity.

In its first year, we believe that "Save-A-Watt" reduced our summertime peak by about 200,000 KW and reduced the predicted consumption of electric energy during summer months by more than 100,000,000 KWh.

Upward pressure on rates.   Electricity is still a good bargain compared to other necessities of life.

It will continue to be.

In the past 25 years, our average residential rates have risen about 35%. By comparison, the cost of living has risen about 100% in that period, subway fares 600%, bridge and tunnel tolls 50 to 150%, newspapers 400%, and even City water bills have gone up as much as 250%.

To finance the new facilities that people require, and pay the increasing wages and the taxes that can be expected in New York, will require substantial rate increases. We regret that this is necessary. We will do our best to minimize further increases by operating as efficiently as possible.

Our present electric rates are based on adjusted 1970 costs, and average 1970 investment in electric plant. Both are far below 1972 costs and investment. Specifically, 1972 average investment in electric plant will be $500,000,000 greater than 1970 average investment, and 1972 electric operating expenses, including fuel costs and taxes, will exceed 1970 by nearly $300,000,000. Revenue increases have not been as large proportionately.

Most of the same cost factors that push electric rates up are also pushing gas rates up. An extra cost-push factor for gas arises from the necessity to develop substitutes for declining supplies of natural gas from Louisiana and Texas. These new substitutes will cost 80 cents to $1.00 per thousand cubic feet, or more, as against 45 cents for gas we buy now.

Leadership in equal employment.   In the utility industry we have won national recognition for our achievements in employing and training minorities and the disadvantaged. Since 1966 we have increased the minority members in our work force from 8% to 17%. In cooperation with the U.S. Department of Labor we are training our third group of disadvantaged youngsters, and helping them advance their academic skills at the same time.

We invite you to visit "Con Edison Prep," where 140 young men are now learning trade skills while improving their reading and math.

Customer billing and accounting.   We regret that our performance in customer billing and accounting has not been better. Our computer system has been outdated, and we were not prepared for the tremendous surge of customer telephone calls and letters when we changed from bi-monthly to monthly billing. Customer inquiries have jumped from 2,800 to 3,700 per day since we made that change.

Improvements in this area have top priority in our 1972 budgeting and planning. Among other things, we are installing an entirely new computer system which will enable our customer service people to do a much better job. With this new system, the employee who takes your call will be able to answer your question in most cases without referring it to another employee.

With some 3 million customers, and 36 million billing transactions per year, we know that we won't get out of the woods overnight. *We know, too, that machinery alone won't solve all the problems. It will take commitment by each employee to treat every customer's inquiry as though it were his own.*

The gas system.   Much of the above report on our electric system applies as well to the gas and steam divisions.

In the gas division we have taken action to increase supply, especially our peaking capability to meet cold weather heating loads; to maintain our system at maximum safety conditions; and to modernize our distribution system through replacement of old cast-iron mains.

Our over-all gas supply situation is as favorable as any along the East Coast, but all gas distributors, including us, must be planning for future supplies, whether of traditional pipeline gas, liquified natural gas from foreign sources, synthetic natural gas from petroleum products, or gasification of Eastern coal deposits. *Reflecting concern for state-wide supplies of natural gas, the PSC recently has placed rather severe limitations on providing gas service to new customers throughout the state.*

We will continue to need your help.   Almost everything we do in constructing and operating energy supply systems unavoidably causes inconvenience or annoyance to someone. But an adequate supply of energy to New York City and Westchester is absolutely essential for the welfare of the people. If we do not receive the necessary permits to build and operate new facilities on time, there will not be an adequate energy supply.

We, the men and women of Con Edison, will plan the necessary new facilities as intelligently as we know how, and we will go about the essential work of building and operating them with due regard to the people we are privileged to serve. We hope that, in turn, you will continue to extend to us your helpful understanding and your support. We will need it.

January 1972

Charles F. Luce

PART IV

Unions and other interest groups

Organization of New York City's hospitals[1]

In early 1958, only one of New York City's 85 voluntary hospitals[2] dealt with a union representing its employees. By the close of 1960, 12 voluntary hospitals recognized a union as the representative of their employees, another handful were in the process of being organized by a union, and 37 were signatories to an agreement which required them to abide by the recommendations in regard to employee relations, of a board on which there was labor representation.

Voluntary hospitals operated without profit, with revenue derived from patients (15 percent)[3], Blue Cross (50 percent), city patients (15 percent), gifts and endowments (10 percent), and other sources (10 percent). They were generally managed by professional administrators and directed by a board of trustees whose members were of considerable stature and financial means. These hospitals were tax exempt and were excluded from the jurisdiction of minimum wage laws and other measures designed to provide employee benefits such as disability and unemployment insurance. It is important to recognize that voluntary hospitals

---

[1] This case is taken from a longer version prepared by Roy Penchansky, research associate, under the direction of Professor E. Robert Livernash as the basis for class discussion rather than to illustrate either effective or ineffective handling of an administrative situation.

[2] New York City's 157 hospitals were divided into three groups: 85 voluntary hospitals having 24,000 beds; 27 municipal hospitals having 19,000 beds; and 45 proprietary hospitals having 5,000 beds.

[3] Approximate figures for 1957.

417

are not covered by the Taft-Hartley Act or by corresponding labor laws in New York or in most states. The legal position of workers and management was therefore essentially what it had been before the legislation of the 1930s which encouraged the growth of unions. Basically, workers could organize, but the law did not require management to recognize the union as their bargaining agent and to bargain in good faith, even though the union was properly elected by a majority of the workers.

In 1958, wage rates for unskilled workers in voluntary hospitals in New York City were between $30 and $40 per week for a 44-hour week. The municipal hospitals, which were part of the city government and financed through taxation, followed the city's policy of recognizing their employees' right to organize into unions and bargained with these unions. The minimum hiring rate in these hospitals was $53 per week. The two unions representing the municipal hospital employees were the International Brotherhood of Teamsters and the American Federation of State, County, Municipal Employees.

Proprietary hospitals were privately owned and operated for profit, frequently by doctors. As such, they were subject to the same tax legislation, protective labor legislation, and labor-management relations legislation as any other business. In 1960, the employees of a large number of the proprietary hospitals were represented by the Hotel and Allied Service Employees Union. Most of these contracts had been negotiated initially during the two previous years.

During the depression and World War II numerous attempts had been made to organize the workers in voluntary hospitals in New York City. The unions attempting organization were generally weak and had little ability to oppose management or support the workers in a strike; many of these unions have since ceased to exist. Therefore, although the nonprofessional hospital workers were not reluctant to join unions, the organizing attempts had been largely unsuccessful. Since 1945, there had been little in the way of union activity in the hospitals.

In the mid-1950s, the one voluntary hospital under contract with a union was Maimonides in Brooklyn. This was a small hospital supported by the Federation of Jewish Philanthropies. The union at Maimonides had changed its affiliation as different unions representing government and nonprofit institution employees were established, merged with other organizations, or died. In 1957, the employees at Maimonides were represented by Local 237 of the Teamsters, which represented workers in the New York City municipal hospitals, and which later attempted to organize the New York City Police Force and the hospitals in Miami, Florida.

The key person in the Maimonides situation was Eliot Godoff, a pharmacist, who had been involved in the original attempts to organize the voluntary hospitals. When the Maimonides local, which had about

200 members, affiliated with the Teamsters, Godoff became a Teamster organizer.

In about 1957 it became obvious to Godoff that little could be done for the Maimonides workers as long as no other voluntary hospitals were organized; also he was not particularly happy with his role within the Teamsters Union. For these reasons, Godoff visited Leon Davis, president of Local 1199, Drug Employees Union, with whom he was familiar, to seek assistance in finding work as a pharmacist.

Local 1199, Drug Employees Union, was affiliated with the Retail, Wholesale and Department Store Union, AFL-CIO. This local represented 2,100 registered pharmacists, who were mainly Jewish, and 4,900 drugstore employees, which included a substantial number of Blacks and Puerto Ricans, in 1,800 retail drugstores in metropolitan New York and Long Island. This membership represented the workers of over 85 percent of New York City's drugstores. The local was an extremely democratic one, with a high level of member participation in the local's operations as well as its educational, social, and cultural activities.

The Retail, Wholesale and Department Store Union represented mainly unskilled workers drawn from poorly educated, minority groups. The International's largest unit was District 65 in New York City, with over 30,000 members. Local 1199 and District 65 operated in a similar manner and had a history of cooperation and mutual assistance.

Leon Davis, as well as the other officers of Local 1199 and similar unions such as the Building Service Employees and the RWDSU, had long been interested in the workers in the voluntary hospitals and the possibility of organizing the hospitals, though no real effort had been made to do so. These individuals were interested in the hospital workers because of the extremely low wages and poor working conditions, and felt it the responsibility of the trade union movement, as well as the general populace, to attempt to alleviate such situations. Also, the hospital work forces were composed largely of members of minority groups, as were the memberships of these other unions, and their leaders felt a responsibility toward these groups. There was also the factor that large numbers of low-paid hospital workers, who were frequently changing employment or unemployed, made it more difficult for other unions representing unskilled workers to bargain for their memberships and raise their employment standards.

Davis told Godoff that he would be interested in seeing if his union could do something to organize the hospitals. He suggested that if Godoff could get permission to bring the Maimonides workers into Local 1199, then they would use this group as a core, and Godoff could work at organizing other voluntary hospitals.

The Teamsters were willing to release the Maimonides workers, and they were transferred to Local 1199. The Teamsters Union had not been equipped to do much for these workers and the workers were pleased to become part of a union that could better handle their problem.

Godoff and an organizer from the drugstore staff were assigned to the job of surveying the hospital situation, the employment conditions, and the approaches to organizing as well as the best place to start organizing.

Early in 1958 it was decided that Montefiore in the Bronx would be the first voluntary hospital Local 1199 would attempt to organize. Montefiore, a large institution with about 850 nonprofessional employees, was chosen because the organizers had contacts with a number of employees who were interested in having the union come into the hospital.

A number of earlier attempts had been made to organize Montefiore was to develop a corps of 60 workers who would form the organizing were of the opinion that most of the employees felt that there was no sense in joining a union as it would only fold and because little could be done to improve their position. This attitude was generated by the previous unsuccessful organizing attempts and the complete demoralization of the workers due to their overwhelming economic and social problems. For these same reasons, some unionists felt that these workers could not be organized as they would not band together or be willing to fight to improve their position.

In April of 1958, Local 1199 began its organizing attempts. The union people felt that their most important job was to instill a feeling in the workers that there was some chance of victory. The union's first task was to develop a corps of 60 workers who would form the organizing committee and be the center of operations within the hospital. According to union sources, a tremendous amount of field work over many weeks was necessary to form a group of people who showed leadership abilities and were accepted by their fellow workers; this group had to have the feeling "that we can break through."

As soon as the organizing committee of 60 was established, these individuals began a person-to-person campaign within the hospital. By early June, 500 to 600 workers, comprising a majority of the employees, had joined the union.

Local 1199 then attempted to devise tactics to show management the feeling of the workers and to indicate that, unless recognition was to come from management, the workers, in desperation, would be willing to strike. They also wanted to show that for once there was a union willing to put money and manpower behind the workers.

To show their strength as well as give the workers a feeling of unity, the union began to call demonstrations before and after work; the workers would come in early, march up and down for an hour or so, and then march into work. The same was done after work. Somewhat later the workers refused to eat lunches in the hospital dining rooms and ate at the union headquarters which had been established near the hospital. According to union sources, nurses, doctors, and interns joined in the union boycott of the dining rooms, and they estimated that the boycott was 95 percent effective. As a third approach to show their power, the union had the workers picket in mass formation from 6:00 to 10:00 A.M.—a period during which the workers were suppossed to be at work—and then the workers would file en masse into work. The demonstrations during working hours were 95 percent effective, a union leader stated. These activities continued throughout the summer and fall.

The union's position among the workers improved, according to union sources, because management in this hospital was quite liberal. Management did not attempt any direct interference with the activities of the union, such as discharge or other forms of discrimination, which might have increased workers' fear of supporting the unions.

After various pressure tactics and a strike vote by the employees, union and hospital leaders in conjunction with the city's labor commissioner, held a series of meetings. They decided to hold an election to see if the union actually represented the majority of the employees. In December, with 95 percent of the nonprofessional employees voting, 628 voted to support the union and 31 were opposed. The hospital signed a contract recognizing Local 1199 as the bargaining agent for the hospital's 850 nonprofessional, technical, and office employees. The contract included, among other items, a maintenance-of-membership clause; a $30 per month raise over the two-year period of the contract, and an increment system with raises of up to $30 over the two years (this figure varying with the labor grade); a full grievance procedure with arbitration as the final step, seniority provisions, and a 40-hour work week with time and one half for all hours over 40. Under this contract the minimum hiring rate was $40 per week with a $5 per week increase after the first month and another $5 at the end of the sixth month.

The signing of an agreement between Montefiore Hospital and the union had an electrifying effect on the hospital workers in New York City. No longer was there a strong negative feeling or fear among the workers which a union would have to dispel.

The union immediately enlarged its hospital staff. Assisting in the campaign were some 500 drugstore members of Local 1199 who appeared at hospital gates early in the morning to distribute leaflets and talk union with the hospital workers. The response to the union was overwhelming, not unlike the organizing campaigns which took place in the mass production industries in the 1930s. As one union leader stated, "We did a mail-order business in organizing and received 6,000 to 7,000 membership cards in the mail." All of the organizing material was published in both English and Spanish.

Excerpts from an article by Dan Wakefield entitled, "Victims of Charity," which appeared in *The Nation* on March 14, 1959, provide some feeling for the movement that took place among the hospital workers as well as additional material on the hospital campaign:

        ✿   ✿   ✿   ✿   ✿

Local 1199 . . . was distributing cards and leaflets at forty-one of the city's eighty-one voluntary hospitals. Meetings were scheduled nearly every night . . . for workers from hospitals all over the city. Requests for information grew—especially from Puerto Rican workers—as *El Diario de Nueva York,* the largest Spanish language daily in the city, published more stories and editorials on what it called "La Cruzada de Local 1199."

"La Cruzada" in many ways is the only union-organizing drive of the fifties that the word "crusade," in any language, seems appropriate to attach to without provoking a tongue in the cheeks of the organizers, or a flush in the cheeks of the reporters looking on. To walk into one of these organizing meetings is to walk into a time of the five-and-a-half and six-day week, the wages under a dollar an hour, the fears of firing from the boss for "talking union," and the almost revival-meeting enthusiasm of workers suddenly awakened to a way out of their plight.

. . . An organizer . . . was telling them . . . , "It is no secret that till recently workers in this city felt a hospital job was one you come into, save a little, and go on. Everyone felt there was no future in hospitals. Now, for the first time, they know that if they organize well enough they can get decent wages and conditions until they can look on hospital work as a job where they can be treated as respectable human beings."

        ✿   ✿   ✿   ✿   ✿

Before the questioning was over, there arose the problem that comes up in all these sessions—the balking of the white-collar and "professional" workers. Clerks and lab technicians don't fare much better than the other workers, but in the grand old tradition, attempt to supplement their income with pride through distinction from the masses. College-trained lab technicians usually make less than $50 a week in these hospitals, but along with the office workers, they are the last to accept the union. It was the constant task of the organizers to remind the other workers that the white-collar brothers and sisters usually didn't make enough to keep their collars white.

The Lenox Hill meeting was about to break up . . . when a lady hesitantly raised her voice to ask what seemed to be a possibly embarrassing question: "Some of the ladies heard they have to pay dues and a big fee to get in the union, and I don't know what to answer 'em." It was the organizer's pleasure to assure the assemblage that "We're not asking hospital workers to give us one penny for dues or anything else—until the day we get a contract for them with better wages and conditions. Then, our dues are $3 a month; but the rest of the union has decided that the hospital workers are getting so little to begin with that they won't have to pay an initiation fee at all."

. . . There to express the shame of neglect and promise of fulfillment from the city's organized labor movement was Morris Iushewitz, secretary of the Central Labor Union Council of New York, who admitted that the 30,000 unorganized toilers in the voluntary hospitals are the "shame of the labor movement" of this city.

Davis told the hall that they were finally making their way out of the wilderness: "I don't know of any organizing drive that took on the kind of crusading spirit that you have—it's taken exactly three weeks and two days to get the majority signed up at Mount Sinai. . . . This is the beginning of a new day—a new day of dignity and self-respect. The hospitals will never be the same and the workers will never be the same."

✿   ✿   ✿   ✿   ✿

After their long sleep, the hospital workers have awakened with impatience and outrage. There is still a long way to go before the traditional nonunion front of the voluntary hospitals is broken, but the first break has come and thousands of workers are knocking at the white-painted walls. Already a major step toward better conditions has been brought about by the union drive through a $12,000,000 increase in the city's payments to voluntary hospitals, announced last month by the mayor. The city contributes $16 a day for each ward patient in the voluntary hospitals, but the cost of maintaining these patients is $24 a day. The new grant will mean an increase to $20 a day for each ward patient, effective July 1; and in three more years the grant will rise to $24 a day. It has been the argument of the nonprofit voluntary institutions that they already operate at deficit, and can't afford to increase workers' wages. The union can now point to the increase as a source to be used for this purpose.

The union's organizing drive was accompanied by an extensive publicity campaign aimed at impressing the public with the plight of the hospital workers. The *New York Times* editorial for March 7, 1959, part of which follows, is representative of the position taken by the press and the public in general:

✿   ✿   ✿   ✿   ✿

Obviously the nonprofit hospitals face an acute problem in granting wage increases—with all their costs rising ever closer to the limits of income from charitable giving and from charges to their patients. Also, the thought of a strike, even by the nonprofessional employees, is naturally upsetting to the nerves.

But why should workers performing the same kind of jobs as in private employment be asked to be philanthropists by accepting much lower wages and the human sufferings that follow? And why should collective bargaining be denied them when that is a policy overwhelmingly approved by the American public? As for a hospital strike, the likelihood is exceedingly remote. Surely, if one did occur, an outraged public opinion, not to mention action by the courts, would quickly put a stop to it—and hamper further unionization as well.

Those wise in the ways of labor-managment relations know that, given widespread employee dissatisfaction and a truly representative organization, it is far better to deal with a union than to resist it. Formal grievance procedures and two way communications alone can often do a great deal to increase morale and effective job performance. To slam the door shut on such advantages may well have precisely the opposite effect in the voluntary hospitals.

The tremendous reaction of the hospital workers and the wide public attention given to the hospital problems had one serious negative effect on the union; it instigated a unification of the hospitals within their association, the Greater New York Hospital Association, in opposition to the efforts of the union. The hospitals had not unified in support of Montefiore as, according to one hospital official, they felt that unionization would not become a general problem. When the hospitals saw the Montefiore situation turn into a larger movement they consolidated their opposition to 1199.

The union leaders had considered a hospital-by-hospital organizing campaign and this might not have consolidated the opposition. However, they later concluded that the mass movement and widespread organizing was to their benefit because it focused the public's attention on the situation, and the hospital drive became a crusade and not solely "a union's attempt to organize some hospital workers." Also, during the campaign Local 1199 received extensive support from other unions; this support might not have been forthcoming if the campaign had not been as widely publicized or as massive.

Although the union had a large staff to use in organizing and was willing to expend considerable sums of money, it could not carry on a campaign in 30 or 40 hospitals at once. Also, having large numbers of signed membership cards did not mean that the union had a strong operating unit in the hospitals. The union therefore, after the first burst of activity, decided to retrench and consolidate its position.

The union established four subheadquarters near hospitals in which it had strong worker support. Operating through these centers, the union staff developed its local leadership and established an organizing committee for each hospital. Demonstrations, similar to those used at Montefiore, were carried out to show the strength and unity of the workers to the hospital administrators as well as to the workers themselves.

The union concentrated its efforts on about 15 hospitals. As a majority was reached in each of these institutions, Leon Davis sent a letter to the administrators stating that Local 1199 represented a majority of their employees and requesting that they meet with the union to discuss recognition and a contract. The hospital administrators refused to meet with the union. On innumerable occasions the union also attempted personal contacts with various people affiliated with the hospitals to establish conferences with management, but these too were unsuccessful. As one union leader stated, the issue became, "Will they talk to us? The hospital answer was, no, that they would not meet the union and that they would not recognize the union." By April 1, 1959, the union claimed a majority of 15 hospitals and the memberships at five had already voted to strike if union recognition was not forthcoming.

The Greater New York Hospital Association advised its member hospitals to refrain from dealing with the union. According to law the hospitals were not required to recognize the union. A *Wall Street Journal* article on April 2, 1959, reported on the hospitals' position.

✿　✿　✿　✿　✿

"We don't deny that we pay a low wage," says Joseph Terenzio, the tense, dark-haired young executive director of Knickerbocker Hospital. "We want to pay higher wages but we are paying as much as we can right now." He points to a chart sketching in red ink more than five years of ascending deficits. "What do these union people expect us to do, open up a trap door in the floor and pull out a big bag of money?"

Dr. I. Magelaner, executive director of Jewish Hospital of Brooklyn, says flatly, "Wage increases cannot be given when the money does not exist."

✿　✿　✿　✿　✿

. . . So far, most of the hospitals have taken the position that they will not deal with the unions in any way. This stand apparently is based on hospital administrators' contentions that the unions, if recognized, would interfere with the care of patients.

"Everyone in a hospital, from the janitor to the head nurse, has one purpose, the care of patients," argues New York Hospital's Dr. Pratt in a calm, patient voice. "We do not want a third party—a union or anyone else without responsibility—to stand between the patient and the people who are charged with his care."

Unions, some other hospital officials speculate, might want to set up hiring halls where union officials could determine who goes to work in a hospital—or unions might want to have a firm say about whether an employee should or should not be fired.

However, the main ground for opposition to the union drive undoubtedly is financial. Hospital leaders in New York like to point to Minneapolis as an example of what might happen if union demands are granted.

Costs per patient per day, at hospitals where Local 113 of the Building Service Employees Union has obtained a contract, are estimated at $38 to $40, compared with the $27 to $35 in New York City. In Minneapolis, orderlies earn $250 a month to start and $266 after two years. Unskilled workers such as dishwashers earn $235 monthly and $251 after two years. A hospital official in Minneapolis figures this is $60 to $80 a month more than in nonunion hospitals in "comparable cities."

The impact is equally pronounced in Blue Cross rates in Minneapolis. An official of Swedish Hospital there reports, "Our Blue Cross full family group contract is around $10 a month, probably the highest for comparable coverage in the nation." In New York, it is $5.34 and roughly comparable plans cost $9 monthly in Denver, $5.75 in Durham, N.C., and $9.55 in Fargo, N.D., according to other hospital officials. (Blue Cross' health coverage is handled by 25 different regional member associations; benefits offered by these associations often vary slightly so premium comparisons are not completely indicative of the respective costs of coverage.)

Similarly, in the San Francisco-Oakland area about 23 hospitals with a work force of 2,900 employees are unionized. The average in-patient cost is slightly over $40 a day per patient; according to W. J. Kramer, executive secretary of the San Francisco Hospital Conference. He says costs have been rising 4% to 5% a year and he expects them to go up another 4% by 1960. However, Mr. Kramer believes the steady wage increases there are not due so much to unionization as to San Francisco's "generally high wage levels." Hospital wages there start at $58.90 a week for the lowest-scaled employees.

Wage levels comparable to these would have an immediate effect on New York's already deficit-ridden hospitals. Last year, for example, New York Hospital had an operating deficit of more than $1 million. Knickerbocker Hospital, with operating costs of $2 million a year, went into the red by $156,000.

To get cash to cover the deficits, New York hospitals are having to borrow from the principal of their endowment funds, which generally have no restrictions on their use, in addition to using interest on their endowment funds and soliciting contributions from the public.

They also are pushing hard to get a 20% boost in the amount the local Blue Cross plan pays the New York hospitals. This figure now amounts to $26 a day for a patient with Blue Cross coverage.

Blue Cross itself is running into serious money troubles. Last year, New York's plan, known officially as the Associated Hospital Service of New York, asked state authorities for a 40% increase in premiums to cover mounting losses. The state, after hearing strong complaints from consumer groups and some labor unions, trimmed the allowable increase to 22%. The result, according to Blue Cross officials, was a deficit of more than $20 million in the Association's operations. The Association has indicated it will appeal again to the state for a higher premium very shortly.

Because of the swift spread of Blue Cross in recent years, hospitals have become increasingly dependent upon its payments. "About 40% of our in-patient income is from Blue Cross," says Dr. Pratt of New York Hospital.

Most nonprofit hospitals also are charity institutions, with indigent patients taking up a large share of the beds. In New York, the city pays $16 a day to the hospitals to handle these public-charge patients. But this falls far short of actual costs, say the administrators. New York City has promised to boost these payments to $20 a day in July and to make additional $1 and $2 yearly increases in the future.

With so much of their income controlled by the city governments and Blue Cross, hospitals say that a mere increase in their charges to private patients who are able to pay hospital bills will not be enough to solve their problems. "We raised our rates an average of 10% last year, and got only an additional $10,000 of income," says an official of Knickerbocker Hospital.

According to union sources the hospitals attempted to negate their organizing campaign by the following tactics:

1. publicly making promises to improve wages and working conditions;
2. attacking the union as being racketeers whose sole interest was taking money from the workers through dues;
3. firing workers who were active in organizing for the union; and
4. threatening injunctions because of their claim of the illegality of striking hospitals.

Soon after basic organization was established among the hospital workers, Local 1199 established a steward's body, parallel to the steward's body for drug employees, which became the chief policy and operating group within the hospital division. On April 8, after a meeting of this body, Davis announced a strike deadline of April 22 in six voluntary hospitals unless management recognized and bargained with the union. The hospitals involved were Mount Sinai, Jewish Hospital of Brooklyn, Bronx Hospital, Beth David, Beth Israel, and Lenox Hill. The union claimed to represent 3,450 of the 4,500 nonprofessional, technical, and office workers in these hospitals. The strike vote, according to the union, was 2,630 for, 111 against.

The union also claimed majorities at Knickerbocker, Flower-Fifth Avenue, Beth-El, Polyclinic, University, and Long Island Jewish Hospital.

The strike deadline announcement heightened interest in the hospital situation. The press, in general, called upon the hospitals to negotiate with the union. Mayor Wagner became increasingly involved and began a series of conferences with the parties. Since the hospital administrators would not meet with Local 1199's officers, Harry Van Arsdale, Jr., and

Morris Iushewitz, president and secretary respectively, of the City Central Labor Council, and William Michelson of District 65, represented Local 1199 in these conferences.

A number of proposal's were presented for settlement of the strike issues, including one from the *New York Times;* but the hospital administrators rejected any compromise plan that would in any way mean recognition of the union. The position of the hospitals was that they rejected any third party—such as a labor union—which might intervene between hospitals and their patients. Davis stated that he was willing to submit to a representation election and, if the union won, to write a no-strike clause into contracts and submit all contract and contract renewal disputes to arbitration.

On April 21 the mayor held an all-day conference with the parties. At this conference he proposed a three-man fact-finding board which would investigate the issues and make recommendations. The union agreed to a two-week postponement of the strike, and the hospital administrators agreed to present the plan to their boards of trustees for a decision.

During the two-week interval numerous individuals and organizations called upon the hospitals to accept the mayor's fact-finding proposal. Among the individuals were Mrs. Franklin D. Roosevelt, former Senator Herbert A. Lehman, Senator Jacob K. Javits, and representatives of the NAACP and various religious groups.

During this same period the New York Blue Cross added three leading labor officials to its board of directors. At that time the New York City Central Labor Council, which was supporting the demands of the hospital workers, was opposing Blue Cross' attempts to increase its rates.

Another interesting issue was the threat by the Amalgamated Clothing Workers to cut off their normal "substantial" support of the Federation of Jewish Philanthropies if the federation-affiliated hospitals continued to refuse to engage in collective bargaining with the union. All but two of the six strike-threatened hospitals were federation affiliated.

On May 5, three days before the strike deadline, the hospitals, in rejecting Mayor Wagner's plan, stated:

1. That they were not required to bargain,
2. That having a union meant possible strikes which would interfere with the operations of the hospitals,
3. That the hospitals should not and could not bargain because of their financial plight since the union would not take cognizance of this and other hospital problems, and
4. That they would carry out a program to improve the wages and working conditions of their employees.

The program was:

1. *Wages.* The increase of $4 in the payments made by the city to voluntary hospitals would be devoted to increasing wages and hiring rates of hospital employees.
2. *Minimum rates.* No employee would be hired or paid less than $1 an hour.
3. *Hours.* No employee's regular work week would exceed 40 hours.
4. *Overtime.* Overtime rates could be established for any work in excess of 40 hours per week.
5. *Rate ranges.* Job grades would be established with suitable rate ranges and with equitable progressions within the ranges.
6. *Fringes.* Practices in regard to holidays, vacations, sick leave, insurance, etc., vary from hospital to hospital . . . each hospital will review such practices and, in consultation with an advisory committee representing all the voluntary hospitals, will endeavor to improve these practices wherever equitable and feasible.
7. *Discrimination.* The hospitals will make known to their employees their recognition of the right of any employee to join or remain a member of a union without fear of discrimination.
8. *Seniority.* At each hospital a list of employees in accordance with their seniority will be prepared. Seniority is defined as the amount of continuous employment within a job classification.
9. *Grievance procedure.* The hospitals will provide for their employees appropriate grievance and appeal procedures for processing personal grievances regarding working conditions or individual wage adjustments.
10. *Permanent administrative committee.* [With the committee composed of people chosen by the hospitals] to supervise the proper and fair effectuation of the above program; and to engage annually . . . in a review of the wage levels and personnel policies; to engage such professional assistance and advice as it may deem necessary, and to recommend improvements or modifications in light of the various economic developments of the last year and the economic circumstances of the individual hospitals.

Davis answered the hospitals:

> . . . Local 1199 has made it abundantly clear that if the hospitals would submit to arbitration by an impartial board and agree to abide by its recommendations, there need not now or ever be a strike in any hospital . . . if a strike proves necessary as appears likely now, the fault will lie exclusively with the callous and stubborn men whose opposition to unions leads them to endanger the entire community.

The immediate public and press reaction, although there was strong support for the hospital workers, was that there should not be a strike against the hospitals. *The New York Times* editorialized:

> These terms [the improvements proposed by the hospitals] still fall short of what the union has asked—namely, union recognition and collective bargaining. No issue, however, is important enough, or provocation great enough, to justify a strike that would hamper the recovery of helpless invalids.

Upon notifying the mayor of their answer, the hospitals applied for and received court orders staying a walkout at the six hospitals. The order called on the union to show why the stay as well as a temporary injunction should not be issued. The orders were not served, however, as "Davis' whereabouts were unknown."

The mayor continued in his attempts to find a basis of settlement which would avert the threatened strike.

In viewing the question of striking, the leaders of Local 1199 were not concerned with the possibility of personal imprisonment but were reluctant to call a strike as it might involve serious consequences, such as loss of jobs and imprisonment, for some workers. For this reason, the leaders stated, they told the membership of their sentiments and left the final decision on striking to a vote of the stewards' body. On the evening preceding the strike deadline the stewards voted to strike.

On May 8, 1959, the six hospitals were struck. Two weeks later picketing began at Flower-Fifth Avenue Hospital. Union sources stated that this hospital was not struck with the original group because its management was meeting with the union and they felt that an agreement would be reached. The union sources stated further that it was pressure from the hospital association on Flower-Fifth Avenue which thwarted the settlement efforts.

Every major newspaper in New York City, except one, condemned the strike. *The New York Times* called for a law prohibiting strikes by hospital employees and noted that "the union's contemptuous disregard of court injunctions has made an already ugly situation worse. Whatever public sympathy the union may have developed has now been largely wiped out."

Contempt proceedings were started against Davis and other union officials. Davis was still not to be found and there was a series of postponements in the court actions. Since the court orders had not been personally served on union officials, there was disagreement as to whether the strike was illegal. The hospitals claimed "substituted service" of the court orders.

Although there was some feeling that the hospital workers had lost public support by striking, they did receive asistance from many sources; other unionists joined their picket lines, unions lent manpower and gave money, food and money were donated by the public, the building trades unions stopped work on hospital construction, and other unionists such as the laundry workers refused to cross the picket lines. Over the course of the strike, labor contributions amounted to $100,000 with an additional $25,000 from other sources. District 65 lent twelve organizers; Local 3, International Brotherhood of Electrical Workers, lent three organizers; and the regional office of the AFL-CIO, two organizers. No attempt was made to have the Teamsters Union honor the picket lines.

The union claimed that its strike was 90 percent effective, while the hospitals claimed that their service was not affected. It is doubtful that the strike remained 90 percent effective over its entire life. Similarly, hospital service must have been affected, and increasingly so over time, since the hospital staffs were reduced, frozen dinners were served, paper plates were used, little cleaning was done, and deliveries and admissions were reduced. The hospitals did receive a great deal of volunteer assistance to replace the strikers, though union sources claim (and they say that this information was acquired from management) that on the important tasks this assistance was more a hindrance than help.

The union attempted to guard against the consequences of being charged with a calamity that could be traced to the strike by volunteering to have members perform emergency services at the request of any doctor. This offer was accepted in several instances.

The mayor continued in his efforts to promote a settlement. Most of the settlement plans presented excluded any direct union recognition but included grievance procedures in which the union could represent the employees. During the first weeks of the strike the hospitals rejected every proposition which in any way meant the involvement of the union in hospital activities. At one of the mayor's conferences a charge was levelled against management which was to become a recurring theme throughout the strike: that the hospitals were abusing minority groups.

Since five of the strike hospitals were in Manhattan, while one was in Brooklyn, the legal action was taking place in two courts. By May 15, the Manhattan court still had not issued the injunction which was requested by the hospitals. The judge had issued a series of temporary orders and there had been a number of postponements. In Brooklyn, however, an injunction was issued and the judge began hearings on why the officers of the union and strikers should not be held in contempt of court. These hearings were later postponed.

On May 20, the strikers voted on a hospital plan to settle the dispute. This plan included a proposal to arbitrate grievances with the union recognized in the arbitration step and only in that step. The plan also included the economic and fringe benefits which the hospitals had proposed earlier. The strikers vetoed this proposal because it did not include union recognition.

With the rejection of their offer by the strikers, the hospitals attempted to end the strike through legal action. After Davis' attendance at the strikers' meeting, he was served with a legal order from the Brooklyn court to show cause why he should not be cited for contempt of court. The Manhattan judge ordered an immediate trial for a permanent injunction.

The union began a campaign of secondary boycotts at the sites of businesses owned by trustees of the struck hospitals. Such establishments as Macy's, Blumstein's Department Store, and the offices of Webb & Knapp were picketed.

A series of services aside from strike benefits and food packages were arranged for the strikers by the union. The daily strike bulletins, which included news and union announcements, also noted the availability of free medical care through the Health Insurance Plan of Greater New York, reimbursement of bus fare, emergency dental care, and the extension of credit from credit bureaus and landlords for strikers.

In the Brooklyn court action Davis was found guilty of contempt of court, and a 15-day prison sentence was ordered. However, the punishment was never executed. In Manhattan an injunction was issued but was never enforced. It became obvious that no one would act on the court orders. To jail the union leaders would probably only serve to increase the already increasing public support for the strikers, and also there were too many strikers to jail. Similarly, with the strikers composed largely of blacks and Puerto Ricans and the growing charges of "abuse of minorities" and "economic segregation," no one wanted to take responsibility for any action against these groups.

At the beginning of June the mayor established a special committee to study the strike situation. On June 9 this committee made a series of recommendations for settlement of the strike. The report accepted the hospitals' previous economic proposals, which they had already instituted, as well as the plan for a permanent administrative committee, but added, ". . . any interested person, including representatives of any union, will have the right to appear before the permanent administrative committee during its annual review to present his views." In regard to grievances the committee stated:

> . . . There shall be established in each hospital a clearly stated grievance procedure proceeding from the first step in which the aggrieved employee presents his grievance to the appropriate supervisor to a second step in which the aggrieved employee presents his grievance to the personnel manager or administrator or other designated official of the hospital.
> The third step shall be to transfer the grievance to mediation by

two adjusters, one chosen by the hospital management and the other chosen by the employees in the hospital. The adjusters shall meet outside of the hospital unless they mutually agree otherwise.

If the two adjusters are unable to mediate the grievance they may by mutal agreement add a third adjuster chosen from a panel of responsible and experienced persons established by the parties. The function of the adjusters shall be wholly mediatory.

If the dispute is not settled by mediation it shall go on to arbitration and the aggrieved employee shall be entitled to representation before the arbitrator or arbitrators by anyone he may designate. The arbitrator's decision shall be final. This proposal was accepted by the union but rejected by the hospitals.

In Manhattan the withdrawal of the judge from the strike case meant the presiding of a new judge over the hospitals' attempts to acquire contempt citations against the union. On June 13, in a somewhat surprising turn of events, Justice Henry Epstein upheld the right of voluntary hospital workers to organize, engage in collective bargaining, and strike when management refused to resolve their problems. The full text of the decision is found in the Appendix.

On June 22, 1959, an agreement was reached in settlement of the 46-day-old hospital strike. The important clauses are reproduced below:

1. *Wage increases and minimum rates.* No employee will be hired or paid less than $1.00 per hour and a wage increase of at least $2.00 per week shall be given to each employee whose wage rate has not been increased by $2.00 or more per week by lifting the minimum hourly rate to $1.00. All employees will continue to receive the advances in wages already put into effect by the hospitals. Commitments made by individual hospitals prior to and during the strike relative to wages, working conditions and fringe benefits will be full honored and enforced.

2. *Regular work week and overtime.* On and after July 1, 1959, no employee's regular work week will exceed 40 hours. As of July 1, 1959, overtime rates of time and one-half will be established for any work in excess of 40 hours per week.

3. *Permanent Administrative Committee.* A Permanent Administrative Committee of 12 members to be composed of six Hospital Trustees to be named by the Greater New York Hospital Association and six representatives of the public not associated with the Hospitals or Labor to be designated by the Chief Judge of the New York Court of Appeals will be established for the following purposes: (*a*) to supervise the proper and fair effectuation of the above program; (*b*) to engage annually, 60 days prior to July 1, 1960, and July 1 of each year thereafter, in a review of the wage levels, job grades, rate ranges, fringe benefits, seniority rules and personnel policies then prevailing in each of the voluntary hospitals; to engage such professional assistance and advice as it may deem necessary in the furtherance of its task; and to recom-

mend to each of the hospitals on July 1st of each year improvements or modifications in existing wage levels and personnel practices in the light of the various economic developments of the past year and the economic circumstances of the individual hospitals. Any interested person, including representatives of any union, will have the right to appear before the Permanent Administrative Committee during its annual review to present his views.

4. *Grievances.* There shall be established in each hospital a clearly stated grievance procedure proceeding from the first step, in which the aggrieved employee presents his grievance to his appropriate supervisor, to a final step in which he presents his grievance to the Personnel Manager or administrator, or other designated official of the hospital. If unresolved at the final step of the hospital's grievance procedure, a grievance may be submitted to mediation and arbitration outside the hospital before a person, who shall act as mediator and arbitrator, to be appointed as hereinafter provided. In such mediation and arbitration the aggrieved employee may be represented by anyone he may designate. Upon such submission outside the hospital the representative of the aggrieved employee and the designee of the hospital may first jointly attempt to resolve the grievance without the participation of the mediator and arbitrator. The arbitrator's decision shall be final.

The person who acts as mediator and arbitrator shall be selected in accordance with the Voluntary Labor Arbitration Rules of the American Arbitration Association. The arbitrator shall have jurisdiction only over disputes arising over grievances as hereinafter defined and shall not have the power to alter, amend or vary any rules, regulations or provisions established by the hospital.

Grievances, including those subject to arbitration, are defined as individual grievances arising out of the interpretation, application or claimed breach of the rules and regulations in the hospital, including the provisions that are a part of this Statement of Policy, provided, however, that dismissals based upon lack of professional competence or incompetence, including all matters involving relations with or conduct of any employee towards patients, shall not be subject to the grievance procedure nor to arbitration except when the employee claims that the dismissal has been made for reasons other than professional competence or incompetence, in which case that issue, as distinguished from the question of professional competence or incompetence, may be submitted to the grievance procedure, with the burden of proof upon the employee.

5. *Wage structures.* Not later than October 1, 1959, each hospital shall establish job grades with suitable rate ranges and with equitable progression within the ranges, shall review practices in regard to holidays, vacations, sick leave, insurance, etc., endeavoring to improve these practices wherever equitable and feasible, and shall establish seniority rules. Interested persons, including the representatives of any union, may present their views to the Permanent Administrative Committee and the Committee may make recommedations to each hospital on these matters.

The seven struck hospitals signed the Statement of Policy. Some of the other 78 voluntary hospitals indicated that they would sign. This number included many Catholic hospitals in which Local 1199 had no organization. It remained for the other hospitals, most of whom at least had union organization committees among their workers, to predict what the effect of signing or not signing would be, and to decide what course of action they should follow.

APPENDIX

Supreme Court, New York County
Epstein, J.:

Five petitions have been addressed to this court seeking to punish defendants for contempt of court. The contempt charged is willful disobedience to an order of the court. Injunctive relief is also sought against the picketing by defendants and the union. On the argument of these motions this court gave counsel for both sides the following comment of the court with questions to be answered.

REMARKS TO LITIGATING COUNSEL

There have been few issues before the court in recent times as fraught with the public interest, and as likely to have lasting effect on the public welfare as the one now before this court. It is vital, therefore, that the issue be determined so that, within the applicable laws, the public welfare may best be protected.

The interests involved in the instant case are several, though partially overlapping—namely: The Public, The Patients, and The Employees. Obviously, the public embraces the other two categories, which are sections of the public.

The hospitals' Boards of Governors are representatives of the contributors to the voluntary nonprofit hospitals, though they are neither selected by the contributors nor are their acts in any way directed or controlled by the contributors. The members of these boards are, in most instances, public spirited persons who have volunteered to serve.

It is not necessarily a fact that either these Boards or the employees acting jointly are best able to determine the public welfare. But we should be able to assume that the employees acting jointly can determine what is best for their own interests, while the Boards should be able to determine what is best for hospital management.

Those two interests may well be in conflict, and when they are, then the public welfare must be the over-riding consideration. It is, of course, true that in a democracy the rights and welfare of the minority are as important and require as much protection as do the rights and welfare of the majority.

These answers are before the court and have been given consideration in arriving at the determination hereinafter set forth. This court has been most careful in its deliberation and has given the deep respect due the views of colleagues as expressed in granting the relief out of which these contempt proceedings arose.

The Constitution of New York State was amended by the people on November 8, 1938, effective January 1, 1939, by adding section 17 to article I, said article bearing the title "Bill of Rights." Two sentences of that section 17 bear directly upon the issue herein and the impact of that language cannot be mistaken:

> Sec. 17. *Labor of human beings is not a commodity nor an article of commerce and shall never be so considered or construed.*
>
> ❋   ❋   ❋   ❋   ❋
>
> *Employees shall have the right to organize and to bargain collectively through representatives of their own choosing.*

This amendment was voted by the people in the days of a great economic depression and at a time when labor exploitation was a critical issue. It grants a right to "employees"—a right which is in the present proceedings questioned by petitioners. *No legislative enactment; no regulation of statutory bodies or private institutions; no court action can stand in violation of that command of the State Constitution.* Nor should a court permit such explicit language to be rendered meaningless by its action.

This significant amendment was not enacted before, but *after* the Legislature had acted—with what to this court is an equally clear impact—on the subject of labor disputes and the rights of employees. Section 876-a of the Civil Practice Act was adopted in 1935 and was clearly designed to limit the courts in granting injunctions in controversies between management and labor. Subdivision 10, as provided by Chapter 359 of the Laws of 1939 (*immediately after the effective date of the Constitutional provision referred to*) reads:

> 10.   When used in this section, and for the purpose of this section:
>
> a.   A case shall be held to involve or to grow out of a labor dispute when the case involves persons who are engaged in the same industry, trade, craft or occupation or who are employees of one employer; or who are members of the same or an affiliated organization of employers of employees; whether such dispute is between one or more employers or associations of employers and one or more employees or associations of employees; between one or more employers or associations of employers and one or more employers or

associations of employers; or between one or more employees or associations of employees and one or more employees or associations of employees; or when the case involves any conflicting or competing interests in a "labor dispute" (as hereinafter defined) of "persons participating or interested" therein (as hereinafter defined).

b. A person or association shall be held to be a person participating or interested in a labor dispute if relief is sought against him or it and if he or it is engaged in the industry, trade, craft or occupation in which such dispute occurs, or is a member, officer or agent of any association of employers or employees engaged in such industry, trade, craft or occupation.

c. The term "labor dispute" includes any controversy concerning terms or conditions of employment, or concerning the association or representation of persons in negotiating, fixing, maintaining, changing or seeking to arrange terms or conditions of employment, or concerning employment relations, or any other controversy arising out of the respective interests of employer and employees, regardless of whether or not the disputants stand in the relation of employer and employee.

Can there be any doubt that we here are dealing with a bona fide "labor dispute" under the statute and the Constitution? If so, we seek in vain for any express or implied exemption of voluntary hospitals or other like employers. In fact the Court of Appeals has said in unmistakable language: *"Jurisdiction to issue any such injunction is, in so many words, denied to the Courts. It makes no difference who is the plaintiff."* (*Schivera* v. *Long Island Lighting Co.,* 296 N.Y. 26, 31.)

Neither in the Constitution's "Bill of Rights" for labor nor in the statutory enactment of section 876-a of the Civil Practice Act do we find any concept of nonprofit institutions exemption. Nor is there any such exemption to institutional employers who care for indigent sick. *Jewish Hospital of Brooklyn* v. *Doe,* 252 App. Div. 581 does not truly reflect the operation of the Constitutional provision and that of section 876-a of the Civil Practice Act. Nor can the provisions of section 715 of the Labor Relations Act of the State of New York be read into section 876-a of the Civil Practice Act. The exclusion of charitable hospitals from the coverage of section 715 of the Labor Relations Law (enacted by ch. 443, Laws of 1937, amd. by ch. 764, L. 1955) in no manner calls for a cross-reference and exclusion from the clear inclusive language of section 876-a of the Civil Practice Act. All these provisions must be read in the light of employees' unqualified constitutional rights of collective bargaining (*Trustees of Columbia University* v. *Herzog,* 181 Misc. 903 (reversed on other grounds, 269 App. Div. 24); Re New York State Labor Relations Board, 175 Misc. 95).

The city of New York for its own institutions (city hospitals), in a more isolated and protected area, has recognized the value of the collective recognition of employee spokesmen. And the ghost of threatened strikes, raised by petitioners, is laid to rest in the record of the relations of respondent union through contracts with Montefiore Hospital and Maimonides Hospital. These latter have not suffered any impairment in services by virtue of the contractual relations with defendant union on behalf of the member employees.

Nor is the case of *Society of New York Hospital* v. *Hanson,* 185 Misc. 943, affd. 272 App. Div. 998, controlling, because there the employee representatives counsel conceded in that case section 876-a was not applicable. If, as this court in conscience is driven to hold, a real labor dispute exists, then no injunction may be granted without the conditions provided in section 876-a being met. Here the complaint concededly fails so to comply.

There is another, and while possibly regarded as "technical," yet a valid and clear basis for refusing to grant the contempt orders sought. In all but one of the cases here presented, amended complaints were served after the decisions in the injunctive proceedings were rendered. The injunctions ordered on May 25, 1959 were based on the original complaints. On May 21, 1959 amended complaints were served, adding a vital allegation that the defendant-union ratified or authorized the acts complained of. This was essential to jurisdiction for the orders sought (*McCabe* v. *Goodfellow,* 133 N.Y. 89; *Martin* v. *Curran,* 303 N.Y. 276; Carmody-Wait New York Practice, Vol. 10, p. 532; *Wood* v. *Cook,* 132 App. Div. 318). Also in the papers before this court now, defendants Joe Brown (Bronx Hospital), Edward Ayash (secretary-treasurer of defendant Union 1199), William J. Taylor (vice president of defendant Union 1199); George Goodman (division director of defendant Union 1199) swear they were never served with the petitions calling for their being held in contempt. Furthermore the editor of "1199 Drug News," Moe Foner, offers an affidavit pointing out his only duties have no connection with the acts complained of.

Article 19 of the Judiciary Law, section 753, provides that: "3. A part to the action . . . or other person . . . for any disobedience to a lawful mandate of the Court—" may be punished for contempt. If, therefore, defendants were within constitutional and statutory recognized conduct in striking and picketing the instant contempt proceeding must be deemed a nullity. The question is not one of fact, but one of law. The courts must obey the constitution mandate of article I, section 17 of the State of New York's Constitution and directions of section 876-a of the Civil Practice Act.

On the argument of these motions to punish for criminal contempt, counsel for petitioners, speaking for all of them, frankly and courageously admitted that the employees had the full right to organize and to become members of a union of their choice. To make that admission and then to refuse to discuss grievances with such collective representatives of the member-employees' choice, is to render the recognition meaningless. It is in effect telling employees they may freely organize and join a union, pay their dues, but can never have their union speak for them.

There are other vital considerations wholly overlooked by the hospital managements. The State Labor Relations Act expressly preserves to all employees the right to strike (S. 706, subd. 5). The Legislature in enacting section 876-a of the Civil Practice Act gave not the slightest indication of an intent to exempt nonprofit or charitable associations or corporations. Such an exemption could so simply have been written. But with the full impact of the constitutional restriction of 1938 before it, when the statute was amended in 1939, no such limitation was indicated. The courts can neither legislate—nor amend statutes when by decision such judicial amendment would contravene the Constitutional Bill of Rights to labor. This court will not indulge in such action, and its conscience forbids it to do so in the instant proceedings for criminal contempt.

Employees of voluntary hospitals do not have the protection of Civil Service Laws or procedures. Nor do they have the benefits derived from State or City public service. They must work out their own grievances and redress machinery. That must be done through dealings with the directorial and management staffs of the employer hospitals, none of which is subject to governmental control. Yet the City itself and at least two of the private institutions have and do maintain collective bargaining relations with the employees' union. For the management of the hospitals—plaintiffs—to take the course herein which they so forcefully pursue is more an echo of the 19th century than the last half of the 20th century.

Since the court feels impelled to hold that a "labor dispute" is here in issue within the meaning of section 876-a of the Civil Practice Act the complaints are fatally defective and no injunction or contempt orders may properly be issued thereon. (*Boro Park Sanitary Live Poultry Market, Inc.* v. *Heller,* 280 N.Y. 481, 485–486; *Bessert* v. *Dhuy,* 221 N.Y. 342, 365; *Exchange Bakery, etc.* v. *Rifkin,* 240 N.Y. 260.) Picketing is a form of freedom of speech by labor and may not be restricted by injunction absent other compelling factors not here present. (*Senn* v. *Tile Layers Union,* 301 U.S. 468, 478.) Petitioners herein refuse to accept the good faith of defendant-union in its stated willingness to waive any and all right to the strike weapon, if collective representation be accepted by the hospitals. The court cannot so indulge itself. Should such waiver be embodied in an agreement and then be violated—appropriate action can be had from this and other courts. Considerations favorable to this conclusion are found in *Young Women's Christian Asso-*

ciation v. *Jay Rubin,* etc., decided December 24, 1956 by Justice Mc-
Givern and *Railway Mail Association* v. *Corsi,* 293 N.Y. 315, 322–323.
Lest there be any doubts on the question of the employees' wishes
anent their union affiliation, the strike vote was by secret ballot in each
hospital separately, and the vote was overwhelming on the strike itself.
In Mount Sinai the vote was 956 to 59; in Beth Israel, 349 to 8; in
Lenox Hill, 372 to 16; in Bronx Hospital 247 to 6 and in Beth David,
180 to 4.

It is the considered view of this court that the motions to punish
for criminal contempt must be denied as a matter of law. Were the
determination to be reached as an exercise of discretion the same result
would follow.

Orders signed.

Dated, June 1959

EXHIBIT 1
Mt. Sinai management is sick, sick, sick, sick in the head!

Here is one example: Recently the Mt. Sinai Bosses issued a list of rules.
Rule number 7 reads like this: Employees are forbidden to act in "a disrespect-
ful manner toward any supervisor, *at any time, whether on or off hospital
premises.*"

How insane can they get! Of course this rule number 7 presents some
problems: How far off hospital premises should the worker take off his hat
to Management? Does the rule apply to the sea and air as well as land?
What shall we do about the moon? "No disrespect at any time?" Can't we
even dream bad dreams about them?

That isn't all. Mt. Sinai not only tells you how to behave on your own
time. It also regulates your outside income.

Night or week-end work outside of Mt. Sinai is strictly forbidden. How
could we think of another job? Aren't we all getting rich on the Mt. Sinai
salary?

MAYBE IT'S ABOUT TIME FOR A NEW SET OF RULES AT MT.
SINAI. Local 1199 has the following recommendations:

1. Every worker on the job should carry out the directions of supervisors,
   providing they do not directly menace the worker's health or safety.
2. In the case of unfair orders, the workers should obey, under protest, and
   then immediately notify the Union. We have a good supply of grievance
   forms for this purpose.
3. The workers' normal conversation inside the Hospital is not subject to
   Mt. Sinai censorship. He may talk about the weather, or the baseball
   scores or the union with equal freedom. The U.S. Constitution, guarantee-
   ing free speech is an even greater authority than the Mt. Sinai rule book.
4. Within the hospital, supervisors are entitled to normal courtesy and no
   more. No worker is compelled to smile at them, or kiss them, or polish
   their apples.

5. What a worker says, does, thinks, or earns one second after working hours and one fraction of an inch outside of hospital property is 100 percent his own business. SUPERVISORS WHO THEN INTERFERE DO SO AT THEIR OWN RISK.

Local 1199, Hospital Division
300 West 45th Street

oeiu/344
11/13/59

Harry Bridges[1]

ON MARCH 17, 1972, Harry Bridges, president of the International Long-shoremen's and Warehousemen's Union (Independent) considered the policy implications of a ruling made the previous day by the Federal Pay Board. As part of Phase II of the Nixon administration's Economic Stabilization Program, the board had reviewed a contract recently negotiated between the ILWU and the Pacific Maritime Association and ordered a 42 percent reduction in the agreement's first-year wage-increases.

The Pay Board's decision was dramatic because the contract it challenged had ended the longest and most acrimonious dock strike in American history—a 134-day walkout led by the 70-year-old Bridges, who had won the most lucrative settlement in his union's lifetime. Confronted now with the Pay Board decision, Bridges paused to review his position and plan his next move. He faced the immediate question of whether to defy the board, strike again, and risk court action and fines up to $5,000. But he recognized longer-term issues, too, concerning his impending retirement, the economic status of his constituency, the viability of the ILWU as a bargaining agent and political force, and the ability of organized labor to influence national policy.

[1] This case was prepared by Ira Goldstein and Professor James P. Baughman from publicly available materials as the basis for class discussion. It is not intended to illustrate either effectve or ineffective handling of an administrative situation. The cooperation of the International Longshoremen's and Warehousemen's Union (Ind.) and the Pacific Maritime Association are gratefully acknowledged.

Bridges and the ILWU

Alfred Renton ("Harry") Bridges confronted these issues proud of his reputation as a fighter. Articulate and pugnacious, he catapulted to national prominence during the Great Depression and had seldom been off the front page since.

As a dockworker in the 1920s, Bridges experienced the tactics by which employers of that era kept longshoremen dependent and disorganized: hiring by the day through employer-controlled "hiring halls"; enforcing membership in "company unions"; setting wages, hours, and working conditions by the job on "take-it-or-leave-it" terms with no binding precedents or cumulative benefits; "blacklisting" troublemakers; "breaking" strikes; localizing bargaining on a "port-by-port" basis.

Bridges fought this system as a local officer of the International Longshoremen's Association (AFL), but grew restive with that organization's lack of success—a failure he ascribed to elitism in leadership, a craft rather than an industrial orientation, pacifism, and accommodation. Encouraged by the prolabor posture of the Roosevelt administration and the militancy of the newly formed Congress of Industrial Organizations, Bridges took matters into his own hands. Between 1934 and 1938, he instigated and managed two massive West Coast dock strikes and a host of local skirmishes, seceded from the AFL, organized the ILWU within the CIO, and achieved the "coastwise solidarity" he sought when his ILWU (CIO) rather than the ILA (AFL) was certified by the National Labor Relations Board as the duly elected and sole bargaining agent for all Pacific Coast longshoremen. The ILA (AFL) continued to represent the Atlantic and Gulf Coasts.

From 1938 to 1948, Bridges continued to make news: battling employers over wages, hours, and working conditions; squabbling with other unions over jurisdictional and ideological issues; challenging the federal government's interpretations of labor law; and fighting a series of court actions to prevent his deportation as an "undesirable alien."

Bridges' weapon in the war against management was the strike (see Exhibit 1), and he won substantial gains for the ILWU: coastwise collective bargaining and uniform wages, hours, and work rules; abolition of company unions; joint union-management control of hiring halls; union preference in hiring; a six-day standard work week; a standard work day composed of 6 hours of straight time and two hours of overtime; "minimum call pay" (a worker was guaranteed at least four hours of pay if hired to work); a three-year contract; and increased wages which raised the average hourly straight-time wage for longshoremen from $0.956 (1934 settlement) to $1.82 (1948 settlement).

Paralleling Bridges' militant negotiations with employers were feuds with other labor leaders, notably Joe Ryan of the ILA (AFL) and Dave

Beck of the International Brotherhood of Teamsters (AFL). Bridges worked diligently to bring other groups within the ILWU besides the longshoremen, shipclerks, walking bosses (foremen), and watchmen who formed his original constituency. He wooed and won a large following among warehousemen and distribution workers; sugar-planting, harvesting, and mill workers; pineapple growing and processing workers; fishermen and cannery workers in California, Oregon, Washington, British Columbia, Alaska, and Hawaii. This aggressive conglomeration along industrial lines fit the philosophy of the CIO but involved Bridges in incessant jurisdictional warfare with the AFL. His militancy and outspoken support of the international labor movement also put him constantly at odds with the more nationalistic and accommodating posture characteristic of the majority of American labor leaders. (Even his fellow CIO leaders ultimately turned on him and expelled the ILWU in 1950.)

Bridges' differences with the federal government centered around interpretation of the Taft-Hartley Act (1947). The Wagner Act (1935) guaranteed labor's right to bargain collectively without outside interference and bolstered Bridges' cause during the recognition strikes of 1934–38. Taft-Hartley was another matter. In the words of one of its authors, it sought to make labor as "responsible" as the Wagner Act had made management.

Taft-Hartley outlawed the "closed shop," required certified unions to bargain collectively with their employers, made unions subject to "unfair labor practices" suits, created the Federal Mediation and Conciliation Service to "offer services in any dispute affecting interstate commerce or to intervene upon request," and authorized the president to obtain emergency 80-day injunctions restraining strikes while federal officers tried to settle disputes. The act also required unions to register their financial and election procedures with the Department of Labor and ordered their officials to sign affidavits stating that they were not and never had been members of the Communist party.

Bridges ran afoul of almost all of these provisions during the ILWU's strike of 1948. The preference given ILWU members in work assignments and the jointly controlled union-management hiring halls were assailed by employers and other unions as a closed shop. Bridges' view that they were not prevailed. President Truman invoked an 80-day "cooling-off period" in hopes of forestalling a strike. Bridges renamed it a "warming-up period," followed it with a 95-day coastwise walkout, and capped his performance by signing what he called "one of the finest trade union agreements ever made."

The anti-Communist affadavit required by Taft-Hartley was a sticking point. Bridges refused to sign, which only increased his critics' wrath. Since 1934, when his managerial and union opponents had alleged him to be a Communist, he had been under constant investigation by the

Department of Labor, the Department of Justice, and various congressional committees. Because he was Australian born, a lengthy series of deportation proceedings was instituted. Tens of thousands of pages of testimony were taken over an 11-year period, but Bridges won his case on appeal to the Supreme Court in 1945. Justice Frank Murphy wrote on that occasion, "Seldom if ever in the history of this nation has there been such a concentrated and relentless crusade to deport an individual because he dared to exercise that freedom which belongs to him as a human being and is guaranteed him by the Constitution."

Bridges filed for and was granted American citizenship in 1945 only to have it revoked in 1950 and be sentenced to five years in prison for his refusal to sign various anti-Communist affadavits. These matters dragged on (Bridges actually served 21 days in prison) until 1953, when the Supreme Court on appeal found for Bridges and restored his citizenship.

The mechanization and modernization agreements

Bridges' relationships with management pacified after the three-year settlement of 1948. Various employer groups merged into the Pacific Maritime Association in 1949 and a series of amicable settlements with the ILWU followed. Wages, hours, and benefits dominated the negotiations of the 1950s, but by 1960, automation had become the primary concern.

Pressed by rising costs and seeking faster "turnaround" in port, carriers and shippers were experimenting with containerization, bulk loading, and specialized packaging and handling in lieu of traditional piece-by-piece hand loading. Cognizant of the threat to ILWU jurisdiction and jobs, Bridges took the initiative in negotiating an "epochal" Mechanization and Modernization Agreement as part of a five-and-one-half-year contract with the PMA in 1960.

The "M and M Agreement" granted the longshoremen a "fair share" of the yield from automation. In return, they agreed to permit employers to install any new machine or method, provided only that the method was safe, that there was no speedup of the individual, and that the work was not "onerous." Subject to these safeguards, management was free to change any existing work rule which could be shown to prevent or to limit efficiency.

The PMA agreed to contribute into a fund $5 million annually for five and one-half years, beginning January 1, 1961. Three million dollars of each year's contribution was considered to be, in the union's terminology, the men's "share of the machine." This portion of the fund was to be used for early retirement, cash vesting, and death benefits. The remaining $2 million per year represented what the men received for "selling their property rights" in the work rules. This portion of the fund was to guarantee that "if a longshoreman's average weekly earnings fell below the equivalent of 35 straight-time hours as a result of mechanization and modernization, he would be paid the equivalent of 35 straight-time hours anyway."

Maximum possible security for the registered work force was provided in the following ways:

1. There was a flat guarantee against layoffs. Registration was frozen to those on the rolls in 1958 and placed on a coastwide instead of a port-by-port basis, thereby encouraging the movement of men from area to area.
2. The Agreement provided for voluntary early retirement, at age 62, with a monthly benefit of $220. At age 65, when Social Security was payable, the industry pension dropped back to $115. This provision encouraged "shrinking the workforce from the top," leaving more work for the younger men. If a man chose not to retire early, but continued to work until normal retirement, he received a lump sum of $7,920—the equivalent of $220 per month for his 36 months from age 62 to age 65.
3. If a sharp decline in work opportunity made it necessary, the parties could invoke compulsory early retirement. In this event, the men would receive $320 a month; the additional $100 intended to make early retirement more palatable.

The 1960 contract and M & M Agreement terminated on June 30, 1966. After 26 joint negotiating sessions, they were renewed to expire June 30, 1971.

Under the new M and M Agreement, as under the old, ship owners and stevedoring contractors were "freed of restrictions on the introduction of labor-saving devices, relieved of the use of unnecessary men, and assured of the elimination of work practices which impede the free flow of cargo or quick ship turnaround." The longshoremen received benefits designed "to protect them against the impact of the machine on their daily work or on their job security."

The annual contribution by the PMA was increased to $6.9 million and the entire fund was earmarked for early retirement and vesting. The 35-hour wage guarantee was dropped at the suggestion of the ILWU. Tonnage had increased beyond all expectations and the wage guarantee had never been used. Work never dropped to the point that the men earned less than 35 straight-time hours' pay. Indeed, together with the increased attrition rate, the rise in tonnage handled made it necessary to add some 2,000 men to the work force. Over the five and a half years during which the original agreement was in effect, approximately $13 million accumulated in the Wage Guarantee Fund. This money was distributed equally among the registered work force. On December 30, 1966, each man who was on the fully registered list on July 1, 1960 and June 30, 1966, received slightly more than $1,200.

The new agreement increased the early retirement benefit to $13,000, receivable at retirement at any time between ages 62 and 65. Since normal retirement age had been reduced from 65 to 63, it was anticipated that many more men would choose to retire before age 65.

Besides the changes in the M and M Agreement, there were changes in the regular pension plan and improvements in wage rates and fringe benefits. Normal retirement pension (to be paid in addition to any M and M benefits) was increased from $165 to $235 per month, and the age for voluntary retirement was reduced from 65 to 63. The basic straight-time wage rate was increased from $3.38 to $3.88 with additional $0.20 per hour raises to take effect in 1969 and 1970. With the last two hours of the standard eight-hour shift at overtime rates, this increased base weekly earnings for 40 hours from $152 to $193.

Exhibits 2 through 6 summarize trends in the Pacific Coast maritime industry during the lifespan of the M and M Agreements and contracts of 1960 and 1966. They provide a background for understanding subsequent events.

The 1970–71 negotiations

The ILWU (acting for 12,400 longshoremen and 1,900 clerks) and the PMA (acting for 122 shipping, terminal, and stevedoring companies) commenced negotiations eight months in advance of the June 30, 1971 contract expiration date in hopes of reaching an early settlement.

The ILWU's initial proposals included:

1. A $1.60 raise in the 1970 basic rate of $4.28 to be paid in two installments: $0.85 on July 1, 1971, and $0.75 on June 30, 1972.
2. A 40-hour guaranteed work week for all "fully registered" longshoremen.
3. A pension of $500 per month at age 62 after 25 years of service.
4. Expansion of medical and dental benefits.
5. Jurisdiction over all loading and unloading of containerized cargo on the waterfront (work currently done by members of the International Brotherhood of Teamsters).

The PMA countered with a 35-hour weekly guarantee and "substantially smaller" wage increases spread over three years. On the last issue, President Edmund J. Flynn granted that containerization had increased 26 percent over 1969 and had reduced jobs. He felt, however, that management was "in a no-man's land" between rival unions competing for the remaining jobs. He promised to "do our share to alleviate the uncertainties occasioned by fewer job opportunities," but urged Bridges and other union leaders to do their share "by seeking unselfish long-range plans which will avoid the debilitating efforts of jurisdictional strife."

At the ILWU's annual convention in April, the appearance of Thomas W. Gleason of the ILA (AFL) prompted merger speculation and talk of "one down—all down" mutual aid. But no strike resolution was passed. More attention was focused on an open split between Bridges and long-time ILWU treasurer Louis Goldblatt over finances and bargaining tactics.

Immediately after the convention, however, a caucus voted "not to enter into further negotiations unless PMA comes up with an offer which can be recommended to the rank and file . . . and to empower the negotiating committee to call for a strike vote effective July 1, if necessary." The ILWU's Coast Negotiating Committee did so, recommending a "yes." On June 25, by a vote of 9,317 to 343 a strike was approved, and on July 1, the ILWU "went out" coastwide for the first time since 1948.

The 1971–72 strike

Before the end of July, Bridges was reportedly discussing matters of mutual concern with ILA President Gleason, including a possible extension of the walkout to Atlantic and Gulf ports when the ILA's contracts expired on September 30. They clearly expected a lengthy campaign: "It takes a month or two to get everything shut up tight," Bridges said. "Then you've got a strike!"

By mid-August, 145 ships were idle in Pacific Coast ports and costing their owners from $4,000 to $15,000 per day. The Port of Los Angeles estimated its foregone revenues at $27,000 per day and anecdotes of adversely affected shippers were multiplying. Mazda Motors of America reported 3,000 lost sales as of August 3 and extra expenses of $250,000 to import 2,800 cars via Vancouver, Canada, and Ensenada, Mexico. A shipment of 21,000 pounds of Roquefort cheese en route to a Los Angeles producer of salad dressing was also diverted to Vancouver. No refrigerator trucks were available to bring it south and Vancouver's warehouses were full. Ultimately, the cheese went back to France with its buyer liable for three-way shipping costs—and no cheese.

Initial federal interest in the strike was confined to Department of Commerce officials who began to attribute portions of the American trade deficit to the strike's "dampening influence" on exports, and to Department of Defense representatives fearful of an interruption of supply lines to Vietnam. On August 15, however, in the dramatic announcement of his "New Economic Game Plan" and its 90-day wage-price freeze, President Nixon made a special point of asking strikers in the country to "cooperate" by returning to work. In a direct wire to the president, Bridges responded by blasting the Nixon program for putting "the burden of fighting inflation on the backs of the working people of the United States." So there would be no misunderstanding Bridges added: "The ILWU strike against the Pacific Maritime Association will continue in full force and effect until such time as a collective bargaining agreement is ratified by the membership."

On August 25, the ILWU and the PMA began formal negotiations. No progress had been reported by October 1 when the ILA struck Gulf and Atlantic ports. Bridges now stood at the head of the first nationwide dock strike in American history and the White House was threatening to invoke the Taft-Hartley Act to reopen the waterfront.

In an October 3 editorial, A. H. Raskin, the veteran labor reporter of the *New York Times*, offered some perceptive comments. Things were not quite what they seemed, Raskin argued. Underneath the strike "were topsy-turvy factors of a kind likely to be multiplied a thousandfold after November 13, when the country moves out of the present freeze into the vagaries of a still uncharted Phase Two in the long-term battle against inflation." Raskin raised doubts about the nature of Bridges' role:

> The walkout grew out of internal conflict in the ILWU between its president, Harry Bridges—once a symbol of all that was revolutionary in organized labor—and rank-and-file union militants who now consider him a "partner of the bosses" because he traded antiquated work rules for assured jobs, early retirement and other employee benefits when containerization altered traditional methods of cargo loading a decade ago.
>
> For all practical purposes, the Pacific Coast shipping companies were on the sidelines in this family quarrel; they were eager to sign a new pact, but they knew that any agreement would be voted down until Mr. Bridges got his own house in order.
>
> . . . employers in all three areas quickly let the White House know that the last thing they wanted was an invocation of the law.
>
> On the West Coast the employer resistance stemmed from a belief that a back-to-work injunction would be a "disaster" for Mr. Bridges in his efforts to subdue the ultramilitant wing of his union. The hope the Pacific shipping companies relayed to the Administration was that the threat of an injunction would be a spur toward fast agreement, but they cautioned that the issuance of an injunction would ice over the negotiating climate and give the anti-Bridges forces an opportunity to take over.

The same day as Raskin's editorial, President Nixon issued an executive order setting up a five-man board of inquiry "to assess the status of negotiations in the strikes" in accordance with his power under the Taft-Hartley Act. On October 6, he sought and received a 10-day temporary order restraining the ILWU from striking; this order was quickly superceded by an 80-day injunction under the "National Emergency" section of Taft-Hartley, to expire Christmas Day. The ILWU membership returned to work.

Phase two of the economic stabilization program

On October 7, a White House press release revealed the president's "post-freeze economic stabilization program" which would commence November 13. A major portion of that program was a plan to attain "equitable, noninflationary wage and salary adjustments." A Pay Board would regulate "all elements of compensation including wages, salaries, and fringe benefits." The board was "to develop over-all standards for wage and salary increases and selectively review major labor settlements which have a major impact on national wage developments." The board would include five representatives of labor, five representatives of management, and five members representing the public.

The Pay Board was instructed to "give maximum latitude to the exercise of free collective bargaining." However, after agreements had been reached in major bargaining units, the board was to "analyze and review the economic provisions of the contract to see that they are consistent with the guidelines." Where contract terms were found inconsistent with the guidelines, the board was to "secure compliance" or to "recommend the invocation of the sanctions provided by the Economic Stabilization Act of 1970 if the voluntary compliance of labor and management cannot be attained." These sanctions ranged from executive orders through judicial injunctions to fines of up to $5,000.

Presidents Bridges and Gleason responded immediately to President Nixon's announcement with a joint statement: Their membership would strike again if the Pay Board did not approve whatever agreement was ultimately reached and they would see to it "that gains won in collective bargaining are not taken away by governmental action under Phase Two."

Although the Taft-Hartley injunction expired on Christmas Day, the ILWU membership remained voluntarily on the job. On January 17, however, they went back on strike. The reasons for the renewal of the walkout and President Nixon's response are summarized in Exhibit 7. The flavor of the ILWU-PMA bargaining sessions is suggested by Exhibit 8.

On February 8, the PMA and the ILWU announced a tentative settlement. Eight days later, the ILWU's Coast Longshore Caucus (a 110-member executive committee) voted 68 percent in favor and 25 percent against recommending acceptance to the rank and file (7 percent of the caucus abstained). On February 19, the settlement was ratified by

71 percent of the ILWU rank and file. Major economic provisions of the settlement are summarized in Exhibit 9. Some of the economic consequences of the strike are estimated in Exhibit 10.

On February 21, the president signed the bill to force the striking longshoremen back to work, which Congress had approved a week earlier. The measure had no real effect, since the dock workers were back on their jobs. Nevertheless, the White House announced President Nixon's act as an important "symbolic gesture."

Pay Board review

Although the longshoremen were once again at work, Pay Board approval was still required before the new wage and benefit package could be put into effect. Bridges continued to threaten renewal of the strike if the settlement was cut. AFL-CIO president and Pay Board member George Meany also publicly warned the business and public members of the board that new dock strikes could result from their failure to allow the settlement.

ILWU arguments for approval pointed to gains made in productivity over the past decade which would make the raises noninflationary (see Exhibits 5 and 6). The PMA also urged the board to approve the full settlement. The employers' calculations indicated that the first-year wage and benefits package was a 20.6 percent increase over the previous average hourly labor cost (see Exhibit 11). Of this amount, 5.1 percent was argued to be for benefits of a "noninflationary" type, and therefore "excludable" from the board's guidelines.

In its statements to the board, the PMA pointed out that productivity had increased 97 percent (1965–1971); that tonnage had increased 27 percent (1966–1970); but that labor hours had decreased 26 percent. In view of such rapidly increasing productivity, the employers argued, the negotiated increase was not inflationary. Needless to say, the ILWU agreed.

The Pay Board's staff, in an extensive report upon which the board based its decision, disputed various figures of the PMA. The staff's calculations indicated that the first-year settlement was an increase of 25.9 percent, of which 9.5 percent could be considered "excludable" by board standards. Pointing to the extensive productivity gains in the industry, the staff reasoned that the maximum allowable guideline of 7 percent rather than the usual 5.5 percent should be used. Of the 16.4 percent increase subject to board scrutiny, the staff said, "9.4 percent was therefore the amount by which the request exceeds the guideline." The second-year increase was placed at 7.9 percent by the staff.

While refraining from any specific recommendations, the staff suggested that the Pacific Coast situation might meet a "test of uniqueness," permitting a special exemption "because of unusually high productivity gains."

On March 16 the decision of the Pay Board was announced. The Board had made "a number of . . . additions and modifications to the staff's submission," considered various methods of calculating the actual first-year increase, and had concluded that 20.9 percent was the "true" amount of the increase in wages and fringes. Of this amount, the board allowed only 14.9 percent and directed that $0.30 be cut from the negotiated first-year increase of $0.72.

The board's decision stated (by vote of 8 to 6) that the proposed adjustment of wages and salaries submitted by PMA and ILWU was "unreasonably inconsistent with the general wage and salary standard" and was therefore disapproved. It decided that the maximum 7 percent guideline was allowable because "the aggregate percentage of wage and salary increases in each of the five years of the prior employment contract" had been sufficiently less than allowable. In addition to this 7 percent, the board allowed 3 percent in wages and benefits due to "arrangements . . . specifically designed to foster economic growth, and other factors, including productivity." The board calculated the negotiated excludable benefits at 4.9 percent and allowed that full amount. The second-year benefit settlement was not touched.

Reaction to the cut from 20.9 percent to 14.9 percent was immediate. The five labor members of the board, who had voted against the majority, bitterly attacked the decision as the product of an "unholy alliance between public members and employer members of the Pay Board." They also charged that the majority action was "a political move designed to force a strike that would lead Congress to adopt a law requiring compulsory arbitration of labor disputes."

Bridges must decide

It was within this setting that Harry Bridges considered his next move. His immediate problem was what to do about the Pay Board decision. Beyond that lay the need for action concerning the future of the ILWU.

EXHIBIT 1
Losses from coastwise and major local strikes of Pacific Coast longshoremen, 1934–1948

Years	Longshoremen man-days lost by strikes	Percentage of available longshoremen man-days lost by strikes
1934	456,000	23.3
1935	114,000	5.4
1936	411,000	17.9
1937	348,000	14.5
1938	34,000	1.4
1939	225,000	9.0
1940–1945	"No-strike agreements" in effect during World War II	
1946	743,000	21.2
1947	22,000	0.7
1948	847,000	26.5

Note: These figures apply to the 31 coastwise or major local strikes (out of a total of 83) for which length in calendar days and men involved are known. If losses could have been computed for the remaining 52 major local strikes and for the 152 minor local strikes of known extent, totals would be considerably larger.

Source: W. Gorter and G. Hildebrand, *The Pacific Coast Maritime Shipping Industry, 1930–1948*, 2 vols. (Berkeley, 1952–54), Vol. II, pp. 344–49.

EXHIBIT 2
Tonnage moving through Pacific Coast ports, 1960–1970
(millions of revenue tons)

Year	Containers	Total
1960	0.5	28.5
1961	0.7	28.0
1962	0.7	27.8
1963	1.7	32.3
1964	2.6	34.2
1965	3.5	40.2
1966	4.3	45.6
1967	5.2	49.9
1968	6.1	54.5
1969	7.0	57.8
1970	8.7	59.9

Source: Office of Economic Policy and Case Analysis, Pay Board, Executive Office of the President.

EXHIBIT 3
Average number of ILWU registered men in utilization rates

Year	Longshoremen Number (000)	Longshoremen Utilization rate (percent)	Longshoremen Number (000)	Longshoremen Utilization rate (percent)
1960 . . . . 14.2		78.8	1.8	95.9
1961 . . . . 13.5		77.3	1.7	91.9
1962 . . . . 12.7		77.7	1.6	93.3
1963 . . . . 12.9		81.8	1.6	93.4
1964 . . . . 13.4		81.1	1.7	97.5
1965 . . . . 13.2		87.6	1.7	106.4
1966 . . . . 13.2		92.3	1.8	104.9
1967 . . . . 13.2		89.2	1.8	103.9
1968 . . . . 13.0		86.7	1.8	103.5
1969 . . . . 12.6		82.7	1.9	98.6
1970 . . . . 12.4		72.9	1.9	95.2
1971 . . . . 12.0		57.3	1.9	75.9

Source: Calculated from PMA and ILWU data.
Note: Utilization rate equals hours actually worked divided by "full-time hours." Full-time hours defined as 40 hours a week for 49 weeks.

EXHIBIT 4
Hourly wage rates Pacific Coast longshore industry

Year	Longshoremen base rate*	Clerks base rate†	Average rate‡
1960	$2.820	$3.035	$2.913
1961	2.880	3.120	2.973
1962	3.060	3.320	3.153
1963	3.190	3.465	3.283
1964	3.320	3.610	3.413
1965	3.380	3.680	3.473
1966	3.880	4.365	3.973
1967	3.880	4.365	3.973
1968	3.880	4.365	3.973
1969	4.080	4.590	4.173
1970	4.280	4.815	4.405

* In 1971, 51 percent earned the base rate; the remainder earned additional "skill rates" as follows: $0.150 (37 percent), $0.200 (3 percent), $0.250 (one percent), $0.300 (1 percent), $0.400 (7 percent).
† In 1971, 50 percent earned the base rate. The remainder were classified as supervisors or supercargoes at premiums of $0.480 and $1.085.
‡ Computed by weighting the wage rates for a particular year by the number of men working in corresponding categories in 1971. Assume a constant proportion of men in each category for each year.
Source: Office of Economic Policy and Case Analysis, Pay Board, Executive Office of the President.

EXHIBIT 5
Various indexes of Pacific Coast longshore productivity

Year	PMA index*	ILWU index†	PB index‡	CEA index§
1960	100	100	100	100
1961	107	101	103	103
1962	110	111	113	108
1963	124	115	120	112
1964	132	124	131	116
1965	142	131	136	120
1966	149	140	146	125
1967	169	158	165	128
1968	186	179	188	132
1969	197	195	197	132
1970	244	239	233	133

* Total tonnage divided by total shoreside man-hours as calculated by PMA.
† Weighted tonnage (net of containers) divided by longshore man-hours as calculated by ILWU.
‡ Weighted tonnage (net of containers and bulk) divided by total shoreside man-hours as calculated by Pay Board.
§ Output per man-hour in total private economy as calculated by Council of Economic Advisors.

EXHIBIT 6
Various indexes of unit labor cost for Pacific Coast longshore industry

Year	PMA/ILWU index*	PMA index†	ILWU index†	PB index†	CEA index‡
1960	100	100	100	100	100
1961	107	100	106	104	100
1962	112	102	101	99	100
1963	118	96	103	98	100
1964	123	93	99	94	101
1965	129	90	98	94	102
1966	142	96	102	97	105
1967	155	92	98	94	109
1968	155	83	87	82	114
1969	157	80	80	80	122
1970	165	67	70	71	130

* Longshore labor cost per hour as calculated by PMA and ILWU.
† Labor cost per ton as calculated by PMA, ILWU, and Pay Board.
‡ Unit labor cost for total private economy as calculated by Council of Economic Advisors.

EXHIBIT 7
And in This Corner, Harry Bridges*

Harry Bridges was causing more anxiety in the White House last week than he ever had in the years when Presidents Roosevelt, Truman, and Eisenhower were vainly trying to have him deported to Australia as a Communist. A Bridges order renewing last year's hundred-day dock strike in West Coast ports lit a fuse that could blow up the Pay Board, battered guardian of the Nixon Administration's wage-control policy.

All the remedies available under the national emergency provisions of the Taft-Hartley Act were used up in ending the first tie-up, but on Friday President Nixon asked Congress to rush through a special back-to-work law this week submitting the dispute to compulsory arbitration. Passage of such a law, however, would take care of only half the problem even if the longshoremen do go back to the piers, a question that Mr. Bridges left wide open at week's end.

A no less troublesome question for the Administration is whether the already rickety Pay Board can survive if arbitrators appointed by the Sectretary of Labor under mandate from Congress come down with a wage award double or triple the 5.5 per cent set by the official wage regulations as the guide post for noninflationary settlements.

The law recommended by the President calls upon the arbitration board to operate consistently with the Economic Stabilization Act, but it leaves the final decision to the arbitrators without review by the Pay Board. Given the vacillation with which the Pay Board has been monitoring its own standards, most experts in industrial relations are convinced that the most powerful guidepost influencing the umpires is likely to be the high-cost tentative agreement on wages and most other money items that Mr. Bridges and the Pacific Maritime Association had reached before the strike began. Only one issue—a highly technical on involving the method of crediting an automation tax on containerized freight—kept the two sides from a full settlement without any tie-up.

Included in the tentative accord on all other matters was a basic 32.3 per cent direct wage increase in a contract expiring in the middle of next year, plus employer payments of $5.2-million a year into a guaranteed annual wage fund to protect longshoremen against technological displacement. If the arbitrator were to order any substantial scaledown of either of these figures on the ground that they were out of line with the anti-inflation guideposts, it is highly improbable that the Bridges rank and file would stay on the docks, law or no law.

"There are two industries that can't be run by the General Motors manual, the coal mines and the docks," a Bridges aide warned last week. "There would be murder if the longshoremen were ordered back on terms below those they had been offered before the strike."

Thus, an arbitrator's award incorporating most, if not all, of the money demands is expected. Some Administration experts view such an outcome as the best possible under the circumstances: It would avoid a strike showdown, which the Government might well lose, and the responsibility for ap-

* Editorial by A. H. Ruaskin, *New York Times*, January 23, 1972.

EXHIBIT 7 (*continued*)

proving an expensive settlement would rest not upon the shaky Pay Board but upon a transient arbitration panel. What that tidy equation leaves out, however, is that the panel would carry a White House imprimatur.

On top of that, as with every deviation from ceilings, the breach would not stop with one. The International Longshoremen's Association, which is tying up loose ends of a tentative contract providing increases of 41 per cent over three years in New York and other North Atlantic ports, would almost certainly be a hitch-hiker on any above-ceiling authorization the Bridges union won. That would mean two breakthroughs for the price of one, and would probably mean a pullout from the Pay Board of its industry members and perhaps most of its public members as well.

There is a measure of irony in the prospect that Mr. Bridges may prove an icebreaker for the I.L.A. in getting its pact approved. Three weeks ago the West Coast leader brought his executive board to New York to make final arrangements for a full-fledged merger with the I.L.A. The two unions had no trouble agreeing that they would go on a joint strike if either had its contract trimmed by the Pay Board. But other commitments Mr. Bridges wanted were turned down by the East Coast union, and the merger talks collapsed.

Despite that setback Mr. Bridges, 70 years of age and locked in internal union conflict with some of his lifetime power-sharers, was determined to solve his succession problems by merging with someone. He went to Washington and negotiated a tentative unification deal with the giant Teamsters Union—a deal that had the extra attraction of promising to end a bitter jurisdictional fight between dock workers and teamsters over who stuffs containers at waterfront terminals. But when the jubilant Mr. Bridges returned to San Francisco he found he could not sell the merger to his fellow officers. Under the President's bill the arbitrators will now have to rule on the teamster-longshoreman controversy as well as everything else—an extension of Federal authority in union affairs that labor may find even more startling than the wage tangle.

EXHIBIT 8

Excerpts from testimony before Congress of PMA President Flynn and ILWU President Bridges*

". . . Mr. Flynn said that 'no union, no employer—no combination of the two—should be able to impose the widespread financial and human disasters upon helpless third parties that have been fomented by this dispute.'"

"'We are concerned here with a special situation,' Mr. Flynn said. 'We are concerned with such things as national defense, foreign and domestic commerce, balance of payments, the support of the states of Hawaii and Alaska and of Puerto Rico, [and] our ability to remain a maritime power in world affairs.'"

". . . Mr. Bridges dropped many hints that there would be slowdowns on the docks, sympathy measures by maritime unions, and even retaliation by foreign unions if Congress legislated an end to the strike."

* *New York Times*, February 5, 1972.

EXHIBIT 8 (*continued*)

"'One thing about a worker on the waterfront,' he said at one point, 'it's awfully hard to make him work fast and hard.' At another, he jerked his thumb toward Mr. Flynn beside him and said that if the strike was ended by compulsory arbitration, "these employers will be sorry.'"

"'We've got a few friends in other countries,' he said, 'and they will respond to our call for help. It may reach the point where the ships won't come back here.'"

"Mr. Bridges said he understood why the shippers favored the legislation."

"'We have these blokes on the ropes," he said, tilting his head toward Mr. Flynn. 'We're going to whip them and they're depending on you to save them. I don't blame them. I'd do the same.'"

EXHIBIT 9
Major economic provisions of ILWU-PMA agreement of
February 11, 1972

Wages.   Longshoremen's hourly base rate increased $0.720, effective December 25, 1971 and another $0.400, effective July 1, 1972. Skill rates increased as follows: $0.150 to $0.250; $0.200 to $0.350; $0.300 to $0.500; $0.400 to $0.700.

Clerk's hourly base rate increased $0.810 effective December 25, 1971.

Work guarantee.   PMA guarantees $5.2 million of work to ILWU per year. The majority of longshoremen would be guaranteed a minimum of 36 hours of work per week or straight-time pay in lieu thereof if no work is available.

Funds from Container Tax to be spent for additional guarantee payments after the $5.2 million is expended.

Container Tax.   All containers stuffed or stripped within a 50-mile zone in each port to be stuffed or stripped by ILWU longshoremen or taxed $1.00 per long ton, except:

- those containers stuffed or stripped at retail or wholesale warehouses, factories, or processing plants;
- household goods stuffed or stripped by a moving company; or
- containers moving in the coastwise or intercoastal trade.

Retirement.   Increase in monthly pension benefit from $235 to $500 from age 62 to 65. At age 65, when Social Security payments become available, pension benefit reduced to $350.

Compulsory retirement age reduced from 68 to 65. Early retirement possible at age 59 with 25 years of service with pension benefit reduced to $331.

Pay Board approval.   "In the event that the Wage and Price Board approvals are not granted within 30 days after filing of applications, either party may give notice of cancellation and the proposed contract and local agreements shall expire and the union shall be free to take such action, including strike action, as may be necessary to force implementation of the proposed agreement."

EXHIBIT 10

Some of the economic consequences of the longshore strike
May 1971 through January 1972

Item	Pacific Coast only	Atlantic, Gulf, and Pacific Coasts combined
Decline in exports	$ 1 billion	$800 million
Decline in imports	$700 million	$200 million
Net reduction in trade balance	$300 million	$600 million
Longshoremen's earnings lost	$ 41 million	$ 94 million
Seamen's earnings lost	$ 5 million	$ 11 million
Related occupations' earnings lost	?	?
Carriers' earnings lost.	?	?
Shippers' earnings lost	?	?

Source: Estimates made by Office of Economic Policy and Case Analysis, Pay Board, Executive Office of the President, February–March 1972.

EXHIBIT 11
First-year wage and benefits increases per hour as
agreed to by ILWU–PMA

Item	$ amount of increase per hour	Per-centage[1] increase
Includable costs:[2]		
Base wages.	$.720	
Concomitant for clerks[3]	.027	
Skill differentials[4].	.056	
CFS rate change[5]	.003	
Overtime and vacation cost of increase. . .	.257	
Wage guarantee[6].	.105	
	$1.168	15.7
Excludable costs:[7]		
Welfare.	$.204	
Pensions	.473	
M and M discontinuance[8]	(.312)	
	.365	4.9
Total costs and percentage	$1.533	20.6

[1] The previous year's average compensation, including overtime, vacation, skill differentials, and welfare and pension benefits, was $7.428 per hour.

[2] Those costs which are included in the Pay Board's 5.5 to 7 percent guideline calculations.

[3] The clerks' salaries were higher than the longshoremen's. The clerks' concomitant is the total impact of that extra hourly salary, divided by total "shoreside hours."

[4] Skilled men who operated sophisticated equipment were paid an extra amount per hour as a "skill differential."

[5] The CFS, or Containerized Freight Station agreement was the contract clause providing a tax of $1.00 per ton for containers stuffed or unstuffed within 50 miles of the docks.

[6] The estimated total cost of the wage guarantee over the coming year, divided by total shoreside hours guaranteed.

[7] As opposed to "Includable Costs," "Excludable Costs" are those which the Pay Board does not consider within its 5.5 to 7 percent guideline, and are therefore segregated for consideration. These costs are generally considered noninflationary.

[8] The PMA argued that since many of the benefits under the new agreement were replacing those received under the now discontinued Mechanization and Modernization Fund, the discontinued expense of the M and M Fund payments, no longer required, should be credited to the new welfare and pension costs.

Source: PMA.

Individualism, interest groups, contract, and consensus at General Motors, 1908-1972[1]

IF ONE MAN can be said to have made General Motors what it is today, he is Alfred P. Sloan, Jr., chief executive officer of the company from 1923 to 1946. His history of GM from the company's beginning in 1908 until 1962 contains the following statements of his philosophy:[2]

> . . . General Motors could hardly be imagined to exist anywhere but in this country, with its very active and enterprising people; its resources, including its science and technology and its business and industrial know-how; its vast spaces, roads, and rich markets; its characteristics of change, mobility, and mass production; its great industrial expansion in this century, and its system of freedom in general and free competitive enterprise in particular. . . . If in turn we have contributed to the style of the United States as expressed in the automobile, this has been by interaction. (p. xxi)

۰ ۰ ۰ ۰ ۰

> If I have expressed or implied in this book a so-called ideology, it is, I suppose, that I believe in competition as an article of faith, a means of progress, and a way of life. . . . We set out to produce not

---

[1] This case was prepared by Professor George C. Lodge as a basis for class discussion rather than to illustrate either effective or ineffective handling of an administrative situation.

Distributed by the Intercollegiate Case Clearing House, Soldiers Field, Boston, Mass. 02163. All rights reserved to the contributors. Printed in U.S.A.

[2] Alfred P. Sloan, Jr., *My Years With General Motors* (New York: Doubleday & Co., 1964).

for the chosen few but for the whole consumer public on the assumption of a continuously rising standard of living. . . . (p. xxiv)

*   *   *   *   *

. . . It is as I see it the strategic aim of a business to earn a return on capital, and if in any particular case the return in the long run is not satisfactory, the deficiency should be corrected or the activity abandoned for a more favorable one. (p. 49)

*   *   *   *   *

The measure of the worth of a business enterprise as a *business* . . . is not merely growth in sales or assets but return on the shareholders' investment, since it is their capital that is being risked and it is in their interests first of all that the corporation is supposed to be run in the private-enterprise scheme of things. . . . (p. 213)

Mr. Sloan noted that even during the depression from 1929 to 1932, when production fell 75 percent, General Motors' cost control was so effective that it was able to earn $248 million and pay shareholders $343 million. (p. 199)

The rise of the UAW

In 1900 Detroit was already the manufacturing center of the horseless carriage and the internal combustion engines. Its position was strategic. Surrounded by the Pittsburgh-Youngstown steel mills, the rubber plants at Akron, and the Messabi iron range, it was also at the hub of one of the world's great water transport systems. It was the natural place for Henry Ford, Louis Chevrolet, R. E. Olds and the other pioneers of the American automobile industry to open their shops.

Thousands flocked to Detroit to seek work in the new factories. When, in January of 1914, Ford announced that he would pay $5 a day, for example, 5,000 men were lined up outside his gates at 5 A.M. on a bitterly cold morning. By the time the plant opened 12,000 were outside. Soon a riot broke out. The *Detroit News* reported: "The crowd stormed the doors of the plant, hundreds forcing their way through, bricks and other missiles were hurled at the officers and buildings, and the rioters were dispersed only after a drenching with ice-cold water.[3]

But no fire hose was sufficient to stem the flow. From the backwoods of Arkansas, the cotton fields of Georgia and Alabama, the farms of Kentucky and the mountains of Tennessee they came by the thousands—immigrants, illiterates, young, and old. By 1938 more than 150,000 Blacks were jammed into Detroit's "Paradise Valley" slums. Racial violence was common.

---

[3] *Detroit News,* January 12, 1914.

In 1929 some 470,000 men worked in Detroit's auto factories. By 1931 there were 211,000 people on relief and some 150,000 had left the city to return to the land they had come from or to wander.[4]

B. J. Widick has recorded the following interview with John Kelly, an auto worker who recalls the early 1930s:

> We used to get out to the employment gates by six in those days and we would build a fire and wait around. If you knew someone inside you stood a better chance of being called in. Foremen used to come out and pick whom they wanted, and seniority didn't mean a thing. My brother was a superintendent, so I used to get some breaks. I felt sorry for the others, but what could you do? When I started to sign fellows up in the union my superintendent warned me I'd get fired and never get another job. He said he couldn't believe I would do anything like that when I had a brother who was a superintendent. One night my brother came over to the house and begged me to quit. He was afraid of losing his job because I was a union man.[5]

Another worker, Joe Hattley, recalled: "One day I started to complain about a job. My foreman took me over to the window and pointed to all those guys standing outside the employment gate. 'If you don't like your job there's plenty of them outside who want it.' What could I say?"

General Motors management, like that of most other American companies at the time, was firmly opposed to the organization of workers into a union.[6] But organization took place nevertheless. The crisis came with the sitdown strikes of 1935 and 1936 when some 2,000 members of the newly formed United Automobile Workers (CIO) seized several plants, including Chevrolet in Flint, Michigan. Governor Frank Murphy sent 1,200 National Guardsmen to enforce a court injunction against the strikers. The workers refused to vacate the plant. Their leader, John L. Lewis, told Governor Murphy, "I do not doubt your ability to call out your soldiers and shoot the members of our union out of those plants, but let me say when you issue that order I shall leave this conference and I shall enter one of those plants with my people."[7]

The governor backed down to avoid violence and General Motors reluctantly agreed to negotiate with the union. Among the militants at Flint was Walter Reuther with many of those who later became officials and shop stewards of the UAW.

Business Week editorialized as follows:

---

[4] Irving Howe and B. J. Widick, *The UAW and Walter Reuther* (New York: Random House, 1949), p. 29.

[5] Ibid., p. 30.

[6] Ibid., p. 31.

[7] Ibid., p. 61.

By means of sitdown stikes, the country has been put at the mercy of thoroughly irresponsible groups which in effect have no leadership, no control, no authority that can restrain them. Great industries, whose operations affect the daily welfare of millions, are confronted with demands to sign contracts with groups which, day by day and hour by hour, demonstrate that they have almost no control over their own people, no conception of the validity or the sanctity of a contract, no respect for property rights or for rights of any sort except their own.[8]

Mr. Sloan recalled:

. . . One is inclined to forget that unionization in large industries was not then the custom in the United States. The significance of large-scale unionization was not yet clear to us. We knew that some political radicals regarded unions as instruments for the attainment of power. But even orthodox "business unionism" seemed to us a potential threat to the prerogatives of management. As a businessman, I was unaccustomed to the whole idea. Our early experiences with the AF of L unions in the automobile industry were unhappy; the chief issue with these unions became organizational. They demanded that they represent all our workers, even those who did not want to be represented by them. Our initial encounter with the CIO was even more unhappy; for that organization attempted to enforce its demands for exclusive recognition by the most terrible acts of violence, and finally seized our properties in the sit-down strikes of 1937. I have no desire to revive the bitter controversies that arose over these early encounters with labor organizations. I mention them merely to suggest one of the reasons why our initial reaction to unionism was negative.

What made the prospect seem especially grim in those early years was the persistent union attempt to invade basic management prerogatives. Our rights to determine production schedules, to set work standards, and to discipline workers were all suddenly called into question. Add to this the recurrent tendency of the union to inject itself into pricing policy, and it is easy to understand why it seemed, to some corporate officials, as though the union might one day be virtually in control of our operations.

In the end, we were fairly successful in combating these invasions of management rights. There is no longer any real doubt that pricing is a management, not a union, function. So far as our operations are concerned, we have moved to codify certain practices, to discuss workers' grievances with union representatives, and to submit for arbitration the few grievances that remain unsettled. But on the whole, we have retained all the basic powers to manage.

The issue of unionism at General Motors is long since settled. We have achieved workable relations with all of the unions representing our employees.[9]

---

[8] *Business Week*, April 10, 1937.
[9] Sloan, *My Years With General Motors*, pp. 405–6.

By 1946 the United Automobile Workers had become one of the two or three largest and most powerful unions in America with a membership of over a million. The union's organizing effort reached a climax at General Motors in a 119-day strike in 1945 and 1946 during which the entire corporation was shut down over wage demands. The trade union anthem *Solidarity Forever,* which was sung to the tune of the *Battle Hymn of the Republic,* captures the mood of the times:

> When the union's inspiration through the workers' blood
>   shall run,
> There can be no power greater anywhere beneath the sun.
> Yet what force on earth is weaker than the feeble strength
>   of one.
> But the union makes us strong.
> Solidarity forever, solidarity forever,
> Solidarity forever, for the union makes us strong.

For GM management the situation was made worse by the fact that the political order seemed to be singing along with UAW chief Walter Reuther and his militant cohorts. As Mr. Sloan put it,

> . . . the UAW was unable to enlist the support of the government in any great crisis. The government's attitude went back as far as the 1937 sit-down strikes, when we took the view that we would not negotiate with the union while its agents forcibly held possession of our properties. Sit-down strikes were plainly illegal—a judgement later confirmed by the Supreme Court. Yet President Franklin D. Roosevelt, Secretary of Labor Frances Perkins, and Governor Frank Murphy of Michigan exerted steady pressure upon the corporation, and upon me personally, to negotiate with the strikers who had seized our property, until finally we felt obliged to do so.
>
> Again in 1945–46, during the 119-day strike, President Truman formally backed up the union's controversial insistence that our "ability to pay" should affect the size of the wage increase. We successfully resisted this unsound proposition, but there is no doubt in my mind that the President's statement served to strengthen the union's public position and thus prolong the strike.[10]

1948–61—the strengthening of the UAW

With the contract negotiations of 1948, however, came a marked change in the attitude of both General Motors and the UAW. Each had developed a healthy respect for one another's power. They agreed to conduct negotiations in a serious, business-like atmosphere and, most importantly, to do so in private. ". . . In previous years," said Mr. Sloan, "our collective bargaining had come to resemble a public political forum

---

[10] Ibid., p. 393

in which the union fed a stream of provocative statements to the press, and we felt obliged to answer publicly. The privacy of the 1948 negotiations made their tone more realistic from the start."[11]

Although Chrysler was struck for 17 days in 1948, General Motors and the UAW signed an agreement without a work stoppage. This agreement was the first major labor contract in the U.S. to be of two years' duration. It contained two new features: (1) "the annual improvement factor" which called for an automatic annual increase in the base wage rate reflecting the continually improving productivity of the American worker and (2) the cost of living escalator under which wages would rise and fall according to the Government's cost of living index. The details of the new contract were worked out in three days of round-the-clock bargaining by company and union task forces. One troublesome side effect of these innovations was that they tended to narrow the wage differential between skilled and unskilled workers.[12]

In 1950, Chrysler was again shut down, this time for 103 days; but General Motors succeeded in peacefully negotiating an unprecedented five-year contract with the UAW. It included a union shop agreement under which new employees were required to join the union within 90 days of their employment, which management had firmly opposed. Also for the first time pensions and health insurance programs were admitted as proper subjects for collective bargaining and inclusion in the labor-management contract, again over management's firm opposition. Although the company had already unilaterally instituted such programs, in 1948 GM's president held that they were not appropriate for bargaining. He said:

> If we consider the ultimate result of this tendency to stretch collective bargaining to comprehend any subject that a union leader may desire to bargain over, we come out with the union leaders really running the economy of the country; but with no legal or public responsibility and with no private employment except as they may permit. . . .
>
> Only by defining and restricting collective bargaining to its proper sphere can we hope to save what we have come to know as our American system and keep it from evolving into an alien form, imported from East of the Rhine. Until this is done, the border area of collective bargaining will be a constant battleground between employers and unions, as the unions continuously attempt to press the boundary farther and farther into the area of managerial functions.[13]

Somewhat less than a year later, in 1949, the courts ruled that pension and insurance programs were subject to bargaining (*Inland Steel Company* v. *NLRB*).

---

[11] Ibid., p. 398.

[12] Ibid., p. 400.

[13] *New York Times*, March 24, 1948.

Both sides had begun to study pensions and insurance in a joint committee established in October 1949. The committee met 13 times before the formal 1950 contract negotiations began. The corporation gave the union extensive data about the work force to help it in its preparations. The committee activities were only exploratory; both sides realized that it would be foolish to freeze their positions before bargaining actually started.

In 1955, minutes before the strike deadline expired, a collective agreement was signed between GM and the UAW containing a Supplementary Unemployment Benefit plan. It allowed a laid-off worker to receive a total of up to 65 percent of his weekly after-tax pay during the first four weeks of his unemployment and up to 60 percent for 22 weeks thereafter. Skilled workers, who made up 10 percent of the UAW's membership were in many cases dissatisfied with the agreement. Many walked off the job during ensuing weeks, although most returned. Some 800 withdrew from the UAW to join AFL unions and in Flint dissident skilled workers for the Society of Skilled Trades. In 1956 the SST claimed membership of more than 50,000, about 2.5 percent of UAW membership.

1961–72—the beginnings of dissension

Another three-year agreement was reached in 1958 after a four-month no-contract period following the expiration of the 1955 contract. The negotiations were marked by numerous plant level strikes during the no-contract period and by a one-week national strike. 1958 marked the beginning of difficulties with local demands and strikes in General Motors.

In 1961, local bargaining became even more of an issue. Nineteen thousand local plant-level demands were submitted compared to 11,600 in 1958. On September 11, 1961, 90 plants were struck although the parties were not far apart on national contract issues.

On September 20, the UAW's General Motors Council, which is composed of local representatives from GM plants, voted to accept the national agreement but also voted to continue the national strike in support of local unions which had not yet resolved their local issues. The following day the UAW's International Union Executive Board met and overruled the GM Council on the matter of a national strike. The executive board ordered the local unions that had settled their local issues to return to work and permitted those that had not reached local settlements to remain on strike.

Local negotiations at the plant level were even more difficult in 1964. Twenty-four thousand local demands were submitted. A national strike against General Motors began on September 25. Although a tentative national agreement was reached on October 5, local strikes continued at some plants until November 8. General Motors and the UAW signed a new three-year National Agreement on November 9. The following article in the *Wall Street Journal* described the situation:

Auto Union Ferment[14]

Russ Alger's problems as president of a local complicate GM talks; to hold post, he must heed members' pressure to win concessions of work rules—Ann Landers and night calls
(by Norman Miller, staff reporter of the *Wall Street Journal*)

Flint, Michigan—The United Auto Workers Union seems well on the road to winning its biggest contract settlement ever from giant General Motors Corp. But it could still cost UAW executive Russell Alger his job.

Mr. Alger is president of UAW Local 581, representing 5,000 workers at the GM Fisher Body plant here. As such, he knows the men on the assembly line will welcome the record-setting pensions, liberalized vacations and additional relief time likely to come out of this week's bargaining. But he's aware, too, that the gains will mean little if they are not accompanied by some improvements on the hottest issue of all: Work standards. "This is the high point—what we get from the company here is what makes or breaks you in this job," he says.

Gray-haired Russ Alger is hardly in a mood to give up his union job. It took six years of campaigning to capture the post and now he's counting on it to become a springboard to political office; he plans to run for the Michigan House of Representatives in 1966. So Russ Alger this week isn't the affable, easy smiling union boss that he is most of the year—instead, he's a tough, fist-pounding labor bargainer. Along with officials of 130 other GM union locals, Russ is putting intense pressure on UAW president Walter Reuther to seek sizable concessions on the work rules issue. Such determination raises the real possibility that the GM talks may deadlock and a strike ensue.

An early warning

Actually, Mr. Reuther needs no reminder from Mr. Alger and his other local union presidents on the strong feelings over work rules. He has only to look back to last year when rank-and-file restiveness in local elections swept out of office more than one-third of the UAW leaders at auto plants. The upheaval carried with it an implicit warning to the union's leaders in Detroit, and the UAW's top officials are intent on avoiding another big shake-up in the 1965 elections.

The union leadership seems in sight of this goal, having won the biggest contract gains in UAW history in negotiations with Chrysler

[14] Reproduced with permission from *The Wall Street Journal*, September 24, 1964, p. 1.

Corp. and Ford Motor Co. But GM is the big one in the eyes of the UAW, and the union's bargainers are determined to make good on their promise to top the Ford and Chrysler contracts. They must do so to placate the 354,000 UAW workers at GM plants—more than a third again as many workers as at Chrysler and Ford combined.

This will be no easy task. While GM already has offered to match the basic money settlement made at Ford and Chrysler, it has shown little disposition to give in on the work rules question. It traditionally has resisted demands in this area, regarding them as a threat to management prerogatives.

The drums are sounding

But this year Mr. Alger and his cohorts seem equally determined. For months the UAW's propaganda drums have sounded a rising protest against what it charges are "filthy plants," "speedups on the assembly line" and coercion and terror tactics by foremen at GM plants. GM has vehemently denied the allegations, counter-charging that the union is throwing up a smokescreen in an attempt to extend the contract into areas that would infringe upon the company's "right to manage."

Whatever the accuracy of the UAW's charges, the union has emphasized them so much that it cannot sign a contract without broad gains on the explosive working conditions issue—unless it is willing to risk another rout of local union GM leaders in the next intra-union elections. The pressure on local leaders at GM plants was dramatically pointed up as long ago as last March at the UAW convention when the president of one local, after an impassioned protest against "sweatshop" conditions at his GM plant, cried: "Take a good look at us, Brother Reuther, and remember us. We are behind you today but our first loyalty is to the rank-and-file and we don't give a damn who stands in our way. We'll roll over him, but we're going to get a union shop condition at GM."

To emphasize their concern about work rules, some local leaders at GM plants warn they will ignore any national contract and will call their men out on strike if the company doesn't accept their local demands. Such local strikes became so widespread in 1961 that the vast GM vehicle-making complex ground to a halt for two weeks.

*　　*　　*　　*　　*

Now Mr. Alger faces the same problem as his defeated predecessor. There are crucial issues in the negotiations with GM over which he has little leverage on the local level. Probably the most important of these is the "speed-up" issue, a charge by the union that GM constantly pushes workers to increase the amount of work they must perform in a given amount of time. Unless the UAW's top bargainers get GM to agree in the national contract that the union should have a voice in setting work standards, Mr. Alger concedes that he has almost no hope of getting such an agreement from local managers at the Flint plant.

Complicating the problem, says Mr. Alger, is the fact that the speedup issue involves more than a mere argument on how fast a machine or an assembly line should go. Enmeshed in the dispute in a union charge that GM foremen use the work pace of eager young workers as the standard that must be met by all employees.

Aptitude tests play role

"These younger workers come into the plant and the management persuades them to increase their effort by leading them to believe that they are potential supervisors," Mr. Alger contends. "They give them aptitude tests and let these guys think they are the smartest guys that have ever come into Fisher Body. Then these younger guys work exceptionally hard to impress the supervisors and make a name for themselves. But the foremen are just using them so they can use their output as a new standard, and this causes the older employees a real hardship."

The younger vs. older worker issue crops up in other areas as well. It's a constant problem when it comes to assigning workers to newly established high-paying jobs, says Mr. Alger. The company will often assign a younger man to the new job with the expectation it will get more work out of him, he charges. "The net result is that lower seniority employees are receiving higher rates of pay on good jobs while people with higher seniority are stuck on the night shift," he says.

The matter has become an important local issue at the Fisher plant here, both GM and union agree. A GM official argues the company should have the right to make work assignments. He says that the matter has become temporarily magnified because in the past year Fisher plants have begun to build more body models. This has required extensive changes in assembly line operations and brought an abnormal number of job realignments. Often in the realignment, he explains, it's necessary to assign a worker in a low-pay-scale job some duties in a higher-pay category for a few hours a day to "balance out" work on the assembly line. Otherwise, the worker in the lower pay category might be idle part of the time.

"Black eyes and busted heads"

In striving for rank-and-file backing for his program, Mr. Alger admits that he has a major problem with the local's younger workers. "We have a new breed in the plant today," he says. "Probably less than 25% or 30% of the people at Fisher today were there when the UAW won recognition in the Thirties in the sitdown strikes. The younger workers are reaping the benefits brought about by years of head-bumping and even black eyes and busted heads. They accept our gains and don't realize how we had to fight for them." (Mr. Alger was defeated by a Reuther supporter in 1965.)

In 1967 the split within the UAW widened as skilled workers protested the narrowing differential between their wage rates and those of the less skilled. When they threatened to leave the UAW, the union amended its constitution to allow skilled workers the right to vote separately on ratifying new contracts. This effectively gave them the right of veto over any contract. (In 1967 there were 110,000 skilled workers out of the UAW's total membership of 650,000.) Ford sustained a long and costly strike in 1967 but an agreement was signed with GM with only a few minor local walkouts.

The next big strike at GM came in 1970 when the company was shut down for 67 days. Many observers felt that one of the principal causes of the strike was the need for unity and solidarity in the UAW:

> To teach young members who have not known hard times that struggle and unity are necessary;
> Help make expectations more realistic;
> Foster loyalty and pull together warring factions within the union; and to
> Create an escape valve for workers who are frustrated by the boredom of the assembly line routine.[15]

To get the most out of the strike in terms of internal cohesion, the UAW set up a strike school. Strikers could qualify for the $30 to $40 weekly strike benefits by attending the classes. Among other things they learned to sing *Solidarity Forever*.

Lordstown

In March 1972 there was a 22-day strike at General Motors' assembly plant in Lordstown, Ohio, involving 7700 members of the United Auto Workers Local 1112. It also affected 8,800 other workers at the Fisher Body stamping plant at Lordstown and the Chevrolet engine plant at Tonawanda, New York, and the axle plant in Buffalo.

The strike had been a long time brewing. At issue, on the surface at least, was a speedup of work and the layoff of several hundred workers.

In January, according to the *New York Times*,[16] General Motors estimated that it had lost the production of 12,000 Vega automobiles and about 4,000 Chevrolet trucks worth about $45 million. The *Times* reported:

> Management has had to close down the assembly line repeatedly since last month after workers slowed their work and allowed cars to move down the line without performing all operations.
> A. B. Anderson, the plant manager, said in an interview, "We've had engine blocks pass 40 men without them doing their work."
> Management has also accused workers of sabotage, such as breaking windshields, breaking off rear-view mirrors, slashing upholstery, bending

---

[15] Norman Pearlstine, *Wall Street Journal*, October 29, 1970, p. 1.

[16] Agis Salpukas, "Young Workers Disrupt Key GM Plant," *New York Times*, January 23, 1972.

signal levers, putting washers in carburetors and breaking off ignition keys.

In the last four weeks a lot that holds about 2,000 cars has often been filled with Vegas that had to be taken back into the plant for repair work before they could be shipped to dealers. Sales of Vegas in the last two weeks have been cut about in half.

The union, which concedes that there may have been some sabotage by a few angry workers, maintains that the bulk of the problems with the cars were a result of cutbacks in numbers of workers in a drive by management to increase efficiency and cut costs.

According to the union, the remaining workers have had to absorb the extra work and cannot keep up with the assembly line. The result, the union men say, is improperly assembled cars.

The dispute is taking place in one of the most modern and sophisticated assembly plants in the world, built in 1966 on a farm field near Lordstown.

Through better design, a variety of new types of power tools and other automated devices, much of the heavy lifting and hard physical labor has been eliminated in the plant. Even the parking lots were planned in such a way that the long walk to one's car had been done away with.

Workers on the assembly line have easier access to the car body and do not have to do as much bending and crawling in and out as in the older plants in Detroit. The Vega also has 43 percent fewer parts than a full-size car, making the assembly easier.

But as the jobs become easier and simpler, the rate at which they can be done can be increased. On a regular assembly line, which runs at about 55 cars an hours, a worker takes about a minute to perform a task, while workers at the Lordstown plant need only about 40 seconds.

The wages are good. Workers start out on the line at $4.37 an hour, get a 10-cent-an-hour increase within 30 days and another 10 cents after 90 days. Benefits come to $2.50 more an hour.

The plant sits almost in the center of the heavy industrial triangle made up of Youngstown, with its steel plants; Akron, with its rubber industry; and Cleveland, a major center for heavy manufacturing.

The plant, which produces all the Vegas made by General Motors, draws its 7,700 workers, whose average age is 24 years (29 is the correct figure, according to the company), from areas that have felt the sting of foreign competition and where unemployment and layoffs have been heavy.

Many of the fathers of the young auto workers are employed in steel and rubber and have watched their jobs dwindle because foreign products have undercut their industries.

But the threat of unemployment and pressure from mothers and fathers, from the local press and public officials, have so far had little effect on the militant young workers who began their struggle with General Motors last October.

It was then that General Motors Assembly Division (GMAD), a management team that has developed the reputation for toughness in cutting costs and bettering productivity, took over the operation of the Fisher Body Plant and Chevrolet assembly plant here and began to consolidate the operations.[17]

From the point of view of the management, the two plants had not been operating at their peak efficiency.

A major reorganization of work began. According to management it consisted mostly of changing jobs to make them more efficient, although management conceded that about 300 jobs had been eliminated and some workers had been given additional work.

Mr. Anderson explained that changes had to be made to bring the assembly line, which can turn out 100 Vegas in an hour, up to the potential it was designed for.

"If we are to remain competitive, we will have to take advantage of those sections of the contract on making the work more efficient," he said.

Curtis Cox, GMAD's supervisor of standards and methods, commenting on the sabotage on the Lordstown line said: "We shut down to maintain quality." More generally, his view was, "the worker must take responsibility for productivity for this country to remain competitive."[18]

Irving Bluestone, director of the UAW's GM department, said that he had proposed to GM a method for settling the labor tension at Lordstown, but indicated "that the plan was scuttled when local union officials wouldn't go along."[19]

George Morris, GM's industrial relations vice president, said: "It is unfortunate that this local cannot go along with agreements that other GM-UAW locals have used to settle comparable disputes."[20]

According to Nat Weinberg of the UAW, Lordstown "is a phenomena that goes on every year," noting that auto workers have always struck over work standards. "Management at Lordstown was trying to increase the work pace to intolerable levels, which was exactly the reason the UAW was created over 35 years ago," he said.[21]

In late March, however, other GM plant locals at Wilmington, Delaware; St. Louis, Missouri; and Norwood, Ohio, either gave notice of impending strikes or voted to strike if long lists of grievances were not settled.

Motivation

In recent years GM, like many other U.S. companies, has encountered increasing problems associated with workers' motivations which do not

---

[17] Homemade signs around the plant read: "Get rid of GMAD," "Beat GMAD." *Iron Age,* February 3, 1972, p. 39.

[18] *Iron Age,* February 3, 1972, pp. 38–39.

[19] *Wall Street Journal,* March 7, 1972.

[20] Ibid.

[21] *Labor Relations Reporter,* May 29, 1972, p. 93.

seem susceptible to collective bargaining or contractual arrangements. In some GM assembly plants absenteeism in 1972 ran as high as 13 percent compared with 3 percent several years ago. Mondays and Fridays were particular problems with workers apparently eager for long weekends. There has also been increased turnover and workers are pressing for early retirement. All this results in higher labor costs and lower productivity.

Lee A. Iacocca, speaking in 1971 as president of Ford, put the productivity problem of the U.S. auto industry. During the 1960s, he said, "Japan's productivity gain was 188.5%. Ours was 34.7%."[22] (See the Appendix for other comparative figures.)

Workers at Lordstown and elsewhere object to the boredom and to the repetitive nature of assembly line work. Although this complaint is by no means new, it appears to be taking on greater intensity. Weinberg said, "We are creating more jobs for imbeciles than there are imbeciles to fill them." Others have noted: "Like it or not, the availability of welfare benefits makes it possible to refuse to take a job that involves excessive drudgery. The fear of drudgery has replaced the fear of unemployment."[23]

"A revolution is starting now—it has to come," 31-year-old Jerry Cook, an exterior trim repairman at GM's Linden, N.J., plant. He pointed out that workers are now better educated, many with college training, and that they have the capacity to know and understand more about their jobs and the company. "Workers should have the right to decide who's going to do the job and how they're going to do it. The supervisor can tell them what to do but not how to do it."

> Gary B. Bryner, 29, president of UAW Local 1112 at Lordstown, said: The attitude of young people is going to compel management to make jobs more desirable in the workplace and to fulfill the needs of man. . . . The management concern is for productivity and profits. Ours is for the employee. There's got to be a blending. . . . The attitude that a guy goes to work and slaves to get his $4 an hour is passe. The guys want to feel like they're making real contributions. They don't want to feel like a part of a machine.[24]

George Gallup, Jr., pollster, said in September 1972, that about 19 percent of American workers of all ages are unhappy with their jobs. Some 33 percent in the 18- to 29-year-old age bracket find their work unsatisfactory. Fully 70 percent of young workers feel they are not producing at full capacity.[25]

---

[22] *New York Times,* September 11, 1971.

[23] Morris Abrams, *Labor Relations Reporter,* May 29, 1972.

[24] *Business Week,* September 9, 1972, p. 108.

[25] *Wall Street Journal,* September 12, 1972.

Nick Schecodonic summed up his feelings after six years on the line by saying:

> It's going to take something, somewhere to change that. Where a guy can take an interest in his job. GM can say to us, 'You're crazy,' but a guy can't do the same thing eight hours a day, year after year. And it's got to be more than just saying to a guy 'Okay, instead of six spots on the weld you'll do five spots.'
>
> I was reading about Sweden where they're going to bring parts together and then have a team of 20 guys put the whole part together. That's the kind of thing I'm talking about.[26]

Volvo and Saab announced in April 1972 that they were eliminating the traditional assembly line and instead would bring parts to teams of men who would assemble the whole car. Work tasks have been expanded, workers are expected to take part in planning sessions concerning work rationalization, workers are encouraged to learn several different jobs to allow for a breakdown in the division of labor.[27] Most Swedish firms also involve unions in the decision-making process. In addition, worker-management councils have been established at different levels of operation to allow those affected by changes to examine them ahead of time.[28]

In Germany a new labor law was enacted in January 1972, greatly strengthening the union's voice in determining company policies regarding such matters as mergers, plant shutdowns and hiring and firing. German labor leader, Heinz-Oskar Vetter, said: "West Germany's work force will no longer be satisfied with a few more concessions. It demands control and participation in economic power."[29]

U.S. auto companies are experimenting with new ways of relating workers to the company. At Chrysler workers are being brought into management decisions and consulted on how new cars should be built and plants organized.[30] GM has initiated a systematic study of worker motivation, and *Business Week* reported that:

> Last fall, it established a new personnel administration and development staff and hired Stephen Fuller, an associate dean of the Harvard Business School, to head it as vice-president. Fuller says he has been told to be the "vice-president of tomorrow." "If someone says, 'that's the way we've done it for 10 years,' that in and of itself should make it suspect," he says.

---

[26] *New York Times*, February 3, 1972, p. 38.

[27] Ibid.; "Job Design Experiment at Saab-Scania's Automotive Plants in Sodertalje" (ARB 710708).

[28] "Concepts of Organization Development in Sweden," Dr. Larry E. Greiner, Harvard Business School case 3-472-118, p. 3.

[29] *Business Week*, July 8, 1972, p. 34.

[30] *New York Times*, April 2, 1972, p. 40.

A former GM plant manager, Frank Schotters, was named last fall to assist Fuller because of innovative worker motivation techniques he employed in the Atlanta area. Schotters believes that communication may be the most important solution. At GM's Lakewood (Ga.) assembly plant, workers and management get together for "rap" sessions on absenteeism and how to improve assembly processes.

GM experiments with "enlarging" jobs—by giving the worker four functions instead of one, for example—have not been very successful. Workers often found they had less rest time and the job was not more interesting. Workers, however, have responded favorably to experiments in giving them responsibility for deciding how their simple tasks will be performed.

Sometimes it takes more than that. The Lordstown dispute showed that some young workers went through their assembly line routine without knowing what parts they were handling; the job was entirely mechanical.

Many auto union officials see no real way that can be changed substantially enough to make assembly line jobs seem more worthwhile. The solution may be, they say, to pay workers to accept the unpleasantness—and cut their work time so that they will have shorter hours and fewer years to work.[31]

One GM personnel man believes "the assembly line is here to stay. We must get at the attitudes of people. The real problem is communications between supervisory people and the workers." The company now has about 60 organization development (OD) specialists working on this problem in about 30 plants.

The UAW has mentioned that "alternatives to the assembly line" will be an issue in 1973 bargaining.[32]

APPENDIX A

	U.S.	Japan	France	U.K.	Germany
Annual average rate of growth in output per man-hour (1965–70)	2.1%	14.2%	6.6%	3.6%	5.3%
Increase in labor costs in manufacturing* (1965–70)	3.9	0.8	2.7	3.8	3.2
Average annual increase in GNP (constant prices)† (1960–70)	4.2	11.3	5.6	2.7	4.7
Exports as percent of GNP†	4.0	9.6	11.5	16.0	19.2

* Arthur Neef, "Unit Labor Costs in Eleven Countries," *Monthly Labor Review,* August 1971, p. 5.
† Source: OECD.

[31] *Business Week,* March 4, 1972, p. 70.
[32] *Business Week,* September 9, 1972, p. 108.

The automotive workforce and its contract[1]

On September 15, 1970, 343,600 members of the United Automobile, Aerospace, and Agricultural Implement Workers of America (UAW) walked off their jobs at 145 American and Canadian plants of the General Motors Corporation. At stake was a new employment contract and a considerable amount of face. The UAW had not struck GM since a 119-day walkout in 1946. Also, 1970 was the debut of Leonard Woodcock, Walter Reuther's successor as president of the UAW. While heading up his union's General Motors Department for 15 years under Reuther, Woocock had been turned down several times when he had urged a strike against GM. His elevation to the presidency was popular with those local leaders and rank and file who had perennially shouted at UAW conventions for a "showdown" with GM—only to be told by Reuther, "Brothers, that would take a helluva lot of money."

Since World War II, the UAW has pursued a policy of bargaining with the entire automobile industry through a "target" company. One of the three big automotive manufacturers has been selected and efforts concentrated on this target until a settlement has been reached. This settlement has then been held out as precedent to the other companies, all of which generally agree to similar settlements. The unwritten rule has been that the UAW will not force demands upon nontarget com-

---

[1] This material was prepared from public sources as the basis for class discussion. Distributed by the Intercollegiate Case Clearing House, Soldiers Field, Boston, Mass. 02163. All rights reserved to the contributors. Printed in U.S.A.

panies that are substantially different from those accepted by the target. If settlement with the target is delayed, existing contracts with the non-target companies are unofficially extended until settlement with the target company is reached.

Some observers have also detected an additional pattern in the UAW's target selection process. Whenever the union wishes to win a large increase in wages or benefits, it chooses GM. Ford is used to win policy victories. Chrysler is chosen when neither a large increase nor a major policy issue is at stake and then only following periods in which the company has experienced good performance. Smaller companies, such as American Motors, are generally not selected as targets.

Whatever the reason, GM was the target for 1970. Woodcock assured the company that the UAW was "deadly serious" and would suspend work until all local and national issues were resolved. He also stated that because of "distortion in the economy," the UAW would concentrate on shoring-up past contract gains rather than forge into new areas of dispute with the automobile manufacturers.

At the national level, the UAW generated 41 position papers on wages, hours, and working conditions. At the plant level, 155 UAW locals produced 38,900 demands in 85 categories (for example, 3,061 re seniority; 1,863 re overtime; 1,534 re wages; 1,432 re grievance and representational procedures; 1,229 re skilled-trade jurisdictional disputes; 1,012 re shift assignments; 703 re production standards; 362 re relief time; 172 automation grievances; etc.). As in past rounds, negotiations were carried on simultaneously at both national and local levels so that changes in work rules and grievances procedures at the plants would neither undermine nor contradict national agreements. Also, as always, all national agreements were subject to local ratification.

Who are these people and what is on their *collective* mind? Exhibits 1 through 6 present selected characteristics of the automotive production workforce just prior to the GM strike of 1970. What are the central tendencies of this population in terms of attributes, propensities, and behavior? Do these central tendencies have any predictive value? How much elasticity is there in wages? In productivity? In demand? These exhibits should be used in conjunction with the reading "Blue-Collar Blues on the Assembly Line" (IM 1954) to answer the question of who are the automotive workers and what options are available to them if they aspire to improve their collective lot.

Exhibits 7 through 14 summarize the strike and subsequent events. The UAW ratified a contract with GM that bound 400,000 workers. Similar contracts were ratified with Ford (binding 161,000 workers) and Chrysler (binding 110,000 workers). These contracts will expire on September 15, 1973. A contract with American Motors (binding 11,000 workers) followed, to expire on September 15, 1974. How responsive were these settlements to the needs and aspirations of the automotive production work force? What are likely to be the UAW's bargaining objectives in 1973? If these questions seem unanswerable, what data would you like to have in order to answer them? Would that data permit you to track the automotive work force sufficiently to project who will comprise it and what will be on its collective mind in 1983?

EXHIBIT 1
Earnings distribution for production workers, April 1969
(percent distribution of production and related workers by straight-time hourly earnings.* United States, Michigan, and selected regions†)

Average hourly earnings	United States	Mich-igan	North Central (except Mich-igan)	South	West	Remain-der of United States
Under $3.35	0.2	0.3	0.3	0.1	0.1	0.1
$3.35 and under $3.40	1.8	1.8	1.9	1.9	2.3	1.5
$3.40 and under $3.45	1.2	1.4	1.0	.7	.5	1.3
$3.45 and under $3.50	4.0	5.0	1.7	1.7	.9	9.0
$3.50 and under $3.55	6.9	6.1	9.0	5.0	2.5	8.0
$3.55 and under $3.60	12.6	13.5	13.1	9.6	8.7	9.7
$3.60 and under $3.65	22.9	22.4	21.4	31.0	33.1	20.8
$3.65 and under $3.70	10.1	11.0	10.4	6.5	6.8	7.7
$3.70 and under $3.75	11.3	10.0	11.3	16.9	19.7	11.7
$3.75 and under $3.80	2.2	2.5	2.2	2.2	1.4	1.4
$3.80 and under $3.85	7.6	6.3	8.1	13.5	12.2	8.3
$3.85 and under $3.90	1.8	1.5	1.7	2.1	2.8	2.9
$3.90 and under $3.95	1.3	1.2	1.0	2.2	2.1	1.3
$3.95 and under $4.00	.2	.2	.2	.1	.2	.2
$4.00 and under $4.10	.4	.4	.4	.3	.4	.3
$4.10 and under $4.20	.2	.2	.4	.1	§	.2
$4.20 and under $4.30	.1	.1	.2	–	–	.3
$4.30 and under $4.40	.2	.2	.4	§	§	.3
$4.40 and under $4.50	.5	.4	.7	.1	.2	.6
$4.50 and under $4.60	1.0	1.1	1.1	.4	.5	1.0
$4.60 and under $4.70	2.8	3.0	2.6	1.4	1.5	3.1
$4.70 and under $4.80	4.4	4.8	4.4	2.4	2.3	4.6
$4.80 and under $4.90	2.0	2.0	2.3	1.3	1.4	1.8
$4.90 and under $5.00	2.7	2.8	3.2	.4	.5	2.9
$5.00 and over	1.4	1.9	1.0	.2	–	.9
Total‡	100.0	100.0	100.0	100.0	100.0	100.0
Number of workers	605,556	317,717	177,447	38,617	19,850	51,925
Average hourly earnings	$3.82	$3.83	$3.83	$3.73	$3.74	$3.81

* Excludes incentive payments and premium pay for overtime and for work on weekends, holidays, and late shifts.
† The regions used in this study are: *North Central (except Michigan)*—Illinois, Indiana, Iowa, Kansas, Minnesota, Missouri, Nebraska, North Dakota, Ohio, South Dakota, and Wisconsin; *South*—Alabama, Arkansas, Delaware, District of Columbia, Florida, Georgia, Kentucky, Louisiana, Maryland, Mississippi, North Carolina, Oklahoma, South Carolina, Tennessee, Texas, Virginia, and West Virginia; and *West*—Arizona, California, Colorado, Idaho, Montana, Nevada, New Mexico, Oregon, Utah, Washington, and Wyoming.
§ Less than 0.05 percent.
‡ Because of rounding, sums of individual items may not equal 100.
Source: U.S. Dept. of Labor, Bureau of Labor Statistics, *Industry Wage Survey: Motor Vehicles and Parts, April 1969*, Bulletin 1679 (1971).

EXHIBIT 2
Occupational averages—production workers
(number and average straight-time hourly earnings of workers in selected occupations, United States, Michigan, and selected regions°)

Occupation	United States		Michigan	
	Number of workers	Average hourly earnings†	Number of workers	Average hourly earnings†
Maintenance:				
Carpenters	802	$4.62	506	$4.63
Electricians	7,079	4.74	3,582	4.75
Machine repairmen (maintenance mechanics)	7,090	4.79	4,056	4.78
Millwrights	7,039	4.64	3,762	4.64
Pipefitters	4,701	4.64	2,266	4.64
Sheet-metal workers (tinsmiths)	1,427	4.63	783	4.63
Toolroom:				
Die sinkers, drop-forge dies	201	5.58	102	5.68
Machine-tool operators, toolroom	3,564	4.76	2,128	4.76
Patternmakers, metal and wood	1,433	5.44	913	5.44
Tool and die makers	17,181	4.91	9,236	4.91
Custodial, material movement, and plant clerical:				
Checkers, receiving and shipping	6,554	3.62	3,679	3.61
Janitors, porters, and cleaners	10,633	3.37	5,533	3.37
Laborers, material handling	7,229	3.53	3,786	3.52
Truckers, inside, gas and electric	18,663	3.57	10,386	3.57
Truckdrivers, outside (semi)	1,356	3.91	1,206	3.91
Truckdrivers, outside (other than semi)	1,011	3.66	609	3.65
Other selected occupations:				
Assemblers, major	94,859	3.62	39,968	3.62
Assemblers, minor	19,527	3.52	12,374	3.53
General foundry laborers	4,829	3.58	3,137	3.59
Heat treaters, furnace (control men)	520	3.72	304	3.72
Heat treaters, furnace (load and unload)	2,075	3.55	732	3.60
Inspectors, final	10,404	3.76	4,172	3.75
Inspectors, floor	6,809	3.73	3,920	3.72
Inspectors, general	15,189	3.61	8,717	3.61
Inspectors and checkers, production	3,470	3.66	2,325	3.65
Machine-tool operators, production	30,315	3.64	18,728	3.64
Bar stock screw-machines	1,814	3.87	946	3.88
General (except set-up men)	17,825	3.61	10,115	3.61
Special (except set-up men)	10,676	3.66	7,667	3.66
Metal finishers	4,538	3.78	1,977	3.79
Moulders, machine	568	3.79	378	3.79
Punch-press operators (except set-up men)	29,191	3.62	17,548	3.63
Body stampings	12,295	3.69	6,890	3.68
General	14,119	3.57	8,649	3.58
Heavy	2,777	3.66	2,009	3.66
Sewing-machine operators	5,445	3.55	4,890	3.56
Sprayers, body, fender, and hood	4,658	3.78	1,711	3.79
Trimmers	5,799	3.72	2,134	3.72
Welders, hand	5,605	3.78	3,405	3.78
Welders, machine (resistance)	22,348	3.67	9,715	3.65

* The regions used in this study same as Exhibit 1.
† Excludes incentive payments and premium pay for overtime and for work on weekends, holidays, and late shifts.
Note: Dashes indicate no data reported or data that do not meet publication criteria.
Source: *Industry Wage Survey: Motor Vehicles and Parts.*

North Central (except Michigan)		South		West		Remainder of United States	
Number of workers	Average hourly earnings†	Number of workers	Average hourly earnings†	Number of workers	Average hourly earnings†	Number of workers	Average hourly earnings†
188	$4.60	35	$4.63	29	$4.61	44	$4.62
2,219	4.74	425	4.75	199	4.76	654	4.72
2,179	4.79	48	4.81	16	4.78	791	4.80
2,223	4.63	278	4.66	144	4.68	632	4.63
1,541	4.63	322	4.66	159	4.65	413	4.63
425	4.63	17	4.69	8	4.69	194	4.63
83	5.40	—	—	—	—	16	5.90
1,086	4.76	—	—	—	—	349	4.77
365	5.44	—	—	—	—	155	5.46
5,889	4.91	361	4.90	193	4.87	1,502	4.91
1,750	3.62	388	3.64	239	3.64	498	3.68
3,328	3.36	689	3.37	401	3.37	682	3.37
2,379	3.54	367	3.50	168	3.49	529	3.56
5,245	3.57	1,096	3.57	522	3.58	1,414	3.58
101	3.96	10	3.90	—	—	39	3.90
268	3.68	29	3.63	29	3.68	76	3.65
28,976	3.60	11,992	3.62	5,711	3.62	8,212	3.62
5,130	3.54	156	3.54	—	—	1,867	3.47
1,186	3.58	116	3.52	54	3.52	336	3.56
184	3.72	—	—	—	—	32	3.75
371	3.60	—	—	—	—	972	3.48
3,696	3.75	1,217	3.78	671	3.79	648	3.80
1,973	3.75	261	3.81	74	3.80	581	3.70
4,111	3.59	524	3.68	295	3.67	1,542	3.61
987	3.67	90	3.66	14	3.67	54	3.73
10,179	3.65	16	3.66	—	—	1,392	3.62
775	3.86	—	—	—	—	93	3.91
6,756	3.61	—	—	—	—	954	3.54
2,648	3.67	16	3.66	—	—	345	3.61
1,440	3.78	435	3.78	266	3.78	420	3.78
165	3.77	—	—	—	—	25	3.81
8,933	3.63	95	3.62	—	—	2,615	3.59
4,525	3.70	—	—	—	—	880	3.72
3,793	3.55	—	—	—	—	1,677	3.52
615	3.64	95	3.62	—	—	58	3.61
553	3.46	—	—	—	—	—	—
1,416	3.77	711	3.78	449	3.78	371	3.78
1,877	3.72	798	3.72	421	3.73	569	3.74
1,225	3.78	360	3.79	194	3.78	421	3.74
7,747	3.67	1,854	3.69	1,041	3.70	1,991	3.72

EXHIBIT 3
Occupational earnings—production workers
(number and average straight-time hourly earnings of workers in selected occupations, April 1969)

			Number of workers receiving straight-time hourly earnings of:							
Occupation	Number of workers	Average hourly earnings*	$3.20 and under $3.30	$3.30 — $3.40	$3.40 — $3.50	$3.50 — $3.60	$3.60 — $3.70	$3.70 — $3.80	$3.80 — $3.90	$3.90 — $4.00
Maintenance:										
Carpenters	802	$4.62	–	–	–	–	–	–	–	–
Electricians	7,079	4.74	–	–	–	–	–	–	–	–
Machine repairmen (maintenance mechanics)	7,090	4.79	–	–	–	–	–	–	–	–
Millwrights	7,039	4.64	–	–	–	–	–	–	–	–
Pipefitters	4,701	4.64	–	–	–	–	–	–	–	–
Sheet-metal workers (tinsmiths)	1,427	4.63	–	–	–	–	–	–	–	–
Toolroom:										
Die sinkers, drop-forge dies	201	5.58	–	–	–	–	–	–	–	–
Machine-tool operators, toolroom	3,564	4.76	–	–	–	–	–	–	–	–
Patternmakers, metal and wood	1,433	5.44	–	–	–	–	–	–	–	–
Tool and die makers	17,181	4.91	–	–	–	–	–	–	–	–
Custodial, material movement, and plant clerical:										
Checkers, receiving and shipping	6,554	3.62	–	1	788	1,952	3,385	81	346	1
Janitors, porters, and cleaners	10,633	3.37	189	9,889	553	2	–	–	–	–
Laborers, material handling	7,229	3.53	–	15	1,649	3,440	2,125	–	–	–
Truckers, inside, gas and electric	18,663	3.57	–	–	3,356	9,415	5,891	1	–	–
Truckdrivers, outside (semi)	1,356	3.91	–	–	–	3	–	–	6	1,323
Truckdrivers, outside (other than semi)	1,011	3.66	–	–	–	78	904	–	–	29
Other selected occupations:										
Assemblers, major	94,859	3.62	–	–	425	22,827	67,013	4,448	146	–
Assemblers, minor	19,527	3.52	225	95	6,747	12,359	100	1	–	–
General foundry laborers	4,829	3.58	–	–	376	2,378	1,608	467	–	–
Heat treaters, furnace (control men)	520	3.72	–	–	–	5	364	98	7	6
Heat treaters, furnace (load and unload)	2,075	3.55	–	–	880	618	574	1	1	1
Inspectors, final	10,404	3.76	–	–	–	199	967	3,488	5,698	52
Inspectors, floor	6,809	3.73	–	–	–	860	2,007	169	3,759	14
Inspectors, general	15,189	3.61	105	12	1,642	3,546	8,422	323	1,139	–
Inspectors and checkers, production	3,470	3.66	–	–	–	99	2,751	301	268	6
Machine-tool operators, production	30,315	3.64	–	28	1,337	3,812	21,531	1,875	772	960
Bar stock screw-machines	1,814	3.87	–	–	–	–	99	5	750	960
General (except set-up men)	17,825	3.61	–	28	1,337	3,339	12,662	458	1	–
Special (except set-up men)	10,676	3.66	–	–	–	473	8,770	1,412	21	–
Metal finishers	4,538	3.78	–	–	–	–	90	1,911	2,537	–
Molders, machine	568	3.79	–	–	–	–	15	261	274	18
Punch-press operators (except set-up men)	29,191	3.62	–	574	223	7,522	14,346	6,433	93	–
Body stampings	12,295	3.69	–	–	–	211	6,378	5,706	–	–
General	14,119	3.57	–	574	223	7,217	5,882	223	–	–
Heavy	2,777	3.66	–	–	–	94	2,086	504	93	–
Sewing-machine operators	5,445	3.55	–	110	212	3,971	1,152	–	–	–
Sprayers, body, fender, and hood	4,658	3.78	–	–	–	–	49	2,378	2,231	–
Trimmers	5,799	3.72	–	–	–	74	383	5,217	124	1
Welders, hand	5,605	3.78	–	–	–	3	297	2,813	2,397	93
Welders, machine (resistance)	22,348	3.67	–	–	3	5,267	7,575	9,184	319	–

* Excludes incentive payments and premium pay for overtime and for work on weekends, holidays, and late shifts
Source: *Industry Wage Survey: Motor Vehicles and Parts.*

						Number of workers receiving straight-time hourly earnings of:									
$4.00 – $4.10	$4.10 – $4.20	$4.20 – $4.30	$4.30 – $4.40	$4.40 – $4.50	$4.50 – $4.60	$4.60 – $4.70	$4.70 – $4.80	$4.80 – $4.90	$4.90 – $5.00	$5.00 – $5.10	$5.10 – $5.20	$5.20 – $5.30	$5.30 – $5.40	$5.40 – $5.50	$5.50 and over
–	–	–	–	27	61	714	–	–	—	–	–	–	–	–	–
–	–	–	–	–	143	577	4,209	1,970	177	1	1	1	–	–	–
–	–	–	–	–	36	406	4,612	1,576	460	–	–	–	–	–	–
–	–	–	–	149	657	3,957	2,276	–	–	–	–	–	–	–	–
–	–	–	–	113	357	2,943	1,287	–	–	–	–	–	–	–	–
–	–	–	–	26	114	1,046	241	–	—	–	–	–	–	–	–
–	–	–	–	–	–	–	20	–	36	–	–	–	–	–	145
–	–	–	–	–	13	269	3,269	6	6	–	–	–	–	–	–
–	–	–	–	–	–	–	–	–	–	7	5	–	68	1,351	–
–	–	–	–	–	–	–	318	4,293	11,032	1,538	–	–	–	–	–
–	–	–	–	–	–	–	–	–	–	–	–	–	–	–	–
–	–	–	–	–	–	–	–	–	–	–	–	–	–	–	–
–	24	–	–	–	–	–	–	–	–	–	–	–	–	–	–
–	–	–	–	–	–	–	–	–	–	–	–	–	–	–	–
–	–	–	–	–	–	–	–	–	–	–	–	–	–	–	–
–	–	–	–	–	–	–	–	–	–	–	–	–	–	–	–
–	40	–	–	–	–	–	–	–	–	–	–	–	–	–	–
–	–	–	–	–	–	–	–	–	–	–	–	–	–	–	–
–	–	–	–	–	–	–	–	–	–	–	–	–	–	–	–
–	–	–	–	–	–	–	–	–	–	–	–	–	–	–	–
45	–	–	–	–	–	–	–	–	–	–	–	–	–	–	–
–	–	–	–	–	–	–	–	–	–	–	–	–	–	–	–
–	–	–	–	–	–	–	–	–	–	–	–	–	–	–	–
–	–	–	–	–	–	–	–	–	–	–	–	–	–	–	–
–	–	–	–	–	–	–	–	–	–	–	–	–	–	–	–
–	–	–	–	–	–	–	–	–	–	–	–	–	–	–	–
–	–	–	–	–	–	–	–	–	–	–	–	–	–	–	–
–	–	–	–	–	–	–	–	–	–	–	–	–	–	–	–
–	–	–	–	–	–	–	–	–	–	–	–	–	–	–	–
–	1	1	–	–	–	–	–	–	–	–	–	–	–	–	–
–	–	–	–	–	–	–	–	–	–	–	–	–	–	–	–

EXHIBIT 4
Supplementary wage provisions, U.S. auto manufacturing, April 1969

Information is presented in this section on shift differential payments for production workers and on selected supplementary wage benefits for production and office workers, including paid holidays and paid vacations; health, insurance, and pension plans; and supplemental unemployment benefits. Data for these items were obtained from collective bargaining agreements and company publications.[1]

Shift differentials. Premium pay for production workers assigned to late-shift work was the same for each of the companies covered by the survey. It amounted to 5 percent of day-shift rates for second-shift work and 10 percent for third-shift work.

Definitions of late shifts, however, varied among the companies. Second-shift work, for example, was defined in one company as work beginning on or after 10:30 A.M. but before 7 P.M., whereas corresponding hours in the other companies were 11 A.M. and 7 P.M., 12 noon and 7 P.M., and 2 P.M. and 10 P.M. Third-shift work was defined to begin when second-shift work ended and extended into the morning hours. Information was not obtained on proportions of workers actually employed on various shifts at the time of the survey. Employment on late shifts tends to fluctuate throughout the year as the volume of production changes.

Paid holidays. Paid holiday provisions were similar for plant and office workers in each of the four companies. Three companies provided 10 full-day holidays in 1969 (New Year's Day, Good Friday, Memorial Day, July 4, Labor Day, Thanksgiving Day, December 24, Christmas Day, December 26, and December 31) and 11 holidays in 1970. The other company provided 11 holidays, including the day after Thanksgiving Day, in 1969.

Paid vacations. Production workers qualified under eligibility rules in collective bargaining agreements in effect in 1969 were entitled to paid vacations or to payments in lieu of vacations. The companies provided the following schedule of vacation payments for eligible employees with 1 year of service or more:

Years of seniority	Vacation payment
1 and under 3	40 hours
3 and under 5	60 hours
5 and under 10	80 hours
10 and under 15	100 hours
15 and over	120 hours

Vacation payments were based on an employee's straight-time hourly rate, excluding shift and overtime premiums, but including cost-of-living allowances. In addition to vacation benefits specified above, the companies provided a paid absence allowance, to be used in units of not less than 4 hours and

[1] For more detailed information on supplementary wage benefits for production workers in the industry, see the Bureau's Wage Chronologies for the Chrysler Corp., Ford Motor Co., and General Motors Corp.

EXHIBIT 4 (*continued*)

not to exceed 40 hours annually, that employees could use for various purposes (e.g., personal leave, illness, additional vacation).

Vacation provisions for office employees varied somewhat among the companies. All companies provided 2 weeks of vacation pay for employees with at least 1 year of service. One company provided 3 weeks' paid vacation after 10 years of service, and another granted 3 weeks after 3 years and 4 weeks after 10 years. Two companies gave 2½ weeks after 3 years, 3 weeks after 5 years, 3½ weeks after 10 years, and 4 weeks after 15 years.

Health, insurance, and retirement plans. Provisions for health, insurance, and retirement benefits for production workers were included in collective bargaining agreements of all companies. Generally, similar benefits applied to office workers in these companies. The entire cost of benefits was borne by employers.

Three of the four companies, accounting for a large majority of the workers, provided life insurance (including total and permanent disability feature and accidental death and dismemberment benefits) and sickness and accident insurance. The amount of life insurance coverage and sickness and accident payments varied according to the individual's basic hourly rate for production workers and according to base salary for office workers. Hospitalization, surgical, and medical insurance benefits were provided to production and office workers in all companies. These plans covered both employees and their dependents. In 1969, a prescription drug program, covering employees and their dependents, was established in three companies. It required that the subscriber pay the first $2 for each separate prescription, original or refill, and that the plan pay the additional cost to participating pharmacies.

Production and office workers of all companies were provided retirement pension benefits (in addition to those available under Federal social security). With few exceptions, the major features of these plans were identical. For normal retirement, employees were required to be age 65 and have a minimum of 10 years of service. Depending on an employee's base wage rate or salary, monthly annuities amounted to $5.50, $5.75, or $6 multiplied by the individual's years of credited service. All plans provided for early retirement benefits, disability retirement benefits, and vesting (rights to accrued benefits deferred until age 65).

Supplemental unemployment benefits. Each of the companies had supplemental unemployment benefit plans for their production and related workers. These plans, essentially identical, were financed by company payments to trust funds from which benefits were paid to laid-off workers with at least 1 year of service and who met certain other tests of eligibility. The duration of benefits up to a maximum of 52 weeks for each benefit year, depended on the "credit units" accumulated by each eligible employee and the position of the fund at the time of layoff. Employees with 7 years or more of eligible service were guaranteed a full year's layoff benefits. In general, laidoff employees could receive cash benefits ranging up to a maximum of $70 a week (plus $1.50 a week for each dependent up to four) when not receiving State unemployment compensation benefits. The supplemental unemployment

EXHIBIT 4 (*concluded*)

benefits, when combined with State unemployment compensation, are designed to give the employee an amount equal to a maximum of 95 percent of his weekly straight-time pay (after taxes) for a 40-hour week, less $7.50 for work related expenses not incurred.

Office employees of one company were covered by the provisions of the supplemental unemployment benefit plan.

Short workweek benefits. Short workweek benefits for production workers were included in the supplemental unemployment benefit plans. Workers with 1 year of service and meeting other eligibility requirements were provided 80 percent of their base hourly wage rate times the difference between the number of paid hours and 40.

Separation allowances. Companies typically provided monetary allowances for both production and office workers who were laid off or separated from work under certain conditions. Production workers were covered by plans requiring 1 year of service for eligibility and providing lump-sum payments ranging from 50 to 2,080 hours' pay, depending on years of service. Eligibility requirements and the schedule of benefits for office workers varied among the companies.

Moving allowances. Allowances toward expenses incurred by production workers when transferring from one plant location to another were provided by all companies. Maximum benefit depended on mileage and marital status, ranged from $170 to $370 for single employees and from $445 to $795 for married employees. The incidence of such benefits was not determined for office workers.

Source: *Industry Wage Survey: Motor Vehicles and Parts.*

EXHIBIT 5

Output per man-hour, unit labor requirements, and related data, production workers, 1957–70
(indexes, 1967 = 100)

Year	Output per...		Unit labor requirements in terms of...		Related data		
	Production worker	Production worker man-hours	Production workers	Production worker man-hours	Output*	Production workers	Production worker man-hours
1957	67.7	67.6	147.7	148.0	65.0	96.0	96.2
1958	67.3	69.2	148.6	144.4	48.6	72.2	70.2
1959	73.0	72.5	137.1	138.0	62.6	85.8	86.4
1960	78.9	78.5	126.8	127.4	70.9	89.9	90.3
1961	80.4	81.9	124.4	122.1	61.5	76.5	75.1
1962	91.2	87.2	109.7	114.7	77.7	85.2	89.1
1963	94.9	90.4	105.4	110.6	86.8	91.5	96.0
1964	96.8	91.9	103.4	108.8	89.5	92.5	97.4
1965	103.9	96.0	96.2	104.1	109.3	105.2	113.8
1966	102.6	97.9	97.4	102.2	109.7	106.9	112.1
1967	100.0	100.0	100.0	100.0	100.0	100.0	100.0
1968	112.6	106.6	88.8	93.8	122.3	108.6	114.7
1969	106.2	104.0	94.2	96.2	120.2	113.2	115.6
1970†	98.9	100.1	101.1	99.9	96.7	97.8	96.6
Average annual rates (percent)							
1957–70	3.8	3.6	−3.7	−3.4	6.2	2.3	2.6

* The measures of output used in this table represent the total production of the industry resulting from all employees and do not represent the specific output of any single group of employees.
† Preliminary.
Source: U.S. Dept. of Labor, Bureau of Labor Statistics, *Indexes of Output Per Man-Hour, Selected Industries, 1939 and 1947–70*, Bulletin 1692 (1971).

EXHIBIT 6

Growth in output per man-hour in selected industries, 1957–70

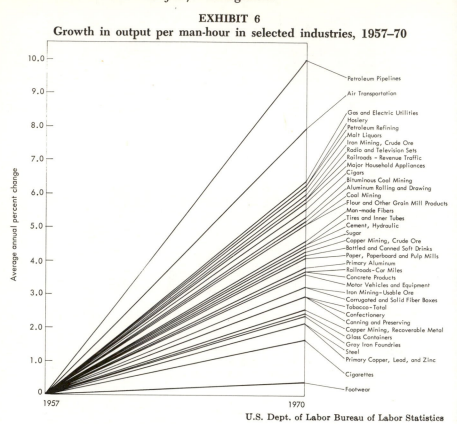

U.S. Dept. of Labor Bureau of Labor Statistics

EXHIBIT 7
The UAW National Convention, April 20–24, 1970

UAW sets collective bargaining goals for 1970°

Delegates to the 22d Constitutional Convention of the United Auto Workers union (UAW) met in Atlantic City, N.J., April 20–24, to set their union's 1970 bargaining goals at Chrysler, Ford, and General Motors. Contracts covering about 700,000 workers employed by the "Big 3" expire on September 15.

The following items won top priority as bargaining proposals: (1) A substantial wage increase and a year-end cash bonus; (2) revision of the cost-of-living adjustments from an annual to a quarterly basis, with the remainder of the 1967 contract cost-of-living bonus paid in cash; (3) improvements in the pension plan to provide a minimum of $500 a month after 30 years; and (4) optional overtime.

In calling for a substantial wage increase, the UAW leadership rejected pleas for wage restraint to help curb inflation. Some indication of their wage demand was given in a constitutional amendment ratified by the delegates

* Written by Lucretia Dewey, economist, Division of Industrial Relations, Bureau of Labor Statistics.

to raise the salary of officers and staff members by 8 percent, including fringe benefits, after completion of the 1970 auto negotiations, and by 7 percent effective August 1971. President Walter P. Reuther warned newsmen that these increases should not be taken as a guide to the UAW demands and commented that "we expect to do a lot better than that for the guy in the shop." A year-end cash bonus, similar to compensation for corporation executives, will also receive priority.

During the 1967 auto negotiations, the UAW agreed to change the cost-of-living formula from quarterly increases to a minimum of 8 cents, based on a yearly review for 1968 and 1969. Current bargaining proposals call for the restoration of unlimited quarterly increases along with an improvement in the ratio of adjustment—one cent for each 0.3 rise in the Consumer Price Index, instead of the current 1 cent for each 0.4 rise.

Under the 1967 contract, the UAW members have received 17 cents in cost-of-living adjustments. On September 15, 1970, the contract expiration date, an additional allowance becomes due, an amount which represents the difference between the 17 cents already received and the adjustment that would have been received under the formula in existence prior to 1967. Whether UAW members will receive the amount, 21–26 cents (depending on the level of the Consumer Price Index by September), in wages, in fringe benefits, or in some combination of the two was left open for discussion in 1970. Representatives of the Auto National Councils have decided that the entire amount ought to be paid in wages. This payment, the UAW maintains, is due under the contract and has nothing to do with bargaining demands.

Delegates voiced strong support for pension revisions. Currently, the pension plans with the auto companies provide for a $400-a-month minimum at age 60 with 30 years of service. The new proposal would eliminate the age requirement and raise the minimum by $100. At the UAW Skilled Trades meeting in March, Mr. Reuther had been reluctant to commit himself to the "30 and out" proposal, preferring to remain flexible at the bargaining table. Membership sentiment, however, swayed Mr. Reuther to make it a top priority item.

Enthusiastically supported by the delegates and made part of the package proposal is what the union calls a "Bill of Rights" for workers. Based on the premise that when a worker contracts to work for a company he does so for 8 hours a day and 40 hours a week, the UAW would give each worker the choice of accepting or rejecting overtime work.

Other bargaining proposals ratified by the delegates include inverse seniority at local option, improvement of supplementary unemployment benefits for low seniority workers, higher insurance benefits (including a dental program), restriction of subcontracting, group auto insurance, and longer vacations with a vacation bonus.

Mr. Reuther emphasized that collective bargaining would play a role in ending pollution in the environment and in auto plants.

In an effort to establish sufficient funds during a work stoppage, the convention adopted a constitutional change granting a local union or intracorporation

EXHIBIT 7 (*concluded*)

council—with executive board authorization—the right to double monthly dues up to 4 months preceding the termination of a contract or following ratification of a new agreement. Each local authorized to double its monthly dues will be required to place half of the payment in trust. The additional dues would be applied against future dues or refunded to each member. This process will insure dues collection if a company refuses to continue dues checkoff after a contract expires.

For the first time since 1949, Mr. Reuther was challenged for the presidency. An opposition group, the United National Caucus, presented a full slate of candidates and a collective bargaining program. Included in the opposition's proposals were a call for the establishment of a 30 hour workweek, a minimum hourly rate of $5 and a 50-percent wage increase in 1970, payment of $1,000 lost under the 1967 cost-of-living gap, 25 years and out retirement. and referendum vote for election of officers. Art Fox, a member of the bargaining committee of Local 600, Dearborn, Mich., was the caucus nominee for the international presidency. At the completion of the roll call of delegates, no United National Caucus candidate received as many as 300 votes. Just 2 weeks after being reelected to his 13th term, Mr. Reuther was killed in a plane crash.

Source: U.S. Bureau of Labor Statistics, *Monthly Labor Review*, June 1970.

EXHIBIT 8
The Death of Walter Reuther, May 9, 1970

Walter P. Reuther, 62, one of the most dynamic and innovative leaders in American labor annals, died in a plane crash on May 9. His death came just 2 weeks after his reelection to a 13th consecutive term as president of the 1.6 million member United Auto Workers union (UAW) and increased the possibility of turbulence in the fall bargaining between the union and the major auto and agricultural implement companies.

President Nixon called Mr. Reuther's death "a deep loss not only for organized labor, but also for the cause of collective bargaining and the entire American process." The loss may have a profound effect on the future direction of the American labor movement, particularly the Alliance for Labor Action (ALA), founded by Mr. Reuther and Teamsters' Acting President Frank E. Fitzsimmons to "revitalize" the movement. (The ALA was formed in July 1968 shortly after the UAW "formally disaffiliated" from the AFL-CIO and held its founding convention in May 1969.)

Walter Reuther left behind him a trailblazing set of collective bargaining innovations. He was one of the first major labor leaders to demand that company increases in profits and productivity be translated into increased wages and to insist that higher wages do not justify price increases. He was concerned with overall economic planning as well as bread-and-butter unionism, voicing equal consideration for productivity, pricing, profits, consumer interests, and wages. He felt that labor unions should be an active force for community betterment in civil rights, minimum wages, and similar areas—rather than conveying the image of a self-centered power bloc.

Collective bargaining firsts often associated with Mr. Reuther include cost-of-living escalator clauses, annual improvement factors (deferred wage in-

EXHIBIT 8 (*concluded*)

creases based on productivity), Supplemental Unemployment Benefits, fully funded pension plans, profit sharing (at American Motors Corp.), and the guaranteed annual wage—won in 1967 and providing SUB payments of 95 percent of takehome pay, when combined with State unemployment benefits.

Although sometimes accused of a political philosophy that matched his hair color, the "fiery redhead" was instrumental in purging the UAW executive board of communist elements when he assumed the UAW presidency and later in expelling CIO affiliates for alleged communist leanings.

Shortly after Mr. Reuther's death, the UAW international officers appointed secretary-treasurer Emil Mazey acting president. The union's 25-member international executive board met on Friday, May 22 to select a permanent successor to Mr. Reuther. Besides Mr. Mazey, strong candidates for the job had included vice-presidents Douglas Fraser, 53, director of the union's Chrysler and skilled trades departments; chief organizer Duane (Pat) Greathouse, 54; and Leonard Woodcock, 59, head of the General Motors department. Mr. Fraser is one of 5 new vice-presidents voted in on the Reuther slate at the UAW's recent convention. (Mr. Reuther was eligible for only one more 2-year term under the UAW constitution—which prohibits a man from running for the presidency after reaching age 65—and backed the plan to boost the number of vice-presidents from 2 to 7. Observers felt this indicated his desire to provide for an orderly transition for his eventual successor.) The board chose Mr. Woodcock.

The upcoming negotiations are expected to be particularly difficult, and Mr. Reuther's absence may make the bargaining even harder. The auto companies have suffered increased costs and declining sales and are expected to take a "tough" bargaining approach. The Auto Workers want to offset the rise in the cost of living, and convention delegates approved a bargaining demand for "substantial" wage hikes.

Prepared by Leon Bornstein and other members of the staff of the Division of Trends in Employee Compensation, Bureau of Labor Statistics, and based on information from secondary sources available in April.
Source: U.S. Bureau of Labor Statistics, *Monthly Labor Review*, June 1970.

EXHIBIT 9
The election of Leonard Woodcock, May 25, 1970

UAW election

On May 25, Leonard Woodcock, 59, was elected president of the 1.6-million member United Auto Workers Union, succeeding Walter Reuther who died in a plane crash on May 9. Mr. Woodcock was elected unanimously by the union's 25-man executive board, after Douglas Fraser announced that he had decided to withdraw as a candidate and support Mr. Woodcock. Mr. Fraser said that his action was based on a poll of the executive board, which indicated that 13 members favored the new president, while 12 favored Mr. Fraser. Both UAW executives were among the union's seven vice presidents. Mr. Woodcock headed its GM and aerospace departments; Mr. Fraser heads the Chrysler Department and the UAW's skilled tradesmen.

The election of Mr. Woodcock lent some support to speculation that the UAW would choose General Motors Corp. as its prime target for the first

EXHIBIT 9 (*concluded*)

time since 1945–46 in the auto negotiations scheduled for the fall. Referring to the coming bargaining with the "Big 3" auto makers, Mr. Woodcock said that the UAW "is determined to win a settlement that will get equity for our members and that Walter Reuther would have been proud of." He also indicated that the UAW's concern for social causes would not change. Shortly after his election, he spoke at the General Motors Corp.'s annual meeting in support of a proposal to create a committee for corporate responsibility at GM, called for a full-scale Congressional investigation of "senseless killings of American citizens by American military and police" at Kent State University, Jackson State College, and Augusta, Ga., and repudiated his earlier support of the Viet Nam war by calling on the United States "to disentangle itself from the morass of Indochina."

Source: U.S. Bureau of Labor Statistics, *Monthly Labor Review*, July 1970.

EXHIBIT 10
The UAW Strikes GM, September 15, 1970

September song

The United Auto Workers may have found new meaning in the lyrics of a familiar song. At the beginning of May 1970, the Auto Workers had just completed their 22d constitutional convention, during which bargaining goals were formulated for the approaching auto negotiations. Three-year contracts covering 700,000 employees of the "Big 3" automakers expired on September 15. As "the days dwindled down to a precious few," union members voted to strike General Motors Corp. and Chrysler Corp. (The union had earlier decided not to strike Ford.) On September 13, the UAW dropped Chrysler as a strike target and 2 days later struck General Motors for the first time since a 119-day walkout in 1946. With both sides adamant and far apart on bargaining issues, observers saw little hope of a quick settlement.

A primary issue in the dispute is the 26 cents an hour that Auto Workers would have received in the last 2 years if there had not been an 8-cent annual ceiling on cost-of-living adjustments in the prior contract. In 1967, the parties had agreed that any excess over 16 cents would automatically become part of the 1970 agreement. The union asserts that the 26 cents is really back pay and should not be considered part of the immediate wage increase resulting from any 1970 settlement, as the auto makers desired. The union also wants to remove ceiling of future escalator adjustments.

Early retirement is another issue. Under the union's "30-and-out" proposal, members could retire after 30 years with a pension of $500 a month (including social security benefits), regardless of age. The company proposed a minimum age of 58, with an 8 percent a year reduction for earlier retirement. About 325,000 production workers struck GM (plus 22,000 in Canada), but the union permitted 75,000 others to continue work because they make parts for other auto firms, farm implement makers, or the Government.

Prepared by Leon Bornstein and other members of the staff of the Division of Trends in Employee Compensation, Bureau of Labor Statistics, and based on information from secondary sources in September.

Source: U.S. Bureau of Labor Statistics, *Monthly Labor Review*, November 1970.

EXHIBIT 11
The UAW-GM settlement, November 11–23, 1970

UAW negotiations

Nearly 400,000 Auto Workers at General Motors Corp., including 320,000 workers who went on strike September 15, were covered by a tentative 3-year national agreement reached on November 11. The UAW's 350-delegate General Motors Council approved the pact on November 12 and on November 20 the union announced the contract had been ratified by the members. Full-scale production did not resume immediately, pending settlement of local disputes involving working conditions.

The contract provided a first-year wage boost of 49 to 61 cents and hour (averaging 51 cents an hour), with a 3-percent increase effective in both the second and third years. Included in the first-year increase was the 26 cents in cost-of-living adjustments that the workers would have received under the prior 3-year agreement if it had not been subject to a 16-cent cost-of-living ceiling over the term. (The union had reportedly demanded 61 cents in the first year, while the company's final prestrike offer was 38 cents.)

A feature of the agreement was a return to the unlimited quarterly escalator adjustments that prevailed prior to the 1967 settlement, which provided for annual reviews in 1968 and 1969. The first adjustment was set for December 6, 1971, calculated at a 1-cent-an-hour wage change for each 0.4-point rise in the Consumer Price Index (determined by subtracting the August 1970 index level from the average of the levels for August, September, and October 1971), followed by quarterly adjustments in March 1972, June 1972, and so on.

A compromise was reached on another major bargaining issue. Workers are to be permitted to retire at a $500 a month pension at age 58 after 30 years of service, beginning October 1, 1971, with the age requirement dropping to 56 on October 1, 1972.

The $500, which is subject to reduction if the retiree has outside earnings, drops to $450 at age 62, when the retiree becomes eligible for early Social Security benefits. (Under its "30-and-out" demand, the UAW had sought a $500-a-month pension, including Social Security benefits, after 30 years of service, regardless of age). Previously, employees were eligible for a $400-a-month early retirement benefit at age 60 after 30 years of service. Other pension improvements included a $1.75-a-month increase in the normal rate, bringing it to $7.25–7.75 a month for each year's credited service, depending on the workers' wage scale. The rate for present retirees was also increased $1 a month for each year of service.

Other terms included additional paid holidays, an additional week of vacation after 20 years of service, extension of the employees' prescription drug plan to retirees and their spouses, continued company payment of the full fee (recently increased to $5.30 a month) for Part B Medicare coverage for retirees, and a 5-to-10-cent-an-hour company financing of supplemental unemployment benefits (SUB), instead of 5 to 7 cents depending on the position of the fund.

Earlier a special UAW convention had approved a temporary dues increase

EXHIBIT 11 (*concluded*)

for 900,000 of the union's 1.4 million members still employed (that is, those not striking GM and not laid off at other firms as a result of the strike). Some 350,000 Auto Workers still employed at other auto and auto parts firms and at agricultural implement companies were assessed an extra $20 a month on top of their normal dues of $7 to $8 a month. Dues of UAW members employed by other industries were doubled to $15–$16 a month.

The special assessment was also necessitated by the UAW's decision to pay the insurance premiums of the strikers. Earlier, GM had agreed to pay the $23-million-a-month premiums. The union would then reimburse the company.

Prepared by Leon Bornstein and other members of the staff of the Division of Trends in Employee Compensation, Bureau of Labor Statistics, and based on information from secondary sources available in October.

Source: U.S. Bureau of Labor Statistics, *Monthly Labor Review*, December 1970.

EXHIBIT 12
The Ford and Chrysler settlements, December 7, 1970 and January 19, 1971

Ford and UAW settle

Ford Motor Co. and the Auto Workers reached accord December 7 on a 3-year agreement nearly identical to the union's new contract with General Motors. (See *Monthly Labor Review*, December 1970, p. 51.) On December 15, the union announced ratification of the agreement, covering 161,000 workers at Ford. By early January, the last of the 99 bargaining units had settled on local issues. The final national issue resolved was the effective date of the initial wage increase. Ford and the UAW had agreed earlier that 26 cents in cost-of-living catchup money would be retroactive to September 15, termination date of the previous agreement. The UAW contended that the 23 to 35 cents in new money should also be effective on that date; Ford maintained it should not be effective until the Monday after the union formally notified the company that the national and all local agreements had been ratified. The contract set November 2 as the effective date. At GM, the entire 49 cents to 61 cents was effective November 23, except that 26 cents was retroactive to September 15 for UAW members not included in the walkout because they produce parts for other auto manufacturers.

There were two other differences between the Ford and General Motors agreements. At GM, the fund set up to finance November 1971 wage inequity adjustments is equal to $1.25 cents an hour for each worker (396,051) in the bargaining unit in April 1970; at Ford, funding was set at 0.5 cent an hour for each worker. Ford also agreed to check off dental care premiums from workers' pay if the UAW establishes such a plan. Some union officials view this as a first step toward the company-financed dental plans the union had attempted to win from GM and Ford.

Meanwhile, GM and the UAW were continuing to resolve local issues. As of January 1, 3 of the 155 bargaining units were still on strike.

At Chrysler, negotiators were unable to meet their December 18 target date for settlement, and talks were recessed until January. After talks resumed, the union set a strike deadline of January 19.

EXHIBIT 12 (*concluded*)

Settlements were also reached in the automotive parts and farm and construction industries, where UAW contracts traditionally are patterned after agreements with the Big Three auto makers.

Chrysler, UAW reach accord

The round of bargaining for the Big Three auto producers' production workers ended on January 19 as Chrysler Corp. reached a 3-year settlement for 110,000 Auto Workers (bargaining was continuing for 10,000 white-collar employees). Terms were similar to those negotiated with General Motors Corp. and Ford Motor Co. (See *Monthly Labor Review*, December 1970, p. 51, and February 1971, p. 74.

The last issue for production workers was resolved when the parties agreed that the 23-cent to 35-cent "new money" portion of the initial 49-cent to 61-cent wage increase would be effective November 2. The company had been seeking to have the increase become effective after the contract was ratified. The parties had earlier agreed that the 26 cents "spillover" of cost-of-living adjustments accrued during the previous agreement (but not paid because of a 16-cent limit on adjustments) would be effective September 15.

A unique feature of the new contract is a provision for a study of the feasibility of switching from a 5-day, 40-hour week to a 4-day, 40-hour week. Auto Workers' President Leonard Woodcock said a 4-day week could alleviate the substantial increase in absenteeism (particularly on Fridays and Mondays) that the industry has been experiencing in recent years.

At General Motors, bargaining on local issues ended on January 26, when UAW members at the Atlanta assembly plant approved a settlement, ending their 133-day walkout. More than 1,000 issues were involved. The unit was 1 of about 24 that remained on strike after the November 11 agreement on national issues.

Meanwhile, bargaining was continuing at American Motors, where work was continuing under an extension of the 2-year agreement that expired October 15.

Source: U.S. Bureau of Labor Statistics, *Monthly Labor Review*, February–March 1971.

EXHIBIT 13
The Chrysler Settlement is Modified and American Motors Settles

Workweek study shelved

The Chrysler Corp. and the United Auto Workers union agreed to terminate their feasibility study of the 4-day, 40-hour workweek. Provision for the study was included in the 3-year agreement reached in January 1971 (*Monthly Labor Review*, March 1971, p. 78). At that time, the 4-day week was suggested as a method of alleviating increased employee absenteeism in the auto industry, particularly on Mondays and Fridays. After a final meeting with the union on the subject on December 13, Chrysler issued a statement citing "the many obstacles" which led to the decision to terminate the study. Chrysler said that plants with three-shift operations could not be included in a 4-day program, thus eliminating over half of its employees. Also cited

EXHIBIT 13 (*concluded*)

as obstacles were the Walsh-Healey Act, which requires time-and-a-half pay after 8 hours a day on Federal contract work; a union demand for time-and-a-half for Friday work; and the "substantial" investment required to increase storage facilities and to modify receiving docks at various plants. The union had reportedly requested that the plan be tried out at an assembly plant. Prior to the December 13 meeting. UAW Vice President Douglas A. Fraser said. "We think the time has come for the studies to end and the experiment to begin. We therefore view this next meeting as a last chance to get a commitment from Chrysler to designate one or more plants of the corporation at which the 4-day week experiment will be conducted." Mr. Fraser added that if agreement on an experiment were not reached on December 13 discussion would not be resumed until the "current contract expires" (in September 1973).

American Motors accord

Continuing its recent history of contract concessions to American Motors Corp., the Auto Workers union agreed to a 47-month pact (from October 16, 1970, to September 15, 1974) containing the same provisions as the 3-year contracts at the Big Three but delaying the effective date of some benefit improvements. Wages were increased by 51 cents an hour effective immediately and by 3 percent at the beginning of each of the other contract years. Twenty-six cents was retroactive to October 16, 1970 (representing the additional cost-of-living increases the employees would have received during the two previous agreements if there had not been a 16-cent maximum, and 25 cents in "new money" retroactive to mid-March. In the Big Three contracts, the 25 cents was retroactive for longer periods. The American Motors' agreement covers 11,000 workers.

Source: U.S. Bureau of Labor Statistics, *Monthly Labor Review*, March–July 1971.

EXHIBIT 14
The UAW National Convention, April 22–27, 1972

United automobile workers' 23d constitutional convention

Job security and unemployment were the paramount issues confronting the 2,976 delegates to the 23d Constitutional Convention of the United Automobile Workers' Union, the first since the death of its longtime president Walter P. Reuther. The convention was held in Atlantic City, N.J., April 22–27. In keeping with the union's socially conscious posture of the past, the delegates adopted a wide-ranging social, economic and political program.

Many observers of the labor movement felt that with the death of Walter Reuther a change would occur in the direction of the UAW. President Leonard Woodcock, although stressing the importance of "bread and butter" issues, assured the delegates that the UAW would not withdraw its sponsorship of social causes. In his major address, he emphasized that "the passing of the leader had not meant the passing of the spirit."

With negotiations in the automobile and agricultural implement industries

EXHIBIT 14 (*continued*)

scheduled for mid-1973, and recognizing the unsettled conditions in the present national economy, the delegates decided to hold a special convention in Detroit, Mich., from March 22–24, 1973 to establish bargaining objectives.

Secretary-Treasurer Emil Mazey pronounced the union on the way back to fiscal health, after the costly ($160 million) strike at General Motors in 1970. Although still $3.5 million in debt, the union has reduced its General Fund deficit by over $7 million since April 1971, while repaying loans of $10 million from the Steelworkers and $3 million from the Rubber Workers. A substantial loan from the Teamsters' Strike Fund is expected to be repaid by March 1973, at which time the Teamsters will also be engaged in negotiating new agreements. Mr. Mazey estimated the Auto Workers would have a strike fund of $47 million when current contracts end in 1973, compared to $120 million prior to negotiations in 1970. In commenting on the financial report, President Woodcock emphasized that the size of the strike fund would not influence next year's bargaining strategy. In his words, "this union will be ready and able to take on anyone, any company that is foolish enough to want to test us again."

Job security

The pervasiveness of the job security issue reflected rank and file uneasiness about reduced employment opportunities in the automobile and aerospace industries—which had resulted in a drop of 128,000 in dues-paying members between fiscal 1969 and 1971.

Recognizing the multidimensional nature of the problem, the union proposed three approaches to protect jobs: (1) collective bargaining, (2) Congressional legislation, and (3) effective control of multi-national corporations. Specifically, the leadership proposed the continuance and extension, in collective bargaining agreements, of fair standards clauses designed to protect workers adversely affected by plant shutdowns or transfers. This protection, Mr. Woodcock noted, would be in the form of relocation and retraining payments to the displaced worker.

The Federal Government was also called upon to play an increasing role in protecting job security. The union will work for national legislation to provide pension reinsurance, severance pay, moving allowances, allowance for losses from the sale of homes due to transfers, and full income and fringe benefit maintenance, "to protect the workers and his family against the hazards of job loss caused by plant shutdown or transfer of operation."

Mr. Woodcock cited the precedent set when Amtrak took over rail operations. For example, railroad workers who lost their jobs due to a reduction in passenger operations are to receive their former wage as well as future increases and existing fringe benefits and any improvement for up to 6 years. In speaking to newsmen afterwards, Mr. Woodcock noted that "what's good for railroad workers is certainly good enough for automobile workers."

A further legislative proposal, perhaps the most radical adopted by the convention, would require a company to obtain Federal permission before it may relocate a plant, close a plant, or relocate work from one area to another. The resolution would require legislation to include criteria for a permit that

EXHIBIT 14 (*continued*)

would protect the social and economic needs of all individuals and institutions affected.

The third approach to protecting jobs in the United States was to achieve some measure of equality in wages and working conditions for workers in automobile plants abroad. Mr. Woodcock attributed the loss of auto workers' jobs to multinational corporations, who buy human labor in the cheapest markets ("worldwide sourcing"), and sell the products elsewhere.

Two approaches have been pursued by the UAW to combat this "worldwide sourcing" policy: First, through the Automotive Department of the International Metalworkers' Federation, the Auto Workers have sought to bring together union representatives of the three major international automobile corporations, "to coordinate their efforts against their respective corporations." Second, the union has supported efforts to amend the General Agreement on Tariffs and Trade to provide international fair labor standards which would require all exporting firms to pay fair wages.

According to Mr. Woodcock, however, the only effective means for meeting the challenge presented by multinational corporations was the establishment of a worldwide labor organization. Fair wages and just working conditions could be achieved universally, the union leader stated, if workers could unite and "seek common solutions to their common problems."

Controlling the power of international corporations is basic to the UAW's program. Delegates overwhelmingly endorsed a proposal to seek national legislation that would require a company to obtain a Federal license to export capital and thus (in the opinion of the union leaders) jobs. This license would be issued only if the company could prove that the export was "in the national interest of the United States." Further, these licenses would contain a code of "good behavior" relating to the corporation's foreign employees and a guarantee to provide their American employees full protection against loss of wages or fringe benefits.

Employment and unemployment

A number of resolutions dealt with the restoration of full employment and full production while maintaining effective restraints on inflation. In his State of the Union address, President Woodcock urged Congress to enact an amendment to the Emergency Employment Act of 1971 creating a "Jobs Now" program which would produce 500,000 public service jobs. Second, he proposed an increase in social security benefits, contending that a high proportion of the recipients are below the poverty level and that higher monthly payments would boost beneficiaries' purchasing power, hence increase employment.

Another resolution sought to increase overtime pay under the Fair Labor Standards Act from time-and-a-half to at least double time. This requirement would encourage the employment of additional workers and discourage the use of overtime.

Other resolutions related to employment called for increased emphasis on Federal manpower programs to train disadvantaged workers, and for the creation of an agency equivalent to NASA that would coordinate America's

EXHIBIT 14 (*concluded*)

scientific, technical, and production resources to fulfill high-priority civilian needs.

Other proposals

National Health Insurance. The UAW urged all candidates for public office to commit themselves to support the principle of comprehensive national health insurance, and called for passage of the Griffiths-Corman-Kennedy Health Security Program. Congresswoman Martha Griffiths (D., Mich.) and Senator Edward Kennedy (D., Mass.) spoke in support of their program, stating it was the only one which could "effectively make health care available to all, at a price every American could afford."

Education. The convention unanimously called for equal and quality education for all, committing itself to the following goals: nondiscriminatory school systems, progressive tax bases, more and better qualified teachers and guidance counselors, curriculum improvements, greater community involvement, and increased security in terms of administrative and police protection.

Busing was endorsed as usable "with the effort for quality education but not before it." The issue was vigorously debated, with a considerable number of delegates against it. President Woodcock ended debate by stating that quality education was the major issue, not busing, which he cited as a peripheral and temporary issue.

The convention also supported civil rights for all, tax reform, revenue sharing, and an immediate end to the Vietnam war.

Other convention affairs

A constitutional amendment raising certain salaries by 5 percent on January 1, 1973, and again on January 1, 1974, was adopted without discussion. Offices included were the international president, international secretary-treasurer, international vice-presidents, international executive board members, and international representatives.

As expected, President Woodcock easily won election for his first full term over United National Caucus candidate Jordan U. Sims of Local 961, Detroit, Mich. With the exception of Paul Schrade, Director of Region 6 (west coast), all members of the Executive Board were reelected to 2-year terms.

Social Justice awards were presented to Victor Reuther, retiring director of the International Affairs Department, Cesar Chavez, President of the United Farm Workers Union, and Roy Wilkins, Executive Secretary of the NAACP.

Written by Sheldon M. Kline. Mr. Kline is a labor economist in the Division of Industrial Relations, Bureau of Labor Statistics.
Source: U.S. Bureau of Labor Statistics, *Monthly Labor Review*, July 1972.

Food Mart, Inc. (A)[1]

JOHN BERGER was vice president of Food Mart, Inc., a nationwide super-market chain. He was in charge of the company's northeast region, which included 200 stores with some 5,000 employees in the New York–New Jersey metropolitan area. At 35 years of age he was proud of his achievement; he was particularly pleased by the outcome of events during the past 18 months.

Berger had been in his present position for four years. The profit margin of his stores was among the highest in the country. He had come to Food Mart after six years of experience in various administrative posts at another large supermarket chain, bringing with him a variety of new managerial techniques which he had been able to introduce successfully. Foremost among these was a decentralization scheme which followed a theory which he had been taught at business school and which left to local and district managers primary authority for handling day-to-day operating problems, including personnel and labor relations.

Food Mart's general labor policies had been laid down by Herbert P. Llewellyn III, chairman and chief executive of the company. Berger remembered well his interview with Llewellyn at the Chicago headquarters when he had been hired. Llewellyn had contended forcefully that if Food Mart's personnel men did their job properly, there was no need for a union.

---

[1] This case was prepared by Charles Biderman and Professor George C. Lodge. Although it is based upon facts revealed in congressional and court investigations, it is not intended to represent or relate to any specific individuals, organizations, or actions.

"Our wages are higher than or consistent with the competition; our benefits more generous; and we are able to know and handle our workers' problems better than some crooked union leaders," Llewellyn had said. "There is no reason why a union should interfere with our ability to manage and control our stores efficiently."

Berger had been somewhat concerned by Llewellyn's views, since it had been his experience that a well-run union saved management many headaches and that a bargaining relationship with workers was in general more satisfactory than one based on an individual connection between an employee and the personnel department. He was also somewhat puzzled because he knew that under his predecessor some 15 percent of the work force in his region—butchers and meat warehouse employees—had been organized by the United Meat Workers after a bitter strike which shut down operations for more than a month. Llewellyn explained that Food Mart had had no choice in that situation. Although the union only had about 600 members, it was well organized and had been able to persuade other employees into joining the strike. "They seemed to have a lot of friends," Llewellyn said. "We finally reached agreement when the union compromised on some of its more unreasonable demands. Since then, we have had no trouble at all."

Berger remembered reading in the newspapers that the United Meat Workers was mixed up with organized crime. It had been reported that the head of the union, Leonard T. Fiedler, was in some way connected to the Borleone family of the Cosa Nostra in New Jersey. He asked Llewellyn about this.

"They're no more crooked than the rest of those union guys," Llewellyn had said. "We'd be better off without any of them, but in this case we had no choice."

The interview had ended with Llewellyn's strong admonition to John to avoid getting himself into a position of having to choose between a strike or a union.

Several years later John Berger confronted his biggest challenge as a Food Mart vice president. It began the day that Anthony Luzo, president of Local 656 of the Associated Grocery Clerks and Warehouse Employees of America (AGCWE), AFL-CIO, walked into Berger's New York office to inform him that the union was going to seek election as the bargaining representative of Food Mart's 4,000 unorganized employees, including clerks, checkers, warehouse and maintenance workers. Berger told him that another union was unnecessary; the unorganized workers were happy at Food Mart. Luzo had replied that his efforts were part of a nationwide organizing drive by the AGCWE.

Berger was impressed by Luzo's forthright sincerity; also, he was doubtful about the ability of Food Mart to withstand further organization indefinitely. It was, therefore, with considerable reluctance that he called his staff together to plan the defeat of the union in the coming election. The campaign was to be under the direction of Dana Thomas, Berger's personnel chief, who had been in his job for some ten years. Berger ordered a public relations program aimed at informing the workers why they were better off without a union, but specifically prohibited intimidation or threats of dismissal. From time to time in the past he had heard sporadic complaints that some employees had been fired for promoting the idea of organization under the AGCWE. He had found that most of these stories were apparently untrue, but they had caused unfavorable publicity for Food Mart in the local press.

As the election drew near, Berger learned, while lunching with a friend from his old company, that the clerks' union was going to get a 40-hour week at the same pay in their new contract with that company and, indeed, that the union had succeeded in negotiating a 40-hour week in recent bargaining throughout the country. "The chances are that they'll want the same from you," his friend said.

Previously, Berger had thought that talk of a 40-hour week was union propaganda to gather worker support, but this news caused him to consider seriously the costs of such a change for his stores which were then working a 45-hour week. He estimated that the change would cost him about $4 million a year before taxes. This compared with total earnings after taxes of some $12 million a year. The high cost was due to the fact that Food Mart stores were open six days a week and the work force would have to be substantially expanded if the 40-hour work week were introduced.

With a week to go before the election, therefore, Berger told Thomas to redouble his efforts.

The election resulted in a victory for Food Mart: 1,824 votes to 1,263. Llewellyn called from Chicago with congratulations.

Several weeks later Berger picked up his newspaper at the train station on the way to work and was dumbfounded by what he saw on page one. Local 656 had requested the National Labor Relations Board to call a new election, charging the company with violations of the National Labor Relations Act during the recent elections: intimidation of prounion employees, threats of reprisals by store managers and assistant managers if the union won the election, and illegal harassment of organizers.

Berger called a meeting of his staff and district managers as soon as he got to his office. Although there was general denial of the union's charges, some said that they had heard rumors about antiunion activity in some stores. Then Dana Thomas spoke up and said, "We had assumed that if there were such goings on, it was with your approval and Mr. Llewellyn's blessing. We know how strongly you felt about the 40-hour week business." When pressed by Berger, Thomas admitted that he had "talked with Chicago" and that they had informally approved the stronger measures.

Food Mart's lawyers told Berger that the position did not look good. The NLRB would almost certainly order a new election. With all the publicity it appeared certain that the Clerks would win.

Berger was deeply concerned. A union victory would not only bring down the wrath of Llewellyn, it would almost certainly cause pressure for a 40-hour week which would threaten Food Mart's healthy profit line. To make matters worse, at the very time that these labor problems plagued him, three stores in Newark reported sharp increases in enforcement activity by city building and traffic authorities. The stores had suddenly been charged with a number of violations of building codes, and trucks which had generally been allowed to double park while delivering their load were being ticketed and heavily fined.

It was at this point that Berger received the following letter from Leonard Fiedler, National President of the United Meat Workers:

> Dear Mr. Berger:
>
> There is a matter which we consider of great importance as affects our organization and Food Mart which we would like to personally discuss with you.
>
> We will not bring many people and we do not feel the meeting should take much of our time. There are some things which we feel will be very advantageous to Food Mart as well as to our organization. It would be a good idea to talk it over, I assure you.
>
> You will let me know if you are in agreement to meet us and we can set a definite date for the conference.
>
> Very sincerely,
>
> Leonard T. Fiedler

Berger wondered why the letter was from the national head of the union and not the local secretary-treasurer with whom the company generally dealt. He was further puzzled because as far as he knew there were no problems with the Meat Workers, although he was aware that a new two-year contract would be up for negotiation soon. He had never met Fiedler; all dealing with the union until now had been conducted by Thomas. As he thought about it, he had not wanted to meet Fiedler. In part, he supposed, his reluctance had stemmed from the reports of an underworld tie which he had read. On several occasions he had thought of investigating further, but he had decided it would just get him into trouble. There was nothing he could do about it anyway.

Pressed as he was now, however, and eager to avoid any further labor difficulties, Berger told his secretary to make an appointment with Fiedler. For reasons of which he could not be entirely sure, he decided to meet with him and his group alone and away from the office. The meeting was set for the following week at a Holiday Inn outside of Newark.

Fiedler was a heavy-set man who looked as though he would have been more comfortable in his butcher's apron than the expensive suit he was wearing. Three men were with him, one of whom was introduced as the head of the Food Mart local. They were silent during the meeting, showing deference to their boss.

Fiedler began the conversation, reminiscing about the amicable relations which had prevailed between his union and the company during the years of their association.

Berger replied, somewhat facetiously, "You haven't got much to complain about, getting $4 a month dues from 600 Food Mart employees, not to mention the administration of the $7 million meat workers pension fund."

Fiedler looked across the table at Berger. His large, full face was impassive; tinted glasses shaded his eyes.

"We're doing all right, Mr. Berger, but we could do better and so could you," said Fiedler. "We got problems and you got problems. My union is a big organization. Like any big organization we got big expenses. That's my problem. Your problem is the Clerks, the 40-hour week and all. And my friends in City Hall tell me you have been violating the law over there a good bit. It seems to me and my associates here that in a case like this your interests are pretty close to ours. I was thinking maybe we could help each other."

Berger said nothing as Fiedler went on to outline his plan. Prior to the new election, certain to be ordered by the NLRB, the Meat Workers would "let it be known" that a "no" vote—against the Clerks' union—would be in effect a vote for organization by the Meat Workers. The AGCWE would thus lose the election a second time. The company would then agree to allow the Meat Workers to circulate cards as prescribed by the NLRB to the 4,000 unorganized clerks, checkers, warehouse and maintenance employees for them to sign declaring their desire to join the Meat Workers. The cards would read: "In accordance with my legal rights, guaranteed by the National and State Labor Relations Act, I hereby designate the United Meat Workers as my collective bargaining agent." The company would agree to put no obstacle in the union's way. In return the union would give the company a guarantee that all employees would continue to work a 45-hour week for the next five years. The guarantee would be included in the forthcoming bargaining agreement with the Meat Workers.

"How can you make such a guarantee when Local 656 will offer the 40-hour week immediately?" asked Berger.

"There are two reasons," said Fiedler. "Our shop stewards will make clear to the retail and warehouse people that they will be represented by a strong, competent union which may give a little at first in order to make big gains later. And then when the word gets around that you are favorably inclined towards us, it will make a big difference. Your workers think a lot of you."

"Is that legal? It wouldn't sit well with the NLRB if we forced our people to join your union."

"No force," countered Fiedler. "Just don't hinder my men. Just keep out of the way."

Berger told Fiedler he would let him know his answer in a few days. Driving back to his New York office, he regretted not having asked Fiedler to be more explicit about the building code and traffic violation problem. He also wondered what would happen if he turned down the proposition. The AGCWE would undoubtedly be successful and there was always the chance of another strike by the Meat Workers. He knew he would have to call Llewellyn. The chairman would not like the deal but neither would he like a 40-hour week and another strike.

Berger called Chicago and found that Llewellyn was cruising off the coast of Mexico on his schooner. The executive vice president took the matter under advisement and called Berger back the following day, telling him to do what he thought best.

Berger decided to agree to Fiedler's conditions. The second election was held as ordered by the NLRB. The AGCWE was soundly defeated and the Meat Workers quickly secured the necessary majority of signed cards. Shortly thereafter a new contract was signed with the Meat Workers as Fiedler had promised, providing for the 45-hour week. Although the agreement was for five years, wages were to be renegotiable after two years.

The Clerks protested that workers had been coerced into joining the other union and that there had been collusion between the company and the Meat Workers.

After a few weeks, however, the protests subsided and all was going smoothly. Even the Newark violation problem had disappeared. Berger's Newark district manager reported at a regular management meeting that it had "apparently solved itself."

Berger didn't pursue the matter, glad that he was relieved of one more worry.

Thomas reported that relations with the new, expanded union were very good and that he expected no difficulties in the forthcoming negotiations.

Llewellyn's ideas are old fashioned, thought Berger. Managers must change with the times, respond to environmental pressures, act with realism.

FIGHT and Eastman Kodak[1]

RACIAL EXPLOSION marked the summer of July 1964 in Rochester, New York. Four days of rioting and violence, set off by the arrest of a 17-year-old Black on charges of drunkenness ended with four dead, hundreds injured, a thousand arrested and property damages of $1 million.

Many local citizens did not understand what caused the riots, especially given Rochester's image as a city "proud of its tradition of abundant, locally provided social services, proud of its reputation as a clean, progressive community."[2] Outsiders tended to focus on the resentment which many alienated Blacks felt toward the prosperous White community. The frustrations of poverty, run-down ghetto housing, lack of education, job skills and motivation, and an animus against the police were seen as a complex of causes which created and fostered a "new, angry, combustible force" in Rochester. In contrast one civic leader diagnosed the problem as follows:

[1] This case is an extension of "Eastman Kodak and FIGHT," International Clearing House 12H68, which was prepared from public sources at Northwestern University by Frances Sheridan under the direction of Professor Howard F. Bennett. It incorporates new material prepared at Harvard University from public sources by Linda Waters under the direction of Professor George C. Lodge and from an interview conducted with Bernard R. Gifford in February 1972 by Professor Lodge. This case is intended to serve as a basis for class discussion rather than to illustrate effective or ineffective handling of an administrative situation.

[2] Patrick Anderson, "Making Trouble Alinsky's Business," *The New York Times Magazine,* October 9, 1966, p. 30.

This city seems to have become a victim of its own generosity. Rochester is known as a soft touch for welfare and relief chiselers. As a result
there has been a large influx of shiftless people with no real desire
to work for a living. . . . Many of the newcomers are ne'er-do-wells.
They are the people who live in squalor, who won't try to better themselves, whose main interest seems to be where the next bottle of booze
is coming from.[3]

Thriving in industry, with such firms as Eastman Kodak, Xerox,
Bausch & Lomb, Taylor Instruments, and divisions of General Motors
and General Dynamics offering well-paid jobs to highly skilled workers,
the city promoted itself as:

a community . . . with the highest percentage of skilled, technical,
and professional employees of any major U.S. metropolitan area; more
engineers than any one of 23 States; the highest median family income
of any city in the State, sixth highest in the nation. . . . 67 percent
of the residents owning their own houses.[4]

But Rochester, along with the rest of urban America, has mounting
"inner city" problems. From 1950–1964 the Black population increased
by 24,000, but the total population decreased by 26,000 with a White
population loss of 51,000. Statistics on census tract changes reflect the
growth of segregated enclaves in those years. While in 1950 no Blacks
lived in census tracts that were more than 50 percent Black, by 1964
60.4 percent of the Black population lived in areas that were more than
50 percent Black, and 25.7 percent of the Black population lived in
tracts that were 75 percent Black or more.

In 1964, Rochester's 35,000 Blacks accounted for about one tenth
of the city's population. Living largely in a slum area, they worked
at construction or low-pay service jobs, or were on welfare.[5] While the
city's major industries upheld equal opportunity policies most Blacks
had minimal educational and vocational skills, and could not meet industry's job requirements. Eastman Kodak, the largest employer of all, had
begun to actively recruit Black workers. But after the July riot Kodak's
industrial relations director stated: "We're not in the habit of hiring
bodies. We need skills. We don't grow many peanuts at Eastman
Kodak."[6]

After the summer's riot, the Rochester Area Council of Churches
(a Protestant group) brought in two members of Dr. Martin Luther
King's Southern Christian Leadership Conference to see what could

---

[3] *U.S. News & World Report,* August 10, 1964, p. 38.

[4] From a full-page ad in the February 5, 1967 issue of *The New York Times*
and quoted in Raymond A. Schroth, "Self-Doubt and Black Pride," *America,* April
1, 1967, p. 503.

[5] *Business Week,* August 1, 1964, p. 24.

[6] Quoted in *Newsweek,* August 10, 1964, p. 27.

be done to ease conditions in the Black poverty areas. A few weeks later, for reasons which have never been clearly explained, the SCLC representatives departed. The council then invited Saul Alinsky, the "middle-aged deus ex machina of American slum agitation,"[7] to Rochester. Predictably, a cry of civic outrage went up. The city's two Gannett-owned newspapers immediately denounced the church leaders' move; a local radio station rescinded the clergymen's free Sunday morning radio time, and the Community Chest hastened to invite the Urban League to set up shop in Rochester.

Saul Alinsky and FIGHT

Mention of the late Saul Alinsky's name alone was sufficient to set the teeth of dozens of American communities on edge.[8] Alinsky, who believed that the poor (because they are not a power bloc) are cut off from any meaningful participation in the democratic process, spent 30 years organizing slum communities in the United States. In 1940, backed financially by Marshall Field III, he set up the Industrial Areas Foundation, "a kind of training school for agitators," in Chicago. Soon other philanthropists, foundations, and several church groups (such as the Catholic Archdiocese of Chicago)[9] contributed money to IAF's work. Alinsky borrowed many of his techniques from the American labor movement, and spent the 40s and 50s organizing Mexican-American slums in California and other slum districts in Chicago, Detroit, and New York. He became nationally prominent in the early 60s when he set up The Woodlawn Organization on Chicago's south side.

Alinsky's projects aim to create a "disciplined, broad-based power organization capable of wringing concessions—better jobs, better schools, better garbage collection, better housing—from the local establishment."[10] By organizing, the IAF seeks to replace slum resident alienation with participation in the decision-making process. "The hell with charity," said Alinsky, "it's self-determination that counts."

Once invited to a community, an IAF representative scouts churches, barbershops, and poolhalls for potential slum leaders and any existing organizations which might be welded into a power bloc. After an effective combination is set up, (this generally takes two to three years) the organization is on its own.[11] "One thing we instill in all our organizations," Alinsky said, "is that old Spanish civil war slogan 'Better to die

[7] *The New York Times Magazine,* October 9, 1966, p. 28.

[8] Mr. Alinsky died of a heart attack in 1972.

[9] Bishop Bernard Sheil of Chicago was a strong Alinsky supporter, and it was he who introduced Alinsky to Marshall Field.

[10] *The New York Times Magazine,* October 9, 1966, p. 28.

[11] IAF charges $50,000 a year for its services. Alinsky drew a $25,000-a-year salary; organizers are paid $15,000.

on your feet than to live on your knees.' Social scientists don't like to think in these terms. They would rather talk about politics being a matter of accommodation, consensus—not this conflict business. This is typical academic drivel. How do you have a consensus before you have a conflict? There has to be a rearrangement of power and then you get consensus."[12] Alinsky disclaimed any interest in imposing values or political goals on slum residents—"We're just technicians trying to organize people," he said.

Rochester's IAF project became known as FIGHT (Freedom, Integration, God, Honor—Today).[13] Alinsky sent Edward Chambers, his top organizer, to the city in the spring of 1965. In June of that year, FIGHT adopted a constitution[14] and elected its first president, the Reverend Franklin Florence. Florence, a Church of Christ minister, is:

> very much the New Negro. He is angry and articulate. He wears a "Black Power" button, reveres the memory of Malcom X and is studiously rude to most whites. . . . Florence's relationship with Alinsky and Chambers is a delicate one. He clearly resents the fact that he needs their help. In Rochester, as elsewhere, the days are numbered when white men can lead the black man's revolt. [15]

But Alinsky believed that Blacks need White allies, and so a "separate but not quite equal" group, the Friends of FIGHT, was organized to provide money, legal expertise, and tutors for various FIGHT programs.

FIGHT soon succeeded in impacting the city's urban renewal plan and won provision for new housing construction on vacant land, nonprofit housing corporations, and 250 units of public housing (only two units had been planned), before old public housing on scattered sites was torn down.

In its first efforts to tackle unemployment, FIGHT arranged an on-the-job training program with Xerox for 15 Blacks. By September 1966, it broadened its sights considerably and began negotiating with Eastman Kodak for the recruitment, training, and hiring of 600 Blacks. Taking on Kodak was something that just wasn't done in Rochester. "But we knew if we could get Kodak in line every other business would follow,"[16] said Reverend Florence.

---

[12] *The New York Times Magazine*, October 9, 1966, p. 102.

[13] The publisher of the Gannett newspapers offered some "less offensive" acronyms such as W-O-R-K, L-O-V-E, T-R-Y, D-E-E-D-S. See the *New Republic*, January 21, 1967, pp. 11–13. The "I" in FIGHT was subsequently changed to stand for "Independence."

[14] FIGHT's constitution guarantees that leadership be selected annually through the convention process. Each local organization that joins FIGHT selects 15 member delegates, who attend the annual convention. No FIGHT president can be elected for more than two consecutive terms.

[15] *The New York Times Magazine*, October 9, 1966, p. 82.

[16] The Binghampton, New York, *Sunday Press*, April 23, 1967.

The company

Rochester has often been called Kodak City. Eastman Kodak, with 44,400 people on its local payroll, is by far the largest employer in the Rochester area and a dominant influence on community life.[17] Kodak has an established quality image in product and in management, and has long been known as a good place to work. Personnel turnover is one fourth the national industrial average, and no Kodak U.S. plants have ever been unionized.

Much of "the Kodak way" derives from founder George Eastman's approach to company management; and at his death in 1932, "his three closest associates took over more or less as a team, with considerable commingling of responsibility and a singularity of purpose: to do as Mr. Eastman would have done."[18] A "philosopher-tinkerer," Eastman pioneered in several areas of industrial relations.[19] By 1903, his company had an employment stabilization program to overcome seasonal variations in labor needs and to cut down on layoffs; in 1911, it created an employee benefit, accident, and pension fund; and in 1912 it established its unique wage-dividend policy whereby the rate of dividends to workers is scaled to the rate of cash dividends paid to stockholders. In 1966, for example a $69.3 million wage dividend was paid to some 63,000 U.S. Kodak employees, or contributed to the employees' savings and investment plan.[20] George Eastman's policy was to hire the best brains available; and with some 450 of its employees holding doctorates, Kodak may have more Ph.D.'s running around the shop than office boys.[21] Financially, too, Kodak is an impressive company. It is the world's largest supplier of photographic materials and a leading manufacturer of chemicals, plastics, and synthetic fibers. It ranked 35th in size among U.S. industrial corporations in 1966.

Kodak under fire

In the fall of 1966, seemingly imperturable Eastman Kodak found itself in the midst of a mushrooming controversy. In September, FIGHT asked Kodak to consider setting up a training program (to include such

---

[17] Kodak employs about 13 percent of the area's labor force and about one out of three in industry.

[18] Robert Sheehan, "The Kodak Picture—Sunshine and Shadow," *Fortune*, May 1965, p. 129.

[19] Mr. Eastman was also a philanthropist par excellence. In 1924, he gave away half of his fortune. His total gifts amounted to more than $75 million with the University of Rochester and the Massachusetts Institute of Technology the leading beneficiaries. Kodak has continued the philanthropic tradition. In the last decade the company has given $22 million to Rochester's hospitals, schools, and Community Chest (of which Eastman was a founder).

[20] This was $39.50 for each $1,000 earned over the previous five-year period.

[21] Philip A. Cavalier, "Kodak's Growth: Never Out of Focus," *The Magazine of Wall Street,* November 26, 1966, p. 246.

fundamentals as reading and arithmetic) for some 500 to 600 Blacks. "We're not talking about the man who can compete," Reverend Florence pointed out to Kodak officials. "We're talking about the down-and-out, the man crushed by this evil system, the man emasculated, who can't make it on his own. He has a right to work."[22] Florence proposed that FIGHT recruit and Kodak train these unemployables over an 18-month period for entry-level jobs with the company. FIGHT made clear its feeling that Kodak should give favored treatment to Blacks, whatever the expense, and argued that Kodak in the past had hired White workers from other cities while ignoring local Blacks. "If Kodak can take pictures of the moon," Florence contended, "it can create 500 jobs for our people."

William Vaughn, Kodak's president in 1966, did not expressly turn down FIGHT, but agreed to further talks. Said Vaughn, "This is a civic problem and a national problem that has to be solved."[23] At a meeting on September 14, FIGHT presented a written proposal, while Vaughn distributed a statement outlining Kodak's plans to expand training programs and invited FIGHT to refer applicants. After this meeting, Vaughn turned future dealings with FIGHT over to Kenneth Howard of the industrial relations department.[24]

Kodak and FIGHT representatives met twice more in September with no outcome. While letters between the two organizations went back and forth, neither side agreed on what had taken place.[25] Florence would only discuss the FIGHT proposal and Kodak continued to argue that FIGHT should cooperate and refer candidates to Kodak's expanding training programs for the unskilled and uneducated, as other organizations were doing.

In the previous spring, Kodak had issued a management letter describing both its existing special training programs and those under development. The letter set forth a change in emphasis in company employment policies:

> . . . our policy had been simply to try to employ the person best fitted to do the work available without regard for his or her background. We have moved actively beyond that position. We now seek to help the individual who lacks the necessary qualifications to become qualified . . . . we are contributing to the training of the individual so that he or she can qualify for employment.

❋   ❋   ❋   ❋   ❋

> Overall, it appears that industry must look less critically at the individual's school record and work experience and more at his potential.

---

[22] *Business Week*, April 29, 1967, p. 38.

[23] Ibid., pp. 38–39.

[24] Nonunion Kodak carefully avoided using the word "negotiations" to describe its exchanges with FIGHT.

[25] See Appendix A for copies of two of the letters included in this correspondence.

> Frustration and unfavorable circumstances in early life often result in a school record far below the person's actual potential.

Throughout September's meetings, neither Kodak nor FIGHT would budge an inch, and

> the situation was aggravated by the fact that the FIGHT negotiators did not trust Howard. The formidable Rev. Florence is quick to sense when a white man is ill at ease in his presence, and he could not respect a man who seemed to be afraid of him. But perhaps non-union Kodak was not accustomed to bargaining with another "power" organization.[26]

Meanwhile, in television and newspaper conferences, Florence promised to keep pressuring Kodak until it "woke up and came into the 20th century," while Saul Alinsky called Kodak's attitude "arrogant" and typical of Rochester's "self-righteousness." Alinsky further accused the company of playing a public relations "con-game" with FIGHT, when, in October, it announced the hiring of the Indiana-based Board of Fundamental Education to help expand its remedial education programs. The new programs were to have an initial enrollment of 100, but as it turned out, the trainees had already been selected. Sixty had recently been hired by Kodak and 40 were regular employees.[27]

Kodak upheld its position on FIGHT's proposal, and in November, sent a letter to company supervisors explaining its stand:

> We [cannot] enter into an arrangement exclusively with any organization to recruit candidates for employment and still be fair to the thousands of people who apply on their own initiative or are referred by others.
> We [cannot] agree to a program which would commit Kodak to hire and train a specific and substantial number of people in a period which would extend so far into the future.
> . . . we [told] FIGHT that we would expand and broaden certain special training activities, and we expressed the hope that they would refer candidates to us. . . . [But] we cannot delegate decisions on recruitment, selection, and training for Kodak jobs to any outside group. Other organizations with whom we have worked readily understand this.

Despite a background of deadlocks, discussions were eventually resumed in December when John G. Mulder, a Kodak assistant vice president,[28] and an acquaintance of his, the Rev. Marvin Chandler, a

---

[26] *America,* April 1, 1967, p. 503.

[27] See the *Rochester Democrat,* October 26, 1966, and the *Rochester Times-Union,* October 24, 1966.

[28] Mr. Mulder, the assistant general manager of Kodak Park Works, the company's largest installation in the Rochester area, was also president of the city's Council of Social Agencies. His wife is a member of the Friends of FIGHT.

FIGHT official, met for lunch. In discussing possible ways to resolve the dispute, Chandler indicated that FIGHT would prefer a new negotiating team. The two men next discussed the matter at an unannounced meeting in Kodak's board room on December 16, and Vaughn (who hoped "there was a new deal here") gave Mulder the go-ahead to meet with FIGHT representatives. Kodak had expected to deal with Chandler, but Florence attended the two-day meetings which followed. On December 20, he and Mulder signed a joint statement indicating that FIGHT and Kodak had agreed to "an objective of the recruitment and referral (to include screening and selection) of 600 unemployed people over a 24-month period, barring unforeseen economic changes affecting the Rochester community. FIGHT, at its own expense, would provide counseling for the employees selected by Kodak." (For the full text of the statement, see Appendix B.)

According to reports, Kodak's president-elect Louis Eilers[29] exploded when he heard of the signing. The next morning Kodak's executive committee voted to repudiate the agreement, and the following day the board of directors agreed. A statement was then drafted, and Eilers informed reporters that the agreement was invalid because Mulder had no authority to sign any document on Kodak's behalf. He said that Kodak had neither intended nor authorized the FIGHT arrangement and that management "expressed the greatest of displeasure at the signing." Asked why Mulder would sign the statement without authority to do so, Eilers replied that Mulder had "apparently not been informed of company policies."[30] He added, however, that he "didn't envision any change in Mulder's job." Mulder himself declined to comment on the dispute, saying he was "in no position to talk," but he personally went to Reverend Chandler's home to break the news that Kodak would not honor the agreement. Meanwhile, Florence announced that FIGHT would demand that the agreement be put into effect. He insisted that he had asked Mulder three times if he had authority to sign the agreement. "They've shown they're no good and deceitful. Obviously, there are hard-line people who don't care a thing about partnership with the poor."

In the midst of the uproar that followed, Kodak ran a conciliatory two-page ad in the local morning and afternoon newspapers stating it "sincerely regret[ted] any misunderstanding," but it could not "discriminate by having an exclusive recruiting arrangement with any organization. Nor, owing to the uncertainties of economic conditions [could]

---

[29] In November 1966, Kodak had announced Eilers' election to the presidency.

[30] *The New York Times*, January 7, 1967. While the public probably will never know what Vaughn's directions to Mulder were, Vaughn insists that the assistant vice president exceeded his instructions, feeling that "he got trapped, or rather trapped himself." See *Business Week*, April 29, 1967, p. 40.

the company commit itself on a long-term basis to employ a specific number of people." Kodak was "deeply concerned to do all that [it] reasonably can to meet a pressing social need in this community, namely, to try to develop employment opportunities," and management was taking "many positive steps" in this direction.

But the tone of Eilers' remarks at a news conference on January 6 was decidedly bitter. Eilers fired off a succession of charges against FIGHT. Its "talk about employment," he said, was "being used as a screen for making a power drive" in the community, and its demands were "arbitrary and unreasonable."

> Since the Alinsky forces were brought to Rochester, FIGHT has run a continuing war against numerous Rochester institutions that help build Rochester—the school system, the community chest, the city government and even organizations especially set up to help solve minority group problems. Kodak's turn came last September. A savage attack has been directed at us since that time.[31]

Eilers charged that FIGHT's attempt to gain an exclusive hold on 600 jobs, required Kodak management to surrender its prerogative to determine whom and when to hire. This, the company neither could nor would do. He noted that Kodak employed some 1,200 to 1,500 Blacks in Rochester, several hundred of whom had been hired in the last few months,[32] and that the company already had special training and employment programs for the unskilled and uneducated, with which FIGHT had repeatedly refused to cooperate. Later, Eilers was to say:

> To tell the truth, I don't know what they want. Certainly not jobs—they could have had those, and still can. Every one of the other 10 referring agencies in Rochester has placed people in jobs at Kodak and none has asked for an exclusive deal.
>
> This year we'll have about 300 more in our training program. It's too bad FIGHT doesn't want to participate.[33]

A community divided

From 1960 to 1967, Rochester accomplished far more than the country as a whole in increasing Black employment, but an unrelenting influx of unskilled and uneducated Southern Blacks had completely wiped out the city's gains. While Black employment in the area had risen 43 percent (more than four times the national average), the Black population of working age increased 46 percent. Availability of jobs was not the problem. In January 1967, 10,000 job openings existed in the

---

[31] *The New York Times,* January 7, 1967.

[32] Kodak's Vaughn grants that FIGHT pressure led Kodak to hire more Blacks. *Business Week,* April 29, 1967, pp. 39–40.

[33] The Binghampton *Sunday Press,* April 23, 1967.

Rochester area, but 60 percent of these required a high school education and over 15 percent required a college degree. Fifty-four percent of Rochester's unemployed Black males had not completed the ninth grade.

The Rochester community, confronted with the conflict and the specter of more racial explosion, was splintered in its reaction to the dispute. "Kodak made FIGHT look good," a University of Rochester professor said. "If I were Alinsky," said the acting president of the Friends of FIGHT, "I would have bribed Eilers to repudiate the agreement."[34] A number of Kodak employees were members of Friends of FIGHT and there were rumors of an ideological split within the company itself. For weeks after Kodak's repudiation of the agreement, sermons for and against FIGHT and the Council of Churches were heard at Sunday services. The publisher of Rochester's newspapers excoriated the Council for widening the "gulf between pulpit and pew," by bringing in a divisive force which attacked a "company famed the world over for its sometimes ponderous but ever humane approach to all things." The council's president (a Kodak employee) and two members of the board of directors resigned in protest against its continued support of FIGHT. But the council gained an ally in Fulton J. Sheen, newly appointed bishop to the Rochester Catholic diocese; in his first appointment he named a highly vocal FIGHT supporter and Kodak critic as his special vicar to minister to the city's poor. And, representatives of the National Council of Churches, the United Presbyterian Church, and the United Church of Christ came out in support of FIGHT.

Within the Black community itself, there was mixed reaction to FIGHT's abrasive tactics. The head of the local Urban League attacked Florence's "irresponsibility" and questioned whether "FIGHT" and only FIGHT should be the spokesman for the 'poor' Black man in the Rochester community." A supporter of FIGHT ("Negroes must have a militant organization"), he objected to Florence's followers calling him a traitor to the cause because he did not "necessarily follow the FIGHT philosophy as projected by Minister Florence."[35] The Urban League also took strong exception to Florence's statement that it would be joining a "conspiracy" if it referred any applicants to Kodak's training programs.

On the whole, most citizens seemed anxious to get Kodak and FIGHT "unhooked" from their dispute, and a group of industrial and religious leaders set about organizing Rochester Jobs, Inc. to provide work for 1,500 hard-core unemployed. The organization received commitments from 40 companies (including Kodak) to provide on-the-job training, remedial education, and counseling, with jobs to be divided on a quota basis.

---

[34] Barbara Carter, "The FIGHT Against Kodak," *The Reporter*, April 20, 1967, p. 30. There was some feeling in Rochester that FIGHT would have been hard put to produce the 600 Blacks its proposal called for.

[35] Ibid., p. 31.

But Florence was determined to hold Kodak to the signed agreement. He did nothing to lessen the mounting tension of the uneasy winter. In January, he invited Stokely Carmichael to speak to a FIGHT rally. Promising a national boycott which would bring Kodak to its knees, Carmichael predicted; "When we're through, Florence will say 'Jump,' and Kodak will ask 'How high?' "[36] Florence next fired off a telegram to Eilers, warning: "The cold of February will give way to the warm of spring, and eventually to the long hot summer. What will happen in Rochester in the summer of 1967 is at the doorstep of the Eastman Kodak Company. . . . You'll be hearing from us, and it won't be in black and white."[37]

Kodak did hear from FIGHT—at its annual meeting on April 25. The entire two-and-three-quarter hours meeting (except for a brief review of operating results) was devoted to the Kodak-FIGHT dispute. Florence, who owned one share of Kodak stock,[38] took the floor to demand that Kodak reinstate the December 20 agreement. When Chairman Vaughn refused, Florence, together with 25 FIGHT supporters, walked out of the meeting, declaring, "This is war—and I state it again—war." Florence told 600 demonstrators waiting outside, "Racial war has been declared on American Negroes by Eastman Kodak. Kodak has shown American Negroes that powerful companies can't be trusted." He announced that FIGHT would conduct a national campaign against Kodak, including a "candlelight service" in Rochester on July 24, the third anniversary of the city's race riot.[39]

To stockholders remaining in the meeting (including representatives of several church groups who had withheld their proxies from management),[40] Vaughn explained that Kodak refused to honor the December 20 agreement because it was unauthorized. "In his overzealousness to resolve the controversy, Mr. Mulder put his name to a document prepared by FIGHT," the chairman said. "The incident was most unfortunate and regrettable. We have acknowledged it was a mistake and have apologized for it ever since." (Vaughn later told reporters that Mulder was still an assistant vice president and wouldn't be penalized for his action.)

---

[36] Ibid., p. 28.

[37] Ibid., p. 31.

[38] In anticipation of the annual meeting, Florence and nine other FIGHT officials had purchased a share of Kodak stock, for a total of ten shares.

[39] No service was held; however a minor riot occurred on July 24, 1967 which ended with three persons dead and damage of several hundred thousand dollars.

[40] FIGHT had succeeded in getting stockholders to withhold proxies for about 40,000 shares. At the meeting, 84 percent of Kodak's 80,772,718 shares outstanding were voted for management. Reverend Florence had also filed suit to get the company to give him access to its list of stockholders, but a New York State court denied the request.

Meanwhile, FIGHT, augmented its request to Kodak and asked the company to provide 2,000 jobs, while Alinsky warned Kodak of what to expect in the future. "The battle," said he, "will be in Eastman Kodak's arena—the nation from Harlem to Watts."

A settlement

Two months later, on June 23, protagonists on both sides of the bitter Kodak-FIGHT dispute "swallowed a small chunk of their black and white pride. In doing so, they gave new status to the ghetto's black poor, salvaged the national reputation of a locally revered industry and most likely rescued their city from threatened summer violence."[41]

Kodak made the first move in late May by calling in Daniel P. Moynihan, the director of the Joint Center for Urban Studies of the Massachusetts Institute of Technology and Harvard University, and a former assistant secretary of labor. Moynihan met separately with Kodak and FIGHT officials, then brought both sides together to thrash out their differences. After a week of meetings, accord was finally reached. FIGHT emerged from the dispute with its sense of pride intact, and Kodak management lost none of its "prerogatives."

By the settlement (the terms were stated in a telegram from Eilers to Florence), Kodak recognized that FIGHT "speaks in behalf of the basic needs and aspirations of the Black poor in the Rochester area," and Kodak planned to send interviewers into the city's slums, accompanied by FIGHT representatives, to provide "special guidance and advice" about "special problems and perspectives of hard-core unemployed persons."[42] Kodak also agreed to meet periodically with FIGHT officials to discuss the economic problems of the city's slum dwellers.

Notably absent from the arrangement,[43] which FIGHT persisted in calling an "agreement" and Kodak referred to as an "understanding," was any mention of Kodak's hiring a specific number of employees from among the city's unemployed: All hiring decisions were left to Kodak.

With the imbroglio at an end, Eilers told Kodak employees: "It was apparent right along that a resolution of community tensions was highly desirable." That, for most Rochesterites, said *Business Week,* was the understatement of their year.

A perspective

Neither Florence nor Eilers are organization presidents these days.[44] John Mulder, the Kodak official who signed the ill-fated December 20

---

[41] *America,* July 8, 1967 (inside cover).

[42] *Business Week,* July 1, 1967, p. 22.

[43] Eilers' telegram noted that neither side considered the relationship exclusive.

[44] Mr. Eilers is chairman of the board and chief executive of Kodak.

agreement is still assistant general manager of the Kodak Park Works but failed to be reelected as assistant vice president when Kodak's board of directors met in May 1967.

FIGHT has now had four presidents in office (each can serve only a two-year term). Former President Bernard R. Gifford (1969–71)[45] was acting, nonpaid "dean" of FIGHT's job training program on December 20, 1966 when the agreement was signed. Looking back on that day, some five years later he states:

> We all knew that FIGHT and Kodak would eventually have to get together. It was inevitable. The question was not how or why, but when. When the agreement was signed, I felt that we had won and lost at the same time. We had won recognition from Kodak and maybe six hundred jobs, but we had also put ourselves in a position where we promised services that I knew we could not deliver. The December 20 agreement stated that FIGHT "at its own expense, would provide counseling for the employees selected by Kodak." . . . I knew that FIGHT did not have the capacity to deliver such services. All I thought of was two thousand Black men and women looking for work, desperate for a shot at Kodak, lining up outside the job training program which had *no* money to perform the services that had been agreed to.
>
> I was also happy for the Black community. I knew of John Mulder's reputation, and I knew his wife, who worked for me as a volunteer tutor in the job training program. They were good people, so I knew that he would see to it that Kodak would provide the best atmosphere for the success of the agreement.
>
> I was also confused by Kodak's new progressive stance. "Maybe," I thought, "Rochester could really make it." I daydreamed about Kodak's president going on television the next day and stating: "By God, this is the best thing that ever happened to Rochester. We want to make Rochester a model city for racial progress. FIGHT and Kodak can do it. Black Power is a picture developed by Kodak." (I even began to think about going back to work for Kodak after graduation.)
>
> I also thought about the new political power that FIGHT would have. If Kodak could sit down with us, could General Dynamics be far behind? I felt that FIGHT had developed a patronage mechanism without selling out on its principles.

Asked if Kodak deliberately excluded Blacks prior to the 1966 confrontation, Gifford felt that

> That is not the real question. The question is: What were the results of Kodak's hiring policy on its work force composition? Issuing great policy papers on equal employment opportunities without supplying the back-up muscle to enforce those policies is like feeding a hungry man the sizzle rather than the sausage, or telling a baby that the cow's "moo" is as important and as nourishing as its milk, or my wife telling

---
[45] See Appendix C for biographical sketch.

me at the dinner table the chicken's "cock-a-do-da-do" will be served rather than the chicken.

In physics if you have two forces acting on an object you would be a fool if you tried to predict the motion of the object by describing the two forces as if they were independent of each other. Instead you must look at the resultant of those two forces which, mathematically speaking, is an imaginary line. But the impact is real and predictable. If you know how it is constructed, you're in great shape. If not, then make sure you're never in a position where two forces are pulling at you.

In Rochester, the Black community was saying to Kodak, "What's your resultant?"

We knew that Kodak did not plan on bombing the ghetto, but if it did not provide jobs for people who lived in the ghetto, then maybe it would have been more merciful if it in fact did bomb the ghetto.

The December 20 victory was a good one, but it was to be short-lived. . . . We knew that it meant new power to bring other people to the bargaining table. But at no time were we overcome with a "power high." Kodak later made the charge that all of our efforts were aimed exclusively at gaining power. In fact we became more aware of the need for power and the importance of what Saul Alisky had been saying after Kodak broke one agreement on December 23.

Looking back over the long, drawn-out dispute, Kodak's president Eilers opined: "I think we used too much patience."[46]

FIGHT since 1967

FIGHT pressures caused both the formation of Rochester Jobs, Inc., and the Rochester Business Opportunities Corporation (RBOC), "a coalition of established Rochester businesses,"[47] which, since 1967 has helped start minority businesses.

In 1968 FIGHT and the Xerox Corporation became partners and established FIGHTON, an electronics subcontracting plant, as a community owned inner city business. RBOC acquired a plant through a SBA loan, and leased it to FIGHTON, but despite this aid, a two-year training grant from the Department of Labor, and a $250,000 loan granted by the SBA, the enterprise began undercapitalized. In its first two years of operation, FIGHTON showed sales respectively of $97,176 and $678,635 and went from a deficit of $32,000 to a profit of $46,000. Xerox's pledge to take $400,000 of output in fiscal 1970, and $730,000 in both 1971 and 1972 has helped FIGHTON to succeed initially.

FIGHT Square, a $3.5 million project to create 149 units of low and

---

[46] *Business Week,* April 29, 1967, p. 41.

[47] *CDCs: New Hope for the Inner City* (Report of the Twentieth Century Fund Task Force on Community Development Corporations, The Twentieth Century Fund, New York, 1971) p. 74.

moderate income housing was completed in 1971. It is part of a five-stage plan for the development of Rochester's inner city Third Ward, and "is designed to take advantage of the opportunities that exist for obtaining available, and within this limitation to attempt to locate, projects that will maximize the impact upon the surrounding area, giving it additional development 'leverage.' "[48]

APPENDIX A

Text of letter sent to Pres. Franklin Florence of FIGHT on September 28, 1966 from Pres. W. L. Vaughn of Kodak

Dear Minister Florence:

I have your letter of September 26 from which I note that apparently considerable misunderstanding still exists as to what we tried to convey to you and your associates in FIGHT at our meeting on September 14.

In the first place, Kodak's program and plans described at that meeting, in response to your verbal proposal of September 2, were *not* simply "a repeat of your limited special training programs," as you state in your letter. If you will reread, closely and carefully, the second paragraph on page 2 of the statement handed to you at our meeting on September 14 you will see that we are talking of "an *expanded* concept of on-the-job training," which we go on to describe in general terms. We went on to say that we hoped "to benefit from suggestions which FIGHT may offer," as well as from those of other organizations interested in these matters.

Since the goals of "the FIGHT proposal" seemed to be so close to the aims of our programs, we assumed that you wanted to cooperate in making our efforts more successful.

We have indicated to you on several occasions that we cannot accept your "proposal," which is, quoting from your September 14 memorandum, as follows: "Kodak would train over an 18-month period between 500 and 600 persons so that they qualify for entry level positions across the board. FIGHT would recruit and counsel trainees and offer advice, consultation, and assistance in the project." Your memorandum also states that the project ". . . would be geared to individuals with limited education and skills . . ." and that ". . . areas to be worked out would include selection criteria, recruitment, training needs . . ." and that "programs should include remedial reading, arithmetic; industrial orientation and training to afford a basic understanding of industrial processes, tools, machinery, and work rules; basic skills training like

---

[48] Ibid., p. 77.

material handling, blueprint reading, and mechanical principle; others." In addition, you have indicated that you expected this company to undertake all this exclusively in cooperation with FIGHT.

We have tried to make clear to you why we cannot accept the "FIGHT proposal." Apparently, it is necessary at this time for me to restate our position.

1. In light of the company's legal obligations and its responsibilities to Kodak customers, employees, stockholders, other applicants for employment, and the community, the company obviously cannot discriminate by granting any one organization an exclusive or monopolistic position in the recruitment, selection, or training of Kodak people.
2. We are not in a position to establish any statistical objective or quota for any special training programs which we undertake. Our ability to hire a person at Kodak depends first on the existence of job opening, and second, on the availability of a person qualified to fill that opening.

During the last several months, we have hired a good many people, among whom were many Negroes. We hope we can continue to provide additional job opportunities in the future. But it is impossible for us to say how many, if any, such opportunities will be available at Kodak six months, a year, or 18 months hence. It would be an inexcusable deception on our part to promise something we cannot be sure of honoring.

You are quoted in this morning's paper as having said last evening, "I hate to believe a company of this stature would misguide poor people." We have no intention of misguiding anyone, and it is precisely for this reason we cannot promise a given number of jobs at some future date when we do not control the economic and other factors which create the job opportunities.

I think both you and we are concerned with a problem to which no one has yet found a satisfactory solution—that is, how to motivate people to prepare themselves for job openings, and how to train people for industrial jobs who are lacking in such fundamental skills as reading, writing, and arithmetic. Certainly it would be dishonest and unfair to the people involved if we were to suggest that we have the knowledge or manpower to take on such a complete job where, so far as I know, no others have succeeded. However, as we have told you, we are planning to expand our special training efforts to see what further we can do. We are naturally anxious that any program we undertake have some reasonable chance of success.

What we are trying to do is to see what we can accomplish, by special training programs, to upgrade persons who are willing to try to improve themselves so they can qualify for the kinds of jobs we have. In doing this, we will seek the assistance of interested organizations which are willing to cooperate in constructive ways.

If FIGHT is interested in cooperating on this basis by making suggestions for the programs or referring applicants for them, I would again suggest that you resume discussions with Mr. Howard. If, on the other hand, your interest is solely in talking further about "the FIGHT proposal," I doubt that anything very useful could come from just going over the same ground that has been covered in the several talks that have already taken place.

Text of letter sent to Pres. W. L. Vaughn of Kodak on October 7, 1966 from Pres. Franklin Florence of FIGHT

Dr. Mr. Vaughn:

I have your letter of September 28th and offer at this time the following observations.

An American economy which is in the first stages of inflation and which has shown an accompanying rising employment rate finds itself threatened by an alarming increase in unemployment among Negroes. The last figure issued by our government pointed to 8.3% of all employable Negroes were unemployed. It is clear to all students and observers of economic conditions among the Negroes of America that the employment rate in the various ghettos from Harlem to Watts are substantially higher. This dangerous condition not only for the Negro population but the general American public becomes particularly ominous since it follows on the heels of civil rights legislation, extensive job retraining programs, and a convergence of public opinion and government pressure upon private industry and organized labor to drop their discriminatory hiring practices and to open jobs for Negro fellow Americans. So, we are confronted with the strange and frightening anomaly of increasing employment for whites occurring simultaneously with decreasing employment for Negroes.

There are a number of reasons for this kind of economic sickness and one of the major ones is the fact that large industries such as Eastman Kodak persist in employing the same testing procedures for hiring eligibility to Negro applicants as they do with white applicants. The pursuit of this practice indicates an extraordinary insensitivity to the social and educational circumstances which have prevailed in our country for many years: Circumstances of limited opportunities, economy-wise, education-wise, and in almost every other sector of our life which all Americans today are fully cognizant of and are moving toward their correction. It is clear that a Negro of the same age as that of a white has not had the academic opportunities to qualify for the same test. It is clear that if there is to be an intelligent approach to this issue that those factors must be taken into consideration in terms of equity as well as the practical politics of keeping a healthy American way for all people.

The obvious remedy lies in avoidance in the trap of this discriminatory test and hiring of Negroes for jobs where they will not only receive on-the-job training, but also special educational programs to bring them up to the point where they could then qualify under the test. Any employer who would regard this as discrimination in reverse would be guilty of an extraordinary shortsightedness and unawareness of the general situation prevailing in our nation today.

This has been the issue in our approach to Eastman Kodak. With it has gone our own feelings that if private industry does not meet this challenge that we will of necessity have to assume that there is no other recourse but massive governmental public projects and we have nowhere else to turn except to our government. Paradoxically, major industries in America, including Eastman Kodak, have always expressed concern for the ever-expanding encroachment by government in various areas of our life. They have regarded this with a great deal of alarm. Some of the most conservative of them have denounced it as creeping socialism. We, ourselves, believe that the democratic way of life would hold to most problems being met and resolved on a local community basis and that there is that kind of free initiative in various sectors of our society: that government should not move in unless local communities are obviously unable, incapable, or unwilling, to meet their own problems. Eastman Kodak has the opportunity to make a significant contribution by cooperating with FIGHT's proposal. But, if FIGHT continues to be stalled and politely rejected as it has been to this date, then we must conclude that while industry talks about government encroaching upon all spheres of the American scene that in fact, it is just talk and that it is coming because industry refuses to act. We, like all other Americans, prefer to be employed by our government, to have our dignity, to have a job and to have an economic future rather than to have a basket full of empty generalities and unemployment by private industry which is immobilized by its own straightjacket, by antiquated definitions of discrimination and by an astounding blindness to their own self-interest.

Use of terms like "exclusively," "monopolistic," "arbitrary demands," etc. in reference to the FIGHT proposal does an injustice to the careful thought and consideration that has gone into our suggestions. We have not even had the opportunity to discuss the details of our approach with Eastman Kodak.

APPENDIX B

December 20, 1966

A special committee appointed by Eastman Kodak president, William Vaughn, has been meeting Monday and Tuesday with officers of the FIGHT organization.

Kodak representatives stated that they have not employed traditional standards of hiring for the last two years. FIGHT hailed this as a step in the right direction as well as Kodak officers' statement that they will deal with the problem of hard core unemployed.

Job openings, specifications and hourly rates were discussed and agreed upon by the joint group.

January 15th was agreed upon as the date for a beginning of the referral of 600 employees, the bulk of which would be hard core unemployed (unattached, uninvolved with traditional institutions).

Under the agreement, the FIGHT organization and Kodak agreed to an objective of the recruitment and referral (to include screening and selection) of 600 unemployed people over a 24-month period, barring unforeseen economic changes affecting the Rochester community. FIGHT, at its own expense, would provide counseling for the employees selected by Kodak.

Kodak agrees to the following: join with FIGHT in a firm agreement to

a.   Continue semi-monthly meetings between Kodak and FIGHT to increase the effectiveness of the program.

b.   Kodak will familiarize FIGHT counselors with the foremen and work skills required, and in turn FIGHT will familiarize Kodak foremen with the life and environment of poor people.

c.   Kodak and FIGHT will share information on the referrals.

d.   Kodak and FIGHT will issue a 60-day community progress report.

John Mulder
Asst. Vice President, Eastman Kodak
Asst. General Manager, Kodak Park Works

Franklin D. R. Florence
President of FIGHT

APPENDIX C

Bernard R. Gifford was recently named president of The Rand Institute in New York. At the age of 29, he holds a Ph.D. in radiation biophysics from the University of Rochester Medical School, which he attended as a U.S. Atomic Energy Commission Fellow in Nuclear Science. Mr.

Gifford grew up in Brooklyn, New York in a family of six children. His father died when he was seven, and his family was on and off welfare for many years. He first went to Rochester in 1950 under the New York Herald Tribune "Fresh Air Fund" program, which was designed to get poor children out of the city during the summer. In 1963, at age 20 he organized Brooklyn's Brownsville Community council, which in 1967 became involved in the struggle for community control of schools in the Brownsville–Ocean Hill district of New York. During the summer of 1965 he was employed by Kodak as an optical engineer and worked on the Lunar Orbiting Program. At this time he joined FIGHT.

Affirmative action at Aldrich[1]

ON FEBRUARY 5, 1973, John Cooke, manager of the Evanston Radar Division of the Aldrich Electronics Corporation, was disturbed by his meeting with Frank Stearns, field director of Progress Now, a Chicago-based Black Power group (see Exhibit 1 for a list of case participants). Cooke wondered whether he and Stearns had been talking about the same company when they were discussing the Evanston facility. Stearns had demanded that Cooke promote immediately the 23 Black women on the Evanston transistor line to the next pay level. Each of the women had more than six years' seniority. Stearns threatened to file suit on behalf of the women with the Equal Employment Opportunity Commission (EEOC).[2]

Cooke realized that his frame of mind had been fairly negative even before the meeting. That morning he had received a memo from corporate headquarters detailing new procedures for hiring and promoting women throughout the Aldrich organization. The memo also mentioned that a special corporate task force would study all job classification grades and pay scales in order to determine whether women and minorities were being discriminated against, either overtly or covertly.

Cooke liked to think he had come up the hard way. He had made his name at Aldrich initially as chief management-labor negotiator for

---

[1] This case was written by Rikk Larsen, associate in research, under the direction of Professor George C. Lodge to serve as the basis for classroom discussion. It is not intended to illustrate either effective or ineffective handling of an administrative situation.

[2] See Exhibit 6 for an explanation of the EEOC court process.

526

the Chicago area. He prided himself on being a tough but fair team player, empathetic to labor's legitimate demands. The International Electrical Workers (IEW), who represented 90 percent of Aldrich's blue-collar workers, had a reputation as a hard bargainer; locals were vigilant, insisting upon the letter of the contract. Cooke respected the union's approach; he liked to play by the rules of the game.

After ten years as manager of the Evanston plant, Cooke feared that his job would be very different in coming years, that the old measurement criteria for success in the corporation would probably change. He was not sure, however, what to do.

Company background

Aldrich Corporation, based in and around Chicago, Illinois, was principally an electronic equipment manufacturer with some 50 percent of its business in contracts with the Defense Department. It manufactured components for sophisticated defense systems as well as for civilian uses. The corporation was divided into four divisions: the Radar Division at Evanston, employing 5000; the Equipment Division, specializing in self-contained components; the Guidance Systems Division, making guidance instruments for both defense and civilian aircraft; and the Aerospace Division, designing systems for NASA. Aldrich had total sales of $950 million in fiscal 1971.

The company had achieved its greatest growth immediately after World War II. It had located its main Midwest plants in six suburban communities that surrounded Chicago. At the time, management felt that this was advantageous because the semiskilled and skilled labor needed for successful business operations was readily available in these communities. All were within an hour's drive of corporate headquarters in downtown Chicago. (Exhibit 2 provides basic demographic data for each community as well as Aldrich's employment figures.)

The Evanston plant

The Evanston plant consisted of three groups: design research, engineering, and manufacturing. Historically, a product was conceived in design research, modified for production in engineering, and then manufactured in the main building of the plant. Cooke had been with the Aldrich Corporation for 34 years, the last 22 having been at Evanston. He had risen to his present position because he was known as a "production man" who had been able to meet production deadlines at least cost. Although Aldrich prided itself on its many technological achievements over the years, often industry giants like Raytheon or General Dynamics would introduce innovations which required Aldrich to rush a new design into production. Cooke had always done well when the pressure was on.

Contract compliance review at the Evanston plant

Cooke's troubles in the equal employment opportunity area began in November 1971, when, one day with little notice, the Defense Department contract compliance people swarmed over his facility, checking through the details of his Affirmative Action Plan. No other Aldrich plant either before or after had undergone such scrutiny. At the time, in fact, he had felt discriminated against. He told Charles Hogen, Aldrich's director of equal employment programs, that as far as he could see, he had done everything the corporation had asked him to do in the personnel area. His plant managers had attended the sensitivity training sessions run by Hogen's department; he himself had gone to the senior management seminars where corporate affirmative action programs were discussed. His Affirmative Action Plan had been accepted by Hogen's department. He just could not understand all the fuss.

The transistor line protest

The Stearns issue had begun early in June 1972, when three young Black female employees in pay grade 4 had bypassed the normal union-management grievance procedures provided for in the contract to bring a complaint about unequal pay for men and women on their assembly line. They insisted on talking to Cooke personally. They said that only women were assigned to the transistor preassembly line and that their pay grades went only from 3 to 7, while men on the intermediate and final assembly lines, who were doing virtually the same kind of work, started at grade 5 and could go to grade 11. (Exhibit 3 shows the job breakdown on the transistor line.) The women went on to state that the union, the IEW, did not seem to be interested in their problems. The union had said it would consider their problems when the contract was renegotiated in two years. The local president had said that the women had agreed to it when it was signed so they would have to live by it until the next bargaining session. He also noted that any kind of revision would, of course, have to be carefully considered so that it did not work to the disadvantage of other workers. The women said they were not willing to wait that long and wanted some quick action. Cooke had planned to smooth the incident over, relying on the support of the union. But when he happened to mention the incident to Hogen while they were discussing some other matter, Hogen had been very interested, had cut the conversation short, and the next day had brought two corporation lawyers and a job classification specialist to Cooke's office. They urged Cooke to make the women happy. Hogen said that if they took Aldrich to court, the problem could escalate. Much against his better judgment, Cooke called the women back and transferred them to a new, all-female line in the wiring department at the next pay grade. It had taken a whole day of heated discussions with the union to explain the extraordinary action. The union reluctantly accepted the shift when Cooke told them about the danger of court and possible government action.

A month later, in early August, he received a memo signed by the 23 remaining Black females on the transistor line all with six years' or more seniority, stating that they wished for pay increases without transfers. They were happy on the line, but felt they were doing virtually the same work as White males on the intermediate and final assembly lines who had higher pay classifications. Given the contract seniority system, the women could not transfer without losing all seniority. Cooke had told Hogen: "This is exactly what I feared when you asked me to make those other three girls happy. We had a fine situation here before. The transistor line has been a model of what Black workers can do—and women too. Most of my people on that line have been there for ten years or more. We never had any trouble."

Hogen had come down, and a series of meetings with the women and the union had taken place. Cooke thought he and the union had placated the women when Stearns entered the picture in November with the demands he was now voicing.

Aldrich and contract compliance

Since Aldrich had such extensive dealings with the U.S. government, management was eager to maintain a corporate posture that would insure the company's ability to bid successfully on government contracts. Contract compliance was a major component of this posture since a company that fulfills past contracts to the letter of the law has a better chance in the future. In recent years that part of contract compliance which had been of most concern to Aldrich was the Affirmative Action Program required under Order No. 4 (revised) of the Office of Federal Contract Compliance (OFCC). (See Exhibit 4.) Other areas of contract compliance, such as safety and security, were not so troublesome. Accepted and established procedures had long since been adopted in these areas. Affirmative action, on the other hand, was a major new thrust of the government. No one knew just what the requirements were, how literally they should be taken, or how they would evolve.

Order No. 4

The Office of Federal Contract Compliance (OFCC) of the U.S. Department of Labor determines contract compliance requirements for all contracting agencies and departments of the federal government (for example, HEW, Defense Department, Atomic Energy Commission). Each agency is then responsible for enforcing the OFCC orders through its own separate contract compliance divisions.

In January of 1970, OFCC spelled out in Order No. 4 what the government contracting agencies required in order to judge the adequacy of contractors' written affirmative action programs. These requirements dealt mainly with the hiring and training of members of minority racial groups. They applied to each prime or subcontractor with 50 or more employees and a contract of $50,000 or more. The contractor had 120 days from the commencement of the contract to develop a written affirmative action compliance program for each of his establishments.

In December of 1971, OFCC published a revision of Order No. 4 requiring contractors to commit themselves to goals and actions to remedy *sex* as well as minority discrimination. Contractors had 120 days to revise existing programs to include the changes under the new Order No. 4.

Written affirmative action programs must contain the following:

1. A detailed analysis of all major job classifications at the facility, with an explanation if minorities or women were currently being underutilized in any one or more job classifications.
2. Goals and timetables for affirmative action commitments must be established to correct any identifiable deficiencies.
3. Such goals and timetables with supporting data and analysis must be compiled and maintained as part of the written affirmative action programs.
4. Contractors must direct special attention in their analyses and goal setting to specific categories of employees.
5. These programs must contain among other things:
    a. Identification of problem areas (deficiencies) by organizational units and job classification;
    b. Establishment of goals and objectives by organizational units and job classification, including timetables for completion;
    c. Development and execution of action-oriented programs designed to eliminate problems and attain established goals and objectives.

If, for whatever reason, the contractor was not in compliance, there was a penalty process:

1. If the concerned government agency chose to prosecute and not accept the company's explanation, a letter asking the company to "show cause" why their name should not be eliminated from the agency bidding list would be sent.

2. A company had 30 days in which to make a reply.
3. If the reply was again not judged satisfactory, the regional office could again reject it.
4. The company would have ten days to prepare for a hearing in Washington.
5. At the hearing, if the company again was judged to be grossly negligent, they could be barred completely from all future government contracts.
6. The company then had access to the courts to try to overrule the decision.

A multi-facility corporation was required to have an affirmative action program for each facility; and a "show cause" letter to one plant automatically barred all other plants of the corporation from any government business.

Revised Order No. 4 was the latest step in a process that began in 1965 with President Johnson's Executive Order No. 11246, which called for all government contractors to develop affirmative action plans in "good faith" for the hiring and training of minorities. At that time there was no machinery set up to define what "affirmative action" meant or to make it effective. It quickly became apparent within the Labor Department that rules and regulations were needed to guide contractors as well as compliance officers in the fulfillment of the spirit of Executive Order No. 11246. In May of 1968 the Labor Department issued, under Chapter 60–1 of Title 41 of the code of Federal Regulations, rules and regulations regarding procedures that contractors should follow in developing goals as well as a penalty schedule. The major difference between Chapter 60–1 and Order No. 4 (Chapter 60–2) was the fact that under Chapter 60–1 there was no provision that required companies to put in writing their affirmative action plans and goals. This was seen as a major weakness of 60–1 by OFCC and was the main reason for Order No. 4.

The political evolutionary process that resulted in Revised Order No. 4 occurred primarily in the Department of Labor with pressure from minorities and women. It was not the result of legislative initiative.

Aldrich's response to Order No. 4

In 1970 the responsibility for handling minority affairs and contract compliance at Aldrich was assigned to the Industrial Relations Department (IR). IR handled community relations and legislative lobbying in addition to general labor relations, while the Public Relations Department dealt with press and financial relations. (Aldrich had generally chosen the low-profile approach to public relations and recognized that few nonbusiness-oriented people could identify with what Aldrich was or did.)

Senior management was aware of the potential explosiveness of Order No. 4 in particular and the whole minority hiring situation in general. As a consequence, Hogen was hired in early 1970 to be director of equal opportunity programs for Aldrich. The new job was placed in IR.

Hogen was hired at the personal suggestion of the president and chairman of the board of directors, Ronald Fleming, a fact that was generally known in the company.

Hogen and his tactics

Hogen had been director of human relations for the Manufacturer's Association of Illinois, a progressive lobbying organization. Fleming had been closely involved with Hogen at the association and had supported his efforts to educate businessmen that their own self-interest was served by staying ahead of social demands, particularly as concerned human resources.

Hogen came to Aldrich with definite views about the role of corporations as effective agents of social change. He felt that a corporation should try to stay out in front of guidelines and governmental requirements and that in the long run it was "cheaper to lead." He saw his new job at Aldrich as an opportunity to test whether he could be effective in a corporate situation. He was excited because he believed strongly that "Fleming had a deep ethical feeling about life and a commitment that things ought to be better." His immediate boss, M. A. Bergmeyer, the senior vice president in charge of industrial relations, seemed to hold similar views although his background was quite different. Bergmeyer had risen in the IR department because of his abilities as a labor negotiator. (He and Cooke had entered Aldrich at the same time and worked closely together in early contract negotiations.) He was primarily responsible for Aldrich's history of relatively good labor relations. While other corporations dealing with the IEW had often found it difficult to come to reasonable terms, Aldrich had a history of quick settlements that did not "give away the shop."

In January 1970, after moving into the Aldrich executive office building in Chicago, Hogen quickly realized that to be effective in creating change in the area of equal opportunity, he would have to work through the established system. He had no staff and no specific line authority. His only influence resulted from his close relationship with Fleming and the general awareness of that fact in the company. He realized that this implicit access would only be effective in the organization as long as he was not publicly overruled. Thus he was very cautious in his initial approach to contract compliance. As he put it:

> Ron Fleming is as sincere about equal opportunity as any man in the U.S. But we have some very conservative divisions here. We have a lot of managers who are very good at production and do not really see the jeopardy. The line people are inclined to say, "If I can produce, you have got the lawyers to keep me out of trouble." No man in the company can get canned for not doing well in the employee relations area. I have Fleming's support, but I use it very judiciously.

Hogen knew Fleming was the type of manager that preferred traditional channels. During his 20 years as chief operating officer, Fleming had built a solid organizational structure with a defined chain of command. He prided himself on not having any "unnecessary frills" at Aldrich. He had placed his managerial stamp on the many charitable and civic organizations in which he involved himself. When something needed to be done by the business community for Chicago nonprofit organizations, Fleming was the one everyone invariably turned to first. Hogen went on to say:

> It was soon very obvious to me that there was little I could do at Aldrich as an individual, unless I could generate some support. I'm a specialist, a counselor, a salesman if you will. So it seemed to me that my first goal was to develop a local competence in this area (contract compliance). The best way to do that was through the Industrial Relations Office because it has to deal with contract compliance. This is a fixed responsibility for the IR people, and they were nervous about handling it. Instead of selling programs to them, I was supporting them in a function that they already had responsibility for, and I tried very hard to articulate whatever I wanted to have done in a way that took on the appearance of being of assistance to them. That was my general tactic.

Attracting managerial attention

Hogen felt that the first step toward changing Aldrich's attitudes and organization with regard to Blacks and women was to focus increased attention by top management on the problem. Change would not come unless it were given a higher priority. Everyone was too busy with day-to-day business to make the necessary additional effort required to alter traditional practices. He decided that the most effective way to obtain increased management attention was to encourage the intensification of affirmative action review by the Defense Department.

Tim Dorman, contract compliance chief for the Defense Department in the Midwest area, respected Hogen's intentions and was only too glad to cooperate.

Before Dorman came to the Defense Department Contract Compliance Division by way of army contract compliance, he had been Cultural Attaché in the U.S. embassy in India. Previously, he had been executive director of the Urban League in Chicago, where in the early 50s he had run a controversial radio show that dealt with racial matters. Dorman had received numerous personal threats during this period.

He preferred to work "nose to nose" with companies in his jurisdiction, seeking to persuade rather than coerce. He regarded the "show cause" letter as a last resort.

Dorman believed, as did Hogen, that one of the greatest values of the affirmative action programs was the complete self-evaluation process it forced a company to go through. Not only did the company have to identify its weaknesses and deficiencies but it also had to set goals and declare how it planned to achieve them. The company knew the review team would come back and say "why didn't you?" if the goals were not met.

Dorman was responsible for all of the 4,700 companies in the Midwest area which had contracts with the Defense Department. He had a non-clerical staff of 24 officers.

Dorman felt that contract compliance was most effective in the period between 1966 and 1969 when substantial gains had been made in minority hiring at the blue-collar level. Since 1969, however, blue-collar hiring had remained static, with gains for minorities and women coming mostly at white-collar levels.

Both he and Hogen knew that during the last five years only six companies in the nation had actually received the "show cause" letter. No company had ever been disbarred from bidding lists or had a contract cancelled. As a member of Dorman's staff remarked, "Most companies reach an agreement with us before this stage, and in actual fact, if we issued a 'show cause' letter to every company not in compliance, the economy would stop in a month."

Hogen gave one example of a review team he had recently dealt with as illustrative of Dorman's style:

> This was an interesting team because it had one old-line reviewing officer who had been with the Defense Department for five or six years under this program but who had a background in labor relations. He was familiar with the whole process of reviewing industry under various legislative and administrative requirements. With him at this in-depth review were two so-called trainees who were new to the Defense Department and part of Tim Dorman's effort to step up the quality of the people he's getting there. One was a girl and one was a young Black guy with counseling background. Both were extremely articulate, extremely on the ball, almost overly agressive. I mean I think they got my dander up a few times by nit picking over what they called "missed

opportunities for affirmative action." You know—that's a ball park you could fill any day because there's no limit to the missed opportunities that you have!

But anyway, they lent a very real atmosphere to this thing. They brought it into interracial and female terms. They were defending a cause rather than just being government interviewers. It was a very effective team. We found that, in a way, the veteran review officer was in a position of defending the company quite a bit. He took my role in many cases. "Calm down, Aldrich has been doing this," etc. They worked well together. There was a stepped-up militancy on the part of the group, and I think it's going to continue.

Hogen wanted to demonstrate to senior management that there was a need for defined positions in Aldrich, that is, organizational structure, to deal specifically with affirmative action's plans and minority affairs. He felt, though, that it was important to keep these activities separate in the organization since he was sure that minorities would achieve more gains at Aldrich initially if they had separate definable managers to handle their problems and needs.

With Dorman's cooperation the process of institutionalization came quicker than Hogen expected. In November 1971, at Hogen's initiative, an in-depth contract compliance review took place at the Evanston facility. Neither Cooke nor other members of the corporate staff were aware of Hogen's tactics. The review and disclosures shocked Cooke. Immediately thereafter he told Hogen that he needed a full-time manager of affirmative action programs and requested help in describing the job and finding someone to fill it.

News of the Evanston review passed quickly to other facilities in the Aldrich organization. Some plant managers asked Bergmeyer for advice. He said that each plant would have to examine its own requirements for additional IR staffing.

Women in Order No. 4

When the Revised Order No. 4 came out on December 4, 1971, Hogen was happy because the revision helped prove his point about the need for specialized positions in the Aldrich organization to deal specifically with changes in affirmative action requirements.

The revision demonstrated to senior management that the future could bring more sudden changes in government policy, and that it paid to have an institutionalized means of dealing with these changes.

Hogen said of the change at Aldrich, "Again, the key to change was pressure from the government. This is the way we respond—to pressure. I've been kind of a mediator between the government and the problems and interests of the IR men at our facilities."

The revision of Order No. 4, as well as the Evanston situation, forced management to focus attention on their women employees.

Women and the courts

Aldrich was especially mindful of recent back-pay settlements. Employees at Wheaton Glass Company had recently won a court decision costing $900,000 when they proved that there were dual lines of progression in the organization for men and women in violation of Title VII of the 1964 Civil Rights Act. Executives at Aldrich also knew that courts were no longer ruling that job content had to be "absolutely" the same under the Equal Payment Act in order to prove discrimination in pay but only "substantially" the same. Accordingly, Fleming authorized the formation at Aldrich of an eight-man, one-year task force commissioned to look at job descriptions throughout the organization that might tend to discriminate against either minorities or women. Hogen was on the committee that would oversee the task force's work and was of the opinion that substantial revisions in Aldrich's personnel and hiring practices would be needed if Aldrich was to be adequately protected from the possibility of adverse court action. The memo detailing the goals of the task force had arrived on all division managers' desks on February 5, 1973.

Minority affairs commitment

At the same time Fleming decided that Aldrich should commit itself to a stepped-up minority affairs program. To implement this commitment, he ordered the creation of six new jobs in the company in addition to the corporate manager of minority manpower development (reporting to Hogen) which had previously been created in August. The six new positions were as follows: four division managers of minority affairs, one for each Aldrich division, one special training coordinator to report to the corporate director of equal opportunity programs (Hogen); and a manager of minority vendor programs.[3] (Exhibit 5 shows a partial Aldrich organization chart.)

Hogen had always contended that the implementation of affirmative action plans should remain distinct and separate from minority affairs functions.

---

[3] Vendor, in this instance, is defined as any minority enterprise that Aldrich might purchase items from. Aldrich's procurement program approached one-half billion dollars and ranged from hardware items for specific products to furniture, window cleaning, leasing and trucking services. The manager of minority vendor programs had specific authority to seek out and develop more business with minority enterprises in all procurement areas. He reported to the Purchasing Department and was not in Hogen's IR area.

The maintenance of our affirmative action program entails a great deal of statistical and mechanical work and is increasingly concerned with problems of women employees. I believe that Fleming's action was a commitment to a full-time effort to create an employment climate that would attract and keep larger numbers of minority employees at all levels in the company.

Hogen found that he had difficulty maintaining the distinction between a stepped-up commitment to affirmative action and a stepped-up commitment to minority affairs. By August 1972, contrary to Hogen's hopes, three division managers of minority affairs, at the direction of division IR managers, had been told they were responsible for affirmative action programs. While this reflected budgetary pressures at the division level, it appeared that the company had not implemented the commitment by Fleming.

Cooke had been one of the first managers to combine the two positions. Hogen tried to persuade him that it was necessary to keep the jobs separate, since women would represent an increasing problem in the implementation of Aldrich's affirmative action programs. Women comprised 80 percent of Aldrich clerical workers and 13 percent of the blue-collar workers. Cooke responded, "That is all well and good, but until I am given an increased budget for two extra positions, I will combine them. Besides, I don't feel that Blacks should be treated separately. They are treated fairly, and if they don't like the system, they can go somewhere else for work."

Progress Now and its demands

Because of its location, the Evanston plant had been experiencing a hard time recruiting qualified Blacks to meet its affirmative action goals. As a result, the minorities in the labor force at Evanston (3 percent) were primarily in low-paying clerical or assembly line jobs.

Progress Now, a new Chicago-based Black Power group, had come into existence in order to help publicize and otherwise help minorities in large corporations who felt the system discriminated against them. In articles in *The Chicago Tribune* Frank Stearns had been quoted as saying:

> We see many corporations in and around Chicago practicing overt and covert racism. There is supposed to be machinery in the form of affirmative action programs that is supposed to be helping Black people throughout America, but it is a sham. Anyone remotely familiar with affirmative action knows that it is another case of big business getting into bed with government to talk a good game but to go on with "business as usual."

Progress Now had publicized a number of cases of alleged racism in the Chicago area, but as far as Cooke could tell, no substantive actions either in the courts or through any other agency had resulted.

Stearns had sent Cooke a letter of November 6, 1972, stating that he knew exactly how many Blacks were in what positions at Evanston and that their affirmative action plans were a sham to hide Aldrich's racist hiring and promotion practices. He then gave surprisingly accurate figures to prove he knew what he was talking about. He went on to note that a number of Black women at Evanston had come to his organization complaining that they were denied promotion and access to high pay scales.

Cooke, alarmed at the publicity potential, started to pay more attention to the equal employment program bulletins that Hogen had been sending out. Two articles especially caught his eye (see Exhibits 5 and 6). He was also aware of Labor Secretary Hodgson's recent decision concerning Bethlehem Steel's Sparrows Point plant where Blacks had become concentrated in certain departments with short pay-grade ladders and held there by departmental seniority rules. It seemed to him that Evanston might indeed have the same kind of situation, but he did not know how to proceed.

The meeting with Stearns of February 5 only upset Cooke more. He felt that if there was a problem, it was not his responsibility. Departmental seniority had been a cornerstone of labor contracts for as long as he could remember. He thought he might as well let this task force he had read about that Hogen was behind take care of the situation.

EXHIBIT 1
Case participants

Ronald Fleming —President and Chairman of the Board of Aldrich Electronics Corporation

M. A. Bergmeyer—Vice President of Industrial Relations of Aldrich Electronics Corporation

John Cooke —Manager of the Evanston Radar Division of Aldrich Electronics Corporation

Charles Hogen —Director of Equal Opportunity Programs of Aldrich Electronics Corporation

Tim Dorman —Contract Compliance Chief for the Defense Department

Frank Stearns —Field Director of Progress Now

EXHIBIT 2

	Total population 1970	Percent minority in the community	Aldrich plant size
Oak Park	62,000	4.2	3,800 (Equipment Division)
Evanston	80,000	3.0	5,000 (Radar Division)
Maywood	29,000	4.8	1,600 (Equipment Division)
Evergreen Park	25,000	3.2	2,400 (Guidance System Division)
Skokie	68,000	5.0	3,500 (Guidance System Division)
Dolton	25,000	4.1	2,100 (Guidance System Division)

Note: The Aerospace Division, the only one not located near Chicago, was in Los Angeles, California with one plant of 4,800.

EXHIBIT 3
Transistor line

Pay grade	Seniority requirements for grade	Males	Females
Preassembly			
3–$2.70	0-1 yrs.	–	2
4– 2.80	1-2	–	1
5– 2.90	2-4	–	2
6– 3.00	4-6	–	8
7– 3.10	6-	–	23
Intermediate assembly			
5–$2.90	0- 1 yrs.	4	–
6– 3.00	1- 2	3	–
7– 3.10	2- 4	5	–
8– 3.25	4- 6	3	–
9– 3.40	6- 8	4	–
10– 3.65	8-10	10	–
11– 3.90	10-	15	–
Final assembly			
5–$2.90	0- 1 yrs.	6	–
6– 3.00	1- 2	4	–
7– 3.10	2- 4	3	–
8– 3.25	4- 6	2	–
9– 3.40	6- 8	5	–
10– 3.65	8-10	11	–
11– 3.95	10-	13	–

EXHIBIT 4

Title 41—PUBLIC CONTRACTS AND PROPERTY MANAGEMENT

Chapter 60—Office of Federal Contract Compliance, Equal Employment Opportunity, Department of Labor

PART 60–2—AFFIRMATIVE ACTION PROGRAMS

On August 31, 1971, notice of proposed rule making was published in the *Federal Register* (36 F.R. 17444) with regard to amending Chapter 60 of Title 41 of the Code of Federal Regulations by adding a new Part 60–2, dealing with affirmative action programs. Interested persons were given 30 days in which to submit written comments, suggestions, or objections regarding the proposed amendments.

Having considered all relevant material submitted, I have decided to, and do hereby amend Chapter 60 of Title 41 of the Code of Federal Regulations by adding a new Part 60–2, reading as follows:

Subpart A—General

Subpart B—Required Contents of Affirmative Action Programs

Subpart C—Methods of Implementing the Requirements of Subpart B

Subpart D—Miscellaneous

Authority: The provisions of this Part 60–2 issued pursuant to sec. 201, Executive Order 11246 (30 F.R. 12319).

EXHIBIT 4 (*continued*)

Subpart A—General

§ 60–2.1 Title, purpose and scope.

This part shall also be known as "Revised Order No. 4," and shall cover nonconstruction contractors. Section 60–1.40 of this Chapter, Affirmative Action Compliance Programs, requires that within 120 days from the commencement of a contract each prime contractor or subcontractor with 50 or more employees and a contract of $50,000 or more develop a written affirmative action compliance program for each of its establishments, and such contractors are now further required to revise existing written affirmative action programs to include the changes embodied in this order within 120 days of its publication in the *Federal Register*. A review of agency compliance surveys indicates that many contractors do not have affirmative action programs on file at the time an establishment is visited by a compliance investigator. This part details the agency review procedure and the results of a contractor's failure to develop and maintain an affirmative action program and then set forth detailed guidelines to be used by contractors and Government agencies in developing and judging these programs as well as the good faith effort required to transform the programs from paper commitments to equal employment opportunity. Subparts B and C are concerned with affirmative action plans only.

Relief for members of an "affected class" who, by virtue of past discrimination, continue to suffer the present effects of the discrimination must either be included in the contractor's affirmative action program or be embodied in a separate written "corrective action" program. An "affected class" problem must be remedied in order for a contractor to be considered in compliance. Section 60–2.2 herein pertaining to an acceptable affirmative action program is also applicable to the failure to remedy discrimination against members of an "affected class."

§ 60–2.2 Agency action.

(a) Any contractor required by § 60–1.40 of this chapter to develop an affirmative action program at each of his establishments who has not complied fully with that section is not in compliance with Executive Order 11246, as amended (30 F.R. 12319). Until such programs are developed and found to be acceptable in accordance with the standards and guidelines set forth in §§ 60–2.10 through 60–2.32, the contractor is unable to comply with the equal employment opportunity clause.

(b) If, in determining such contractor's responsibility for an award of a contract it comes to the contracting officer's attention, through sources within his agency or through the Office of Federal Contract Compliance or other Government agencies, that the contractor has not developed an acceptable affirmative action program at each of his establishments, the contracting officer shall notify the Director and declare the contractor-bidder nonresponsible unless he can otherwise affirmatively determine that the contractor is able to comply with his equal employment obligations or, unless, upon review, it is determined by the Director that substantial issues of law or fact exist as to the contractor's responsibility to the extent that a hearing is, in his

EXHIBIT 4   (*continued*)

sole judgment, required prior to a determination that the contractor is nonresponsible: *Provided,* That during any pre-award conferences every effort shall be made through the processes of conciliation, mediation and persuasion to develop an acceptable affirmative action program meeting the standards and guidelines set forth in §§ 60–2.10 through 60–2.32 so that, in the performance of his contract, the contractor is able to meet his equal employment obligations in accordance with the equal opportunity clause and applicable rules, regulations, and orders: *Provided further,* That when the contractor-bidder is declared nonresponsible more than once for inability to comply with the equal employment opportunity clause a notice setting a timely hearing date shall be issued concurrently with the second nonresponsibility determination in accordance with the provisions of § 60–1.26 proposing to declare such contractor-bidder ineligible for future contracts and subcontracts.

(c)   Immediately upon finding that a contractor has no affirmative action program or that his program is not acceptable to the contracting officer, the compliance agency representative or the representative of the Office of Federal Contract Compliance, whichever has made such a finding, shall notify officials of the appropriate compliance agency and the Office of Federal Contract Compliance of such fact. The compliance agency shall issue a notice to the contractor giving him 30 days to show cause why enforcement proceedings under section 209(b) of Executive Order 11246, as amended, should not be instituted.

(1)   If the contractor fails to show good cause for his failure or fails to remedy that failure by developing and implementing an acceptable affirmative action program within 30 days, the compliance agency, upon the approval of the Dierector, shall immediately issue a notice of proposed cancellation or termination of existing contracts or subcontracts and debarment from future contracts and subcontracts pursuant to § 60–1.26(b), giving the contractor 10 days to request a hearing. If a request for hearing has not been received within 10 days from such notice, such contractor will be declared ineligible for future contracts and current contracts will be terminated for default.

(2)   During the "show cause" period of 30 days every effort shall be made by the compliance agency through conciliation, mediation, and persuasion to resolve the deficiencies which led to the determination of nonresponsibility. If satisfactory adjustments designed to bring the contractor into compliance are not concluded, the compliance agency, with the prior approval of the Director, shall promptly commence formal proceedings leading to the cancellation or termination of existing contracts or subcontracts and debarment from future contracts and subcontracts under § 60–1.26(b) of this chapter.

(d)   During the "show cause" period and formal proceedings, each contracting agency must continue to determine the contractor's responsibility in considering whether or not to award a new or additional contract.

Subpart B—Required Contents of Affirmative Action Programs

§ 60–2.10   Purpose of affirmative action program.

An affirmative action program is a set of specific and result-oriented procedures to which a contractor commits himself to apply every good faith effort.

EXHIBIT 4 (*continued*)

The objective of those procedures plus such efforts is equal employment opportunity. Procedures without effort to make them work are meaningless; and effort, undirected by specific and meaningful procedures, is inadequate. An acceptable affirmative action program must include an analysis of areas within which the contractor is deficient in the utilization of minority groups and women, and further, goals and timetables to which the contractor's good faith efforts must be directed to correct the deficiencies and, thus to increase materially the utilization of minorities and women, at all levels and in all segments of his work force where deficiencies exist.

§ 60–2.11 Required utilization analysis.

Based upon the Government's experience with compliance reviews under the Executive order programs and the contractor reporting system, minority groups are most likely to be underutilized in departments and jobs within departments that fall within the following Employer's Information Report (EEO–1) designations: officials and managers, professionals, technicians, sales workers, office and clerical and craftsmen (skilled). As categorized by the EEO–1 designations, women are likely to be underutilized in departments and jobs within departments as follows: officials and managers, professionals, technicians, sales workers (except over-the-counter sales in certain retail establishments), craftsmen (skilled and semiskilled). Therefore, the contractor shall direct special attention to such jobs in his anslysis and goal setting for minorities and women. Affirmative action programs must contain the following information:

(a) An analysis of all major job classifications at the facility, with explanation if minorities or women are currently being underutilized in any one or more job classifications (job "classification" herein meaning one or a group of jobs having similar content, wage rates and opportunities). "Underutilization" is defined as having fewer minorities or women in a particular job classification than would reasonably be expected by their availability. In making the work force analysis, the contractor shall conduct such analysis separately for minorities and women.

(1) In determining whether minorities are being underutilized in any job classification the contractor will consider at least all of the following factors:

(i) The minority population of the labor area surrounding the facility;

(ii) The size of the minority unemployment force in the labor area surrounding the facility;

(iii) The percentage of the minority work force as compared with the total work force in the immediate labor area;

(iv) The general availability of minorities having requisite skills in the immediate labor area:

(v) The availability of minorities havng requisite skills in an area in which the contractor can reasonably recruit;

(vi) The availability of promotable and transferable minorities within the contractor's organization;

(vii) The existence of training institutions capable of training persons in the requisite skills; and

EXHIBIT 4 (*continued*)

(viii)   The degree of training which the contractor is reasonably able to undertake as a means of making all job classes available to minorities.

(2)   In determining whether women are being underutilized in any job classification, the contractor will consider at least all of the following factors:

(i)   The size of the female unemployment force in the labor area surrounding the facility;

(ii)   The percentage of the female workforce as compared with the total workforce in the immediate labor area;

(iii)   The general availability of women having requisite skills in the immediate labor area;

(iv)   The availability of women having requisite skills in an area in which the contractor can reasonably recruit;

(v)   The availability of women seeking employment in the labor or recruitment area of the contractor;

(vi)   The availability of promotable and transferable female employees within the contractor's organization;

(vii)   The existence of training institutions capable of training persons in the requisite skills; and

(viii)   The degree of training which the contractor is reasonably able to undertake as a means of making all job classes available to women.

§ 60–2.12   Establishment of goals and timetables.

(a)   The goals and timetables developed by the contractor should be attainable in terms of the contractor's analysis of his deficiencies and his entire affirmative action program. Thus, in establishing the size of his goals and the length of his timetables, the contractor should consider the results which could reasonably be expected from his putting forth every good faith effort to make his overall affirmative action program work. In determining levels of goals, the contractor should consider at least the factors listed in § 60–2.11.

(b)   Involve personnel relations staff, department and division heads, and local and unit managers in the goal setting process.

(c)   Goals should be significant, measurable and attainable.

(d)   Goals should be specific for planned results, with timetables for completion.

(e)   Goals may not be rigid and inflexible quotas which must be met, but must be targets reasonably attainable by means of applying every good faith effort to make all aspects of the entire affirmative action program work.

(f)   In establishing timetables to meet goals and commitments, the contractor will consider the anticipated expansion, contraction and turnover of and in the work force.

(g)   Goals, timetables and affirmative action commitments must be designed to correct any identifiable deficiencies.

(h)   Where deficiencies exist and where numbers or percentages are relevant in developing corrective action, the contractor shall establish and set forth specific goals and timetables separately for minorities and women.

(i)   Such goals and timetables, with supporting data and the analysis thereof shall be a part of the contractor's written affirmative action program and shall be maintained at each establishment of the contractor.

EXHIBIT 4 (*continued*)

(j) Where the contractor has not established a goal, his written affirmative action program must specifically analyze each of the factors listed in 60–2.11 and must detail his reason for a lack of a goal.

(k) In the event it comes to the attention of the compliance agency or the Office of Federal Contract Compliance that there is a substantial disparity in the utilization of a particular minority group or men or women of a particular minority group, the compliance agency or OFCC may require separate goals and timetables for such minority group and may further require, where appropriate, such goals and timetables by sex for such group for such job classifications and organizational units specified by the compliance agency or OFCC.

(l) Support data for the required analysis and program shall be compiled and maintained as part of the contractor's affirmative action program. This data will include but not be limited to progression line charts, seniority rosters, applicant flow data, and applicant rejection ratios indicating minority and sex status.

(m) Copies of affirmative action programs and/or copies of support data shall be made available to the compliance agency or the Office of Federal Contract Compliance, at the request of either, for such purposes as may be appropriate to the fulfillment of their responsibilities under Executive order 11246, as amended.

§ 60–2.13 Additional required ingredients of affirmative action programs.

Effective affirmative action programs shall contain, but not necessarily be limited to, the following ingredients:

(a) Development or reaffirmation of the contractor's equal employment opportunity policy in all personnel actions.

(b) Formal internal and external dissemination of the contractor's policy.

(c) Establishment of responsibilities for implementation of the contractor's affirmative action program.

(d) Identification of problem areas (deficiencies) by organizational units and job classification.

(e) Establishment of goals and objectives by organizational units and job classification, including timetables for completion.

(f) Development and execution of action oriented programs designed to eliminate problems and further designed to attain established goals and objectives.

(g) Design and implementation of internal audit and reporting systems to measure effectiveness of the total program.

(h) Compliance or personnel policies and practices and the Sex Discrimination Guidelines (41 CFR Part 60-20).

(i) Active support of local and national community action programs and community service programs, designed to improve the employment opportunities of minorities and women.

(j) Consideration of minorities and women not currently in the workforce having requisite skills who can be recruited through affirmative action measures.

EXHIBIT 4 (*continued*)

§ 60–2.14   Compliance status.

No contractor's compliance status shall be judged alone by whether or not he reaches his goals and meets his timetables. Rather, each contractor's compliance posture shall be reviewed and determined by reviewing the contents of his program, the extent of his adherence to this program, and his good faith efforts to make his program work toward the realization of the program's goals within the timetables set for completion. There follows an outline of examples of procedures that contractors and Federal agencies should use as a guideline for establishing, implementing, and judging an acceptable affirmative action program.

Subpart C—Methods of Implementing the Requirements of Subpart B

§ 60–2.20   Development or reaffirmation of the equal employment opportunity policy.

(a)   The contractor's policy statement should indicate the chief executive officers' attitude on the subject matter, assign overall responsibility and provide for a reporting and monitoring procedure. Specific items to be mentioned should include, but not limited to:

(1)   Recruit, hire, train, and promote persons in all job classifications, without regard to race, color, religion, sex, or national origin, except where sex is a bona fide occupational qualification. (The term "bona fide occupational qualification" has been construed very narrowly under the Civil Rights Act of 1964. Under Executive Order 11246 as amended and this part, this term will be construed in the same manner.)

(2)   Base decisions on employment so as to further the principle of equal employment opportunity.

(3)   Insure that promotion decisions are in accord with principles of equal employment opportunity by imposing only valid requirements for promotional opportunities.

(4)   Insure that all personnel actions such as compensation, benefits, transfers, layoffs, return from layoff, company sponsored training, education, tuition assistance, social and recreation programs, will be administered without regard to race, color, religion, sex, or national origin.

§ 60–2.21   Dissemination of the policy.

(a)   The contractor should disseminate his policy internally as follows:

(1)   Include it in contractor's police manual.

(2)   Publicize it in company newspaper, magazine, annual report and other media.

(3)   Conduct special meetings with executive, management, and supervisory personnel to explain intent of policy and individual responsibility for effective implementation, making clear the chief executive officer's attitude.

(4)   Schedule special meetings with all other employees to discuss policy and explain individual employee responsibilities.

EXHIBIT 4 (*continued*)

(5)   Discuss the policy thoroughly in both employee orientation and management training programs.

(6)   Meet with union officials to inform them of policy, and request their cooperation.

(7)   Include nondiscrimination clauses in all union agreements, and review all contractual provisions to ensure they are nondiscriminatory.

(8)   Publish articles covering EEO programs, progress reports, promotions, etc., of minority and female employees, in company publications.

(9)   Post the policy on company bulletin boards.

(10)   When employees are featured in product or consumer advertising, employee handbooks or similar publications both minority and nonminority, men and women should be pictured.

(11)   Communicate to employees the existence of the contractors affirmative action program and make available such elements of his program as will enable such employees to know of and avail themselves of its benefits.

(b)   The contractor should disseminate his policy externally as follows:

(1)   Inform all recruiting sources verbally and in writing of company policy, stipulating that these sources actively recruit and refer minorities and women for all positions listed.

(2)   Incorporate the Equal Opportunity clause in all purchase orders, leases, contracts, etc., covered by Executive Order 11246, as amended, and its implementing regulations.

(3)   Notify minority and women's organizations, community agencies, community leaders, secondary schools and colleges, of company policy, preferably in writing.

(4)   Communicate to prospective employees the existence of the contractor's affirmative action program and make available such elements of his program as will enable such prospective employees to know of and avail themselves of its benefits.

(5)   When employees are pictured in consumer or help wanted advertising, both minorities and nonminority men and women should be shown.

(6)   Send written notification of company policy to all subcontractors, vendors and suppliers requesting appropriate action on their part.

§ 60–2.22   Responsibility for implementation.

(a)   An executive of the contractor should be appointed as director or manager of company Equal Opportunity programs. Depending upon the size and geographical alignment of the company, this may be his or her sole responsibility. He or she should be given the necessary top management support and staffing to execute the assignment. His or her identity should appear on all internal and external communications on the company's Equal Opportunity Programs. His or her responsibilities should include, but not necessarily be limited to:

(1)   Developing policy statements, affirmative action programs, internal and external communication techniques.

(2)   Assisting in the identification of problem areas.

(3)   Assisting line management in arriving at solutions to problems.

EXHIBIT 4 (*continued*)

(4)   Designing and implementing audit and reporting systems that will:

(i)   Measure effectiveness of the contractor's programs.

(ii)   Indicate need for remedial action.

(iii)   Determine the degree to which the contractor's goals and objectives have been attained.

(5)   Serve as liaison between the contractor and enforcement agencies.

(6)   Serve as liaison between the contractor and minority organizations, women's organizations and community action groups concerned with employment opportunities of minorities and women.

(7)   Keep management informed of latest developments in the entire equal opportunity area.

(b)   Line responsibilities should include, but not be limited to, the following:

(1)   Assistance in the identification of problem areas and establishment of local and unit goals and objectives.

(2)   Active involvement with local minority organizations, women's organizations, community action groups and community service programs.

(3)   Periodic audit of training programs, hiring and promotion patterns to remove impediments to the attainment of goals and objectives.

(4)   Regular discussions with local managers, supervisors and employees to be certain the contractor's policies are being followed.

(5)   Review of the qualifications of all employees to insure that minorities and women are given full opportunities for transfers and promotions.

(6)   Career counseling for all employees.

(7)   Periodic audit to insure that each location is in compliance in area such as:

(i)   Posters are properly displayed.

(ii)   All facilities, including company housing, which the contractor maintains for the use and benefit of his employees, are in fact desegregated, both in policy and use. If the contractor provides facilities such as dormitories, locker rooms and rest rooms, they must be comparable for both sexes.

(iii)   Minority and female employees are afforded a full opportunity and are encouraged to participate in all company sponsored educational, training, recreational and social activities.

(8)   Supervisors should be made to understand that their work performance is being evaluated on the basis of their equal employment opportunity efforts and results, as well as other criteria.

(9)   It shall be a responsibility of supervisors to take actions to prevent harassment of employees placed through affirmative action efforts.

§ 60–2.23   Identification of problem areas by organizational units and job classifications.

(a)   An in-depth analysis of the following should be made, paying particular attention to trainees and those categories listed in § 60–2.11(d).

(1)   Composition of the work force by minority group status and sex.

(2)   Composition of applicant flow by minority group status and sex.

(3)   The total selection process including position descriptions, position titles, worker specfications, application forms, interview procedures, test ad-

EXHIBIT 4 (*continued*)

ministration, test validity, referral procedures, final selection process, and similar factors.

(4) Transfer and promotion practices.

(5) Facilities, company sponsored recreation and social events, and special programs such as educational assistance.

(6) Seniority practices and seniority provisions of union contracts.

(7) Apprenticeship programs.

(8) All company training programs, formal and informal.

(9) Work force attitude.

(10) Technical phases of compliance, such as poster and notification to labor unions, retention of applications, notification to subcontractors, etc.

(b) If any of the following items are found in the analysis, special corrective action should be appropriate.

(1) An "underutilization" of minorities or women in specific work classifications.

(2) Lateral and/or vertical movement of minority or female employees occurring at a lesser rate (compared to work force mix) than that of nonminority or male employees.

(3) The selection process eliminates a significantly higher percentage of minorities or women than nonminorities or men.

(4) Application and related preemployment forms not in compliance with Federal legislation.

(5) Position descriptions inaccurate in relation to' actual functions and duties.

(6) Tests and other selection techniques not validated as required by the OFCC Order on Employee Testing and other Selection Procedures.

(7) Test forms not validated by location, work performance and inclusion of minorities and women in sample.

(8) Referral ratio of minorities or women to the hiring supervisor or manager indicates a significantly higher percentage are being rejected as compared to nonminority and male applicants.

(9) Minorities or women are excluded from or are not participating in company sponsored activities or programs.

(10) De facto segregation still exists at some facilities.

(11) Seniority provisions contribute to overt or inadvertent discrimination, i.e., a disparity by minority group status or sex exists between length of service and types of job held.

(12) Nonsupport of company policy by managers, supervisors or employees.

(13) Minorities or women underutilized or significantly underrepresented in training or career improvement programs.

(14) No formal techniques established for evaluating effectiveness of EEO programs.

(15) Lack of access to suitable housing inhibits recruitment efforts and employment of qualified minorities.

(16) Lack of suitable transportation (public or private) to the work place inhibits minority employment.

(17) Labor unions and subcontractors not notified of their responsibilities.

EXHIBIT 4 (*continued*)

(18)   Purchase orders do not contain EEO-clause.

(19)   Posters not on display.

§ 60–2.24 Development and execution of programs.

(a)   The contractor should conduct detailed analyses of position descriptions to insure that they accurately reflect position functions, and are consistent for the same position from one location to another.

(b)   The contractor should validate worker specifications by division, department, location or other organizational unit and by job category using job performance criteria. Special attention should be given to academic, experience and skill requirements to insure that the requirements in themselves do not constitute inadvertent discrimination. Specifications should be consistent for the same job classification in all locations and should be free from bias as regards to race, color, religion, sex, or national origin, except where sex is a bona fide occupational qualification. Where requirements screen out a disproportionate number of minorities or women such requirements should be professionally validated to job performance.

(c)   Approved position descriptions and worker specifications, when used by the contractor, should be made available to all members of management involved in the recruiting, screening, selection, and promotion process. Copies should also be distributed to all recruiting sources.

(d)   The contractor should evaluate the total selection process to insure freedom from bias and, thus, aid the attainment of goals and objectives.

(1)   All personnel involved in the recruiting, screening, selection, promotion, disciplinary, and related processes should be carefully selected and trained to insure elimination of bias in all personnel actions.

(2)   The contractor shall observe the requirements of the OFCC Order pertaining to the validation of employee tests and other selection procedures.

(3)   Selection techniques other than tests may also be improperly used so as to have the effect of discriminating against minority groups and women. Such techniques include but are not restricted to, unscored interviews, unscored or casual application forms, arrest records, credit checks, considerations of marital status or dependency or minor children. Where there exist data suggesting that such unfair discrimination or exclusion of minorities or women exists, the contractor should analyze his unscored procedures and eliminate them if they are not objectively valid.

(e)   Suggested techniques to improve recruitment and increase the flow of minority or female applicants follow:

(1)   Certain organizations such as the Urban League, Job Corps, Equal Opportunity Programs, Inc., Concentrated Employment Programs, Neighborhood Youth Corps, Secondary Schools, Colleges, and City Colleges with high minority enrollment, the State Employment Service, specialized employment agencies, Aspira, LULAC, SER, the G.I. Forum, the Commonwealth of Puerto Rico are normally prepared to refer minority applicants. Organizations prepared to refer women with specific skills are: National Organization for Women, Welfare Rights Organizations, Women's Equity Action League, Talent Bank from Business and Professional Women (including 26 women's organizations), Professional Women's Caucus, Intercollegiate Association of

EXHIBIT 4 (*continued*)

University Women, Negro Women's sororities and service groups such as Delta Sigma Theta, Alpha Kappa Alpha, and Zeta Phi Beta; National Council of Negro Women, American Association of University Women, YWCA, and sectarian groups such as Jewish Women's Groups, Catholic Women's Groups and Protestant Women's Groups, and women's colleges. In addition, community leaders as individuals shall be added to recruiting sources.

(2) Formal briefing sessions should be held, preferably on company premises, with representatives from these recruiting sources. Plant tours, presentations by minority and female employees, clear and concise explanations of current and future job openings, position descriptions, worker specifications, explanations of the company's selection process, and recruiting literature should be an integral part of the briefings. Formal arrangements should be made for referral of applicants, followup with sources, and feedback on disposition of applicants.

(3) Minority and female employees, using procedures similar to subparagraph (2) of this paragraph, should be actively encouraged to refer applicants.

(4) A special effort should be made to include minorities and women on the Personnel Relations staff.

(5) Minority and female employees should be made available for participation in Career Days, Youth Motivation Programs, and related activities in their communities.

(6) Active participation in "Job Fairs" is desirable. Company representatives so participating should be given authority to make on-the-spot commitments.

(7) Active recruiting programs should be carried out at secondary schools, junior colleges, and colleges with predominant minority or female enrollments.

(8) Recruiting efforts at all schools should incorporate special efforts to reach minorities and women.

(9) Special employment programs should be undertaken whenever possible. Some possible programs are:

(i) Technical and nontechnical co-op programs with predominately Negro and women's colleges.

(ii) "After school" and/or work-study jobs for minority youths, male and females.

(iii) Summer jobs for underprivileged youths, male and female.

(iv) Summer work-study programs for male and female faculty members of the predominantly minority schools and colleges.

(v) Motivation, training and employment programs for the hard-core unemployed, male and female.

(10) When recruiting brochures pictorially present work situations, the minority and female members of the work force should be included, especially when such brochures are used in school and career programs.

(11) Help wanted advertising should be expanded to include the minority news media and women's interest media on a regular basis.

(f) The contractor should insure that minority and female employees are given equal opportunity for promotion. Suggestions for achieving this result include:

(1) Post or otherwise announce promotional opportunities.

EXHIBIT 4 (*continued*)

(2)   Make an inventory of current minority and female employees to determine academic, skill and experience level of individual employees.

(3)   Initiate necessary remedial, job training and workstudy programs.

(4)   Develop and implement formal employee evaluation programs.

(5)   Make certain "worker specifications" have been validated on job performance related criteria. (Neither minority nor female employees should be required to possess higher qualifications than those of the lowest qualified incumbent.)

(6)   When apparently qualified minority or female employees are passed over for upgrading, require supervisory personnel to submit written justification.

(7)   Establish formal career counseling programs to include attitude development, education aid, job rotation, buddy system and similar programs.

(8)   Review seniority practices and seniority clauses in union contracts to insure such practices or clauses are nondiscriminatory and do not have a discriminatory effect.

(g)   Make certain facilities and company-sponsored social and recreation activities are desegregated. Actively encourage all employees to participate.

(h)   Encourage child care, housing and transportation programs appropriately designed to improve the employment opportunities for minorities and women.

§ 60–2.25   Internal audit and reporting systems.

(a)   The contractor should monitor records of referrals, placements, transfers, promotions and terminations at all levels to insure nondiscriminatory policy is carried out.

(b)   The contractor should require formal reports from unit managers on a schedule basis as to degree to which corporate or unit goals are attained and timetables met.

(c)   The contractor should review report results with all levels of management.

(d)   The contractor should advise top management of program effectiveness and submit recommendations to improve unsatisfactory performance.

§ 60–2.26   Support of action programs.

(a)   The contractor should appoint key members of management to serve on Merit Employment Councils, Community Relations Boards and similar organizations.

(b)   The contractor should encourage minority and female employees to participate actively in National Alliance of Businessmen programs for youth motivation.

(c)   The contractor should support Vocational Guidance Institutes, Vestibule Training Programs and similar activities.

(d)   The contractor should assist secondary schools and colleges in programs designed to enable minority and female graduates of these institutions to compete in the open employment market on a more equitable basis.

(e)   The contractor should publicize achievements of minority and female employees in local and minority news media.

EXHIBIT 4 (*concluded*)

(f) The contractor should support programs developed by such organizations as National Alliance of Businessmen, the Urban Coalition and other organizations concerned with employment opportunities for minorities or women.

Subpart D—Miscellaneous

§ 60–2.30   Use of goals.

The purpose of a contractor's establishment and use of goals is to insure that he meet his affirmative action obligation. It is not intended and should not be used to discriminate against any applicant or employee because of race, color, religion, sex, or national origin.

§ 60–2.31   Preemption.

To the extent that any State or local laws, regulations or ordinances, including those which grant special benefits to persons on account of sex, are in conflict with Executive Order 11246, as amended, or with the requirements of this part, we will regard them as preempted under the Executive order.

§ 60–2.32   Supersedure.

All orders, instructions, regulations, and memoranda of the Secretary of Labor, other officials of the Department of Labor and contracting agencies are hereby superseded to the extent that they are inconsistent herewith, including a previous "Order No. 4" from this Office dated January 30, 1970. Nothing in this part is intended to amend 41 CFR 60-3 published in the *Federal Register* on October 2, 1971 or Employee Testing and other selection Procedures or 41 CFR 60-20 on Sex Discrimination Guidelines.

Effective date. This part shall become effective on the date of its publication in the *Federal Register* (12-4-71).

Signed at Washington, D.C., this 1st day of December 1971.

J. D. HODGSON,
Secretary of Labor.
HORACE E. MENASCO,
Acting Assistant Secretary
for Employment Standards.
JOHN L. WILKS
Director, Office of
Federal Contract Compliance.
[FR Doc. 71–17789 Filed 12–3–71; 8:51 am]

Reprinted from the *Federal Register*, Vol. 36, No. 234 (Washington, D.C.: December 4, 1971), pp. 17–21.

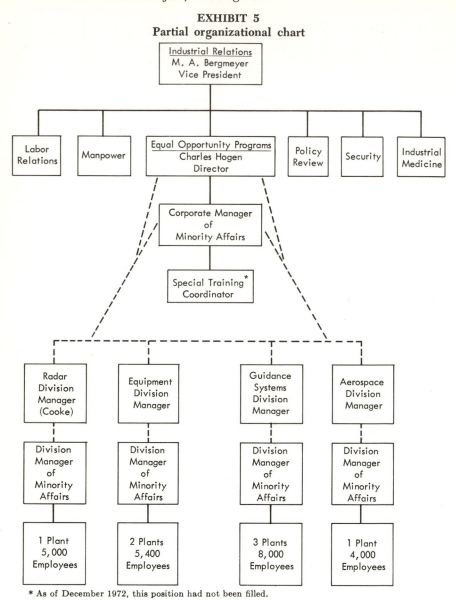

EXHIBIT 5
Partial organizational chart

* As of December 1972, this position had not been filled.

EXHIBIT 6

The courts back woman on job equality

Elizabeth G. McDonald, a witty 23-year-old graduate student at California State University in San Francisco, gets a lot of laughs during her Women's Lib show on a cable television station in the Bay area.

The show is called "The Second Sex Scene."

EXHIBIT 6 (*continued*)

Ms. McDonald may also get some chuckles—including the last laugh—out of a law suit she has filed against 32 companies, many of them nationally known, charging that they refused to interview her for executive trainee and sales openings in 1970, when she was about to graduate from Sacramento State College at San Francisco. She did get an interview with J. C. Penny Co.'s personnel man after she had set up an appointment for "my brother, Edward G. McDonald."

Ms. McDonald is suing Penney, Goodyear Tire & Rubber, Boise Cascade, Phillips Petroleum, Western Electric, and 27 other companies on behalf of herself and other women for allegedly violating the 1964 Civil Rights Act by interviewing only men for the executive trainee and sales jobs. She seeks $640,000 in back pay and compensatory damages, or about $20,000 per company.

Whether or not Ms. McDonald wins her case, other cases filed by individuals and federal law enforcement agencies under the Civil Rights Act and the 1963 Equal Pay Act are producing some distinctly unfunny consequences for company managements. Some of the nation's best-known corporations have lost cases costing hundreds of thousands of dollars in back pay and higher wage scales for women workers. More basic to management policy, court decisions have repeatedly erased hiring and promotion practices designed to keep women out of "men's jobs," whether blue-collar, white-collar, or executive. Every indication points to much more of the same.

Winning streak. All told, some 400 equal pay cases have been filed by the U.S. Labor Dept., and the results should gladden a feminist's heart. The department has won 178 of 208 lower court decisions handed down to date. It has won 14 of the 30 "losers" when they were appealed to higher courts.

The most important decision under the Equal Pay Act—from a standpoint of the money it involved and the precedent it set—was the 1970 U.S. Circuit Court ruling against the Wheaton Glass Co., of Millville, N.J. The court ruled that jobs need not be identical, just "substantially equal," for the equal pay law to apply. It ordered Wheaton to pay close to $1-million in back pay to women inspector-packers. The U.S. Supreme Court refused to hear an appeal, in effect confirming the decision.

This summer, Congress broadened the Equal Pay Act to cover an estimated 15-million executive, administrative, and professional employees, and outside salespeople. From 4-million to 5-million of this group are women. Among jobs newly covered are professor, engineer, chemist, buyer, programmer, writer, and editor.

AWARDS IN EQUAL PAY CASES

Wheaton Glass	$901,062
G. C. Murphy	648,000
Pacific Telephone & Telegraph	593,457
Midwest Mfg.	238,695
Daisy Mfg.	209,905
Hayes Industries	206,214
American Can	149,927
RCA	100,432

EXHIBIT 6 (*continued*)

Pace quickens. If the cases involving equal pay appear sure to increase, those involving equal hiring, promotion, and other job patterns appear headed for a quantum jump. Last spring, Congress amended the Civil Rights Act to enable the Equal Employment Opportunity Commission to take employers to court for violations of the fair employment provisions of the act, a change that quickened the pace of litigation considerably. Formerly, only individuals and the Justice Dept. had possessed this power—an arrangement expensive to individuals and apparently uncongenial to the Justice Dept., which had filed only four sex discrimination suits in the eight years of its jurisdiction. EEOC has begun 12 legal actions since receiving its new power last March.

An individual's suit produced the Supreme Court's one decision on sex discrimination under the 1964 rights act: Phillips vs. Martin Marietta. The court forbade Martin Marietta to reject women with preschool children, since the company had no bar against employing men with preschool children. Lower court rulings in cases by individuals included one that opened the job of airline cabin attendant to men.

Of the Justice Dept.'s four sex discrimination cases, three—against Libbey-Owens-Ford, Obear-Nester Glass, and Household Finance—were settled by consent decrees. The first and most important suit charged Libbey-Owens-Ford with keeping women out of supervisory positions and with limiting their overtime work. Justice's fourth case, which is against Philadelphia Electric Co., is in the courts.

In the first of EEOC's 12 legal actions, the commission took Liberty Mutual Life Insurance Co. to court to restore the job of a woman fired after she had filed sex discrimination charges against the company. The court ordered the employee reinstated with back pay, pending an EEOC investigation of her substantive charges against Liberty Mutual. The other cases deal with matters ranging from sex-segregated help-wanted ads to the use of stiffer promotion criteria for women than for men.

The deluge. In a series of tough speeches, EEOC Chairman William H. Brown III has warned employers that these moves are only the beginning. Many more cases will be filed, he says, once the commission's general counsel, William A. Carey, builds up his staff of 57 lawyers to the more than 200 permitted by the EEOC's 50% budget increase for fiscal 1973.

"Many people consider sex discrimination rather comical," says Brown. "But it is not funny—certainly not to the 5,800 people who filed charges of sex discrimination with our commission in fiscal 1971 and the 10,400 who filed charges in fiscal 1972."

Though similar in most ways, race and sex discrimination assume different forms, Brown says. "Today racial discrimination is subtler than in the past," he says. "Women, however, are often excluded by frank, overt discrimination. They are denied certain types of work and those responsible are quite candid about the reasons. They say that women are simply unacceptable in high pressure management, as supervisors, in heavy construction work, or in jobs that require travel. The same people say that women are good as bookkeepers and switchboard operators and things like that because they are good at detail and don't mind monotony."

EXHIBIT 6 (*concluded*)

When management men act on these preconceptions about the capabilities of women to deny or restrict job opportunities, they are being just as unlawful as when they exclude minorities, Brown stresses. The EEOC chairman notes that some women do reach top jobs even though sex discrimination exists in almost every business in America—"and some people argue that this shows if a women works hard, she can achieve success as easily as a man." All it really shows, Brown says, is that women may be as competent as men when given the chance.

Guidelines. Employers preparing for what apparently lies ahead are finding their handiest guide in the revised version of *Guidelines on Discrimination Because of Sex,* issued by the EEOC last March and often cited in judicial decisions on sex discrimination cases. The guidelines narrow almost to the vanishing point the kinds of jobs for which sex is a "*bona fide* occupational qualification"—BFOQ in lawyers' shorthand.

For instance, the guidelines say that an employer cannot refuse to hire a woman because of the assumption "that the turnover rate among women is higher than among men" or that women are less capable than men of aggressive salesmanship; similarly, a man cannot be denied a job because of "stereotyped characterizations" that men are less capable than women of assembling intricate equipment.

That leaves actor or actress as examples of jobs for which sex might be a BFOQ. Another example, as one court decision suggested, is wet nurse.

The guidelines also say that state laws barring women from jobs that require lifting loads of certain weights, or barring them from jobs that require night work and overtime work "do not take into account the capacities, preferences, and abilities of individual females," and therefore must yield to the federal antidiscrimination law.

Pregnancy. The same principle applies to state laws requiring special rest periods and meal periods for women—unless they cover men, too. And any rule restricting the employment of married women is illegal unless it also applies to married men.

The guidelines are equally explicit about fringe benefits. A pension or retirement plan is unlawful if it specifies different retirement ages or benefits because of sex. Disability benefits related to pregnancy must be available "on the same terms and conditions as are applied to other temporary disabilities." A series of cases has been filed against companies (and, on behalf of teachers, against school boards), challenging requirements that pregnant women must quit work by a certain stage in their pregnancy.

The probable outcome of the pregnancy cases is suggested by the action taken last January by General Electric Co. The company responded to a suit by the International Union of Electrical Workers by changing its policy and allowing pregnant women to work for as long as the women's physicians certify that they are physically able to work.

EXHIBIT 7

Lackawanna case[1]

Bethlehem's Lackawanna plant, located near Buffalo, New York, was one of the largest steel-making facilities in the United States. At full capacity, the plant employed about 20,000 people. Covering 5,000 acres, it consisted of several distinct, interrelated operations: receiving raw materials, producing coke and iron, making the steel, rolling it in various shapes and forms and finishing it. The plant was divided into 74 production and maintenance departments with about 280 seniority units. Associated with these departments and units was a wide variety of working conditions, each demanding particular skills and each involving certain hazards. Consequently, for efficient and safe operations, definite job progressions were established in each unit. In the course of doing a job, an employee acquired the skills and training needed for higher jobs in the same unit. Promotions and, in slack periods, demotions were effected along these lines of progression. Work in one unit was usually different enough from that in another unit that a transferee to a unit was hardly more knowledgeable than a person recently hired.

Prior to October 1, 1967, it was the unofficial practice to assign newly hired black workers to certain departments in the plant. As a result, about 80 percent of the Blacks ended up in one of eleven departments: Brickmason Labor, Yard, Sintering Plant, Coke Ovens, Blast Furnace, Steelmaking, 44″ Mill, Billet Yard, Bar Mills, 28″ Mill, and 14″ Mill. The jobs in these departments were among the hottest and dirtiest in the plant. Almost all of the employees in five of these departments were black: Blast Furnace, Brickmason Labor, Coke Oven, Sintering Plant, and Steelmaking. In the other six departments, more than 20 percent of the employees were black.

Representatives of the Department of Justice arrived unannounced at the plant on September 7, 1967, to investigate the employment and other personnel practices there. A week later the assistant attorney general for the Civil Rights Division wrote the company stating that, in his judgment, its practices were not consistent with Title VII of the Civil Rights Act of 1964. Section 703(a) of Title VII prohibited discrimination against any employee "with respect to his compensation, terms, conditions, or privileges of employment, because of such individual's race." Further, employers could not limit, segregate, or classify employees "in any way which would deprive or tend to deprive any individual of employment opportunities or otherwise adversely affect his status as an employee, because of such individual's race." On September 29 the company replied that it was anxious to comply with the objectives and the spirit of the act; it asked about the steps to be taken to bring it into compliance with the act. Among other things, the company was most cooperative with governmental investigators, opening its records to them, providing them with computerized data, and putting its employees and equipment at the government's disposal.

On December 6 the Justice Department brought action against the company in the federal district court. The following May 15 the United Steelworkers

[1] This exhibit was prepared by Kim Kehoe, research assistant, as part of an unreleased case study in 1972.

EXHIBIT 7 (*continued*)

of America and five locals at the plant were named as defendants. At that time the attorney general alleged that provisions of the collective bargaining agreement served to perpetuate the effects of past discriminatory practices.

In his findings, the judge said in part:

> The court finds as fact that the transfer and seniority system negotiated in the 1962, 1965, and 1968 Master Agreements by the company and the union operates (as described above) in such a way as to tend to lock an employee into the department to which he has been assigned. This lock-in effect becomes stronger as an employee's length of service increases in the department. This means that the longer a Negro has worked in the hot and dirty department to which he was admittedly discriminatorily assigned, the more he has to lose by transfer.

In its order the court expanded the seniority and transfer rights of the employees who had been assigned and limited to the eleven departments mentioned above. All of these employees hired before October 1, 1967, were given priority transfer rights to move into any other department, provided they had the ability and skills requisite for the job. However, the judge did not grant the full relief sought by the government: retention of both their prior pay rate and their seniority for purposes of promotion and demotion. The judge did not grant rate retention and seniority carry-over because he held that the present system was not a complete deterrent to transfer and that the changes requested by the Government would disrupt operations and disturb the other employees at the plant. This decision was rendered April 13, 1970.

The government appealed the decision to the U.S. Circuit Court of Appeals. The case was heard in December and the three-judge panel issued its findings and decree the following June. The court commented on the relationship between the seniority and transfer system and the discriminatory assignment of Blacks in the past.

> Although these overt practices were finally discontinued after October 1, 1967, . . . the seniority and transfer provisions perpetuated their effects in two ways. First, they tended to lock discriminatorily assigned employees into their jobs. In order to transfer to a formerly "white" department, these employees were required to suffer an economic penalty: forfeiture of seniority rights and pay levels earned in the "black" departments. The former was due to the use of departmental seniority, the latter to the fact that the transferee's new job was at a low-paid entry level in the new department. Thus, to obtain an opportunity that had been denied them because of race, these employees had to be willing to give up what was already theirs because of service in the plant. Second, a transferee to a white department would never be able to reach the level of a white employee already there. For example, if a Black and a White had been hired at the same time and the latter had been assigned to the more desirable white department but the Black had not been so assigned, the White started to accumulate department or unit seniority in that department but the Black did not.

EXHIBIT 7 (*continued*)

Even if the Black were given the chance years later to transfer to the white department, the earlier discriminatory job assignment had denied him the chance to earn seniority up to that time in the white department. Therefore, the use of departmental or unit seniority for purposes of promotion in the formerly white department continued the effect of the earlier discriminatory practice.

The court went on to address the question of the effect of the remedy, rate retention, and seniority carry-over, on the seniority system and on employee morale. The company and the union had argued that the seniority system insured orderly and efficient job mobility so that "after transfer the employee will advance in his new line of progression in an orderly manner, developing and building on new skills as he moves from job to job." In this way the seniority system served both safety and efficiency. The court went on to say:

> . . . Therefore, the crucial question must be whether the basic goal of the seniority system will necessarily be frustrated by these remedies. It is perfectly clear that this will not be the case. An unqualified worker need not be promoted whether or not he is a transferee under the district court's order. . . . Transferees will not move directly to high or middle level jobs or displace workers from jobs presently held nor jump from low to higher jobs.
>
> Under the government's proposals, a transferee has priority rights only with respect to jobs in formerly "white" departments that are not otherwise filled in the normal seniority procedures. Accordingly, transfers will be to low-skilled, entry-level jobs. A transferee will be promoted from those jobs in the normal job-by-job fashion, moving up the progression line only as a job immediately above him becomes vacant.

Appellees also argue that the morale of employees who did not suffer discrimination will suffer if rate retention and seniority carry-over are ordered. But in the context of this case that possibility is not such an overriding business purpose that the relief requested must be denied. Assuming *arguendo* that the expectations of some employees will not be met, their hopes arise from an illegal system. Moreover, their seniority advantages are not indefeasibly vested rights but mere expectations derived from a collective bargaining agreement subject to modification.

The court returned the case to the district court with the request for a revision of the order. The revised order was to include the following provisions:

1. A transferee shall receive, in his new position, pay equal to the pay in his former permanent position and shall continue to be so paid until he reaches a position whose pay scale is greater. If no job in his new department or unit has a rate as high as his former position, then he shall receive the rate of the highest level job in that department or unit. Because the rate retained is that of the transferee's permanent job, he shall not

EXHIBIT 7 (*concluded*)

retain any temporary pay increase if he transfers after a temporary promotion.

2. A transferee shall be permitted to exercise plant seniority for all purposes following transfer, except as otherwise set forth herein. When a transferee competes on the basis of seniority for vacancies occurring in the normal course of business, seniority for all bidders shall be computed on the basis of plant, rather than unit or department, seniority. Only workers qualified to fill a higher job may use plant seniority to advance. As workers are recalled after a layoff, all employees shall assume the same positions relative to each other as they held immediately prior to the layoff.

3. A transferee's right to transfer with seniority carry-over and rate retention may be exercised only once and only during the next two years. If he exercises that right within that period, the transferee's protection of seniority carry-over and rate retention shall continue in accordance with the other provisions in the order.

4. A transferee shall lose his privilege of rate retention if he refuses a promotion in his new unit or department.

The revised order was issued by the district court judge on October 14, 1971.

Note on the public relations campaign of the eastern railroads

THE FOLLOWING PAGES contain excerpts from the record and opinion in suits brought by certain trucklines and trucking interests against the Eastern Railroads President Conference and their public relations counsel, Carl Byoir and Associates.

SUMMARY

The court has found as a fact that the railroads and Byoir entered into a conspiracy in unreasonable restraint of trade, the nature and purpose of which was to injure the truckers in their competitive position in the long-haul freight industry in the northeastern section of the United States. This, of course, involves interstate commerce. The immediate purpose was to create public resentment to the truckers, not only in the minds of the general public but in the minds of those who utilized the services of the trucks and in such a manner as to interfere with business relations between shippers and truckers. There is no doubt that the railroads prior to the development of the long-haul truck industry had an actual monopoly of that field. A new industry in competition had appeared. That industry by reason of more flexibility and faster service had made great inroads in that particular competitive field and its business has increased a thousand fold. Both were regulated industries. The truckers could not operate without a certificate from the Interstate Commerce Commission showing the need for the service in a particular locality. Instead of meeting the competition in the field and

562

giving the shippers what the shippers wanted, they determined upon another course of action—to injure and/or destroy the truckers and thereby force the shippers to their detriment to continue to use the railroads. This, of course, would be to the shippers' disadvantage in this great area of flexibility which was clearly so vital to the shipper, but would eliminate the fundamental cause of the railroads' loss of revenue. It was with this very thought in mind that the combination of Byoir and the railroads occurred in August of 1949 and a definite program for accomplishing this desired result was instituted with the full knowledge and consent both of Byoir and every defendant railroad. Briefly restated, the plan was first to create hostility to the truckers. With that as a base the rest of the plan evolved. This plan generally had ten fundamental objectives:

1.   To seek out or create "independent" organizations favorable to the railroads' point of view and opposed to the truckers.

2.   Through Byoir and the ostensible independent organizations create a hostile public using the method detailed under the heading. "Campaign of Vilification."

3.   Through the organizations and at the instigation of Byoir create a demand for more tax revenues by government at all levels, particularly the local level.

4.   Through Byoir and railroad contacts have one of these organizations hire a recognized and ostensibly impartial statistical group to make a study of revenue-producing methods most palatable to the public; the statistical group would be supplied by Byoir with the questions to be asked the public and the answers to these questions would form the basis for the conclusions in the study. These questions by Byoir would be so framed that only the desired answers would be forthcoming—that the truckers must be more heavily taxed. Another use of these so-called independent survey organizations was to focus attention upon the trucks as destroyers of the highways and emphasize by "statistics," based on the false premise that truckers are the prime users of roads, that the truckers were the recipients of enormous public subsidies.

5.   With these statistics on hand have the "independent" organizations through Byoir publicize them from one end of the United States to another, through speeches, magazines, and news releases.

6.   Interest writers of important magazines in articles attacking the truckers and present the writers with all the statistics compiled by the "independent sources."

7.   With an outstanding magazine article have the organizations, through Byoir, intensify their campaign and then seek further articles with the ever-growing research material as a basis.

8. While all of the above was being carried out to aid financially and in every other way legislators disposed to the railroads' point of view.

9. Present the research packages and a hostile and aroused public to the legislature and then propose the type of legislation determined by the associated railroads of that particular state as the type of legislation desired, and which to the associated railroads appeared feasible under the circumstances.

10. Make absolutely certain that the general public attributed the entire campaign to public-spirited organizations only, keep the railroads in the background, and conceal particularly from objective-minded public officials interested in the problem the fact that the entire campaign was a creature of the railroads, the whole cost of the campaign being borne by the railroads, and for the purpose of hindering and destroying the trucking industry as a competitor to the railroads in the long-haul transportation industry.

It is clear from the above, regardless of the success or failure of legislation proposed by the railroads unfavorable to the truckers, that a real private injury to the truckers was accomplished. There was definitely a loss of goodwill to the trucking industry and in some instances that loss of goodwill was extreme.

The defendants' actions destroyed to a large extent the public confidence which the truckers had earned by their own efforts and which they might have won additionally, especially in the light of the innumerable beneficial accomplishments of the truckers in the field of long-haul transportation. We must assume that most people are honest, law-abiding citizens, and that includes those engaged in the trucking field. It certainly has not been proved in this case that all or even a substantial number of truckers are lawbreakers. To the contrary, the evidence in this case clearly shows that, except for a small segment, the truckers are decent, law-abiding citizens, but as a result of this campaign they were categorized as lawbreakers, road-hoggers, completely indifferent to the safety of others on the highway, and moochers on the public through failure to pay their way.

As a final note it can be remarked at this point that, although not outlined above, overt acts to accomplish the objectives of this conspiracy were committed among others in the states of Connecticut, Indiana, and Illinois. This feature is mentioned at this point to show that this was not a series of individual conspiracies but was one large, ever-growing conspiracy with the single objective of "improving the competitive position of the railroad in the field of transportation," but by the illegal means of limitation of or destruction of the trucking industry. Restated in extremely simple form I have found the following:

1. That the defendants combined in and about May 19, 1949 with the intent and object of substantially lessening competition in the long-haul carriage of freight in unreasonable restraint of trade.
2. That they were joined in this combination by the Byoir organization on or about August 15, 1949 for the same purpose and with the same intent and for a handsome remuneration.
3. The instrumentality or means by which this object was to be achieved was primarily by a campaign designed to destroy the good-will of the truckers and, secondly, by fomenting governmental restrictions obtained by virtue of the methods outlined in the factual phase of this decision.
4. Hundreds of overt acts in furtherance of this plan were carried out throughout the country, and all in furtherance of the same object and design.

New York activities

When Byoir undertook to represent the railroads in the summer of 1949, it found in New York State that the railroads had already enlisted the aid of many civic organizations and were themselves utilizing the "third-party technique." Outstanding were two organizations: The Citizens Tax League of Rochester, New York, whose secretary A. J. Menzie apparently delighted in public controversy, and The Citizens Public Expenditure Survey, Inc., an independent public-spirited organization originally formed for the purpose of scrutinizing the budgets of all governmental political divisions and subdivisions from the state itself to the smallest municipality.

Through agricultural agents employed by them, the railroads had been able to enlist the sympathetic cooperation of many prominent Grange members to present their viewpoint against the truckers to the public. But they were in need of statistics to bolster their contentions, and it was important that any review come from an apparently independent source. They decided that should a survey of highway users and the revenue derived from them for road construction and maintenance be sponsored by the railroads it would be of little, if any, value. Therefore, it was determined to have such a survey made by an independent source. Griffinhagen & Associates, consultants in public administration and finance, with offices in Chicago, New York, Boston, and Los Angeles, were chosen to make the survey. The sponsor was The Citizens Public Expenditure Survey, Inc. This survey which was completed and documented in February of 1950 again had no apparent railroad relation and seemingly was what it purported to be, a completely objective independent analysis of the highways and highway use and revenue conditions in the state of New York. To put it in its proper perspective, however, the evidence in this case discloses that during the years 1951, 1952, and 1953, substantial "subscriptions" in uneven amounts were made to the Citizens Public Expenditure Survey, Inc. by the Pennsylvania Railroad. The evidence also discloses that Mr. Little-field, after the passage of the weight-distance tax bill on trucks in New York, sought a vote of thanks for Mr. Dugan of the New York Central for his efforts in bringing Griffinhagen to New York for the survey and the results of the survey. Over and above that, weekly reports of Kiely, Byoir's New York representative for the ERPC, clearly indicated that Kiely directed the activities of both Walter Howe, executive director of Citizens, and one Finke, head of its so-called research department. The closely knit cooperation of these three individuals was such, together with the "subscriptions" which appear rather to be "assessments," that the inference is inescapable, and the court so finds, that the railroads paid for the survey and subsidized the activities of Messrs. Howe and Finke.

With the Griffinhagen report as a basis, Kiely toured New York State and "sold the railroad story to editors, the Mayors Conference, County Supervisors, Chief of Police Associations, Rural Letter Carriers, Members of the Grange, and other organizations. He also worked closely with The Citizens Tax League of Rochester, New York, and used that organization for the dissemination of literature unfavorable to the truckers. Byoir absorbed all of the costs of this distribution and paid the secretary, Menzie, a substantial fee of several hundred dollars for the so-called research, which the court finds was for the use of his position. In order to obtain more extensive publicity Byoir formed the Empire State Transport League, a strictly paper organization, with its principal office at a desk in a public stenographer's office in Albany, New York. Byoir induced many prominent New Yorkers to lend their names to this paper organization. The amount of antitruck literature and news releases critical of the truckers put out by this organization was prodigious. Of course, it was all at the expense of the railroads without any attribution of responsiblity to the railroads.

While there is naturally a scarcity of evidence as to the connection of Byoir with the Legislative Committee of the New York State Senate, which had the weight-distance bill before it in the year 1950, it is significant that when Senator Manning, the head of that committee, came up for election in a later year he became extremely resentful of rumors that Byoir had written the Senate report recommending the weight-distance tax and refused to let Byoir relate any further remarks to him. The inference is again inescapable, and the court so finds, that Byoir's representatives were working in close contact with his office during the pendency of this particular piece of legislation and were responsible for many of the news releases which came out under his authorship.

As in the case of Stull in Ohio, who will be later discussed, and Hardy with Pevler and Mackie in New Jersey, Kiely did a magnificent job of grass-root selling. He persuaded the Rural Letter Carriers, the Grange, and the Mayors Conference to adopt resolutions at their state conventions, several of which were actually written by him, denouncing the truckers and urging strict enforcement of the weight-distance tax. Under the letterhead of the Empire State Transportation League, he urged the sheriffs of every county of the state to enforce the strict penal provisions of the weight-distance tax, particularly with regard to overloading. He sought out legislators, particularly members of the Highway Committee, and solicited the introduction of and urged the passage of an act giving local communities, through their local police organizations, the right to arrest the drivers of overladen trucks and impound the trucks if necessary. The bait held out was that local communities could profit from the high penalties set forth in the weight-distance tax law for overloading. He worked also with his friends in the Grange, in the Mayors Conference, and in other organizations to put pressure upon the political leaders to see that the legislative committees were composed of legislators favorable to the railroad point of view.

In addition to the Griffinhagen report, the Byoir organization was able to obtain further statistics against the heavy trucks by so-called public opinion polls. The media for obtaining this information was Fact Finders, Inc. and the Princeton Polls, the latter headed by Dr. Robert Sly, head of the New Jersey Tax Study Commission. The questions were framed in the light of a demand carefully nurtured by Byoir, through the Grange, the Mayors Conference, and others, to obtain a greater allotment of state funds for local community roads. While very astutely, and apparently innocently, worded, the bold import of the questions presented to individual persons ran substantially as follows: Since more money must be obtained for roads, do you prefer: (1) increase in passenger car registration fees; (2) increase in the motor fuel tax; (3) increase in the charges made for the use of the highways by the heavy trucks? It would certainly be less than human if an overwhelming majority of the people approached would not vote for the third proposition, to wit: Tax the truckers! These public opinion polls at the cost of many thousands of dollars were inaugurated by and subsidized by Byoir on behalf of and at the expense of the railroads. The results of these polls received the widest publicity that Byoir could give them both on the metropolitan level of all the larger cities of the state of New York, in national magazines, where possible, and with particular emphasis on the country weekly newspapers. In that regard it might also be noted that Kiely was also able to obtain the cooperation of a few editors of weekly newspapers who printed strong editorials against the truckers.

Defendants argue that these antitruck statements contained the considered opinion of the editors and that it was merely another facet of the freedom of press and speech guaranteed by the First Amendment to the Constitution of the United States. This argument would certainly carry great weight were it not for the fact that Kiely, a highly placed and highly paid employee of Byoir, had written the editorials himself in furtherance of the Byoir-railroad objective. In accordance with standard operating procedures, these skillfully written diatribes against the truckers received the widest possible publicity and became part of a Byoir kit for presentation to the next editor.

In this posture of the case it might be well to note also that much of the success of Kiely and the others in "planting" these ideas with editors was due to the fact that apparently independent writers of recognized stature had written articles about the damage that truckers did to roads. As will be related hereafter under the headings "Magazine activities" and "Campaign of vilification," these articles in outstanding magazines of national circulation, the names of which will also be hereafter related, were based almost exclusively on data furnished by Byoir and written or edited by Byoir before appearing in these magazines.

To keep the case in proper perspective we must recognize that Kiely, Stull, Hardy, et al., were on the payroll of the ERPC through Byoir; that their entire salaries and expenses were reimbursed by ERPC to Byoir; that their job was to create public dissatisfaction with the truckers, arouse animosity against the truckers, and all to the final purpose that the railroads might at least limit the activities of the truckers in the long-haul industry or, if completely successful, destroy them as a competitive factor with the railroads. Bluntly stated, all were working to accomplish injury to a business competitor within the prohibition of the Sherman and Clayton Antitrust Acts.

The results of Byoir's work in New York in conjunction with Messrs. Littlefield and Deegan were extremely gratifying to the Research Subcommittee of the ERPC. In its report dated June 20, 1951, to Mr. Walter Tuohy, chairman of the Special Transportation Committee, the following pertinent language is found:

> 7. Research Committee has acted more or less as liaison between State Railroad Associations and the Carl Byoir group. In June, 1949, the Policy Committee named the states of New Jersey, New York and Ohio as trial states. The Carl Byoir group, under the direction of Mr. Girdler, placed the facts before state administrations and otherwise gave the states a vast amount of help, resulting in favorable truck legislation in New Jersey and New York.
>
> 8. The Mileage Tax Bill, which passed the New York legislature in April of this year, was of outstanding importance. This is the first state east of the Mississippi to put a substantial mileage tax on trucks.

Other states are watching this development. The New York authorities advise that they expect to build 50 weighing stations scattered throughout the State.

9. After the New York Bill passed, the Carl Byoir people concentrated on Ohio. A Bill was passed increasing truck license fees about 30%. There is much more to be accomplished and the campaign will be resumed at the next session of the legislature.

10. The first of June, the railroads of Pennsylvania unanimously requested the help of the Carl Byoir people, and a man has been assigned.

Ohio activities

The State of Ohio posed one peculiar problem to the Byoir organization. Representing the Goodrich Tire and Rubber Company, which of course was vitally interested in automotive equipment and the sale of tires, Byoir found itself in the predicament of representing opposing interests. Nevertheless, following the pattern of New Jersey, Byoir threw the weight of its organization behind Donald Stull, who had charge of the Ohio activities. The success of Stull in Ohio in advancing the interests of the Byoir-ERPC plan was little less than phenomenal. T. J. Kauer was director of the Ohio Department of Highways; Harold Cohen was the chief of the Bureau of Public Relations for the Ohio Department of Highways. Kauer was also chairman of the Interregional Council on Highway Transportation which had charge of the Maryland Road Test. Stull had complete access to their offices and worked closely with them. He also, through Kauer, apparently had entree to the office of Governor Lausche. Building up a grass-root campaign against the truckers through the use of "independent factual data" obtained from sources apparently independent, but based completely on Byoir material, he was successful in creating a wave of indignation towards the truckers which resulted in an increase of fees to the truckers in 1951 of approximately 30 percent. Again, through Kauer, he was able to "educate" the members of the Ohio Legislative Highway Investigating Committee. In 1952, according to a Byoir report, Stull had done such "an efficient job of education" that there arose a public demand for taxation on heavy trucks.

There was also a gubernatorial campaign in Ohio last year. Charles Taft, the Republican candidate, adopted the proposition that trucks should pay higher taxes "based on weight carried and miles traveled." Stull reported to Byoir that up to three weeks before Election Day, Lausche, the incumbent, had planned to campaign solely on his record and was backing away from the ton-mile tax as a too-familiar story and one already chosen by his opponent. What he needed, he told his aides, was "a dramatic story that could be told over TV." That was all Stull needed (according to Byoir). Using newspaper clips, editorials, magazine articles, etc., which, as will be demonstrated later, were practically all Byoir-inspired and paid for by ERPC, Stull demonstrated the apparent widespread public interest in the ton-mile tax. He also had available a *Harper's* magazine article by Senator Neuberger of Oregon entitled, "Who Shall Pay for Our Roads?" for the writing of·which Byoir "research" had been made available, and which will be referred to in detail under the heading "Magazine activities." Lausche campaigned just 15 days. According to reports found in Byoir's files, in all but one speech he talked only the ton-mile tax; in every TV program he centered attention on truck taxation; waiving copies of the *Harper's* magazine article before the camera; pointing to placards showing the justice of heavy taxes on trucks; displaying Public Utility Commission records of violations by explosive-hauling truckers (the results of a Byoir-inspired investigation) and repeating the results of the Maryland Road Test (a distorted Byoir interpretation) to prove how badly big trucks damage highways. Again, according to Byoir, the data and, in many cases, the words and props were supplied by Stull. The *Cleveland Plain Dealer* stated categorically "Lausche's astonishing victory, against the political tide, can be construed as an endorsement of his highway program." Stull did his job so well that the truckers were forced to abandon their early charges that the "bills were railroad inspired"— which they were.

In addition and as part of his program Stull introduced into Ohio the "Save Our Highways Club." This was an organization founded by railroad employees in Tennessee and its entry into Ohio was completely financed by Byoir for which it was reimbursed by the railroads. Literature in profusion was mailed to legislators, granges, farmers' organizations and automobile clubs. All of it was calculated to and did bring the trucking industry into public disrepute. Again, a magnificent job was accomplished in keeping any information as to the true position of the railroads in this campaign from the general public. The rise in fees and the campaign for the weight-distance tax in Ohio were two of the outstanding accomplishments of Byoir for the railroads in the entire campaign.

Two other aspects of the Byoir-Stull campaign are worthy of mention. The records of the Byoir organization introduced in this case demonstrate clearly that copies of Governor Lausche's correspondence with protesting truckers were in the hands of Byoir before the correspondence even reached the U.S. mails, and to quote Stull, it "contained our poison." This again points out that Kauer and Cohen were working diligently for the interests of the railroads.

While defendants have vigorously argued that the term "poison" was nothing but public relations jargon, I find that Stull meant exactly what he said and in the ordinary context of the words used. It is clearly apparent that the political campaign against the truckers was based on slanted statistics created by Byoir for the railroads, and that most of the data used in the speeches, if not the speeches themselves on both sides, Republican and Democratic, stemmed directly from the Byoir organization. While the trucking industry and its members were intellectually certain that this apparent grass-root uprising against the industry was definitely railroad-inspired, so well did Stull and Byoir work that it was impossible to document and prove it. The net result was that the trucking industry faced a hostile public opinion in Ohio because of the method of distortion and overemphasis of the admitted shortcomings of the industry on the part of Byoir. This statement will be amplified in the heading "Vilification campaign."

Magazine activities

One of the most unusual of Byoir's employees, the head of the Magazine Department, was Patricia Lochridge Hartwell. Mrs. Hartwell, whose professional name while she was with Byoir was Patricia Lochridge, joined the Byoir organization in November of 1949 and was assigned to the ERPC account. She thereupon set out to develop magazine articles which would portray the railroads' point of view and would be unfavorable to the trucking interests. Her method of operation was to interest an editor of a magazine in a story, and if the editor thought it had sufficient merit, he might assign one of his staff writers or editors to do the piece. In that event Mrs. Hartwell would furnish the writer with the data which Byoir had compiled—data which, of course, was always slanted against the truckers. She also made use of free-lance writers. She would interest them in a particular story and pay them— while they researched the proposed story at Byoir's or at other places— amounts which in many instances ran into several hundreds of dollars. Since the ultimate aim was to hurt the truckers, any such payments were reimbursed by the railroads, and should the free-lance writer be able to sell the article to a magazine the entire fee went to the writer. In other words, Byoir paid the writer during the preparation of the article and the magazine paid him for writing it. In the extremely limited number of instances that a writer contemplated an article which would be favorable to the railroads' point of view with respect to the truckers, Byoir extended every facility it possessed for use by the writer and at no cost to the writer.

The worth of such a project in the attainment of the ERPC goal cannot be minimized. In addition to the ordinary extensive circulation which the magazines themselves possessed, it was possible, at railroad expense, to circulate reprints of the articles widely to civic organizations, state, city, and government officials, as well as to legislators and other individuals who were concerned with public opinion. While it is true that her efforts in every case did not meet with complete success, she was successful in having enough magazine articles released to make an important contribution to the railroads' antitruck campaign. Without attempting to individuate the details of each article, it will be sufficient to recount some of the articles published and Byoir's connection with them.

The first article, "The Giants Wreck Highways" with a subtitle "Heavy Trucks Are Making Their Runs On Your Tax Dollars," appeared in the April 1950 issue of *Everybody's Digest*. It was based almost completely upon Byoir's research and development. In the same month Byoir claimed credit for having furnished minor research and comment for an article by Sen. Joseph C. O'Mahoney entitled, "What Bad Roads Are Costing Us," which appeared in the April 1950 issue of the *American Magazine*.

Early in 1950 Mrs. Hartwell presented an outline of a story about truck damage to roads to the editor of *Harper's* magazine. This outline was very extensive and *Harper's* evinced interest in it. Thereafter Mrs. Hartwell contacted Myron Stearn, an independent free-lance writer, interested him in the story, furnished him with all the Byoir data on the trucks, and the completed product appeared in the September 1950 issue of *Harper's* magazine under the caption, "Our Roads Are Going To Pot." At approximately the same time an article entitled, "The Rape of Our Roads," by ·Frederick Brownell, a Byoir protégé, appeared in the *Reader's Digest*. This article was condensed from a *Buffalo Evening News* story. These two articles became the first authoritative sources of so-called independent public attacks upon the trucking industry.

Through the good efforts of Clinton Johnson, director of publicity for the Maryland Roads Commission and a close associate of the Byoir organization, David G. Wittels, an outstanding writer for the *Saturday Evening Post*, in the September 16, 1950 issue of that magazine wrote a very critical article entitled, "Are Trucks Destroying Our Highways?" Byoir furnished extensive national research in a 5,000-word background memorandum to round out his story on the Maryland State Highway Commission Program. It was the same Clinton Johnson who persuaded Mr. Wittels to go to Maryland and actually research the story in the field, live with the highway crew, meet the highway commissioner, and find out what the problems were for himself. While the article justifiably was critical of a certain class of truckers, it must be realized that the initiative for the article stemmed from railroad-inspired sources and portrayed a particularly venal type of trucker as representative of the entire trucking industry. The distortion, however, was so skillfully done and so subtly written as to make a profound impression upon a casual reader of the article. Again, it is a variation of third-party technique approach, which technique in its application to this case will receive further attention.

Hardy Burke, "a sometime employee of Byoir" and a sometime independent free-lance writer, wrote an article in the April 1952 issue of the *National Grange Monthly* entitled, "History, Trucks and Money." This article was actually authored by a Byoir ghost-writer, James Miller, and, according to Mrs. Hartwell, "skillfully developed all the major points in the ERPC campaign." This article, which pictorially highlighted the collapse of a bridge due to an overladen truck attempting to escape a weighing station on a main highway and the destruction of a detour on a main highway over a country road, was skillfully designed to arouse the farmers in opposition to the trucks.

Again, in the August 1951 Sunday issue of *Parade* magazine, which is a supplement to hundreds of Sunday newspapers throughout the country, Clinton Johnson assisted Byoir in obtaining the insert of an article entitled, "Trucks: Help or Headache?" This article, completely critical of trucks, contained the words and pictures of the Byoir organization.

In the July 30, 1952 issue of *People* magazine appeared an article entitled, "Trucks Wreck Your Roads." This article, again critical of the trucking industry, was not only "planted" by Byoir but extensive circulation of reprints was made with the article appearing as the lead article on the cover of the reprint whereas the original magazine cover contained no such reference.

An article which represented an extremely important item in the railroads' campaign against the truckers was that which appeared in the April 1952 issue of the *Country Gentleman*. This article by Emilie Hall, described as "You Can Have Better Roads" was referred to by the magazine as a "new chapter in the farm roads story." The writer was discovered by Horace Lyon, a Byoir employee assigned to the ERPC account, and Mrs. Hartwell did most of the research and editing for the article, with Jim Miller and Dick Strouse of Byoir helping in some last-minute rewrites. Quoting Mrs. Hartwell's appraisal of the publication of this article: "This was a difficult job to put across, entailing two complete rewrites of the article to satisfy both a pixie author and a difficult editor. This was accomplished without too much pain and the underlying philosophy of the ERPC account came through in the final draft." After various complications, Lyon and Lochridge were able to get the article endorsed in a box which appeared on the first page of the article by the president of the all-important Association of American State Highway Officials. This article received widespread distribution at the hands of Byoir but more importantly a motion picture based on this article was made for distribution to farm groups throughout the country. The story of how this motion picture came into existence, the purpose behind the picture, and the ultimate success of the endeavor is significantly interesting.

For some 17 years one Fred O. Bailey had served as reporter and farm editor of the United Press Association. During the years 1945, 1946, and 1947 he had served as legislative counsel of the National Grange. Subsequent to 1947 he served a number of national magazines in the farm field as a reporter and columnist. According to the testimony of David I. Mackie, one of those magazines served was the *Country Gentleman*. During the year 1951 Bailey had discussed the formation of a Farm Roads Foundation but nothing came of it during that year. However, the general idea of such a Foundation was to cooperate with and assist farm organizations and farm groups in planning for an adequate, balanced-roads program to serve their needs. The first and only function of the Farm Roads Foundation up until May of 1953, the date of Mr. Bailey's disposition in this case, was the distribution of a film, "Highways and Byways, U.S.A.," based upon the story in the *Country Gentleman* magazine, "You Can Have Better Roads." The evidence in this case discloses beyond peradventure of doubt that the moving force in the making of this film was the Western Association of Railroads. Bailey was approached by representatives of that association and offered an outright grant of a picture for distribution. It was not until this offer had been made that the Farm Roads Foundation was incorporated and came into being. The evidence is also crystal clear that Byoir, in conjunction with representatives of the Western Railroads Association, had been working on a script for this picture. In fact, Byoir edited the script. Dudley Pictures of Hollywood was commissioned by the association of railroads to make the picture and the cost of making the picture was divided between the eastern, western, and southern railroads on a basis of 18 percent to the southern railroads and 41 percent each to the eastern and western railroads. The assessment to the eastern railroads was $62,600. Based on the above percentages of assessment it would appear, therefore, that the cost of the film to the three railroad associations exceeded $150,000. This film, the cost of the public distribution of which (and it was most extensive) has always been borne through a grant by the railroads, was exhibited at the trial of this case, and the film and a transcript thereof have been filed of record. The film is professionally and skillfully done. It demonstrates clearly the needs of the farmers for auxiliary roads and suggests united, combined, intelligent, community efforts to obtain the necessary funds to bring about this very desirable result. The lasting impression created by the picture, however, is contained in a very few sentences of the dialogue and as the picture concludes. The lasting impact of the film is that big trucks do not pay their fair share of highway construction and maintenance. While extremely expensive, it constituted a very important piece of propaganda carrying a terrific impact upon its viewers. Mr. Bailey, whose cooperation had been sought in the editing of the script, was completely unaware of the very important role played by Byoir. He had no idea of the cost of the film nor of the cost of distribution which was borne by the railroads. Two distribution companies were employed to distribute the film through their regular agencies to farm groups and other interested parties. It was distributed free of charge for showing in regular moving picture houses. One hundred and eighty-six colored prints were made in 16 mm size and ten black-and-white 16-mm-size copies were made for showing on TV. Four 35-mm copies were made for showing in regular motion picture theatres. To a viewer of the picture it would appear that the sponsors were the *Country Gentleman* and the Farm Roads Foundation. No suggestion either in the title, dialogue, or screen credits indicated the connection of the railroads with this film. Viewed as it was by millions, the effect was most certainly to build up prejudice in the public mind against the trucking industry.

The final article which appeared shortly before the institution of this suit was an article, "Who Shall Pay for Our Roads," by the Honorable Richard L. Neuberger, United States Senator from the state of Oregon. Mr. Neuberger before entering politics was a capable newspaperman and writer. He was also a legislator in Oregon when the first weight-distance tax on heavy trucks was passed in that state. It would follow naturally that he should be an expert in that field. Hearing that *Harper's* magazine had discussed the writing of an article in connection with highway financing with the senator, Mrs. Hartwell telephoned him at his home and discussed the article with him. She suggested that Byoir had splendid material on the national picture and suggested that such material might be useful to him in his article. As a result of this conversation, the Byoir material was mailed to Mr. Neuberger in Oregon where he was working on the article. That he availed himself of the material is clear from a reading of the article. Byoir had been pyramiding data, mostly "planted" material, for a period of approximately three years and this was the authoritative material submitted to Mr. Neuberger. His article included generally the same "statistics" as every other article admittedly planted by Byoir. Byoir, of course, took no part in the reviewing or editing of the article, but the impact of its "help" is clearly discernible throughout.

In commenting upon the above magazine articles, it is not intended to convey the impression that the above represented the sum total of the Byoir efforts in the magazine field. They cannot and do not reflect the further extensive efforts of Byoir's magazine department and its success in putting over the railroads' point of view in other magazines of lesser importance and circulation. They merely outline the importance of the work of the magazine department in this field, since once articles were published they were extensively used by Byoir's representatives in selling their antitruck story to persons concerned with public opinion.

Pennsylvania activities

As stated at the outset of this opinion, after 1943 the attempts of the trucking industry to increase axle loads and gross weights in the legislative sessions of 1945 and 1947 failed. In the 1949 session the then-governor, James A. Duff, ordered the chairman of the Legislative Committee on Highways not to send any bill to his desk increasing the said weights. With complete administrative support the railroads had no difficulty in controlling the restrictions on trucks—and by legally acceptable means.

Pennsylvania had a lower gross weight than all of its surrounding states, and the net result was that many of the trucks could not legally carry through Pennsylvania, loads which would be legal in other states. One incongruity of that situation was that at the western end of the state in shipments from steel mills only the first 60 miles of a trip to surrounding states of many hundreds of miles was off limits for a full load. Naturally it created a considerable problem for the truckers engaged in the long-haul steel industry. That the situation was favorable to the railroads was fully recognized and every attempt was made on behalf of the railroads to keep that weight limitation by statute and, of course, for the express purpose of helping railroad revenues. Again, this was entirely proper. The situation was such that in 1949 Pennsylvania did not need the services of Byoir. William A. Reiter, chairman of the Associated Railroads of Pennsylvania, had a good working team operating in Harrisburg. Joab K. Mahood, secretary of the Grange, together with H. A. Thomson, better known as "Cappy" Thomson, secretary of the Pennsylvania State Association of Township Supervisors, worked in close cooperation with Mr. Reiter. However, improper activities were also present. That the Pennsylvania Railroad used the Byoir third-party technique in creating ill will against the trucks when House Bill 560—The Big Truck Bill of 1949—was pending, is clear from two advertisements printed during the months of March and April of 1949. While it is true that one advertisement designated as 3P-5192 was put out under the Associated Railroads of Pennsylvania, two advertisements—3P-5205, "You Can't Satisfy A Road Hog," showing a big truck in the form of a hog at a large trough marked House Bill 560, and 3P-5203, "Mr. Taxpayer and Motorist We've Had Enough . . . Haven't You?"—were put out under the name of the Pennsylvania State Association of Township Supervisors, H. A. Thomson, secretary. The advertisement 3P-5202, "Road Hog," appeared in 135 Pennsylvania newspapers, while advertisement 3P-5203, "Mr. Taxpayer," was limited to the newspapers of the larger cities of Pennsylvania. The Pennsylvania State Association of Township Supervisors is created by statute. Public monies are appropriated for its support and it would be impossible for that association under statutory budgetary requirements to use public money to pay for advertisements of this sort. Mr. Reiter's naïve explanation was that Mr. Thomson wanted to run the advertisements; and that he had Al Paul Lefton, P.R.R.'s advertising agency, prepare them for the association, had them inserted in the respective newspapers, and did not discuss the payment of the charges until sometime thereafter. Then, out of the goodness of his heart and so as not to embarrass Mr. Thomson, he persuaded the railroad to pay the charges of preparing the ads and inserting them in the newspapers. That explanation the court does not accept. To the contrary it finds that they were prepared with prior financial and academic approval of the same Mr. Reiter. These advertisements were in line with the Byoir technique designed to vilify the trucking industry as such.

It is apparent from the record made in this case that Mr. Mahood and Mr. Thomson were both members of Mr. Reiter's team in opposition to any increase in truck sizes or weights. They had worked together for a good many years and had worked well together. However in 1951, after the introduction of the Big Truck Bill in May of that year in the legislature, it became evident to all three that Senate Bill 615 had a good chance of passing and being signed by the governor of the state, then the Honorable John S. Fine. At a dinner meeting paid for by Reiter, it was decided to call upon the services of a publicity agent to help them in their campaign against the bill. Reiter went to Littlefield and, as a result of that conference, the Carl Byoir organization was called upon to move into Pennsylvania in the fight against The Big Truck Bill. With almost three years of experience in this particular field behind it, Byoir, through Colburn C. Hardy, assisted at times by Kiely, Marine, and Stull, immediately started its third-party technique operations. It was not necessary in Pennsylvania to set up bogus organizations. As aforesaid, Reiter had working closely with him the secretary of the Pennsylvania Society of Professional Engineers, the Pennsylvania Grange, and the Pennsylvania State Association of Township Supervisors. These three organizations, but principally the latter two, were the springboards for the publicity in Pennsylvania. The state was divided into sections: Stull in the western, Hardy in the central, and Marine in the northeast. Every editor of every newspaper was contacted—and personally, wherever possible. The Byoir "kit," a composite of all statistical information created by Byoir, was made available to these editors. Release after release denouncing Senate Bill 615 was given to the newspapers. It was also at this time that it appeared Mr. Mahood would retire as secretary of the Pennsylvania Grange to be succeeded by Dr.

B. H. Dimit, who was retiring from the profession of teaching at one of the State Teachers Colleges. Investigation by Reiter, et al. showed that one of his close, personal friends and associates was Robert K. Fisher, an attorney on retainer by the New York Central lines. Their first connection with Dr. Dimit was through Mr. Fisher, and through Fisher the Byoir "kit" was made available to Dimit. Dr. Dimit was an ideal associate to have join the team since the considered opinion of the "team" was that Dr. Dimit was a person who would be very glad to have someone else do his research for him. From that time Dr. Dimit was putty in the hands of Byoir. Completely unknown to him Byoir so manipulated him that no speech, letter, or news release was delivered, sent out, or released until it had been carefully edited by Byoir and in at least one instance cleared with Mr. Littlefield of the Pennsylvania Railroad.

Hardy took up his quarters in the office of the Grange, used Grange stationery, and the bills for publicity were sent to the Pennsylvania Grange c/o Mr. Hardy. The caption of the bills clearly indicates that the printing houses and newspaper services regarded Hardy as a member of the Grange. Hardy also had an address attacking the bill made over a Lancaster Broadcasting System station under the name Pennsylvania State Association of Township Supervisors. Although the station must have known, since Byoir was billed for the broadcast, that it was made under the auspices of at least Byoir and not the association and in violation of the Federal Communications Act, 47 U.S.C.A. Sec. 151 et seq, no mention was made at the conclusion of the broadcast that it was being paid for by an independent organization. This bill as well as the other bills referred to above were paid in the first instance by Byoir and all reimbursed by the ERPC.

The Trucking Bill had hard sledding, due to this organized opposition. However, on the agenda of the legislature was another bill that caused tremendous difficulty—The Pennsylvania Sales Tax Bill. Controversy over this kept the legislature in session until the end of the year. Despite the terrific resistance created by Byoir and its third-party technique as well as the opposition of the railroads, the bill passed by a resounding majority of each House and was sent to the governor. Exhibit P–53—contained in a memorandum of Reynolds Girdler, the account executive of ERPC, dated February 15, 1952, to John Stahr—summarized Byoir's accomplishments from Byoir's viewpoint in helping to bring about the ultimate veto of the bill. It is well worth repeating it at this point in toto:

To:	John Stahr
From:	Reynolds Girdler
Date:	February 15, 1952
Re:	Nomination for December Award
Achievement:	Defeat of "Big Truck's" bill in Pennsylvania.

The state of Pennsylvania has one of the lowest gross road limits for heavy trucks in the East. Specifically, Pennsylvania will not permit any truck on its highways which weighs more than 50,000 pounds with load, as compared with 73,000 pounds allowed by New York, New Jersey, and most other Eastern states.

This low maximum in Pennsylvania is very irksome to the heavy trucking industry because it keeps them from getting a large share of the very profitable steel hauling business between major cities in Pennsylvania and Ohio.

Consequently, the trucking industry started back in the middle of 1950 to lay the groundwork for a piece of legislation which would increase the Pennsylvania maximum from 50,000 to 60,000 pounds. The trucking industry bought an elaborate system of television and radio programs blanketing Pennsylvania. They went through the major cities of Pennsylvania and worked out promotional special trucking sections with the all important newspapers, thus giving each important newspaper very substantial and profitable advertising. In addition, the trucking industry smartly inveigled the Pennsylvania Railroad into a discussion of their agreeing on an increase in the allowable maximum, and the Pennsylvania Railroad very stupidly agreed not to oppose an increase up to 50,000 pounds. This agreement was thoroughly publicized throughout the political world of Pennsylvania.

The trucking industry went further. It got up a committee and $200,000 for the campaign for the Republican candidate for governor, and he was elected. The trucking industry also heavily subsidized various members of the Pennsylvania legislature during the November 1950, election.

When January 1951, opened there seemed every reason to believe that the truckers would get their bill through, increasing the allowable weight to 60,000 pounds.

The 17 railroads of Pennsylvania then started fighting—without our help. They fought the bill for four months, and then threw in the sponge. They reported to their superiors that they were licked. Even so, the lobbyists in control of the railroad activity continued to oppose allowing the C.B.&A. people to operate in Pennsylvania.

Their superiors then thrust us down their throats.

The team went to work in Pennsylvania beginning in June 1951. Not only did they begin to generate publicity against the bill, but they were successful in getting a long list of organizations and individuals publicly to oppose the bill. Those organizations ranged from the CIO to the Pennsylvania State Grange. The individuals ranged from a "crusading coroner" of Pittsburgh to John L. Lewis. The clamor against the bill grew and grew. Even so, the Republican majority in the Pennsylvania Legislature was so thoroughly committed to the trucking industry that the bill finally went through both the lower and upper houses. However, so violent was the fight that it kept the Pennsylvania legislators in session for nine months—a record in Pennsylvania.

Even after the bill was passed by both houses, the clamor against the bill continued. Day to day went by without the Governor's signing the bill. Finally, he announced that the opposition was so great that he would have to hold a public hearing. He scheduled the public hearing to be held in his own chambers.

The C.B.&A. team thereupon went out and organized 21 witnesses for 21 organizations against the bill. They prepared their statements and the publicity together with it.

The public hearing was one of the biggest news events in Pennsylvania. Major Pennsylvania newspapers placed the eight-column streamers front page, over national and international news involving Truman and Churchill. Six minutes before the bill automatically would become law in the absence of a Governor veto, Governor Fine vetoed the bill.

The repercussions on the trucking industry were nationwide, and embittered comments went into newspapers all over the country. In Ohio the truckers were so stupid as to state publicly that "All the ATA money didn't do [them] any good." They went on to say that they thought they had the bill bought.

Veto of this bill meant that some $5,000,000 worth of freight was retained on the Pennsylvania Railroad, because the trucking limit was not raised.

This represented one of the most dramatic illustrations of the power of organized public opinion that anybody could hope to find. While the award must go to Colburn Hardy as head of the team, he must share the award with Lyon, Stull, Marine, and Kiely, because it was a team job.

I attach as evidence copy of the letter written by the top railroad lobbyist, who originally fought hardest to keep us from being allowed to operate in Pennsylvania. I don't think anybody in the history of Byoir ever received a more impressive tribute.

Reynolds Girdler

RG/et
Enc.

While the record in this case clearly discloses that some of the statements constituted "puffing," Hardy himself admitted on cross-examination that the veto was his greatest accomplishment in the public relations field up until that time and that it constituted "his finest hour." However, the record and the governor's veto message also clearly indicate that Byoir was extremely effective and that its organized opposition had much to do with the governor's veto. And how was that accomplished over and above the use of the third-party technique?

To begin with, Pennsylvania was one of the constituent states of the Maryland Road Test. The governor's veto, P-282, was dated January 21, 1952. It will be recalled that the first tentative draft of the Maryland Road Test Report was to have been issued on January 15, 1951. Byoir had obtained advance copies and had publicized the railroad theory that big trucks alone break roads. The final draft was not printed and distributed until 1952. The State Highway Department of Pennsylvania through the secretary of highways was against the bill. One of the reasons that the chief engineer was against the bill and urged the governor to veto it was based upon statistics drafted by his own department. An objective analysis of the statistics presented, however, finds that they came in the first instance from the desk-space organization created by Byoir in New York, the Empire State Transport League. In the second place, one Mr. Marine—the same Mr. Marine of Byoir, a statistician of great merit in presenting trucking statistics in such a way as to damn the trucking industry—was the chief source to Mr. Van Riper, assistant chief engineer of the Pennsylvania Highway Department, of the trucking statistics upon which Mr. Schmidt, then secretary, relied in urging the veto to Governor Fine. It will be seen that there was here, as there was in the U.S. Bureau of Public Roads, considerably less than complete objectivity in the presentation of facts to public officials, upon which facts public officials were urged and did exercise executive judgment favorable to the railroads and injurious to the truckers.

In addition to the above, Byoir, at the request of Reiter, wrote speeches for legislators in opposition to the bill. Hardy also prepared all of the press releases of Dimit and Thomson when they appeared at the governor's open public hearing on the bill. These releases, skillfully drawn, stressed those elements chosen by Byoir and the railroads for particular attack.

There is no doubt that Dr. Dimit admitted on the stand that he had, without his knowledge, been "used" by the Byoir organization. The effect of the testimony of "Cappy" Thomson on cross-examination, even though he attempted to vehemently deny the fact, was that he, too, had been "used" by the Byoir organization. From his appearance, manner, and testimony, the court was persuaded that Mr. Thomson knew he was being used by the Byoir organization and was perfectly happy in that status.

Having successfully repulsed the truckers in their efforts to clear Pennsylvania as a bridge state for the next year and up until the institution of this suit, the record is abundantly clear that Byoir worked hand-in-hand with Littlefield and with Reiter to promote the introduction and passage of a weight-distance tax, using exactly the same methods that had been used in the other states of the program. While there is no direct testimony on that subject, it is the opinion of the court that it was the institution of the present suit which prevented further action along that particular line of attack. However, up to a few days before the institution of this suit, extensive plans were being made for Byoir to again enter Pennsylvania and to push its campaign with the utmost vigor and backed by whatever funds were necessary. It may be remarked at this point that neither Byoir nor the railroads were ever short on funds in this campaign.

Campaign of vilification

The whole tenor of the antitruck campaign, originated by the railroads in the 30s, abandoned during the war, and thereafter reactivated in 1946, was based upon the use of third parties to "front" for the railroads. As noted, in New Jersey, the New Jersey Automobile Owners, Inc. and the New Jersey Tax Study Foundation were two shining examples. In New York, the Citizens Tax League and the Empire State Transport League were two further examples. In Ohio, Save Our Highways Clubs were used. In Pennsylvania, the good offices of the state Grange and the state Association of Township Supervisors were exploited. The above examples are quoted to demonstrate that Byoir merely accentuated and accelerated the campaign of the railroads by forming bogus front organizations and perfecting the use of existing ones. The base of the pyramid of accomplishment on the part of Byoir for the railroads was the arousing of resentment in the ordinary citizen against the trucks. To this end Byoir shrewdly chose the obvious shortcomings of the trucking industry and by use of dramatic segments of truth distorted them into complete falsehoods. While Byoir chose the appellation of "third-party technique" for its activities, I prefer to treat the whole procedure in its true light, which is the technique of the "Big Lie."

How was public resentment aroused during the period 1949 to 1952? Byoir as early as 1949 had started a collection of photographs of sensational truck accidents. Immediately upon the happening of such an accident, no matter in what part of the country, Byoir would find some person not averse to publicity to issue a news release and use the picture as representative of usual day-by-day traffic events rather than the unusual, which it was. In some few instances, trucks carrying weight far beyond the loaded capacity of a bridge would attempt to cross, would fall through and actually destroy the bridge. While these were few in number, Byoir saw to it that these few were so publicized as to create the impression that it was a matter of great frequency, if not of daily occurrence. Byoir also highlighted the obvious shortcomings of the trucks, which were slow speeds on steep, mountainous grades causing traffic tie-ups; the racing of the truck down the opposite grade thereby preventing the unblocking of the tie-ups; the obstruction of the vision of the motorists following large trucks; the "gunning" of the motors of the trucks in residential areas, and other actions of some drivers in order to bring all truck drivers into disrepute. The breaking down of secondary and country roads by the use of large trucks was highlighted pictorially throughout the country and to the point where the casual motorist was convinced that a tremendous percentage of our secondary roads were being broken down and absolutely destroyed by heavy trucks. While it is true that on occasions some venal truckers did use back roads to escape weighing stations on main roads; in a vast majority of the instances, represented as typical, the damages resulted from detouring by state officials of heavy trucks over roads not capable of carrying the weight and solely for the purpose of making repairs on main highways fully capable of bearing or carrying the weight of the trucks in question. All of these publicity releases, pictures, etc., were furnished by Byoir to all the civic organizations previously mentioned. In addition, and ostensibly as an independent news source, Byoir utilized wholly owned subsidiary corporations which made newspaper mats of a group of pictures which were distributed at nominal cost to thousands of newspapers throughout the country. These newspapers were primarily in the smaller communities and, of course, they could not afford that type of photographic coverage. And what were these photographs so furnished?

Reproductions of a few typical instances were exhibited at the trial. From Byoir's *Central States News Views* in Chicago came sex, sports, and a truck breaking up a road. First, a picture of a plunging neckline; next a picture of the new Notre Dame basketball coach (side-by-side at the top of the mat). On the bottom half of the mat was a truck "bogged down" breaking up a road.

Again, another *Central States News Views* showed at the top of the mat Joe Louis, Jr., age two and a half, being given a boxing lesson by his famous father, retired heavyweight champion at that time. Next, "Miss Continuous Towel of 1949," a shapely model honored by linen-supply industry. In the lower half of the picture was a truck and a broken-up highway caused by heavy trucks on detour.

Finally, *People, Spots in the News,* a New York subsidiary of Byoir sent out for immediate release, exclusive in a particular city, a 2-column 13-EM mat, showing royalty, sports, and trucks. The top of the mat on one side showed the then Queen Elizabeth of England on her 50th birthday. On the other top side is shown a recalcitrant race horse in the starting gate at Detroit's Hazel Park track. Finally at the bottom of the mat appears a picture of the Maryland Road Test showing engineers measuring deflections at a joint and termed in the mat picture "Crackathon"—"Scientific tests to measure road damage inflicted by heavy trucks are underway on this mile-stretch of highway in Maryland, sponsored by 11 states alarmed over road deterioration." In the light of what has been said before about the Maryland Road Test this amounts to almost complete distortion.

Another very effective method of inflaming a large segment of the public which always has been influential in the formation of public opinion was to put on the Byoir payroll for purely propaganda purposes Mrs. Bessie Q. Mott, vice chairman of the New York State Federation of Women's Clubs, and chairman of the Public Affairs Department of that same group. Mrs. Mott, described as "a typical American club-woman," made quite a profitable career out of being the typical American clubwoman. In addition to receiving a sum substantially in excess of $13,000 (reimbursed by ERPC) over a relatively short period of time, she was successful in infiltrating into the programs of most of the important women's groups in New York and New Jersey, programs arranged by Byoir, which included speakers furnished by Byoir, for the purpose of arousing resentment against the truckers. It was necessary to make Mrs. Mott an expert in that field so Byoir made her an author. Byoir wrote a pamphlet entitled, "Are We Being Railroaded Into Social-ism?—a survey of what's wrong with national transportation policy and how it affects each of us." A foreword was written by Charles L. Berg-mann, chairman of the Railroad Securities Committee, Investment Bankers Association of America. This brochure contained all of the favor-able aspects of the railroad story and damned the truckers. While no witness of Byoir at the trial definitely would concede that the entire publication was Byoir's handiwork, and not Mrs. Mott's, the purported author, there is no doubt in the mind of the court that Byoir conceived and executed the entire transaction. Mrs. Mott was not new in the propa-ganda field. Byoir had occasion in the past to use her expensive services in the same field of propaganda in the A&P situation, which will be discussed infra.

By the use of these various media of arousing public resentment, including newspapers, magazines, radio broadcasts, and television, Byoir, in the area of its operation, built a strong base of public resentment. During this period they created so great public resentment against the trucks that it was then a relatively simple problem for Byoir in the public relations field to sell their "poison" against the truckers, and by the use of already existing organizations friendly to the railroad story, and by reactivating and setting up other organizations, as already noted, to convince people and legislators that everything the trucks did was wrong and that any restriction suggested should be placed upon them.

The cap of the pyramid, of course, was the projected legislation, and the cap of the pyramid differed in each state. In New Jersey it was increased license fees and lowering of weights. In New York it was the weight-distance tax. In Ohio it was first a substantial increase in license fees and next the campaign for the weight-distance tax. In Pennsylvania it was the veto by Governor Fine of the so-called Big Truck Bill to be immediately followed by a campaign for the weight-dis-tance tax.

Counsel for all defendants have argued strenuously that since everything done was geared to ultimate legislation, then anything done to accomplish that end was within the protection of the First Amendment to the Constitution of the United States and without the orbit of the Sherman and Clayton Antitrust statutes. But this was more than merely an attempt to obtain legislation. It was the purpose and intent of Messrs. Deegan, Littlefield, and Mackie on the one side, and Byoir on the other, to hurt the truckers in every way possible, even though they secured no legislation; it was their purpose to restrict the activities of the truckers in the long-haul industry to the greatest extent possible; and finally, if possible, to drive them out of that segment of the entire transportation industry. This feature of the action, which must always be carried in mind and represents the considered finding of the court in this case, will be discussed at greater length in the legal discussion to follow. However, this particular section of the opinion is of great importance in the overall consideration of the case since it constitutes the original basis of activity of Byoir and the railroads against the trucking industry.

APPENDIX

Background material on the public relations campaign of the eastern railroads

Motor carriers are subject to regulation by both the federal and state governments. State legislatures control intrastate commerce and federal law governs interstate commerce.

Federal. The Interstate Commerce Commission (ICC), established in 1887, administers regulations affecting all carriers engaged in interstate commerce. Regulations cover rates; rights to operate traffic routes; mergers, acquisitions, and consolidations; stock issues in excess of $1 million; insurance coverage and safety.

Support for federal regulation came originally from both railroads and large motor carriers. They wanted to give a semblance of order to a disorderly and unstable market and to promote reliable, safe, and responsible service. Support came not because of transportation monopoly and monopolistic abuses such as discrimination but rather because of transportation competition and the excesses of a competitive transportation market. Opposition to regulation came from agricultural groups who feared transportation monopoly.[1]

State. State regulation of motor carriers affects the use of highways and provides economic controls to assure adequate service to the public. The latter refers mostly to busses and other forms of public transportation.

---

[1] Roy J. Sampson and Martin T. Farris, *Domestic Transportation: Practice, Theory and Policy* (Boston: Houghton Mifflin, 1966), p. 269.

In regulating the use of highways, state governments are protecting their investment in highways as well as the safety of those who travel upon them. Typically, these regulations prescribe maximum weights of motor vehicles and the licensing of truck rigs. Weight limitations take many forms varying from simple overall gross-weight limitations to complicated axle-weight limitations—weight per inch of tire width, spacing of wheels beneath a load and the like.[2] Substantial differences in regulations among states has impeded the flow of commerce across state lines.

Revenues and expenditures
(in millions)

	1939	1947	1950	1955	1960	1967
Freight revenues in interstate commerce						
Railroad	$3,584		$8,592		$8,701	$ 9,939
Truck	792		3,702		7,155	10,082
Federal and state expenditures for highway facilities		$2,866		$6,941		15,127

Source: Transportation Association of America, *Transportation; Facts and Trends*, April 1969, pp. 22–23.

---

[2] Ibid, p. 267.

PART V

Environmental issues facing management

Clean Air Amendments Act of 1970 (A)[1]

DESPITE the "monumental opposition" of the automobile and oil industries, the bill usually identified with Senator Edmund Muskie for legislating auto emission standards was signed into law by President Nixon as the Clean Air Amendments Act of 1970 on December 31, 1970. (See Appendix A.)

The auto industry's reaction was one unequivocally of dismay. "GM 'knows no way' to meet the standards [for automobile emissions] with the current technology unless an engineering breakthrough is achieved," announced William Agnew, head of the emissions studies at the GM Labs on January 13, 1971. Commenting on the bill on December 17, 1970 prior to the Senate vote, Mr. Lee A. Iacocca, Ford's president, echoed,

> . . . We believe we will be able to manufacture cars in 1975 that will be virtually emission free. Whether we can achieve by 1975 or 1976 the last few percentage points of reduction demanded by the new standards, we still are not sure. We did our best to explain to the Congress the technical problems that we face in trying to meet these requirements and the need for adequate lead time to solve those problems. We have a very difficult task ahead of us. . . . We will do our best and we will come as close as we can as soon as we can.

[1] This case was prepared as the basis for class discussion rather than to illustrate either effective or ineffective handling of an administrative situation.

Some observers expressed concern about the effects of this legislation on the economy in general and several industries in particular. (See Appendix B for general economic and structural data pertaining to the automobile, oil, lead, steel, and natural gas industries.) The futures of already ailing American Motors and somewhat faltering Chrysler began to appear more bleak. Despite the concern about the lack of technology and enormous costs involved in meeting the tighter auto-emission standards contained in the act, Sen. Edmund Muskie of Maine, a 1972 democratic presidential hopeful, defended the bill in the Senate on September 21, 1970:

> Our responsibility in Congress is to say what the requirements of this bill are, what the health of the nation requires and to challenge polluters to meet them.
> The first responsibility of Congress is not the making of technological or economic judgments or even to be limited by what appears to be technologically or economically feasible. . . . This may mean that people and industries will be asked to do what seems to be impossible at the present time. But if health is to be protected, these challenges must be met. I am convinced they can be met.

Senator Griffin disagreed with this philosophy:

> I am deeply concerned about this bill because it introduces a novel concept to automotive emission control—the concept of brinkmanship. An industry pivotal to the U.S. economy is to be required by statute to meet standards which the committee itself acknowledges cannot be met with existing technology. . . .
> Mr. President, brinkmanship is risky business. It is especially risky where it is applied to a key industry,[2] and when it is based upon such questionable premises. . . . This bill, as written, proposes to give the automobile industry from 18 to 30 months to make a technological breakthrough that has withstood more than 15 years of research. . . . We are putting ourselves in the position of scientists and automotive engineers. As Senators, we do not have the expertise that is needed. And obviously, the committee is not willing to delegate any authority to those who do have the expertise.

Air pollution and automobile emissions

Public concern with auto emissions picked up momentum when Professor A. J. Haagen-Smit, professor of biochemistry at Caltech made

---

[2] According to the Congressional Record of September 22, 1970, Senator Griffin indicated: "Cars and trucks generate 10 percent of all taxes collected in federal state, and local governments combined. . . . Expenditures for automotive transportation account for more than 16 percent of our gross national product. Even a slight dip in auto sales, to say nothing of a strike at General Motors, sends shock waves throughout the financial community."

public in 1950 his discovery that automobile exhaust gases contributed significantly to smog formation in particular and air pollution in general in Los Angeles. According to the Department of Health, Education, and Welfare, auto emissions constituted 38.8 percent by weight of all air pollutants on the nationwide basis in 1968. The automobile was by far the largest emitter of carbon monoxide (CO), hydrocarbons (HC) and oxides of nitrogen in 1968 despite some progress to alleviate the problem made during the period 1966–68. (See Exhibit 1.)

Caused by a variety of sources, including furnaces, combustion of fuels to generate power, industrial processes with chemical vapors, and motor vehicle exhausts, air pollution most affects either the very young or the very old and is significantly correlated as a dominant causal factor with emphysema, cancer, heart disease, bronchitis, tuberculosis, and pneumonia, particularly in high-density urban areas. According to the surgeon general of the United States, "The air over most cities and towns contains the kind of ingredients that could produce another London. . . ."[3] There is absolutely no way to predict with confidence that such disasters will not happen again, in the same cities or in any of hundreds of others."[4] (See Exhibits 2 and 3.)

Air pollution carries an economic price tag, as well. Athough costs of cleaning the air and repairing damaged materials are difficult to determine, some cost estimates have been made. As early as 1963, President Kennedy estimated that air pollution resulted in $11 billion worth of damage per year in the United States, including agricultural losses of $500 million. More recently, annual costs of contaminated air were estimated at $20 billion.[5]

Legislative history

Primary responsibility for air pollution control has historically been vested in state and local governments. The Air Pollution Control Act of 1955 established a federal air pollution research and technical assistance program to supplement existing state and local programs.

In the following years, automotive exhaust emissions and their role in air pollution received increasing congressional attention. The Special Subcommittee on Traffic Safety heard testimony and visited automobile manufacturing plants to determine the extent of the industry's air pollution research. By 1960 a law was passed which authorized the surgeon

---

[3] Referring to the famous 1952 smog episodes in London in which 4,000 more deaths occurred than would have normally occurred in the same period. Other episodes have occurred in Donora, Pennsylvania, in 1948; New York City in 1953; and London in 1962 again.

[4] Clean Air Act of 1967, House Report No. 728, p. 1939.

[5] John Wicklein, "Whitewashing Detroit's Dirty Engine," *The Washington Monthly*, June 1970, p. 20.

general to study automobile emissions and report his findings to Congress.

In 1963 Congress passed the Clean Air Act and extended the federal government's power to combat air pollution. In addition to research programs, the act authorized some federal participation in abating specified air pollution problems, including regulatory powers. The attorney general could bring suit against polluters who refused to comply with abatement requests and whose actions caused interstate pollution.

In order to assist industry efforts to decrease harmful automobile emissions, the secretary (of HEW) was empowered to appoint a committee to discuss programs on pollution control devices and to assess the need for further research. One half of the committee was to consist of representatives from the automobile, exhaust control device, and fuel manufacturers; other members were to be appointed from the Department of Health, Education, & Welfare.

The secretary was also made responsible for measuring the extent of pollution caused by automobiles, for developing emission standards and, if necessary, for recommending further vehicle legislation. He was to report his findings to Congress at the end of a year, and twice a year thereafter.

Three years later, on October 20, 1965, Congress passed a law authorizing the secretary of HEW to establish national standards for the emissions of new automobiles. In passing this law, Congress fully recognized the basic rights and responsibilities of the states for control of air pollution but it preferred to enact and enforce federal standards for auto emissions. Exhibit 4 shows various auto emission standards enacted by the federal government.

Congress further extended the federal jurisdiction on air pollution control by passing the Air Quality Act of 1967. This act authorized the Department of HEW to make planning grants to air pollution control agencies, to expand research provisions relating to fuels and vehicles, to provide for interstate air pollution control agencies, and to determine air quality standards.

The secretary of HEW was expected to develop and publish air quality criteria based upon careful and comprehensive analysis of regional conditions which influence air pollution and upon the effects of pollutant levels on public health and welfare. State and regional control agencies had the right to set air quality standards and deal with air pollution problems, but these standards had to be consistent with the criteria issued by HEW.

In November 1969, the scientific advisor to the president recommended more stringent standards for automobile emissions. A special confidential conference, attended by President Nixon, Robert Finch, the secretary of HEW, spokesman from the automobile industry, and other cabinet members, was held to assess the new standards. At that meeting, automobile industry officials stated that they could meet the administration standards (proposed on February 10, 1970) for 1975 car emissions if the present 1970–71 standards remained constant until 1974. Manufacturers could then direct their full energies toward meeting the 1975 goals and would not have to focus attention on interim standards.

On February 10, however, secretary Finch published a notice of new motor vehicle emission standards for 1973 and 1975 car models. According to President Nixon, "These new standards represent our best present estimate of the lowest emission levels attainable by those years."[6]

Since the Air Quality Act of 1967 expired in 1970, new air pollution measures were also discussed in Congress. Separate Air Quality bills were considered in both the House and Senate. On June 10, 1970, a National Air Quality bill passed the House and on the following day was sent to the Senate Public Works Committee. After study by this committee and by the Subcommittee on Air and Water Pollution and testimony on the Senate floor, Senators substituted portions of the Senate bill for parts of the original House bill. They acted on ten amendments, and passed on Air Quality Standards bill by a unanimous vote of 73 to 0.

Due to the substantial Senate revisions of the original House bill, the House requested that a joint conference be held to resolve the differences. The House and Senate appointed conferees in late September, and meetings were held until the middle of December. During one of the sessions of the joint conference, Eliot Richardson, secretary of HEW, asked that the provision for Congress to legislate the setting of automobile emission deadlines be stricken from the bill, and that the determination of such deadlines remain under the auspices of an executive agency which had responsibility for pollution control. Despite his appeal, the Congress voted to keep that and the other provisions of the Senate version of the bill. The Senate version was then resubmitted to the House and the Senate. It passed both houses and "the Clean Air Amendments of 1970" became public law on December 31, 1970.

Environmental Protection Agency

In October 1970, Congress approved the President's Reorganization Plan, creating the Environmental Protection Agency (EPA) that would provide the focus for all the federal antipollution efforts and enforce the provisions of various laws related to pollution. Most of the agency's employees and constituent functions were drawn from the Department of Health, Education and Welfare, Department of Housing and Urban

---

[6] *Congressional Quarterly*, February 13, 1970, p. 436.

Development, Department of Transportation, Department of Interior, and Department of Agriculture. The agency consisted of five divisions—water pollution, air pollution, pesticides, radiation, and solid waste.

The National Air Pollution Control Administration (NAPCA), formerly part of HEW, became the core element of the air pollution division of EPA. When transferred, NAPCA had a staff of 1,100 and a 1971 budget of about $110 million. Exhibit 5 indicates NAPCAs' planned expenditures on air pollution control up to 1973.

According to the Clean Air Amendment's Act of 1970, NAPCA has both the "research" and the "pollution law enforcements" functions. In terms of research, its major purpose is to stimulate activity by the private sector in developing control technology, to fill research gap areas, and develop a technical basis for the establishment of future emission standards.

In 1970, NAPCA's research efforts included: examining of atmospheric and regional conditions which affect air quality, studying of the effects of various pollutant levels in the air on the public welfare, setting air quality standards in measurable terms and testing procedures, monitoring national air pollutant levels, and investigating the sources of air pollution. In 1968, NAPCA had made a proposal to spend $89.1 million on automotive emission problems over a six-year period. It had planned to allocate about half the sum of developing unconventional nonpolluting automotive engines.

In terms of its enforcement function, NAPCA can schedule public hearings against polluters, bring offenders to court, and gain injunctions against actions which pollute the air. William D. Ruckelshaus, the first incumbent as EPA's administrator, underscored the importance of the enforcement function when he announced at a November 1970 White House Conference, "EPA's primary responsibility is enforcement . . . we are going after the polluters."

The auto parts industry

Unlike the oligopolistic automobile industry, the auto parts industry is fragmented and essentially a "cottage industry." Several pertinent facts about the auto parts are described below:

1. The auto parts suppliers, of widely varying size, competence, and degree of diversification, received aggregate orders exceeding $24 billion from the Big Three in 1969.
2. About 1,675 U.S. companies were engaged primarily in the manufacture of parts and accessories of motor vehicles, according to the 1967 Census of Manufacturers by the Department of Commerce. Most of these were small. Some 295 had between 100 and 999 employees,

40 had between 1,000 and 2,499 employees, and 40 had 2,500 employees or more. In 1967, about 365,000 people were employed in producing motor vehicles and parts, with a total payroll of $2.89 billion. The values added by manufacture of $5.7 billion, plus the cost of materials of $5.9 billion, gave a total value of shipments in 1967 of $11.6 billion.

3. In addition to these 1,675 companies, there were many thousands of firms that supplied at least a portion of their total production to the automobile producers. Payments to the more than 37,000 domestic companies directly supplying materials, parts, components, and services to General Motors in 1969 totaled $11.5 billion, or $0.4725 on every dollar GM received during the year. Most of these suppliers to GM were relatively small, with more than 75 percent of them employing fewer than 100 people.

4. Ford paid $8.56 billion, or $0.579 of every $1 received and Chrysler paid $4.295 billion or $0.608 of every $1 for materials, suppliers, services, etc., in 1969.

5. Considerable uncertainty hovered over the auto parts industry for several reasons: (1) possible shifts in accounts among parts suppliers; (2) moves toward greater integration of certain operations by motor vehicle builders; and (3) the possibility that some new development in car building may outmode some sources of revenues of one or more parts companies—that is, substitution of gas turbine engines or batteries for present internal combustion engines, or the widespread replacement of carburetors with fuel injection systems.

6. Unit shipments of automotive batteries for replacement purposes in 1968 accounted for 75.8 percent of the total (48.7 million units), original equipment application for 23.2 percent, and exports for the remaining 1.0 percent.

Considerable research work was being done in the area of electric cars which would be powered by batteries or fuel cells. Such small vehicles would be mostly for use in local, lower- to medium-speed driving, particularly in areas where air pollution is a problem. The most promising power plants appeared to be the costly silver zinc and such high-temperature batteries as lithium chloride and sodium sulphur. The latter can be recharged any number of times with ordinary household current.

Other developments

Prior to the enactment of the Clean Air Amendments Act of 1970, the Department of the Treasury had proposed a lead-user tax of $4.25 per lb. in order to discourage the use of lead in gasoline. The magnitude of the tax was considered excessive by some when compared to the base price for lead of $0.13 per lb. In January 1971, the fate of the proposal was indefinite.

The oil industry appeared to have felt as if it were being treated as "second cousins," according to one oil executive. He was amazed "how Cole (president of General Motors) dumped the problem of emission control on the lead and the oil industry." He felt that the consumer, supposedly the main beneficiary, would end up as the loser eventually.

The oil executive asked: "Who will pay the cost of this unnecessary cleanup? The customers!" According to a confidential simulation study made for the Department of Transportation in 1970, "The national cost of converting refinery, distribution, and gasoline retail outlets in order to supply at least one low-lead or lead-free 91 octane gasoline to the automobile drivers ranged from $2.9 billion to $11.3 billion depending upon the strategy of conversion to be used." These strategies included: a two-pump supply—one leaded and the other unleaded; a three-pump supply—two leaded and one unleaded; and a variety of combinations of octanes in each of the two previous categories. The simulation study had attempted to build a configuration of refineries and distribution outlets of the U.S. mainland into a computer model. For a variety of strategies the annual consumption of crude oil for 1969 auto population was expected to increase between 2.1 percent to 30.6 percent and the cost of gasoline from 0.15¢ per gallon to 11.21¢ per gallon. (See Appendix C and Appendix D.)

EXHIBIT 1

Estimated nationwide emissions: 1966-68
(10^6 tons/year)

Source	CO*			Particulates†			SO_x‡			HC§			Oxides of nitrogen∥			Total emissions ($CO + P + SO_x + HC + NO_x$)		
	1966	1967	1968	1966	1967	1968	1966	1967	1968	1966	1967	1968	1966	1967	1968	1966	1967	1968
Motor vehicles	60.6	61.2	59.2	0.7	0.7	0.8	0.2	0.3	0.3	16.5	16.3	15.6	6.6	6.7	7.2	84.6	85.2	83.1
Other transportation	3.9	3.8	4.6	0.5	0.4	0.4	0.4	0.4	0.5	1.1	1.0	1.0	1.0	0.9	0.9	6.9	6.5	7.4
Fuel combustion in stationary sources	1.9	1.9	1.9	9.2	8.9	8.9	22.5	23.1	24.4	0.7	0.7	0.7	6.7	9.5	10.0	41.0	44.1	45.9
Industrial processes	10.7	9.5	9.7	7.6	7.3	7.5	7.1	7.2	7.3	3.5	4.3	4.6	0.2	0.2	0.2	29.1	28.5	29.3
Solid waste disposal	7.6	7.8	7.8	1.0	1.1	1.1	0.1	0.1	0.1	1.5	1.6	1.6	0.5	0.6	0.6	10.7	11.2	11.2
Miscellaneous	16.9	16.9	16.9	9.6	9.6	9.6	0.6	0.6	0.6	8.2	8.3	8.5	1.7	1.7	1.7	37.0	37.1	37.3
Total	101.6	101.1	100.1	28.6	28.0	28.3	30.9	31.7	33.2	31.5	32.2	32.0	16.7	19.6	20.6	209.3	212.6	214.2
Percentage distribution																		
Motor vehicles	59.7	59.2	59.2	2.5	2.5	2.8	0.6	0.9	0.9	52.4	50.7	48.8	39.5	34.2	34.9	40.5	40.2	38.8
Other transportation	3.8	3.8	4.6	1.7	1.4	1.8	1.3	1.3	1.5	3.5	3.1	3.1	5.9	4.6	4.4	3.3	3.1	3.5
Fuel combustion in stationary sources	1.9	1.9	1.9	32.2	31.8	31.4	72.9	72.9	73.5	2.2	2.1	2.2	40.2	48.5	48.5	19.6	20.7	21.4
Industrial processes	10.5	9.6	9.7	26.5	26.1	26.5	23.0	22.7	22.0	11.1	13.3	14.4	1.2	1.0	1.0	13.9	13.2	13.7
Solid waste disposal	7.5	7.8	7.8	3.5	3.9	3.9	0.3	0.3	0.3	4.8	4.9	5.0	3.0	3.0	2.9	5.1	5.2	5.2
Miscellaneous	16.6	16.9	16.9	33.6	34.3	33.9	1.9	1.9	1.8	26.0	25.9	26.5	10.2	8.7	8.3	17.6	17.6	17.4
Total	100.0	100.0	100.0	100.0	100.0	100.0	100.0	100.0	100.0	100.0	100.0	100.0	100.0	100.0	100.0	100.0	100.0	100.0

* Carbon monoxide (CO)—a colorless, odorless, poisonous gas—is produced by the incomplete combustion of carbon in fuels. Exposure to ten parts per million of CO for approximately eight hours may dull mental performance. In heavy traffic situations, levels of 70-100 parts per million are not uncommon for short periods.

† Particulates include particles of solid or liquid substances in a very wide range of sizes, from those that are visible, as soot and smoke, to particles too small to detect except under an electron microscope. According to a study made at Buffalo, the overall death rate rises in areas with an annual average concentration ranging from 80 to 100 micrograms of particulates per cubic meter and that there is a correlation between the incidence of gastric cancer in men 50 to 69 years old and these levels of particulate matter.

‡ Sulfur Oxides (SO_x) are acrid, corrosive, poisonous gases. Sulfur dioxide can irritate the upper respiratory tract. It may imperil health when its annual mean concentration in the air rises above 0.04 parts per million. The annual mean concentration of SO_x in the air was 0.12 parts per million in Chicago in 1968; in Philadelphia it was 0.08.

* Hydrocarbons (HC), like carbon monoxide, represent unburned and wasted fuel. Unlike carbon monoxide, gaseous hydrocarbons at concentrations normally found in the atmosphere are not toxic, but they are a major pollutant because of their role in forming photochemical smog.

* Nitrogen Oxides (NO_x) are produced when fuel is burned at very high temperatures. Nitrogen that is ordinarily inert combines with oxygen in high temperature flames and tends to stay combined if the exhaust gases are cooled too quickly. Control of nitrogen oxides from automobiles is quite difficult because reducing other pollutants can increase the output of NO_x. Under the influence of sunlight, nitrogen oxides combine with gaseous hydrocarbons to form a complex variety of secondary pollution called photochemical oxidants. These oxidants, together with solid and liquid particulates in the air, make up what is commonly known as smog.

Source: Prepared by Harvard Business School Staff from U.S. Department of Health, Education and Welfare, Nationwide Inventory of Air Pollutant Emissions, August 1970.

EXHIBIT 2
Estimates and projections of the population of states: 1960–1985

Region, division and state	Series I-D*				Series II-D†			
	1970	1975	1980	1985	1970	1975	1980	1985
United States	203,940	214,384	226,681	240,747	203,940	214,384	226,681	240,747
Regions:								
Northeast	49,490	51,361	53,544	56,040	49,513	51,441	53,731	56,404
North Central	55,488	57,192	59,607	62,742	55,594	57,462	60,059	63,337
South	63,691	67,160	71,008	75,159	63,671	67,135	71,027	75,315
West	35,271	38,670	42,522	46,807	35,162	38,346	41,865	45,691
Northeast:								
New England	11,571	12,027	12,598	13,280	11,579	12,047	12,634	13,333
Middle Atlantic	37,919	39,334	40,946	42,759	37,934	39,393	41,097	43,070
North Central:								
East North Central	39,470	40,927	42,895	45,388	39,533	41,082	43,141	45,682
West North Central	16,018	16,265	16,712	17,354	16,061	16,381	16,918	17,655
South:								
South Atlantic	30,828	32,887	35,193	37,708	30,783	32,761	34,955	37,343
East South Central	13,254	13,661	14,125	14,634	13,275	13,731	14,282	14,921
West South Central	19,609	20,612	21,690	22,817	19,614	20,643	21,790	23,051
West:								
Mountain	8,346	9,012	9,785	10,652	8,336	8,985	9,731	10,559
Pacific	26,925	29,659	32,737	36,154	26,825	29,361	32,134	35,132
New England:								
Maine	986	993	1,015	1,052	991	1,005	1,036	1,081
New Hampshire	723	771	820	870	721	765	812	861
Vermont	413	425	442	465	414	428	447	470
Massachusetts	5,484	5,636	5,861	6,157	5,495	5,664	5,907	6,219
Rhode Island	910	926	945	968	912	931	957	989
Connecticut	3,055	3,276	3,514	3,769	3,046	3,254	3,476	3,713
Middle Atlantic:								
New York	18,952	19,739	20,564	21,416	18,958	19,776	20,679	21,688
New Jersey	7,330	7,864	8,437	9,053	7,308	7,805	8,331	8,893
Pennsylvania	11,637	11,731	11,945	12,291	11,668	11,813	12,087	12,489
East North Central:								
Ohio	10,599	11,033	11,621	12,364	10,611	11,058	11,649	12,369
Indiana	5,035	5,212	5,457	5,766	5,043	5,230	5,482	5,792
Illinois	10,987	11,395	11,953	12,667	11,003	11,435	12,012	12,732
Michigan	8,604	8,903	9,277	9,728	8,622	8,956	9,381	9,897
Wisconsin	4,246	4,383	4,588	4,863	4,254	4,403	4,617	4,892
West North Central:								

Iowa	2,718	2,706	2,741	2,822	2,730	2,736	2,791	2,889
Missouri	4,584	4,692	4,845	5,042	4,589	4,706	4,870	5,080
North Dakota	651	650	657	670	654	661	676	701
South Dakota	678	674	681	697	682	685	699	724
Nebraska	1,469	1,480	1,502	1,533	1,473	1,493	1,529	1,579
Kansas	2,278	2,309	2,355	2,414	2,284	2,327	2,391	2,475
South Atlantic:								
Delaware	548	592	642	696	546	589	635	685
Maryland	3,867	4,186	4,525	4,876	3,855	4,155	4,471	4,801
District of Columbia[1]	840	895	968	1,052	842	895	964	1,044
Virginia	4,747	5,036	5,331	5,618	4,741	5,027	5,328	5,640
West Virginia	1,747	1,696	1,669	1,667	1,760	1,728	1,725	1,747
North Carolina	5,167	5,373	5,588	5,801	5,172	5,394	5,637	5,902
South Carolina	2,653	2,742	2,842	2,947	2,660	2,765	2,891	3,035
Georgia	4,679	4,928	5,172	5,400	4,678	4,933	5,200	5,477
Florida	6,579	7,438	8,458	9,650	6,528	7,275	8,105	9,012
East South Central:								
Kentucky	3,227	3,271	3,329	3,399	3,236	3,301	3,391	3,505
Tennessee	4,025	4,181	4,339	4,492	4,024	4,185	4,358	4,541
Alabama	3,624	3,763	3,930	4,125	3,629	3,777	3,959	4,171
Mississippi	2,379	2,445	2,525	2,618	2,386	2,468	2,574	2,705
West South Central:								
Arkansas	2,027	2,097	2,160	2,216	2,027	2,100	2,176	2,257
Louisiana	3,766	3,979	4,232	4,523	3,769	3,988	4,249	4,549
Oklahoma	2,507	2,559	2,619	2,686	2,510	2,569	2,643	2,731
Texas	11,309	11,977	12,678	13,392	11,307	11,986	12,722	13,514
Mountain:								
Montana	716	734	762	800	719	740	773	816
Idaho	708	731	767	817	710	735	773	821
Wyoming	331	340	361	392	332	343	362	389
Colorado	2,099	2,250	2,420	2,607	2,096	2,241	2,404	2,582
New Mexico	1,075	1,159	1,277	1,432	1,079	1,164	1,278	1,420
Arizona	1,804	2,037	2,295	2,581	1,795	2,010	2,244	2,496
Utah	1,073	1,155	1,249	1,353	1,073	1,157	1,253	1,361
Nevada	540	605	653	[2]669	533	594	644	[2]674
Pacific:								
Washington	3,064	3,185	3,366	3,607	3,070	3,197	3,378	3,607
Oregon	2,055	2,162	2,270	2,378	2,050	2,152	2,257	2,367
California	20,761	23,224	25,972	28,998	20,657	22,913	25,343	27,937
Alaska	293	311	329	349	294	314	337	362
Hawaii	752	777	799	822	754	785	819	858

* Series I–D. Assumes migration rates would continue within the range observed in 1955–60 and national fertility continues to decline from present levels.
† Series II–D. Assumes migration rates will change from recent levels resulting in no net migration among states in 50 years and national fertility continues to decline from present levels.
Source: U.S. Dept. of Commerce, *Population Projections of the Populations of States—1970 to 1985*, Series P–25 No. 375.

EXHIBIT 3a

Population of selected Standard Metropolitan Statistical Areas

	1960	*1970*	*1975 (projected)*
The ten biggest:			
New York, N.Y.	10,694,633	11,409,739	11,920,700
Los Angeles–Long Beach.	6,038,771	6,974,103	7,468,700
Chicago, Ill.	6,220,913	6,892,509	7,278,200
Philadelphia, Pa.	4,342,897	4,777,414	5,050,300
Detroit, Mich.	3,762,360	4,163,517	4,396,100
S.F.–Oakland, Cal.	2,648,762	3,069,797	3,294,100
Washington, D.C.	2,076,610	2,835,737	3,297,700
Boston, Mass.	2,595,481	2,730,228	3,468,100
Pittsburgh, Pa.	2,405,435	2,383,753	2,376,000
St. Louis, Mo.	2,104,669	2,331,371	2,470,400
The ten fastest growing:			
Anaheim–Santa Ana–Garden Grove, Calif.	703,925	1,409,335	1,761,500
San Jose, Calif.	642,315	1,057,032	1,264,400
Phoenix, Ariz.	663,510	963,132	1,112,900
San Bernardino–Ontario, Calif.	809,782	1,122,041	1,288,600
Houston, Tex.	1,418,323	1,958,491	2,230,000
Dallas, Tex.	1,119,410	1,539,372	1,750,500
Washington, D.C.	2,076,610	2,835,737	3,297,700
Atlanta, Ga.	1,017,188	1,373,629	1,564,700
Miami, Fla.	935,047	1,259,176	1,421,300
Fort Worth, Tex.	573,215	757,105	849,000

Source: Compiled from *Sales Management*, Nov. 10, 1970.

EXHIBIT 3b

Projected car population in the United States

Year	*No. of pre-1971 cars on the road (thousands)*	*No. of post-1970 cars on the road (thousands)*	*Total number of cars on the road (thousands)*
1970	85,255	0	85,255
1971	81,723	7,000	88,723
1972	75,067	17,050	92,117
1973	68,026	27,230	95,256
1974	60,610	37,570	98,180
1975	52,909	48,190	101,099
1976	44,896	58,820	103,716
1977	37,131	69,230	106,361
1978	28,538	79,300	107,838
1979	22,695	88,550	111,245
1980	16,753	96,950	113,703

Source: *The Economics of Lead Removal*, prepared by the Panel on Automotive Fuels and Air Pollution, p. 54.

EXHIBIT 3c

Projected emissions from motor vehicles based on the 1970–71 standards

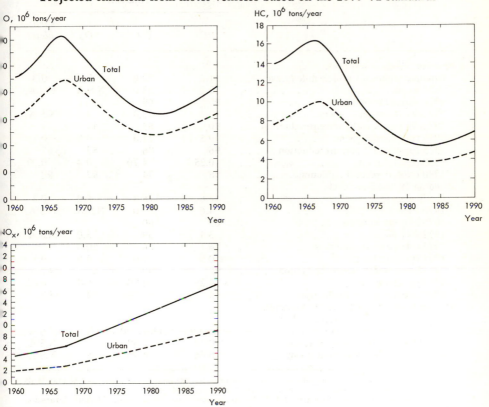

Source: National Air Pollution Control Administration, Department of Health, Education and Welfare.

Current and proposed exhaust emission standards

	Pollutant			
	HC	CO	NO_x	Partic-ulates
Based on 1968–71 test cycle				
Baseline: Grams per vehicle mile (g.v.m.)*..	11.2	73.0	5.4	0.3
1970 g.v.m.	2.2	23.0	N.S.A.	N.S.A.
1970 percent reduction	80	69		
1972–74 (proposed)† g.v.m.	2.2	23.0	3.0	N.S.A.
1972–74 (proposed)† percent reduction. . .	80	69	44	
1975 (proposed)† g.v.m.	0.5	11.0	0.9	0.1
1975 (proposed)† percent reduction	96	86	83	67
1980 (goals)† g.v.m.	0.25	4.70	0.4	0.03
1980 (goals)† percent reduction	98	94	93	90
Based on 1972–75 test cycle				
Baseline g.v.m.	14.6	116.3	6.0	0.3
1970 g.v.m.	4.6	47.0	N.S.A.	N.S.A.
1970 percent reduction	69	60		
1972–74† g.v.m.	3.4	39	3.0	N.S.A.
1972–74† percent reduction	76	66	50	
1975 (proposed)† g.v.m.	0.5	11.0	0.9	0.1
1975 (proposed)† percent reduction	97	90	85	67
1980 (goals)† g.v.m.	0.25	4.70	0.4	0.03
1980 (goals)† percent reduction	98	94	94	90
Standards for 1975 approved by Congress under Clean Air Amendments 1970				
Percent reduction from 1970	at least 90	at least 90	†	N.S.A.
Based on 1968–71 test cycle g.v.m.	0.22	2.30	†	N.S.A.
Based on 1972–75 test cycle g.v.m.	0.46	4.7	†	N.S.A.

* Exhaust Emissions from vehicles manufactured prior to 1968 model year when the first standards set under the 1965 Amendments to the Clean Air Act wereapplied.

† Originally proposed on February 10, 1970, by the then secretary, Department of Health, Education and Welfare.

‡ A reduction of at least 90 percent from 1971 model year vehicles to be applicable to vehicles for the 1976 model year and thereafter.

N.S.A. = No standards applicable.

Note: This exhibit shows current and future exhaust emission standards as initially proposed on February 10, 1970, by the then secretary of the Department of HEW, and the ones actually legislated by Congress under the Clean Air Amendments of 1970. These standards are based on two different testing procedures: (1) 1968–71 Test Cycle—the testing procedure used in testing cars for the model years 1968–71; (2) 1972–75 Test Cycle—the testing procedure to be used for cars for the model years 1972–75. The latter testing procedure is based on a comprehensive measurement system of a more representative sample reflecting actual operating conditions more accurately.

Emission requirements for California

	Prior to control	1966	1970	1971	1972	1974	Proposed 1975
HC	11.0	3.4	2.2	2.2	1.5	1.5	0.5
CO	80.0	34.0	23.0	23.0	23.0	23.0	12.0
NO_x	4.0	–	–	4.0	3.0	1.3	1.0
Evap. control	–	–	Yes	Yes	Yes	Yes	Yes

Source: John H. Ludwig, U.S. Department of HEW, *U.S. Government Air Pollution Control Program,* and paper prepared for the U.S. Conference on Air Pollution, sponsored by the Dept. of Health, Republic of South Africa, October 14–15, 1970.

EXHIBIT 5

Estimate of resources needed to implement proposed admendments
to clean air act as contained in senate bill
(dollars in thousands)

	Fiscal year 1971		Fiscal year 1972		Fiscal year 1973	
	Position	Amount	Position	Amount	Position	Amount
Air quality monitoring	85	$ 3,700	205	$ 3,750	205	$ 3,750
Production car testing	30	1,070	80	3,330	100	3,900
National emission standards . .	107	2,210	130	3,300	130	3,300
Fuels/fuel additives regulation	20	980	30	1,100	30	1,100
Control program assistance:						
(1) Technical assistance . . .	254	6,100	402	11,170	410	11,415
(2) Control program grants	26	12,900	12	6,300	16	8,000
(3) State vehicle inspection						
grants	2	2,500	29	32,500	50	75,000
Mobile source standards	7	655	11	660	12	240
Used vehicles	16	1,275	16	1,800	19	1,800
Instrumentation.	4	1,200	20	5,800	20	5,800
Fuels conversion	1	500	2	1,000	10	10,000
Vehicle R/D	3	750	3	750	3	1,000
Federal facilities and						
procurement.	15	500	35	1,200	50	1,700
Subtotal*	570	34,340	975	72,660	1,055	127,005
Forward planning estimate; im-						
plement current legislation. .	1,141	112,018	1,450	160,500	1,755	186,100
Subtotal cost to implement						
new legislation	1,711	146,358	2,425	233,160	2,810	313,105
Effects research, sec. 107. . . .	30	3,000	110	5,000	120	7,000
Grand total	1,741	149,350	2,535	238,160	2,930	320,105

* Excludes Sec. 107 effects research.
Source: Estimates proposed by John G. Veneman, acting secretary of the Department of Health, Education and Welfare on August 27, 1970, at the hearings of the Senate Public Works Committee, p. 595.

APPENDIX A

Selected provisions of the Clean Air Amendments of 1970 are as follows:

Section 104(a)   The [Administrator] shall give special emphasis to research and development into new and improved methods, having industry wide application, for the prevention and control of air pollution resulting from the combustion of fuels. In furtherance of such research and development, he shall—

(1) conduct and accelerate research programs directed toward development of improved, low cost techniques for (A) control of combustion byproducts of fuels, (B) removal of potential air pollutants from fuels prior to combustion, (C) control of emissions from the evaporation of fuels, (D) improving the efficiency of fuels combustion so as to decrease atmospheric emissions, and (E) producing synthetic or new fuels which, when used, result in decreased atmospheric emissions.

(2) provide for Federal grants to public or non profit agencies . . . for payment of (A) part of the cost of acquiring, constructing, or otherwise securing for research and development purposes, new or improved devices or methods having industry wide application of preventing or controlling discharges into the air of various types of pollutants; (B) part of the cost of programs to develop low emission alternatives to the present internal combustion engine; (C) the cost to purchase vehicles and vehicle engines, or portions thereof, for research, development and testing purposes.

Section 104(c)   For the purposes of this subsection there are authorized to be appropriated $75,000,000 for the fiscal year ending June 30, 1971, $125,000,000 for the fiscal year ending June 30, 1972, and $150,000,000 for the fiscal year ending June 30, 1973. Amounts appropriated pursuant to this subsection shall remain available until expended.

Section 105(a)(1)(A)   The Administrator may make grants to air pollution control agencies in an amount up to two-thirds of the cost of planning, developing, establishing, or improving, and up to one-half of the cost of maintaining, programs for the prevention and control of air pollution or implementation of national primary and secondary ambient air quality standards.

Section 108(a)(1)   For the purpose of establishing national primary and secondary ambient air quality standards, the Administrator shall within 30 days after the date of the enactment of the Clean Air Amendments of 1970 [Dec. 31, 1970] publish . . . a list which includes each air pollutant (A) which in his judgment has an adverse effect on public health or welfare; (B) the presence of which in the ambient air results from numerous or diverse mobile or stationary sources. . . .

Section 118   Each department, agency, and instrumentality of the executive, legislative, and judicial branches of the Federal Government (1) having jurisdiction over any property or facility, or (2) engaged in any activity resulting, or which may result, in the discharge of air pollutants, shall comply with Federal, State, interstate, and local requirements respecting control and abatement of air pollution to the same extent that any person is subject to such requirements. The President may exempt any emission source of any department, agency, or instrumentality in the executive branch from compliance with such a requirement if he determines it to be in the paramount interest of the United States to do so, except that no exemption may be granted from section 111, and an exemption from section 112 may be granted only in accordance with section 112(c). No such exemption shall be granted due to lack of appropriation unless the President shall have specifically requested such appropriation as a part of the budgetary process and the Congress shall have failed to make available such requested appropriation. Any exemption shall be for a period not in excess of one year, but additional exemptions may be granted for periods of not to exceed one year upon the President's making a new determination. The President shall report each January to the Congress all exemptions from the requirements of this section granted during the preceding calendar year, together with his reason for granting each such exemption.

Section 202(a)   Except as otherwise provided in subsection (b)—

(1)   The Administrator shall by regulation prescribe (and from time to time revise) in accordance with the provisions of this section, standards applicable to the emission of any air pollutant from any class or classes of new motor vehicles or new motor vehicle engines, which in his judg-

ment causes or contributes to, or is likely to cause or to contribute to, air pollution which endangers the public health or welfare. Such standards shall be applicable to such vehicles and engines for their useful life (as determined under subsection (d)), whether such vehicles and engines are designed as complete systems or incorporated devices to prevent or control such pollution.

(2) Any regulation prescribed under this subsection (and any revision thereof) shall take affect after such period as the Administrator finds necessary to permit the development and application of the requisite technology, giving appropriate consideration to the cost of compliance within such period.

(b)

(1) (A) The regulations under subsection (a) applicable to emissions of carbon monoxide and hydrocarbons from light duty vehicles and engines manufactured during or after model year 1975 shall contain standards which require a reduction of at least 90 per centum from emissions of carbon monoxide and hydrocarbons allowable under the standards under this section applicable to light duty vehicles and engines manufactured in model year 1970.

(B) The regulations under subsection (a) applicable to emissions of oxides of nitrogen from light duty vehicles and engines manufactured during or after model year 1976 shall contain standards which require a reduction of at least 90 per centum from the average of emissions of oxides of nitrogen actually measured from light duty vehicles manufactured during model year 1971 which are not subject to any Federal or State emission standard for oxides of nitrogen. Such average of emissions shall be determined by the Administrator on the basis of measurements made by him.

(4) On July 1 of 1971, and of each year thereafter, the Administrator shall report to the Congress with respect to the development of systems necessary to implement the emission standards established pursuant to this section. Such reports shall include information regarding the continuing effects of such air pollutants subject to standards under this section on the public health

and welfare, the extent and progress of efforts being made to develop the necessary systems, the costs associated with development and application of such systems, and following such hearings as he may deem advisable, any recommendations for additional congressional action necessary to achieve the purposes of this Act. In gathering information for the purposes of this paragraph and in connection with any hearing, the provisions of section 307(a) (relating to subpoenas) shall apply.

(5) (A) At any time after January 1, 1972, any manufacturer may file with the Administrator an application requesting the suspension for one year only of the effective date of any emission standard required by paragraph (b)(1)(A) with respect to such manufacturer. The Administrator shall make his determination with respect to any such application within 60 days. If he determines, in accordance with the provisions of this subsection, that such suspension should be granted, he shall simultaneously with such determination prescribe by regulation interim emission standards required to be prescribed by paragraph (b)(1)(A) to emissions of carbon monoxide or hydrocarbons (or both) from such vehicles and engines manufactured during model year 1975.

(B) At any time after January 1, 1973, any manufacturer may file with the Administrator an application requesting the suspension for one year only of the effective date of any emission standard required by paragraph (b)(1)(B) with respect to such manufacturer. The Administrator shall make his determination with respect to any such application within 60 days. If he determines, in accordance with the provisions of this subsection, that such suspension should be granted, he shall simultaneously with such determination prescribe by regulation interim emission standards which shall apply (in lieu of the standards required to be prescribed by paragraph (b)(1)(B)) to emissions of oxides of nitrogen from such vehicles and engines manufactured during model year 1976.

(C) Any interim standards prescribed under this paragraph shall reflect the greatest degree of emission control which is achievable by application of technology which the Administrator determines is available, giving appropriate consideration to the cost of applying such technology within the period of time available to manufacturers. (D) Within 60 days after receipt of the application for any such suspension, and after public hearing, the Administrator shall issue a decision granting or refusing such suspension. The Administrator shall grant such suspension only if he determines that (i) such suspension is essential to the public interest or the public health and welfare of the United States, (ii) all good faith efforts have been made to meet the standards established by this subsection, (iii) the applicant has established that effective control technology, processes, operating methods, or other alternatives are not availble or have not been available for a sufficient period of time to achieve compliance prior to the effective date of such standards, and (iv) the study and investigation of the National Academy of Sciences conducted pursuant to subsection (c) and other information available to him has not indicated that technology, processes, or other alternatives are available to meet such standards. (E) Nothing in this paragraph shall extend the effective date of any emission standard required to be prescribed under this subsection for more than one year.

(c) (1) The Administrator shall undertake to enter into appropriate arrangements with the National Academy of Sciences to conduct a comprehensive study and investigation of the technological feasibility of meeting the emissions standards required to be prescribed by the Administrator by subsection (b). . . .

(4) The Administrator shall furnish to such Academy at its request any information which the Academy deems necessary for the purpose of conducting the investigation and study authorized . . . For the purpose of furnishing such information, the Administrator may use any authority he has under this Act (A) to obtain information from any person, and (B) to require such person to conduct such tests, keep such records, and make such reports respecting research or other activities conducted by such person as may be reasonably necessary to carry out this subsection.

(*d*)

. . . Useful life shall . . . in the case of light duty vehicles and light duty vehicle engines, be a period of use of five years or of fifty thousand miles (or the equivalent) whichever first occurs . . .

Section 205

Any person who violates Section 203(a) (i.e. manufacturing and/or distributing new vehicles, engines that are in violation of the regulations promulgated under Section 202) . . . shall be subject upon conviction to a civil penalty of not more than $10,000 . . . Any such violation . . . shall constitute a separate offence with respect to each . . . vehicle. . . .

Section 206(a)

(1) The Administrator shall test, or require to be tested in such manner as he deems appropriate, any new vehicle or new motor vehicle engine submitted by a manufacturer to determine whether such vehicle or engine conforms with the regulations prescribed under section 202 of this Act. If such vehicle or engine conforms to such regulations, the Administrator shall issue a certificate of conformity upon such terms, and for such period (not in excess of one year), as he may prescribe.

(2) The Administrator shall test any emission control system incorporated in a motor vehicle or motor vehicle engine submitted to him by any person, in order to determine whether such system enables such vehicle or engine to conform to the standards required to be prescribed under section 202(b) of this Act. If the Administrator finds on the basis of such tests that such vehicle or engine conforms to such standards, the Administrator shall issue a verification of compliance with emission standards for such system when incorporated in vehicles of a class of which the tested vehicle is representative. He shall inform manufacturers and the National Academy of Sciences, and make available to the public, the results of such tests. Tests under this paragraph shall be conducted under such terms and conditions (including requirements for preliminary testing by qualified independent laboratories) as the Administrator may prescribe by regulations.

(*b*)

(1) In order to determine whether new motor vehicles or new motor vehicles engines being manufactured by a manufacturer do in fact con-

form with the regulations with respect to which certificate of conformity was issued, the Administrator is authorized to test such vehicles or engines. Such test may be conducted by the Administrator directly or, in accordance with conditions specified by the Administrator, by the manufacturer.

(c)   For purposes of enforcement of this section, officers or employees duly designated by the Administrator, upon presenting appropriate credentials to the manufacturer or person in charge, are authorized (1) to enter, at reasonable times, any plant or other establishment of such manufacturer, for the purpose of conducting tests of any plant or other establishment of such manufacturer, or (2) to inspect at reasonable times, records, files, papers, processes, controls, and facilities used by such manufacturer in conducting tests under regulations of the Administrator. Each such inspection shall be commenced and completed with reasonable promptness.

(d)   The Administrator shall by regulation establish methods and procedures for making tests under this section.

Section 207(a)   Effective with respect to vehicles and engines manufactured in model years beginning more than 60 days after the date of the enactment of the Clean Air Act Amendments of 1970, the manufacturer of each new motor vehicle and new motor vehicle engine shall warrant to the ultimate purchaser and each subsequent purchaser that such vehicle or engine is (1) designed, built, and equipped so as to conform at the time of sale with applicable regulations under section 202, and (2) free from defects in materials and workmanship which cause such vehicle or engine to fail to conform with applicable regulations for its useful life. . . .

(2)   . . . . The warranty . . . shall run to the ultimate purchaser and each subsequent purchaser and shall provide that if (A) the vehicle or engine is maintained and operated in accordance with instructions [provided by the manufacturer], (B) it fails to conform at any time during its useful life [fifty thousand miles or 5 years whichever comes first] to the regulations pre-

scribed in section 202, and (C) such non conformity results in the ultimate purchaser (or any subsequent purchaser) of such vehicle or engine having to bear any penalty or other sanction (including the denial of the right to use such vehicle or engine) under State or Federal law, then such manufacturer shall remedy such nonconformity under such warranty with the cost thereof to be borne by the manufacturer.

(c)   Effective with respect to vehicles and engines manufactured during model years beginning more than 60 days after the date of enactment of the Clean Air Amendments of 1970—

(1)   If the Administrator determines that a substantial number of any class or category of vehicles or engines, although properly maintained and used, do not conform to the regulations prescribed under section 202, when in actual use throughout their useful life . . . he shall immediately notify the manufacturer thereof of such nonconformity, and he shall require the manufacturer to submit a plan for remedying the nonconformity of the vehicles or engines with respect to which such notification is given. The plan shall provide that the nonconformity of any such vehicles or engines which are properly used and maintained will be remedied at the expense of the manufacturer. If the manufacturer disagrees with such determination of nonconformity and so advises the Administrator, the Administrator shall afford the manufacturer and other interested persons an opportunity to present their views and evidence in support thereof at a public hearing. Unless, as a result of such hearing the Administrator withdraws such determination of nonconformity, he shall, within 60 days after the completion of such hearing, order the manufacturer to provide prompt notification of such nonconformity in accordance with paragraph (2).

(2)   Any notification required by paragraph (1) with respect to any class or category of vehicles or engines shall be given to dealers, ultimate purchasers, and subsequent purchasers (if known) in such manner and containing such information as the Administrator may by regulations require.

(d)   Any cost obligation of any dealer incurred as a result of any requirement imposed by subsection (a), (b), or (c) shall be borne by the manufacturer. The transfer of any such cost obligation from a manufacturer to any dealer through franchise or other agreement is prohibited.

Section 211(a)   The Administrator may by regulation designate any fuel or fuel additive and . . . no manufacturer or processor of any such fuel or additive may sell, offer for sale, or introduce into commerce such fuel or additive unless the Administrator has registered such fuel or additive. . . .

(c)   (1)   The Administrator may, . . . by regulation, control or prohibit the manufacture, introduction into commerce, offering for sale, or sale of any fuel or fuel additive for use in a motor vehicle or motor vehicle engine (A) if any emission products of such fuel or fuel additive will endanger the public health or welfare, or (B) if emission products of such fuel or fuel additive will impair to a significant degree the performance of any emission control device or system which is in general use, or which the Administrator finds has been developed to a point where in a reasonable time it would be in general use were such regulation to be promulgated.

(d)   Any person who violates subsection (a) or the regulations prescribed under subsection (c) or who fails to furnish any information required by the Administrator under subsection (c) shall forfeit and pay to the United States a civil penalty of $10,000 for each and every day of the continuance of such violation. . . .

Section 210   The Administrator is authorized to make grants to appropriate State agencies in an amount up to two-thirds of the cost of developing and maintaining effective vehicle emission devices and systems inspection and emission testing and control programs . . .

Section 212(b)   (1)   There is established a Low-Emission Vehicle Certification Board to be composed of the Administrator or his designee, the Secretary of Transportation or his designee, the Chairman of the Council on Environmental Quality or his designee, the Director of the National Highway

Safety Bureau in the Department of Transportation, the Administrator of General Services, and two members appointed by the President. The President shall designate one member of the Board as Chairman.

(e)   (1)   Certified low-emission vehicles shall be acquired by purchase or lease by the Federal Government for use by the Federal Government in lieu of other vehicles if the Administrator of General Services determines that such certified vehicles have procurement costs which are no more than 150 per centum of the retail price of the least expensive class or model of motor vehicle for which they are certified substitutes.

(2)   In order to encourage development of inherently low-polluting propulsion technology, the Board may, at its discretion, raise the premium . . . to 200 per centum of the retail price of any class or model of motor vehicle for which a certified low-emission vehicle is a certified substitute, if the Board determines that the certified low-emission vehicle is powered by an inherently low-polluting propulsion system.

(i)   There are authorized to be appropriated for paying additional amounts for motor vehicles pursuant to, and for carrying out the provisions of, this section, $5,000,000 for the fiscal year ending June 30, 1971, and $25,000,000 for each of the two succeeding fiscal years.

Section 304(a)   . . . Any person may commence a civil action on his own behalf (1) against any person . . . who is alleged to be in violation of (A) an emission standard or limitation under this Act or (B) an order issued by the Administrator or a State with respect to such a standard or limitation, or (2) against the Administrator where there is alleged a failure of the Administrator to perform any act or duty under this Act which is not discretionary with the Administrator. The district courts shall have jurisdiction, without regard to the amount in controversy or the citizenship of the parties, to enforce such an emission standard or limitation, or such an order, or to order the Administrator to perform such act or duty, as the case may be.

(e)   Nothing in this section shall restrict any right which any person (or class of persons) may have under any statute or common law to seek enforcement of any emission standard or limitation or to seek any other relief (including relief against the Administrator or a State agency).

Section 307(a)   (1)   In connection with any determination under . . . section 202(b)(5) or 202(b)(4) . . . the Administrator may issue subpoenas for the attendance and testimony of witnesses and the production of relevant papers, books, and documents, and he may administer oaths. . . . In case of contumacy or refusal to obey a subpoena served upon any person under this subparagraph, the district court of the United States for any district in which such person is found or resides or transacts business, upon application by the United States and after notice to such person, shall have jurisdiction to issue an order requiring such person to appear and give testimony before the Administrator to appear and produce papers, books, and documents before the Administrator, or both, and any failure to obey such order of the court may be punished by such court as a contempt thereof.

Section 308   Whenever the Attorney General determines, upon application of the Administrator (1) that—(A) in the implementation of the requirements of section . . . 202 of this Act, a right under any United States letters patent, which is being used or intended for public or commercial use and not otherwise reasonably available, is necessary to enable any person required to comply with such limitation to so comply, and (B) there are no reasonable alternative methods to accomplish such purpose, and (2) that the unavailability of such right may result in a substantial lessening of competition or tendency to create a monopoly in any line of commerce in any section of the country, the Attorney General may so certify to a district court of the United States, which may issue an order requiring the person who owns such patent to license it on such reasonable terms and conditions as the court, after hearing, may determine. Such certification may be made to the district court for the district in which the person owning the patent resides, does business, or is found.

APPENDIX B

TABLE 1a

General auto related economic data

Items	1945	1950	1955	1960	1965	1966	1967	1968	1969
Auto-related consumer expenditures (10^6):									
Gas and oil	$1,809	$5,431	$9,000	$12,252	$15,094	$16,220			
Repairs, greasing and washing	957	2,509	3,619	5,198	6,080	6,555			
Tires and tubes		801	568	922	1,184	1,343			
Accessories and parts		744	1,013	1,431	1,971	2,191			
Highway motor fuel consumption (10^6 gallons):									
Gasoline		N.A.	46,527	55,429	66,979	69,938	72,639	77,249	81,269
Other		N.A.	1,203	2,449	4,126	4,690	5,053	5,689	6,221
Wholesale value of vehicles produced in U.S. plants (10^6):	$1,239	$10,176	$14,474	$14,515	$22,114	$21,508	$19,245	$24,022	$23,700
Cars	57	8,468	12,453	12,164	18,380	17,554	15,653	19,352	18,700
Trucks and buses	1,182	1,708	2,021	2,351	3,734	3,953	3,592	4,670	5,000
Vehicles sold—domestic and imported (10^3):									
Domestic total		8,003	9,169	7,869	11,057	10,329	8,976	10,718	10,142
Cars		6,666	7,920	6,674	9,305	8,598	7,437	8,822	8,224
Trucks and buses		1,337	1,249	1,194	1,752	1,731	1,539	1,896	1,919
Imported total (new cars only)		21.7	59.5	494.7	598.3	976.4	1,114.4	1,759.2	2,026.4
Trucks and buses		.08	1.3	23.8	30.9	57.4	88.4	129.1	171.1
Taxes on motor vehicles ($ millions):									
Cars—State	$1,252	$2,615	$4,026	$5,320	$7,007	$7,519	$7,899	$8,631	$9,341
—Federal	557	1,479	2,736	4,397	5,716	5,716	5,524	6,055	6,728
Trucks—State	412	782	1,311	1,709	2,296	2,466	2,599	2,830	3,055
—Federal	187	345	555	1,121	1,548	1,707	1,682	1,822	2,025

TABLE 1b

1969	Manufacturing	Wholesale	Retail	Selected services
Total automotive manufacturing (number of businesses) . . .	3,505	65,698	307,271	197,018
Total U.S. manufacturing (number of businesses).	311,125	311,464	1,763,224	1,187,814
Percent automotive.	1.1	21.1	17.4	16.6
Total automotive sales ($000).	64,979,600	78,751,289	75,580,714	10,323,256
Total U.S. manufacturing sales ($000)	557,767,200	459,475,967	310,214,393	60,542,218
Percent automotive.	11.6	17.3	24.4	17.1
Total automotive employees.	961,300	65,698	1,739,035	745,550
Total U.S. employees.	19,339,200	3,640,879	11,005,067	4,755,822
Percent automotive.	5.0	15.1	15.8	15.7

TABLE 1c
Automotive materials consumption
(1968)

	Steel	Aluminum (000 lbs.)	Copper and alloys (000 lbs.)	Cotton (500 lb. bales)	Lead (short tons)	Zinc (tons)	Rubber (long tons)	Nickel (000 lbs.)	Gray and ductile iron (tons)
Automotive consumption	19,269,373	1,045,000	521,000	153,140	723,443	566,000	1,756,754	48,460	2,927,000
Percent of total consumption used by cars	21.0	10.4	8.2	1.8	54.7	36.5	N.A.	14.3	19.4

Source: Compiled by Automobile Manufacturers Association from various trade sources.

TABLE 1d
Cars in fleets by type of business, 1969

Type of fleet	Automobiles
Business fleets—25 or more cars:	
Salesman owned	438,000
Company owned	243,000
Leased by companies by lease type	
Finance and management	638,000
Partial or full maintenance	381,000
Net or fixed.	84,000
	1,103,000
Individually leased	697,000
Business fleets—10–24 cars	
owned and leased	641,000
Total business fleets	3,122,000
Government	594,000
Utilities.	404,000
Police.	191,000
Taxi.	169,000
Rental	297,000*
Driver schools	27,000
Total—Other than business fleets.	1,682,000
Total.	4,804,000

* Includes double cycling registrations.
Note: Estimate of total number of cars in fleets of four or more vehicles: 9,780,000.
Source: Edward J. Babit, publisher, *Automotive Fleet and Trucking Business* magazines.

TABLE 1e
Distribution of trips and vehicle-miles of travel by cars and trucks

Trip length (miles)	Trips		Vehicle miles	
	Cars	Trucks	Cars	Trucks
Under 5	59.6%	53.0%	13.2%	9.4%
5–9	19.9	20.8	15.4	13.0
10–14	8.1	9.3	11.2	10.3
15–19	4.2	5.1	8.2	8.0
20–29	3.7	5.1	10.4	11.1
30–39	1.6	2.3	6.5	7.0
40–49	0.8	1.1	4.3	4.7
50–99	1.3	2.0	10.8	12.0
100 and over.	0.8	1.3	20.0	24.5
Total.	100.0%	100.0%	100.0%	100.0%

Note: Based on motor-vehicle-use studies 1951–56, covering 19 states for passenger cars and 18 states for trucks.
Source: U.S. Department of Commerce, Bureau of Public Roads, *Highway Transportation*.

89 percent of intercity travel is by motor vehicle
(intercity passenger miles by mode of travel)

	Automobiles	Motor coaches	Total motor vehicles	Railways, revenue passengers	Inland waterways	Airways, domestic revenue services	Total
Passenger-miles, in billions							
1950	438.3	26.4	464.7	32.5	1.2	10.1	508.5
1955	637.4	25.5	662.9	28.7	1.7	22.7	716.0
1960	706.1	19.9	726.0	21.6	2.7	34.0	784.3
1962	735.9	21.3	757.2	20.2	2.7	27.6	817.7
1963	765.9	21.9	787.8	18.6	2.8	42.8	852.0
1964	801.8	22.7	824.5	18.4	2.8	49.2	894.9
1965	817.6	23.8	841.4	17.6	3.1	58.1	920.2
1966	856.4	24.6	881.0	17.3	3.4	69.4	971.0
1967	889.8	24.9	914.7	15.3	3.4	87.2	1,020.6
1968	936.4	26.2	962.6	13.3	3.5	101.2	1,080.6
1969*	977.0	26.0	1,003.0	12.0	4.0	111.0	1,130.0
Passenger-miles, percent by mode of travel							
1950	86.19	5.20	91.39	6.39	0.23	1.99	100
1955	89.02	3.56	92.58	4.01	0.24	3.17	100
1960	90.03	2.54	92.57	2.75	0.34	4.34	100
1962	90.00	2.60	92.60	2.47	0.33	4.60	100
1963	89.89	2.57	92.46	2.18	0.33	5.03	100
1964	89.60	2.53	92.13	2.06	0.31	5.50	100
1965	89.33	2.48	91.81	1.83	0.32	6.04	100
1966	88.19	2.53	90.72	1.78	0.35	7.15	100
1967	87.18	2.44	89.62	1.50	0.33	8.54	100
1968	86.66	2.42	89.08	1.23	0.32	9.37	100
1969*	86.46	2.30	88.76	1.06	0.35	9.83	100

* Estimated.

TABLE 2a
Structure of the automobile industry
(dollars in millions)
AMERICAN MOTORS CORPORATION

Year	Net sales	Net income	Capital exp.	Profit margin	Current ratio	Percent domestic market share
1969*. . . . . . $ 737.4		$ 4.93¶	$47.04	1.7	1.7	3.0
1968	761.1	3.31	19.05	3.0	1.5	3.0
1967	651.2	d70.53	38.84	deficit	1.2	3.1
1966	870.4	d30.92	57.78	deficit	1.3	3.2
1965	990.6	7.36	47.57	1.6	1.5	3.7
1964	1,095.4	44.48	67.50	4.5	1.7	5.1
1963	1,132.4	74.56	19.96	6.5	1.7	6.3

* Total number of domestic dealers in 1969—27,775: 2,375 or 8.5 percent of total for American Motors, or 21.7 percent of total for Chrysler; 6,850 or 24.7 percent of total for Ford; and 12,500 or 45.1 percent of total for General Motors.

¶ The depreciation and plant amortization expense for 1960 for American Motors $10.3 million; for Chrysler $170.3 million; for General Motors $76.7 million; for Ford $385.2 million.

Sources: Compiled by the Harvard Business School Staff from (a) Standard & Poor's *Industry Surveys*; (b) *Survey of Current Business*; (c) *Handbook of Labor Statistics 1969*; and (d) *Ward's Automotive Reports*.

TABLE 2b
GENERAL MOTORS CORPORATION
(dollars in millions)

Year	Net sales	Net income	Capital exp.	Profit margin —op. income sales	Current ratio	Percent domestic market share
1969*. . . . . $24,295‡		$1,711.0¶	$1,043.8‖	16.7	2.3	53.7
1968	22,755	1,731.9	860.2	18.1	2.4	51.9
1967	20,026	1,627.3	912.6	18.0	2.4	55.5
1966	20,209	1,793.4	1,188.1	18.7	2.5	51.7
1965	20,734	2,125.6	1,322.0	21.6	2.7	53.0
1964	16,997	1,734.8	929.6	21.3	3.0	51.1
1963	16,495	1,591.8	647.2	22.4	3.3	53.3

* Total number of domestic dealers in 1969—27,775: 2,375 or 8.5 percent of total for American Motors, or 21.7 percent of total for Chrysler; 6,850 or 24.7 percent of total for Ford; and 12,500 or 45.1 percent of total for General Motors.

‡ 19.5 percent of all the G.M. automobiles were manufactured in England, West Germany, Australia, Argentina, Brazil, Mexico, and South Africa.

¶ The depreciation and plant amortization expense for 1960 for American Motors $10.3 million; for Chrysler $170.3 million; for General Motors $76.7 million; for Ford $385.2 million.

‖ The General Motors Corporation spent $65 million on automotive emission control research, engineering, and testing. It planned to spend $115 million in 1970 on these activities.

Sources: Compiled by the Harvard Business School Staff from (a) Standard & Poor's *Industry Surveys*; (b) *Survey of Current Business*; (c) *Handbook of Labor Statistics 1969*; and (d) *Ward's Automotive Reports*.

TABLE 2c
CHRYSLER CORPORATION
(dollars in millions)

Year	Net sales	Net income	Capital exp.	Profit margin —op. income sales	Current ratio	Percent domestic market share
1969*. . . .	$7,052.2†	$ 88.77¶	$374.50	5.0	1.3	16.9
1968	7,445.3	290.73	217.03	10.1	1.5	17.9
1967	6,213.4	200.43	191.19	8.3	1.4	18.4
1966	5,649.5	189.22	306.19	8.7	1.4	16.8
1965	5,299.9	233.38	292.00	10.4	1.6	15.7
1964	4,287.3	213.77	313.00	11.1	1.5	16.0
1963	3,505.3	161.60	78.00	10.9	1.7	13.7

* Total number of domestic dealers in 1969—27,775: 2,375 or 8.5 percent of total for American Motors, or 21.7 percent of total for Chrysler; 6,850 or 24.7 percent of total for Ford; and 12,500 or 45.1 percent of total for General Motors.
† 27.6 percent of all the Chrysler automobiles were manufactured in France, England, Australia, Spain, and other countries.
¶ The depreciation and plant amortization expense for 1960 for American Motors $10.3 million; for Chrysler $170.3 million; for General Motors $76.7 million; for Ford $385.2 million.
Sources: Compiled by the Harvard Business School Staff from (a) Standard & Poor's *Industry Surveys;* (b) *Survey of Current Business;* (c) *Handbook of Labor Statistics 1969;* and (d) *Ward's Automotive Reports.*

TABLE 2d
FORD MOTOR COMPANY
(dollars in millions)

Year	Net sales	Net income	Capital exp.	Profit margin —op. income sales	Current ratio	Percent domestic market share
1969*. . . .	$14,755.6§	$546.5¶	$533.5¶	10.1	1.4	26.3
1968	14,075.1	626.6	462.4	11.7	1.4	27.1
1967	10,516.0	84.1	661.1	4.9	1.6	22.9
1966	12,240.0	621.0	692.5	12.0	1.6	28.2
1965	11,536.8	703.0	629.1	13.4	1.7	27.5
1964	9,670.8	505.6	463.1	12.7	1.7	27.7
1963	8,742.5	488.5	352.1	14.4	1.6	25.7

* Total number of domestic dealers in 1969—27,775: 2,375 or 8.5 percent of total for American Motors, or 21.7 percent of total for Chrysler; 6,850 or 24.7 percent of total for Ford; and 12,500 or 45.1 percent of total for General Motors.
§ 30.6 percent of all the Ford automobiles were manufactured in England, West Germany, Australia, Argentina, Brazil, and Mexico.
¶ The depreciation and plant amortization expense for 1960 for American Motors $10.3 million; for Chrysler $170.3 million; for General Motors $76.7 million; for Ford $385.2 million.
Sources: Compiled by the Harvard Business School Staff from (a) Standard & Poor's *Industry Surveys;* (b) *Survey of Current Business;* (c) *Handbook of Labor Statistics 1969;* and (d) *Ward's Automotive Reports.*

TABLE 2e
Structure of the automobile industry
(selected industry data)

Year	Hourly earnings 1957–59 = 100	Principal raw matl. cost 1957–59 = 100	Consumer price index – 1957–59 = 100 New automobiles	All items	U.S. imports percent of total domestic factory sales
1969	158.9	115.9	102.4	127.7	22.5
1968	151.2	109.8	100.8	121.2	18.4
1967	138.0	106.3	98.1	116.3	13.8
1966	133.7	104.4	97.2	113.1	10.6
1965	129.8	104.1	99.0	109.9	6.0
1964	124.7	102.2	101.2	108.1	6.9
1963	120.5	100.2	101.5	106.7	5.4

Sources: Compiled by the Harvard Business School Staff from (a) Standard & Poor's *Industry Surveys;* (b) *Survey of Current Business;* (c) *Handbook of Labor Statistics 1969;* and (d) *Ward's Automotive Reports.*

TABLE 2f
Structure of the automobile industry
(market penetration of domestic automobiles by car groups for 1969—by percent)

Car groups	G.M.	Ford	Chrysler	A.M.C.	Total
Luxury	86.3	11.4	2.4	0.0	100
Medium	74.2	8.5	17.3	0.0	100
Regular	40.6	43.3	12.3	3.8	100
Intermediate	63.3	20.4	12.7	3.6	100
Compact	37.2	25.2	27.0	10.6	100
Specialty	50.0	28.1	14.0	7.5	100

* Total number of domestic dealers in 1969—27,775: 2,375 or 8.5 percent of total for American Motors, or 21.7 percent of total for Chrysler; 6,850 or 24.7 percent of total for Ford; and 12,500 or 45.1 percent of total for General Motors.

† 27.6 percent of all the Chrysler automobiles were manufactured in France, England, Australia, Spain, and other countries.

‡ 19.5 percent of all the G.M. automobiles were manufactured in England, West Germany, Australia, Argentina, Brazil, Mexico, and South Africa.

§ 30.6 percent of all the Ford automobiles were manufactured in England, West Germany, Australia, Argentina, Brazil, and Mexico.

‖ The General Motors Corporation spent $65 million on automotive emission control research, engineering, and testing. It planned to spend $115 million in 1970 on these activities.

¶ The depreciation and plant amortization expense for 1960 for American Motors $10.3 million; for Chrysler $170.3 million; for General Motors $76.7 million; for Ford $385.2 million.

Sources: Compiled by the Harvard Business School Staff from (a) Standard & Poor's *Industry Surveys;* (b) *Survey of Current Business;* (c) *Handbook of Labor Statistics 1969;* and (d) *Ward's Automotive Reports.*

TABLE 3a
Use of lead in the United States*
(in thousands of short tons)

	White lead	Red lead and litharge	Storage batteries	Cable covering	Building	Tetra-ethyl	Ammunition	Foil	Bearing metal	Solder	Type metal	Calking	Other uses	Total
1969	7	80	583	54	45	271	79	6	17	73	26	45	103	1,389
1968	6	85	500	53	44	262	81	6	17	67	26	48	124	1,319
1967	8	77	467	63	47	247	79	6	20	69	29	49	100	1,261
1966	8	90	472	66	49	247	78	6	22	79	30	63	114	1,324
1965	8	80	455	60	47	225	57	5	22	78	33	67	104	1,241
1964	9	75	429	56	50	223	56	4	23	71	25	74	107	1,202

* Includes scrap which accounts for difference between this table and Table 3c.

TABLE 3b
World consumption of primary lead
(in thousands of short tons)

	U.S.	Canada	Belgium	France	West Germany	Italy	Sweden	U.K.	Japan	Australia and New Zealand	Russia*	Free World	World total
1969	943	74	85	219	467	134	51	175	212	50	490	2,582	3,802
1968	857	67	71	198	355	116	50	178	199	45	469	2,609	3,482
1967	779	65	71	181	322	125	50	184	180	50	460	2,461	3,331
1966	815	72	62	186	324	105	53	214	163	47	420	2,481	3,236
1965	716	63	69	159	365	70	45	216	162	43	400	2,355	3,080
1964	740	58	66	190	334	77	44	222	181	52	386	2,371	3,068

* Estimated.

TABLE 3c

World production of lead on mine bases

(in thousands of net tons)

	U.S.	Canada	Mexico	Peru	West Germany	Italy	Spain	Yugo-slavia	Morocco	S.W. Africa	Aus-tralia	Russia*	Free World	World total
1969 . . .	502	305	188	177	43	41	77	130	78	79	467	550	2,561	3,518
1968 . . .	359	355	192	166	58	39	82	123	79	64	406	629	2,374	3,282
1967 . . .	317	314	185	183	65	43	69	119	87	73	412	520	2,302	3,196
1966 . . .	327	304	201	160	61	40	69	113	88	94	400	485	2,269	3,103
1965 . . .	301	296	187	170	53	39	62	117	85	97	398	460	2,162	2,961
1964 . . .	286	201	193	102	54	36	64	112	78	104	412	452	2,013	2,776

* Estimated.

TABLE 3d
World reserves of lead
(measured and indicated in thousands of short tons)

Country	Reserves
United States	35,000,000
Australia	13,000,000
Canada	14,000,000
Communist Countries	10,000,000
Latin America	9,000,000
Other	14,000,000
Total	95,000,000

Source: American Bureau of Metal Statistics;
Commodity Data Summaries, U.S. Bureau of Mines.

TABLE 3e
Secondary lead recovery, total imports, and average annual price of lead

Year	Secondary lead recovered (short tons)	Total imports (short tons)	Average annual price—New York (cents/lb.)
1969	550,500	403,352	14.895
1968	550,879	432,587	13.212
1967	553,772	498,706	14.000
1966	572,834	439,088	15.115
1965	575,819	350,110	16.000

Note: Lead price has fluctuated by as much as ±20 percent in a given year.
Source: American Bureau of Metal Statistics; Commodity Data Summaries,
U.S. Bureau of Mines.

TABLE 3f
Selected direct requirements of lead industry

Input-output tables code	1963 direct requirements of the lead industry per $ of its output from:	Dollars	Value added per $ of output of the industry indicated in the row
27.01.	Industrial inorganic and organic chemicals	0.02001	0.43481
38.02.	Primary lead	0.17275	0.06575
38.03.	Primary zinc	0.07189	0.24093
38.06.	Secondary nonferrous metals	0.39923	0.23310
65.01.	Railroad and related services	0.01714	0.67468
69.01.	Wholesale trade	0.01159	0.67589
	Others	0.34164	
	Value added	0.06575	
	Total	1.00000	

Source: "Input-Output Structure of the U.S. Economy: 1963," U.S. Department of Commerce, December 1969.

TABLE 4
Salient features of the natural gas industry*

1. *Domestic industry:* Approximately 95 percent of the natural gas marketed in the United States was used as a gaseous fuel. The industrial sector accounted for 44 percent of the demand; the household and commercial sector made up 32 percent of the demand; electric utilities required 16 percent of the demand; other uses consumed 8 percent of the total demand. The wellhead value of the natural gas production was approximately $3.2 billion.

   Natural gas demand over the last ten years has averaged a 5.8 percent annual growth rate. During this period, proved reserves (AGA) increased at an average annual rate of 1.3 percent. As a result, the natural gas proved reserves production ratio has declined to 14.9 percent by 1968. A sustained high demand growth rate and a low reserves replenishment rate could result in a short fall in supplies in the future.

2. *Salient statistics—United States:*

	*1969**
Production marketed	20,602
Imports	782
Exports	80
Domestic consumption	20,822

3. *World production and proved reserves:*

	Production 1969	*Proved reserves*
United States	19,322	287,350
Canada	1,643	47,666
Netherlands	514	69,000
Italy	360	6,700
Other Free World	2,141	568,454
Communist countries (except Yugoslavia)	7,049	165,000
World total	31,029	1,144,170

* Billion of Cubic Feet, 14.73 psi @ 60°F.
† Estimated.
‡ Imported from Canada and Mexico.
Source: American Bureau of Metal Statistics; Commodity Data Summaries, U.S. Bureau of Mines.

TABLE 5
Salient features of the crude petroleum industry*

1. *Domestic industry:* Texas, Louisiana and California are the three largest oil producing States, accounting for some 70 percent of the total U.S. domestic production. Alaska is gaining rapidly in importance as an oil producing state. Total value of domestic production in 1968 was approximately $9,795 million. Principal end uses and their percentages of total consumption were: fuel 89.4 percent; petrochemical feedstocks 5.2 percent; asphalt anl road oil 3.0 percent; and miscellaneous uses, including lubricants, 2.4 percent. The largest consuming sector in 1968 was transportation, which accounted for 55.1 percent of all petroleum products consumed; the household and commercial sector was second with 23.4 percent. Electric Utilities consumed 3.8 percent. Petroleum made up 43.3 percent of total energy resources consumed in the United States.

2. The outlook for petroleum demand, during the next 10 to 15 years is for an average growth rate between 3 to 3.5 percent annually. Possible demand levels by year 2000 could range between 7.3 and 16.4 billion barrels annually, depending on economic and technological factors which will determine the mix of energy fuels.

3. The $900 billion Alaska State lease sale portends increasing supplies from large discoveries on the north slope. Plans were announced for a large-diameter pipeline to transport crude oil to the southern part of Valdez.

4. *Salient statistics—United States:*

	1969†
Production	3,362
Imports	516
Exports	3
Domestic demand	3,882
Value: Average at wellhead ($/bbl.)	3.06

5. *World production and proved reserves:*

	Production 1969†	Proved reserves
United States	3,362	31,000
Iran	1,234	50,000
Kuwait	940	71,000
Libya	1,148	25,000
Saudi Arabia	1,092	78,000
Venezuela	1,300	16,000
Other Free World	3,449	112,000
Communist Countries (except Yugoslavia)	2,635	39,000
World Total	15,160	422,000

* Volumes in million barrels (1 barrel contains 42 gallons).
† Estimated.
Source: American Bureau of Metal Statistics; Commodity Data Summaries, U.S. Bureau of Mines.

TABLE 5 (*concluded*)
Petroleum refining and related products

Input–output tables code	1963 direct requirements of the lead industry per dollar of its output from:	Dollars	Value added per dollar of output of the industry indicated in the row
8.00.	Crude petroleum and natural gas	0.47044	0.56475
12.02.	Maintenance and repair construction	0.01655	0.60425
27.01.	Industrial inorganic and organic chemicals	0.02413	0.43481
31.01.	Petroleum refining and related products	0.06775	0.23214
65.04.	Water transportation	0.01233	0.38027
65.06.	Pipe line transportation	0.02514	0.78931
68.02.	.Gas utilities	0.01140	0.35396
69.01.	Wholesale trade	0.01381	0.67589
71.02.	Real estate	0.01982	0.65896
73.02.	Advertising	0.01276	0.09331
	Others	0.09003	
	Value added	0.23214	
	Total	1.00000	

Source: "Input-Output Structure of the U.S. Economy; 1963," U.S. Department of Commerce, December 1969.

1. *Domestic industry:* Over the last several years the domestic steel industry has suffered from low capacity utilization, heavy capital outlays, low-cost European and Japanese imports, and rising labor costs. The total U.S. steel production as a percentage of the world total has also declined from 25.9 percent in 1963 to 22.5 percent in 1969.
2. McLouth Steel Corporation sells some three quarters of its output to the auto industry. The National Steel Corporation, the nation's fourth largest steel maker, relies primarily on automobile and container industries.

TABLE 6
Salient features of the steel industry

1. *Domestic industry:* Over the last several years the domestic steel industry has suffered from low capacity utilization, heavy capital outlays, low-cost European and Japanese imports, and rising labor costs. The total U.S. steel production as a percentage of the world total has also declined from 25.9 percent in 1963 to 22.5 percent in 1969.
2. McLouth Steel Corporation sells some three quarters of its output to the auto industry. The National Steel Corporation, the nation's fourth largest steel maker, relies primarily on automobile and container industries.

Breakdown of 1969 steel product shipments to major markets
(in thousands of net tons)

	Semi-finished steel	Shapes and piling	Plates	Rails	Other railroad products	Bars and tool steel	Pipe and tubing	Wire products	Tin mill products	Hot rolled	Cold rolled	Galvanized	Electric sheets strip	Strip	Net total steel products
Converting and processing	307	27	94	2	1	290	43	1,220	36	652	316	164		85	3,237
Forgings	722		12			514		5		3	8				1,256
Bolts, nuts, rivets, etc.			48			478		443		73		1		39	1,090
Warehouse and distributors	65	1,404	1,342	22	5	1,942	4,545	790	236	2,616	3,005	1,277	32	284	17,565
Const. incl. maint.	125	3,336	2,054	47	13	2,664	2,143	78	26	455	90	335		36	11,402
Contractors' products	6	31	166			416	160	582	37	715	974	1,491		189	4,767
Automotive	502	184	292			2,850	185	273	110	4,625	7,281	1,155	8	811	18,276
Rail transportation	7	405	886	708	644	307	11		1	293	15	41	1	22	3,344
Shipbuilding	3	151	643			43	7	5		43	3	7		1	906
Agriculture	6	38	146			315	35	19	1	266	43	216	20	82	1,167
Machinery and equipment	252	238	1,745	5	8	1,497	462	446	26	454	264	73		200	5,690
Elec. mach. and equip.	1	17	190			163	367	27	22	277	823	136	615	175	2,813
Domestic and comm'l. equip.	2	7	31			151	34	344	174	331	2,411	470	6	225	4,186
Containers	7	1	14			7	5	64	5,618	421	642	54		312	7,145
Other classification	2,745	405	575	46	13	2,717	1,235	580	268	1,247	552	227	43	380	11,033
Total all groups.	4,750	6,244	8,238	830	684	14,354	9,232	4,879	6,555	12,471	16,427	5,647	725	2,841	93,877

Source: Standard and Poor's Industry Analysis, 1970.

APPENDIX C*

Simulated, estimated, incremental national investment and costs related to various strategies for supplying at least one unleaded 91-octane gasoline

Simulated incremental national investment and costs	Case A†	Case B	Case C
Approximate total U.S. differential refinery investment at 1970 gasoline consumption level	$272 million	$6,946 million	$148 million
Approximate total U.S. differential refining cost at 1970 gasoline consumption level. .	$166 million	$5,371 million	$157 million
Increased gasoline refining cost at various refinery capacities			
@ 200,000 barrels/day...........	+0.10 ¢/gal	+4.45 ¢/gal	+0.12 ¢/gal
@ 15,000 barrels/day...........	+0.75 ¢/gal	+11.21 ¢/gal	+0.56 ¢/gal
@ 80,000 barrels/day...........	−0.15 ¢/gal	+4.50 ¢/gal	−0.07 ¢/gal
National average	+0.18 ¢/gal	+5.82 ¢/gal	+0.17 ¢/gal
National average incremental raw material requirements and variable products outputs at 1970 gasoline consumption level.			
a. Total crude demand would increase by (percent)	+2.1	+30.6	1.2
b. Fuel gas output would decrease by (percent)	96.2	207.5	94.2
Economic sensitivities, according to the model, on the basis of national average due to:			
a. An increase of 10¢ bbl on crude oil	+.01 ¢/gal	+0.12 ¢/gal	0
b. 3 percent inflation for 10 years . . .	+.07 ¢/gal	+1.01 ¢/gal	+.04 ¢/gal

* This appendix summarizes the results of a simulation study made for the Department of Transportation. This study analyzes three different gasoline strategies for the simulated configuration of the nation's refineries and retail outlets. The actual costs and investments for each of these cases and their inherent assumptions are described below.

† *Case A* (*a three-pump strategy*): 36 percent 100-octane premium with 2 gm/gal lead max.; 24 percent 94-octane premium with 2 gm/gal lead max.; 40 percent 91-octane unleaded.

‡ *Case B* (*a two-pump strategy, present octanes and unleaded*): 45.8 percent 100-octane unleaded premium; 54.2 percent 94-octane unleaded regular.

§ *Case C* (*alternate two-pump strategy*): 45.8 percent 100-octane premium with 3 cc/gal lead max.; 54.2 percent 91-octane regular with 0.5 cc/gal lead max.

Note: Selected assumptions are (*a*) National average was computed by assigning appropriate weights to 3 typical refinery configurations in 3 U.S. locations assumed to be representative of the present U.S. scene. These weights were 0.60 for a 200,000 barrels per day (BPD) refinery located on the U.S. Gulf Coast, 0.20 for a 15,000 BPD, refinery located on the mid-continent, 0.20 for a 80,000 BPD located on the West Coast; (*b*) 91-octane unleaded gasoline was chosen as the desirable gasoline in the future because it represents, according to the state of current technology, the only method currently available for the control of No_x; (*c*) 20 percent ROI, 10-year straight-line depreciation.

Source: An interim draft of a Special Report, Office of Science and Technology, U.S. Department of Commerce, Washington, D.C.

APPENDIX D
TABLE A°

Changes 1970–80	Case A	Case C
Net increase in sales cost ¢/gallon	0.34	0.84
Refinery investment in $ billion.	1.42	1.21
Lead consumed (billion lbs.).	1.95	3.37
Lead tax† ($ billions).	$5.78	$9.94

TABLE B

Case A–(three pumps)	1971–73	1974–76	1977–80
100 octane	2.0	2.0	0
94 octane	2.0	2.0	0
91 octane	0.5	0	0

Allowable lead levels–gms/gallon

Case C–(two pumps)	1971–73	1974–76	1977–80
100 octane	3.0	3.0	2.0
91 octane	0.5	0	0

* Table A describes for the decade of 1970–80 increase in costs, refinery investment, consumption of lead and the economic effect of proposed lead tax for each of the two strategies that appear to be most economical on the basis of the simulation study shown in Appendix C. These strategies, in terms of Appendix C, are Case A and Case C, with the phasing out of lead gradually between 1971 and 1980. The specific scale for phasing out lead for each of these strategies is shown in Table B.

† Calculated, and discounted to 1970 dollars, (1) on the basis of a lead tax $4.25 per pound as sold by the manufacturer, and (2) permit to use additives containing up to 1 million pounds of lead tax free the first year, that amount to decline by 20 percent per year to expiration.

Source: An interim draft of a Special Report, Office of Science and Technology, U.S. Dept. of Commerce, Washington, D.C.

Volkswagen of America, Inc.[1]

On May 12, 1972, Environmental Protection Agency administrator William D. Ruckelshaus denied requests by Volvo, Inc., International Harvester Co., Chrysler Co., General Motors Corp., and Ford Motor Co. for a one-year suspension of the effective date of emission limitations applicable to 1975 model year automobiles under the Clean Air Amendments Act of 1970.

Ruckelshaus' decision created particularly troublesome problems for Volkswagenwerk AG and its American distribution subsidiary, Volkswagen of America. The unique configuration of the VW engine and its position in the car made pollution-reduction modifications very difficult; and, lack of excess space in the engine compartment prohibited the installation of all pollution-control attachments in current development.

Volkswagen was already burdened by "import surcharges" and currency exchange expenses which were depressing American profits. It now faced increased pressure to reengineer its best-selling vehicle within the 31-month lead-time required to incorporate new design items into its 1975 models.

The clean air amendments act of 1970

On December 31, 1970, the Clean Air Amendments Act of 1970 was signed into law. The act requires a reduction of 90 percent in emissions

[1] This case was prepared by Ira Goldstein and Professor James P. Baughman as the basis for class discussion and is not intended to illustrate either effective or ineffective handling of an administrative situation.

of carbon monoxide (CO) and hydrocarbon (HC) in all newly manufactured vehicles of the 1975 model year, when compared to 1970 standards. In addition, oxides of nitrogen (NOx) are to be cut by at least 90 percent of their 1971 actual average levels by 1976. In recognition that such low levels of these emissions were not obtainable under technology available at the time the act was passed, any manufacturer was given the right to request a one-year suspension of either year's standards. Such a request was to be received and ruled upon by the administrator of the Environmental Protection Agency. Further background on the Clean Air Amendments Act of 1970, the standards and penalties which it sets for noncompliance and police powers granted to the EPA are described in Clean Air Amendments Act of 1970 (A), 9-371-482.

By early 1972, significant industry progress had been made toward development of systems which could filter the proscribed pollutants out of the 1975 vehicles. However, two-year lead-times for America's major manufacturers made decisions necessary in mid-1972 for the 1975 model year, and no system had been even close to successful for the 50,000-mile life required by the act.

By early April the EPA had received requests for one-year suspension of the 1975 standards for Ford, Chrysler, General Motors, Volvo, and International Harvester. Volkswagen of America, Inc., American Motors Corp., Nissan Motors Corp., British Leyland Motors, Inc., Daimler Benz of North America, Toyo Kogyo, Saab-Scania of America, and Toyota Motor Co., Ltd. announced that they would await the outcome of the first set of requests. It was generally agreed that the same decision would apply to all requests, as any single successful system had to be made available to all manufacturers.

Administrator Ruckelshaus described the EPA's job as a bit like "running the 100-yard dash while undergoing an appendectomy." While the American people want cleaner air, no one wants to pay for it. Determining whether the industry had exercised "all good faith efforts . . . to meet the standards," was a difficult question at any time, but nearly impossible to debate in an election year. Additionally, the law required that all available potential power plants be studied by the manufacturers in their efforts to minimize pollutant emission, not just improvements on the gasoline internal combustion engine.

The technology

While investigating other, more radical changes, all major manufacturers' near-term hopes lay with the "catalytic converter." This device attaches to the exhaust of the standard engine, cleaning up the emitted CO and HCs by chemical reaction, before allowing the exhaust's escape into the air. Converters consist of a housing, which encloses a ceramic "substrait" or support on which the actual catalyst, an active metal, is adhered.

The most successfully tested active metal was platinum, which showed the potential to last long enough and remove enough of the pollutants to meet the law's requirements. Englehard Minerals and Chemicals Corp., by the end of May 1972, had received the first major purchase commitment for the devices—a "firm commitment" from Ford Motor Co. for half of Ford's anticipated 1975-model requirements. Although each device uses only 0.1 ounce of platinum, industry adoption of the converter would create a demand for an estimated 1.2 million ounces for 1975 cars; over 25 percent of the current annual world supply of platinum. The converter alone was expected to cost the auto manufacturers about $50 each.

The Diesel engine was considered as one of the potential auto power plants which might yield cleaner exhausts. However, its larger size (for a given horsepower engine), heavier construction (to handle higher pressures), slightly degraded performance, and greater initial expense quickly discouraged major manufacturers.

As early as 1970, the industry had begun paying considerable attention to "the most promising successor to the piston engine," a rotating combustion engine developed by inventor Felix Wankel.

The Wankel engine is an internal combustion, gasoline-fueled engine, but uses a "rotating piston" instead of the standard "up and down" type. Since the apexes of the engine's triangular rotor are always in contact with the housing, they create three separate, variable volumes, each of which undergoes the equivalent of the conventional engine's complete four-stroke cycle in one revolution of the rotor. On the intake stroke a fresh charge of fuel and air enters one of the chambers through the intake port, which is always open. As the rotor turns clockwise the charge is sealed off and compressed as the housing's "epitrochoid" shape causes the compartment volume to shrink. When the charge is fully compressed, it is ignited by the firing of the spark plug (or plugs). The exploding combustion gases drive against the rotor until the exhaust port is uncovered, allowing the spent gases to escape.

For equivalent horsepower, a Wankel engine is only about half the size and weight of a conventional engine because it delivers one power stroke for each rotation of the crankshaft; twice the power-stroke frequency of the conventional piston engine.

The Wankel engine's smaller size and half the number of moving parts carry many advantages. When in mass production it should cost about half as much per horsepower as a conventional engine and will be quieter. "Overall, the Wankel-powered car is expected to weigh from 600 to 1,000 pounds less than the standard car, equivalent to a savings of $600 to $1,000, on the basis that present cars retail at about $1 per pound."

Emission data from existing Wankel engines show that they release only about half as much NOx as piston engines, and comparable amounts of HC and CO. As significant, however, is the new space available for the emissions control devices as a result of the engine's reduced size. Additionally, catalytic converters work better with the Wankel than with the piston engine because it heats up "almost instantly" and burns hotter, thereby letting the cleaning device "burn off" pollutants more efficiently.

In 1970, General Motors negotiated a nonexclusive licensing agreement for development and production of Wankels, paying $50 million to Curtiss-Wright for the license. By early 1972 plans were being made for a test run of 1974 Vegas, and a limited Wankel production run, possibly by 1976.

Other solutions to the emissions dilemma were being discussed within the industry, although none seemed to hold the short-term promise of the catalytic converter or long-term potential of the Wankel. These longer-term possibilities are summarized in *Note on Automotive Engine Technology* 9-372-266.

Volkswagenwerk AG and emission controls

Volkswagen of America, along with other major world auto and emissions control manufacturers and experts, was subpoenaed to appear before the EPA hearings into Ford, Chrysler, General Motors, Volvo, and International Harvester's requests for a one-year extension.

The hearings were held during April and May 1972 and investigated each manufacturer's test program and results in depth. Of prime importance to the EPA hearing examiners were the questions: Will any single company or device have the capability to satisfy the standards by 1975? Have the applicants shown "all good faith efforts to meet the standards," regardless of expense or impact upon other aspects of their business? The Volkswagen test program was discussed relative to both questions. Because the company was not then an applicant, major emphasis was placed on the former question.

On April 10 and 11 Arthur Railton represented Volkswagen of America at the hearings, accompanied by his Manager for Emissions and Development. Because VW of America manufactures no cars itself, but is a wholly owned importing and distributing subsidiary of Volkswagenwerk AG (Germany), Mr. Railton was also accompanied by the parent's Managers of the Engine and Emission Control Systems Testing (also Senior Engineer) and Government Liaison for Environmental Affairs.

·In the six months prior to the hearing, VW had made 250 low-mileage emission tests on the four systems under consideration to meet 1975 and 1976 U.S. standards. A "fuel injection"[2] system with NO_x and HC/CO converters and a "VW reactor" was considered, as well as a carburetor with the same devices. The "VW reactor" was a device to heat up the converters, thereby increasing their efficiencies. The third system considered was transfer to a water-cooled engine with carburetor and NO_x and HC/CO converters. No reactor would be required here. The fourth system was an "advanced" fuel-injection system with one combined NO_x/HC/CO converter. Primary focus had been placed on the carburetor, NO_x and HC/CO Converter with VW reactor.

Volkswagen had concluded that power sources other than internal combustion engines would not be ready "in the immediate future." Although electric and gas turbine power had been considered, neither showed short-term promise. Volkswagen was spending $6 million a year developing the Wankel engine for use in its cars, a major internal change expected in the near future, but not in time for the 1975 and 1976 standards. Volkswagenwerk AG, through its ownership of Audi-NSU Auto Union AG held the patent rights to the engine, and was therefore "in the middle of Wankel development."

It is commonly accepted in mass-production industries that prototype vehicles' performance will generally exceed actual production-line models by some "slippage percentage" attributable to the difference in care taken in manufacture and assembly. Although no figures were available on the proposed automobiles' expected "prototype to production slippage" relative to emissions controls, VW was using 30 percent, based on past VW historical data. In addition, the converters were expected to deteriorate 40 to 55 percent over their 20,000-mile life (VW would require replacement each 20,000 miles). Thus, the prototypes currently tested would have to *exceed* the emission standards by 70 to 85 percent in order to assure that most production units met the standards.

Time was a major consideration: 1975 models had to be ready for production by mid-1974. To reach that point, new design items required 24 months after management approval, which had to be preceded by 7 months of required durability testing. Thus, new systems intended for 1975 models had to be designated by the beginning of 1972. At the time of the hearings no emissions control system had come close to being ready to begin durability testing.

By the beginning of 1972, VW emission testing was being performed on 35 cars for 1975 requirements. Of these, however, only three were being run to test the converter itself. Greater quantities had been run at earlier times; however, mechanical failure of the catalyst's support

---

[2] "Fuel injection" is an advanced method of mixing fuel and air into the cylinders, and replaces the standard carburetor on many "high-performance" type cars.

material (substrate) at lower mileage ranges continually forced an end to the testing below 2,000 miles. Breakage of the ceramic substrate had become the principal problem impeding progress of the test program, and was all the worse because it was a problem uniquely VW's. Because the VW exhaust system was part of the engine, which was located to the rear of the car, the emissions controls had to be placed directly on the engine. However, VW's engine was a unique, four-cylinder "opposed piston" engine, which vibrated much more than most others. It was this vibration which was causing the ceramic supports to crumble. While other "foreign" companies had achieved much better results, VW was "stopped" at 2,000 to 3,000 miles until a solution could be found. (Volvo, for instance, reported good results up to 22,000 miles.)

VW engineers reported that they required successful testing up to 50,000 miles, proven by at least 20 cars, before a catalyst would be "acceptable." Checking of emissions had been stopped, however, as a solution to the mechanical support problem was sought. Although 35 cars were currently equipped with catalysts for testing, only 3 of these were "on the track," being driven 24 hours per day to test the new support systems for the catalyst. The three cars had put on 10,000 to 15,000 kilometers by the time of the hearing. Emissions measurement would begin on the 32 remaining cars when the original 3 completed "about 40,000 to 50,000 kilometers," estimated to take an additional three months.

Volkswagen could do little of its own research into the support problem, as most of the ceramics skill was held exclusively by the suppliers. Their substrate supplier, American Lava Corp., a subsidiary of Minnesota Mining and Manufacturing, had recently developed an improved support substrate. However, industry testing demands in America made it difficult for a European manufacturer such as VW to obtain. By early April none of the improved substrates had been received.

VW's emissions controls laboratory testing had indicated that many other less technical but highly critical problems remained to be solved. There were major space problems—little space remained available for required devices without cutting into passenger or luggage room, and heat dissipation was very difficult within the small confines of the VW engine compartment. Fuel consumption was expected to increase 20 percent over 1974 models, with an accompanying performance decrease of 10 to 25 percent (hestitation during acceleration was a major concern). The fire hazard, previously mentioned, had to be dealt with. Finally, extensive and thorough maintenance of the emissions system would be essential, and the act seemed to place the burden for this on the manufacturer for the first 50,000 miles.

Other auto manufacturers gave testimony similar to, and generally almost as pessimistic as Volkswagen's. Supporting their requests for an extension, the companies pointed to two government studies which suggested that extensions be granted.

In January 1972, The National Academy of Sciences, in it study required by Section 202(c)(1) of the Clean Air Act, reported: "While there is no certainty today that any 1975 model year vehicles will meet the requirements of the act, the status of development and rate of progress make it possible that the larger manufacturers will be able to produce vehicles that will qualify." The NAS stated that this possibility depended upon three actions by the federal government: (1) "The Government must alter its regulations for testing . . . to allow for replacement before 50,000 miles;" (2) "The Government must guarantee the availability of gasoline with 'suitably low levels' of lead and other elements that 'poison' the catalyst;" (3) "The Government must allow for an 'averaging' of emissions [rather than testing each one] . . . , because some engines may emit slightly more pollution than the law allows and some slightly less." By the time of the hearings, the first two actions had been taken by the EPA. However, averaging was still seriously in question.

But the NAS report also warned that the emissions controls could increase 1975 car prices $200 over 1973 retail prices, increase maintenance costs and fuel consumption, and impair engine performance. Therefore, the report suggested a year's postponement of the standards to allow manufacturers to prove performance with the antipollution devices.

A month later, the White House Office of Science and Technology issued a report entitled *Cumulative Regulatory Effects on the Cost of Automotive Transportation,* which was also welcomed by Detroit as support for the postponement requested. The report estimated that pollution control and safety requirements will add $722 to the average retail price of 1976 models, compared with 1971 cars: $317 for emissions control and $405 for safety features. Specifically, the White House study recommends that:

> Instead of requiring auto makers to meet the strict emission ceilings slated for 1975 and 1976 models on a nationwide basis, "a sounder approach" for Congress would be to adopt a "two-car strategy." This would permit the sale of lower-cost, higher-emission cars in regions where air pollution is less critical, in addition to the low-emission models that would be required for California and more urbanized zones with the dirtiest air.
>
> Alternatively, control costs could be reduced if Congress raised the nitrogen oxides ceiling of 0.4 gram a mile currently required of 1976 models. The study says a limit of one to two grams a mile wouldn't appear to materially harm air-quality-improvement efforts "in many regions."

The report claims that the auto costs will outweigh the benefits, under present law. It concludes:

> A regulatory attitude of establishing standards beyond the known state of the art on the theory that industry can do anything if enough pressure is put on it isn't likely . . . to provide the greatest net benefits to society. While regulatory agencies shouldn't hesitate to push reluctant industries to make use of available technology, they shouldn't presume that major breakthroughs in technology are there simply for the taking if enough money is expended.

An Environmental Protection Agency official disagreed strongly with study's conclusions, saying, "there are a lot of uncertainties" in the assumption underlying the emission control findings.

The economics of auto pollution control

The question of the actual economic impact of controls on auto costs and the ultimate result which price changes would have on Volkswagen's position in the U.S. market was subject to extensive debate, depending on one's sources and estimates. However, since 558,029 of Volkswagen and subsidiaries' total 2,317,385 unit sales in 1971 were in the United States,[3] the question was of significant concern to the company.

Although the catalyst itself would reputedly cost $50 or less, the entire emissions-control system, was estimated, would add from $317 to $500 to the purchase price of a 1976 automobile, over its 1972 price. The EPA estimated that regulation would increase 1972 prices by about $400 by 1976, causing a decrease of 3 percent (or approximately 420,000 units) in what 1976 sales would otherwise be, and slipping the rate of real GNP growth from an expected 5.2 percent to 4.9 percent, with the emission controls, over the next five years. Charles Heim, Chrysler Corporation's top emission specialist, catalogued his company's expected price increase as follows:

```
For engine changes required to accommodate controls  . . . . . .  $125
For catalyst materials  . . . . . . . . . . . . . . . . . . . . . . . . .    50
For catalyst system development and manufacturing  . . . . . . .   325
   Total impact  . . . . . . . . . . . . . . . . . . . . . . . . . . . . .   500
```

Business Week reported that the replacement cost of the Englehard catalyst and system favored by Ford and Chrysler would be as much as $300 per car.

Even the available technology for testing the cars prior to delivery from the factory was expected to be exceptionally costly. Eric O. Stork, director of the EPA's Division of Mobile Source Pollution Control estimated that, with 1972 capabilities, each car will take at least 12 hours

---

[3] Figures include VW, Audi, and Porsche sales.

preparation time plus 1 hour testing labor to be tested for emissions. Not only would this put a terrific burden on the manufacturers, but the EPA's current staff would have to be expanded by several orders of magnitude. The EPA laboratory staff at Ann Arbor, assigned to monitor certification of hundreds of cars for 50,000 miles each numbered ten in 1972. They were charged with testing the output of the four U.S. manufacturers and "scores" of importers.

In a report prepared for the Council on Environmental Quality, Department of Commerce, and EPA, the Chase Econometric Associates investigated the expected impact of auto emission controls through 1977. They estimated that controls would be $351.50 of the 1976–1977 auto manufacturer's cost per car, an increase of $317 over his 1972 cost (Exhibit 1 details the controls plus costs).

Because the change in cost for emissions control will be roughly constant for all cars, the marginal impact will be greater the cheaper the car price. According to the Chase study, for Volkswagen's "Subcompact" category the change in marginal cost for emissions systems was expected to average almost 13 percent of the 1976 car price, requiring that the manufacturer absorb about 16 percent of the cost increase himself (Exhibit 2). This inequity, according to the study, is expected to alter individual segments' shares of market as well as total market size (Exhibits 3 and 4). The authors even predicted a new class of car, "class zero," possibly beginning to sell in 1974–1975. This "sub-sub compact" would be expected in accordance with trends of the last 15 years, and in response to pressures for cheaper cars as a result of safety and emissions price impact. A "motorcycle with a roof" might have an engine small enough to meet pollution requirements with no added controls and might be suitable for downtown or station driving.

The "throwaway car" is another possibility. It would last only 10,000 to 15,000 miles, enabling great manufacturing and maintenance saving due to lack of durability requirements. Any of the "sub-sub compacts" were sure to pose tremendous competition for Volkswagen.

The Ruckelshaus decision

The industry had many reasons to expect that EPA administrator Ruckelshaus would grant their requested extension. Not only was he considered a "friend and protégé" of Attorney General John Mitchell, who was expected to be a prime force in President Nixon's reelection bid that year, but Ruckelschaus himself was reportedly considering running for governor of Indiana on the Republican ticket in November. This would be an unwise time to "clamp-down" on big business, especially with the excess of data and government reports supporting the requests.

However, Ruckelshaus rejected the five companies' requests on May

12, stating that they had failed to substantiate their contentions that "present control technology is not available to meet the act's requirements for 1975 cars." The administrator said: "Although auto manufacturers demonstrated difficulties in their efforts to reduce exhaust pollutants, they haven't established that the technology doesn't exist. Impressive progress has been achieved in controlling auto emissions by a variety of control systems employing catalysts. Our analysis of all data suggests the technology may well be available for the 1975 cars to meet these standards." One key concession was made, however—the EPA reiterated its assurance that it would allow the replacement of catalysts "at least once during 50,000 miles of vehicle operation if that is necessary." Averaging of emissions was still not to be allowed.

The postponement denial was based upon several less-pessimistic test reports uncovered at the hearings, testimony of various catalyst manufacturers, and the question of whether the industry had exercised "all possible efforts" to meet the standards. Five Ford and two Chrysler test cars had shown very promising results in road testing with catalytic converters. The Chrysler cars, in particular, fell "well within the standards" after 40,000 and 43,000 miles, respectively. The 43,000-mile vehicle, a Plymouth Fury with a V-8 engine, was fitted with a catalyst made by Engelhard and was still operating below 1975 emission ceilings at the end of the 43,000-mile test.

During their testimony before the EPA panel Chrysler officials downgraded the test's importance. They said the car had been "babied" to provide the most favorable conditions for catalyst performance. Vice president S. L. Terry claimed that technicians had made "special carburetor adjustments and spark plug changes every 5,000 miles," and that a device had been installed that warned the driver when the catalyst was overheating, so he could reduce the speed of the car.

The optimistic testimony of both major catalyst manufacturers, as well as Toyo Kogyo Company, manufacturer of the Japanese Mazda, were also instrumental in Ruckelshaus' decision. Executives of Engelhard testified that they already had a device good for 1975 standards up to 23,000 miles; and Mathey Bishop Inc., a subsidiary of Johnson Mathey and Company of England, boasted a device good for 20,000 miles.

Testimony of Toyo Kogyo was significant, as the company's Wankel-powered Mazda provided the only actual data base for the new rotary engine. Based upon their experience and data from 20,000 Mazdas with thermal reactor emission controls systems sold to date in North America, the company said that it "may be able to meet 1975 standards with the Wankel engine."

The industry, Mr. Ruckelshaus said, had failed to meet the Clean Air Amendments Act's "good faith" clause on two counts: (1) The industry didn't build adequate test facilities to capably test at the required quantities; and (2) the catalyst manufacturers had not received sufficient "support" from the auto industry, on whose shoulders the legal responsibility fell.

The "Big Three" had reportedly decided to seek a federal court review of the EPA decision. Any manufacturer was still free to submit its own request for a one-year postponement, despite the denial of the first five requests. Those five could reapply any time new information materially changed the situation.

Volkswagenwerk AG

As Volkswagenwerk and its U.S. subsidiary faced the emission decision they sat in the midst of their worst year for both American and world sales in recent memory. A five-year condensed statement of earnings and balance sheet is presented in Exhibit 5: 1972 sales within the United States were expected to number between 420,000 and 470,000 VWs, plus 45,000 Porsches and Audis, as compared to 520,630 VWs and 37,400 Porsches and Audis the previous year. Competition among imports during 1968–1971 is summarized in Exhibit 6.

VW profit continued to decline in the first quarter of 1972, after a sharp plunge from $126.2 million in 1970 to $45.6 million in 1971. Despite continued claims that "the company isn't in a crisis," production was halted in January for five days due to lagging worldwide sales, and price increases were seen as "almost certain" in an attempt to keep the company out of the red. Higher labor costs, declining domestic and U.S. demand and declining foreign revenues were blamed.

More specific to U.S. sales, VW's price advantage over domestic U.S. manufacturers virtually disappeared in 1971. As a result of the May revaluation of the Deutsche Mark its value rose over 10 percent relative to the dollar. This together with the August introduction of President Nixon's import surcharge increased the German imports' U.S. price by approximately $200. Removal of the 7 percent auto excise tax dropped the average U.S. domestic price by $50, thus leaving a $250 increase in the VW's price relative to its U.S. domestic competition. VW's 1971 auto operations ran at a loss, saved from the income statement by "peripheral" operations which covered the deficit. By the middle of 1972 a decrease of almost 6 percent in plant manpower was announced and attributed to sales declines.

The impact of U.S. safety and emissions regulation upon VW operations was considerable. While no estimates were available for potential emissions control systems, because no system was yet considered satisfactory, the company's chairman estimated that U.S. safety requirements alone will increase 1975 VW prices 25 percent in the United States.

"Safety requirements were already boosting the costs of each car about $186," Chairman Rudolf Leiding said. "A good third of the more than 300 detail changes to the VW for the 1972 model year was concerned with improvements in this field [auto emissions and safety]."[4]

Volkswagen hoped that the recent lifting of the U.S. import surcharge, allowing the "Beetle" model to be bought for under $2,000, would help 1972 U.S. sales. The Beetle, and recently the Super Beetle, were the "bread and butter" of the VW line. Although least expensive and, therefore, offering lowest margins, the worldwide quantity of "Bug" sales sustained the organization. The Beetle sold for $1,999; the Super Beetle for $2,159. The organization was attempting to move sales into more expensive Porsches and Audis, retailing as low as $3,900 and $3,085, in an attempt to increase profit margins. The rest of the three lines were VW's Karmann Ghia ($2,750) and VW-411 ($3,275); Porsche's 911-T ($7,367), 911-E ($7,995), and 911-5 ($9,495); and Audi's Super 90 ($3,085), 100 ($3,595), 100-LS ($3,745), and 100-GL (4,245).[5] Major competition was expected to continue from those makes summarized in Exhibits 6–8. Chairman Leiding had good reason to ponder the future of his company's American market share.

---

[4] Volkswagen of America Company 1971 annual report.

[5] East Coast U.S. Port of Entry prices, March 1, 1972.

EXHIBIT 1
Estimated investment costs for alternative mobile source emission controls
for automobiles and light-duty trucks

Model year	Controls added	Cost per new vehicle (dollars)	Cumulative costs (dollars)
1967	None	0.00	0.00
1968–69	Closed PCV system (above cost of open system)		
	Carburetor changes		
	Ignition timing changes.		
	Inlet air temperature control	5.40	
			5.40
1970	Additional carburetor changes.		
	Idle control solenoid		
	Ignition timing changes.	7.40	
			12.80
1971	Evaporative emission control		
	Improved idle control solenoid with overheat protection (above 1968–70 costs) including transmission spark control		
	Lower-compression ratios		
	Additional carburetor changes.	19.70	
			32.50
1972	Valve and valve seat changes for unleaded gasoline . . .	2.00	
			34.50
1973–74	Exhaust gas recirculation for NO_x control, fixed orifice system		
	Speed controlled spark advance	48.00	
			82.50
1975	Catalytic oxidation of exhaust HC and CO (includes long-life exhaust system).		
	Unitized ignition systems for 50,000-mile service-free performance.		
	Air injection for catalytic unit needs	164.00	
			246.50
1976–77	Dual catalyst units for HC, CO oxidation and NO_x reduction (additional cost above previous controls which are supplanted)		
	Modified manifold reactors to reduce catalyst load. . . .	105.00	
			$351.50

Source: Report on "Automobiles" by Chase Econometric Associates in *The Economic Impact of Pollution Control: A Summary of Recent Studies.* Prepared for the Council on Environmental Quality, Department of Commerce, and Environmental Protection Agency (Washington: GPO, March 1972).

EXHIBIT 2
Pass-along proportions by size-price classification

Class number and name	Change in marginal cost as a percent of 1976 price	Pass-along proportion of price increase for unit cost increase (percent)
I. Subcompact	12.8	84
II. Compact	10.3	90
III. Standard-size regular	9.3	90
IV. Intermediate	8.1	90
V. Luxury	5.4	98

Note: Volkswagen automobiles compete primarily in Class No. 1.
Source: Report on "Automobiles."

EXHIBIT 3
Macroeconomic and auto sales projections, 1970–1980

Year	GNP baseline	P baseline	UN baseline	NPCR baseline	NPCR impact
1970	720.0	116.3	5.0	8.44	8.44
1971	741.9	121.2	5.9	10.32	10.32
1972	785.7	124.8	5.4	11.17	11.17
1973	836.1	129.8	4.9	11.91	11.83
1974	875.5	135.5	4.7	12.37	12.30
1975	906.6	141.5	4.8	12.68	12.36
1976	952.8	147.0	4.4	13.31	12.89
1977	996.2	153.0	4.4	13.60	13.27
1978	1038.4	159.0	4.4	13.90	13.65
1979	1083.4	164.6	4.4	14.24	14.04
1980	1131.1	169.9	4.5	14.53	14.35

Note: GNP = Gross national product, 1958 dollars
P = Consumer price index, 1967 = 100
UN = Unemployment rate (percent)
NPCR = New passenger car registrations (millions)
Baseline = Projections assuming *no* emission control standards
Impact = Projections assuming emission control standards
Source: Report on "Automobiles."

EXHIBIT 4
Impact of emission-control standards on new passenger car
registrations by size-price classification

Class by year	Baseline registrations (millions)	Net gain (loss) due to change in share	Net loss due to decline in total market	Registrations after emission controls (millions)
Class I (subcompact)				
1970	1.698	0	0	1.698
1971	1.773	0	0	1.773
1972	1.606	0	0	1.606
1973	1.847	−.007	−.013	1.827
1974	2.062	−.006	−.012	2.044
1975	2.156	−.024	−.054	2.078
1976	2.289	−.036	−.071	2.182
1977	2.366	−.035	−.057	2.274
1978	2.446	−.036	−.043	2.367
1979	2.536	−.036	−.036	2.464
1980	2.615	−.036	−.032	2.547
Class II (compact)				
1970	2.083	0	0	2.083
1971	2.619	0	0	2.619
1972	2.979	0	0	2.979
1973	3.174	.010	−.021	3.163
1974	3.297	.010	−.019	3.288
1975	3.380	.037	−.085	3.332
1976	3.550	.057	−.113	3.494
1977	3.627	.057	−.089	3.595
1978	3.704	.057	−.067	3.694
1979	3.794	.056	−.054	3.796
1980	3.872	.058	−.048	3.882
Class III (standard-size regular)				
1970	2.169	0	0	2.169
1971	2.658	0	0	2.658
1972	2.953	0	0	2.953
1973	3.064	−.036	−.021	3.007
1974	3.095	−.036	−.018	3.041
1975	3.094	−.155	−.074	2.865
1976	3.160	−.232	−.092	2.836
1977	3.135	−.288	−.071	2.836
1978	3.115	−.229	−.052	2.834
1979	3.093	−.231	−.040	2.822
1980	3.059	−.234	−.035	2.790
Class IV (intermediate)				
1970	1.674	0	0	1.674
1971	2.215	0	0	2.215
1972	2.443	0	0	2.443
1973	2.548	.005	−.017	2.536
1974	2.572	.005	−.015	2.562
1975	2.537	−.001	−.064	2.472
1976	2.619	−.008	−.083	2.528
1977	2.564	.005	−.062	2.507
1978	2.487	.019	−.045	2.461

EXHIBIT 4 (*continued*)

Class by year	Baseline registrations (millions)	Net gain (loss) due to change in share	Net loss due to decline in total market	Registrations after emission controls (millions)
1979	2.411	.038	−.034	2.415
1980	2.341	.037	−.029	2.349
Class V (luxury)				
1970	.816	0	0	.816
1971	1.055	0	0	1.055
1972	1.188	0	0	1.188
1973	1.276	.011	−.009	1.278
1974	1.343	.011	−.008	1.346
1975	1.404	.042	−.036	1.410
1976	1.487	.076	−.048	1.515
1977	1.545	.063	−.038	1.570
1978	1.608	.060	−.029	1.639
1979	1.679	.058	−.024	1.713
1980	1.741	.058	−.022	1.777

Source: Report on "Automobiles."

EXHIBIT 5
VOLKSWAGEN OF AMERICA, INC.
Condensed balance sheet and earnings statement
Volkswagenwerk AG, subsidiaries, and affiliates
BALANCE SHEET (condensed)

	1967	1968	1969	1970	1971
Assets:					
Property, plant, and equipment	3,137	3,188	3,639	4,187	4,905
Investments	100	101	230	427	584
Inventories	1,229	1,352	1,710	2,128	2,496
Receivables and the like	529	637	987	1,265	1,457
Liquid funds	623	1,141	1,142	1,035	673
Own stock	—	—	—	—	40
Total Assets	5,618	6,419	7,708	9,042	10,155
Liabilities:					
Capital stock	750	750	750	900	900
Reserves	1,891	2,237	2,588	2,578	2,627
Minority interest in consolidated					
subsidiaries	97	113	272	238	189
Old-age pensions	285	338	433	519	630
Other undetermined liabilities	649	883	1,071	1,345	1,596
Liabilities payable within more than					
4 years	311	281	292	305	413
within 1 to 4 years	141	102	217	281	268
within 1 year	1,339	1,538	1,908	2,696	3,442
Net earnings after reserve transfers					
of VW AG	150	171	167	167	81
Minority interest in earnings to be					
distributed	5	6	10	13	9
Total Capital	5,618	6,419	7,708	9,042	10,155

STATEMENT OF EARNINGS (condensed)

Gross output	9,289	11,837	14,250	16,263	17,925
Cost of materials	5,347	6,619	7,855	9,356	10,072
Labor cost	1,898	2,319	2,920	3,646	4,416
Depreciation and write-down	496	619	691	836	912
Taxes	734	1,128	1,476	1,161	1,113
on income, earnings, and property	305	687	820	538	421
Sundry expenses less sundry income	491	612	828	857	1,265
Net earnings	323	540	480	407	147
Dividend of VW AG	150	150	167	167	81

Note: Figures in millions of DM. DM per U.S. dollar (spot rate at year end except for 1972 which is at end of first quarter) = 4.000 (1968); 3.690 (1969); 3.648 (1970); 3.268 (1971); 3.168 (1972).

Source: Volkswagen of America, Inc., annual company reports.

EXHIBIT 6
Sales of imported cars in United States

1963		1969		1970		1971	
Volkswagen	563,522	Volkswagen	537,933	Volkswagen	569,182	Volkswagen	509,207
Opel	80,366	Toyota	117,384	Toyota	184,898	Toyota	270,512
Toyota	68,779	Opel	91,161	Datsun	100,541	Datsun	182,058
Datsun	40,219	Datsun	58,569	Opel	83,189	Opel	85,554
Volvo	38,335	Fiat	41,519	Volvo	44,630	Capri	53,219
Fiat	28,377	Volvo	36,448	Fiat	36,642	Volvo	47,012
Mercedes Benz	23,724	Mercedes Benz	24,693	MG	30,548	Fiat	42,621
English Ford	22,983	MG	21,806	Mercedes Benz	28,743	Mercedes Benz	32,651
Renault	19,359	English Ford	20,750	Renault	19,589	MG	30,950
Standard Triumph	18,600	Renault	17,735	Capri	15,628	Colt	26,503
All others	81,503	All others	93,619	All others	117,371	All others	185,386
Total	985,767	Total	1,061,617	Total	1,230,961	Total	1,465,673

Source: *Ward's Automotive Yearbook* analysis of new car registrations based on R. L. Polk & Co.'s statistical reports.

EXHIBIT 7
"Captive" import car sales
(includes U.S. and European deliveries)

Make	Distributor	1970	1971
Capri	Lincoln-Mercury	17,316	56,118
Colt.	Dodge	0	28,381
Cortina	Ford	10,328	757
Cricket	Chrysler-Plymouth	0	27,682
Opel	Buick	85,995	87,712
Pantera	Lincoln-Mercury	0	130
Simca	Chrysler-Plymouth	6,670	4,778
Rootes	Chrysler-Plymouth	3,192	330
Total		123,501	205,888

Source: *Ward's Automotive Yearbook.*

EXHIBIT 8
New car registrations of U.S. domestically produced Class I
automobiles retailing under $2,630

Make	1968	1969	1970	1971
Compact size:				
Pontiac Ventura II	0	0	0	47,896
Chevy II/Nova.	187,515	263,981	246,553	251,223
Chevrolet Corvair	12,977	4,280	0	0
Ford Falcon	139,944	97,990	35,596	19,885
Plymouth Valiant	81,815	90,001	246,013	246,417
Dodge Dart	159,180	165,047	202,890	231,618
AMC Hornet	84,208	88,476	84,000	67,052
Ford Maverick	0	213,784	342,198	247,626
Mercury Comet 72	0	0	0	62,373
Total	665,639	923,559	1,157,250	1,174,090
Percent of total U.S. registrations				
(including imports)	7.1	9.8	13.8	12.1
Subcompact size:				
Chevrolet Vega	0	0	22,520	323,443
Ford Pinto	0	0	76,038	328,275
AMC Gremlin	0	0	39,701	70,096
Total			138,259	721,814
Percent of total U.S. registrations				
(including imports)	0.0	0.0	7.4	1.6

Note: Ford's Torino, although it lists for under $2,630 is omitted because it is neither compact nor subcompact.

Sources: *Ward's Automotive Yearbook* and *Automotive News 1972 Almanac.*

EXHIBIT 9
U.S. total new car registrations, 1955–1971

Year	Total	Foreign market share
1955	7,169,908	0.8
1956	5,955,248	1.7
1957	5,982,342	3.4
1958	4,654,515	8.1
1959	6,041,275	10.2
1960	6,576,650	7.6
1961	5,854,747	6.5
1962	6,938,863	4.9
1963	7,556,717	5.1
1964	8,065,150	6.0
1965	9,313,912	6.1
1966	9,008,488	7.3
1967	8,357,421	9.3
1968	9,403,862	10.5
1969	9,446,524	11.2
1970	8,388,204	14.7
1971	9,729,109	15.1

Source: *Ward's Automotive Yearbook.*

A case study in resource development: The Trans-Alaska Pipeline[1]

Everything about Alaska is extreme. It is physically as big as Texas, California and Montana combined—586,000 sq. mi. . . . Alaska's 33,000 mile coastline doubles that of all the co-terminous United States. While Port Walter in the southern panhandle is flooded by 18 feet of annual rainfall, the wind dried North Slope is an Arctic desert that gets only four inches of precipitation per year. At Fort Yukon in the vast central plateau region temperatures plummet from 100° in the summer to 75° below zero in the winter. To travel from the state capital of Juneau to the outermost Aleutian island of Attu is to span 2,000 miles and four time zones. Yet Alaska has fewer people than any other state: 293,000. . . . [2]

Described both as America's newest and last frontier, the state of Alaska has served as the locus for one of the most significant and controversial issues facing the United States. Since 1969 the State of Alaska, the federal government, the oil industry, and environmentalists have endeavored to influence the development of Alaska's vast untapped resources, particularly its oil reserves. The eventual resolution of this issue will embody enormous implications both for the state of Alaska and for the course of future resource development in the United States and, perhaps, the world.

---

[1] This case was prepared by Michael C. Brooks, under the direction of Howard W. Pifer, lecturer on Business Administration, as the basis for class discussion rather than to illustrate effective or ineffective handling of an administrative situation.

[2] "The Great Land: Boom or Doom," *Time,* July 27, 1970.

History of Alaska

That Alaska provided a focus for so major an issue was ironic considering its virtually anonymous existence as a territory of the United States. Purchased from Russia in 1867 for the sum of $7.2 million (less than two cents per acre) the area was derided as "Seward's Folly" and "Seward's Ice Box" by those members of Congress who opposed its acquisition by Secretary of State Seward. Some assumed that the United States bought the area but actually the purchase agreement gave the federal government the right to govern and tax the inhabitants, leaving the land ownership in the hands of the natives. This provision had particular significance over a century later.

Alaska, lacking a government at the time of purchase, was administered successively by the Department of War, the Department of the Treasury, and the United States Navy. In 1884 the laws of Oregon were extended to the "district" as part of the Organic Statute, but the area remained virtually ignored until the Yukon and Nome gold rushes at the turn of the century. Followed by the Cordova copper rush, this ruthless prospecting put Alaska on the map and Congress formally declared Alaska a United States territory in 1912 and authorized the establishment of a limited territorial government.

Alaska had the status of an "organized territory" yet its powers were far more limited than those of the previous continental territories. Alaskans exerted pressure for changes but Congress remained reluctant to alter the situation. Finally, responding to increasing pressure and an awareness of the area's natural resources, Congress passed the Alaska Statehood Act in 1958, enabling Alaska to become the 49th state on January 3, 1959. One of the act's major provisions granted the state of Alaska the right to withdraw from the federal domain 103 of the 365 million acres within the state, subject to federal approval.

The congressional intent of this land selection provision was to provide the state with land from which it could derive revenues to finance the state government. The state would receive 100 percent of the revenues and royalties from mineral leases on its own lands, but only 90 percent from those on federal lands. Accordingly Alaska has endeavored to select the prime mineral areas for itself, but with limited success. There was a wealth of untapped mineral resources in the form of significant deposits of coal, iron, chromite, lead, tungsten, tin, and platinum. However, despite the state's mineral wealth, fishing provided the greatest revenues and the military remained the biggest employer.

The construction of military bases during World War II provided Alaska with a new source of income. During the 1950s defense investment continued with the construction of DEW (Distance Early Warning) stations along Alaska's coast. The fishing and timber industries grew stronger during the postwar period, but the federal government soon became the biggest employer in Alaska providing over 60 percent of the state's funds, employing over 50 percent of its labor force, and controlling 97 percent of the land.

There were no formal explorations for oil in Alaska until World War II. Responding to security considerations, the United States government delegated the Navy to develop a local supply of crude oil to support the military forces within the territory. This led to the initiation of exploratory efforts on Naval Petroleum Reserve #4, a large federally owned area due west of Prudhoe Bay on the North Slope of Alaska (see map of Alaska Exhibit 1).

After the war a number of oil concerns commenced exploratory efforts for oil throughout the territory. Some of the wildcat efforts produced oil and gas discoveries, but they were never large enough to justify large scale activity. The first breakthrough occurred in 1957, when Richfield Oil Corporation discovered substantial reserves on the Kenai Peninsula. This discovery led to the first commercial production of Alaskan oil, and the news of the discovery attracted other oil companies. Although the discovery scarcely improved Alaska's weak, regional economy it facilitated the fight for statehood: "Oil led the way for statehood. Washington pundits note that for the first six years of the Fifties, statehood for Alaska was a dead issue. Oil was discovered in 1957, and statehood was granted in 1959.[3] The next decade represented a period of considerable growth, both in population and economic development. (See Exhibit 2 for detailed demographic comparison.)

The economy and the people

Alaskans had exhibited a unique sense of independence, a provincial self-sufficiency which distinguished the state from the "lower 48." This perspective evolved as much from Alaska's remote location as from the distinctive life style which the severe climate forced upon its inhabitants. This independence served both as a source of pride and a cause for resentment. Whereas most other states were able to join together for specific projects, particularly in the transportation, communications, and energy fields, the State of Alaska was generally compelled to "go it alone." Providing services for an area one fifth the size of the continental United States, with a population density of only 4 people per square mile (the national average was 60 people per square mile), was both demanding and costly, resulting in Alaska's debt burden, the state's debt per capita becoming one of the highest in the country. The state budget, relatively consistent during the 1960s, more than doubled in

---

[3] "Alaska's $50-Billion Boom," *Forbes*, November 15, 1969. p. 30.

1970, and in 1971 Alaska spent $300 million while receiving less than $200 million in taxes and investment income.

Alaska's economy, despite the growth of the service and oil industries, remained underdeveloped and highly seasonal with small-scale industrial growth. The federal government remained the largest employer, and renewable resources such as harvesting, fishing, and timber dominated the private sector. However, both the fishing and timber industries encountered difficulties: The state's "father and son" fishing fleet was being outmoded by the Russians and Japanese, and the state did not yet possess facilities for producing building materials to meet the standards of the Federal Housing Administration. Traditionally, capital accumulated in Alaska moved out of the state, leaving insufficient funds to finance home-grown industry. Ted Stevens, Alaska's Republican senator, expressed the hope that oil money could be used as "seed capital to get industries moving within the state." Additionally, the state had promising mineral extraction and tourist industries, which also could be enhanced by the investment of oil money. However, despite recent interest from the "lower 48," Alaska's major trading partner was neighboring Japan, which accounted for 87 percent of Alaska's $100 million in annual exports.

To judge Alaska by its median per capita income, which ranked seventh among the United States was misleading, for its cost of living exceeded the national average by nearly 25 percent. One sixth of Alaska's inhabitants, nearly 60,000 natives, lived in poverty, unaided by the state's inadequate social programs. Compounding this exorbitant cost of living was persistent unemployment, structural in nature, which exceeded 10 percent. State officials understandably perceived Alaska's top priority as "uplifting human resources."

Discovery of North Slope oil

Although Richfield Oil discovered a second reserve of considerable size in the Cook Inlet during 1963, the company entertained more ambitious hopes. Allying itself with Humble Oil and Refining Company, it proceeded to explore the northern part of the state. During the 1950s and 1960s eight wildcat wells had been drilled on the North Slope; six by British Petroleum and Sinclair and one each by Colorado Oil and Gas and Union Oil. In 1966 Atlantic Richfield (ARCO)[4] and Humble decided to drill a wildcat well on North Slope leases they had acquired from the state of Alaska. Their first effort was inland from Prudhoe Bay, where they sunk $4.5 million into a well before abandoning it as dry. In a final effort the companies moved north to Prudhoe Bay,

---

[4] On January 3, 1966 Richfield Oil was merged with the Atlantic Refining Company to form Atlantic Richfield.

where the drilling was successful. ARCO then proceeded with a second rig located seven miles southeast of the first well, which confirmed the presence of a significant oil reserve in May 1968. On the basis of these two wells, the independent consulting firm of DeGolyer and MacNaughton described the field as "potentially one of the largest petroleum accumulations known to the world today." Recoverable reserves were estimated at five to ten billion barrels, making the field potentially one of the worlds largest. In July 1968 ARCO reported the opinion of De-Golyer and MacNaughton in announcing its discovery of oil on the North Slope.

ARCO's dramatic announcement thrust the North Slope onto center stage. Companies possessing acreage in the area proceeded to transfer equipment to the North Slope and nine other drilling tests were in progress by March 1969. At this time the state of Alaska announced plans to conduct a public lease sale for the area in September. By June ten wells were completed and twenty-one others were in various stage of development.

While oil companies prepared for the September bidding with extraordinary secrecy, the state of Alaska conducted its own research on the minimum bids which it would accept for the 179 tracts to be offered, each of approximately 2,500 acres. An aura of uncertainty pervaded bidding preparations:

> Considering the enormous sums of money involved, preparation of the Alaskan oil bids was based on an incredible amount of pure guesswork. Oilmen point out that lease sale bidding on any piece of untried property begins with the inexact science of petroleum geology, proceeds to judgements on major economic and political uncertainties, and ends up in a poker-like effort to size up the intentions of the competition. But we've never been in a lease sale before that involved so many unknown factors as this one. [5]

On September 11, 1969, the State of Alaska offered, through competitive sealed bidding, leases on nearly 450,000 acres of the North Slope's Prudhoe Bay area. The lease sales netted $900 million, for which the successful bidders received ten-year leases over the mineral rights, renewable indefinitely. This $900 million was immediately placed in the state's "General Fund."

Immediately following the lease sales, ARCO announced that five of their nine wells, completed since the initial discovery, were productive. However, despite their exploratory success, the oil companies encountered significant obstacles. The climactic conditions were harsh and unforgiving, reducing human efficiency to less than a third of what

---

[5] "North Slope Gamble," *Wall Street Journal*, November 17, 1969.

it would be in more temperate climates, and significantly impairing the reliability of machinery:

> Strangely, it is the equipment that quits before the men. Engines are left running rather than attempting to restart them. A shutdown plane engine takes 4 or 5 hours to restart at 50° below. When temperatures reach 40° below, the rule of thumb is not to do anything which would put a strain on equipment. At those temperatures high-grade steel can shatter like glass.[6]

However, the difficulties in economically transporting oil to the domestic United States market in the "lower 48" proved to be the major obstacle to successful exploitation of the Prudhoe Bay discoveries. (See Exhibit 3 for a summary of the major events concerning the Trans-Alaska Pipeline controversy.)

TRANS-ALASKA PIPELINE

In an attempt to develop transportation alternatives, eight of the oil companies involved in the North Slope explorations established the Trans-Alaska Pipeline System (TAPS) as a joint enterprise.[7]

Prior to the lease sale, ARCO, Humble and British Petroleum announced in February 1969 plans for the proposed construction of a crude-oil pipeline extending from Prudhoe Bay to Valdez, an ice-free port on Alaska's southern coast. TAPS had hoped to begin during the fall months, starting in the south where access roads already existed. Heavy equipment would be transferred to the north over frozen ground during the winter of 1969–70, enabling TAPS to commence work on the northern segment during the summer of 1970. If construction had adhered to this schedule, the pipeline could be completed by mid-1972. Accordingly in April 1969, TAPS filed, with the United States Department of the Interior, for a permit to commence construction of the pipeline and an access road. However, by the completion of the lease bidding the permit had still not been approved.

---

[6] "Alaska: Land of Challenge," *The Oil and Gas Journal*, August 11, 1969 p. 117.

[7] The oil companies included and their respective shares of the pipeline venture were:

Company	Percent share
Atlantic Richfield	28.08
British Petroleum	28.08
Humble Oil (Standard Oil of N.J.)	25.52
Mobil Oil	8.68
Phillips Petroleum	3.32
Union Oil	3.32
Amerada Hess	3.00

The Secretary of the Interior, Walter J. Hickel, former governor of Alaska, refused to issue the permits until he was satisfied that the oil companies had formulated a program which would protect the land both during and after the construction period. Upon receipt of the permit application, the Department of the Interior established the Task Force on Alaskan Oil Development, under the leadership of Interior Undersecretary Russell E. Train, to study the problems inherent in developing the North Slope and hold public hearings.

Perhaps of greatest importance to Secretary Hickel was the likely environmental impact of a pipeline or road project which had not been subjected to considerable scientific scrutiny and analysis. As a resident and former governor of Alaska, Secretary Hickel was acutely aware of the havoc which an inadequately planned pipeline could wreak upon the Alaskan environment and its "fragile tundra." The extreme, hostile climate of the Arctic rendered the northern regions of the state extremely vulnerable. This area received limited solar radiation during the year, resulting in retardation of plant and animal growth and the existence of permafrost.[8] Although permafrost may be any kind of frozen subsurface material, like gravel or solid rock, which remains stable when thawed, much of the Alaskan permafrost was of the "ice-rich" variety containing a high water content. Typically, only a few feet of surface soil thawed during the North Slope's "summer" months, leaving the subsurface material frozen and quite stable. Altering the nature of the tundra by disturbing the soil and vegetation which insulated the permafrost, exposed the frozen subsurface to radiation, which could quickly transform an area into a bog. This thawing, combined with erosion-causing summer rains and the region's limited natural restorative powers, could cause the entire process to sustain itself and be virtually impossible to reverse. In short, it was essential to keep permafrost frozen, yet the "simple passage of a tracked vehicle that destroys the vegetation mat is enough to upset this delicate balance."[9]

Hickel's fears were not unfounded. On at least two occasions imprudent construction techniques resulted in severe environmental damage to the state's arctic regions. During World War II the navy's exploratory efforts at the Naval Petroleum Reserve #4 left unhealed scars from bulldozers and seismic tests. In March 1972, *Business Week* reported that "one imprint left by a Caterpillar tractor is now a 56-foot gorge."

More serious were the effects of the state's efforts to construct a 400-mile highway from the Fairbanks area to the oil rigs at Prudhoe Bay. The road, proposed by Hickel and ultimately begun under his successor Governor Keith Miller, was aptly dubbed the "Walter J. Hickel

[8] The U.S. Geological Survey defined permafrost as "rock or soil material that has remained below 0°C. continuously for two or more years."

[9] Tom Brown, *Oil on Ice,* p. 60

Highway." Many Alaskan roads had previously been constructed, with little environmental damage, by heaping snow upon the tundra and compacting it into a raised berm. However, for this project the state used bulldozers to scrape off the snow and gouge out the road in the tundra. The road proved adequate during the winter but, during the spring breakup, the highway didn't survive nearly as long as a snow berm. As the exposed permafrost began to melt, and the water from surrounding areas drained into the roadbed, the highway soon assumed more characteristics of a canal than a road.

Native claims

The reluctance of the Interior Department to approve the construction permits was only one of a number of problems impeding the pipeline. Equally significant was a general land freeze declared in 1966 by then Secretary of the Interior Steward Udall, which blocked further state selections until December 1970, or until Congress resolved native claims that the state had leased land to the oil companies which it did not rightfully own.

Eager to take advantage of the provisions of the 1958 Statehood Act, the state initially selected 2 million acres on the oil-rich North Slope, claiming that the area was "free of aboriginal use and occupancy." In actuality, much of the land lay under existing native villages or their hunting and fishing grounds, but the state avoided the problem by publishing the legal notice in an obscure newspaper, read by few natives, and ultimately claiming possession when no native claimants appeared to dispute it.

Forming a coalition of 18 organizations, the Alaskan Federation of Natives elected delegates to present their case in Washington before Secretary Udall. The natives relied on two legislative acts to support their case: (1) the Alaska Organic Act of 1884, in which Congress stipulated that Alaska natives "shall not be disturbed in the possession of any lands actually in their use or occupation or now claimed by them but the terms under which such persons may acquire title to such lands is reserved for future legislation by Congress"[10] and (2) the 1958 Alaska Statehood Act which not only gave the new state "the right to select 103 million acres from federally held lands . . . but also restricted the state's right to take land claimed by the natives."[11]

The native claims controversy was finally resolved in December 1971 by congressional passage of the Alaska Native Claims Settlement Act. The legislation provided Alaska's estimated 53,000 natives with $462.5

---

[10] "Resources Report," *CPR National Journal*, April 17, 1971 p. 842.
[11] Ibid.

million in grants, a 2 percent royalty upon the gross value of minerals extracted from state or federal lands (maximum of $500 million), and native ownership claims to 40-million acres. In addition, it eliminated a major obstacle to obtaining right-of-way for the pipeline by resolving the natives' ownership claims to the land through which the pipeline would pass. The right-of-way for the proposed pipeline was to be reserved under the supervision of the Interior Department. Although nearly 95 percent of Alaska's 365 million acres were under federal control at the time of the act's passage, the legislation authorized additional land selections by the state which would eventually reduce federal control to 60 percent. Another provision of the act established a joint federal-state land use planning commission to provide a systematic approach to the selection of federal lands and the state's resource development programs. Consequently, the Native Claims Settlement Act facilitated the approval of a trans-Alaska oil pipeline and contributed to orderly planning for the development of Alaska's other resources.

Environmental issues

On October 5, 1969 the Department of the Interior published certain guidelines with which the builders of the pipeline would have to comply. These ground rules were developed by the enlarged Task Force on Alaska Oil Development under the direction of Russell Train, who stated, "To my knowledge, no private construction project has ever been asked to accept such strong constraints or such continuing direct control by the Federal Government."

The oil companies were required to post a $5 million security deposit to provide payment for any environmental damage. The guidelines also included the following stipulations:[12]

a. Federal monitors must accompany all construction crews.
b. The contractor must train construction personnel in avoiding damage to the environment.
c. Detailed contingency plans must be made for controlling possible oil spills or pipeline leaks.
d. Pollution abatement controls must meet established federal standards for Alaska.
e. The pipelines must go under stream beds unless otherwise authorized by the Interior Department.
f. Permanent installations such as oil pump stations must be designed to harmonize with the natural setting.

For specific protection of fish and wildlife, the agreement included a ban on construction during fish spawning and wildfowl nesting in migra-

---

[12] "Pipeline Builders Consent to Wildlife Rules," *New York Times,* November 1, 1969, p. 20.

tion periods; required uninterrupted passage of fish and big game animals; banned blasting within a quarter mile of streams and lakes without a permit; and restricted the use of pesticides and herbicides.

Any significant alteration of lakes or streams of the quality of their water must be cleared in advance with the Alaska director of the Bureau of Land Management. Though not financially liable for aesthetic or ecological damage, TAPS was made liable for any damage caused by spilled oil. The stipulations were subject to further amendment at any time. If violations occurred, the Alaska director of the Bureau of Land Management, or his superior, the United States secretary of the interior could "suspend or terminate" construction or operation of the pipeline.

Despite the Interior Department's stipulations, environmental groups strenuously opposed the initial TAPS permit request. Led by the Sierra Club, environmentalists challenged the wisdom of constructing either a pipeline or the 370-mile access road, on a number of grounds:

1. *Permafrost.* The immediate concern was the possible damage which might result from construction of the access road, similar to what happened with the Hickel Highway. However, an inadequate pipeline design could result in far greater damage to the environment. Oil experts estimated that the crude oil would enter the pipeline at temperatures ranging to 145°F, and the hydraulic friction would sustain this temperature while it was pumped over the 789 miles. Conservationists feared that the TAPS design, which called for 90 percent of the line buried, involved a substantial risk of this heat being dissipated and melting the adjacent permafrost, thereby causing the line to sag and, possibly, snap. Subsurface experiments confirmed the environmentalist's fears that effective insulation would be extremely difficult to achieve.

2. *Earthquakes.* The proposed pipeline route passed in the vicinity of three major fault systems (the Fairweather, Chugach-St. Elias, and Castle Mountain) and actually crossed two major faults (the Kaltag and Titina Fault, near Fairbanks, and the Denali Fault of the Alaska range). The major fear was that seismic activity, similar to the earthquake which destroyed Valdez in 1964, would cause multiple ruptures in the pipeline and inundate areas with hot crude oil.

3. *Pipeline spills.* Landslides, erosion, and other natural events could also rupture the pipeline, damaging vegetation, waterfowl, and fresh-water industries. Additionally, environmentalists were apprehensive that minor leaks, up to 31 barrels per hour, could continue undetected for days.

4. *Wildlife.* Of particular concern to environmentalists was the impact of pipeline construction upon fish and wildlife. In order to construct supports and insulation material for the line, it would be necessary to dredge nearby rivers and streams; thereby endangering the char, burbot, pike, and grayling populations of the area. Additionally, the

possibility of a pipeline break at one of the 350 streams crossing the projected route was a major consideration. With regard to wildlife, it was feared that above-ground construction of the line might alter or inhibit the migration of the Arctic and Porcupine caribou herds, and the activities of moose and Dall sheep. Naturally, any melting of permafrost and its resulting erosion posed serious obstacles to wildlife migration and mobility. Other concerns included the possible retardation of small vegetation, upon which arctic animals fed, and the presence of oil in Valdez harbor, which would affect marine life. In all, environmentalists claimed that at least 60 square miles of bird habitat would be destroyed or modified, ground and air traffic would drive large mammals away, and that marine life would be affected by river siltation and oil spillage.

5. *Tanker spills.* Environmentalists also expressed reservations about the possibility of oil spills both in Valdez Harbor and enroute to the West Coast ports. Average figures for worldwide maritime accidents seemed to support claims that oil spills might be a likely occurrence once oil production began. In actuality, these accident rates were for worldwide traffic, which were much higher than those for United States flagships, which the Jones Act required for traffic between domestic ports. It was also feared that the tankers might gradually pollute Prince William Sound and Valdez Harbor by discharging oily ballast water directly into Alaskan waters.

National Environmental Policy Act (NEPA)

On January 1, 1970, in the midst of the pipeline controversy, President Nixon, signed into law the National Environmental Policy Act of 1969 (42 U.S.C. 4321). Largely the result of legislation proposed by Representative John D. Dingell (Democrat, Michigan), and Senators Henry M. Jackson (Democrat, Washington) and Edmund S. Muskie (Democrat, Maine), this act was virtually unopposed when enacted by Congress late in 1969 and was promptly signed by the president as the first act of the 1970s. Sections 101 and 102 of the act are contained in Appendix A. The law declared, as a national policy, the safeguarding of the environment by requiring that environmental impact must figure in governmental decision making. In effect, the NEPA was largely a disclosure and planning statute, requiring only that the particular department assess environmental problems and weigh alternatives. However, it became a major tool for opponents of the pipeline and some contend, subject to its interpretation by the courts, that it might establish "a new judicial veto power over the executive branch based upon an open-ended definition of the environment."

In January 1970, after evaluating the guidelines stipulated by the

Task Force on Alaskan Oil Development, both the Senate and House Interior Committees voted to permit the Interior Department to grant the right-of-way for the Trans-Alaska oil pipeline. The committees reached this decision despite reservations about the environmental impact and native claims expressed during congressional hearings on the issue. Nevertheless, the decision enabled the Interior Department to approve the permit and lift land restrictions, and make specific decisions concerning the right-of-way and other issues.

On January 7, 1970, Secretary Hickel ordered an exception to the freeze on federal lands in Alaska for construction of the oil pipeline, explaining that the action "does not constitute approval of the right-of-way application by TAPS," but that a permit would be granted when protection of the environment was assured. Perhaps the reason for delaying approval was a startling article which expressed considerable reservations about the project's environmental safety. Arthur H. Lachenbruch, of the U.S. Geological Survey, prepared an alarming report entitled "Some Estimates of the Thermal Effects of a Heated Pipeline in Permafrost," in which he seriously questioned the design of the pipeline and offered discouraging predictions with regard to its environmental impact. In any event, the Interior Department concluded that it needed additional data to make a decision on the TAPS permit application.

Involvement of the courts

With the Interior Department still deliberating over the TAPS permit, the courts became involved in the pipeline controversy. Reacting to the vote of the House and Senate Interior Committees, the Alaska Federation of Natives, whose representatives included former California Senator Thomas Kuchel and former Supreme Court Justice Arthur Goldberg, brought suit against the Interior Department (*Alaska* v. *Hickel*) claiming that the department could not grant the right-of-way without the consent of tribal leaders of the villages along the route. On April 3, 1970, Federal Judge George L. Hart granted a preliminary injunction, blocking construction on a 20-mile stretch of land claimed by Stevens Village, one of the native communities.

During April, the courts became further involved when another suit was filed in the same court by the Wilderness Society, the Friends of the Earth, and the Environmental Defense Fund, Inc. (*Wilderness* v. *Hickel*). The three environmental groups contended that Secretary Hickel had not complied, in full, with Section 102 of the NEPA, which required that a statement of environmental impact be submitted to the Council on Environmental Quality. The Interior Department acknowledged that no statement had been submitted, explaining that the delay was due to Hickel's evaluating the advice of Lachenbruch and other scientists. On April 14, Judge Hart issued a second injunction, barring the Department of Interior from issuing permits for either the road or the pipeline. Under the terms of the injunction the Interior Department was required to give the three environmental groups 14-days' notice prior to the issuance of a right-of-way permit for the pipeline.

Alaskan legislative action

The events of the Trans-Alaska Pipeline controversy developed with increasing rapidity after the successful lease sales of September 1969. Within six months efforts by the Interior Department, environmentalists, and the courts had effectively delayed an imminent resolution of the situation. Consequently, the prevailing optimism of January 1970, which accompanied the convening of the state legislature, gradually yielded to an atmosphere of frustration and desperation by April. Governor Miller and the legislature leaders initially anticipated a short session, devoid of partisan politics, to deal with the allocation of the $900 million from leases. To assist with this project, both the Brookings Institution and the Stanford Research Institute were employed to analyze the needs of the state and provide recommendations. However, increasing opposition to the pipeline by interests outside the state, and the issue of partisan politics ultimately transformed the session into a confusing one, less productive than anyone anticipated:

> The session did not run for a mere 90 or 100 days; it dragged on interminably. Partisan politics, as usual, did become an issue. There were crackpot schemes; there was irresponsible handling of state money. It was not until 147 days after convening, in the small hours of June 7, that the session finally ended. The legislators were boneweary, and optimism had long since evaporated. Indeed, 1970 turned out to be a year of false hopes raised only to be dashed by reality.[13]

Governor Miller's original state budget proposal of $242 million uncontrollably balooned to $314 million before the close of the session, more than double the $154 million budget of the previous year. Contributing to this increase was passage of an ill-prepared access-road bill which antagonized both politicians and oil interests. Aware that chances for immediate approval of the pipeline permit were becoming exceedingly remote, the governor and 120 other Alaskans, hoping to secure approval for the project, embarked upon an unsuccessful lobbying expedition to Washington. Judge Hart's first injunction, issued shortly thereafter, limited the state's alternatives to contesting the injunction through some legal loophole. Such a loophole existed, an 1866 statute which provided the state with the right to grant road right-of-ways on federal land

---

[13] T. Brown, *Oil on Ice,* p. 117.

not specifically reserved for other uses. Responding to pressure from Fairbanks business interests, Governor Miller announced on April 6 his intention to assume control of the right-of-way and authorize construction of a road to support the pipeline;

> It is absolutely imperative that we dispense with the red tape and get on with the opening of the permanent highway to the North Slope. The road will be among the most important elements in both the development and conservation of the Arctic and reliable year-round surface transportation is a necessity.[14]

One week later Judge Hart issued his second injunction, expanding the restriction to include the entire 350-mile stretch from the Yukon River to Prudhoe Bay, which effectively blocked the state action.

The governor's plan proposed that the state build the road, using the TAPS contractors who were already in Alaska, with a guarantee that the oil companies would reimburse the full $120 million cost if the pipeline construction permit were approved by June 1, 1971. However, this plan substantially reduced the risk to the oil companies, requiring only partial repayment if the permit were not approved. This controversial provision was attacked by members of the legislature and the proposal was subsequently rewritten. The alternative bill proposed in the legislature also provided for state construction, contingent upon settlement of the native claims situation, but with full repayment within five years, by the oil industry, regardless of whether or not the permit were approved. Additionally, a few legislators who opposed any concessions for the oil industry, attached to the bill an increase in the oil and gas severance tax from 16 to 20 percent.

Not only was this tax increase unpopular with oil companies, but there was no guarantee that the ultimately approved right-of-way would parallel the road. Moreover, the bill obligated them to repay the $120 million construction cost, even if the pipeline were never built. The legislature passed the bill, as expected, dramatically inflating the state budget. The oil companies, reacting to the unwanted legislation, promptly rejected it. Thus the 1970 session of the Alaskan legislature resulted in a frustrating and unsuccessful attempt to commence development of the pipeline. Governor Miller's subsequent effort at reconvening the legislature to formulate alternative legislation was futile.

Although 1970 began with excitement and optimism over the North Slope discoveries, this boom atmosphere rapidly evaporated. Events clarified that approval and construction of the proposed pipeline would have to await resolution of the environmental and legal controversy by the Interior Department (and Council of Environmental Quality) and the federal courts. The waiting period would be a costly one not

---

[14] Ibid. p. 13.

only for the oil companies, now combined into the Alyeska Pipeline Service Company (formerly TAPS),[5] but particularly for the State of Alaska whose Legislature, despite the aforementioned problems, enacted considerable public works and social welfare legislation during 1970. These programs increased expenditures to a level nearly double that of state's tax receipts, which left the state no alternative but to liquidate a portion of its "General Fund."

Evaluating of the environmental and security considerations

During the first months of 1971, the Department of the Interior held public hearings in Washington and Anchorage to gather information on which to base a preliminary environmental impact statement to comply with the NEPA. A principal participant was E. L. Patton, president of Alyeska Pipeline Service Company, who testified at length on the environmental ramifications of the proposed project:

> All our studies point to the conclusion that the proposed pipeline is technically and economically feasible and that, with adequate safeguards and careful planning, it can and will be constructed in a way which will result in minimum impact on the Alaskan environment.[16]

However, the new Secretary of the Interior Rogers Morton was not totally convinced. In late February he issued a preliminary environmental impact statement and requested that Alyeska file, with the department, a comprehensive description of the project. In July and August Alyeska produced a 29-volume *Project Description*, which was then evaluated by a 60-man task force from the Interior Department. The conclusions of this group were compiled in the *Technical Review* of the *Project Description*, which raised serious doubts as to whether a pipeline could be constructed without causing "major and irreparable damage to the Alaskan landscape." The Sierra Club ultimately obtained a copy of the *Technical Review* and brought it to the attention of the press in December.

Meanwhile, the State of Alaska published a study of their own. *Comments on the Proposed Trans-Alaska Pipeline*, in response to a request by the Department of the Interior, which analyzed the project's impact on Alaska's wildlife, transportation and energy systems, and the social and economic situation of the state. The study supported the proposed project on the basis of its limited environmental impact and the potential economic benefits it would provide the state of Alaska.

---

[15] TAPS was reorganized as the Alyeska Pipeline Service Company on August 31, 1970.

[16] Hearing testimony from Department of the Interior Public Hearings, Washington, D.C. and Anchorage, Alaska, February 1971.

The first favorable break for pipeline proponents occurred in December 1971 when the Department of the Interior issued *An Analysis of the Economic and Security Aspects of the Trans-Alaska Pipeline*. This publication discussed alternative methods of transporting North Slope oil to domestic ports, evaluating each in light of Alaskan and national security considerations. Of the three major alternatives proposed, the Mackenzie River Valley Pipeline (MVPL) had received the most publicity. This line was to extend approximately 2500 miles, three times the length of the Alyeska design, along the Mackenzie River of Canada's Northwest Territory to Edmonton, Alberta. Although the study indicated that MVPL would provide the lowest-cost means of transporting oil to Midwest markets, it concluded that national security considerations favored the construction of a pipeline located solely within the United States. Additional reservations were expressed about the complexities of financing, ownership and control of the project. Two other alternative methods, utilizing ice-breaking tankers through the Northwest Passage and constructing a trans-Alaskan railroad, were rejected for financial and efficiency reasons. In essence, the report concluded that, on the basis of national security considerations, the Trans-Alaska route was the preferable alternative, stating among its major findings: "No transportation alternative is economically more efficient than the Trans-Alaska pipeline system . . . The early completion of the Alaska pipeline must be considered an important national security objective."[17]

The environmental impact statement

By February 1972 there were reliable indications that the Department of the Interior favored approval of the pipeline project. That month the department issued documents establishing certain stipulations which would govern any pipeline construction and the transportation of North Slope oil by tankers. In remarking on the report, Secretary Morton described the stipulations as "The most stringent and comprehensive set of terms and conditions dealing with environmental protection ever attached to the granting of a permit to use public lands."[18]

On March 20, 1972, Secretary Morton submitted to the Council on Environmental Quality and the public the *Final Environmental Impact Statement Proposed Trans-Alaska Pipeline*. Consisting of six volumes, plus three volumes of appendices, this statement was prepared by a special inter-agency task force, under the Federal Task Force on Alaskan Oil Development, at a cost of over $9 million. This statement was de-

---

[17] *An Analysis of the Economic and Security Aspects of the Trans-Alaska Pipeline*, U.S. Department of the Interior, December 1971, p. 1.

[18] Alaskan Oil: Powerful Interests in Pipeline Battle," *Congressional Quarterly*, March 11, 1972, p. 530.

scribed by Max Brewer, commissioner of Alaska's Department of Environmental Conservation as "perhaps the most comprehensive statement of environmental impact this country will ever produce." Supplementing a thorough analysis of the project's probable impact upon the environment, the study included 64 pages of stipulations governing pipeline construction and operation. Appendix B provides a summary of the impact as contained in the final statement.

Edward Patton, president of the Alyeska Pipeline Service Company, reacted enthusiastically to the study: "The report clearly confirms our conclusion that the Trans-Alaska pipeline is the preferable means of transporting oil from Alaska's North Slope."[19] Since the initial discoveries of 1968, the oil companies had spent more than $35 million in researching methods to limit the project's environmental impact, ranging from the development of rapidly growing erosion-controlling vegetation to a study on the spawning habits of Alaskan fish. Consequently Alyeska maintained a comprehensive public relations program aimed at convincing the public of the environmental safety of the project. Responding to allegations by the Sierra Club that the *Project Description* and the *Final Environmental Impact Statement* left many "unanswered questions," Alyeska sought to enlighten the public about the environmental safeguards incorporated into the new design of the proposed pipeline. A summary of Alyeska's claims is presented in Appendix C.

Recent developments

On May 11, 1972 Secretary of the Interior Rogers Morton approved construction of the Trans-Alaska pipeline, announcing his intention to issue the permits to Alyeska when Judge Hart rescinded the injunction. Although he acknowledged that the project involved environmental risks, Morton explained:

> I am convinced that it is in our best national interest to avoid all further delays and uncertainties in planning development of Alaska North Slope oil reserves by having a secure pipeline located under the total jurisdiction and exclusive use of the United States. . .A bilateral arrangement with Canada for a pipeline is impractical at this time.[20]

This statement elicited response from the Alyeska Pipeline Service Company, who added that they would delay construction preparations until the legal situation was resolved.

That same month the state of Alaska published *Comments on the Trans-Alaska Pipeline and its Alternatives* which assessed the proposed

---

[19] "Alaska: Closer to Cashing Oil's Riches," *Business Week*, March 25, 1972, p. 78.

[20] "Morton Approves Alaska Pipeline: Court Fight Seen," *New York Times*, May 12, 1972, p. 1.

route through Canada's Mackenzie Valley. Believing the *Final Environmental Impact Statement's* analysis of the alternative to be inadequate, the state examined it in greater detail, arriving at conclusions similar to those expressed by Secretary Morton before the Congressional Joint Economic Committee the following month (see Exhibit 4).

Although the Department of Interior decision improved the prospects for eventual approval of the pipeline, the passage of two acts by the Alaskan legislature has severely impaired cooperation between Alyeska and the state. A proposal to modify the Severance Tax Law, the "cents per barrel amendment," raised taxes on oil production regardless of market price, thereby establishing a floor for revenues to the state. The Right-of-Way Leasing Act levied an increased tax on oil production, charging more for oil from the North Slope than from the south. In effect, this taxed the users of the pipeline for use of the right-of-way. The oil companies, claiming this altered the original lease terms and that the pipeline was subject solely to federal control, under the Interstate Commerce Commission, threatened to contest the legislation by suing the state.

On August 16, 1972, Judge Hart finally terminated his injunction of April 1970 citing that: 1) The *Final Environmental Impact Statement* "reasonably set forth alternatives" to the proposed system, fulfilling the requirements of the NEPA, and 2) that the right-of-way, leasing, and forest permits requested for the project were legal. However, Judge Hart added that he could "confidently anticipate that the final decision rests with the Supreme Court." If the pipeline project were approved by the Supreme Court it was anticipated that it could be in full operation by 1977 or 1978.

IMPLICATIONS OF THE TRANS-ALASKA PIPELINE CONTROVERSY

The eventual decisions relating to the construction of a Trans-Alaska Pipeline will contribute substantially towards resolving a number of important local, regional, and national issues. The environmental concerns have been widely publicized, but the proposed pipeline would have a significant impact upon critical social and economic issues, and dramatically influence the pattern of future resource development in the United States. A shortsighted or unreasonable solution could lead, in the words of Alaska's current Governor William Egan, to "a disaster of the first order."

The state of Alaska

Of primary concern to Alaska were the immediate economic benefits to be derived from construction of the proposed pipeline. Alaskan politicians referred to the priority of the state's "human resources" and cited that the royalty and rights revenue from North Slope oil would provide the resources to develop them. As Governor Egan explained before the Congressional Joint Economic Committee in June 1972:

> Alaskans are burdened by some of the greatest extremes of poverty, unemployment and high cost of living experienced anywhere in this nation. However, as owner of some of the greatest undeveloped oil and gas resources anywhere in the world, including the oil which will be shipped in the Trans-Alaska Pipeline, the State of Alaska has the means of alleviating these burdens.[21]

The first benefits from North Slope oil had already been realized: the $900 million lease payments received in September 1969. However, this had been insufficient to cover the costs of the social programs enacted by the Alaskan legislature. With oil revenues uncertain in their timing or existence, the Alaskan officials were no longer so sanguine about the state's future.

> The fact is that the sale of the leases in 1969 did produce moneys permitting the state to make a start on meeting some of the desperate housing and health needs of Alaskans. But the delay of North Slope production revenues is seriously undermining the State's ongoing programs. . . . If oil is not flowing on the tentative completion dates of 1976 or early 1977, but instead is delayed several more years, the State will find itself in a condition of economic distress and unable to provide *a minimum level* of services to Alaskans. North Slope revenues no later than 1976 or 1977 are essential to the viability of Alaska as a state.[22]

The North Slope oil revenues, if forthcoming, would be a percentage of the wellhead value of the oil (the market value of the oil less the transportation costs), rendering the future revenue highly vulnerable to changes in transportation costs. The Alaskan administration had concluded, based on a thorough analysis of all feasible transportation alternatives, that the proposed pipeline was not only "the logical, most economical, and safest route" but that "maximum revenues can only be realized from the Trans-Alaska route." Few disagreed with this contention, but there remained additional factors which could affect future revenues. For example, the state derived full royalties on minerals extracted from state land and only 90 percent from those on federal lands. Therefore a key consideration would be the success of Alaska's claims for the remainder of the 103 million acres allotted to the state.

Other developments could also alter Alaska's share of revenues. First the proposed increase in severance taxes, the legality of which is in

---

[21] United Stated Congress: Hearings of the Joint Economic Committee, June 22, 1972.

[22] Ibid.

question, would significantly increase Alaska's oil revenues. However, what remained uncertain was the point at which such state legislation might effectively discourage the oil companies from continuing their development efforts. A more complex issue was whether or not the state of Alaska could pursue the project independently, assuming ownership of the pipeline.

In November 1971, Governor Egan announced that he was considering a proposal whereby the state would assume the financing and ownership of the pipeline. The proposal was inspired by an alarming study which concluded that, given existing taxation and budget growth rates, state revenues from a privately owned pipeline would not be sufficient to prevent total depletion of the $900 million "General Fund" by 1978. Moreover, Alaskan officials realized that they could influence transportation costs only through equity control of the pipeline. Since transportation costs influenced wellhead values, and the Interstate Commerce Commission ensured a regulated return on pipeline operations, state officials feared that Alaska's revenues might be limited by inflated costs of private ownership and operation of the pipeline. Governor Egan also hoped that state ownership might allay criticism by environmentalists and that the Internal Revenue Service might declare Alaska's pipeline profits tax free.

Although the governor seemed confident that the state could raise the necessary funds independent of the oil companies, oil spokesmen strongly opposed the plan and questioned the assumption that state financing would not encumber the credits of their companies. Raymond Gary, a Morgan Stanley representative, expressed serious reservations about the State's proposal:

> We reluctantly come to the conclusion that the State on the basis of its present resources cannot, CANNOT finance the construction of this pipeline . . . it has to have the unconditional backstopping of the oil companies . . . if it (the plan) doesn't encumber the oil companies, its no good as securities.[23]

As a result of the financing uncertainties and other factors, the state-private ownership issue was never resolved, but the Alaskan legislature did enact higher severance taxes to increase the state's oil revenues.

The Trans-Alaska Pipeline controversy has dramatically influenced the state's programs for developing other resources, which were largely contingent upon obtaining revenues from North Slope oil. For example, the state intended "to invest oil revenues to develop commerce in the renewable resource areas which have historically been the backbone of the Alaskan economy." Since the North Slope discovery, more than

---

[23] State of Alaska Hearings on Proposed Pipeline Legislation, March 6–10, 1972, p. 571.

1,400 outside companies had registered in Alaska to meet state requirements for doing business, particularly those interested in mineral explorations. Kennecott Copper and American Smelting were among the concerns operating in the state for whom an adverse decision on the pipeline issue could prove a serious blow.

The uncertainties of the Statehood Act land selection and the legal controversy made land planning for resource development difficult, if not impossible. As Larry Eppinbach, Investment Officer of the Alaska Department of Revenue explained: "We have a good idea of where the mineral resources are but how can we plan for developing them if we don't even know what land we own?" An important benefit of the Native Claims Act was the establishment of a joint federal-state, land-use planning body whose cooperative effort P. T. Davis, a state development planner, described as "imperative." As a result of the National Environmental Policy Act, various development projects within the state had been thwarted. U.S. Plywood–Champion Papers Inc., planned to build a $100 million pulp plant at Berner's Bay, near Juneau, and committed sizeable funds to research the environmental impact of the project. Although the company published the findings well before enactment of the act, a suit by conservationists effectively stalled the project. The eventual outcome of this and other resource development projects will hinge upon the resolution of the pipeline issue.

Of particular importance to a significant minority of citizens opposing the pipeline was the fear of what effect oil might have upon their Alaskan way of life. The most remote of the 50 states, Alaska had been a frontier which bred tough, resourceful, independent people. A common apprehension was that the North Slope oil would destroy Alaska's special attraction and "condemn Alaskans to a state of common, dull ordinariness." Gene Guess, Speaker of the Alaska House of Representatives expressed this feeling during an interview with *Business Week:* "Most Alaskans want an opportunity to maintain our way of life that brought us up here—that is, small population and preservation of our wilderness."[24]

National considerations

However, the impact of the Trans-Alaska Pipeline issue far transcended the state and regional considerations. Concomitant with a growing number of development projects delayed by environmentally related legal injunctions was a dramatic increase in energy needs within the United States. Estimates for the 1970s projected sustained economic growth and a doubling of the country's demand for petroleum. In *Eco-*

[24] "Alaska: Closer to Cashing Oils Riches," *Business Week,* March 25, 1972, p. 81.

nomic and Security Aspects of the Trans-Alaska Pipeline the Interior Department stressed the importance of the security considerations and recommended the development of domestic oil reserves to reduce dependence upon foreign sources. The oil import quota had effectively been rescinded for the West Coast, which dramatized the need for new petroleum sources.

At stake was no less than the future of the National Environmental Policy Act. James Moorman, the attorney for the Environmental Defense Fund, underscored the importance of the pipeline controversy: "Even if we don't stop the pipeline we're going to change the ballgame as far as the National Environmental Policy Act is concerned. What comes out of this case will determine the requirements of the NEPA."[25] The economics reflected the significance of the issue the Interior Department study cost $9 million, Alyeska had spent over $35 million in research, and the new environmental safeguards would add $300 million to the cost of the pipeline. Nevertheless, environmentalists continued to express doubts about the project and the adequacy of the Final Environmental Impact Statement and hoped to persuade the courts to order additional studies.

Max Brewer, commissioner of the Alaska Department of Environmental Conservation foresaw the court's interpretation of the NEPA as crucial, yet an unnecessary and regrettable circumstance:

> The NEPA approaches the problem of man's interaction with other aspects of the environment in a very positive, not a negative way. There is nothing in the NEPA that prohibits wise development of resources. Unfortunately the NEPA often is not used as intended . . . and they can be sowing the seeds of destruction. What the political processes have given us in the NEPA, the political processes can also take away. Not all environmental decison making should be made by the courts ruling on the legal gymnastics of two antagonists, neither of whom is required to be trained in the natural, social or economic sciences. [26]

The possibility that improper interpretation and use of the statute could destroy its effectiveness was not altogether remote, and indiscriminate use of the NEPA in the Alaskan situation would provide its opponents with a banner cause.

Governor Egan attacked the current interpretation of the NEPA from another perspective, a view which was gaining credence. Contending that the federal government did not possess the resources or the expertise to sustain the act in its present form, he warned:

> We interpret the NEPA as requiring the federal administrator to exercise the same scope of inquiry and review into the granting or

---

[25] "Resources Report," *CPR National Journal*, April 17, 1971, p. 843.

[26] Max C. Brewer, "Environmental Credibility—Do Alaskans Believe That It Exists?" p. 2.

witholding of a permit as he would for an action initiated by the federal government itself . . . Congress has not given the Executive Branch the substantive standards it would need to have for the decision making attempted through the NEPA . . . The federal government is totally incapable of performing with comparable excellence the same task in thousands of other major federal actions. The realities of federal capabilities suggest a more restrained interpretation of the NEPA.[27]

Considering the amount of litigation based on the NEPA, sustaining the current interpretation could well result in excessive delays for significant national development projects.

20th century federalism

In a broader context the Trans-Alaska Pipeline controversy raised the larger issue of federalism within the United States. Article V of the *Bill of Rights* stated: "The powers not delegated to the United States by the Constitution, nor prohibited by it to the States, are reserved to the States respectively, or to the people." This implied the importance of the court's ultimate interpretation of the NEPA. Alaskans had raised the issue of state's rights by questioning whether or not the NEPA empowered the federal government to determine how and in what manner resources should be developed within the United States. Historical precedent seemed to justify increasing the role of the federal government in this country's resource development. However, empowering the federal government with broad powers carried with it the potential for abuse, and excessive centralized planning under the pretext of environmental protection. Governor Egan expressed reservations about this trend during his testimony before the Joint Economic Committee in June 1972:

> It now appears that the federal government intends to exercise a much larger role in the management of the State's petroleum resources than had earlier been realized. For the past year and a half that role has loomed increasingly larger relative to the role of the State and of private industry. The net effect, whether good or bad for the national economy or the national environment, is a restructuring of American enterprise, public and private, based upon a highly centralized planning and decision making.[28]

Neither Governor Egan nor other Alaskan officials would stand by idly while the federal government ursurped what they considered to be the lawful rights of the state of Alaska:

> The government of the state of Alaska does have primary responsibility for both the economic welfare of its citizens and the development

---

[27] United States Congress, Hearings of the Joint Economic Committee, June 22, 1972.

[28] Ibid.

and conservation of its resources. Since the demonstration of profound interest and willingness to intervene in the management of our resource development by national interest groups, we have had to assess our policies and programs in light of the concern that the interest of the people of Alaska might be lost in the play of such interests. Alaska will not again let her resources be developed without a fair return to her people. Nor will the state allow its political processes or economic life to be dominated by an absentee interest.[29]

John Werner, deputy commissioner of the Alaska Department of Economic Development best expressed the frustration which many Alaskans shared: "The fact which is most difficult to accept is that, at this point, we aren't the masters of our own destiny."

A view of the future?

It was evident that the Trans-Alaska Pipeline controversy might have a substantial impact upon the course of future resource development within the United States. The ultimate resolution could largely determine the function and importance of environmental planning and protection in future projects as well as clarify further the respective roles of the federal government, the state, and private industry in the development of national resources. However, in future controversies the jurisdictional boundaries between the major participants might be even less clearly defined. For example, oil interests planned to exploit what were believed to be sizeable oil reserves along the Alaskan coastline, which would undoubtedly raise the issue of how and by whom resource development projects on the Continental Shelf should be administered. The resolution of the Trans-Alaska Pipeline controversy might provide the foundation for closer cooperation between entities within the United States, and perhaps between countries in harvesting the vast international resources of the sea.

The discovery of North Slope oil had set in motion the dynamics of change. Alaskans could not ignore the presence of this rich resource nor would they ignore the lessons of the gold and copper rushes, when outsiders exploited the resources without giving Alaska its fair share. It was universally accepted that the delay had resulted in a pipeline design which was infinitely superior to the initial version, but it had been at a substantial economic cost. What had become clear was that the remaining challenges for industry, the state, and the United States were as formidable as they had ever encountered.

---

[29] United States Congress, Hearings of the Joint Economic Committee, June 22, 1972.

EXHIBIT 1
Map of Alaska*

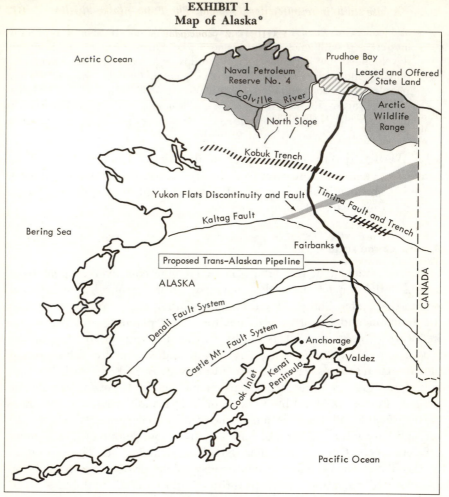

* Reproduced from *Environment*, Vol. 12, No. 70, September 1970 p. 17.

EXHIBIT 2
Percentage distribution of persons by age:
United States 1900–1970 Alaska 1900–1970

	United States			Alaska		
	1900	1950	1970	1900	1950	1970
Total	76,212,168	151,325,798	203,211,926	63,592	128,643	300,382
Percentage by age:						
0–14	34.4	26.9	28.4	17.0	26.5	34.3
15–24	19.6	14.7	17.5	12.4	21.7	20.7
25–34	15.9	15.7	12.2	17.8	20.6	16.4
35–44	12.1	14.3	11.4	14.6	14.4	12.6
45+	18.0	28.4	30.5	38.2	16.8	16.0
Median age.	22.9	30.2	28.1	29.1	25.8	22.9

EXHIBIT 2 (*concluded*)

	United States	Alaska	Rank among states
Percentage of population employed in:			
Manufacturing	25.9	7.1	45
White-collar occupations.	48.2	55.3	3
Government work	16.1	36.5	2
Percentage of employed persons by industry:			
Agriculture, forestry, and fisheries	3.7	2.0*	
Mining	.8	2.6	8
Manufacturing	25.9	9.4	50
Construction	6.0	9.4	1
Other transportation (that is, marine)	1.4	5.2	1
Insurance, real estate, and other finance.	3.3	2.1	41
Public administration	5.5	16.4	2
Percentage of employed persons by occupation:			
Farmers	3.1	0.4	49
Service workers	11.3	13.3	6
Health service workers	1.5	.9	50
Operatives—manufacturing	10.4	1.9	50
Operatives—nonmanufacturing	3.3	4.2	13
Salaried managers and administrators—manufacturing . . .	1.3	.4	50
Salaried managers and administrators—nonmanufacturing	4.0	7.3	1
Physicians, dentists, and related practitioners.	.7	.5	50 (tied)
Technicians (except health)	1.3	3.1	1
Teachers	3.3	4.9	1
Poverty status—for those receiving income below poverty levels:			
Percentage receiving social security.	19.0	4.6	50
Mean size of family	3.88	4.82	1
Percentage of persons in their state of birth	68.0	31.7	49

* Census was taken during April which accounts for low figures for these seasonal activities. A recent state study estimates the number of fisherman at about 7,000 or roughly 7 percent of the work force.

Note: Per capita indebtedness in $ millions (based on outstanding bonds): state of Alaska, $1,073; average of the 50 states, $207. Alaska's present authorized general obligation bonds: $324,427,000; Alaska's current bond rating, BAA-1.

State and local tax collection per $1000 personal income:

Year	United States	Alaska	Rank among states
1966.	106.63	91.68	46
1967.	105.50	93.52	41
1968.	198.10	91.23	45
1969.	112.20	96.93	41
1970.	116.58	100.14	41

Source: United States 1970 Census.

EXHIBIT 3
Summary of major events in the Trans-Alaska Pipeline controversy

January 1968	Atlantic Richfield and Humble and Refining discover oil at Prudhoe Bay on the North Slope of Alaska. Reserves estimated at ten billion barrels.
February 1969	ARCO, Humble, and British Petroleum announced plans for construction of a 48-inch, crude-oil pipeline to run 789 miles from Prudhoe Bay to the ice-free port of Valdez.
April 1969	Pipe worth $100 million ordered from Japan. Delivery completed in October 1971.
August–October 1969	Interior Department held public hearings in Alaska and issued preliminary requirements for environmental protection.
September 1969	Alaska auctioned off North Slope leases to oil companies for $900 million.
December 1969	Congress passed National Environmental Policy Act (NEPA), which President Nixon signed into law on January 1, 1970.
January 1970	Senate and House Interior Committees voted to permit the Interior Department to grant right-of-way for the pipeline.
March 1970	Three environmental groups sued the Department of Interior, claiming the agency had failed to comply with NEPA. Five Alaskan villages sued the Department of Interior, claiming the pipeline would cross their land without permission.
April 1970	Judge George L. Hart upheld both suits and enjoined the Interior from issuing a pipeline permit without resolving the natives' claims and issuing a satisfactory impact statement.
January–February 1971	Interior Department issued a preliminary impact statement and held public hearings.
July 1971	Alyeska Pipeline Service Company issued a 29-volume *Project Description*. Alaska published *Comments on the Proposed Trans-Alaska Pipeline* in response to the preliminary impact statement.
December 1971	Interior Department published *An Analysis of the Economic and Security Aspects of the Trans-Alaska Pipeline,* supporting the project. Congress passed The Native Claims Act, which resolved the controversy over native ownership claims.
March 1972	Interior Department issued nine-volume *Final Environmental Impact Statement.*
May 1972	Secretary of the Interior, Rogers Morton, approved

EXHIBIT 3 (*concluded*)

	construction of the pipeline project in the "national interest." Alaskan legislature passed the Severance Tax Law (the "cents per barrel amendment") and the Right-of-Way Leasing Act. Oil companies threatened to sue the state over the legislation.
August 1972	Judge Hart lifted the injunction imposed in April 1970, stating that the Interior Department had complied with the NEPA. However, he anticipated "that the final decision rests with the Supreme Court."

Source: *Business Week*, March 25, 1972, p. 80.

EXHIBIT 4

On June 22, 1972, during his testimony before the Joint Economic Committee of the United States Congress, the Secretary of the Interior, Rogers Morton, supported his contention that the Trans-Alaska Pipeline was a preferable alternative to a Canadian pipeline through the Mackenzie River Valley:

1. A Canadian pipeline would cross twelve rivers of a half-mile or more in width, whereas the Alaskan route would involve only one such crossing.
2. The proposal to construct crude-oil and gas pipelines along the same Canadian route was impractical. The engineering and environmental factors dictated that they should be constructed "a considerable distance apart" and were sufficiently different to preclude significant economies of scale in the project.
3. The Canadian project, three times as long as the Alaskan alternative, would require 320 million cubic yards of gravel for construction, the availability of which was uncertain.
4. It would take between three to five years longer to complete the Canadian project, a delay which would be "substantial and unacceptable." The delay would be to drill core tests, in the 700 miles of continuous permafrost along the route, and to prepare environmental impact studies.
5. The Canadian project would cost approximately $6–8 billion as compared with $3–4.5 billion for the Trans-Alaska Pipeline. Moreover, Canada was expected to demand 51% ownership, which would require raising over $3 billion in Canada's capital markets. Secretary Morton doubted this could be accomplished in addition to the $2.2 billion financing for a gas pipeline.
6. The proposed Canadian line might give rise to needless conflict between the United States and Canada.

Source: *Wall Street Journal*

APPENDIX A

NATIONAL ENVIRONMENTAL POLICY ACT OF 1969

For Legislative History of Act, see p. 2751

PUBLIC LAW 91–190; 83 STAT. 852

[S. 1075]

An Act to establish a national policy for the environment, to provide for the establishment of a Coun cil on Environmental Quality, and for other purposes.

Be it enacted by the Senate and House of Representatives of the United States of America in Congress assembled, That:

This Act may be cited as the "National Environmental Policy Act of 1969".

PURPOSE

Sec. 2.   The purposes of this Act are: To declare a national policy which will encourage productive and enjoyable harmony between man and his environment; to promote efforts which will prevent or eliminate damage to the environment and biosphere and stimulate the health and welfare of man; to enrich the understanding of the ecological systems and natural resources important to the Nation; and to establish a Council on Environmental Quality.

TITLE I

DECLARATION OF NATIONAL ENVIRONMENTAL POLICY

Sec. 101.   (a)   The Congress, recognizing the profound impact of man's activity on the interrelations of all components of the natural environment, particularly the profound influences of population growth, high-density urbanization, industrial expansion, resource exploitation, and new and expanding technological advances and recognizing further the critical importance of restoring and maintaining environmental qual-ity to the overall welfare and development of man, declares that it is the continuing policy of the Federal Government, in cooperation with State and local governments, and other concerned public and private organizations, to use all practicable means and measures, including financial and technical assistance, in a manner calculated to foster and promote the general welfare, to create and maintain conditions under which man and nature can exist in productive harmony, and fulfill the social, economic, and other requirements of present and future generations of Americans.

(b)   In order to carry out the policy set forth in this Act, it is the continuing responsibility of the Federal Government to use all practicable means, consistent with other essential considerations of national policy, to improve and coordinate Federal plans, functions, programs, and resources to the end that the Nation may—

> (1)   fulfill the responsibilities of each generation as trustee of the environment for succeeding generations;
>
> (2)   assure for all Americans safe, healthful, productive, and esthetically and culturally pleasing surroundings;

Jan. 1   NAT'L. ENVIRONMENTAL POLICY ACT P.L. 91–190

> (3)   attain the widest range of beneficial uses of the environment without degradation, risk to health or safety, or other undesirable and unintended consequences
>
> (4)   preserve important historic, cultural, and natural aspects of our national heritage, and maintain, wherever possible, an environment which supports diversity and variety of individual choice;
>
> (5)   achieve a balance between population and resource use which will permit high standards of living and a wide sharing of life's amenities; and
>
> (6)   enhance the quality of renewable resources and approach the maximum attainable recycling of depletable resources.

(c)   The Congress recognizes that each person should enjoy a healthful environment and that each person has a responsibility to contribute to the preservation and enhancement of the environment.

Sec. 102.   The Congress authorizes and directs that, to the fullest extent possible: (1) the policies, regulations, and public laws of the United States shall be interpreted and administered in accordance with the policies set forth in this Act, and (2) all agencies of the Federal Government shall—

> (A)   utilize a systematic, interdisciplinary approach which will insure the integrated use of the natural and social sciences and the environmental design arts in planning and in decision-making which may have an impact on man's environment;
>
> (B)   identify and develop methods and procedures, in consultation with the Council on Environmental Quality established by

title II of this Act, which will insure that presently unquantified environmental amenities and values may be given appropriate consideration in decisionmaking along with economic and technical considerations;

(C)   include in every recommendation or report on proposals for legislation and other major Federal actions significantly affecting the quality of the human environment, a detailed statement by the responsible official on—

>   (i)   the environmental impact of the proposed action,
>
>   (ii)   any adverse environmental effects which cannot be avoided should the proposal be implemented,
>
>   (iii)   alternatives to the proposed action,
>
>   (iv)   the relationship between local short-term uses of man's environment and the maintenance and enhancement of long-term productivity, and
>
>   (v)   any irreversible and irretrievable commitments of resources which would be involved in the proposed action should it be implemented.

Prior to making any detailed statement, the responsible Federal official shall consult with and obtain the comments of any Federal agency which has jurisdiction by law or special expertise with respect to any environmental impact involved. Copies of such statement and the comments and views of the appropriate Federal, State, and local agencies, which are authorized to develop and enforce environmental standards, shall be made available to the President, the Council on Environmental Quality and to the public as provided by section 552 of title 5, United States Code, and shall accompany the proposal through the existing agency review processes:

D)   study, develop, and describe appropriate alternatives to recommended courses of action in any proposal which involves unresolved conflicts concerning alternative uses of available resources:

(E)   recognize the worldwide and long-range character of environmental problems and, where consistent with the foreign policy of the United States, lend appropriate support to initiatives, resolutions, and programs designed to maximize international cooperation in anticipating and preventing a decline in the quality of mankind's world environment;

(F)   make available to States, counties, municipalities, institutions, and individuals, advice and information useful in restoring, maintaining, and enhancing the quality of the environment;

(G)   initiate and utilize ecological information in the planning and development of resource-oriented projects; and

(H)   assist the Council on Environmental Quality established by title II of this Act.

Sec. 103.   All agencies of the Federal Government shall review their present statutory authority, administrative regulations, and current policies and procedures for the purpose of determining whether there are any deficiencies or inconsistencies therein which prohibit full compliance with the purposes and provisions of this Act and shall propose to the President not later than July 1, 1971, such measures as may be necessary to bring their authority and policies into conformity with the intent, purposes, and procedures set forth in this Act.

Sec. 104.   Nothing in Section 102 or 103 shall in any way affect the specific statutory obligations of any Federal agency (1) to comply with criteria or standards of environmental quality, (2) to coordinate or consult with any other Federal or State agency, or (3) to act, or refrain from acting contingent upon the recommendations or certification of any other Federal or State agency.

Sec. 105.   The policies and goals set forth in this Act are supplementary to those set forth in existing authorizations of Federal agencies.

APPENDIX B

Excerpts from the *Final Environmental Impact Statement*

Summary of environmental impact and adverse environmental effects

Environmental impact would result from the construction, operation, and maintenance of the proposed oil pipeline system (including the accompanying haul road), of a gas transportation system of some kind, from oil-field development, and from operation of the proposed tanker system. Because of the scale and nature of the project, the impact would occur on abiotic, biotic, and socioeconomic components of the human environment far beyond the relative small part (940 square miles out of 572,000 square miles of land area) of Alaska that would be occupied by the pipeline system and oilfield. The impact paths between the project and the affected parts of the environment would be of varying complexity and length, and would involve linkage factors that are not all well known.

Of the impact effects that would occur, some, like those that would be associated with the wilderness intrusion and public access north of the Yukon River, could be considered either beneficial or adverse, depending on the value framework used. Some effects would occur on socioeconomic parts of the environment which many would classify as beneficial. Most of the remaining impact effects would in some way decrease the existing quality of the parts of the environment affects and would in that sense be adverse. Such effects would occur on both natural physical systems and on the superposed socioeconomic systems.

Some impact effects are unavoidable and can be evaluated with some certainty. Other effects would result from the occurrence of a threatened event which impacts the oil transportation system; these cannot be evaluated with as much certainty.

The principal unavoidable effects would be those disturbances of terrain, fish and wildlife habitat, and human environs during construction, operation, and maintenance of the oil pipeline, haul road, oil field, and of the gas pipeline that would probably follow; the effects of the discharge of effluent from the tanker ballast treatment facility into Port Valdez and of some indeterminable amount of oil into the ocean from tank cleaning operations at sea; and those associated with increased human pressures of all kinds on the environment. Other unavoidable effects would be those related to increased State and Native corporation revenues; accelerated cultural change of the Native populace; and the extraction of the oil and gas resource.

Changes in stable terrain caused by construction and maintenance procedures could produce rapid and unexpected effects, including slope failure, modifications of surface drainage, accelerated erosion and deposition, and other terrain disturbances as a result of the thawing that would follow destruction of the natural insulating properties of tundra vegetation. Placement of gravel pads and berms would especially affect surface drainage. The excavation of borrow materials and pipeline ditch in and near flood plains and stream beds would also cause some changes in stream erosion and deposition. About 83 million cubic yards of construction material, mostly gravel, would be required. The general noise, commotion, and destruction of local habitat could cause many species of wildlife to leave the construction sites, which amount to an area of about 60 square miles for the oil pipeline.

Socioeconomic effects during construction would include accelerated inflation; increased pressures on existing communities for acommodations and public services; and job opportunity for perhaps 25,000 persons at peak times (including multiplier effects), but unemployment would probably continue to be relatively high.

The main operational disturbances would be heat loss from the hot-oil pipeline and resulting changes in permafrost when the ice present (particularly if in segregated masses) thaws and causes possible instability and differential settlement; some barrier effects of aboveground oil pipeline sections on large mammal (especially caribou) migrations in the Brooks Range, Arctic Coastal Plain, and Copper River Basin areas and similar effects of any aboveground sections of gas pipeline that would eventually be built; and adverse but unquantifiable effects on the marine ecosystem of Port Valdez and perhaps Valdez Arm and Prince William Sound proper from the discharge of an estimated 2.4 to 26 barrels of oil per day from the ballast treatment facility at the terminal and on the marine ecosystem in general from discharge of an indeterminate amount of oil from tank cleaning operations at sea. These last effects would in turn affect the fishing industry to some unquantifiable extent.

Other main operational effects would include the gradual conversion of about 880 square miles of the North Slope wildlife habitat to an area with widely spaced drilling pads, roads, pipelines, and other structures with accompanying adverse effects on the tundra ecosystem; the many diverse effects on wilderness, recreational resources (including hunting and fishing), and general land use patterns that would result from increased public access to the relatively inaccessible region north of the Yukon River; acceleration of the cultural change process that is already underway among Alaska Natives and some adverse modification of local Native subsistence resource base as a result of secondary effects; and State revenues of about $300 million per year from extraction of the oil and subsequent expenditures of those revenues for public works and activities throughout Alaska. Immediately after the end of construction unemployment would probably increase.

The main threatened environmental effects would all be related to unintentional oil loss from the pipeline, from tankers or in the oil field. Oil losses from the pipeline could be caused by the direct effects of earthquakes, destructive sea waves, slope failure caused by natural or artificial processes, thaw-plug instability (in permafrost), differential settlement of perma-frost terrain, and bed scour and bank erosion at stream crossings. Any of these processes could occur at some place along the route of the proposed pipeline. Oil loss from tankers could be caused by accidents during transfer operations at Valdez and at destination ports like Puget Sound, San Francisco Bay, and Los Angeles, and by tanker ship casualties due to collision, grounding, ramming, or other cause.

The potential oil loss from pipeline failure cannot be evaluated because of the many variables involved, but perfect no-spill performance would be unlikely during the lifetime of the pipeline. Various models of oil loss from the tanker system indicate that an average of 1.6 to 6.0 barrels per day could be lost from the whole system during transfer operations and an average of 384 barrels per day or about 140,000 barrels per "average" year could be lost from tanker casualties. This modeled amount would occur in incidents of undetermined size at unknown intervals and at unknown locations. This is considered to be a maximum or "worst case" casualty discharge volume.

Oil spilled from the pipeline as a consequence of one of the threats mentioned, could, depending on location, volume, time or year, and other factors. result in adverse effects on all of the biota involved; not all of the linkage factors are known, but vegetation, waterfowl, and freshwater fisheries could all be affected and in turn affect Native subsistence use to some unquantifiable extent.

Oil spilled in tanker casualties or transfer operations would affect the marine ecosystem to an extent that would be determined by many variable factors. The salmon and other fishery resources of Prince William Sound would be especially vulnerable to such spills. Over the long term, however, persistent low-level discharge from the ballast treatment facility and tank cleaning operations at sea could have a greater adverse effect than could short-lived larger spills.

The probable eventual construction and maintenance of a gas pipeline would, if it were not in the oil pipeline corridor, result in a separate corridor with some of the same effects described for the proposed oil pipeline corridor.

APPENDIX C

Alyeska's claims based upon the *Project Description* and public relations material distributed by Alyeska Pipeline Service Company

Permafrost.   Disappointed by the inability to develop adequate insulation for the pipeline, Alyeska deviated from the original design which called for burial of 90 percent of the line. Based upon over 15,000 samplings of subsurface ice wedges and soil conditions, Alyeska altered the design to provide for three modes of construction. Along 50 percent of the route, where soil was either bedrock or well drained gravel, the line would be conventionally buried at depths ranging from 18 inches to several feet. Along approximately 40 percent of the route, where melting of permafrost could produce pipe deformation or hazardous soil conditions, the line would be constructed above ground. This would necessitate construction of supporting pile bents or gravel berms, spaced approximately 50 to 70 feet apart to ensure that the pipe would remain at least two feet above the ground. The pipe would be thermally insulated along this suspension system. Over the remainder of the route the design called for a special burial technique, for economic or safety reasons, even though underground construction was feasible. The construction technique utilized would either be heat sinks or heat extraction piles to insulate the pipeline. Where neither of these methods adequately prevented thawing, pumped convention or mechanical refrigeration would provide efficient heat extraction. Alyeska contended that the modified design eliminated any risk of permafrost thawing.

Earthquakes. Alyeska designed the pipeline to withstand the effects of "contingency earthquakes," which were defined as equal to, or greater in magnitude than, any known earthquake which had occurred in the fault areas through which the line would pass. Additionally, the pipeline was designed to remain functional during "operational earthquakes," defined as one half the magnitude of contingency earthquakes. The route was nearly perpendicular to the Denali Fault, the only active zone along its course, which limited potential displacements to a few miles. The special above ground construction techniques enabled the pipeline to sustain, without rupturing, a horizontal movement of 20 feet and a vertical movement of 3 feet. Additionally, the pipeline would be laid in a trapezoidal zig-zag pattern to withstand maximum stress. A monitoring system with remote control valves provided an additional safety feature in the event of seismic activity.

Pipeline activity. Alyeska contended that a complex automatic monitoring system, presenting updated data every ten seconds, would be capable of detecting leaks much less than one percent of the line flow. Four separate automatic alarm systems would be integrated in a computerized system to monitor pressure deviation, flow deviation, flow balance deviation and line volume balance. The line volume balance method could detect a leak as small as 31 barrels per hour. Additionally, a leak detector "pig" would be utilized to travel through the line to determine leaks as small as five barrels per hour. In the event that a leak was detected, Alyeska's system of block and check valves, spaced no further than 20 miles apart, could halt the oil flow in less than four minutes.

Wildlife. Alyeska explained that aboveground sections of the pipeline would be short enough so that animal migration would not be impaired. Where vegetation was disturbed, it was believed that new experimental strains would enable Alyeska to revegetate the route rapidly and effectively, thus providing food and habitat for wildlife. With regard to fish life, the construction would occur at such a time that spawning activities would not be disturbed and in such a way that siltation would be minimized. Additionally, the route crossed streams, the pipeline would be buried at 120 percent of maximum depth ("scour depth") encased in several inches of concrete.

Tanker spills. Alyeska contended that Port Valdez, the northern most ice-free Alaskan port, was one of the world's safest harbors. The channel depth exceeded 100 fathoms, and was 3000 feet in width, which compared favorable with most other shipping channels, and Alyeska explained that "never in the history of the port has a ship failed to dock or undock because of tides, wind, fog, sea conditions, ice or any condition relating to weather." The marine terminal was located on bedrock 250–400 feet above sea level in an area undisturbed by the earthquake which destroyed old Valdez. In the event of a tsunami (seismically generated tidal wave) the Alaskan Tsunami Warning System could provide sufficient warning to docked ships and the operating platforms were designed to withstand 12-foot waves, equivalent to those experienced during the 1964 earthquake. Incorporated in the terminal design were steel loading arms, which eliminated the need for hoses, sophisticated navigational aids, and a ballast treatment unit which could reduce the oil content in ballast water one part per million by the time it was flushed into the harbor. Additionally, tankers calling on Valdez would not be permitted to load oil if inspection of their ballast tanks indicated that they had dumped ballast at sea prior to entering the harbor. Alyeska also cited that the Jones Act would prohibit the use of foreign carriers, that the U.S. shipping had a better safety record than most other countries.

Atlantic Richfield Company (ARCO)[1]

IN THE SPRING of 1972 Thornton F. Bradshaw, president of Atlantic Richfield Company, discussed the problems facing the energy industry and its major segment, the petroleum industry, during the 1970s. One of Mr. Bradshaw's primary concerns was planning for future refining capacity needs on a regional basis. Although the location of refineries depended to some extent upon the final selection of the transportation alternative for crude oil from the North Slope of Alaska, site selection and construction feasibility studies should begin as soon as possible in order to provide sufficient lead-time for the anticipated opposition to refinery construction by local residents. Atlantic Richfield's development of energy alternatives (oil shale, tar sand, and nuclear energy) was also conditional upon the availability of North Slope oil to reduce the energy gap projected for 1980.

Corporate history

Growth through mergers during the late 1960s vaulted Atlantic Refining Company from the 15th largest petroleum firm in the 1965 Fortune 500 to the 8th largest in 1970.[2] Prior to its mergers with both Richfield

---

[1] This case was prepared by Howard W. Pifer, lecturer on Business Administration as a basis for class discussion rather than to illustrate either effective or ineffective handling of an administrative situation.

[2] Domestic petroleum firms which ranked above Atlantic Richfield in 1970 were Standard Oil of New Jersey, Mobil, Texaco, Gulf, Standard Oil of California, Standard Oil of Indiana, and Shell. In 1965 the list included the above plus Phillips, Continental, Sinclair, Union, Cities Service, Sun, and Tidewater.

Oil (1966) and Sinclair Oil (1969), Atlantic Refining was declining in relative size among major U.S. corporations. Selected financial and operating data since 1950 are provided in Exhibit 1.

Mr. Thornton F. Bradshaw joined Atlantic in 1956 as assistant general manager of accounting and analytical services. In 1958 Mr. Bradshaw was elected vice president and general manager of finance and accounting and a member of the Board of Directors. Four years later he was promoted to the newly formed position of executive vice president in charge of finance and accounting, research and development, chemicals and diversification. The 1963 acquisition of Hondo Oil Company brought its president, Robert O. Anderson into the Atlantic Refining Company as a member of the Board of Directors. In 1965, Messrs. Anderson and Bradshaw were promoted to their current positions of chairman of the board/chief executive officer and president, respectively.

During the 1960–65 period, Atlantic's assets grew at an annual rate of less than 4 percent; its operating revenue, 4.6 percent. Production, refining, and petroleum sales grew slowly while the two refineries at Philadelphia and Port Arthur, Texas were expanded from 210,000 to 239,000 barrels per day capacity. Retail outlets were limited to the 18 states in the New England, Middle Atlantic and Southeast regions.

Richfield Oil merger

The rapid growth in the late 1960s began with the January 3, 1966 announcement of the merger of Richfield Oil into Atlantic Refining, forming the Atlantic Richfield Company. Richfield operated from a single 165,000 barrel per day refinery in Carson, California and distributed only on the West Coast. With assets in excess of $1.6 billion, Atlantic Richfield ranked thirteenth among major oil companies after the merger. It marketed automotive products through some 13,000 service stations in 24 states.

The merger increased the likelihood of Atlantic Richfield's achieving complete domestic crude oil self-sufficiency. Other advantages included a more efficient complex of refineries strategically located for availability to ocean tanker transportation, marketing in the two fastest growing regions and a new chemical company.

Sinclair Oil merger

On March 4, 1969 Sinclair Oil Corporation was merged into the Atlantic Richfield Company. Prior to the merger, the Justice Department commenced an antitrust suit in the U.S. Second District Court. Atlantic Richfield agreed to sell Sinclair's marketing outlets which overlapped with Atlantic's markets in New England, Middle Atlantic and Southeast regions and two refineries (Atlantic Richfield's in Port Arthur, Texas and Sinclair's in Marcus Hook, Pennsylvania) to British Petroleum.

After the merger and the above divestitures, the new Atlantic Richfield Company had assets of more than $4 billion and five refineries with a refining capacity of 702,000 barrels of crude oil per day. Atlantic's markets were expanded to some 24,000 retail outlets throughout the continental United States with the exception of Maine and Montana. It also had a more diversified chemical business as well as a limited stake in the production of nuclear energy. The justification for the Sinclair merger was linked to ARCO's 1968 oil discovery in Alaska at Prudhoe Bay on the North Slope. Sinclair had a relative imbalance with a large refining and retailing capacity and a shortage in crude oil production.

In August 1970, a final agreement was reached with the Justice Department to divest itself within three years, of former Sinclair assets in the Midcontinent area, including approximately 2,500 marketing outlets in 14 states, the 32,000 barrel per day refinery in Sinclair, Wyoming and oil producing leases in seven Wyoming fields. In 1971 a proposed sale to American Petrofina was found unacceptable by the Department of Justice. Efforts to sell these assets were continuing in the Spring of 1972.

Post-merger developments

The operating segments of the petroleum industry can be defined as exploration for new oil reserves, production and transportation of crude oil from known reserves, refining of crude into petroleum products, and the marketing of these products through industrial and consumer markets. Throughout these operations, crude oil can be processed into final petroleum products with little, if any, change in volume. Thus, one barrel of crude oil can be assumed to yield one barrel of final products. In 1970, crude oil was refined into final products in roughly the following proportions: motor fuel 40 percent, kerosene and jet fuel 8 percent, distillate fuel oil 17 percent, residual fuel oil 15 percent and miscellaneous products (lubricants, waxes, asphalt, etc.) 20 percent. Within each of these segments, independent nonintegrated corporations competed directly with self-sufficient, fully integrated oil companies.

Prior to the mergers Atlantic was a strong regional marketer of petroleum products within the first Petroleum Administration for Defense (PAD) District (see Exhibit 2 for the definition of geographical regions) with production concentrated in the third PAD District and refineries in both regions. After the mergers ARCO was a nationwide oil major with production, refining, and marketing capabilities in all five PAD districts. Exhibit 3 summarizes the recent regional position of Atlantic Richfield in net proved reserves, production, refining, and sales.

Some observers believed that the potential impact of Atlantic's oil discovery on the North Slope of Alaska might overshadow its previous growth through mergers. At year end 1971, ARCO's net proven reserves of petroleum liquids, excluding North Slope, were 2.6 billion barrels of which 1.5 billion were located in North America. At current production levels, this represented an eleven-year supply worldwide and a 9.6-year supply in North America. ARCO's 20 percent share in the North Slope (1.9 billion barrels) increased these life indices by approximately 70 percent worldwide and 125 percent in North America. As reported by the American Petroleum Institute, proved reserves in the main Prudhoe Bay field totaled 9.6 billion barrels of recoverable oil.

During 1971 Atlantic Richfield completed a sixth refinery in the state of Washington, increasing its refining capacity to 802,000 barrels per day. The plans for a Washington refinery had been delayed for more than a decade by local zoning issues. The location of the refinery complemented ARCO's growing West Coast market. In addition, it was strategically placed to be supplied by Canadian petroleum and, if the Trans-Alaska Pipeline were completed, oil from the North Slope.

ENERGY OUTLOOK

Historically, the United States had enjoyed a relative abundance of domestic fuels. Although in the past some petroleum had been imported, the United States could have met all of its needs. This situation had significantly changed by 1970. The United States was no longer self-sufficient in energy supply and would soon become dependent on foreign sources as the increase in the consumption of energy outstriped the development of both new and established domestic energy sources. The demand for energy would nearly double by 1985, and would require the development of alternative sources of supply (see Exhibit 4).

Petroleum

Crude oil was the largest single source of energy in the United States and was expected to retain this position. In 1970 crude oil provided more than 40 percent of the total energy supplied and had in the past been able to make up the energy deficit between demand and other sources of supply. At current rates of consumption, the United States was using up her crude oil reserves faster than the oil industry was able to develop new sources. In the late 1960s, crude oil production in the United States exceeded 3 billion barrels annually whereas additions to reserves were approximately 2 billion barrels per year (excluding the North Slope of Alaska). To encourage domestic exploration, imports of foreign crude by any oil company were originally limited in PAD Districts 1 through 4 to 12.2 percent of their domestic production. These quotas had been increased to higher levels in recent years. Lagging domestic production again forced President Nixon to increase these quotas by approximately 15 percent in May 1972. Under the new restrictions, daily imports excluding Canada were 1,165,000 barrels; Canadian allotment, 570,000 barrels. Residual fuel oil imports were not subject to quota limitations and amounted to 2.3 million barrels per day in 1970.

Future U.S. reliance upon Eastern Hemisphere crude oil was almost certain to occur by 1980, although the level was uncertain. In January 1970 known, world crude oil reserves consisted of 534 billion barrels. Although U.S. interests owned, leased, or held under concessions more than 50 percent of these reserves, the majority of existing reserves were located in the Middle East (330 billion barrels) and not in the United States (30 billion barrels excluding the North Slope). Most oil companies doubted that major new finds would be made with the possible exception of the Continental Shelf off the East Coast of the United States and the Arctic shores of North America, including Alaska's North Slope.

In order to gauge the possible magnitude of forecasted U.S. crude oil deficits by 1980, ranges for domestic supply and final product demand have been estimated in Exhibit 5. If the demand for crude oil products in 1980 was low and the crude oil supply from the United States, Canada, and other Western Hemisphere sources was high, then the deficit excluding the North Slope would only be 3.2 million barrels per day, or 16 percent of demand. On the other hand, if the demand was high and the alternative supply sources low, the daily need for Eastern Hemisphere oil would be 13.2 million barrels, approximately 53 percent of demand.[3] The unstable political situation and demands by Middle East countries for equity participation affected the reliability of Eastern Hemisphere crude. North Slope oil could decrease the 1980 daily deficit by 2 million barrels.

More than two thirds of oil reserves in the "lower 48" states were found in the third PAD District, primarily in West Texas and offshore Louisiana—nearly 40 percent of the demand coming from the first PAD District. Only PAD Districts 3 and 4 produced more crude oil than they consumed. These regional differences resulted in significant interdistrict flows as summarized in Exhibit 6. Most exports entered along the East Coast, primarily from Venezuela in the Western Hemisphere.

---

[3] These estimates were based upon the forecasted 1980 U.S. supply and demand as well as a forecast of future daily Canadian (low, 1.0 million; medium, 1.4 million; high, 1.6 million) and other Western Hemisphere (low, 2.0 million; medium, 2.4 million; high, 3.3 million) imports.

1980 forecasts of petroleum supply and demand by region accentuate the current petroleum deficits on both coasts and in the Midwest. The size of these deficits would depend upon the resolution of the Trans-Alaska Pipeline decision and the destination of Alaskan crude oil.

Nuclear

Progress in commercial applications of nuclear power had been far slower than had been anticipated only five years ago. The commercial operation of nuclear power plants was running two or three years behind original schedule, and overall lead times of six to seven years were being forecasted for new plants. Previous forecasts published by the Atomic Energy Commission had not anticipated the magnitude of delays that have resulted from technical problems and environmental concern over the possibility of radiation hazards and thermal pollution.

In April 1967, Atlantic Richfield acquired the assets of Nuclear Materials and Equipment Corporation (NUMEC) which produced uranium and plutonium-bearing fuels for nuclear reactions. To enhance its position in the field. Atlantic Richfield sought and won in 1967 a five-year contract to operate the AEC's Hanford plant near Richland, Washington which included facilities for separating plutonium, uranium, and other fission products from irradiated reactor fuels. This complex was operated by a subsidiary, Atlantic Richfield Hanford Company. In 1971 Atlantic Richfield, prompted by unsatisfactory expected returns, sold its subsidiary NUMEC but continued to be active in the nuclear field through the operation of the Atlantic Richfield Hanford Company.

Coal

Over-optimistic estimates of nuclear power capacity deterred the development of new coal mining during the 1960s. Air-quality regulations applying to the burning of fuels prevented consumers in the East and Midwest from using abundant local supplies because of their high sulfur content. Low-sulfur coals were generally located in the Rockies at significant distances from these markets. Although ample secure supplies of coal were available, expanded use of coal as a solid fuel was relatively undesirable at current levels of technology. ARCO controlled significant coal reserves in the Rocky Mountains and Illinois.

Natural gas

Demand for natural gas had grown at an average rate of 6 percent a year and potential demand was expected to exceed domestic supplies by a significant margin in the near future. Gas suppliers were reluctant to expand exploration and production in the face of price regulation by the Federal Power Commission. In the context of present regulatory procedures and supply conditions, the National Petroleum Council expected domestic production to decline sharply through 1985 with an increasing contribution of synthetic gas from naptha by 1975 and from coal by 1985. ARCO was a substantial producer of natural gas with 1970 North American sales amounting to more than 2 billion cubic feet per day.

Synthetics

While it was possible to derive crude oil from coal, tar sands, and oil shale, economic viability at current market prices had not been demonstrated except possibly for Canadian tar sands. Tar sands and oil shale were likely to become significant sources of crude oil although there was considerable uncertainty concerning the timing of such development. If by 1980 the North Slope could provide 2 million barrels of crude oil per day and the development of synthetics proceeded as currently planned, a few hundred thousand barrels of synthetics per day would be available.

If, on the other hand, an all-out effort were undertaken to develop synthetics, shale oil might yield 1 million barrels per day, coal liquefaction 2 million barrels daily, and tar sands supplementing Canadian supplies by 1 or 2 million barrels per day. In this case, synthetics could become a real alternative by 1980. Such development could reduce dependence on foreign sources, but would require enormous investments for plants and equipment.

Oil shale was any type of rock containing a solid organic material which, when heated, became liquid and could be separated from the shale. Extensive reserves of oil shale have been located in the Rocky Mountains. Currently, Colony Development Company, 30 percent owned and operated by Atlantic Richfield, was analyzing results of engineering and economic feasibility studies directed towards construction of a 50,000 barrels per day shale oil plant to come on-stream in 1976. The very low sulfur residual fuel output would be of interest to utilities. It was expected that further commercial development of this alternative would be delayed until the 1980s to allow for an economic evaluation of this initial study.

Tar sands contained oil of such high viscosity that it would not flow to a conventional oil well. Sun Oil's initial development of this technology had been in the Athabascan region of Alberta, Canada and had reached the breakeven point at its 45,000 barrels per day pilot plant. Atlantic Richfield Canada, Ltd. held the largest position in Canadian tar sands. Syncrude Canada, Ltd., in which ARCO owned a 30 percent interest, received approval in 1971 to construct a 125,000-barrels-per-day plant along the Athabasca River which was expected to be in operation by 1976. Again, full-scale development of this alternative awaited economic evaluation.

ALASKAN OIL

On March 20, 1972, the Department of Interior published the "Final Environmental Impact Statement, Proposed Trans-Alaska Pipeline." This report, which was required under the provisions of the National Environmental Policy Act (NEPA), comprehensively investigated the major issues in the transportation of North Slope oil to markets in the "lower 48" states. Exhibit 7 summarizes the major events since Atlantic Richfield discovered oil at Prudhoe Bay on the North Slope of Alaska.

History of Alaska

Alaska, with its wealth of untapped natural resources, might very well be America's last frontier. Purchased from Russia in 1867 by then Secretary of State Seward, the state owed its name to Senator Charles Sumner of Massachusetts, whose three-hour speech back in 1867 helped persuade the Senate to vote 27–12 in favor of investing in "Seward's Folly." It name, a corruption of the native Aleut word "Alyeska" meaning the great land, was an appropriate one. Alaska was twice the size of Texas and nearly one fifth the size of the rest of the continental United States—586,000 square miles, encompassing four time zones and five distinct weather zones. However, the population of this vast expanse was only 293,000 in 1970.

Except for the gold and copper rushes in the Yukon Valley around the turn of the century, most Americans ignored Alaska. Many politicians did not want to become associated with the controversial land purchase, so it was not until 1912 that Alaska became a U.S. territory. At that time fish, furs, and minerals were the principal products of Alaska, but even then inhabitants were pinning their hopes on oil.

Oil had been discovered in Alaska prior to its purchase by the United States. Russians sent to explore Alaska for the Czar found oil seeps in scattered locations along Gulf of Alaska shores. In 1902, a successful well was drilled by American prospectors and a number of subsequent shallow wells provided small quantities of crude oil which was refined for local needs, primarily lamp oil.

During World War II, the government concluded that oil exploration in Alaska would be necessary in order to obtain a local supply of petroleum products to support military forces in Alaska. The U.S. Navy undertook exploration efforts to develop this desired new source of oil on Naval Petroleum Reserve No. 4, a large tract of federally owned land on the North Slope of Alaska. The navy exploration efforts resulted in discovery of the Umiat Field which had reserves of around 100 million barrels of oil. Had the oil industry discovered Umiat in the "lower 48" states, the field would have quickly gone into production. But, having spent $45 million to find the oil and with no solution for getting it out of the Arctic economically, the Navy could not afford the additional expense of exploiting the discovery.

The oil industry was convinced that if the navy could find oil in Alaska, it could too. So, after World War II, the oil industry began wildcatting and found some oil and gas, but not enough to warrant any large-scale activity until 1957 when the Richfield Oil Corporation discovered the Swanson River Field in the Cook Inlet area of southern Alaska. This marked the first major commercial production in Alaska and signalled a new era of development. Two years later Alaska became the 49th state. The next decade represented a period of some growth, both in population and economic development.

Discovery of oil

As operator for itself and Humble Oil and Refining Company, Atlantic Richfield drilled two wells in a jointly held block of leases covering 90,000 acres in the Prudhoe Bay area of the North Slope. The first of these wells discovered oil in February 1968. The second well, drilled seven miles away, confirmed the oil discovery of the first well in June 1968. On the basis of these two wells, the independent consulting firm of DeGolyer and MacNaughton was quoted as estimating the structure to contain some 5 to 10 billion barrels of oil. In July 1968, the company reported the opinion of DeGolyer and MacNaughton regarding its discovery of oil on the North Slope of Alaska.

News of the Prudhoe Bay strike resulted in a rush by other oil producers to obtain lease rights on the North Slope. On September 10, 1969, the state of Alaska offered for sale oil leases on 179 tracts, each approximately 2,500 acres. The leases were let by competitive, sealed bids and netted the state more than $900 million. Based on an economic analysis of the 179 tracts and its substantial North Slope acreage position prior to the sale, ARCO bid on the tracts being sold. Nineteen of these bids encompassing 47,000 acres were accepted at a cost of $32 million. Many companies without a position in the North Slope apparently entered bids in excess of the economic value of certain tracts.

Prior to the Atlantic Richfield discovery, leases in the area brought between $13 and $15 per acre. In addition to the Atlantic Refining Company, other oil companies which investigated the North Slope before 1968 were Humble, British Petroleum, and Atlantic's partners through mergers, Richfield and Sinclair.

Shortly after the oil lease sale, ARCO announced that five of the nine exploratory wells completed since the first discovery were productive. The drilling cost for the initial well exceeded $4.5 million. Subsequent wells each required $1 million, far in excess of the average drilling cost in the "lower 48."[4] In addition, oil companies faced harsh climate conditions in their search for and extraction of oil. But the major obstacle in large-scale, commercial development had been the difficulty in transporting the oil at economical cost from the frozen North Slope to markets in the "lower 48" states.

In an attempt to develop transportation alternatives, eight oil companies established the Trans-Alaska Pipeline System (TAPS) as a joint enterprise. Subsequently, TAPS was succeeded by the Alyeska Pipeline Service Company. Participation included Atlantic Richfield (interest, 28.08 percent), British Petroleum (28.08 percent), Humble Oil (25.52 percent), Mobil Oil (8.68 percent), Phillips Petroleum (3.32 percent), Union Oil (3.32 percent) and Amerada Hess (3.00 percent). In April 1969, the oil companies applied for a permit to build an access road and an 800-mile pipeline from the North Slope to Valdez, an ice-free port on the Gulf of Alaska (see Exhibit 8). The pipeline design called for an initial capacity of 650,000 barrels per day and an ultimate capacity of 2 million barrels per day. Originally, the haul road and the pipeline were projected to be in operation by the summer of 1972.

Various conservation groups raised objections to building the access road, the first step toward the actual pipeline construction. Some were worried that the heated oil in the pipeline would melt the terrain, upsetting the delicately balanced tundra environment which was thought to be incapable of regenerating itself in the harsh Arctic climate. They feared caribou migrations would be upset by the large percentage of pipe above ground (TAPS had originally planned to lay 15 percent of the pipe above ground). Ecologists feared pollution from oil spills in Alaskan waters. And some have challenged projections of domestic need for the oil and suggested the oil would actually find its way to Japanese markets.

Environmental issues

In the midst of the Alaskan pipeline controversy, President Nixon signed the National Environmental Policy Act (NEPA). The law, which required that environmental impacts must figure in governmental decision making, had become a major tool for the opponents to the pipeline. In a move which held up construction of the pipeline, three plaintiffs

---

[4] The average drilling cost on the North Slope was $150 per foot compared with $15 per foot in West Texas; the cost of operating a rig was $23,000 per day compared with $3,700 per day in West Texas; rig-up time on the North Slope was about 18 days compared to 5 days in West Texas.

(the Wilderness Society, Friends of the Earth, and the Environmental Defense Fund, Inc., of New York) won a preliminary injunction from U.S. District Court Judge George A. Hart Jr. in Washington, D.C. on April 13, 1970. Judge Hart enjoined the Interior from issuing a construction permit for the proposed pipeline until it had satisfied the stipulation under NEPA which required a comprehensive report on the environmental impact of the pipeline, assessing the problems and weighing the alternatives.

In mid-March of 1972, Secretary of the Interior Rogers C. B. Morton issued the report which discussed in considerable detail the issues raised by environmentalists.

> With so many potential hazards, more environmental planning has gone into the pipeline than into any other construction project in history. The Interior study cost $9 million, while Alyeska has spent more than $35 million on research. Among scores of projects, Alyeska has studied the spawning habits of salmon, developed new species of fast-growing vegetation to reduce erosion, and excavated 189 archeological sites. In all environmental safeguards will boost the pipeline cost by more than $300 million.

> Much of this work has been spurred by the requirements of the NEPA, backed by vigilant environmental groups. Moreover, the Interior has used the impact statement to list 64 pages of stipulations governing pipeline construction and operation—ranging from fish protection to soil standards.

> Yet several major environmental worries persist:

> *Permafrost stability.* In areas where the permafrost has a high ice content, the pipeline will be elevated, so that the oil flowing at 145 degrees does not melt the ice and cause the line to sag and possibly break. Originally, only 15% of the line was to be elevated (a raised line is vulnerable to sabotage), but hundreds of test borings convinced Alyeska that it should raise fully half of the line. The other half will be buried in permafrost that remains stable whether frozen or thawed. The Interior report agrees that proper siting and design can avoid permafrost problems, but it urges government inspection during and after construction.

> *Earthquakes.* A "large-magnitude earthquake," the Interior says, is "almost a certainty" during the lifetime of the line. But Alyeska claims that the pipeline is designed to withstand the severest quakes ever recorded in Alaska, and the Interior report apparently agrees. The department also calls for plans to limit spills, if the line does rupture.

> *Pipeline spills.* Landslides, river bank erosion, and other events could also trigger pipeline leaks, the report says, damaging vegetation, waterfowl, and fresh-water industries. Though Alyeska can shut the line within minutes of a large rupture, up to 64,000 bbls. would escape at some points. Moreover, chronic leaks of up to 31 bbls. an hour could go undetected for days. Alyeska says it is committed to cleaning up any spills and rehabilitating the land.

Tanker spills. Some 140,000 bbls. a year—an average of 384 bbls. a day—can be expected to spill from tanker collisions and groundings, the report says. And small but steady discharges at Valdez could have a greater adverse effect, says the report, than short-lived larger spills. Alyeska claims that tidal action and bacterial degradation will reduce the oil content at Valdez to 10 parts per billion—"essentially zero." If a major spill occurs, Alyeska will deploy an array of absorbents, booms, skimmers, and separators to contain and remove the oil. But, says John Dienelt of the Environmental Defense Fund: "As long as they put the oil into boats, we'll be opposed to the pipeline."

Wildlife. The elevated sections might block caribou, moose, and sheep migrations, pipeline construction would destroy or modify at least 60 square miles of bird habitat, and ground and air traffic would drive large mammals from part of their habitat. Fish, too, might be affected by excessive siltation of rivers. Alyeska concedes that nature will be disrupted, but it believes that the overall impact is small and mostly temporary.[5]

On May 11, 1972, Secretary of the Interior Rogers Morton approved the construction of the Trans-Alaska Pipeline. In approving the pipeline, Secretary Morton noted that balance of payments and national security outweighed environmental factors. This announcement was in accordance with Judge Hart's injunction which required advance notice prior to issuing the construction permit. The Environmental Defense Fund, one of a number of organizations opposing the pipeline, vowed it would take its case to the Supreme Court if necessary. Their arguments rested heavily upon the refusal by the Department of the Interior to hold public hearings after publishing the final impact statement.

If Judge Hart rejected these arguments, the next judicial review would be the Federal Court of Appeals. In a May 1972 opinion this court overruled Judge Hart on a procedural question, permitting both a member of the Canadian Parliament and the Canadian Wildlife Federation to intervene in the pipeline permit case. Both parties opposed the trans-Alaska route on the basis that heavy tanker traffic southward from Valdez would threaten the Canadian Pacific coast with harmful oil spills.

Following the favorable decision by the Interior, Alyeska stated that it would not start construction until the courts settled the pipeline issue. In an earlier assessment, Alyeska expected further litigation to be resolved by the end of 1972 which would permit construction to begin in March 1973 and to be completed by 1976.

Oil transport alternatives

In addition to environmental issues, the Interior's impact statement evaluated alternative methods of transporting North Slope oil to markets

---

[5] *Business Week,* March 25, 1972, pp. 79–80.

in the "lower 48" states. Although many transportation modes and routes have been proposed, only three alternatives could be justified economically.

1. *Trans-Alaska Pipeline.* This proposal had received most of the attention with a comprehensive engineering evaluation completed by the Alyeska Pipeline Service Company. This pipeline would transverse the state of Alaska from Prudhoe Bay on the North Slope to the southern ice-free port of Valdez. The crude oil would then be transported by tankers either to West Coast ports or the East Coast via tankers and a pipeline across the Isthmus of Panama (see Exhibit 8). Transportation expenses per barrel for each segment of this proposed system had been estimated to be:

Pipeline:
Prudhoe Bay to Valdez $0.45
Isthmus of Panama 10
Tanker:
Valdez to Seattle 40
Valdez to Los Angeles 45
Valdez to Panama 55
Panama to New York 30

These pipeline costs were based on the original investment required to build the pipeline, operating costs for the pipeline, and a fair return on the pipeline investment. The rate of return on pipelines was controlled by the Interstate Commerce Commission (ICC) and currently ranged from 7 to 8 percent. Current estimates of the investment required were $3 billion and could increase the pipeline tariffs by a factor of two or three.

Although the construction of the Trans-Alaska Pipeline had not begun, ARCO's investment in North Slope oil was estimated to be approximately $200 million—$100 million in oil leases and exploration expenses, and $100 million in the Alyeska Pipeline Service Company.

2. *MacKenzie Valley Pipeline (MVPL).* This alternative to the Trans-Alaskan Pipeline would link Prudhoe Bay with Inuvik, Canada and then follow the MacKenzie River Valley from Inuvik to Edmonton, Canada. From Edmonton, existing pipelines to either Seattle or Chicago would bring the oil to the West Coast and Midwest markets (see Exhibit 8). Construction of a pipeline between Chicago and New York would permit North Slope oil to reach the East Coast. The per barrel transportation costs for pipeline segments which originally had been estimated on the basis of a $3 billion MVPL investment were:

Pipeline:
Prudhoe Bay to Inuvik $0.20
Inuvik to Edmonton 50
Edmonton to Seattle 40
Edmonton to Chicago 38
Chicago to New York 25

Many of the environmental issues cited for the Trans-Alaska Pipeline would apply to the MVPL except that the impacts would affect Canada rather than Alaska. This 2,500-mile route through the MacKenzie River Valley would be three times as long as the Alaska pipeline, transversing twice as much permafrost. However, the threat of oil spills from North Slope crude and other marine pollution would not, of course, apply to this land route. Supporters of the Trans-Alaska Pipeline pointed out that construction of the MVPL would not necessarily eliminate the problem of oil spillage. If the MVPL were developed and the oil were transported to PAD Districts 1 or 2, future West Coast deficits would most likely be met by ocean-borne imports of Eastern Hemisphere oil, transported in foreign-flag tankers which might not have the navigational and other safety features required of U.S.-flag tankers.

The major drawbacks of this route centered on the expected delays in bringing Alaskan oil and gas to market. First, engineering evaluation of the Canadian route would be required. Second, complicated international negotiations with the Canadian government would delay construction. Finally, insufficient rigging crews were available to complete simultaneously the MVPL oil pipeline and the proposed natural gas pipeline planned for this route. It was estimated that a decision to transport oil via MVPL would delay North Slope production until 1978.[6]

The MacKenzie Valley Pipeline is estimated to require a $5 to $6 billion investment, an amount which would exceed the financing capability of major oil companies. Thus, some portion of the capitalization of this alternative would have to come from public sources, among them the Canadian government. Nationalism had become a significant political issue in Canada and, even if the MVPL could be financed by private U.S. sources, some observers believed that financial participation by Canadians, not necessarily the government, would be required.

The Canadian government had a significant interest in this route. MVPL would open up the Canadian Northwest Territory, an area which promised additional energy sources. But Canadian sources, by themselves, could not support a pipeline. In light of this, the Canadian government had expressed a strong desire to leave open a certain proportion of the MVPL pipeline (approximately 50 percent) for future transport of oil from Canadian fields. In addition, construction of the pipeline through Canada would, by government stipulations, be required to use both Canadian steel and Canadian workers. These constraints on labor and raw material inputs could adversely affect the United States balance of payments.

---

[6] Because the expected life of the Prudhoe Bay field was several decades, the discounted value to the oil industry of delayed production would approximately equal the profit margin from 2 million barrels a day multiplied by the length of delay. This opportunity cost would also apply to environmental delays.

3. *Northwest Passage route.* The desire to find an all-water route through the Northwest Passage, coupled with a prospect of economic feasibility, had induced Humble with limited participation by Atlantic Richfield and British Petroleum to fit an icebreaking bow to the 150,000 deadweight ton tanker, Manhattan. The Manhattan, escorted by two icebreakers, completed the passage between New York and the North Slope in 1969 and 1970, returning with two holes in its hull (see Exhibit 8). After the test Humble concluded that the route would be possible with tankers specifically designed for ice passage.

The Jones Act (Merchant Marine Act of 1920) required that cargo between American ports be carried in American-flag ships. Mr. Louis F. Davis, executive vice president of Atlantic Richfield's North American Producing Division, estimated that the Jones Act added 40 percent to tanker costs. The transportation cost from Prudhoe Bay through the Northwest Passage to New York by American-flag icebreakers had been estimated at $1.30 per barrel.

Economic comparison of transportation alternatives

The relative economic attractiveness of the above-mentioned alternatives depended strongly on the markets to which the crude oil was transported and upon the pricing structure within those markets. Crude-oil market prices represented the value of the resource at the wellhead plus the cost of gathering and transportation. Petroleum imports were subject to an additional import duty of $.105 per barrel.

The average wellhead price of domestically produced crude was $3.18 per barrel in 1970, significantly higher than the world market price (see Exhibit 9 for historical wellhead prices). Since more than 60 percent of domestic production was in Texas and Louisiana, regional variations in delivered prices were due primarily to transportation charges. Shipment of crude oil from PAD District 3 to New York by tanker cost $0.45 per barrel and pipeline charges to Chicago averaged $0.28 per barrel.

Recent negotiations with the Organization of Petroleum Exporting Countries (OPEC) had resulted in significant increases in the future wellhead price of foreign crude oil. Representative prices for Eastern Hemisphere oil were currently estimated to increase from $1.59 in 1970 to $2.51 by 1975. Venezuela, the largest source of crude oil imported into the United States, increased its wellhead price to $2.66 per barrel in 1971 and future crude prices were subject to governmental decrees effective January 1972.

A partial offset to this increased wellhead price was the expected decrease in transportation charges. Supertankers now under construction could decrease international tanker charges to 60 percent of their nominal levels. Tanker charges from the Middle East to either coast of the United States were now $0.74 per barrel. Venezuelan oil could be transported to New York for $0.23 a barrel or to the West Coast for $0.48.

The alternative routes proposed for delivery of North Slope oil assumed that the crude oil would enter the "lower 48" states on the East Coast (New York area), the West Coast (Los Angeles or Seattle), or the Midwest (Chicago). Because of supply/demand patterns within these areas, regional variations in the 1971 average delivered price of crude oil were:

PAD District	*Delivered price (barrel)*
I (New York)	$3.63–3.74
II (Chicago)	3.40–3.51
V (Los Angeles, Seattle)	3.29–3.33

The comparative economics of different methods of transporting North Slope crude oil could be determined by computing the netback value at the wellhead, that is, the delivered price less the transportation expense and a gathering charge of $0.05 a barrel.

For example, based upon the above-mentioned transportation costs, the netback for crude oil transported to New York by the Trans-Alaska Pipeline from Prudhoe Bay to Valdez, tanker to Panama, pipeline across the Isthmus of Panama, and tanker to New York would be:

Delivered price		$3.63–3.74
Less:		
Alaskan pipeline	$0.45	
Tanker to Panama	0.55	
Panama pipeline	0.10	
Tanker to New York	0.30	
Gathering charge	0.05	1.45
Netback value at wellhead		$2.18–2.29

Netback values for other transportation alternatives are summarized in Exhibit 10.

The royalty payments and severance taxes to the state of Alaska would depend on the netback value, amounting to slightly more than 20 percent of the value at the wellhead ($0.45–$0.47 in the above example). Increases in the transportation costs or decreases in the delivered price of crude oil would adversely affect the royalty payments to the state. Realizing this, Alaskan Governor William A. Egan proposed that the state should construct the pipeline itself rather than the Alyeska Pipeline Service Company.

Since the state of Alaska's financial position in the crude oil would equal their tariffs and severance fees, the oil industry was divided on Alaskan participation. Atlantic Richfield's position was that it would not oppose complete state government financing if (a) the state could finance the pipeline without recourse to ARCO's credit (that is, the loan or bond issue would not depend upon an oil throughput agreement), and (b) the state would post a schedule of tariffs and severance fees for the next 20 years.

REFINING CAPACITY

In 1970 approximately 300 domestic refineries had the capacity to process more than 12 million barrels of crude oil per day. Given the current level of demand for petroleum products, this resulted in a daily shortage of approximately 2 million barrels—primarily in the form of No. 6 residual fuel oil imported from Venezuela. Recurring industrial shortages of residual oil on the East Coast prompted the lifting of import quotas for this specific product in 1965. The low levels of domestic supply of residual fuel oil was an indirect result of the federal government's control of the price for natural gas, a close substitute for utilities and some large industrial consumers. In response to the low, competitive price, oil refiners changed their product mix to maximize the yield of lighter hydrocarbons (for example, motor fuel and kerosene) and producing heavier products (for example, asphalt and coke) in place of No. 6 residual fuel oil.

To meet the future need for refined products Shell Oil Corporation had estimated that a total of 76 new refineries, averaging 160,000-barrel capacity, would be needed in the United States by 1980. In response to this need for additional refining capacity, only one new domestic refinery was currently under construction, although many existing refineries were undergoing expansion. The primary delay in constructing new refineries involved environmental issues. An example of the difficulty in siting refineries was highlighted in the Machias, Marine controversy.

Machias proposals[7]

For several years the state of Maine had been in an uproar over the efforts of oil companies to develop large refinery complexes and deep-water ports capable of accommodating the great new supertankers. Some of their proposals would entail competitive challenges to many of the big, internal oil companies.

Potential victims of oil spills—the coastal property owners, the tourist industry, and the lobstermen, clam diggers, and fishermen who constitute the native backbone of coastal Maine—also had a stake in the outcome. The potential beneficiaries of the proposals included the taxpayers of the state and the residents of its chronically depressed areas.

Maine possessed the only natural harbors in the eastern United

[7] This section, with minor modifications, is a condensation of "Oil and the Environment: The View from Maine," *Fortune*, April 1971, pp. 84 ff.

States with water a hundred or more feet deep. Of the tankers on order or under construction at the beginning of 1971, 85 percent were ships of more than 200,000 tons. A number of different ports on the coast of Maine were able to receive these mammoth ships, whereas no existing port elsewhere on the East Coast could dock a tanker of over 80,000 tons.

The siting of the proposed refineries centered on Machias, a small town in Washington County at the northeastern tip of the United States. Its fine harbor made it a thriving port in tht 19th century, but it was now pretty quiet except for a few skiffs and lobster boats. The whole county had been officially designated a "depressed area" by the Commerce Department's Economic Development Administration.

An oil refinery was almost invariably followed by a surrounding petrochemical complex. Maine looked forward to the associated development of ore-reduction plants, pulp and paper mills, and shipbuilding in the Machias area.

In June 1968, the Maine Port Authority applied to the Foreign Trade Zone Board in the Department of Commerce for a zone at Machias in which there would be an oil refinery with a capacity of 300,000 barrels a day and a deep-water terminal. Foreign trade zones had a unique legal status. They were foreign territory so far as customs were concerned and thus could receive raw material without having to respect any quota or pay any duty. Only when goods were "imported" from a zone into the United States were they subject to any quotas or other restrictions. A zone had another advantage from the point of view of the state: As landlord the state had complete control over decisions affecting the environment.

Shortly thereafter, a plan was submitted to then Secretary of the Interior Stewart Udall which proposed a special authorization for Occidental Oil Company to ship 300,000 barrels a day of foreign crude into the zone. It also requested a quota that would permit shipping of 100,000 barrels a day of refined product out of the zone to U.S. markets without being restricted by existing oil import quotas. The other 200,000 barrels of crude could either be made into No. 6 residual fuel, which is used industrially, and shipped to U.S. markets since it is exempt from the quota, or it could be refined into some other kind of petroleum product and shipped abroad. Use of low-priced foreign crude could provide New England with industrial fuel and residential heating oil at a lower price. The governors of the six New England states immediately supported the project and declared it vital to the whole region.

Many of the major oil companies, which saw Occidental's bid as a serious breach in the quota system, fought it from the beginning in Washington, D.C. Confronting pressures from the industry on one side and spokesmen for New England on the other, President Johnson let the issue go over to the Nixon administration. But President Nixon awaited the report of an oil task force of cabinet rank, appointed in March 1969, and charged with reviewing the whole import program. The task force did not report until February 1970, and when it did the president overrode its recommendations (a majority favored ending the quota system and replacing it with a tariff on oil). Recent reexamination of the task force findings have shown that the conclusions were based on assumptions that have proved contrary to actual experience. As of May 1972, Nixon had not taken action on the requests for either a zone or a quota exemption.

Another entry in the siting of a refinery in Maine was Atlantic Richfield. In July 1969, ARCO announced that it had taken options on land in the Machias area and had tentative plans to build a 100,000-barrel-per-day refinery. The company requested neither a zone nor a quota, and so did not have to wait upon the decisions of the federal government as Occidental did.

Atlantic Richfield's primary concern appeared to be the large volume of foreign crude which would be imported to the East Coast. If the Northwest Passage proved feasible, Alaskan crude could be brought to this site. The company viewed Machias as the prospective site of a new refinery using some combination of regular domestic, Alaskan, and foreign crude and serving the New England and other eastern markets. After taking options on a refinery site, the company demonstrated its intent when consulting engineers were engaged to make a study of the feasibility of constructing a marine oil terminal in Machias Bay. In 1972 Atlantic Richfield continued to maintain its option on the land in Machias.

Up to this point, no environmental interests had entered the issue. Different groups affected by the oil projects began to perceive their varied, conflicting, and overlapping interests, and environmental issues were raised. At the time the first oil proposals were made in 1968, the state had no effective laws that would restrict or control oil development. But in 1969 the state legislature came under strong pressure to enact some such laws, and it did so in February 1970 when it created an independent State Environmental Improvement Commission with authority to veto industrial sites. When a company selected a site for an industrial plant, it had to apply to the commission for a permit before construction began.

In addition to this site act designed to minimize damage, the legislature passed a conveyance tax of one-half cent on each barrel of incoming oil. The receipts would go to build and maintain a $4 million fund, which was to be spent on research, cleaning up oil spills, and paying damages. Although the oil-conveyance act was aimed at proposed new ports, it also applied to existing operations at Portland. That city was the second largest crude oil port on the East Coast. Portland had this distinction, not because of oil brought in for local or regional distribution, but because it was the terminus of a pipeline to Montreal; oil from abroad was taken from tankers and passed on through the pipeline. Neither Occidental nor Atlantic Richfield had existing operations in Maine which were affected by this conveyance tax.

Refining alternatives

Difficulties with environmental organizations had led some oil companies to consider refining crude oil in foreign refineries for shipment into the United States. In 1970 nearly 60 percent of all imported petroleum was in the form of refined products (primarily No. 6 residual oil) shipped into the first PAD District. The higher costs associated with transporting refined petroleum products rather than crude could be offset by lower world crude prices and the use of foreign-flag tankers. Lower operating costs of foreign refineries also would be enjoyed. Use of foreign-flag tankers might be restricted by requirements to ship some minimum quantity in U.S.-flag tankers. These imports would be restricted by quotas if the crude oil were from foreign sources.

If, for example, the Trans-Alaska Pipeline were completed and the crude oil were destined for the East Coast, it would be economically feasible to refine the crude in Central America or the Caribbean for shipment as final produce to Atlantic ports. The Jones Act would not allow such an operation, nor would present oil import regulations.

In planning for additional refining capacity, Atlantic Richfield constrained itself to refineries between 100,000 and 200,000 barrels per day. Refinery size was related to the size of market and other variables to produce acceptable economics. Although ARCO's Sinclair, Wyoming 32,000-barrel refinery was its most efficient in terms of unit operating costs, larger refineries generally were required to support a profitable marketing area. (Because of the market size, all Rocky Mountain refineries were relatively small.) On the other hand, diseconomies in the distribution of the refined product limited the size of refineries.

EXHIBIT 1
Selected financial and operating data 1950–1971

	1950	1955	1960	1965	1970	1971
Total assets ($ millions)	433	612	820	994	4,442	4,704
Sales and other operating revenues ($ millions)*.	478	513	661	827	3,444	3,658
Net income before extraordinary items ($ millions).	40.8	39.5	46.6	66.2	209.5	210.5
Crude oil and NGL production (thousand barrels/day).	83	102	153	200	658	647
Crude oil refined† (thousand barrels/day).	159	196	193	218	717	737
Crude oil refining capacity in U.S. (thousand barrels/day).	167	210	210	239	702	702
Petroleum product sales‡ (thousand barrels/day).	172	195	197	236	872	871
Underground reserves§ (million barrels).	507	515	884	1,141	2,713	2,592

* Excludes excise taxes prior to 1960.
† Excludes blending stock runs prior to 1970.
‡ Includes chemical sales prior to 1970.
§ Excluding North Slope, Alaska. In 1971, DeGolyer and MacNaughton, independent consultants, estimated that Atlantic Richfield's net proved reserves in the original Jurassic-Triassic reservoirs of the main Prudhoe Bay Field on the North Slope of Alaska amount to 1.9 billion barrels of oil and gas liquids.
Source: Atltanic Richfield (and Atlantic Refining) Annual Reports—1970 values restated to include Brazilian operations.

EXHIBIT 2
Petroleum administration for defense (PAD) districts

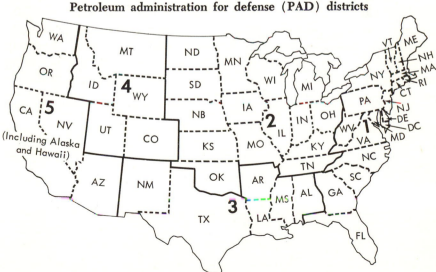

Source: *Final Environmental Impact Statement Proposed Trans-Alaska Pipeline.*

EXHIBIT 3
Atlantic Richfield Petroleum product supply, demand and refining capacity—1970
(thousand barrels daily)

PAD District	Proved reserves*	Crude oil production	Refining capacity	Crude oil refined	Final product sales	Arco's share of final product market (percent)
1	N.A.	0	160	N.A.	275	4.7
2	N.A.	38	135	N.A.	206	5.1
3	N.A.	241	210	N.A.	66	2.7
4	N.A.	36	32	N.A.	21	5.7
5	N.A.	91	165	N.A.	195	10.0
Canada	N.A.	36	0	0	0	–
North American total.	1,595	442	702	678	763	–
Other	1,118	216	N.A.	39	68	–
World total	2,713	658	N.A.	717	831	–

* Millions of barrels excluding North Slope, Alaska.
N.A. = Not available.
Source: Atlantic Richfield Annual Reports.

EXHIBIT 4
U.S. demand for energy by major sources, 1970–1985

	Actual 1970	1975	Projections 1980	1985
Total demand (quadrillion BTUs)	67.8	83.5	102.6	124.9
Percentage distribution:				
Coal	20.0	–	19.4	–
Petroleum	43.0	–	46.1	–
Natural gas.	32.8	–	21.9	–
Nuclear	0.3	–	9.3	–
Hydroelectric	3.9	–	3.3	–

Source: National Petroleum Council, "U.S. Energy Outlook: An Initial Appraisal, 1971–1985," July 1971.

EXHIBIT 5
United States petroleum product supply, demand, and refining capacity*
(thousand barrels daily)

	PAD district 1	PAD district 2	PAD district 3	PAD district 4	PAD district 5	Total
Proved reserves† 1970 actual . .	120	2,803	20,147	1,868	4,675	29,613
Crude-oil production	34					
1970 actual	34	1,490	7,947	711	1,417	11,599
1980 forecasts: Low	81	1,038	6,278	504	899	8,800
1980 forecasts: Medium	95	1,227	7,419	596	1,062	10,400
1980 forecasts: High	109	1,404	8,489	682	1,215	11,900
Refining capacity 1970 actual. .	1,509	3,404	4,881	441	1,939	12,074
Final product demand						
1970 actual	5,853	4,041	2,478	370	1,954	14,696
1980 forecasts: Low	7,842	5,345	3,503	515	2,795	20,000
1980 forecasts: Medium	8,626	5,880	3,853	567	3,074	22,000
1980 forecasts: High	9,802	6,682	4,378	644	3,493	25,000

* Excluding North Slope, Alaska.
† Millions of barrels.
‡ Includes processing gains, inventory accumulation, and crude loss.
Source: *Final Environmental Impact Statement Proposed Trans-Alaska Pipeline* and DeGolyer and MacNaughton's *20th Century Petroleum Statistics*, 1971.

EXHIBIT 6
Inter-district petroleum product flows 1970
(thousand barrels daily)

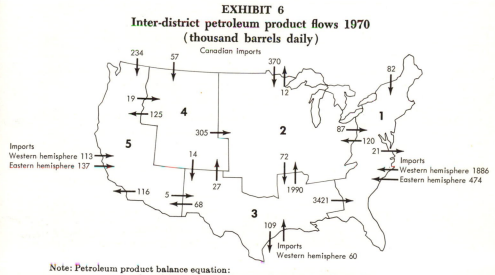

Note: Petroleum product balance equation:
1 barrel of crude oil = 1 barrel of final product demand
Production + Inflows = Final product demand + Outflows
PAD District 1: 34 + (87 + 3431 + 82 + 1886 + 474) = 5853 + (120 + 21)
Source: *Final Environmental Impact Statement Proposed Trans-Alaska Pipeline.*

EXHIBIT 7
Summary of major events since discovery of North Slope oil

January 1968	Atlantic Richfield and Humble Oil and Refining discover oil at Prudhoe Bay on the North Slope of Alaska. Reserves now estimated at ten billion barrels.
February 1969	ARCO, Humble, and British Petroleum announce plans for a 48-inch crude-oil pipeline to run 789 miles from Prudhoe Bay to the ice-free port of Valdez.
April 1969	Pipe worth $100 million ordered from Japan. Delivery completed in October 1971.
August–September 1969	Interior Department holds public hearings in Alaska and issues preliminary requirements for environmental protection.
September 1969	Alaska sells North Slope leases to oil companies for $900 million.
December 1969	Congress passes National Environmental Policy Act (NEPA). Interior required to consider ways to minimize environmental impact of pipeline and weigh alternatives.
March 1970	Three environmental groups sue Interior, claiming agency's environmental impact statement fails to comply with NEPA. Five Alaskan villages sue Interior, claiming pipeline will cross their land without permission.
April 1970	Federal court upholds both suits, enjoins Interior from issuing pipeline permit without court-approved impact statement.
August 1970	Alyeska Pipeline Service Company formed to design, build, and operate Alaskan pipeline.
January–February 1971	Interior issues preliminary impact statement, holds public hearings, then starts more studies.
July 1971	Alyeska Pipeline submits 29-volume description of project and environmental safeguards.
December 1971	Congress passes Native Claims Act, giving natives 40 million acres of land, $462.5 million in cash over 11 years, and $500 million in mineral royalties.
March 1972	Interior issues nine-volume environmental impact statement, probably clearing the way for pipeline construction.

Source: *Business Week*, March 25, 1972, p. 80.

EXHIBIT 8
Transportation alternatives for North Slope crude oil

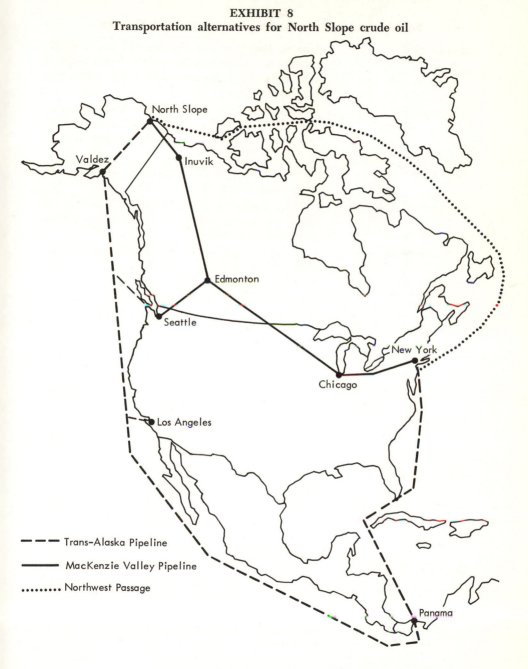

EXHIBIT 9
Historical comparison of wellhead prices, 1950–70

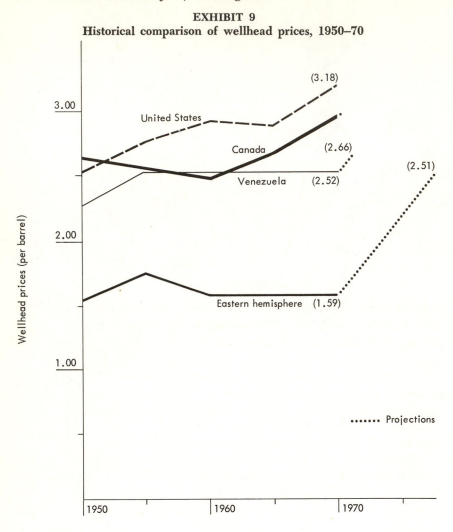

····· Projections

EXHIBIT 10
North Slope netback values for selected transportation alternatives
(per barrel)

Shipment to PAD District	Transportation alternatives		
	Trans-Alaska Pipeline System	MacKenzie Valley Pipeline	Northwest Passage
1 New York	$2.18–2.29	$2.25–2.36	$2.28–2.39
2 Chicago.	–	2.27–2.38	–
5 Los Angeles	2.34–2.38	–	–
Seattle	2.39–2.43	2.14–2.19	–

List of cases